Combined with the resources you have trusted throughout the years to provide you with the best business resources available:

- **In the News**—New current events articles are added throughout the year. Each article is summarized by our teams of experts, and fully supported by exercises, activities, and instructor materials.

- **Online Study Guide**—Three quizzes are linked to each text chapter and include "hints" for each question. Each quiz is graded immediately upon submission, provides immediate feedback on each given answer, and enables students to e-mail results to the instructor.

- **Research Area**—Your own personal resource library includes tutorials, descriptive links to virtual libraries, and a wealth of search engines and resources.

- **Internet Resources**—provide discipline-specific sites, including preview information that allows you to review site information before you view the site, ensuring you visit the best available business resources found by our learning community.

For the professor

- **Teaching Resources** provide material contributed by professors throughout the world—including teaching tips, techniques, academic papers, and sample syllabi—and **Talk to the Team,** a moderated faculty chat room.

- **Online Faculty Support** includes downloadable supplements, additional cases, articles, links, and suggested answers to current events activities.

- **What's New** gives you one-click access to all newly posted PHLIP resources.

For the student

- **Talk to the Tutor** schedules virtual office hours that allow students to post questions from any supported discipline and receive responses from the dedicated PHLIP/CW faculty team.

- **Writing Resource Center** provides an online writing center that supplies links to online directories, thesauruses, writing tutors, style and grammar guides, and additional tools.

- **Career Center** helps students access career information, view sample résumés, even apply for jobs online.

- **Study Tips** provides an area where students can learn to develop better study skills.

www.prenhall.com/russell

KLEPPNER'S
Advertising Procedure

Fifteenth
Edition

KLEPPNER'S

Advertising Procedure

**Fifteenth
Edition**

J. THOMAS RUSSELL
Piedmont College

W. RONALD LANE
University of Georgia

Prentice
Hall

Upper Saddle River, New Jersey 07458

Library of Congress Cateloging-in-Publication Data

Russell, Thomas
    Kleppner's advertising procedure/J. Thomas Russell, W. Ronald Lane.–
15th ed.
        p.cm.
    Includes bibliographical references and index.
    ISBN 0-13-032877-4
    1. Advertising.   I. Lane, W. Ronald,   II. Kleppner, Otto, Advertising
    procedure. III. Title.
HF5823.K45 2001

659.1–dc21
2001024676

Acquisitions Editor: Whitney Blake
Assisstant Editor: Anthony Palmiotto
Editorial Assisstant: Melissa Pellerano
Media Project Manager: Cindy Harford
Marketing Manager: Shannon Moore
Marketing Assistant: Kathleen Mulligan
Mamaging Editor (Production): Judy Leale
Production Editor: M. E. McCourt
Permissions Coordinator: Suzanne Grappi
Associate Director, Manufacturing: Vincent Scelta
Production Manager: Arnold Vila
Buyer: Diane Peirano
Design Manager: Patricia Smythe
Art Director: Kevin Kall
Cover Design: Ox & Company, Inc.
Interior Designer: David Levy
Associate Director, Multimedia Production: Karen Goldsmith
Manager, Print Production: Chisty Mahon
Full-Service Project Management: TECHBOOKS
Printer/Binder: Courier, Inc.

Credits and acknowledgments borrowed from other sources and reproduced, with permission, in this textbook appear on appropriate page within text.

10 9 8 7 6 5 4 3 2
ISBN 0-13-032877-4

Brief Contents

Contents

Preface

The fifteenth edition of *Kleppner's Advertising Procedure* continues its long tradition of concise coverage of the fields of advertising and promotion with a marketing foundation. At the same time, the current edition has incorporated a number of new sections dealing with the expansion and convergence of technology as well as some dramatic changes in the practice and management of advertising by agencies, clients, and the media. The primary aim of the authors is to offer students a road map for the future of advertising while at the same time emphasizing the enduring concepts of ethics, social responsibility, and consumer benefits that should be a primary concern of all advertisers.

The reader will note that the basic organization of the text has remained essentially the same, although the content of each chapter has been significantly updated with new examples and data. More importantly, the text has expanded sections reflecting issues such as the Internet, Web selling, digital production, and interactive television, to name only a few. The text discusses the various areas of advertising and marketing communication in a manner that relates them to the overall planning and strategy of marketing and advertising goals. It is the integration of these relationships among the various marketing and advertising functions that distinguishes the fifteenth edition of *Kleppner's Advertising Procedure* from earlier editions as well as similar texts.

While the text recognizes the synergy between marketing and promotion, it is fundamentally a book about advertising and how the field of advertising complements and is enhanced by related business functions. In a complex business environment, the fifteenth edition recognizes that there is no single-right or wrong-approach to advertising problem solving. With this in mind, the authors have included a number of approaches that will address unique issues faced by every company. The text demonstrates that advertising must function within a matrix of variables including product quality, consumer perceptions, pricing policies, distribution, and competitive pressures. Successful advertising demands more than just a knowledge of business, marketing, and communication. Central to successful advertising is an understanding of consumers and the sociological, psychological, and cultural factors that lead them to accept or reject specific products and services.

In order to accomplish the challenge of providing students with the latest information in an organized and compelling format, the authors have divided the text into six sections to provide a logical and understandable overview of advertising. Part I includes a historical overview of the roots of advertising with special emphasis on the early twentieth century development of modern marketing communication. In Chapter 2, the text provides an overview of the many roles of advertising and the ways in which companies from the local merchant to giant multi-national conglomerates utilize advertising.

The second part of the text reviews the means by which advertisers establish specific brands in the face of sometimes daunting competition and numerous product options available to consumers. In Chapter 3, the text introduces a theme that is a benchmark of *Kleppner's* past and present—that advertising must provide a benefit to both the seller and the buyer. Successful advertising must begin with a worthwhile product provided at a competitive price with benefits that solve a consumer problem. The consumer is the keystone for successful advertising and it is the consumer, not the product, that must be the focus for successful advertising. Chapter 4 develops the concept that there is no single consumer group with unified tastes and needs. Instead, advertisers must deal with a fragmented marketplace that is represented by distinct segments of consumers, products, and media, each with their own unique characteristics.

Like any business enterprise, advertising requires sophisticated management and oversight. In the third part of the text, the coordination of the advertising and marketing process is discussed. Chapter 5 views the role of the advertising agency and related media and creative services are examined. Special emphasis is given to the manner in which the modern advertising agency is being force to reengineer its basis philosophy to react to client issues such as globalization, the role of new technology, and demands for greater returns on investments. In Chapter 6, advertising is examined from the corporate/client perspective where issues of overall marketing and advertising strategy are paramount concerns.

In part four of the fifteenth edition, the various media vehicles are examined. In Chapter 7, we discuss the convergence of the different media into coordinated marketing communication outlets including the complementary nature of sales promotion, public relations, and advertising. In Chapters 8-14, the various media vehicles are examined individually, but with a priority of linking these media in a manner that demonstrates the complementary manner in which each supports the others. In a world of audience fragmentation, it is rare that any single medium can reach the majority of a product's market. Likewise, this section addresses the communication strengths and weaknesses of each media to show that the various media serve distinctly different roles in the typical advertising campaign.

Part five begins the review of the creative function. Chapter 15 begins this discussion of the creative function with an analysis of the role that research plays in developing consumer-oriented campaigns. The key to successful creative executions is the ability to direct messages to the core concerns of consumers. Successful advertising creativity flows from a thorough knowledge of the consumer, the product, and the marketplace. Chapters 16 and 17 show how research data are interpreted and translated into creative advertisements and commercial themes. In Chapters 18 and 19, the various techniques of print and broadcast advertising production are discussed. It is important to remember that the best ideas, if poorly presented, will probably fail to accomplish the intended marketing task. With consumers bombarded daily with thousands of promotional messages, presentation is as important as the message to gain awareness and interest of potential prospects.

In Chapter 21, the text continues to emphasize the importance of an integrated plan for all aspects of marketing communication with a discussion of trademarks and packaging. To a degree, the package is the last opportunity to influence the customer and it also provides an opportunity for synergy between a product and its advertising. This section concludes with an overview of the planning and strategy necessary for a complete campaign. In many respects, Chapter 22 is a capstone chapter that brings together many of the issues discussed throughout the text. The organization of an advertising campaign can only be accomplished when all aspects of research, budgeting, media planning, and creative execution are assimilated into a single coordinated advertising program.

The final part of the text examines some specialized areas of advertising. In Chapter 23, retail advertising and marketing are addressed from the perspective of the ultimate consumer. While retail marketing and advertising has many similarities with other type of promotion, it also demonstrates a number of unique characteristics. The fast-paced immediacy of retailing and the ability for short-term consumer feedback makes the retail sector fundamentally different from other forms of advertising. From the local retailer, we move to the world of multi-national marketing and advertising with its special opportunities and challenges. From it roots in the post-World War II era, international business has become the norm for most firms. Chapter 24 examines the role that multi-national companies play in every aspect of American advertising. It is a rare company that does is not influenced in some respect by the global marketplace. As the Internet and new technology makes the world even smaller, American advertising will continue to be influenced by global marketing.

No business function is more regulated and comes under more scrutiny than advertising. Chapter 25 examines the numerous legal, regulatory, and industry controls of the advertising process. Despite the many formal regulations imposed on advertising, it is the public perception of the industry that may be of more long-term importance. In Chapter 26, the text concludes with a review of the economic and social aspects of advertising. It is obvious that advertising can only be effective if the public trusts it to provide truthful and constructive information that will allow consumers to make rational decisions about the goods and services they purchase.

While the purpose of the text is to offer students an overview of the business of advertising, the authors hope that we also have been able to convey the excitement and fun of this dynamic area. Whether you are entering a career in advertising, interested in the field as it relates to some other discipline, or simply interested in advertising as a consumer, our goal is that *Kleppner's Advertising Procedure* has introduced you to the concepts, theories, and pragmatic operation of this challenging, but never dull, field.

J. THOMAS RUSSELL
W. RONALD LANE

Acknowledgements

Over the years, *Kleppner's Advertising Procedure* has benefited from the advice and expertise of hundreds of professional advertisers. Media Planners, account executives, creative personnel and brand managers at numerous companies have combined their knowledge to offer students the latest information about the changing fields of advertising and promotion. Although the authors are solely responsible for the content of the text, we are indebted to the following people who have offered their counsel in the fifteenth edition of the text.

Gary H. Knutson, Exec. V.P. Creative Director, *Howard, Merrel & Partners, Raleigh NC*

Robert Shaw West, Exec. Creative Director, *West & Vaughan, Inc*, Durham, NC

Neil Aronstam, *Independent Media*

David Dean Jacobs, J*acobs Outdoor*

Val Onyski, *Yellow Pages Publishers Association*

Lisa Dalsin, *Transtop*

Ronald W. Waggener, *Waggener & Associates*

Don Varner, *Billboard Connection*

Jim Mountjoy, Executive Creative Director, *Loeffler Ketchum Mountjoy*, Charlotte, NC

Bradford P. Majors, President, *Socoh Marketing*, Greenville, SC

Sheri L. Bevil, President, *Sheri Bevil Advertising*, Atlanta

Thomas Y. Robinson, President, *Robinson & Associates*, Tupelo, MS

Thanks also go to the helpful personnel at:

Television Bureau of Advertising

Nielsen Media Research

Radio Advertising Bureau

Newspaper Association of America

Magazine Publishers of America

Outdoor Advertising Association of America

Advertising Council

Kleppner's Advertising Procedure is one of the best-selling advertising books and has been for many years. Each edition has benefited from valuable feedback from our adopters around the world. During the fourteenth edition, students sent us their comments and suggestions through the MyPHLIP web site which supports the text. (www.prenhall.com/myphlip). We would like to thank a group of individuals who offered detailed comments during the process of developing the fifteenth edition. They are:

Howard S. Cogan, *Ithaca College*

Lee S. Wenthe, *University of Georgia*

Jennifer Gregan-Paxton, *University of Delaware*

Carolyn F. Stringer, *Western Kentucky University*

Dennis J. Ganahl, *Southern Illinois University*, Carbondale

Jon P. Wardrip, *University of South Carolina*

A book such as this could not be produced without the assistance of many people at Prentice Hall, especially the editorial team of Whitney Blake, Executive Editor, Anthony Palmiotto, Assistant Editor, Melissa Pellerano, Editorial Assistant, and Mary Ellen McCourt, Production Editor. In addition, Suzanne Grappi managed a challenging permissions process, and the team in manufacturing, Arnold Vila, Vincent Scelta and Diane Pierano, produced a beautiful book.

INSTRUCTOR SUPPORT MATERIAL

Where can professors and students find a huge array of resources for teaching and learning in advertising? All of the resources can be found in one place-at www.prenhall.com/myphlip. Professors and students can register their class and receive access to all the resources found on the inside covers of the fifteenth edition. In addition, the following supplementary materials are available for instructor's:

Instructor's Manual

Prepared by John Brooks of Houston Baptist University, this complete manual contains (for each chapter) learning objectives, chapter overview, lecture outline, key terms, answers to end of chapter questions, suggestions for class projects and internet exercises and suggested video clips from the advertising video library.

TEST ITEM FILE

Prepared by John Brooks, this test item book contains 150 questions per chapter including true false, multiple choice and essay, organized by chapter.

PH CustomTest

The electronic test generator is available in Windows and Mac versions.

PowerPoint Lecture Presentations

A brand new set of dynamic PowerPoint slides, many of which include advertisements and other animations and graphics. These slide lectures do not duplicate text material, and many of the slides are available in the overhead transparency package.

Full Color Acetate Transparencies

A new set of lecture and ad transparencies in acetate form, over 200 in all.

Advertising Transparencies

An additional 75 print advertisements in acetate form, complete with lecture suggestions.

Advertising Video Library

A set of 15 video segments, averaging eight to ten minutes in length, showcase a wide variety of concepts in advertising and promotion. Clips includes Blair Witch (Internet

Promotion), House of Blues, Mad Dogs and Englishmen (Agencies), New Product Showcase, Nike (international), Kodak, NASCAR (sponsorhip), Got Milk, and Intel (comparative advertising). In addition, the ever popular NY Festivals award winners are included in the library.

Online Course Solutions

The new fifteenth edition is available in three on line course formats, WEB CT, Blackboard and Course Compass. Adopters can order these on line courses free with the text. Contact you Prentice Hall representative for the correct ordering ISBN number. (See inside covers for a list of features!) Full communication and gradebook features, and much more.

OTTO KLEPPNER
(1899–1982)

A graduate of New York University, Otto Kleppner started out in advertising as a copy-writer. After several such jobs, he became advertising manager at Prentice Hall, where he began to think that he, too, "could write a book." Some years later, he also thought that he could run his own advertising agency, and both ideas materialized eminently. His highly successful agency handled advertising for leading accounts (Dewar's Scotch Whisky, I. W. Harper Bourbon and other Schenley brands, Saab Cars, Doubleday Book Clubs, and others). His book became a bible for advertising students, and his writings have been published in eight languages.

Active in the American Association of Advertising Agencies, Mr. Kleppner served as a director, a member of the Control Committee, chairman of the Committee of Government, Public and Educator Relations, and a governor of the New York Council. He was awarded the Nichols Cup (now the Crain Cup) for distinguished service to the teaching of advertising.

J. THOMAS RUSSELL

Thomas Russell is Phil Landrum Professor of Communications and Dean of the Athens Center of Piedmont College, Demorest, Georgia. He also is Dean Emeritus of the College of Journalism and Mass Communication at the University of Georgia. Tom received his Ph.D. in communications from the University of Illinois and has taught and conducted research in a number of areas of advertising and marketing. He was formerly editor of the *Journal of Advertising*.

In addition to his academic endeavor, Tom has worked as a retail copywriter as well as been a principal in his own advertising agency. He is a member of a number of academic, professional, and civic organizations. He also has served as a judge and faculty member for the Institute of Advanced Advertising Studies sponsored by the American Association of Advertising Agencies.

W. RONALD LANE

Ron has worked in most aspects of advertising. He began in advertising and promotion for a drug manufacturer. Ron has worked in creative and account services for clients including Coca-Cola, National Broiler Council, Minute-Maid, and Callaway Gardens Country Store.

He is a professor of advertising at the University of Georgia and has served as advertising manager of the *Journal of Advertising*. He was coordinator of the Institute of Advanced Advertising Studies sponsored by the American Association of Advertising Agencies for six years. He is also a partner in SLRS Communications, an advertising-marketing agency.

Currently, Ron is a member of the American Advertising Federation's (AAF) Academic Division, Executive Committee. He has been the AAF Academic Division Chair and served as a member of the AAF Board of Directors, Council of Governors, and Executive Committee. He has been an ADDY Awards judge numerous times and has been a member of the Advertising Age Creative Workshop faculty. He is a member of the Atlanta Advertising Club, American Academy of Advertising, American Marketing Association, and the ACEJMC Accrediting Council.

PART 1

The Place of Advertising

Chapter 1

Background of Today's Advertising

The history of advertising can only be studied from the perspective of the social and economic environment in which it functions. This chapter traces the relationship between advertising and the economic and social conditions that made it possible including the development of mass media, a rising middle class, effective transportation, and the growth of mass production. After reading this chapter you will understand:

>> the earliest forerunners of modern advertising

>> advertising and the development of mass media

>> the rise of advertising as a major business

>> government regulation and the fight for responsible advertising

>> advertising growth during the post–World War II era

>> global advertising in the twenty-first century

Modern advertising is a product of the last 100 years, and most sophisticated elements of the industry such as in-depth research into consumer behavior and media analysis have come into their own in the last 30 years. However, the exchange of goods and the need to link buyers and sellers dates to prehistoric times. Some of the earliest cave drawings refer to the makers of primitive objects. In order to understand the origins of modern advertising, we must examine the conditions that made it possible.

The study of advertising demonstrates that it does not function in a void. Not only is advertising a product of the society and business environment in which it operates, but it is only one of a number of marketing and communication tools that combine to market a product or service effectively. Regardless of the specific objective of a particular advertisement, the basic function remains the same. "The institutional aspects of advertising are to be found in its performance of the function of supplying market information. . . . Advertising brings buyers and sellers together and possesses utility in facilitating the exchange of property."[1] As we explore the many facets of advertising in coming chapters, we should keep in mind the fundamental role of advertising as a communication tool that functions to promote the exchange of goods in the most efficient manner possible.

As we will see later in this chapter, advertising developed as part of an overall trend toward marketing specialization introduced after the Civil War. Three primary forces were responsible for the environment that created advertising. The first was the beginning of the fulfillment of democratic ideals. While eighteenth-century America had far to go before basic rights such as women's suffrage and full citizenship for Americans of African descent were a reality, public education was creating a literate population and interest in the political process created a need for mass-media outlets.

Second, advertising was part of the industrial revolution that swept over the United States during the latter part of the nineteenth century. Mass production allowed not only the efficient manufacturing of a host of goods, but this same technological expertise created the high-speed presses that enabled the publishing of mass-circulation magazines and newspapers as well as the advertising that supported them.

This period also saw the growth of railroads that resulted in the widespread distribution of both national magazines and national branded products. The railroad, combined with the instant communication of the telegraph, bonded the country into a single entity. Without the railroad, expansion of western markets would have been impossible and marketing and media would have been largely confined to local and regional areas. From a political, economic, and social standpoint, the railroad and the telegraph more than any other elements forged a single nation.

The third significant social development during this period was the movement from a rural to an urban society. By 1900, America had moved from a nation of farmers to one of factory workers living in major industrial centers with different needs than their rural counterparts for products and information.

While all of these elements were crucial to the development of advertising, it is clear that efficient transportation and the initiation of widely distributed branded goods of consistent quality set the stage for twentieth-century advertising. "National advertising developed when businesses in several important industries decided that branding and promoting their products would be profitable."[2]

Prior to the American industrialization revolution, most trade took place in a limited area through locally owned retailers receiving goods from local or regional producers. The producers of goods had little or no contact or relationship with their ultimate customers. They were totally dependent on local merchants for their sales.

Branded, nationally distributed goods radically changed this relationship. "Branding offered manufacturers a new kind of control when supported by effective advertising, by altering the balance of power in the traditional chain from manufacturer to . . . customer. No longer were customers to rely on the grocer's opinion about the best soap . . . . People asked for Ivory, which could only be obtained from Procter and Gamble."[3]

The convergence of the availability of branded products, the ability to provide national distribution, and a growing middle class as a market for these products had evolved sufficiently by 1920 to support the creation of an advertising industry that demonstrated most of the basic functions found among modern agencies and corporate advertising departments today.

---

[1] James W. Carey, "Advertising: An institutional approach," in C. H. Sandage and Vernon Fryburger, *The Role of Advertising* (Homewood, IL: Richard D. Irwin, 1960), 14.
[2] Daniel Pope, *The Making of Modern Advertising* (New York: Basic Books, 1983), 62.
[3] Susan Strasser, *Satisfaction Guaranteed* (New York: Pantheon Books, 1989), 30.

The two elements missing in most advertising during the early years of this century were (1) an ethical framework for creating promotional messages and (2) valid and reliable research to measure advertising effects. Despite efforts as early as 1890 to insure honest advertising, it would be many years before the industry adopted a formal structure for self-regulation.

Likewise, the pioneering work of early advertising researchers such as Claude Hopkins would not gain widespread acceptance until the latter half of this century. "Several agencies boasted of . . . research into consumer attitudes in the late 1920s, but their crude, slapdash methods made these 'surveys' of questionable value in providing accurate feedback. One agency reported that it could obtain quick, inexpensive results . . . by having all members of the staff send questionnaires to their friends."[4]

Generally, the advertisers of the period thought that an intuitive "feel" for the consumer was quite sufficient to produce effective advertising. However, research opportunities did exist in the many mail order ads of the day that could measure results by coupon returns. In spite of a few attempts at consumer feedback, pretesting of advertising was largely unknown.

Let's begin our discussion of the exciting business of advertising by examining its history, which we will divide into three broad periods and the prediction of a fourth:

premarketing era
The period from prehistoric times to the eighteenth century. During this time, buyers and sellers communicated in very primitive ways.

1. *The **premarketing era.*** From the start of product exchange in prehistoric times to the middle of the seventeenth century, buyers and seller communicated in very primitive ways. For most of this period "media" such as clay tables, town criers, and tavern signs were the best way to reach potential prospects for a product or service. Only in the latter decades of the period did primitive printing appear.

mass communication era From the 1700s to the early decades of this century, advertisers were able to reach large segments of the population through the mass media.

2. *The **mass communication era.*** From the 1700s to the early decades of the twentieth century, advertisers were increasingly able to reach large segments of the population, first with faster presses and later through broadcast media.

research era In recent years advertisers increasingly have been able to identify narrowly defined audience segments through sophisticated research methods.

3. *The **research era.*** During the last 50 years advertisers have methodically improved the techniques for identifying and reaching narrowly targeted audiences with messages prepared specifically for each group or individual (in the case of direct mail).

interactive era
Communication will increasingly be controlled by consumers who will determine when and where they can be reached with promotional messages.

4. *The **interactive era.*** A fourth era, which we are just embarking on, is one of interactive communication. Soon, consumers will use communication on a interactive basis. Rather than mass media sending one-way messages to the audience, the audience will control when and where the media can reach them and this change in control will have major implications for both the mass media and advertising.

As we begin our discussion of the development of advertising, we must keep in mind the interrelationships among marketing, the general business climate, social mores and conventions, as well as public attitudes toward advertising. As advertising has become an integral part of our economy, advertising practitioners have come under close public scrutiny and they find themselves working within a complex legal and regulatory framework. Perhaps the most important change in the last 20 years has been a growing sense of social responsibility within the advertising community. Many advertising practices that were routine a century ago are universally condemned by the industry today. Advertisers realize that public trust is the key to successful advertising. The remainder of this chapter discusses the forces that have shaped contemporary advertising.

---

[4] Roland Marchand, *Advertising the American Dream* (Berkeley, CA: University of California Press, 1985), 76.

BEGINNINGS

The urge to advertise seems to be a part of human nature, evidenced since ancient times. Of the 5,000-year recorded history of advertising right up to our present television satellite age, the part that is most significant begins when the United States emerged as a great manufacturing nation about 100 years ago. The early history of advertising, however, is far too fascinating to pass by without a glance.

It is not surprising that the people who gave the world the Tower of Babel also left the earliest known evidence of advertising. A Babylonian clay tablet of about 3000 B.C. bears inscriptions for an ointment dealer, a scribe, and a shoemaker. Papyri exhumed from the ruins of Thebes show that the ancient Egyptians had a better medium on which to write their messages. (Alas, the announcements preserved in papyrus offer rewards for the return of runaway slaves.) The Greeks were among those who relied on town criers to chant the arrival of ships with cargoes of wines, spices, and metals. Often a crier was accompanied by a musician who kept him in the right key. Town criers later became the earliest medium for public announcements in many European countries, and they continued to be used for centuries. (At this point, we must digress to tell about a promotion idea used by innkeepers in France around A.D. 1100 to tout their fine wines: They would have the town crier blow a horn, gather a group—and offer samples!)

Roman merchants, too, had a sense of advertising. The ruins of Pompeii contain signs in stone or terra-cotta, advertising what the shops were selling: a row of hams for a butcher shop (Exhibit 1.1), a cow for a dairy, a boot for a shoemaker. The Pompeiians also knew the art of telling their story to the public by means of painted wall signs like this one (tourism was indeed one of advertising's earliest subjects):

- Traveler
- Going from here to the twelfth tower
- There Sarinus keeps a tavern
- This is to request you to enter
- Farewell

Outdoor advertising has proved to be one of the most enduring forms of advertising. It survived the decline of the Roman empire to become the decorative art of European inns in the seventeenth and eighteenth centuries. That was still an age of widespread illiteracy, so inns vied with one another in creating attractive signs that all could recognize. This accounts for the charming names of old inns, especially in England—such as the Three Squirrels, the Man in the Moon, the Hole in the Wall (Exhibit 1.2). In 1614, England passed a law, probably the earliest on advertising, that prohibited signs from extending more than eight feet out from a building. (Longer signs pulled down too many house fronts.) Another law required signs to be high enough to give clearance to an armored man on horseback. In 1740, the first printed outdoor poster (referred to as a "**hoarding**") appeared in London.

hoarding First printed outdoor signs—the forerunner of modern outdoor advertising.

Exhibit

1.1

One of the oldest signs known. It identified a butcher shop in Pompeii.

Chapter 1   Background of Today's Advertising   **5**

Three Squirrels

Hog in Armour

King's Porter and Dwarf

Harrow and Doublet

The Ape

Hole in the Wall
"A Guide for Malt Worms"

Barley Mow

Bull and Mouth

Man in the Moon

Goose and Gridiron

Exhibit

1.2

Signs outside seventeenth-century inns.

ORIGINS OF NEWSPAPER ADVERTISING

Johann Gutenberg
Began the era of mass communication in 1438 with the invention of movable type.

The next most enduring advertising medium, the newspaper, was the offspring of **Johann Gutenberg's** invention of printing from movable type (about 1438), which, of course, changed communication methods for the whole world. About 40 years after the invention, William Caxton of London printed the first ad in English—a handbill of the rules for the guidance of the clergy at Easter. This was tacked up on church doors. (It became the first printed outdoor ad in English.) But the printed newspaper was a long time coming. It really emerged from the newsletters, handwritten by professional writers, for nobles and others who wanted to be kept up to date on the news, especially of the court and important events—very much in the spirit of today's Washington newsletters.

The first ad in any language to be printed in a disseminated sheet appeared in a German news pamphlet in about 1525. And what do you think this ad was for? A book extolling the virtues of a mysterious drug. (The Food and Drug Administration did not exist in those days.) But news pamphlets did not come out regularly; one published in 1591 contained news of the previous three years. It was from such beginnings, however, that the printed newspaper emerged. The first printed English newspaper came out in 1622, the *Weekly Newes of London*. The first ad in an English newspaper appeared in 1625.

Siquis—Tack-Up Advertisements

The forerunner of our present want ads bore the strange name of *siquis.* The clergy were apparently the first to make use of the written word for the purpose of bringing together the forces of supply and demand. A candidate seeking a clerical position would post a notice setting forth his qualifications, while someone having an appointment to make would post a notice specifying the requirements. These early "want ads" were usually in Latin and began *si quis* ("if anybody"): hence the name siquis. The name continued, although soon these notices covered a variety of subjects, including lost-and-found objects, runaway apprentices, and so on.[5]

Advertising in the English newspapers continued to feature similar personal and local announcements. The British have, in fact, shown so much interest in classified ads that until a few years ago the *London Times* filled its first page with classified advertising.

siquis Handwritten posters in sixteenth- and seventeenth-century England—forerunners of modern advertising.

Advertising Comes to America

The Pilgrims arrived on American shores before the *Weekly Newes of London* was first published, so they had had little chance to learn about newspapers. But later colonists acquainted them with the idea, and the first American newspaper to carry ads appeared in 1704, the *Boston Newsletter* (note the newsletter identification). It printed an ad offering a reward for the capture of a thief and the return of several sorts of men's apparel—more akin to the ad offering a reward for returned slaves written on Egyptian papyrus thousands of years before than to the advertising printed in the United States today. By the time the United States was formed, the colonies had 30 newspapers. Their advertising, like that of the English newspapers of the time, consisted mostly of ads we would describe today as classified and local.

THREE MOMENTOUS DECADES: 1870–1900

Neither those ads nor all the ads that appeared from ancient Egyptian days until the American industrial revolution explain the development of advertising in the United States. The history of advertising in the United States is unique because advertising took hold just as the country was entering its era of greatest growth: Population was soaring, factories were springing up, railroads were opening the West. Advertising grew with the country and helped establish its marketing system.

---

[5] George Burton Hotchkiss, *An Outline of Advertising* (New York: Macmillan, 1957), 10.

The United States entered the nineteenth century as an agricultural country, following European marketing traditions, and ended the century as a great industrial nation, creating its own patterns of distribution. A new age of advertising had begun.

We pick up the story in about 1870, when this era of transition was crystallizing. Among the major developments, transportation, population growth, invention, and manufacturing ranked high.

Transportation

Here was a country 3,000 miles wide. It had sweeping stretches of rich farmland. It had minerals and forests. It had factories within reach of the coal mines. It had a growing population. But its long-distanced transportation was chiefly by rivers and canals.

Railroads today are fighting for survival, but 100 years ago they changed a sprawling continent into a land of spectacular economic growth. In 1865, there were 35,000 miles of railroad trackage in the United States. By 1900, this trackage was 190,000 miles. Three railroad lines crossed the Mississippi and ran from the Atlantic to the Pacific. Feeder lines and networks spread across the face of the land. Where railroads went, people went. No longer limited to the waterways, they established farms, settlements, and cities across the continent. The goods of the North and East could be exchanged for the farm and extractive products of the South and West. Never before had a country revealed such extensive and varied resources. Never since has so vast a market without a trade or language barrier been opened. This was an exciting prospect to manufacturers.

People

In 1870, the population of the United States was 38 million. By 1900, it had doubled. In no other period of American history has the population grown so fast. This growth, which included those recently freed from slavery, meant an expanding labor force in the fields, factories, and mines; it also meant a new consumer market. About 30 percent of the new population were immigrants. But all the settlers before them had been immigrants or descendants of immigrants who had had the courage to pull up stakes and venture to the New World, a land far away and strange to them, in search of a new and better life. The result was a people who were mobile, both in their readiness to move their homes and in their aspirations to move upward in lifestyle.

Inventions and Production

The end of the nineteenth century was marked by many notable inventions and advances in the manufacture of goods. Among these were the development of the electric motor and of alternating-current power transmission, which relieved factories of the need to locate next to waterpower sources, thus opening the hinterland to development and growth. The internal combustion engine was perfected in this period; the automobile age was soon to follow.

It was the age of fast communications; telephone (Exhibit 1.3), telegraph, typewriter, **Mergenthaler linotype,** high-speed presses—all increased the ability of people to communicate with one another.

In 1860, there were 7,600 patent applications filed in Washington. By 1870, this number had more than doubled to 19,000; by 1900, it had more than doubled again, to 42,000.

Steel production has traditionally served as an index of industrial activity. Twenty *thousand* tons of steel were produced in 1867, but 10 *million* tons were pro-

Mergenthaler linotype Ottmar Mergenthaler invented the linotype, which replaced hand-set type by automatically setting and distributing metal type.

duced in 1900. There is also a direct correlation between the power consumption of a country and its standard of living. By 1870, only 3 million horsepower was available; by 1900, this capacity had risen to 10 million. More current means more goods being manufactured; it also means that more people are using it for their own household needs. Both types of use form a good economic index.

The phonograph and the motion-picture camera, invented at the turn of the century, enhanced the American lifestyle.

The Columbian Exhibition in Chicago in 1893 was attended by millions, who returned home to tell their friends breathlessly about the new products they had seen.

Media

Advertising is specialized communication. While its purpose and execution may differ from other types of communication, it uses the same channels of linking senders to receivers available to other communicators. Whether using Greek parchment, Egyptian papyrus, the Gutenberg press, Marconi's wireless, or the Internet, advertisers are part of the communication process. They look for ways to reach an audience in need of a product or a service. In doing so, advertising has historically been part of the development and support of most communication technology and will remain so in the future. Later chapters will discuss the development of major media and their relationship to advertising. However, here the development of media is examined as part of the emergence of both advertising and a literate, middle class.

Newspapers As early as 59 B.C., the Romans posted daily, government-published news sheets known as acta diurna and the first English newspaper, *The Oxford Gazette,* was published in 1665. The first colonial newspaper, Benjamin Harris's *Publick Occurrences,* was published in Boston in 1690 and it was promptly banned by the governor after one issue. However, many newspapers followed over the next century and by 1800 every major city in the United States had several publishers.

With the introduction of Richard Hoe's rotary press during the 1830s, *The New York Sun* ushered in the era of the so-called **penny press,** which provided inexpensive newspapers to the general population. For the first time, both readers and advertisers had extensive access to inexpensive newspapers. By 1900, newspapers such as the *New York World* and the *Chicago Tribune* had circulations of more than 500,000. These high circulation publications and many more like them were supported by advertisers seeking more and more buyers for their goods. The newspapers of the era established the model for financial support from advertising that continues for the majority of media to the present.

Magazines

The earliest colonial magazines gave little promise that they would grow into a major mass medium. The first magazine in America was published by William Bradford in 1741. Aptly named the *American Magazine,* it lasted all of three issues. Its major competitor, Benjamin Franklin's *General Magazine,* started in the same year, died a quiet death after only six issues.

From these humble beginnings, there were more than 100 magazines by 1800. Most of these publications carried literary, political, or religious content. The cost was prohibitive for most readers and these early magazines appealed only to the educational and financial elite. Magazines such as *Harper's Monthly, Atlantic Monthly,* and *Century* were typical of the popular magazines of the mid-1800s.

During the 1890s the editorial and advertising foundations of the modern consumer magazines took shape. Supporting a populist agenda, many magazines of the day began to speak to the concerns of the American family with articles on health, fashion, and food. In addition, some of the major writers of the time such as Mark Twain and Sir Arthur Conan Doyle were frequent contributors to these magazines.

In many respects, the magazine was a unifying means of communication and, serving as a slower version of the telegraph, gave the far flung country a sense of common purpose after the Civil War. "The magazine was a vehicle which could present simultaneously identical facts, uniformly treated, in every locality. Men and women, North, South, East, and West, could read and judge the same materials, instead of forming their beliefs and reaching their decisions on the basis of varied accounts published in different sections and often distorted by regional prejudice."[6]

By the turn of the century, *Ladies Home Journal* passed a milestone with one million circulation and other major magazines of the day such as *Munsey's* and *McClure's* had circulations of more than a half million. Support for these publications came from manufacturers who were enjoying success with the distribution of national brands such as Quaker Oats and Uneeda Biscuit. It was very common for magazines of the time to carry 100 pages or more of advertising. For advertisers, magazines provided the only means of reaching buyers throughout the country.

Religious Publications Religious publications today represent a small part of the total media picture; but for a few decades after the Civil War, religious publications were the most influential medium. They were the forerunners of magazines. The post–Civil War period was a time of great religious revival, marking also the beginning of the temperance movement. Church groups issued their own publications, many

---

[6] James Playsted Wood, *Magazines in the United States* (New York: The Ronald Press, 1949), 99.

with circulations of no more than 1,000; the biggest ran to 400,000. But the combined circulation of the 400 religious publications was estimated at about 5 million.

Religious publications had great influence among their readers, a fact that patent-medicine advertisers recognized to such an extent that 75 percent of all religious-publication advertising was for patent medicines. (Many of the temperance papers carried advertisements for preparations that proved to be 40 percent alcohol. Today we call that 80 proof whiskey.)

Patent-Medicine Advertising

Patent-medicine advertisers had been around for a long time, and by the 1870s, they were the largest category of advertisers. After the Civil War, millions of men returned to their homes, North and South, many of them weak from wounds and exposure. The only kind of medical aid available to most of them was a bottle of patent medicine. As a result, patent-medicine advertising dominated the media toward the end of the nineteenth century, its fraudulent claims giving all advertising a bad name (Exhibit 1.4).

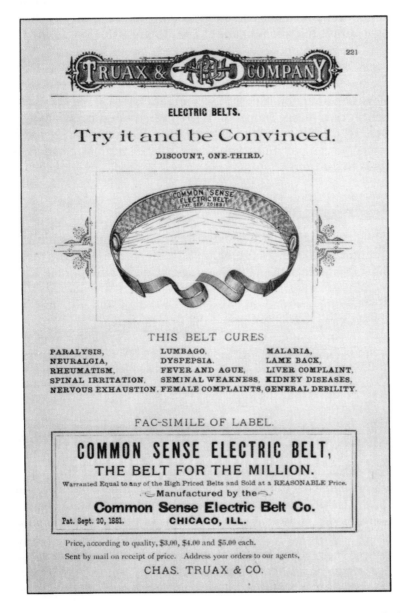

Exhibit

1.4

One of the more restrained ads in the patent-medicine category. Electricity, the new, magic power of the 1890s, was offered in a curative belt.

National Advertising Emerges

Meanwhile, legitimate manufacturers saw a new world of opportunity opening before them in the growth of the country. They saw the market for consumer products spreading. Railroads could now transport their merchandise to all cities between the Atlantic and Pacific coasts. The idea of packaging their own products carrying their own trademarks was enticing, particularly to grocery manufacturers: It allowed them to build their businesses on their reputations with the consumer instead of being subject to the caprices and pressures of jobbers, who had previously been their sole distributors. Magazines provided the missing link in marketing—magazine advertising easily spread the word about manufacturers' products all over the country; Quaker Oats cereal was among the first to go this marketing route, followed soon by many others (Exhibit 1.5).

This was the development of national advertising, as we call it today, in its broadest sense, meaning the advertising by a producer of his or her trademarked product whether or not it has attained national distribution.

Mass Production Appears

The words *chauffeur, limousine,* and *sedan* remind us that some of the earliest motor cars were made and publicized in France. In the United States, as in France, they were virtually handmade at first. But in 1913, Henry Ford decided that the way to build cars at low cost was to make them of standardized parts and bring the pieces to the worker on an assembly-line belt. He introduced to the world a mass-production technique and brought the price of a Ford down to $265 by 1925 (when a Hudson automobile cost $1,695 and the average weekly wage was $20). But in a free society, mass production is predicated upon mass selling, another name for advertising. Mass production makes possible countless products at a cost the mass of people can pay and about which they learn through advertising. America was quick to use both.

The Advertising Agency

While the media and the advertising that supported them were becoming major communication forces throughout the nineteenth century, we should not overlook the importance of the advertising agency during this period. The forerunners of the modern advertising agency were space brokers such as Volney Palmer who bought bulk newspaper space at a discount and then sold it to individual advertisers. By 1869 George Rowell published the first newspaper directory of rates and circulation. In 1917, the American Association of Advertising Agencies (4As) was founded with 111 charter members. Today, the 4As has more than 500 member agencies who place approximately 75 percent of all advertising dollars. Chapter 5 will be devoted to the role of the advertising agency.

AMERICA ENTERS THE TWENTIETH CENTURY

The moral atmosphere of business as it developed after the Civil War reflected laissez-faire policy at its extreme. High government officials were corrupted by the railroads; the public was swindled by flagrant stock market manipulations; embalmed beef was shipped to soldiers in the Spanish-American War. Advertising contributed to the immorality of business, with its patent-medicine ads offering to cure all the real and imagined human ailments. There was a "pleasing medicine to cure cancer," another to cure cholera. No promise of a quick cure was too wild, no falsehood too monstrous.

LEADERS IN NATIONAL ADVERTISING IN 1890's

A. P. W. Paper
Adams Tutti Frutti Gum
Æolian Company
American Express Traveler's Cheques
Armour Beef Extract
Autoharp
Baker's Cocoa
Battle Ax Plug Tobacco
Beardsley's Shredded Codfish
Beeman's Pepsin Gum
Bent's Crown Piano
Burlington Railroad
Burnett's Extracts
California Fig Syrup
Caligraph Typewriter
Castoria
A. B. Chase Piano
Chicago Great Western
Chicago, Milwaukee & St. Paul Railroad
Chicago Great Western Railway
Chocolat-Menier
Chickering Piano
Columbia Bicycles
Cleveland Baking Powder
Cottolene Shortening
Cook's Tours
Crown Pianos
Crescent Bicycles
Devoe & Raynolds Artist's Materials
Cuticura Soap
Derby Desks
De Long Hook and Eye
Diamond Dyes
Dixon's Graphite Paint
Dixon's Pencils
W. L. Douglas Shoes
Edison Mimeograph
Earl & Wilson Collars
Elgin Watches
Edison Phonograph
Everett Piano
Epps's Cocoa
Estey Organ
Fall River Line
Felt & Tarrant Comptometer
Ferry's Seeds
Fisher Piano
Fowler Bicycles
Franco American Soup
Garland Stoves
Gold Dust

Gold Dust Washing Powder
Gorham's Silver
Gramophone
Great Northern Railroad
H–O Breakfast Food
Hamburg American Line
Hammond Typewriter
Hartford Bicycle
Hartshorn's Shade Rollers
Heinz's Baked Beans
Peter Henderson & Co.
Hires' Root Beer
Hoffman House Cigars
Huyler's Chocolates
Hunyadi Janos
Ingersoll Watches
Ives & Pond Piano
Ivory Soap
Jaeger Underwear
Kirk's American Family Soap
Kodak
Liebeg's Extract of Beef
Lipton's Teas
Lowney's Chocolates
Lundborg's Perfumes
James McCutcheon Linens
Dr. Lyon's Toothpowder
Mason & Hamlin Piano
Mellin's Food
Mennen's Talcum Powder
Michigan Central Railroad
Monarch Bicycles
J. L. Mott Indoor Plumbing
Munsing Underwear
Murphy Varnish Company
New England Mincemeat
New York Central Railroad
North German Lloyd
Old Dominion Line
Oneita Knitted Goods
Packer's Tar Soap
Pearline Soap Powder
Peartltop Lamp Chimneys
Pears' Soap
Alfred Peats Wall Paper
Pettijohn's Breakfast Food
Pittsburgh Stogies
Pond's Extract
Postum Cereal
Prudential Insurance Co.
Quaker Oats

Exhibit

1.5

Leaders in national advertising in the 1890s.

Source: Reproduced from Presbrey, *History and Development of Advertising*, p. 361.

The Pure Food and Drug Act (1906)

As early as 1865, the *New York Herald-Tribune* had a touch of conscience and eliminated "certain classes" of medical advertising, those that used "repellent" words. In 1892, the *Ladies' Home Journal* was the first magazine to ban *all* medical advertising. The *Ladies' Home Journal* also came out with a blast by Mark Sullivan, revealing that codeine was being used in cold preparations and that a teething syrup had morphine as its base. Public outrage reached Congress, which in 1906 passed the Pure Food and Drug Act, the first federal law to protect the health of the public and the first to control advertising.

The Federal Trade Commission Act (1914)

The Federal Trade Commission's (FTC) original mandate was to protect one business owner from the unscrupulous practices of another. At the time that the FTC Act was passed, Congress and the public were increasingly alarmed over antitrust violations by big business. It was clear by the early 1900s that the antitrust actions of John D. Rockefeller and other business titans soon would drive their competitors into bankruptcy and create monopolies in vital industries such as oil and steel. Basically, the law stated that unfair business practices were now illegal and would no longer be tolerated.

By the 1930s, the FTC mandate was extended to offer protection to consumers as well as businesses. By combining both business and consumer protection activities, the FTC "seeks to ensure that the nation's markets function competitively, and are vigorous, efficient, and free of undue restrictions. The Commission also works to enhance the smooth operation of the marketplace by eliminating acts or practices that are unfair or deceptive."[7]

Chapter 25 discusses in detail not only the role of the FTC, but also other regulatory and legal bodies that are concerned with truthful advertising. In addition, the advertising industry's self-regulatory mechanisms will be examined. In Chapter 26, a number of criticisms of advertising's social effects will be addressed.

ADVERTISING COMES OF AGE

In about 1905, there emerged a class of advertising executives who recognized that their future lay in advertising legitimate products and in earning the confidence of the public in advertising. They gathered with like-minded peers in their communities to form advertising clubs.

These clubs subsequently became the Associated Advertising Clubs of the World (now the American Advertising Federation). In 1911, they launched a campaign to promote truth in advertising. In 1916, they formed vigilance committees that developed into today's Council of Better Business Bureaus, which continues to deal with many problems of unfair and deceptive business practices. In 1971, the bureaus became a part of the National Advertising Review Council, an all-industry effort at curbing misleading advertising. The main constituency of the American Advertising Federation continues to be the local advertising clubs. On its board are also officers of the other advertising associations.

In 1910, the Association of National Advertising Managers was born. It is now known as the Association of National Advertisers (ANA) and has about 500 members, including the foremost advertisers. Its purpose is to improve the effectiveness of advertising from the viewpoint of the advertiser. In 1917, the American Association of Advertising Agencies was formed to improve the effectiveness of advertising and of the advertising agency operation. Over 75 percent of all national advertising today is placed by its members, both large and small.

Printer's Ink Model Statute (1911) The act directed at fraudulent advertising, prepared and sponsored by *Printer's Ink*, which was the pioneer advertising magazine.

In 1911, *Printers' Ink*, the leading advertising trade paper for many years, prepared a model statute for state regulation of advertising, designed to "punish untrue, deceptive or misleading advertising." The ***Printers' Ink* Model Statute** has been adopted in its original or modified form by a number of states, where it is still operative.

Up to 1914, many publishers were carefree in their claims to circulation. Advertisers had no way of verifying what they got for their money. However, in that year, a group of advertisers, agencies, and publishers established an independent auditing organization, the Audit Bureau of Circulations (ABC), which conducts its

---

[7] From the Federal Trade Commission Mission Statement.

own audits and issues its own reports of circulation. Most major publications belong to the ABC, and an ABC circulation statement is highly regarded in media circles. The ABC reports of circulation are fully accredited in most areas. (Today, similar auditing organizations are operating in 25 countries throughout the world.)

In June 1916, President Woodrow Wilson, addressing the Associated Advertising Clubs of the World convention in Philadelphia, was the first president to give public recognition to the importance of advertising. Advertising had come of age!

Advertising in World War I

World War I marked the first time that advertising was used as an instrument of direct social action. Advertising agencies turned from selling consumer goods to arousing patriotic sentiment, selling government bonds, encouraging conservation, and promoting a number of other war-related activities. One of the largest agencies of the era, N.W. Ayer & Sons, prepared and placed ads for the first three Liberty Loan drives and donated much of its commission to the drive.[8]

Soon these efforts by individual agencies were coordinated by the Division of Advertising of the Committee of Public Information, a World War I government propaganda office. This wartime experience convinced people that advertising could be a useful tool in communicating ideas as well as in selling products.

The 1920s

The 1920s began with a minidepression and ended with a crash. When the war ended, makers of army trucks were able to convert quickly to commercial trucks. Firestone spent $2 million advertising "Ship by Truck." With the industry profiting by the good roads that had been built, truck production jumped from 92,000 in 1916 to 322,000 in 1920. Door-to-door delivery from manufacturer to retailer spurred the growth of chain stores, which led, in turn, to supermarkets and self-service stores.

The passenger car business boomed, too, and new products appeared in profusion: electric refrigerators, washing machines, electric shavers, and, most incredible of all, the radio. Installment selling made hard goods available to all. And all the products needed advertising.

Introduction of Radio   Radio was invented by Guglielmo Marconi in 1895 as the first practical system of wireless communication. In its early years, radio was viewed as a means of maritime communication using Morse code and, with the first voice transmission in 1906, as a diversion for hobbyists. Prior to 1920, few investors saw any commercial potential for the medium. KDKA, the first commercial station, was established in Pittsburgh by Westinghouse to provide programming to buyers of its radio sets.

The modern era of radio as a mass medium can be traced to the heavyweight title fight between Jack Dempsey and Georges Carpentier in 1921. It was estimated that some 200,000 listeners tuned in to the fight and by the time Dempsey knocked out Carpentier in the fourth round, radio had become a national phenomenon.[9]

Less than five years after Dempsey claimed the title, the first radio network was founded by AT&T (with its sale a year later in 1927, it became NBC). Today, Americans average more than five radio sets per household and it is difficult to find an automobile or workplace without at least one set. Today, radio advertisers spend more than $15 billion annually.

---

[8]Ralph M. Hower, *The History of an Advertising Agency* (Cambridge, MA: Harvard University Press, 1949), 180.
[9] Edward Robinson, "Businessman of the century," *Fortune*, 6 September 1999, 227.

The 1930s Depression

The stock market crash had a shattering effect on our entire economy: Millions of people were thrown out of work; business failures were widespread; banks were closing all over the country (there were no insured deposits in those days). There was no Social Security, no food stamps, no unemployment insurance. Who had ever heard of pensions for blue-collar workers? There were bread lines, long ones; and well-dressed men on street corners were selling apples off the tops of boxes for five cents (Exhibit 1.6). The Southwest was having its worst windstorms, which carried off the topsoil and killed livestock and crops. Farmers abandoned their farms, packed their families and furniture into old pickup trucks, and headed west. (John Steinbeck wrote his *Grapes of Wrath* around this experience.) The government finally launched the Works Progress Administration (WPA) for putting people to work on public-service projects, but the bread lines continued to be long.

Out of that catastrophe came three developments that affect advertising to this day:

1. Radio emerged as a major advertising medium. In March 1933, President Franklin D. Roosevelt made the first inaugural address ever to be broadcast by radio, giving heart and hope to a frightened people. His line "We have nothing to fear except fear itself," spoken to the largest audience that had ever at one time heard the voice of one man, became historic. In one broadcast, radio showed its power to move a nation. Radio had arrived as a major national advertising medium. It quickly became part of the life of America. The 1930s began with 612 stations and 12 million sets and ended with 814 stations and 51 million sets.

2. The Robinson-Patman Act (1936) was passed to help protect the small merchant from the unfair competition of the big store with its huge buying power. This law is still operative today.

3. Congress passed the Wheeler-Lea Act (1938), giving the FTC more direct and sweeping powers over advertising, and the Federal Food, Drug and Cosmetic Act (1938), giving the administration authority over the labeling and packaging of these products. These laws, which are discussed in Chapter 25, are a pervasive consideration in advertising today and a forerunner of the government's increasing interest in advertising.

Advertising During World War II

With World War II, industry turned to the production of war goods. Because all civilian material was severely rationed, many firms curtailed their advertising. Others felt that though they were out of merchandise, they were not out of business, and they wanted to keep the public's goodwill, so they applied their advertising efforts to rendering public service. The Goodyear Tire & Rubber Company's advice on how to take care of tires in days of product shortages was akin to ads that were to appear in 1974 and 1975 during the Arab oil embargo.

THE WAR ADVERTISING COUNCIL

War Advertising Council Founded in 1942 to promote World War II mobilization. It later evolved into the Advertising Council.

By the 1940s, the power and persuasive ability of advertising was acknowledged by both businesses and consumers. Therefore, it is not surprising that government leaders would turn to the advertising industry to gain public cooperation in the war effort. The **War Advertising Council** was formed in 1942. The first campaign from the Council was developed by J. Walter Thompson to encourage women to enter the workforce. The "Rosie the Riveter" campaign successfully overcame prejudices toward women in the workforce and added significantly to a labor pool depleted by

SPECIAL	PRICES TODAY	PRICES A YEAR AGO	CHANGE IN PRICE
POTATOES MAINES 100 lb. bag — PRINCE EDWARD ISLES 90 lb. bag	$2.35	3.17	—82¢
PEACHES CALIFORNIA	2 lge. cans 25¢	2 for 46¢	—21¢
UNEEDA BAKERS MACAROON SANDWICH	3 pkgs. 25¢	NEW PRODUCT	....
STRING BEANS STANDARD QUALITY	3 No. 2 cans 28¢	3 for 30¢	— 2¢
TOMATOES STANDARD QUALITY	3 No. 2 cans 20¢	3 for 30¢	—10¢
AUNT JEMIMA PANCAKE FLOUR	2 pkgs. 25¢	2 for 30¢	— 5¢
AUNT JEMIMA BUCKWHEAT FLOUR	2 pkgs. 25¢	2 for 34¢	— 9¢
DEL MONTE FRUIT SALAD	lge. can 29¢	41¢	—12¢
MILK WHITEHOUSE BRAND	3 tall cans 22¢	3 for 23¢	— 1¢
CATSUP BLUE LABEL	sm. bot. 13¢	15¢	— 2¢
CATSUP BLUE LABEL	lge. bot. 19¢	23¢	— 4¢
ORANGE JUICE	2 .. 15¢	2 for 20¢	— 5¢

	PRICES TODAY	A YEAR AGO	CHANGE IN PRICE
Red Circle Coffee....................lb.	29c	39c	—10¢
Eight O'Clock Coffee.................lb. ..	25c	35c	—10¢
Bokar Coffee.....................lb. tin...	35c	45c	—10¢
Grandmother's Bread..........20 ounce loaf.	7c	8c	— 1¢
Jack Frost Sugar...........5 lb. cotton sack...	25c	29c	— 4¢
Pure Lard.........................lb....	15c	17c	— 2¢
Nucoa...........................lb....	23c	25c	— 2¢
Salt....................4 lb. sack ..	8c	10c	— 2¢
Pea Beans..............lb. package	10c	17c	— 7¢
Lima Beans.............lb. package..	17c	23c	— 6¢
Sunnyfield Flour............24½ lb. sack...	75c	89c	—14¢
Sunsweet Prunes............2 lb. package..	15c	29c	—14¢
Puffed Wheat...............package..	12c	13c	— 1¢
Puffed Rice ....package..	14c	15c	— 1¢

FRESH MEATS & FOWL AT A&P MARKETS

	PRICES TODAY	A YEAR AGO	CHANGE IN PRICE
PORK LOINS HALF OR WHOLE ......lb....	25¢	31c	— 6¢
Prime Ribs of Beef (CUT FROM FIRST 6 RIBS) ....lb..	35c	41c	— 6¢
Sirloin Steak ....lb. ..	49c	55c	— 6¢
Loin Lamb Chops ....lb. ..	35c	51c	—16¢
Roasting Chickens (3½ to 4 lbs.) ... lb..	39c	42c	— 3¢

wartime service. Among the many themes and projects promoted by the Council were conservation of items such as fuel, fat, and tires, planting victory gardens, buying war bonds, promoting rationing, and encouraging communications from home to our troops. War Bond sales efforts that resulted in the selling of $35 billion worth of bonds and a "victory garden" initiative that encouraged the planting of some 50 million gardens were among the most successful wartime campaigns of the Council.

Advertising's success during the war moved President Franklin Roosevelt to urge peacetime continuance of the organization as the Advertising Council. Today, the Council annually produces more than 35 campaigns ranging from environmental issues, educational concerns, family preservation, and anti-drinking promotions. Each year member advertising agencies create campaigns on a pro bono basis and media outlets donate more than $1 billion in time and space for Council messages. During the last 25 years, Council campaigns have been instrumental in addressing crucial issues to Americans. In doing so, it has created a number of slogans and characters that have become advertising icons such as Smokey the Bear and McGruff the Crime Dog.

Advertising after World War II to 1975: The Word Was Growth

Advertising, like every aspect of American society, took a backseat to the war during the early 1940s. The advertising that did run was largely confined to reminding the public of trademarks and logos in anticipation of the end of the war. Even institutional advertising (e.g., "Lucky Strike Green Has Gone to War") had a wartime or patriotic theme.

With the end of World War II, advertising and consumer goods began to reach out to a public ready to get on with their lives and spend, spend, spend. With ". . . the end of the war pent-up demand led to an unprecedented acceleration in the rate of growth of advertising media investment—so much so that ad media volume by 1950 was almost three times what it had been only ten years earlier!"[10]

By 1950 Americans were living better than at any time in their history. Moreover, it is doubtful that any nation had ever experienced the rate of economic expansion as the United States during the decade after World War II. Consumer goods purchases grew at an unprecedented rate and advertising was the fuel that fed this consumer buying spree. In 1947 America discovered television and began a love affair that still continues. From its crude beginnings in a few major markets, television set ownership grew from less than 10 percent household penetration in 1950 to more than 90 percent in 1960. At the same time, television's advertising share increased 400 percent from 4 percent to 17 percent. As millions of viewers gave up playing bridge, going to the movies, and even talking to each other to tune in to Milton Berle and *The $64,000 Question*, national advertising dollars poured into television.

By the 1960s, television had forever changed both magazines and radio as advertising media. Television also had major influences on both sports and politics. In its insatiable appetite for programming, television brought thousands of hours of sports into the living room. It was the lure of television dollars that created the American Football League and the American Basketball Association and it allowed even mediocre players to become millionaires.

But perhaps television of the period had its greatest impact on politics. As television's popularity continued to grow, it soon became apparent to politicians that the same formula used so successfully in selling soap and cigarettes might be

---

[10] Herbert Zeltner, "Proliferation, localization, specialization mark media trends in past fifty years," *Advertising Age*, 30 April 1980, 148.

adapted to selling candidates. Rosser Reeves is generally credited with introducing the 60-second commercial to American politics during the 1960 election campaign of Dwight Eisenhower. In a series of commercials, Reeves converted the reserved, rather stiff and awkward candidate into the personable "Man from Abilene." For better or worse, politics would never be the same again.

The Figures Also Said Growth   Between 1950 and 1973,[11] the population of the United States increased by 38 percent, while disposable personal income increased by 327 percent. New housing starts went up by 47 percent, energy consumption by 121 percent, college enrollments by 136 percent, automobile registrations by 151 percent, telephones in use by 221 percent, number of outboard motors sold by 242 percent, retail sales by 250 percent, families owning two or more cars by 300 percent, frozen-food production by 655 percent, number of airline passengers by 963 percent, homes with dishwashers by 1.043 percent, and homes with room air-conditioners by 3,662 percent.

Advertising not only contributed to the growth but was part of it, rising from an expenditure of $5,780 million in 1950 to $28,320 million in 1975—a growth of 490 percent. There were many developments in advertising during this time:

- In 1956, the Department of Justice ruled that advertising agencies could negotiate fees with clients rather than adhere to the then-required 15 percent commission on all media placed. This encouraged the growth of specialized companies, such as independent media-buying services, creative-only agencies, and in-house agencies owned by advertisers.
- The voice of the consumer became more powerful.
- Congress passed an act limiting outdoor advertising alongside interstate highways. Cigarette advertising was banned from television.
- The FTC introduced corrective advertising by those who had made false or misleading claims. Comparison advertising (mentioning competitors by name) was deemed an acceptable form of advertising.
- The magazine-publishing world saw the disappearance of the old dinosaurs— *The Saturday Evening Post, Collier's,* and *Women's Home Companion.* There was no vacuum at the newsstand, however, for there was an immediate upsurge in magazines devoted to special interests.
- Newspapers felt the effect of the shift of metropolitan populations to the suburbs. Freestanding inserts became an important part of newspaper billings.
- Radio took a dive when television came along. The story of how it came out of that drastic decline is a good example of turning disadvantages into advantages.
- Direct-response advertising soared from $900 million in 1950 to $8 billion in 1980, reflecting the growth of direct marketing.
- The two biggest developments to emerge were television and electronic data processing. Television has changed America's life as well as the world of advertising. Data-processing systems have brought before the eyes of management a wealth of organized information. This, together with the syndicated research services, has revolutionized the entire marketing process and the advertising-media operation.

Advertising in the Fragmented 1980s

As we have seen in this chapter, advertising is rarely a stable business. It changes with business conditions, technology, and the social and cultural times. In some cases, it has a role in causing these changes; in others, it simply follows. The 1980s

---

[11] We select 1973 as the last full year before the high inflation brought on by the oil embargo of 1974.

were a period of significant change in American society, and certainly advertising was affected by many of these changes.

Let's briefly discuss some of the major developments during this period:

1. *New technology.* Changes in technology and diversification of the communication system had profound effects on advertising during this period. Cable television, home video recorders, a proliferation of specialized magazines, the success of direct mail and home shopping techniques, and the growth of sales promotion changed the practice of advertising in fundamental ways. The advertising practitioners of today are much more likely than their predecessors to be marketing generalists, competent in evaluating research and understanding the psychology of consumer behavior.

2. *Audience fragmentation.* The 1980s may have marked the end of the traditional mass market. Advertisers no longer identified markets by households or size, but rather by demographics and number of heavy users of specific products. Television, which at one time offered three channels, now offered fifty; newspapers, rather than appealing to a single homogeneous readership, were positioned more as cafeterias where readers choose only what they want to read; and the VCR and home computers began to let the audience control the media.

3. *Consolidation.* Paradoxically, as the media and audience proliferated, ownership of brands, ad agencies, and media was consolidated among a few giant companies. Firms such as Procter & Gamble, American Home Products, and Philip Morris provided corporate umbrellas for dozens, even hundreds, of separate brands. With their billion-dollar-plus budgets, they held tremendous control over the advertising agencies vying for their accounts. Like their clients, ad agencies also merged into so-called mega-agencies designed to offer greater service to these giant conglomerates. Often as not, these agency mergers led to as many headaches as benefits, starting with unmanageable client conflicts. Finally, the media were increasingly under the control of fewer and fewer communication companies. The Turner empire of cable networks, Time Warner's ownership of a bewildering array of media, and Gannett's interest in everything from newspapers to TV production were only a few examples of the changing media landscape during the 1980s.

4. *Credit.* Perhaps the greatest long-term legacy of the 1980s was the buy now, pay later mentality that pervaded every facet of American life from the federal government to the individual household budget. The leveraged buyouts of corporate America and the overuse of consumer credit created an atmosphere in which living within one's income was an illusion. By 1990, when companies and consumers began the slow process of paying for the excesses of the past decade, advertising was often the first victim of any cutbacks. Media saw advertising revenues fall; advertising was harder to sell even with deep discounts; merchants began to deal with a reluctant consumer more interested in deals than fancy advertising; and some of the most famous names in American business faced serious trouble, if not outright bankruptcy.

Advertising and the Twenty-First Century

If the past 25 years have been the age of television, will the next 25 be the age of the Internet? In the past, advertising executives have been able to predict with some accuracy significant trends that impacted the industry. As we look ahead, we find it is much more difficult to determine the related and codependent elements that will determine the future of advertising. Realizing that predicting the future of media and advertising is precarious, let's briefly examine several of the trends that will define advertising in the twenty-first century.

One of the most talked-about phenomena in advertising media is convergence, that is, the combining of several technologies or services to provide a unique synergism. For example, convergence is the blending of technologies such as television, cable, and the computer to create Internet interactivity with the technical speed of cable and the sight, sound, and motion of television. Such convergence is characterized by the ability to reach audiences on a one-to-one basis and greater control of communication channels by the audience.

Obviously, more personal communication with prospects is an exceptional advantage for advertisers. However, offsetting this advantage of narrowly defined audiences is a loss of control over the communication process. Rather than listeners or readers having to accept whatever advertising accompanies their favorite medium, they now determine what messages they receive. The fact that interactive media becomes an invited guest has resulted in a new concept of advertising called *permission marketing*. The term refers to the fact that when consumers control communication channels, they determine which messages, including advertising, they will receive. Presumably, permission is granted because the advertiser has a product or service that either has solved a consumer's problems in the past or has the potential to do so in the future.

With the advent of permission marketing, companies will find that brand loyalty is crucial. It will be harder to develop new markets by sheer weight of advertising. On the other hand, smaller companies with superior products will have a much better chance than in the past to gain market share by providing unique product benefits. If current technology has put us on the doorstep of customized communication, can customized products be far away? Procter & Gamble (P&G) is one of the leaders in studying the feasibility of interactive marketing. P&G is looking into the ways in which it can customize even common household products. For example, by dealing one-on-one with loyal customers, the company might tailor laundry detergent for the water hardness, mineral content, and fragrance preferences of each household. In exchange for product loyalty (perhaps through long-term purchase agreements), customers are guaranteed a product developed specifically for them.[12]

Another area of concern for advertisers in coming years will be globalization and diversity. One only has to look at the population projections for Latin America, the Far East, and Africa to see the magnitude for potential sales of virtually any goods, but particularly consumer package goods. The smallest increase in the market share of Coca-Cola, Tide detergent, Huggies diapers, Gerber Baby Food, or Charmin toilet tissue in India or China would create a profit windfall for these brands.

Understanding the language, culture, economy, and political environment of countries throughout the world is already a prerequisite for most marketing executives. It will become even more important as new global markets are opened to foreign investment. Multinational marketers will find that a locally oriented strategy for global marketing is essential. Corporations such as Coca-Cola, Sony, Ford, and Procter & Gamble will continue to increase their expansion into every part of the world. However, global strategies increasingly will be geared to each country or region of the world.

An advertiser does not have to go abroad to see the necessity for marketing plans that consider a diversified marketplace. Marketing executives and advertisers must realize that in our own country Hispanic, Asian-American, and African-American consumers are part of the fabric of the country and must be reached through messages that are sensitive to their needs. This sensitivity means supporting minority media owners with advertising dollars, hiring a diverse workforce in

---

[12] Jack Neff, "E-goods," *Advertising Age: The Next Century,* 1999, 66.

the advertising industry, creating advertising and commercials that fairly reflect the various ethnic and cultural groups within this country and, when appropriate, developing products specifically for these markets. Chapter 24 discusses the globalization of advertising as well as the need for greater sensitivity to the issue of diversity in domestic advertising.

SUMMARY

Advertising is currently undergoing fundamental changes. A few years ago, the development of e-commerce was looked upon as a new and revolutionary chapter in retailing, advertising, marketing, and even social interaction. Today, many of the most enthusiastic proponents of the "new media" are taking a second look at issues such as profitability, customer service, and product satisfaction.

While new media entrepreneurs are facing an uncertain future, it is clear that the next decade will bring fundamental changes to marketing and mass communication not seen since the advent of high-speed presses and the introduction of broadcasting. Nevertheless, it is difficult to determine exactly when and in what form this new marketing and media revolution will take place. In the current edition of this text, we have tried to explain the current practice of advertising while offering insights into this fast-changing field.

REVIEW

1. What is the primary regulatory body concerned with advertising?
2. Discuss the four broad periods of advertising.
3. Why was the introduction of radio so important to advertisers?
4. What role did national brands play in the growth of advertising?
5. How did federal legislation such as the Sherman Act and the Pure Food and Drug Act indicate a change in the relationship between advertisers and consumers?
6. How did the railroad contribute to the growth of national brands and media?

TAKE IT TO THE NET

We invite you to visit the Russell/Lane page on the Prentice Hall Web site at **www.prenhall.com/myphlip** for end-of-chapter exercises and applications.

Chapter 2

Roles of Advertising

Advertising is a marketing communication tool used to convey information about products, services, or ideas to a targeted audience. Specific advertising executions vary widely, but regardless of message content, media vehicles, or the precise objective of a campaign, it must be measured against communication goals. Advertising is used by companies to reach customers on a global basis or around the corner. After reading this chapter you will understand:

>> how advertising is used as a marketing communication tool
>> advertising and its role in the marketing mix
>> the primary objectives of advertising
>> advertising in consumer and trade promotion
>> advertising of ideas and nonprofit organizations

Advertising is among the most flexible and adaptive elements of marketing communication. It is used for a number of purposes by industrial giants, nonprofit organizations, and the smallest retail establishments. While advertising has undergone a number of changes in recent years, successful advertisers must still ask four basic questions:

1. What is my advertising being asked to accomplish?
2. Who are the prime prospects for my product?
3. What message am I trying to convey?
4. What media are best suited for my message and my prospects?

This chapter answers these questions, which will vary widely depending on the product, consumers, distribution channels, advertising budget, competition, and a host of other factors. However, the key to successful advertising is to answer each of these basic questions within the context of a firm's marketing plan. The advertising program must be geared to accomplish the business priorities set out in a company's overall strategy. This means that communication decisions must be made as part of an overall marketing strategy, not as an afterthought.

> To make key communication decisions while ignoring the impact of strategy is to make decisions in a vacuum and risk being blind-sided by the realities of the marketplace. . . the failure to make communications part of the strategic thinking is like trying to run a car with three wheels.[1]

While advertising should be executed as part of the basic marketing plan, it must be viewed as a *communication* tool. When we stray from this fundamental concept, we are placing unrealistic burdens on advertising and setting ourselves up for failure. Let's look at the steps in a typical marketing plan. As we do, consider those aspects that can be addressed by marketing communication and in what ways communication could complement the implementation of the plan:[2]

1. *Overall goal(s) of the plan.* Usually, marketing goals are expressed in financial terms such as expected sales revenues at the end of the first year or percentage increases over previous years.
2. *Marketing objectives.* Here the objective and rationale of the plan is stated. For example, we may want to show a significant increase in market share relative to specific competitors.
3. *Marketing strategy.* The strategy outlines the steps to achieve our goals and objectives. We might suggest a greater investment in advertising or promotion or a switch in distribution outlets. The strategy offers only a general overview of primary marketing considerations.
4. *Situational analysis.* This analysis is a statement of the product benefits and the pertinent data available concerning sales trends, competitive environment, and industry forecasts.
5. *Problems and opportunities.* At this point, we outline the major problems and opportunities facing the brand. For example, a major manufacturer of lawn tools found that it was losing sales because its major competitors had signed exclusive contracts with major retail chains. However, the company soon found that there were numerous opportunities to sell through local, independent retailers who did not have access to several brands sold exclusively through chains.
6. *Financial plan.* The financial plan is an outline of the expected profit or loss that will be experienced over various time frames. It is here that the company projects the extent of investments that will be made before a product shows a provide. As we have seen recently, a number of e-commerce companies grossly underestimated the extent of this investment and potential profitability.
7. *Research.* Ideally, a company wants to answer questions from available data, but sometimes the marketing plan suggests that primary research is needed. In these cases, a research plan must be suggested. In any case, the research section should include how the plan will be evaluated on the basis of measurable results.

---

[1]Gary Grates, "Of communications and root canals," reprint from GCI Boxenbaum Grates.
[2]Adapted from David W. Schropher, *What Every Account Executive Should Know About a Marketing Plan* (New York: American Association of Advertising Agencies, 1990).

In the ideal situation, advertising objectives flow directly from the marketing strategy. For example, Lever Brothers developed the following marketing strategy for Dove soap.

> The name "Dove" fits a beauty bar. The oval shape is more feminine than the traditional soap rectangle. Dove comes in a box, like a cosmetic, instead of a paper wrapper. It is clearly a product for women.

From this basic marketing strategy, the creative theme was to demonstrate that Dove "creams your skin while you wash." The basic marketing and creative strategies have remained essentially the same since 1957.[3]

ADVERTISING AND PROFITABILITY

While advertising alone rarely creates sales, like any marketing function, it must demonstrate a contribution to profits. Generally, this contribution is expressed as the **return on investment** (ROI), which measures revenues against expenditure of resources.[4]

The measure of advertising's contribution to profitability can be shown in three steps:

1. *Advertising and brand awareness.* Research suggests, if not causality, a strong relationship between brand awareness and market share (see Exhibit 2.1). Perhaps the most significant role that advertising plays is its contribution to the creation of brand awareness. Generally, studies show that the more businesses spend on advertising and promotion as a percentage of sales, the higher their levels of brand awareness.

return on investment (ROI)
One measure of the efficiency of a company is the rate of return (profits) achieved by a certain level of investment in various business functions including advertising.

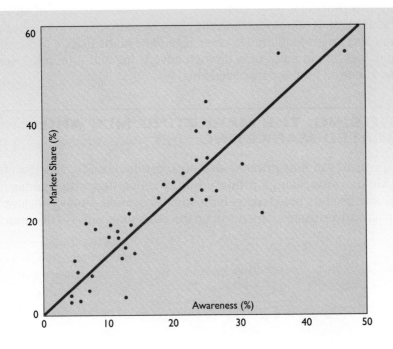

Exhibit

2.1

The relationship between brand awareness and market share is strong.

From: Cahners Advertising Research Report, No. 2000.6, p. 2.

---

[3]Kenneth Roman and Jane Maas, *How to Advertise* (New York: St. Martin's Press, 1976), 2.
[4]This section is adapted from "Brand Awareness as a Tool for Profitability," from *Cahners Advertising Research Report*, No. 2000.6.

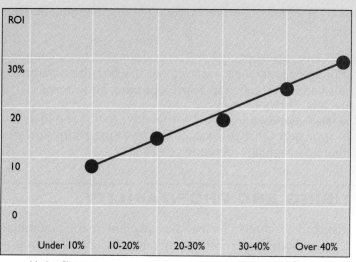

ROI

30%

20

10

0

Under 10%   10-20%   20-30%   30-40%   Over 40%

Market Share

Exhibit

2.2

The relationship between
market share and pretax ROI.

*From: Cahners Advertising Research
Report,* No. 2000.6, p. 3.

2. *Market share and return on investment.* The market share for a brand has been shown to be one of the primary contributors to ROI (see Exhibit 2.2). Businesses demonstrating high levels of market share benefit from economies of scale in production, marketing, and so forth, which has the effect of increasing profitability. By producing and marketing greater product volume, these businesses tend to be more efficient and have lower costs. The conversion of brand awareness into market share and finally into profitability is shown in Exhibit 2.3.

Clearly, this process is not a guarantee of success. The quality of advertising, continuing product development, and the entry of competitors into a market will all have an effect on profitability. However, regardless of the market circumstances, maintaining high brand awareness through advertising and promotion demands continuing attention from top management.

ADVERTISING, THE MARKETING MIX, AND INTEGRATED MARKETING

marketing mix
Combination of marketing
functions, including advertising,
used to sell a product.

Marketing consists of four primary elements: product, price, distribution, and communication. Advertising's primary role is concerned with building brand awareness and product preference—both communication functions. However, in many respects, advertising is dependent on the other three areas of the "**marketing**

Exhibit

2.3

How brand awareness
aids profitability (the
sequence of events).

*From: Cahners Advertising Research
Report,* No. 2000.6, p. 6.

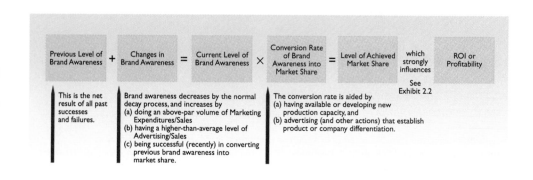

mix" for its success.[5] Not only is advertising dependent on success in areas such as distribution and pricing, but, increasingly, it works in concert with other promotional and sales tools.

To understand the complex relationships among advertising and other forms of marketing communications options, we need to briefly review the following four elements:

1. *Personal selling.* Personal communication is the most effective means of persuading someone. However, it is also the most expensive and impractical as a means of mass selling. Personal selling is most often used as a follow-up to mass communication to close the sale or develop a long-term relationship that will eventually result in a sale. In business-to-business marketing this means opening doors for personal salespeople and in consumer marketing it means steering customers to retailers where the final sales takes place.

2. *Sales promotion.* Sales promotion is an extra incentive for a customer to make an immediate purchase. Sales promotion may consist of a special sales price, a cents-off coupon, a colorful point-of-purchase display, or a chance to win a trip to Hawaii in a sweepstakes. Whereas advertising creates awareness and brand preference, sales promotion's goal is to close the sale. Ideally, advertising builds long-term brand loyalty, while promotion acts as a short-term boost to sales.

3. *Public relations.* According to the Public Relations Society of America, "**Public relations** helps an organization and its publics adapt mutually to each other." Public relations is one of the most familiar forms of business communication, but only in recent years has it been fully integrated into the marketing communication plans of most companies. Public relations differs from advertising in that the advertiser directly pays for exposure of the message, controls in what medium and how often it will appear, and controls the exact content of the message. The public relations communicator can influence all these elements, but has no direct control over them. However, public relations has the advantage of being presented as news rather than promotion messages and therefore often has more credibility with the audience. Some marketing executives view public relations as useful to set the stage for advertising, especially for new product introductions. "Publicity is the nail, advertising is the hammer. Publicity creates the credentials that provide the credibility for the advertising."[6]

> **public relations**
> Communication with various internal and external publics to create an image for a product or corporation.

4. *Advertising.* Advertising is a message paid for by an identified sponsor and usually delivered through some medium of mass communication. Advertising is persuasive communication. It is not neutral; it is not unbiased; it says, "I am going to sell you a product or an idea." Advertising is increasingly dealing with sophisticated consumers who understand the advertising process and its goals. And yet, even with the number of advertisements consumers are exposed to each day, it remains the major promotional method that buyers cite as a motivation to try new products and services (see Exhibit 2.4).

In the past, the various promotional techniques, including advertising, were treated as discrete elements of the marketing plan and often little attention was given to coordinating the overall communication process. Advertising was handled by an advertising agency under the direction of a marketing vice president; public relations was done in-house or outsourced to a public relations firm; and personal selling was directed by the sales department. The not unexpected result was that often the various elements of marketing communication spoke to consumers with different voices.

---

[5] A term coined in the early 1930s by Professor Neil H. Borden of the Harvard Business School to include in the marketing process such factors as distribution, advertising, personal selling, and pricing.
[6] Al Ries and Laura Ries, "First do some great publicity," *Advertising Age*, 8 February 1999, 42.

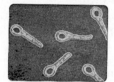

MUSIC UP AND UNDER THROUGHOUT ANNCR V/O:These captivating

designs are not part of a painting,

they are part of you.

For all our scientific knowledge,

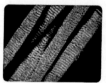

the wondrous intricacies of the human body

never cease to amaze and inspire us.

We also understand

that every part of you

goes to form a beautiful whole

that should never be treated as anything less.

Georgetown University Medical Center.

The Art of Medicine.

Exhibit

2.4

New medical technology is presented in an interesting manner.

Courtesy: Howard, Merrell & Partners.

---

integrated marketing communication (IMC) The joint planning, execution, and coordination of all areas of marketing communication.

In the 1980s, a number of companies began to organize the total communication program under a concept known as **integrated marketing communications (IMC).** While the implementation of IMC varied with individual firms, its core mission was to integrate and coordinate all forms of marketing communication produced by a company. The integration of all communication functions leads to another benefit. IMC allows a central department to gather marketing information and research from numerous sources at a centralized decision point.

The IMC of the 1980s was a much needed and welcomed innovation in marketing communication. However, as we move into the 2000s, the demand for even greater integration of marketing communication has become apparent. Media fragmentation, more narrowly targeted prospects, and the prospect of generally available interactive technology have combined to create a complex promotional landscape.

This new promotional environment has created significant uncertainty for both advertisers and their customers. "It's by no means clear what people want to do where, which technologies to bet on, what alliances to pursue. Do people want stock quotes on their cell phones? E-mail on a TV screen? Interactive game shows? Smart refrigerators?"[7]

Predicting the future role that advertising will play in the marketing communication mix is difficult. However, it is obvious that two areas of the mix will change dramatically in the near term. Both will have monumental significance for the practice of advertising.

1. Neither businesses nor their customers will make relevant distinctions among the channels over which they receive a company's messages.

---

[7]Marc Gunther, "These guys want it all," *Fortune*, 7 February 2000, 78.

2. The consumer will have significant control of the communication channel. In a day of on-line, one-to-one promotions, fragmented communication, interactive television, and wireless communication we must now spend our time finding products for our customers instead of finding customers for our products.[8]

In the opinion of many forward-looking marketing executives, we are spending too much time debating technology. It is clear that the media of the next decade will be digital, interactive, and wireless.

> Marketers . . . should be platform agnostic. It's not that important to handicap what sort of cable and Internet service America Online will deliver in 2005 . . . . It's more important for marketers to integrate interactive programs across their marketing and advertising. The future is not about interactive marketing. It's about marketing.[9]

Advertising will have to find a niche among competing means of reaching customers. In a world of interactive media, the consumers will choose what they are willing to listen to. The click of the Internet user determines whether or not a company will have an opportunity to deliver its sales message.

We will soon be at a point where the convergence of media and messages will create a holistic communication mix. In this mix, defining types of communication or even media is both difficult and, to a great extent, irrelevant. For example, is an on-line newspaper viewed through WebTV a print medium? If a person buys a product as a result of seeing an advertisement in the on-line version of a magazine does anyone care? As one marketing executive observed, "Research, promotion, advertising and PR 'all have their place,' what's been absent is a disciplined examination of consumers and their specific needs, versus what you're going to cram down their throats."[10]

Obviously, agencies cannot operate in this new world of integrated marketing without significant adjustments. IMC is client driven, but agencies must adapt to service those companies that have adopted the IMC concept while simultaneously serving traditionally organized clients. One approach to integration used by some agencies is to create separate units to handle clients' needs beyond traditional advertising. These units will service clients in areas such as sales promotion, direct response, and product sampling as well as advertising.

As integration of the various promotional functions becomes more typical, the advertising person of the future will be required to make decisions about the role that both advertising and other promotional tools will play in any particular campaign. This assessment will include an evaluation of marketing goals and strategies, identification of prime prospects, product characteristics, and the budget available for all areas of the communication mix.

ADVERTISING AS AN INSTITUTION

Throughout this text, we will discuss the various functions of advertising. However, before we examine the basic advertising strategies and tactics used by businesses to promote their products and services, we need to briefly explore advertising from an economic and social perspective. The basic function of advertising is to disseminate product information that allows consumers to know that products exist, give

---

[8]Seth Godin, "Three unexpected side effects of permission," *Marketing News*, 24 September 1999, 13.
[9]Bradley Johnson, "It's just the future," *Advertising Age: The Interactive Future*, 11.
[10]Betsey Spethmann, "Procter's gamble," *Promo*, July 1999, 48.

them information about competing brands, and, finally, permit consumers to make intelligent choices among product options.

However, beyond these strictly utilitarian functions, advertising is both a persuasive agent and a communicator of social standards and mores. For example, product differentiation includes much more than a list of the physical attributes of products. If the communication of physical product characteristics was advertising's only role, then it would be largely confined to technical lists of product ingredients. Toothpaste advertising would offer consumers the chemical components used to whiten teeth rather than the prospect of an enhanced social life.

Ideally, advertisers would like for their products to have physical product attributes to set their brands apart from others. Yet, in most product categories, differences are often very slight and, in these cases, differentiation is often made on the basis of psychological rather than physical attributes.

> Not all product differentiation has been of a material character. Through advertising, psychological values have been built into a particular brand which is physically different from some other brand only in name and package design. Through advertising the psychological values of products are often developed and enhanced. The orchid is physically comparable to the iris, but the psychological qualities are certainly different.[11]

Advertising has an ethical and moral responsibility to provide product information honestly. On the other hand, it is obvious that consumers make purchase decisions on the basis of psychological and social factors as well as strictly utilitarian considerations. People buy Cadillacs instead of Chevrolets, not just for basic differences in transportation needs, but because the Cadillac brand satisfies a need for prestige, social status, and a number of other psychological factors.

It can be argued that advertising creates these wants (as opposed to needs). But, in fact, advertising mirrors the society in which it functions and over time probably contributes to subtle changes in the mores and behavior of the public who are exposed to it.

Advertising's role as an institution has been studied for most of this century by both critics and proponents. These perspectives about the roles of advertising generally fall into one of three categories:

What Advertising Does for Consumers

Effective selling must start with a consumer orientation. It moves from product development that meets consumer demand to advertising and promotion that shows how a product fulfills a need better than other alternatives, distribution channels that make the product conveniently available, and a price that offers customers perceived value for their money. Effective advertising planning must ask the question, "Does my product help people solve a problem better than competing brands?"

By asking the question from the consumer's perspective, advertising is already beginning to develop a creative strategy. Advertising should address the way a product relates to consumer concerns. What are the customers for my product thinking about, worrying about, crusading for? What are the primary benefits they hope to gain from a product category and from my brand (see Exhibit 2.5)?

Within the next decade, perhaps sooner, interactive technology will usher in fundamental changes in the seller/buyer relationship. The most important market-

---

[11]C. H. Sandage and Vernon Fryburger, *The Role of Advertising* (Homewood, IL: Richard D. Irwin, 1960), 261.

Exhibit 2.5

Consumer benefits are the key to this advertising message.
Courtesy: West & Vaughan, Inc.

ing trend in the last 25 years has been to make the consumer the focus of the communication process. Interactive media will make promotional techniques that consider this new relationship and make the consumer the focus of the marketing process even more important.

A consumer focus creates an environment where products are designed for the consumer rather than forcing consumers to accept what is available. Obviously, this process also will result in fundamental modifications in advertising.

With permission marketing, ". . . customers will be rewarded with targeted advertising . . . . Everywhere you go, ads will find you. If you let them. But they'll be your ads—for you and nobody else."[12]

What Advertising Does for Business

Chapter 1 discussed some of the reasons why advertising is only useful in a reasonably developed society. In a society of surplus where overall supply is greater than demand, businesses must use marketing communication techniques to efficiently meet competition. Without advertising, businesses would not be able to bring new products to the attention of enough consumers fast enough to make the enormous cost of creating, developing, manufacturing, and distributing these products practical. In other words, advertising is both a tool and requirement of an abundant economy.

Advertising is important for launching new products, increasing the sale of existing brands, and maintaining the sale of mature brands. Markets are not static. Brands have been characterized as leaky buckets. "They lose customers all the time. Mass advertising helps to keep the buckets full. It fixes leaks by reminding existing buyers, and it tops off the bucket by attracting new ones. It also builds brand awareness among those that aren't even in the bucket yet."[13]

What Advertising Does for Society

Advertising has both intended and unintended consequences. Obviously, the intended result of most advertising is to contribute to the profitable sale of products. In addition to its economic role, advertising revenues support a diverse and

---

[12]Matt Carmichael, "This ad's for you," *Advertising Age: The Interactive Future*, 2000, 107.
[13]Erwin Ephron, "Requiem for a heavyweight?" *Advertising Age*, 13 December 1999, 25.

independent press system protected from government and special interest control. As a key communication link in the marketing process, it also is a major stimulant to vigorous economic growth and stability.

However, there is a growing awareness that advertising must move beyond single-minded concerns with profitability. There is increasing agreement that advertising must be created in an atmosphere that considers a number of ethical factors. For example, not only must advertising be truthful, but it should portray a fair picture of society and the various groups within the population. Sophisticated research allows advertisers to identify groups and subgroups of current and potential buyers with increasing accuracy. A negative result of this data is the temptation for advertisers to stereotype these target markets.

> Persons . . . that are similar . . . tend to be grouped together. The greater the similarity, the greater the probability that we will tend to perceive them as a common group. Women, blacks, or members of any other group that has clearly distinguishable characteristics in terms of features or color will tend to be perceived as alike in other, unrelated characteristics as well.[14]

The move to interactive and one-on-one marketing may have the positive effect of forcing advertisers to view customers individually rather than as part of a stereotyped group. Certainly it is to the benefit of advertising and society in general if this is the case.

ADVERTISING TO DIVERSE PUBLICS

A particular advertisement simultaneously communicates its message to various groups and individuals who in turn interpret this message in a context of their own experience. When designing an advertisement or advertising campaign, firms must consider the many publics that will be reached by their messages and take into account the perception of each of these groups will have of the advertising. Often an advertising campaign is intended to carry out several functions at once.

A single advertisement might be directed to a number of publics:

1. *The distribution channel.* With the growth of huge national retailers such as Wal-Mart and Kmart, national advertisers must demonstrate to retailers that they are offering brands with high consumer demand and ones they are willing to support with significant advertising dollars.
2. *Employees.* A company's product advertising is a means of instilling pride and loyalty in its employees. Sometimes this is done overtly by mentioning the quality workmanship that goes into a product. More often, the message to employees is less overt, but nevertheless an important function of advertising.
3. *Customers.* Present customers are a vital audience for any advertising. Current customers can be encouraged to use more of a product, not consider a competitor, and have previous purchase of the product reinforced as a good decision.
4. *Potential customers.* As discussed earlier, one of the primary objectives of advertising is to create awareness among those who are unfamiliar with a brand. Obviously, a person who doesn't know about a product will not buy it. For most products, advertising provides the lifeblood for continued success by encouraging prospects to become customers.
5. *Stockholders.* Most large national companies are publicly held and depend on stockholders as a major source of operating revenue. Studies have shown that

---

[14]Stephen P. Robins, *Organizational Behavior* (Upper Saddle River, NJ: Prentice-Hall, 1998), 93.

high brand awareness and a company's positive reputation are contributing factors to keeping stock prices higher than might otherwise be the case. Stockholders are a major reason why companies such as airplane manufacturers and utilities advertise in consumer and business magazines.

6. *The community at large.* Many companies operate local plants throughout the country. Advertising is often used to influence public opinion so that when the inevitable disputes about local tax assessment, excessive noise, or zoning ordinances arise, the company is viewed as a good neighbor.

Advertising is only one of the many marketing communication tools available to a company. In fact, advertising planning starts by determining whether, and in what proportion, advertising can be used profitably. At this point, our marketing situation analysis will tell us if the marketing conditions are conductive to the use of advertising alone, or more likely in concert with other marketing communication tools.

Manufacturers, even those marketing similar products, demonstrate markedly different approaches to advertising. A particular advertisement should be designed to single out those consumers who are interested in the particular product features and benefits that you can offer. Successful advertising is built around a specific marketing plan. An advertisement is not created in a vacuum; rather, its message is intended to carry out the specific marketing goals and objectives of the firm. A company's advertising must be viewed as unique to each brand and product category.

Even with the most meticulous planning, advertising success is not guaranteed. If advertising could wield the influence ascribed to it by both critics and proponents, we would not have seen some of the marketing failures of the last decade. When a product is introduced without a clear consumer benefit or differentiation from competing brands, even the most creative advertising usually fails.

Brand Name

Building brand value or equity is one of the most important elements of advertising (see Exhibit 2.6). Whether introducing a new product or maintaining the vitality of a mature one, brand identity is crucial to a product's success. Products are concrete objects; brands, on the other hand, represent attitudes and feelings about products. Branding allows companies to position favorably products and companies by creating unique identities. Brand identity is increasing in importance as companies try to differentiate their products in increasingly crowded fields.

An established brand is among the most important assets of a company. It has been estimated that a **brand name** is worth half or more of the market value of many companies. There are hundreds of fast-food outlets, but how many have the instant visibility and customer loyalty of McDonald's? The value of a brand is directly related to the recognition and loyalty it engenders in buyers. In fact, it is only because of brands that advertising exists. Brands allow a consumer to buy a product with the assurance of consistency from one purchase to another. Without brand identification, advertising could serve only a limited function in promoting generic goods.

brand name The written or spoken part of a trademark, in contrast to the pictorial mark; a trademark word.

The competitive challenge for businesses is to keep their brands on a top-of-mind basis with consumers. According to *Advertising Age,* the top five brands in terms of advertising spending are:

Chevrolet   Dodge cars and trucks
MCI Telephone Services   McDonald's[15]
Ford cars and trucks

---

[15]"The top 100 megabrands," *Advertising Age,* 12 July 1999, S1.

Volkswagain.

Remember everything you heard about the new Volkswagen Beetle in the '50's?

This time it's even better. See for yourself at Southern States Volkswagen. 2421 Wake Forest Road. (919)828-0901.

Remember everything you heard about the new Volkswagen Beetle in the '60's?

This time it's even better. See for yourself at Southern States Volkswagen. 2421 Wake Forest Road. (919)828-0901.

Remember everything you heard about the new Volkswagen Beetle in the '70's?

This time it's even better. See for yourself at Southern States Volkswagen. 2421 Wake Forest Road. (919)828-0901.

Exhibit

2.6

The brand name is a critical element in the reintroduction of the Volkswagen Beetle.

Courtesy: West & Vaughan, Inc.

Each year they each spend more than $3 billion despite the fact they are already among the most recognized names in the world.

Basically, there are two types of brand strategies: (1) focused and (2) diversified.[16] Focused brands such as Coca-Cola concentrate on a core product category and branch out only among narrow brand-related opportunities. For example, Diet Coke is simply an extension of the core soft drink business of the company. Diversified brands leverage their names across a broad range of product and market opportunities. For example, the Sears name is associated with a range of products and services from retail stores to pest control. Both models can work well, but they entail very different marketing strategies.

Major marketing strategies for focused brands include the following:

1. *Owning and broadening a category.* Focused brands expand more by capturing, broadening, and redefining a niche within a product category than by significantly extending the product line. For example, in the apparel category Levi is outdoorsy and Victoria's Secret is romantic in terms of perception and both of their product lines and their advertising seek to maintain these positions.

---

[16]David Court and Mark Loch, "Capturing the value," *Advertising Age*, 8 November 1999, S12.

2. *A focused brand captures all venues.* Coca-Cola has strength in vending machines, grocery and convenience stores, and so forth. It also has a presence not only in traditional advertising, but in event sponsorship from rock concerts to stock car races. Consumers have come to expect to see the brand everywhere.

3. *A focused brand is open to alliances with complementary brands.* To reach outdoor enthusiasts, L.L. Bean and Subaru co-branded a special L.L. Bean/Subaru Outback all-wheel-drive vehicle.

Major marketing strategies for diversified brands include the following:

1. *Creating the "golden thread."* Companies develop a central theme or product characteristic that unifies a number of different products in the mind of the consumer. Sony is known for quality and simplicity of design regardless of the diversified products that carry its logo.

2. *Diversified brands need high-credibility personalities.* Companies such as IBM score very highly on dimensions such as trustworthiness, leadership, and imagination compared to their competitors. When a new product or service comes on the market carrying the IBM brand, it immediately has greater visibility and importance than other brands with the buying public.

3. *Aggressively leveraging the brand.* Diversified brands tend to be risk takers and readily expand into new market opportunities using their already established public recognition as a competitive tool in product categories that have low brand loyalty among existing consumers. For example, Bayer uses the power of its brand on products as different as aspirin and yard chemicals.

The importance of brand image is so important that few companies fail to include brand enhancement as a primary role of their advertising strategy. Companies know that brand image must be continually protected. For example, the problems that Coca-Cola faced with product recalls in Belgium, replacement of its CEO after only two years, and declines in profits and stock prices all contributed to a temporary erosion of brand equity. For Coca-Cola, and other businesses, the development, protection, and maintenance of brand value will continue to be one of the driving forces in modern advertising.

A GOOD PRODUCT THAT MEETS A PERCEIVED NEED

It has been said that a product is not a physical object as much as it is a bundle of consumer benefits. The physical characteristics of a product are generally much less important to consumers than the benefits it offers. Consumers are not interested in products; they are interested in solving problems. In their book *Clicks and Mortars,* David Pottruck and Terry Pearce point out that marketers must listen to consumers' frustrations, disappointments, and objections to come up with products and services that overcome them.[17]

Even when customers clearly enunciate their problems, it may not lead to breakout products. As the authors demonstrate, it is impossible to ask consumers questions about products that don't exist. Products often come from intuitions resulting from research data rather than the data itself. For example, before the

---

[17]"Listening to customers in the electronic age," *Fortune,* 1 May 2000, 318.

invention of the microwave oven, consumers couldn't say they wanted a device that would stir up water molecules and provide a hot dinner in minutes. They could say when they were tired and hungry, and they didn't want to wait 45 minutes for a conventional oven.

Likewise, General Electric listened to patients who expressed claustrophobic reactions to closed MRI machines and doctors who demanded quality resolution of images. The result was open MRI equipment that met the demands of both groups and has been a great sales success. In another example, when Oldsmobile introduced its sports utility vehicle (SUV) Bravada, it faced the challenge of breaking into a crowded market with no track record in the product category. Oldsmobile marketing strategy was to develop a creative theme that addressed the reality that few drivers use SUVs off-road or for sport. Rather than pushing a sports theme, Bravada targeted realistic messages about traffic jams and inclement weather driving on radio traffic and weather reports. As an Oldsmobile executive explained, ". . . radio sponsorship gave us an opportunity to communicate the on-road benefits of the Bravada in a unique, highly relevant environment."[18]

Sophisticated computer software also aids companies in determining consumer perceptions of products. Whirlpool, the giant appliance manufacturer, continually analyzes customer requests for service on washers and refrigerators. Statistical trends gathered from these data can warn of defective product designs, bad parts, or faulty assembly procedures and enable the company to respond before a problem spins out of control.[19]

As seen in these examples, the key to successful advertising begins with product development from the consumer's perspective. Product quality and consumer research go hand in hand. Product development is largely dependent on consumer research to determine the most important attributes consumers are looking for in a product. Likewise, research is crucial in prioritizing the qualities that are most important in influencing purchase decisions.

Every product is unique. A brand's position in the product life cycle, quality perceptions by consumers, distribution channels, and a number of other factors will determine specific marketing and advertising strategies that will contribute to the long-term success of a brand. For example:

1. *Nature of the product.* A new product will require different strategies than an established one. An expensive product will require a different advertising approach than an inexpensive one just as a product with inherent consumer interest will have an advantage over more pedestrian products.

2. *Product purchase cycle.* Obviously, package goods bought on a weekly or biweekly cycle will use different advertising methods compared to durable goods such as appliances, which are purchased every five or ten years.

3. *Product awareness and market position.* Coca-Cola has a much different marketing strategy than RC Cola and it is reflected in both its advertising budget and its creative approach.

4. *Product seasonality.* Suntan lotion is marketed in a fundamentally different way than toothpaste.

5. *Short-term advertising tactics.* Short-term advertising plans may be designed to accomplish targeted objectives within a brand's long-term marketing goals. For example, a particular campaign might be designed to gain initial consumer trial, encourage higher purchase levels from current customers, or change established buying patterns.[20]

---

[18]"Oldsmobile Bravada drives home sales with radio!" a case study from the Radio Advertising Bureau.
[19]Lisa Manning, "Keep the 0010001 happy," *Fortune Technology Guide*, May 2000, 66.
[20]*Radio for the Advertiser*, a publication of the Radio Marketing Bureau, 4.

Unfortunately, even the most focused and marketing-oriented company cannot guarantee success for all its products. The estimates for new product failures run as high as 90 percent. Behind each of these failures is a company that took a wrong turn. Sometimes the error occurs at the very beginning by overestimating consumer demand; sometimes a good product idea is wrecked by inferior quality or service; sometimes an indifferent or untrained sales staff is the culprit; and sometimes unrealistic or poorly executed advertising must take the blame. Regardless of the reason for the failure of a particular product, some marketing mistake almost always plays a role. The concept of matching product quality with consumer demand is one that is fundamental to advertising and marketing success.

Sales, Revenues, and Profit Potential

Throughout the text we discuss the need for marketing and advertising to satisfy consumer needs. However, a company can only fulfill consumer needs as long as it is doing so profitably. Advertising must address consumer preferences and be integrated into the overall marketing strategy. At the same time, advertising will only be used if it contributes to corporate profits. Consequently, it is important that we continue to link the idea of sales, revenues, and, most importantly, *profits* with advertising.

The manner in which advertising contributes to profitability can take a number of forms. In some cases, it may create a favorable corporate image, it may complement short-term sales promotion, or it may introduce new products or improved features for old ones. However, in almost every case, advertising's role is relatively long term. Even in retail advertising, it usually has an element of long-term institutional promotion for the store in addition to short-term sales of specific merchandise.

Regardless of specific advertising objectives, it usually works in concert with other promotional elements and always within a broader marketing context. In the current environment of cost management by many firms, it is more incumbent than ever that advertisers be able to justify their contributions to the bottom line.

The pressure to justify the advertising function has led many businesses to call for greater accountability. This move to measure more precisely the contributions of advertising has led to a broader view of what advertising can and should accomplish. For example, advertisers are focusing on the role of advertising in *maintaining* sales and market share as a major goal. It is difficult to measure the value of advertising in terms of sales not lost versus sales gained. However, given the cost involved in finding new customers versus keeping present customers, the overall contributions to profitability may actually be greater in the former case.

Advertising functions differently at different stages of the product life cycle. During the introduction and growth phase of a product, businesses advertise to establish a beachhead against competition and gain a level of consumer awareness. As products enter more mature stages of development, advertising strategies take longer perspectives and its goals are likely to be involved in brand equity and a longer horizon for sales development. With this in mind, businesses are looking at advertising's contribution to long-term profits. The key is to measure advertising against long-term communications objectives rather than in terms of short-term sales.

Finally, never make the mistake of viewing sales and revenues as substitutes for profits. A review of the last decade demonstrates that some of the largest companies in America (in terms of sales volume) experienced the largest financial losses. Anyone can devise a marketing plan that will result in greater sales, if profits are not considered.

Product Timing

Products can rarely be forced on consumers before the public is ready to accept them. Sometimes the catalyst for product acceptance is price. When the cost of video cassette recorders (VCRs) was reduced to approximately $300, consumer demand skyrocketed. The home computer market was spurred by price reductions, but even more so by the introduction of the Internet, which gave people a reason to buy a computer—in this case, instant (and free) communication with friends and relatives.

In other cases, product timing is a matter of change in lifestyles that move categories from niche products to the mainstream. For example, yogurt and granola were originally introduced to health-conscious consumers. However, in recent years, both product categories have moved into the general market. With the introduction of items such as chocolate chip yogurt and high-fat granola, it is obvious that a significant number of buyers are more interested in taste than content. Following this trend, executives at Gardenburger, a vegetarian hamburger substitute, broadened distribution to meat eaters looking for a unique taste. The product boosted sales from $18 million in 1997 to $100 million in 1999, far greater than what would have been achieved by marketing only to a vegetarian market.[21] It is unlikely that any amount of promotion could have resulted in sales success for these products a decade ago when they had a "health-food-only" connotation.

Another element of timing is an attempt to expand the seasonal purchases for a product or service. For example, theme parks have tried, with some success, to extend their traditional June–August peak season by incorporating a number of indoor amusements such as arcades, theaters, and simulator rides. In other cases, businesses such as Vlasic pickles have simply promoted product usage to overcome their "picnic-season" image. Even television, especially cable networks, have combated the "summer season" viewer declines with more first-run programs and aggressive selling to season advertisers such as suntan lotion makers.[22]

In other cases, a product introduction seems to run on a time schedule of its own with as many coincidences as good planning contributing to its success. For example, Post-it Notes were discovered in 1968 by a 3M Company scientist, Spencer Silver, but he could find no particular use for it. Seven years later, Art Fry, another 3M employee, used the Post-it as a bookmark in his choir hymnal. He saw the commercial potential for the product and Post-its were test-marketed in 1978 (as "Press and Peel" notes) and finally went national in 1980—12 years after the original discovery. They were an immediate best-seller for 3M and, no doubt, would have been in 1968, but product timing had to wait for marketing insight.[23]

While some products can influence timing, most businesses know that product categories sales must take into account when buyers are most likely to make certain purchases and plan their advertising accordingly. The RAB reports that according to the U.S. Department of Commerce, the best months for buying various product categories are:

Product Category	Best Month	% of Sales
All Stores	Dec.	10.2
Life Insurance	Dec.	12.2
Music Stores	Dec.	15.9
Book Stores	Jan/Aug.	11.3
New Cars (domestic)	May	10.6
Florist	May	11.9

---

[21]Judann Pollack, "Gardenburger," *Advertising Age*, 28 June 1999, S2.
[22]Judann Pollack, "Dog days," *Advertising Age*, 26 April 1999, 16.
[23]Liz Stevens, "Read this story today," *The Atlanta Journal*, 24 April 2000, D-1.

While seasonality studies are helpful, they don't provide fail-safe solutions. They can provide only general guidelines and directions. Inventory clearances, unusual weather, general economic conditions, and a number of unpredictable factors can all affect the best time to advertise. In fact, off-timing from competitive advertising patterns is a method of differentiation if consumers will purchase during nontraditional periods. Still, it is rare for any product category to have consistent sales throughout the year and advertisers are taking a major risk when they run counter to established consumer buying patterns and preferences.

Product Differentiation

In the contemporary marketing environment, one of the major challenges for businesses is to separate their products from competitors in the minds of consumers. The key for advertising is to find differences among often similar brands that are relevant to consumers. The primary element in successful **product differentiation** is consumer perception. If consumers *perceive* your product as differentiated from competitors, then it is.

The successful marketer generally follows four steps in gaining meaningful differentiation.[24]

1. *Context.* The differentiating strategy must be meaningful in the context of the product category. Nordstrom's department stores emphasized service when other competitors were cutting back on salespeople.

2. *Differentiating idea.* Remember that differentiation does not have to be product related. It can be a feature such as service, leadership, or innovation, but preferably not price, which is the easiest factor for a competitor to match.

3. *Credentials.* A differentiation should have credibility with the public. It should be based on a feature, service, or product difference that is believable by the average consumer. Sometimes, product differentiations are obvious and consumers immediately see their importance. More often they require some proof. Comparison advertising is a common method of providing this type of credibility. Remember that consumers are skeptical and an unsupported claim of differentiation may do more harm than good to a brand.

4. *Communicate differences.* Don't be bashful; better products don't always win, better perceptions do. Robert Prentice, a marketing consultant, emphasizes the importance of **Consumer Franchise Building** (CFB) ideas.[25] He says that advertisers must concentrate on messages and ideas, either rational or emotional, that set a brand apart from its competitors. Every promotion theme should be measured against the CFB concept. Otherwise, you may be investing dollars in messages that are not registering unique ideas to the public and, therefore, are not creating a unique sales environment in a competitive marketplace.

One of the most important elements of differentiation is keeping an open mind about how to achieve it. Differentiation can involve product styling. Nokia broke out of the wireless telephone pack with an option of 20 distinctive rings and a variety of colorful face plates. Most importantly, it developed new technology that extended the battery life of its phones. Nokia gained attention with a redesigned package and then sold a meaningful product differentiation. Similarly, Apple Computer, sensing that most consumers aren't technical experts, marketed its iMac computer in a colorful, translucent case. It was an immediate hit and gained significant market share for Apple.

product differentiation Unique product attributes that set off one brand from another.

Consumer Franchise Building Creating promotional messages that allow consumers to differentiate one brand from others in the product category.

---

[24]Jack Trout, "Being different is where it's at," *Advertising Age*, 22 November 1999, 27.
[25]Bernard Ryan, Jr., *It Works!* (New York: American Association of Advertising Agencies, 1991), 19.

The Gillette Mach3 razor is an example of very obvious product feature differentiation. The first three-blade razor was marketed on the premise of providing a cleaner, closer shave with fewer strokes. Obviously, it was a difference that men saw as a benefit as the Mach3 became one of the most successful product introductions in history. Sometimes, product differentiation results from changes in neither the package nor the product. For example, the Honda CR-V sports utility vehicle was advertised as a fun car for both men and women as opposed to the macho messages of many of its competitors.

Most advertising has at least some element of product differentiation as a primary theme. Product differentiation usually highlights either product features or product benefits. Let's look at some headlines to demonstrate the use of each type:

Differentiation based on product features

Height-adjustable front seats	VW Jetta
A new Irish Spring with a wee bit of aloe	Irish Spring soap
The Wide Track Gran Prix. Wider Is Better.	Pontiac

Differentiation based on consumer benefits

Less Drag. Less Pull. Less Irritation.	Mach3 razor
We deliver to more international cities than anyone	UPS
Fly First Class for the Price of Coach.	Northwest Airlines
It's Healthy and It Tastes Good	Post Shredded Wheat

As we set about to differentiate our brand, we should remember that product differentiation also is a means of target marketing. In this chapter three approaches used to sell SUVs have been discussed. Honda used a fun approach aimed at both men and women; Subaru allied with L.L. Bean for an outdoors approach; and the Oldsmobile Bravada developed an urban "realistic" theme. Each of these methods of differentiation appealed to a specific prospect group. However, by appealing to one segment of the total SUV market, each company surrendered most of those consumers who are interested in features featured by the other manufacturers. Before embarking on a specific product differentiation strategy, you must make sure that it is featuring elements that are important to enough prospects that you will be able to sustain a profitable niche.

Advertisers also have a responsibility to promote meaningful product differences. Much of the criticism of modern advertising is that it tries to make obscure and inconsequential product differences important. There is no question that some advertising promotes inconsequential product features. However, the best and most successful products can demonstrate an obvious difference from their competitors.

Price

Obviously, the cost of producing and marketing a product has to play a major role in pricing strategy. The greater the gap between a product's cost and its price, the greater the profit. However, a pricing strategy that concentrates solely on cost recovery and ignores consumer demand is overlooking an important element of the marketing process.

It also is important to note that, in spite of the importance of pricing in current marketing, it would be a mistake to suggest that a low price is necessarily going to be a successful marketing strategy. For example, a recent study of the reasons that consumers buy certain makes of automobiles shows a wide disparity among brands in terms of the role that price plays in purchase decisions.[26]

Brand	% Price Factor	% Reputation Factor
Escort	23.7	10.4
Lincoln	7.3	24.4
Cavalier	27.9	11.0
Pontiac Grand Am	32.1	11.3
Saturn	18.1	44.3
Volvo	13.6	36.9

A cursory examination of this list gives some idea of the advertising and marketing strategy that can successfully be adopted for each of these brands. It also is interesting to note that while some brands such as Escort and Cavalier have a "price" orientation, another lower priced brand has been able to position itself as a "quality" brand that insulates it from much of the price competition facing other similarly priced brands.

A primary function of advertising is to create, or enhance, a positive gap between the price of a product and the value the average consumer ascribes to the product (see Exhibit 2.7). The greater this "value gap," the more insulated the product is from competitive inroads into its market. The concept of the value gap underscores the notion that price alone is not a particularly safe means of establishing a long-term, competitive advantage.

Regardless of how pricing strategy is used as a marketing tool, it is one of the most important elements of the marketing process. Depending on business, advertising can play a number of roles in terms of pricing strategy. For example, price is both a means of market entry and product differentiation for mature products. A new product can gain immediate visibility with a price advantage. Likewise, for both new and mature products, price is an obvious point of differentiation. As a rule-of-thumb, the more mature a product, the more likely it is to adopt other marketing themes in addition to price. For example, Men's Warehouse was established primarily on a low-price strategy. For more than 20 years, George Zimmer has promised customers low cost and value in men's clothing with his famous "I guarantee it" slogan. However, in recent years, Men's Warehouse has gone slightly more upscale, broadened its inventory into casual clothes, and toned down its advertising. It still emphasizes price, but also distances itself from other discount clothiers with a style and service message.

A similar change has taken place at Red Lobster seafood restaurants. For years, the chain skewed toward an older audience and promoted value pricing with an entreé-of-the-month advertising strategy. More recently, Red Lobster has modernized both the atmosphere of its outlets and its advertising. New advertising campaigns emphasize Red Lobster as a fun dining experience with less emphasis on price.

Generally, smaller and/or less well-known brands tend to use price as their primary marketing tool. Airlines, such as AirTran, compete with their major competitors Delta or Northwest almost solely on the basis of price. The problem with a price-only strategy is that it can often be easily matched. In addition, when price becomes a primary focus on a product category such as airlines and automobiles, consumers resist paying retail price and simply wait for the next enviable price cut, sale, discount, or rebate program.

Pricing strategy is often used as a means of temporary inventory control. Obviously, end-of-season sales at the retail level are an obvious means of clearing out inventory from Christmas cards and wrapping paper in January to swimsuits in

---

[26]From *1998 Auto Market Profiles*, a publication of the Radio Advertising Bureau.

Exhibit 2.7

Price and value are an important theme in many advertisements.

Courtesy: Howard Merrell & Partners.

yield management
A product pricing strategy to control supply and demand.

September. Many marketers have long adopted a concept known as **yield management** to even out supply and demand. Hotels offer special weekend rates to offset the loss of business travelers. Car rental companies offer specials based on seasonal demand and telephone companies cut long distance rates on weekends and evenings as a form of yield management.

Pricing is one of the most studied areas of marketing and advertising. Proper pricing strategy is necessary for profitability and the continued existence of a business. However, the method of pricing used for a brand determines to a significant degree the type of marketing strategy that can be used and the success that advertising will have in promoting and selling a specific brand.

VARIATIONS IN THE IMPORTANCE OF ADVERTISING

As mentioned earlier, businesses are more interested in marketing communication synergism than ever before. Marketers are continually looking for the proper mix of marketing communication techniques that will best reach their prime prospects. The determining factors that move a company or product category to a particular communication option are both diverse and complex. However, a number of factors will determine the degree to which advertising is used. Among the more important ones are the following:[27]

1. The faster a market is growing, the higher the advertising expenditures as a share of total market sales. Businesses in growing markets take advantage of these opportunities by spending significantly more on advertising than businesses in stagnant markets.

2. Advertising expenditures as a share of sales tend to be higher when production capacity is low. During periods of high demand the ratio of advertising to sales is lower than when there is low demand for a product category. The rate of advertising tends to be related to the number of competitors in a shrinking market. For example, cigarette companies spend a great deal on advertising since there is so much brand switching as opposed to market expansion.

3. The less frequently a product is purchased, the higher the advertising to sales ratio. Basically, high ticket, but infrequently bought, products such as automobiles and household appliances must keep their brands before consumers even though the purchase cycle is very long. Often, media advertising is supplemented by direct response advertising to people who owned a car for three or four years to try to estimate the purchase cycle.

4. The earlier a product is in the life cycle, the higher advertising to sales ratios. Advertising tends to be much greater in the introductory and growth stages of development as the process of building brand awareness and equity demand high promotional expenditures.

5. The higher the perceived product quality of a brand in a product category, the higher the expenditure of advertising to sales. Competing brands with perceived lower product quality often depend on price as a primary sales tool. Product quality must be promoted continually through advertising to maintain brand equity.

6. Businesses with major new competition have higher advertising expenditures. As discussed in number 3 above, when new competitors come into the marketplace, they usually spend heavily on advertising. Established brands are forced to meet this competitive spending to protect their product franchise.

This list is not intended to be inclusive of all the factors that might determine the place of advertising in a specific marketing communication plan. However, it does demonstrate the many variables that must be considered when a business decides the role that advertising will play.

Advertising and the Marketing Environment

In the contemporary marketing environment, companies must determine the social/psychological/marketing propensities of their prospects and then allocate dollars to the various components of the marketing communication mix. For example, Coca-Cola has a very detailed sports marketing strategy to align its brands with the audiences of sports events:[28]

■ *Assessment.* Coke first determines whether or not a sports team has a unique position in a community and how significant it is to local consumers. For example, the Los Angeles Clippers would be far down on a measure of local interest compared to a team like the San Antonio Spurs or the Milwaukee Bucks who play in relatively small markets.

---

[27]"Advertising and promotion: How much should you spend?" *Cahners Advertising Research Report,* No. 2000.10.
[28]Michael Cothran, "Coke's sports marketing strategy," *The Atlanta Journal,* 5 September 1999, Q-1.

- How does a specific sport's attributes complement different Coke brands? Research shows that the intensity of pro football matches well with Coke Classic; Sprite with pro basketball; and Surge with hockey.
- *Strategy.* Next, Coke develops a specific marketing plan. Depending on the circumstances, advertising might complement in-store promotions for the Super Bowl or a sweepstakes featuring a favorite local baseball star.
- *Implementation and measurement.* Regardless of the strategy, the marketing strategy must be executed in a manner that allows measurement of results through sales increases, survey data, and so forth.

Given the number of marketing communication options, it is not surprising that different product categories and brands demonstrate significant variance in their percentage of advertising to sales ratios. For example, perfume and cosmetics businesses spend 11.9 percent of sales revenues on advertising while insurance companies, with huge investments in personal selling, spend less than 1 percent.[29] As companies continue to examine a wide array of marketing communication tools and new communication technologies, we will probably see advertising expenditures demonstrate an even wider disparity from one product category to another in the future.

ADVERTISING AND THE MARKETING CHANNEL

Most of the advertising that we see every day is called consumer advertising since it is directed to the ultimate consumers of goods and services. However, advertising also plays a major role in moving products through the various levels of production and distribution known as the marketing channel. A typical marketing channel might include some of the items in Exhibit 2.8.

At each level of the channel, marketing decisions must be made about the most effective type of marketing communication to employ. Marketing decisions are not made in a void and decisions in one area of marketing and promotion have an immediate and direct effect on others. For example, when a choice is made to expand a company's personal sales force, a concurrent decision is being made about the availability of funds for advertising, or sales promotion, or public relations.

Marketing decisions not only determine the role of advertising and its budget, but often play a major part in decisions concerning media choices. For example, a strategy to use a coupon promotion will probably dictate a print media strategy. A decision to demonstrate product features may mean that television will get the call. A complex sales message may take us to magazines and a localized advertising strategy may move our product into newspaper advertising.

In the remainder of this chapter, some of the ways advertising functions in various industries and stages of the marketing channel will be examined. While you are most familiar with consumer advertising, it is only one of a number of categories that are used to bring products to market. Effective advertising must be successful on two levels: (1) communication and (2) carrying out marketing goals.

Exhibit

2.8

Industrial advertising often includes a means of interactive communication for prime prospects.

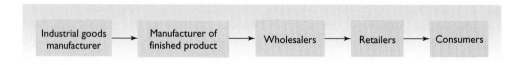

Industrial goods manufacturer → Manufacturer of finished product → Wholesalers → Retailers → Consumers

---

[29]"Ad budget growth to keep going," *Advertising Age*, 28 June 1999, 58.

Unfortunately, it is often the case that you have successful communication on one level (a humorous ad that everyone remembers, but can't identify the brand) without accomplishing marketing goals.

Perhaps the easiest way to evaluate advertising's role in the marketing process is according to the *directness* of the intended communication effect and the anticipated *time* over which that effect is supposed to operate. In other words, how much of the total selling job should be accomplished by advertising and over what time frame should the job be accomplished?

Advertising designed to produce an immediate response in the form of product purchase is called direct-action, short-term advertising. Most retail advertising falls into this category. An ad that runs in the newspaper this morning should sell some jeans this afternoon. Advertising used as a direct sales tool, but designed to operate over a longer time frame, is called direct-action, long-term advertising. This advertising category is used with high-ticket items (washers and tires) where the purchase decision is a result of many factors and the purchase cycle is relatively long.

Another category of advertising includes those advertisements that are used as an indirect sales tool. Such indirect advertising is intended to affect the sales of a product only over the long term, usually by promoting general attributes of the manufacturer rather than specific product characteristics. Included in this category are most institutional or public relations advertising. The exception would be remedial public relations advertising designed to overcome some immediate negative publicity concerning product safety, labor problems, and so forth.

The aim of most advertising is to move a product or service through the various levels of the marketing channel. The objectives and execution of advertising will change from level to level. The intended target audience will result in markedly different advertising strategies. The following sections examine several categories of advertising to both consumers and businesses.

ADVERTISING TO THE CONSUMER

National Advertising The term **national advertising** has a special nongeographic meaning in advertising: It refers to advertising by the owner of a trademarked product (brand) or service sold through different distributors or stores, wherever they may be. It does not mean that the product is necessarily sold nationwide.

Traditionally, national advertising has been the most general in terms of product information. Items such as price, retail availability, and even service and installation are often omitted from national advertising or mentioned in general terms. However, the need to communicate more closely with targeted consumers has significantly changed the messages of national advertising during the last decade.

Beginning in the late 1980s, many national advertisers began to target their advertising on a geographic basis—first regionally and, increasingly, on a market-by-market basis. Then, with a combination of better consumer research and advances in technology, national advertisers have begun to identify and reach more narrowly defined market segments and, in some cases, individual consumers. In coming years, growth of Internet advertising as well as scanner research at the retail level will allow national advertisers to offer specifically tailored messages to consumers based on individual lifestyle and product usage characteristics. However, in the near term, national advertising will continue to emphasize brand introductions of new products and greater brand loyalty for established products.

Retail (Local) Advertising Retail is the workhorse of the advertising world. It usually combines aspects of hard sell messages with institutional advertising. On the one hand, retailers must compete in an extremely competitive business environment to move large volumes of merchandise. At the same time, their advertising

national advertising Advertising by a marketer of a trademarked product or service sold through different outlets, in contrast to *local advertising*.

retail advertising
Advertising by a merchant who sells directly to the consumer.

must enhance the image of the retailer. **Retail advertising** often includes price information, service and return policies, store locations, and hours of operation—information that national advertisers usually cannot provide.

Retail marketing and advertising have changed dramatically in recent years. During the last two decades, the retail environment has been dominated by a few large chains such as Home Depot, Kmart, and Wal-Mart. These huge retailers offer an array of merchandise from clothing to tires and from prescription drugs to sporting goods. It is estimated that more than 55 percent of Americans shop at a mass retailer weekly and of that number, 39 percent go to Wal-Mart and 16 percent to Kmart.[30] It has become so important for manufacturers to gain entry to these megastores that vendors provide a number of product, merchandising, and promotional services specific to each retailer. For example, some products are manufactured to an individual retailer's specifications and both in-store promotion and advertising may be unique to a particular chain.

End-Product Advertising   What do products such as Intel computer chips, Lycra, Teflon, and Nutrasweet have in common? They are rarely purchased directly by consumers. Instead, they are bought as an ingredient in other products. The promoting of such products is called end-product advertising (or *branded ingredient advertising*). **End-product advertising** is most commonly used by manufacturers of ingredients used in consumer products. Successful end-product advertising builds a consumer demand for an ingredient that will help in the sale of a product. The knowledge that such a consumer demand exists will move companies to use these ingredients in their consumer products.

end-product advertising   Building consumer demand by promoting ingredients in a product. For example, Teflon and Nutrasweet.

A number of companies have adopted aggressive end-product advertising campaigns. Long-time brands such as DuPont's Teflon and 3M's Scotchgard have successfully created consumer demand for these and other end products with creative advertising campaigns. Research indicates that end-product advertising is most effective when used as part of a multifaceted campaign coordinated among manufacturers of consumer products, retailers, and consumer end users. This strategy has the advantage of showing the various elements of the trade channel that the end-product manufacturer is supporting them by building consumer demand.

Building demand through end-product advertising is not easy. You must have a recognized ingredient that both manufacturers and consumers perceive as beneficial. In addition, these ingredients usually are not obvious in the product and therefore extensive advertising is required to make consumers aware of their advantages. Successful end products are those that create meaningful differentiation for consumer purchase decisions. End-product advertising is a small part of total advertising, but it is extremely important for a number of product categories.

direct-response advertising   Any form of advertising done in direct marketing. Uses all types of media: direct mail, TV, magazines, newspapers, radio. Term replaces *mail-order advertising. See* Direct marketing.

Direct-Response Advertising   Direct marketing and **direct-response advertising** are not new. In this country, Ben Franklin is credited with the first direct sales catalog, published in 1744 to sell scientific and academic books. The modern era of direct selling was ushered in with the publication of the Montgomery Ward catalog in 1872. While it has grown steadily throughout the last 50 years, the twenty-first century will be the era of direct-response marketing.

Not only will new technology such as the Internet and interactive television provide a catalyst for future growth, but traditional media advertisers increasingly will adopt direct-response techniques. Often companies offer 800-numbers not only to sell a product, but to allow customers to obtain information such as the location of local retailers or more detailed information about an item. In addition, cable television shopping channels and videocassettes give consumers the oppor-

---

[30]"Race you to the checkout," *American Demographics*, May 2000, 9.

tunity to see merchandise "live" before ordering it from their living rooms. The future holds great promise for various forms of interactive media that will provide even more innovative ways of communicating with prospects.

Throughout the next century, direct selling will be an increasingly popular method of reaching consumers. One of the reasons for the growing use of direct response is its flexibility. For example, it can be used to solicit a direct order through a catalog or direct-mail piece; it can generate leads for personal salespersons or follow-up promotions; and it can be used to build store traffic for retailers such as automobile dealers where the final sale is completed on-premise. Direct response also lends itself to a number of media. Telemarketing is the leader in generating overall sales expenditures, followed by direct mail, television, and newspapers. For all media, direct sales revenues will approach $2 trillion during the next decade.

ADVERTISING TO BUSINESS AND PROFESSIONS

Business-to-business (B2B or B-T-B) is one of the fastest growing categories of advertising. The average person doesn't see a very important portion of advertising, because it is aimed at retail stores, doctors, home builders, wholesalers, and others who operate at various stages of the marketing channel.

B2B marketing requires a much different strategy than consumer advertising. The marketing communication options for B2B advertisers are unlike the basic media and promotional plans for consumer advertising. While business publications remain a primary tool of B2B marketing, personal selling, telemarketing, and the Internet occupy a much higher share of expenditures compared to consumer advertising.

Another major difference between B2B and consumer advertising is the type of messages used in each. While all advertising has to gain the audience's interest and attention, B2B tends to be factually oriented with few of the emotional appeals found in consumer advertising. B2B messages are addressed not only to specific industries, but often to particular job classifications within these industries. In addition, B2B advertising appeals are very profit oriented. How a product will eliminate downtime, decrease customer complaints, save time and money, and contribute to the overall efficiency of a business are among the primary themes of B2B marketing.

B2B advertising also has to consider major differences in the buying process compared to consumer purchase behavior. Consumer purchases tend to be fairly straightforward. There may be some external influences on the purchase decision such as children determining a family's fast-food or cereal preferences. But these casual relationships have little similarity with the formal purchasing models used in many B2B buys:[31]

1. *Purchase collaboration.* B2B purchase decisions are usually made by a committee. In many cases, a number of people from different departments within a company make the final decision. These people may have different perspectives and backgrounds and the B2B marketer must account for the various interests among decision makers in making the sale.

2. *Purchase cycles.* In the B2B environment, impulse buying is almost unheard of. In the B2B purchase process, most companies have very formal procedures that must be followed before a major acquisition can be made. These buying cycles can last from weeks to months especially in the case of major capital expenditures. During these long-term purchase cycles, advertising is usually supplemented heavily with personal selling and direct-response techniques.

---

[31]Karen Breen Vogel, "BTB requires new models, strategies," *DM News*, 6 March 2000, 26.

3. *Purchase scale.* Typically, the number of sales opportunities are much less than in consumer purchasing. For this reason, the average time and expense of making a B2B sale is significantly higher than in consumer advertising. Also many of the measures of audience reach are immaterial in B2B. While consumer advertisers generally measure advertising in terms of target audience reach and frequency, B2B measures are much more sales oriented.

THE CATEGORIES OF BUSINESS ADVERTISING

Trade Advertising Manufacturers use trade advertising to promote their products to wholesalers and retailers. **Trade advertising** emphasizes product profitability and the consumer advertising support retailers will receive from manufacturers. In addition, trade advertising promotes products and services that retailers need to operate their businesses. Advertising for shelving, cleaning services, and cash registers are part of trade advertising.

Trade advertising has several objectives:

1. *Gain additional distribution.* Manufacturers are interested in increasing the number of retail outlets that carry their brands.

2. *Increase trade support.* Manufacturers compete for shelf space and dealer support with countless other brands. Trade advertising can encourage retailers to give prominent position to products or to use a manufacturer's point-of-purchase material.

3. *Announce consumer promotions.* Many trade advertisements offer a schedule of future consumer promotions and show retailers that manufacturers are supporting brands with their advertising.

There are approximately 9,000 trade publications—several for virtually every category of retail business. The average consumer probably has not heard of most of these publications, but trade journals such as *Progressive Grocer* and *Drug Topics* play an important role in the advertising plans of most national advertisers.

Industrial Advertising A manufacturer is a buyer of machinery, equipment, raw materials, and components used in producing the goods it sells. Companies selling to manufacturers most often address their advertising to them in appropriate industry publications, direct mail, telemarketing, and personal selling. This method is quite unlike consumer advertising and is referred to as **industrial advertising.** Industrial advertising is directed at a very specialized and relatively small audience.

Industrial advertising rarely seeks to sell a product directly. The purchase of industrial equipment is usually a complex process that includes a number of decision makers. Often industrial advertising is a means of introducing a product or gaining brand name awareness to make it easier for follow-ups from company sales representatives to close a sale. Exhibit 2.9 is an example of an ad that provides an 800-number for information about the chemical suit.

Professional Advertising The primary difference between **professional advertising** and other trade advertising is the degree of control exercised by professionals over the purchase decision of their clients. Whereas, a grocery store encourages consumer purchases of certain goods by the brands it stocks, people can go to another store with more variety, lower prices, or better quality merchandise. On the other hand, a person rarely will change doctors because a physician doesn't prescribe a certain brand of drugs; change banks because the bank orders checks for its customers from a particular printer; or choose an architect based on how designs are reproduced.

Selecting appropriate chemical protective
apparel is not a fleeting responsibility.
That's why at Kimberly-Clark, we've developed HAZARD-GARD.
This line features a lightweight, durable fabric that provides
effective resistance to a broad range of liquid and dry partic-

**Remember when being
chemical-free was the furthest
thing from your mind?**

ulate chemicals. Its exterior is coated with either a 1.3mm
polyethylene film or Saranex 23-P film, while its interior has
a comfortable, cloth-like feel against the skin. For added protection and comfort, HAZARD-GARD apparel also incorporates
our patented REFLEX Coverall Design. This intelligent design
includes a seamless front, a storm flap in the primary splash
area, and a fuller cut in key areas 🔵 **Kimberly-Clark**
areas for enhanced mobility and greater range of motion. Sorry,
not available in tie-dye. For information, call 1-800-835-8351.

**Exhibit
2.9**

Business advertising delivers
specialized message to
knowledgeable audiences.
Courtesy: Howard Merrell & Partners.

Corporate (or Institutional) Advertising While **institutional advertising** remains a long-term image-building technique, in recent years it has taken on a
decided sales orientation in terms of the audiences reached and intent of communication. Like any advertising, corporate advertising reaches an identified target
audience with a specific objective. Among the groups most often targeted for corporate advertising are: ultimate customers, stockholders, the financial community,
government leaders, and employees. Frequently cited objectives of corporate
advertising are the following:

- To establish a public identity
- To overcome negative attitudes toward a company
- To explain a company's diverse missions
- To boost corporate identity and image
- To overcome a negative image
- To gain awareness with target audiences for later sales
- To associate a company with some worthwhile project

These are only a few examples of possible corporate advertising objectives. The
competitive environment of recent years has brought about dramatic changes in
corporate advertising.

**institutional
advertising** Advertising
done by an organization speaking
of its work, views, and problems
as a whole, to gain public
goodwill and support rather than
to sell a specific product.
Sometimes called *public-relations
advertising.*

NONPRODUCT ADVERTISING

Idea Advertising It is not surprising that the same marketing techniques so
successful in selling products would be used to promote ideas. We are living in a
period of conflicting ideas and special-interest groups. Marketing concepts and
advertising have become important elements in swaying public opinion. As we saw
in Chapter 1, advertising propaganda is not a new phenomenon. What is new is the
number of groups using advertising and the sophistication of the communication
techniques being employed. Gun control, abortion, animal rights, and environmental issues are only a few of the topics that have used mass advertising in recent years.

Idea advertising is often controversial. Apart from the emotionalism of many
of the topics being espoused, there are those critics who think that advertising messages are too short and superficial to fully debate many of these issues. Proponents

idea advertising
Advertising used to promote an
idea or cause rather than to sell a
product or service.

counter that advertising is the only practical way to get their messages before a mass audience. They point out that idea advertising may be the most practical means for these groups to use their First Amendment privileges. Regardless of one's position on idea advertising, the increasing ability of media to narrowly target audiences, by ideology as well as product preference, will make this type of advertising more prevalent in the future.

Service Advertising   We are becoming a nation of specialists with more and more Americans seeking advice and services for everything from financial planning to child care. Since services are basically people enterprises, **service advertising** almost always has a strong institutional component. Often service companies keep the same slogan, theme, or identifying mark over long periods of time to increase consumer awareness. Since service industries are so similar (and often legally regulated), it is difficult to develop a distinct differentiation among competitors. Banks and insurance companies have a particularly difficult time in establishing an effective identity.

service advertising
Advertising that promotes a service rather than a product.

Fundamentals of good advertising are the same regardless of whether a product or service is being promoted. However, many marketing experts point out that differences between the two categories require some care in the manner in which service messages are handled. Some basic principles of service advertising include the following:

1. *Feature tangibles.* Since service advertising cannot feature a product, it should be personalized in some way. For example, service advertisements often use testimonials. Service messages should show the benefits of the service such as an on-time plane trip that results in closing a deal or a contented older couple as a result of good investment advice by their broker.

2. *Feature employees.* Since the value of a service largely depends on the quality of a firm's employees, it is important to make them feel that they are an important part of the service. Often service messages feature real employees in their advertisements. This approach has the advantage of personalizing the service to customers and building employee morale.

3. *Stress quality.* Since the quality and performance of services are more difficult to measure than products, advertisements should feature consistency and high levels of competency. Hospitals use terms such as "caring," "professional," and "convenience," in their advertising.

SUMMARY

The roles of advertising are many, varied, and ever changing. The options open to advertisers have never been greater and the costs of errors is significantly magnified compared to only a few years ago. With advertisers dealing with fragmented audiences and media, higher costs of reaching prospects, and the challenges of effectively using new media technology, the demands on advertisers and their agencies have never been greater. However, regardless of the changes in the advertising process, two fundamentals for successful advertising will remain constant:

1. Effective advertising can only function within the context of an organized marketing plan.
2. Advertising is a marketing communication tool and rarely will be successful if directed at noncommunication problems. It is difficult, if not impossible, for advertising to overcome deficiencies in the core marketing program.

An effective advertising plan is an extension of the marketing goals of a firm. Advertising, in addition to other functions, normally is asked to develop or maintain product awareness, build company and brand image, and provide product information that differentiates one brand from another. The execution of advertising will vary by the stage in the trade channel, for example, retail, consumer, industrial, and professional. Furthermore, it can adapt to the primary product benefits and express them in a number of ways, such as testimonials, demonstrations, or long copy. Advertising will also be modified according to funds available as well as the corporate philosophy concerning the value of advertising within the marketing plan.

It is clear that advertising is only one of a number of possible sales tools. The advertising executive of the future will be a marketing communicator, able to utilize an array of marketing communication elements including promotion, public relations, and selling in a coordinated fashion to bring synergy and unity to the overall corporate message.

While major changes in advertising are on the horizon, the specific role of advertising, the key to its success, will continue to be the ability to develop an interesting message that will reach potential customers in an appropriate editorial environment at the proper time.

Planning is the foundation for successful advertising. The remainder of the text will discuss the techniques of advertising against a backdrop of marketing, research, and planning.

REVIEW

1. How do advertising objectives relate to a firm's overall marketing goals?
2. What is the relationship between consumer perception and brand equity?
3. What role does advertising usually play in the total marketing communication plan?
4. Discuss the relationship between generic and brand demand.
5. How does end-product advertising differ from traditional product advertising?
6. What are some of the prime means of making service advertising interesting and distinct?
7. How does the role of advertising differ in industrial and consumer advertising?
8. A product should be viewed not as a physical object, but as a package of consumer benefits. Discuss.
9. Compare and contrast advertising and public relations.

TAKE IT TO THE NET

We invite you to visit the Russell/Lane page on the Prentice Hall Web site at **www.prenhall.com/myphlip** for end-of-chapter exercises and applications.

PART II

Planning the Advertising

Chapter 3

The Advertising Spiral and Brand Planning

CHAPTER OBJECTIVES

One of the critical aspects of marketing communications decision making is developing a strategy. It has been said that strategy is everything. After reading this chapter you will understand

>> the importance of understanding the product life cycle

>> the relationship of the advertising spiral

>> the birth and basics of branding

>> brands and integrated marketing

>> brand equity

>> strategic planning methods

How do you differentiate your product and manage and protect your most important asset—your brand? We've seen a tremendous proliferation of new products over the past decade, not to mention the number of dot.coms created, many of which have ended up as roadkill. How do you know what kind of strategic message is needed? How do you manage advertising or branding for success?

Today's emphasis is being placed on ways to integrate marketing communications, build brand equity, and build better strategies for marketing that product. It doesn't matter whether we're talking about old economy or new economy products—marketing is marketing. Great importance is placed on the development of a product and its marketing objectives as part of a brand's *strategic plan* prior to creating ads. Here we examine several aspects important to creating the strategic plan and their advertising implications. Despite many marketing practices being challenged today, one of the constants is the need to have a clear understanding of the product and consumer wants and needs when making strategic advertising decisions.

The developmental stage of a product determines the advertising message. As products pass through a number of stages—from introduction to dominance to ultimate demise—the manner in which advertising presents the product to consumers depends largely upon the degree of acceptance the product has earned with consumers. The degree of acceptance can be identified as the product passes through its life cycle. It is this degree of acceptance that determines the advertising stage of the product. The life-cycle model discussed in this chapter consists of three primary stages (Exhibit 3.1):

- Pioneering stage
- Competitive stage
- Retentive stage

The nature and extent of each stage are discussed in the next sections.

PIONEERING STAGE

Procter & Gamble introduced a new product category in 1961—the disposable diaper or Pampers, which became a billion dollar product. Recently P&G introduced a product called Dryel. It too created a new consumer category—home dry cleaning. P&G hopes Dryel is a new Tide and projects sales of $500 million, making it as big as Downy or Bounce. But selling a new kind of home dry-cleaning product is not like selling the newest version of Tide; it's much harder. They have to convince consumers they need a kind of product they've never heard of. Their thinking is that Dryel is cheaper than professional dry cleaning (originally the cost was about $9.99 for a box that cleans 16 articles of clothing). It works, but will consumers think it fits their needs?[1]

When manufacturers create revolutionary new products, they may think consumers will flock to buy them. Many times manufacturers have trouble accepting the fact that despite all the money spent in developing and then promoting their product, consumers pay little or no attention to it. There are no guarantees that consumers will see a need for the product. For one thing, it may never have occurred to consumers that they need or want the product, and as a result they don't feel compelled to buy it. Until people appreciate the fact that they need it, a product is in the **pioneering stage.**

pioneering stage
The advertising stage of a product in which the need for such a product is not recognized and must be established or in which the need has been established but the success of a commodity in filling those requirements has to be established. *See* Competitive stage, Retentive stage.

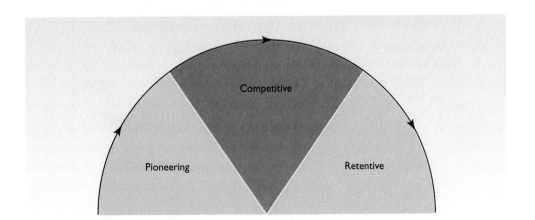

---

[1]Katrina Brooker, "Can Procter & Gamble change its culture, protect its market share, and find the next Tide?" *Fortune*, 26 April 1999, 146–152.

Exhibit

3.1

Primary Stages of the Life-Cycle Model

Advertising in the pioneering stage introduces an idea that makes previous conceptions appear antiquated. It must show that methods once accepted as the only ones possible have been improved and that the limitations long tolerated as normal are now overcome. It may be difficult to believe, but consumers didn't rush out to buy the first deodorants. Many consumers who were concerned with body odor simply used baking soda under their arms. So we can't take for granted the fact that consumers will change their habits. Advertising in this stage must do more than simply present a product—it must implant a new custom, change habits, develop new usage, or cultivate new standards of living. In short, advertising in the pioneering stage of a product's life cycle must educate the consumer to the new product or service.

Almost 30 years ago, Fleischmann's introduced Egg Beaters, a frozen egg alternative made from real eggs but without the yolk. The company had to convince consumers they needed an egg alternative. They had to convert egg eaters into Egg Beaters customers. Their market was concerned about the high cholesterol and fat of egg yolks. Fleischmann's had to change attitudes and habits to be successful. By accomplishing this, they became the dominating force in this new product segment. In the early 1990s, Egg Beaters tried to expand the market with an ad campaign built around the theme "When the Recipe Calls for Eggs" (see Exhibit 3.2).

These ads tried to sell Egg Beaters as a substitute in cooking "because you're using the healthiest part of real eggs. No cholesterol. No fat." Do you and your family use Egg Beaters, or egg substitutes?

The purpose of the pioneering stage of a product's life cycle, reduced to its simplest terms, is

- to educate consumers about the new product or service;
- to show that people have a need they did not appreciate before and that the advertised product fulfills that need; and
- to show that a product now exists that is actually capable of meeting a need that already had been recognized but could not have been fulfilled before.

Pioneering advertising generally stresses what the product can do, offer, or provide that could not have been done, offered, or provided by any product before.

A true pioneering product offers more than a minor improvement. It is important for the advertiser to remember that what determines the stage of the advertising is consumer perception of the product. In the pioneering stage, the consumer is trying to answer the question "What is the product for?" It does not really matter what the manufacturer thinks. Does the consumer think the improved changes in the product are significant? Or, is this really a better way of doing things?

Often the copy focuses on the generic aspect of the product category in an attempt to educate or inform the consumer. In the late 1980s, Interplak introduced a revolutionary new home dental product—an automatic instrument that removed plaque using two rows of counter-rotating oscillating brushes. Interplak had to convince consumers that this product cleaned teeth better than any kind of toothbrush—electric or otherwise (Exhibit 3.3). This was no easy task because the product cost about $100 at introduction. The pioneering Interplak ads suggested that

"Plaque is the real villain in oral hygiene. If not removed daily, its bacterial film can lead to early gum disease and tooth decay. But clinical studies have shown that manual brushing removes only some of the plaque buildup." Twenty years later Interplak is still trying to get the average household to try their product.

Consumer acceptance and understanding may take a long period of time—a few months, a number of years, perhaps never. Yahoo was introduced in 1994 as the first search engine. Both eBay and Amazon.com were introduced in 1995 as the first auction site and on-line bookstore. Priceline.com came along in 1998 selling airline tickets on the Internet with a "name-your-own-price" selling system. These selling concepts became accepted rather rapidly considering they were new business and technology types. Of course, they were enhanced by all the attention to the Web and their leadership.

The original idea behind Snapple was to create an all-natural juice drink line to be sold primarily in health-food stores. It was introduced in 1972, but it didn't become a national beverage company until 1992. The idea of natural beverages, which is common today, wasn't an overnight success with the masses of beverage consumers. Manufacturers may produce a product that does something many consumers instantly desire—a VCR, a cellular phone, or a laptop computer. For these products, advertising will not exhort consumers to raise their standards of acceptance, but rather will aim at convincing them that they can now accomplish something they couldn't before, through the use of the new product. For instance, the cellular phone industry told businesswomen that the cellular phone could keep them in touch not only with their clients, but also the world, as a security device—especially if they had car trouble or were threatened in some way. Now it is a matter of design, color, or size, not if I should own one.

The ad read, "***It mows. You don't. Introducing the Robomower from Friendly Robotics.***" This new product type costs about $800, plus shipping. The deterrent to growth, many times, is the cost. Many people may want the product but are not willing to pay that cost. Decades ago, it was predicted that *every* home would have a microwave in the kitchen. That number leveled off at around 72 percent. We are told that our CDs may soon be replaced by new technology. Are you willing to discard yours and start over with a new system?

Usually during the early introduction of a new product, heavy advertising and promotional expenses are required to create awareness and acquaint the target with the product's benefits. To expand, the manufacturer must gain new distribution, generate consumer trial, and increase geographical markets. At this stage, the product in the pioneering stage is not usually profitable. In other words, there can be a number of factors involved in the acceptance and purchase.

Purell Instant Hand Sanitizer was introduced in 1997 with a $15 million ad budget. Instant hand sanitizers require no soap, water, or towels and claim to be effective against 99.9 percent of all common germs. This was a new concept for consumers who may have used antibacterial soaps to kill germs. Purell was earlier marketed to only health care and food service workers, but the company wanted to grow the consumer market. When a new pain product called Aleve, containing naproxen, was introduced, it created a new category in a very mature analgesic market. Consumers had many analgesic choices to fight pain: aspirin was the first major product (i.e., Bayer) to fight pain, then came aspirin compounds (Anacin, BC tablets, among others), then acetaminophen (Tylenol), then ibuprofen (Advil, Nuprin), and then naproxen. Aleve's advertising support for the introduction was about $50 million. As you can see, pioneering advertisers incur heavy expenses in the process of educating the public about the advantages of a new type of product. If the advertiser has some success with the new idea, one or more competitors will quickly jump into the market and try to grab share from the pioneer.

Usually the main advantage of being a pioneer is that you become the leader with a substantial head start over others. So a pioneering effort can secure customers before the competition can even get started. Think about the hybrid car (gas and electric power). Will it be Toyota or Honda? Or, GM's all electric? Or, will Ford or Mercedes begin to compete? Then the trick is to hold onto your share.

THE COMPETITIVE STAGE

Once a pioneering product becomes accepted by consumers, there is going to be competition. The consumer now knows what the product is and how it can be used. At this point, the main question the consumer asks is, "Which brand shall I buy?" When this happens, the product has entered the **competitive stage,** and the advertising for it is referred to as competitive advertising. (Note that this is a restrictive meaning of the term, not to be confused with the looser meaning that all ads are competitive with each other.)

In the short term, the pioneer usually has an advantage of leadership that can give dominance in the market. Snapple was the dominant leader in ready-to-drink iced tea, but Pepsi and Coke quickly became aggressive with their versions of ready-to-drink iced tea to get a piece of the action. In the ready-to-drink coffee category, Starbucks controls 80 to 90 percent of the market. In 2000, competitors were gearing up for their share of the market including: Havana, Blue Luna, and Planet Java. Coca-Cola Company markets Georgia, a very popular ready-to-drink coffee in Japan. Currently, Starbucks sales are $200 million but predicts it has the potential to reach a billion worldwide. Generally, in the early competitive stage, the combined impact of many competitors, each spending to gain a substantial market position, creates significant growth for the whole product category. If the pioneer can maintain market share during this category, the initial period of competitors' growth, it can more than make up for the earlier expense associated with its pioneering efforts.

Among the many everyday products in the competitive stages are deodorants, soaps, toothpaste, cars, detergents, headache remedies, shaving creams, shampoos, televisions, VCRs, cat food, computers, and packaged foods. The purpose of competitive stage advertising is to communicate the product's position or differentiate it to the consumer; the advertising features the differences of the product.

Competitive slogans and headlines include the following:

Remarkably keeps itself 40% cleaner.
—DuPont Stainmaster Carpet

Every hand lotion stops dryness. This one stops germs.
—Keri antibacterial hand lotion

Acclaimed by French Gourmets since 1908.
—La Cornue stoves

Tungsten: A strong, dense metal used in the production of missles.
And drop shots too.
—Prince tennis racquets

Prudential. All the finest solutions for your home.
—Prudential

How to tell a pair of quality sunglasses from high-priced junk.
—Costa Del Mar

Our eCRM software can beat up your eCRM software!
—MicroStrategy

These one-liners don't educate you as to the product category advantages; that is taken for granted. Instead, each headline and the copy that follows set out to tell you why you should select that particular brand. West & Vaughan advertising said, *"Lee repairmen will fix more than your air conditioning. They'll fix the way you think about repairmen"* (Exhibit 3.4). This retro-layout ad brings back the thought of the quality of yesteryear by talking about the repairmen difference in selling this service.

THE RETENTIVE STAGE

Products reaching maturity and wide-scale acceptance may enter the **retentive stage,** or reminder stage, of advertising.

When a product is accepted and used by consumers, there may not be a need for competitive advertising. At this point, everybody knows about this product and likes or dislikes it—why advertise? The chief goal of advertising may be to hold on to those customers. Over the years, many manufacturers of successful products have stopped advertising and have seen the public quickly forget about them. Therefore, most astute advertisers try to retain their customers by keeping the brand name before them. The third stage through which a product might pass is called reminder advertising—it simply reminds consumers that the brand exists. This kind of advertising is usually highly visual and is basically name advertising, meaning the ad gives little reason to buy the product. Most reminder ads look like posters—they have a dominant illustration of the product and a few words. Generally, there is little or no body copy because there is no need to give consumers this kind of information.

Very few advertisers reach the point where they can consider their product entirely in the reminder stage. There usually are other products in the pioneering and competitive stages challenging their leadership position. In fact, if your product is truly all alone in the retentive stage, that may be cause for alarm. It may mean

Exhibit 3.4

Lee Air Conditioning talks about their competitive advantages.

Courtesy: West & Vaughan.

the product category is in decline, and the competition sees little future in challenging you for consumers.

The advertiser's goal in the retentive stage is to maintain market share and ward off consumer trial of other products. Products in the retentive stage do not necessarily cut back on their advertising expenditures, but they adopt different marketing and promotional strategies than those used in the pioneering and competitive stages. When a brand is used by a large portion of the market, its advertising is intended to keep present customers and increase the total market, on the assumption that the most prominent brand will get the largest share of the increase.

Generally, products in the retentive stage are at their most profitable levels because developmental costs have been amortized, distribution channels established, and sales contacts made. The development of advertising and promotion may often be routine at this stage. Obviously, companies like to maintain their products in the retentive stage as long as possible.

THE ADVERTISING SPIRAL

The advertising spiral (Exhibit 3.5) is an expanded version of the advertising stages of products just discussed. The spiral provides a point of reference for determining which stage or stages a product has reached at a given time in a given market and what the thrust of the advertising message should be. This can be important information for deciding on strategy and giving the creative team a clear perspective on what information they need to communicate to prospects. In many respects, the advertising spiral parallels the life cycle of the product.

Comparison of Stages

Naturally, there are fewer products in the pioneering stage than in the competitive stage. The development of new types of products or categories does not take place frequently. Most advertising is for products in the competitive stage. As already pointed out, such advertising often introduces features of a new product that is in the pioneering stage and gets the spotlight for a period of time.

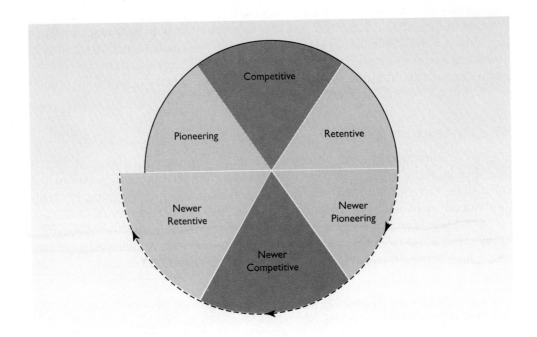

Exhibit

3.5

The Advertising Spiral

In using the advertising spiral, we deal with one group of consumers at a time. The advertising depends upon the attitude of that group toward the product. A product in the competitive stage may have to use pioneering advertising aimed at other groups of consumers to expand its markets. Thus, pioneering and competitive advertising could be going on simultaneously. Each series of ads, or each part of one ad, will be aimed at a different audience for this same product.

Products in the retentive stage usually get the least amount of advertising. This stage, however, represents a critical moment in the life cycle of a product, when important management decisions must be made. Hence it is important to create effective advertising in this stage.

Product in Competitive Stage, Improvement in Pioneering Stage

It is not unusual for a new brand to enter the competitive stage without doing any pioneering advertising. A new product entering an established product category must hit the ground running to differentiate itself from the competition. Every new brand thus enjoys whatever pioneering advertising has already been done in the product category. In 1998, Market Intelligence Service, Ltd., reported 25,181 products were introduced, but most were trivial advances beginning in the competitive stage.[2]

Change is a continuum: As long as the operation of a competitive product does not change, the product continues to be in the competitive stage, despite any pioneering improvements. Once the principle of its operation changes, however, the product itself enters the pioneering stage. Think about the change from the needle record player to compact disc technology. When a product begins to move into more than one stage, the changes are not always easy to categorize.

Whenever a brand in the competitive stage is revitalized with a new feature aimed at differentiating it, pioneering advertising may be needed to make consumers appreciate the new feature. Huggies diapers added a soft elastic band. If this advantage had not been advertised, consumers might have ignored the improvement.

Scramblers and Better'n Eggs, Healthy Choice eggs, and Simply Eggs created nonfrozen egg substitutes to compete with Egg Beaters' frozen product. Egg Beaters developed a refrigerated version to go with its frozen product. Exhibit 3.6 shows a television commercial that tells consumers they can find Egg Beaters in either the frozen food section or the egg section of their grocery. Was this new Egg Beaters in the competitive stage, the pioneering stage, or both?

Gillette has been a master of creating new products with new features. They introduced a two-blade razor (Trac II), adjustable two-blade razors (Atra), shock-absorbent razors (Sensor), and Mach 3, a razor with three blades. On the surface, Mach 3 sounds like a simple new product, but Gillette spent more than $750 million in development of the product.[3]

The Retentive Stage

The life of a product does not cease when it reaches the retentive stage. In fact, it may then be at the height of its popularity, and its manufacturer may feel it can just coast along. But a product can coast for only a short time before declining. No business can rely only on its old customers over a period of time and survive.

As noted earlier, the retentive stage is the most profitable one for the product. But all good things must come to an end. A manufacturer has a choice between two strategies when the product nears the end of the retentive stage.

---

[2]Jack Trout, *Differentiate or Die* (New York: John Wiley & Sons, 2000), 21.
[3]Jack Trout, *Differentiate or Die* (New York: John Wiley & Sons, 2000), 23.

In the first strategy, the manufacturer determines that the product has outlived its effective market life and should be allowed to die. In most cases, the product is not immediately pulled from the market. Rather, the manufacturer simply quits advertising it and withdraws other types of support. During this period, the product gradually loses market share but remains profitable because expenses have been sharply curtailed. This strategy is the one typically presented in textbook descriptions of the product life cycle, but not necessarily the one that corresponds to actual product development.

The problem with the typical life-cycle model in Exhibit 3.7 is that it portrays an inevitable decline in the product life cycle, whereas most long-term products go through a number of cycles of varying peaks and duration before they are finally taken off the market. The advertising spiral depicted in Exhibit 3.5 shows these cycles. The advertising spiral—the second strategy for a product nearing the end of the retentive stage—does not accept the fact that a product must decline. Instead, it seeks to expand the market into a newer pioneering stage. General Mills' CEO's

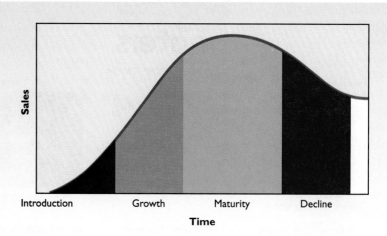

Exhibit

3.7

A Typical Life Cycle Model

advice is, "Do not believe in the product life cycle. Innovate constantly." Tide detergent was introduced in 1946. Since then, Tide has gone through more than 60 product upgrades.

As a product approaches the retentive stage, management must make some important decisions:

■ Can it make some significant improvements in the present product so that it virtually represents a new type of product or category (e.g., Clorox Cleaner)?

■ Is there a possibility for line extensions (e.g., Diet Coke)?

As we have seen, the life cycle of a product can be affected by many conditions. If, however, the product is to continue to be marketed, its own advertising stage should be identified before its advertising goals are set.

The three basic stages of the spiral (pioneering, competitive, and retentive) are straightforward and easy to understand. However, the stages in the bottom half (newer pioneering, newer competitive, and newer retentive) are trickier. To continue to market an established product successfully and profitably, creative marketing is necessary.

The newer pioneering stage attempts to get more people to use the product. Basically, there are two ways to enter this new stage. The first is by-product modification. This can be minor, such as adding a new ingredient to a detergent or a deodorant to a bar of soap, or—in the other direction—taking caffeine or sodium out of a soft drink or fat out of a food product. Alternatively, it may entail a complete overhaul of a product, such as a radical model change for an automobile. In some cases, advertising alone may be enough to get consumers to look at the product in a new light.

Advertisers cannot afford to simply rely on old customers because they die off, are lured away by the competition, or change their lifestyles. Smart advertisers will initiate a change in direction of their advertising when their product is enjoying great success. They will show new ways of using the product and give reasons for using it more often. For instance, if you are a successful soup company and your customers are eating your canned soup with every meal, you have reached a saturation point. How can you increase sales? Simply by encouraging people to use soup in new ways. You create recipe advertising that shows new food dishes and casseroles that require several cans of your product. You now have your customers eating your soup as soup, along with making casseroles from your soup. Of course, this means more sales and a new way of thinking about soup. That's exactly what

Egg Beaters did once they got consumers to switch from eggs to Egg Beaters for breakfast. Then they tried to get cooks to use Egg Beaters in their next recipe and emphasize taste.

New Pioneering Stage and Beyond

A product entering the new pioneering stage is actually in different stages in different markets. Long-time consumers will perceive the product as in the competitive or retentive stage. New consumers will perceive it as being a pioneer. At this point, the advertising spiral will have entered still another cycle (Exhibit 3.8), which we will call the *newest pioneering stage,* where the focus is on getting more people to use this type of product.

The product in this stage is faced with new problems and opportunities. Can you convince segments of your market not using your product that they should? Obviously, you have to understand why they were not interested in the product earlier. Creative marketing and a flexible product help this process.

Nike, Jell-O, Pepsi-Cola, Mountain Dew, Budweiser, ESPN, and Gillette are a few of the brands that reached the retentive stage and began to look for ways to move beyond it. All of these companies moved into new pioneering with product innovations. Hence, products such as Diet Coke, Cherry Coke, Diet Pepsi, Pepsi One, Diet Mountain Dew, and Bud Light were born. New pioneering can be the result of reworking the original product or a line extension—with a new formula and name—that is related to the original version of the product.

Creating product innovation does not always translate into brand share. Royal Crown Cola has been an industry innovator—first with national distribution of soft drinks in cans (1954), a low-calorie diet cola (1962), a caffeine-free diet cola (1980), and a sodium-free diet cola (1983).[4] They had the innovation but didn't effectively manage their advertising against the larger companies of Coca-Cola and Pepsi, nor did they effectively communicate with consumers.

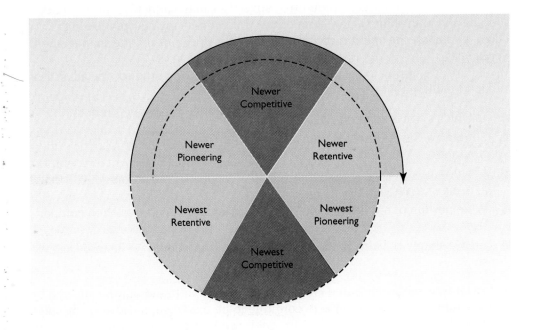

[4]"Royal Crown Plotting a Comeback with New Owners' Financial Support," *The Atlanta Journal* and *The Atlanta Constitution,* 6 March 1994, C8.

Exhibit

3.8

Expanded Advertising Spiral

The advertising focus in newer pioneering must be on getting consumers to understand what the product is about. Advertising in the newer competitive stage aims at getting more people to buy the brand. Current Crest toothpaste ads say, *"New Introducing . . . the most advanced Crest yet, . . . this new formula contains Micro-Cleaning Crystal."* Is this new pioneering or new competitive? The newer retentive stage relies on existing prestige to keep customers.

Moving through these stages—newer pioneering, newer competitive, newer retentive—is not easy. It requires the manufacturer to develop either product innovations or advertising positioning strategies that make the product different in consumers' eyes. Also, as we move to the newer stages of the spiral, there are usually fewer prospects for the product. Therefore, a company must become most efficient at targeting smaller groups of prospects. H.J. Heinz Co. introduced EZ Squirt, a line of colored, vitamin-C fortified ketchup in packaging especially designed for kids. Heinz is trying its hardest to resurrect itself in categories long considered stodgy or outmoded, and help consumers and retailers see them in a new way. EZ Squirt was developed from insight that kids under 12 are the biggest ketchup consumers. The advertising promoted the green-colored ketchup variety plus the product's easy-to-grip, squeezable bottles with a cap that allows kids to control the ketchup stream for drawing.[5] Will this product resurrect ketchup sales?

The Advertising Spiral as a Management Decision Tool

A product may try to hold on to its consumers in one competitive area while it seeks new markets with pioneering advertising aimed at other groups. We must remember that products do not move through each stage at the same speed. In some instances, a product may go quickly from one stage in one cycle to a newer stage in another cycle. This change may also be a matter of corporate strategy. A company may believe it can obtain a greater share of business at less cost by utilizing pioneering advertising that promotes new uses for the product. It is possible that the same results could be obtained by continuing to battle at a small profit margin in a highly competitive market. A retentive advertiser may suddenly find its market slipping and plunge into a new competitive war without any new pioneering work. Like a compass, the spiral indicates direction; it does not dictate management decisions.

Before attempting to create new ideas for advertising a product, the advertiser should use the spiral to answer the following questions:

- In which stage is the product?
- Should we use pioneering advertising to attract new users to this type of product?
- Should we work harder at competitive advertising to obtain a larger share of the existing market?
- What portion of our advertising should be pioneering? What portion competitive?
- Are we simply coasting in the retentive stage? If so, should we be more aggressive?

So far we've shown how the life cycle of a product or brand may be affected by many conditions. If the brand is to continue to be marketed, its advertising stage must be identified before its advertising goals can be set. Next, we examine how to expand on what we have learned to develop a strategic plan for a brand.

---

[5]Stephanie Thompson, "EZ being green: Kids line is latest Heinz innovation," *Advertising Age*, 10 July 2000, 3.

Building Strong Brands and Equity

Every product, service, or company with a recognized brand name stands for something slightly different from anything else in the same product category. If the difference is a desirable one, and is known and understood by consumers, the brand will be the category leader. Today, more than ever before, the perception of a quality difference is essential for survival in the marketplace.[6]

The Birth of Branding   In the mid-1880s, there were no **brands** and little quality control by manufacturers. Wholesalers held power over both manufacturers and retailers. Manufacturers had to offer the best deals to wholesalers to get their products distributed. This created a squeeze of profits. As a result of this profit squeeze, some manufacturers decided to differentiate their products from the competition. They gave their products names, obtained patents to protect their exclusivity, and used advertising to take the news about them to customers over the heads of the wholesalers and retailers. Thus the concept of branding was born. Among the early brands still viable today are Levi's (1873), Maxwell House Coffee (1873), Budweiser (1876), Ivory (1879), Coca-Cola (1886), Campbell Soup (1893), and Hershey's Chocolate (1900).[7] In 1923, a study showed that brands with "mental dominance" with consumers included Ivory (soaps), Gold Medal (flour), Coca-Cola (soft drinks), B.V.D. (underwear), Kellogg's Cornflakes (breakfast food), Ford (automobiles), Del Monte (canned fruit), and Goodyear (tires).[8] Today, we have a whole new generation of interactive brands fighting for value and a permanent place within consumers' lives, including: Yahoo!, America Online, eBay, Amazon.com, Excite@Home, and so on.

brand   A name, term, sign, design, or a unifying combination of them, intended to identify and distinguish the product or service from competing products or services.

Branding as a Financial Decision

Howard, Merrell & Partners of Raleigh, an independent Bozell agency, introduces themselves to clients by saying, "Branding isn't an advertising decision. It's a financial decision. We have learned that creating brand leverage is about dealing correctly with strategic issues and financial commitments at the top management level—then taking the risks necessary to deliver category-dominating creative. It is about risk management. It is about a deep understanding of a brand's one-on-one relationship with people, considered in the context of a macro-competitive environment. We believe that perhaps our most important role is assisting our client partners to achieve the alignment needed to reinforce brand values at all points of human contact. . . ."[9] Spread throughout this text we'll see a number of their ads and campaigns.

Consumer Environment

Today, consumers set the terms of their marketplace relationships because they have more access to information than ever before, and marketers seek to meet terms set by consumers. Advertisers talk in terms of person-to-person. Database marketers talk in terms of customer satisfaction. Information specialists talk in terms of smart systems. This is a new era for brands. It is about consumers telling marketers what they want and marketers responding. It is about interactive, continuous, real-time dialogue replacing traditional models of advertising and consumer communication. Yet consumers have consistently said year after year in

---

[6]David Martin, *Romancing the Brand* (New York: Amacon, 1989), xiv.
[7]Norman Berry, "Revitalizing brands," *Viewpoint*, July–August 1987, 18.
[8]Martin, *Romancing the Brand*, xiv.
[9]Howard, Merrell & Partners, "Introduction," 2000.

Yankelovich's MONITOR research that once they find a brand they like, "it is difficult to get them to change."[10]

Yes, habit is a marketer's biggest challenge. People's past experiences with a brand are consistently the most important factors in their future choices. Despite all the talk about quality, past experiences followed by price, quality, and recommendations from other people lead the reasons people buy a brand. These factors haven't significantly changed over the past two decades; however, price has become more important. Yes, psychological motivations are important, but a brand's most powerful advantage is rooted in the human tendency to form habits and stick to routines. Most people will buy the same brand over and over again if it continues to satisfy their needs.

For marketers to succeed, they must answer three questions: Who buys the brand? What do they want from it? Why do they keep coming back? According to the Roper Organization, many people buy familiar brands even if they believe the product does not have an actual advantage. Only half of Americans think that a specific brand of mayonnaise is different or better than others and worth a higher price. However, 62 percent know what brand of mayonnaise they want when they walk into the store. Another 22 percent look around for the best price on a well-known brand. Brand behavior is complex. Not everyone is brand conscious, and not all brand-conscious people are truly brand driven.[11]

Marketers need to be aware that as consumers' needs change, their purchase behaviors also may change. It is not unusual for needs to change when a life stage changes. For example, a couple may trade in their sports car for a van or SUV when they have a child. A recently divorced parent may be forced to change buying patterns due to less income. Interestingly, 40 percent of the people who move to a new address change their toothpaste. Yes, we need to understand consumers and their relationship to brands. Technology companies live in an even faster changing world. Their products change quickly and often live in a compressed lifecycle. Technology changes and consumer needs change just as quickly. Exhibit 3.9 shows readers an invitation to download their product, *Open Windows Apps on Linux*. Visit www.netraverse.com for free evaluation versions of Win4, a program that lets you open and work with windows software on a Linux 05.

Brands and Integrated Communication

In the past, many marketing functions—advertising, promotion, packaging, direct marketing, public relations, events—were created and managed independently in most organizations. The economic *pressures* facing companies today have created the need to manage these activities more efficiently and to ensure they all reinforce each other. Today a brand's equity is best strengthened through the integrated use of all marketing communication tools. It is imperative to project a single, cohesive brand image into the marketplace and into the consumer's mind. The result has been what is labeled integrated marketing communications.

Integrated communications refers to all the messages directed to a consumer on behalf of the brand: media advertising, promotion, public relations, direct response, events, packaging, Web, and so forth. Each message must be integrated or dovetailed in order to support all the other messages or impressions about the brand. If this process is successful, it will build a brand's equity by communicating the same brand message to consumers.

---

[10]J. Walker Smith and Ann Clurman, *Rocking the Ages* (New York: Harper Business, 1997), 276–286.
[11]Diane Crispell and Kathleen Brandenburg, "What's in a brand?" *American Demographics,* May 1993, 26–28.

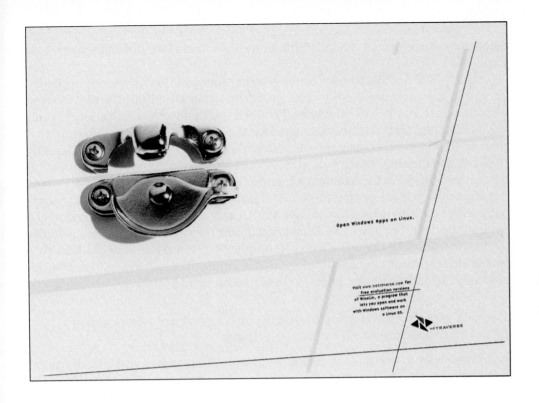

Exhibit

3.9

Netraverse is selling one technology to operate on another technology.
Courtesy: West & Vaughan.

There are those who say integration has been around for decades and decades, but it wasn't as important an issue as it is today.

During the 1980s, too many marketers milked their brands for short-term profits instead of protecting and nurturing their brands. In the 1990s, brand building became fashionable again. Today marketers realize the brand is their most important asset. Because integrated programs and brand building are so important, we discuss a system of integrated communications that builds brand equity. The most important factor in determining the actual value of a brand is its equity in the market. We can define **brand equity** as the value of how people such as consumers, distributors, and salespeople think and feel about a brand relative to its competition. Let us look at how Young & Rubicam assesses brand equity's value.

brand equity The value of how such people as consumers, distributors, and salespeople think and feel about a brand relative to its competition over a period of time.

Young & Rubicam's Brand Asset Valuator

Young & Rubicam (Y & R) has a procedure to evaluate a brand's value called the brand asset valuator (BAV), which explains the strengths and weaknesses of brands on measures of stature and vitality. It believes the relationship between these two factors tells the true story about the health of brand equity and can help diagnose the problems and solutions.

According to Y & R, a brand's vitality lies in a combination of differentiation and relevance. A brand must be distinct, or it simply isn't a brand. But the fact that a brand is highly differentiated doesn't necessarily mean consumers have the desire or means to buy it. Unless a brand is also relevant, the consumer has no reason to select it. One of their studies revealed that U.S. brands with high differentiation are Disney, Dr Pepper, Jaguar, Snapple, and Victoria's Secret. Brands with high relevance include AT&T, Kodak, Campbell's, and the U.S. Post Office.

The two components of brand stature are esteem and familiarity, that is, whether people know and understand your brand and whether they like it. A brand that more consumers know than like is a clear warning signal. Similarly, a brand that is held in high esteem but ranks lower in familiarity suggests that increasing awareness is an appropriate objective. Brands with high familiarity include Coca-Cola, Jell-O, McDonald's, and Kellogg. Among the brands with high esteem are Rubbermaid, Philadelphia brand cream cheese, Reynolds Wrap, and Band-Aid.

Sharon Slade of Marketing Corporation of America says, "Where many people go wrong is to assume there is one answer to evaluating brand equity. Having worked across a variety of categories, I can tell you that you need a variety of tools in your tool box. One of the keys to understanding brand equity is to recognize that there are differences between product categories. People buy computers differently from the way they buy soft drinks. Their relationship to that category is different, so the way you diagnose the health of a brand will be different as well."[12]

Hopefully, you are getting the sense that the development of advertising strategy and building brand equity deals with many complex issues. This discussion has been a little deep, but it has given you a feel for the many issues and terms advertising practitioners face daily. Despite this complexity, the development of advertising isn't brain surgery. It is understanding all the ramifications in the market and the consumer's mind, so we can integrate better, so we build brand equity better.

Brand Equity and Developing Integrated Marketing Communications Strategic Plans

Before you start to think about creating ads for a brand, you need a strategic plan. Before you can develop a strategy, you need an understanding of the marketing situation and a clear understanding of the brand's equity. There are four logical steps in this process resulting in the creative brief or plan:

1. Brand equity audit analysis
2. Strategic options and recommendations
3. Brand equity research
4. Creative brief

Of course, these generally would be followed by evaluation or assessment of some nature. An outline of a strategic planning process is presented next to give you insight into what is required. Some of the concepts and terms are discussed in more detail throughout the text.

Brand Equity Audit Analysis

There are a number of areas to examine in the first step, brand equity audit analysis. For instance, the context of the market, strengths and weaknesses, consumer attitude descriptions, and competitive strategies and tactics are of importance here.

Market Context   We begin by examining the existing situation of both the market and the consumer. What we are looking for are clues and factors that positively or negatively affect brand equity. The whole purpose is to set the scene. The types of questions that are asked include the following:

- What is our market and with whom do we compete?
- What are other brands and product categories?
- What makes the market tick?
- How is the market structured?
- Is the market segmented? If so, how? What segment are we in?

---

[12]Chip Walker, "How strong is your brand?" *Marketing Tools*, January/February 1995, 46–53.

- What is the status of store and generic brands?
- Are products highly differentiated?
- What kind of person buys products in this category?
- In the minds of these consumers, what drives the market or holds it back (needs, obstacles, and so forth)? What are the key motivators?
- Do consumers perceive the brands as very much alike or different?
- Is the product bought on impulse?
- How interested are consumers in the product?
- Do consumers tend to be **brand loyal**?

brand loyalty Degree to which a consumer purchases a certain brand without considering alternatives.

These questions should help us understand the status and role of brands in a given market. For example, when the market is made up of a few brands, the consumer will likely be more brand sensitive than if the market is split up into many brands.

North Carolina's Outer Banks is not a product that consumers pick up off a shelf, but the analysis process is the same. The ad produced by Jim Mountjoy, creative director of Loeffler Ketchum Mountjoy, says, *"The tides are treacherous. The wind sometimes fierce. It's hard to get here. When can we expect you?"* The copy differentiates the area: *"Why sugarcoat it? There is an undertone—the slightest whiff—of danger about this place. Of course, that's what gives the Outer Banks its seductive, otherworldly appeal."* It isn't an easy resort area to reach, but it is worth the trouble, isn't it (Exhibit 3.10)? We must look at the market from varying angles, and select only the relevant ones, so that we can set the scene for understanding and building brand equity.

Brand Equity Weaknesses and Strengths   Now we have a better understanding of the market context and are ready to examine the current brand equity—how strong or weak consumer bias is toward our brand relative to other brands. The following is a list of weakness and strength indicators often used.

- Brand awareness—top of mind is best
- Market share, price elasticity, share of voice, and similar factors
- Brand sensitivity—the relative importance of the brand to other factors involved in the purchase, such as price, pack size, model

Exhibit 3.10

North Carolina Outer Banks says, "Why sugarcoat it? There is an undertone—the slightest whiff—of danger about this place."
Courtesy: Loeffler Ketchum Mountjoy.

- Consistency of the brand's communication over time
- Image attribute ratings, or ranking attributes
- Distribution, pricing, product quality, and product information
- Brand loyalty—the strength of a brand lies in the customers who buy it as a brand rather than just as a product

Once the key weakness and strength indicators have been identified, they are used for future tracking purposes.

Consumer Attitude Descriptions After we understand the **market** in which our brand operates and have a clear understanding of the strengths and weaknesses of our brand equity, we need to identify and describe the consumer's thoughts and feelings that result in their bias toward our brand relative to other brands. This personal relationship between the consumer and the brand provides the most meaningful description of brand equity. To accomplish this, we need to analyze from two points of view.

First, we need to review all the available research to get as close a feeling as possible on how consumers view the brand and how they feel about it. Second, we must analyze in depth our brand's and its competitors' communications over a period of time. It is from these communications that most of the consumer's feelings (emotional elements) and opinions (rational elements) about the brand are derived (see Exhibit 3.11).

A brand equity description for the Golf GTI automobile might be as follows:

Emotional Elements	Rational Elements
My little sports car	Inexpensive
Sets me free	High gas mileage
It makes me feel and look good	Retains value
Simple	Durable
It's there when I want it	Dependable
I'm in control	Handles well
	Easy to park—small

Competitive Strategies and Tactics This area of the analysis is designed to provide a clear summary of the current communication strategies and tactics of our brand and of key competitors. It should include an analysis of all integrated communications in relation to brand equity. Is the strategy designed to reinforce current brand equity? Who is the target audience? Are there different target

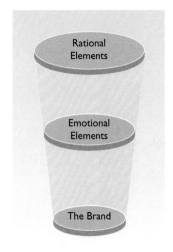

Exhibit
3.11

**The Basic Elements
of a Brand**

audiences? What are the themes and executional approach? How are the marketing funds being spent (consumer pull versus trade push, advertising, promotions, direct marketing, others)? An assessment of problems and opportunities is also in order here.

Strategic Options and Recommendations   The second step draws on the conclusions from the analysis to develop a viable recommendation plan. The strategic options include

- *Communication objectives.* What is the primary goal the message aims to achieve?
- *Audience.* To whom are we speaking?
- *Source of business.* Where are the customers going to come from—brand(s) or product categories?
- **Brand positioning** *and benefits.* How are we to position the brand, and what are the benefits that will build brand equity?
- *Marketing mix.* What is the recommended mix of advertising, public relations, promotion, direct response, and so on?
- *Rationale.* How does the recommended strategy relate to, and what effect is it expected to have on, brand equity?

brand positioning
Consumers' perceptions of specific brands relative to the various brands of goods or services currently available to them.

Brand Equity Research

The third step is where we do the proprietary, qualitative research. It is exploratory and task oriented. Here we need to determine which element(s) of brand equity must be created, altered, or reinforced to achieve our recommended strategy and how far we can stretch each of these components without risking the brand's credibility. This may give us a revised list of rational and emotional elements that describe how we want consumers to think and feel about our brand in the future.

Creative Brief

The final step is a written creative brief (or work plan) for all communications. We synthesize all the information and understanding into an action plan for the development of all communications for the brand: advertising, public relations, promotion, and so forth.

The creative strategy (brief or work plan) is a short statement that clearly defines our audience; how consumers think or feel and behave; what the communication is intended to achieve; and the promise that will create a bond between the consumer and the brand. A typical strategy would include the following:

- *Key observations*—the most important market/consumer factor that dictates the strategy
- *Communication objective*—the primary goal the advertising/communication aims to achieve
- *Consumer insight*—the consumer "hot button" our communication will trigger
- *Promise*—what the brand should represent in the consumer's mind; what the brand is promising the consumer
- *Support*—the reason the promise is true
- *Audience*—to whom we are speaking and how they feel about the brand.

There may be a need for an additional element:

- *Mandatories*—items used as compulsory constraints; for example, if there is a specific legal requirement or corporate policy that impacts the direction of the strategy

Other Examples of Strategic Planning

It is important to understand that there isn't just one approach to developing an integrated strategic plan for a brand. The basic steps are similar, but each agency approaches the process with a little different wrinkle. Let us take a look at the basics of a couple of other strategic planning approaches.

Avrett, Free & Ginsberg's Planning Cycle

Avrett, Free & Ginsberg (AFG) use a seven-step planning cycle that helps create strategic advertising. They use the discipline of account planning at each stage of developing strategy. Briefly, the framework for their strategic planning cycle (see Exhibit 3.12) involves the following steps:

1. *Brand/market status.* AFG evaluates where the brand is in its marketplace and determines strengths, weaknesses, opportunities, and threats.
2. *Brand mission.* After determining brand status, AFG proposes and agrees upon brand goals, that is, where they can take the brand.
3. *Strategic development.* Here they explore various options to determine which of several strategies will empower the brand to achieve the mission. AFG uses a process called needs mapping (Exhibit 3.13). The basic principle is that people respond or bond to products based on a wide range of psychological and rational needs. This process is loosely based on Maslow's Hierarchy of Needs.
4. *Strategy.* AFG formulates a tight strategy to be used in developing a fully integrated marketing communication program.
5. *Creative exploration.* AFG develops, explores, and evaluates a range of executions to ensure that they maximize the relevancy, distinctiveness, and persuasiveness of the strategy and final execution.
6. *Brand valuation.* AFG tracks marketplace performance and progress because it believes it must be accountable for the results its work generates. AFG constantly fine-tunes and improves communications in response to changing market conditions.
7. *Brand vision.* In building equities for a brand through effective communications, AFG plots long-range expansion plans for the base brand. AFG determines if the emerging brand equities can be line extended or translated to serve needs in other related categories.

These seven steps are constantly pursued in the evaluation of a brand's life cycle to ensure long-term growth and brand equity.

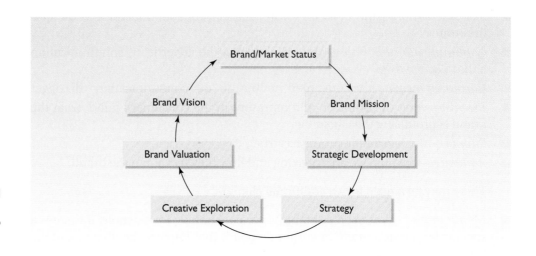

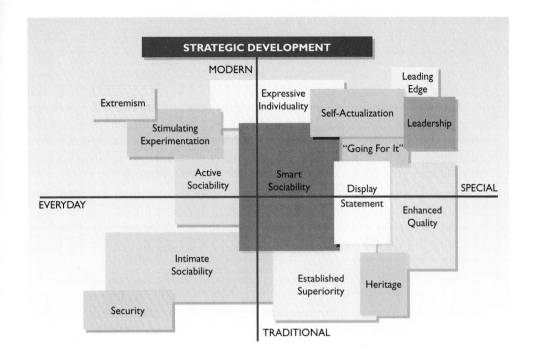

Exhibit

3.13

An Example of AFG's Need-Mapping Process

Courtesy: Avrett, Free & Ginsburg.

Thompson Total Branding

J. Walter Thompson (JWT) approaches what the firm calls Thompson Total Branding.

J. Walter Thompson began a series of organizational changes in 1996 to deliver a broader range of agency services to clients. "More and more clients were coming to us and saying, 'How can we revitalize our brand?' not 'We need a new campaign for this spring,'" according to the New York general manager of JWT. The changes were part of a program the agency calls Thompson Total Branding, a worldwide effort to shift the company's focus from simply creating advertising to broader marketing issues.

Thompson T-Plan

Part of JWT's strategic planning process includes the Thompson T-Plan (see Exhibit 3.14). This planning cycle includes answering five basic questions about the brand: Where are we now? Why are we there? Where could we be? How can we get there? Are we getting there? Let us take a brief look at each step:

1. *Where are we now?* Here the brand is examined in the marketplace, in consumers' minds, in relation to its competitors, and in the client's mind. It attempts to answer a number of questions including: Where do you stand?

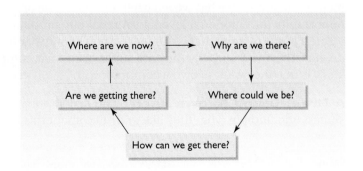

Exhibit

3.14

Thompson T-Plan

Courtesy: J. Walter Thompson/Atlanta.

Which competitors do you really have to worry about? What are the consumers like? How do they feel about the product and the brand? This enables JWT to evaluate and determine the brand's overall appeal.

2. *Why are we there?* The agency uses a series of tools designed to help them develop insights into the reasons behind a brand's current position. They use Key Discoveries about the brand, the category, the consumer, and the communication. These discoveries and the client's attitude and resources all lay the groundwork for identifying what JWT calls the Brand Vision, which serves as a strategic focus for all the brand's communication activities. This is where (SWOT) *strengths, opportunities, weaknesses,* and *threats* are determined.

3. *Where could we be?* Using Key Discoveries as a foundation, the JWT brand team puts itself in the consumer's shoes to identify the most powerful connection between the brand and the consumer. This is the bridge between the insight of planning and the magic of creative innovation. The end product is the Brand Vision.

4. *How can we get there?* The next step is identifying the Brand Idea, which is the creative expression of the Brand Vision. This idea becomes the foundation of all communication briefs. Upon this Branding Idea, JWT builds a communication plan, in which they determine how to reach the consumer target where and when they will be most receptive to the message.

5. *Are we getting there?* An essential aspect of communications planning is accountability. JWT needs to know how well it has accomplished its objectives, and how to improve next time. Thompson Total Branding provides proprietary tools to evaluate and learn from its performance.

What Great Brands Do

Scott Bedbury, former senior vice president of marketing at Starbucks Coffee, said, "I walked through a hardware store last night and I came across 50 brands I didn't know existed. They may be great products, but they're not great brands." Scott should know brands. He's the man who gave the world "Just Do It," Nike's branding campaign. A few of Bedbury's brand-building principles are examined here:[13]

A Great Brand Is in It for the Long Haul For decades there were brands based upon solid value propositions—they had established their worth in the consumers' minds. Then, in the 1980s and 1990s, companies focused on short-term economic returns and diminished in long-term brand-building programs. As a result, there were a lot of products with very little differentiation. Today a great brand is a necessity, not a luxury. By using a long-term approach, a great brand can travel worldwide, speak to multiple consumer segments simultaneously, and create economies of scale, by which you can earn solid margins over the long term.

A Great Brand Can Be Anything Some categories lend themselves to branding better than others, but anything is brandable. For example, Starbucks focuses on how coffee has woven itself into the fabric of people's lives, and that's an opportunity for emotional leverage. Almost any product offers an opportunity to create a frame of mind that is unique. Do you know what Intel computer processors do, how they work, or why they are superior to their competitor? All most people know is that they want to own a computer with "Intel Inside."

A Great Brand Knows Itself The real starting point is to go out to consumers and find out what they like or dislike about this brand and what they asso-

---

[13]Alan M. Webber, "What great brands do," *Fast Company,* August–September 1997, 96–100.

ciate as the very core of the brand concept. To keep a brand alive over the long haul, to keep it vital, you have got to do something new, something unexpected. It has to relate to the brand's core position.

A Great Brand Invents or Reinvents an Entire Category The common ground that you find among brands such as Disney, Apple, Nike, and Starbucks is that these companies made it an explicit goal to be the protagonists for each of their entire categories. Disney is the protagonist for fun family entertainment and family values. A great brand raises the bar—it adds a greater sense of purpose to the experience.

A Great Brand Taps into Emotions The common ground among companies that have built great brands is not just performance. They realize consumers live in an emotional world. Emotions drive most, if not all, of our decisions. It is an emotional connection that transcends the product. And transcending the product is the brand.

A Great Brand Is a Story That's Never Completely Told A brand is a metaphorical story that is evolving all the time. This connects with something very deep. People have always needed to make sense of things at a higher level. Look at Hewlett-Packard and the "HP Way." That's a form of company mythology. It gives employees a way to understand that they are part of a larger mission. It is a company rich in history, a dynamic present, and a bright future.

Levi's has a story that goes all the way back to the gold rush. They have photos of miners wearing Levi's dungarees. Stories create connections for people. Stories create the emotional context people need to locate themselves in a larger experience.

A Great Brand Is Relevant A lot of brands are trying to position themselves as "cool," but most of them fail. The larger idea is to be relevant. It meets what people want; it performs the way people want it to. In the past couple of decades a lot of brands promised consumers things they couldn't deliver. Consumers are looking for something that has lasting value. There is a quest for quality, not quantity.

Brand Development Demystified . . .
Brad Majors, CEO/SOCOH Group

There is a lot of talk about "branding" or "brand development" these days, as if it is the next "new thing" in marketing and sales. "Brand development" is not a new phenomenon. It has been around for at least 100 years.

Any marketer or ad agency worth its salt practices "brand development" every time they perform any marketing function. The history of advertising in America is, essentially, the history of branding. That is what good advertising (and the other communication disciplines) do—create good and consistent reputations for products or services and this consistent imagery is what converts a product into a "brand."

I say "consistent" because one of the greatest sins of marketing these days (especially for smaller businesses) is a lack of "integrated marketing." By this I mean that there may be mixed messages (from media advertising, public relations, the Web site, package copy, or whatever) that go out to consumers from a brand. And with these inconsistent messages comes an inconsistent image for the brand. Developing integrated marketing communications is one of the most important activities that can be done to enhance the value of a client's brand. It is nearly impossible to build a brand with inconsistencies in your marketing communications mix.

Business schools teach "the Marketing Mix," which is pretty basic stuff, but bear with me. This Marketing Mix includes the Four P's of marketing: the Product itself (and its structural packaging), the Price of the product, the Place (of distribution) where the product can be purchased, and the Promotion of the product. Interestingly, the Fourth P, Promotion, is simply the communication of aspects of the first three P's.

What else is critical to the sale other than what the product does, how much it costs, and where you can get it? Only one more "element" I can think of.

Enter the "Fifth P," which isn't discussed in business-school textbooks, but I doubt the idea is mine alone. What does the Fifth P stand for? The Prospect. The person who is going to buy this product or service, based on their perceived needs and wants.

If the Fourth P, Promotion, connects Product, Price, and Place, it also performs another valuable function. Good Promotion, be it in the form of media advertising, packaging graphics, public relations, or in-store merchandising, also has the responsibility of connecting the Prospect to the Product, its Price, and the Place it can be found. In essence, the product is just a collection of features and attributes until the Prospect arrives on the scene. When the Prospect's needs and wants begin to surface, so do the brand's marketing possibilities.

As the Prospect evaluates all the information he or she knows about the Product (what it does, what it costs, where it can be purchased), a relationship may begin to form. However, this will only happen if the brand imagery has been consistently presented. This relationship is based on how the Prospect feels the Product (or service) will meet their needs and wants. I call this "personal relevance." How does the Prospect relate emotionally to those rational product attributes? This "personal relevance" is not a new concept in marketing either. Marketers have been trying to figure out how to achieve the emotional bond between Prospect and brand since the 1920s when Motivational Research was first used by ad agencies. And we are still trying to crack the code on why consumers make the brand choices they make.

A final comment in the Brand Development Demystification process: Sometimes the term "brand development" can suggest some type of inexpensive short cut in marketing. I have spoken with entrepreneurs who wanted to do "brand development" because they didn't have money for advertising. Sorry, it doesn't really work that way. While media advertising may not be the only way to promote your brand, developing a brand takes time and money. Strong brands do not come cheaply. Fortunately, if the "brand development" process is successful, that investment will pay out big as you go down the marketing road.

SUMMARY

Products pass through a number of stages from introduction to ultimate demise, known as the product life cycle. Advertising plays a different role in each stage of product development. Until consumers appreciate the fact that they need a product, that product is in the pioneering stage of advertising. In the competitive stage, an advertiser tries to differentiate its product from that of the competition. The retentive stage calls for reminder advertising.

A product's age has little to do with the stage it is in at any given time. Rather, consumer attitude or perception determines the stage of a product. As consumer perception changes, moving it from one stage to another, the advertising message should also change. In fact, the advertising may be in more than one stage at any given time. Creative marketing may propel a product through new pioneering, new competitive, and new retentive stages. And it is even possible for a product to continue on into the newest pioneering, newest competitive, and newest retentive stages. As a product ages, so do its users, which is why no product can survive without attracting new customers. Long-term success depends on keeping current customers while constantly attracting new ones.

In the mid-1880s there were no brands. Manufacturers differentiated their products and gave them names as the concept of branding was born. Brands are now among the most valuable assets a marketer owns. The product is not the brand. A product is manufactured; a brand is created and is made up of both rational and emotional elements. In today's marketing environment, it is essential that every communication reinforces brand personality in the same manner: advertising, public relations, promotion, packaging, direct marketing, and so forth. The most important factor in determining the actual value of a brand is its equity in the market: how consumers think and feel about the brand.

Advertising agencies have their own unique systems to develop strategic planning for a brand. J. Walter Thompson uses Total Branding, which includes the Thompson T-Plan, to answer five key questions: Where are we now? Why are we there? Where could we be? How can we get there? Are we getting there? The Five P's: Product, Price, Place, Promotion, and Prospect.

REVIEW

1. What is the pioneering stage?
2. What determines the stage of a product?
3. What is the essence of the advertising message in each stage of the spiral?
4. What is brand equity?
5. What are the elements of the creative brief?
6. What are the key elements in the Thompson T-Plan?

TAKE IT TO THE NET

We invite you to visit the Russell/Lane page on the Prentice Hall Web site at **www.prenhall.com/myphlip** for end-of-chapter exercises and applications.

Chapter 4

Target Marketing

Marketers need to determine who their prime prospects are. They need to understand changes taking place in society and their impact on their business. After reading this chapter you will understand:

>> defining prime prospects

>> importance of target marketing information

>> marketing concept

>> planning the advertising

>> niche marketing and positioning

>> beyond demographics: psychographics

In Chapter 3 we examined the brand in the context of market and consumers. In the creative brief we were asked, "Whom are we speaking to?" Here we speak to answering your options.

Who is going to buy your product? Who are you going to aim your advertising and other integrated marketing communications? Men? Women? Men and women? 25- to 49-year-olds? Seniors? Hispanics? Affluents? A lot of possibilities. Has the target changed? Is it going to be profitable? What is the rationale for selecting this target? You need to know the answer to a lot of questions. In the process, does that mean we don't aim at everybody who has money? You know that won't work—that's a shotgun approach. You need to be focused and direct, like a rifle shot, to hit your target. Howard, Merrell & Partners created a terrific series of small ads to target Brookhill Steeplechase prospects, "*The Brookhill Steeplechase. The reason Range Rovers have tailgates*" (Exhibit 4.1) in one of their ads. Another said, "Where else would you go to find a Rolls Royce Corniche convertible with a trailer hitch?" What kind of people do you perceive as their target?

The
Brookhill Steeplechase.
The reason
Range Rovers have tailgates.

🏳 Saturday, May 4, steer your designer 4x4 to the Brookhill Steeplechase.
From tailgate contests to hobnobbing 🏳 with the local gentry, you may
forget there's a race going on. For prime tailgate parking, call 510-7915. 🏳

BROOKHILL ⤚⚬⤚ THE STEEPLECHASE

As we have just indicated, the monolithic mass market of the mid-twentieth century has long been laid to rest, and smaller mass markets have taken its place. Foote, Cone & Belding (FCB) even suggests it is person-to-person advertising.

Marketing Generalization As we discuss many factors and groups used by marketers, a word of caution. Marketers have a tendency to generalize. We talk about baby boomers, seniors, generations X, Y, & Z, or limit discussions to demographics (age, income, sex) as if each is a uniform group of people who live, think, and act exactly the same. Do all 20-year-olds think and act alike? Virtually no generalization encompasses an entire consumer segment, especially age groups. If we stop to think about it, we know better than to generalize. Consider that seniors or matures can be wealthy or not, love the outdoors or not, be inclined to travel or be homebodies, own a vacation home or live in a mobile home. The same considerations apply to virtually each of these catch-all categories. Of course, these groupings or segments can be very useful in assessing potential markets; after all, they do group behavior and lifestyle commonalities. These segments should be considered, but remember they stereotype groups of people. We all know that all Russians drink vodka, Germans drink beer, and the French drink wine, right? Or that all Southerners eat grits? It is okay to start with a premise in narrowing to one of these groups, but it is important to dig deeper.

A cardinal rule in marketing has always been to know your market. That doesn't mean segmenting young and old or rich and poor. It means defining your target in such detail that circumstances allow and necessity requires. There is a reason that reliable market research looks at multiple factors such as age, gender, income, net worth, ethnicity, geography, lifestyle, and family status. It is very appropriate to use "families" as a partial descriptor of a given market, as long as it doesn't become a synonym for the market itself.[1] Now that we have sent up a red flag, let us look at some factors and segments used in target marketing.

Once you ask the obvious questions, you must determine which answers are critical to your decision making. Do you need more information to reach your prospects successfully? Do you understand their problems? Have you thought about what you want people to think and feel about your brand as a result of being exposed to your advertising?

DEFINING PRIME PROSPECTS

One of the keys to success is defining the prime prospects so you do not waste time and money advertising your product to people unlikely to buy it or people you can't make a profit by attracting. This search for the best prospects among all consumers is called **target marketing.**

target marketing
Identifying and communicating with groups of prime prospects.

The process of finding prime prospects can be very complex because there are numerous ways of looking at consumers, many different kinds of information to consider, and a constantly changing consumer environment. Who is the target for the Cybertune.org ad (Exhibit 4.2)?

Where Do We Start?

Different agencies and companies approach the process a little differently, as we saw in the last chapter, but all have to answer the same important questions before advertising can be created. Brand equity research, for instance, seeks to answer a number of questions and examine the existing state of the brand in the context of market and consumers. Today, marketers have a host of informational sources to help plan integrated marketing programs aimed at individual users or groups. Let us look at some of the information sources and trends in America and their implications for advertising planning.

Census Data

Census data offer marketers a wealth of information about people and how they live in the United States. Much of the database is on-line. The Topologically Integrated Geographic Encoding and Referencing system, known as TIGER, is one of the more sophisticated tools. This coding of the country's natural, political, and statistical boundaries includes every street, road, and subdivision. TIGER provides the data for computer maps to plan sales territories and pinpoint direct-marketing prospects. This information can be linked to a number of relevant characteristics, such as age, income, and race. Custom research companies using these data have developed software for marketers to access geodemographic databases.

---

[1]Joe Marconi, "Targets big enough to miss," *American Demographics,* October 1996, 51–52.

We post your music.
They buy it.
We pay you.

cybertunes.org

Minority Markets

African Americans The Census Bureau's statistical profile of African Americans released in 1997 indicated a population of 33.9 million, or 12.8 percent of the nation's total. The black population is younger and faster-growing than the white population. The median income of all black families was $25,970 compared to that of white families at $45,020. However, married-couple black families' median income was similar to the income of white families, $49,752 versus $59,025. Between 2001 and 2010, there will be a slight decline in black students in schools aged 5 to 9, and a decrease of 9 percent for children aged 10 to 14. Census data indicate areas of the country where large concentrations of African Americans live and don't live.

Hispanics Census projections call for Hispanics to overtake blacks as the nation's largest minority in 2009. By 2050, Hispanics will make up a quarter of the U.S. population and blacks less than a sixth. In 1995, there were about 26.5 million Hispanics in this country, or 10 percent of the population. In perspective, this market is comparable to the entire population of Canada. By 2010, the Hispanic population is projected to increase by 8.3 million, which parallels the current populations of Wisconsin, Iowa, and Wyoming combined. Keep in mind there isn't a single Hispanic market because of cultural differences from their countries of origin. Or marketers could look at other implications, between 2001 and 2010, the percentage of Hispanic children aged 5 to 9 will increase by 21 percent and those 10 to 14 years old will increase by 29 percent.

Asians   From 1980 to 1990, the census recorded a 108 percent increase of Asians and Pacific Islanders living in the United States. This marked the highest growth rate for any group in the country. Census projected their population to jump from 12 million in 2000, to 17 million by 2010, and 41 million by 2050. Asians also cannot be lumped together into a single group. There are separate communities to consider: Japanese Americans, Chinese Americans, Filipino Americans, Asian Indians, and others. The percentage increase in Asian children rises faster than Hispanics; 5 to 9 will increase by 22 percent by 2010, and those aged 10 to 14 will increase by 31 percent.

Households

Household Income   The Bureau of Labor Statistics' Consumer Expenditure Survey produces annual estimates of household spending on hundreds of items, cross-tabulated by demographic characteristics. As with most data, you need to use these data wisely. In addition to looking at household income, advertisers often look at disposable and discretionary income. Disposable income is the after-tax income. Discretionary income is the amount of money consumers have after paying taxes and buying necessities such as food and housing.

In September 2000, the Census Bureau reported that the typical U.S. household had a median income of $40,816 in 1999. Women's median earning was $26,324 and men's $36,476. Marketers have to look carefully at the numbers. For example, the Census Bureau reported household non-Hispanic white, $44,366, black $27,910, Asian/Pacific Islander $51,205, and Hispanic 30,735. In the Northeast it was $41,984 and in the Midwest, $42,679; metro areas had a household medium income of $42,785 against nonmetro's $33,021; Alaska was reported at $51,046, Maryland $50,630, Michigan $40,066, Louisiana $32,218, Mississippi $30,628, and West Virginia $28,420. The largest income growth was among blacks and Asian/Pacific Islanders. As you can see marketers need to look beyond the basic numbers to get a better picture if household income is a factor in developing targets. Looking at gender, race, geography, age, and education will paint a different picture.

Spending   American Demographics found that the average U.S. metropolitan household devotes 16 percent of its spending for shelter, 17 percent for transportation, 14 percent for food, 6 percent for utilities, 6 percent for apparel, 5 percent for entertainment, 3 percent for household operations, and 11 percent for personal insurance. Spending patterns depend strongly on the unique age and income characteristics of individual markets.[2] Many products and services depend on disposable income of consumers for their existence. Orange County Speedway depends on attracting people who want to watch races. West & Vaughan created this ad selling the benefit of noise (Exhibit 4.3). Race fans are a growing market.

Marrieds   The U.S. Census Bureau reported in 1997 the continued decline of married households. In 1996, of the 99.6 million households in this country, married couples with or without children accounted for 53.7 percent. In 1990, married households accounted for 56 percent; in 1980, they made up 60.8 percent; and in 1970, they comprised 70.5 percent. Clearly, this decline has had social and marketing ramifications.

Birthrate   To marketers, the number of births in a given year can be important in projecting market size. The birthrate in the United States has been in decline for

---

[2]Marcia Mogelonsky, "America's hottest markets," *American Demographics*, January 1996, 20–27.

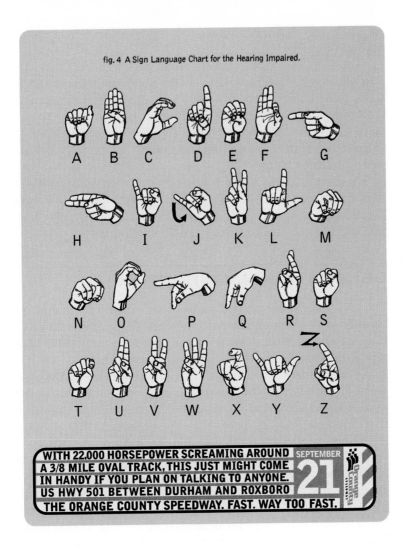

fig. 4 A Sign Language Chart for the Hearing Impaired.

WITH 22,000 HORSEPOWER SCREAMING AROUND
A 3/8 MILE OVAL TRACK, THIS JUST MIGHT COME
IN HANDY IF YOU PLAN ON TALKING TO ANYONE.
US HWY 501 BETWEEN DURHAM AND ROXBORO
THE ORANGE COUNTY SPEEDWAY. FAST. WAY TOO FAST.

SEPTEMBER
21

Orange County

decades. In 1960, the rate was 23.7 per 1,000 population, and it was about 14.2 per thousand in 2000. Just think of the significance to companies selling baby items. If marketers marry knowledge of fluctuations in the birthrate, with an understanding of how consumers tend to act at different stages of their lives, you can get a rough picture of the market challenges that lie in the future.

In recent years there were slightly fewer than 4 million babies a year born; about one-third of children in 1997 were ethnic minorities, and roughly 62 percent of married mothers with preschoolers were in the workforce (in 1965 only 23 percent of married mothers worked).

Population   In the United States, marketers have always had to deal with population growth and shifts that influence advertisers' markets in some way. Obviously, we need to know who is out there in the marketplace. How many of them? Where and how do they live? What do they need? What are their buying patterns? We can't easily reach people if we don't know where they are. But population is more than simple numbers of people. Society tends to group people by age or ethnicity or generation or some factor to help understand better some or all of the people. For instance, *American Demographics* breaks out the generations living in 2000: GI Generation, 71 plus years (9.1%); Depression, 61–70 (6.5%); War Babies, 55–60 years old (5.7%); Baby Boomers, 36–54 years (28.2%); Generation X, 22–34 years (16.4); Generation Y 6–23 years (25.8); and Millennials, 0–5 years (8.3%).[3] How they think,

---

[3]Alison Stein Wellner, "Generational divide," *American Demographics*, October 2000, 56.

act, and spend influences marketers. An advertiser must understand these people beyond numbers.

The U.S. Census Bureau data projections indicate that by the year 2025, 70 percent of the growth will take place in the South and West. By 2025, there will be moderate growth for New York, New Jersey, Pennsylvania, Ohio, and Michigan. California will double its population from 1990 to 2040. But that is only part of the story. California gained 1.3 million immigrants while losing 1.5 million natives to surrounding states. So numbers alone don't tell the picture. But the numbers themselves indicate change.

We are not going to attempt to cover all the demographics that may be important, but these items should give you something to think about, keeping in mind that these may or may not be important to a specific marketing situation. It is very necessary to get a handle on what data are important.

GENERATIONAL MARKETING

The consumer society is really a twentieth-century phenomenon, and for the past century or so, many businesses have made decisions based on the assumptions that one generation will grow up and make the same kinds of choices made by the group that went before them at the same stages of life.

Modern marketing's definition of "generation" is composed of two disparate parts. First, there's the traditional definition used by demographers: the number of people in any age group and what that portends about the size and shape of tomorrow's markets. Second, there's the issue of shared attitudes, a common history, and formative experiences. Both definitions are important to marketers.

Marketers think experiences bind people that are born in continuous years into "cohorts"—a group of individuals that have a demographic statistic in common. Demographers like to package things in a way that's easy to measure, and date of birth is the easiest way to define generations. Generational marketing people take the statistical analysis of births and overlay major world events that occurred during a generation's formative years to construct a picture of a generation's personality.[4] Knowing how many babies are born and then tracing the numbers through different stages of their lives give marketers a rough idea of the challenges and opportunities over 10, 20, and even 30 years.

Researchers have concentrated on four generations mentioned earlier (Matures, Boomers, and Generations X and Y), and are beginning to learn about the Millennials (Gen Z). There are distinct differences in how each generation thinks and buys.

The values of Matures are close to what are considered classic American values: They favor a kind of puritan work ethic, with plenty of self-sacrifice, teamwork, conformity for the common good, and so forth.

The Boomers, on the other hand, are self-assured and self-absorbed. They are much better educated than any generation before them, and they are aware of this. They think they are more sophisticated and believe they know better than their predecessors. They are very self-conscious about changing the world and fixing things.

Generation X Generation Xers were born in the post-Baby-Boom era of 1965 to 1978 with the leading edge approaching their mid-thirties; currently, about 44 percent are married, and almost half are parents. This generation was a long-time media whipping post, once decried as overeducated slackers. Recent Yankelovich Partners research finds Xers to be self-reliant, entrepreneurial, techno-focused, media-savvy, socially tolerant, and slowly, but surely, parents. Growing up with sky-

---

[4]Alison Stein Wellner, "Generational divide," *American Demographics,* October 2000, 52–58.

rocketing divorce rates and with less than family stability, Gen Xers have been more cautious about entering the lifestage of family formation. In 1970, women typically got married before age 21; now, 25 is the median age at first marriage. Men have gone from 23 to 27 over the same period. Today, Xers are reinventing the *Traditionalism* they are bringing to family life.

Survey data shows that Xers are much more likely than their Boomer counterparts were 20 years ago to want to return to traditional standards across a number of domains, especially family life. Their homes will be practical and utilitarian; pragmatic concerns outweigh "home as a showplace" considerations. For instance, the kitchen will be less about kitchen and more about convenience. The dining room is a victim of Xer lifestyle components: fast-paced lives, multi-tasking (consuming food and media at the same time), and the proliferation of "home meal replacement" options. There will be a trend toward "great rooms" that can be used for many purposes. Marketers have begun shifting their views as these shifting self-concepts evolve from carefree kids to obligation-bound parents. A recent ad campaign cleverly highlighted markers of this lifestage transition, focusing on events such as the first time a man is called "sir," and the first time one doesn't get carded at a bar; the ad touts sporty cars that will "make the other soccer moms talk." Regardless of the specifics, the bottom line is that a generation moving to a new lifestage is always a catalyst for social change.[5]

Gen Y (Echo Boomers)   While demographers debate cutoff dates, most calculations place Gen Y (also called echo boomers) as those born from 1979 to 1995. By 2010, the 12 to 19 age group will have expanded to a historic peak of 35 million. Baby Boomers number 77 million, and Gen X are estimated to be about 40 million. However, they outspend all previous generations. According to *USA Today*, they're techno-savvy, coddled, optimistic, prone to abrupt shifts in taste, and tough to pigeonhole. Take music for example: Boomers, embroiled in civil rights battles, anti-war protests and sexual liberation, launched a rock revolution in the sixties. Gen X, mired in a depressed economy, turned to angry, brooding grunge. Gen Y, marinating in financial fitness, fancies peppy rock.[6]

Generation Y is the first generation to come along that's big enough to hurt a Boomer brand simply by giving it a cold shoulder. This generation is more racially diverse: one in three is not Caucasian. Marketers will have to learn to think like they do—and not like the Boomer parents.[7]

Generation Z   Generation Z will defy easy classification. They will come from a wider mix of backgrounds, and will bring different experiences for marketers to understand. By 2010, marketers will have to start all over again to figure out how to impress this new generation.

Why is all this important to advertising people? Without an accurate view of generations, you are likely to misinterpret what you see in the marketplace. Marketers need to know all about generations. The consumer marketplace is no longer the homogeneous marketplace of the 1950s and early 1960s that was dominated by Matures. The Xers' view of convenience has moved from the Matures' "do it quickly" and the Boomers' "do it efficiently" to their own "eliminate the task."[8]

The president of Collegiate Marketing reminds us to be wary of stereotyping as we segment. He points out that Generation X is not a lifestage; it is a birth group ultimately moving through stages of life. Clearly, a generation—usually defined as 30 years—extends past a single decade. Demographers are beginning to agree that Gen Xers were born between 1964 and 1984.[9]

[5]Stephen J. Kraus, "Gen Xers' reinvented Traditionalism," *Brandweek*, 5 June 2000, 28–30.
[6]Edna Gundersen, "Where will teen tastes land next?," *USA Today*, 22 September 2000, E1–E2.
[7]Ellen Neuborne, "Generation Y," *Business Week*, 15 February 1999, 82.
[8]J. Walker Smith and Ann Clurman, *Rocking the Ages* (New York: HarperCollins, 1997), 16.
[9]David Ashley Morrison, "Beyond the Gen X Label," *Brandweek*, 17 March 1997, 23–25.

Marketing Concept and Targeting

Companies cannot operate in every market and satisfy every consumer need. They generally find that it is necessary to divide the market into major market segments, evaluate them, and then target those segments it can best serve. This focus on specific groups of buyers is called market segmentation. It is an extension of the **marketing concept,** defined by Philip Kotler, that achieving organizational goals depends on determining the needs and wants of target markets and delivering the desired satisfactions more effectively and efficiently than competitors. This idea has been stated as "find a need and fill it" or "make what you sell instead of trying to sell what you can make." Advertisers have expressed this concept in colorful ways; for example, Burger King said, "Have It Your Way," and United Airlines said, "You're the Boss."[10]

marketing concept
A management orientation that views the needs of consumers as primary to the success of a firm.

Frederick E. Webster, Jr., however, says the old marketing concept—the management philosophy first articulated in the 1950s—is a relic of an earlier period of economic history. Most of its assumptions are no longer appropriate in the competitive global markets of today. The world is rapidly moving toward a pattern of economic activity based on long-term relationships and partnerships among economic actors in the loose coalition frameworks of network organizations. The concept of customer value is at the heart of the new marketing concept and must be the central element of all business strategy.

As we look at the differences, the old marketing concept had the objective of making a sale, whereas under the new marketing concept, the objective is to develop a customer relationship in which the sale is only the beginning. Under both marketing concepts, market segmentation, marketing targeting, and positioning are essential requirements for effective strategic planning. In the new marketing concept, the focus is sharpened by adding the idea of the value proposition.[11]

Market-driven companies need to understand how customer needs and company capabilities converge to form the customer's definition of value. This is more than a philosophy; it is a way of doing business. It includes customer orientation, market intelligence, distinctive competencies, value delivery, market targeting and the value proposition, customer-defined total quality management, profitability rather than sales volume, relationship management, continuous improvement, and a customer-focused organizational structure.[12]

Marketing databases are helping companies deliver one-to-one relationships not previously available. They include comprehensive data about individual customers' and prospects' sales histories, as well as demographics and psychographics. Interest by marketers has changed from simply getting people to switch brands to figuring ways to keep from losing current customers by continually trying to meet their needs.

What Is a Product?

Seems like a silly question, doesn't it? Let us define it as a bundle of ingredients put together for sale as something useful to a consumer. You don't go into a store to buy water, stearyl alcohol, cyclopentasiloxane, cetyl alcohol, stearamidopropyl

---

[10]Philip Kotler, *Marketing Management,* 8th ed. (Upper Saddle River, N.J.: Prentice Hall, 1994), 18–21.
[11]Frederick E. Webster, Jr., "Defining the new marketing concept," *Marketing Management,* 2, no. 4, 23–31.
[12]Frederick E. Webster, Jr., "Executing the new marketing concept," *Marketing Management,* 3, no. 1, 9–16.

dimethylamine, glutamic acid, dimethicone, benzyl alcohol, fragrance, and so on. Many do, however, go into a store and buy Procter & Gamble's Physique deep hydrating conditioner. It is more than a physical object. It represents a bundle of satisfactions—a product that hydrates hair and helps users achieve the style they imagine.

Some of these satisfactions are purely functional—a watch to tell time or a car for transportation. Some of the satisfactions are psychological—a car may represent status and a watch may represent a piece of beautiful jewelry. Different people have different ideas about which satisfactions are important. Products are often designed with satisfactions to match the interests of a particular group of consumers. We are also judged in large measure by our physical possessions—think of your attitude toward Mercedes, BMW, Jaguars, cellular phones, and so on. The products that we purchase say something about us and group us with people who seek similar satisfactions from life and products. As we match people and benefits, we create product loyalty that insulates us against competitive attack.

The yearly 25,000-plus new products have a difficult time finding a place in the market. The manufacturer must be selective in defining the most profitable market segments because the cost of introducing a new product can be expensive. There are numerous ways to estimate the chances of getting a heavy user of another brand to try a new brand. One technique is to define market segments according to their brand loyalty and preference for national over private brands. Studies of packaged goods brand loyalty found six such segments:[13]

1. *National-brand loyal.* Members of this segment buy primarily a single national brand at its regular price.
2. *National-brand deal.* This segment is similar to the national-brand-loyal segment, except that most of its purchases are made on deal (that is, the consumer is loyal to only national brands but chooses the least expensive one). To buy the preferred national brand on deal, the consumer engages in considerable store switching.
3. *Private-label loyal.* Consumers in this segment primarily buy the private label offered by the store in which they shop (for example, Eckerds, Wal-Mart, Target, Publix, and other store brands).
4. *Private-label deal.* This segment shops at many stores and buys the private label of each store, usually on deal.
5. *National-brand switcher.* Members of this segment tend not to buy private labels. Instead, they switch regularly among the various national brands on the market.
6. *Private-label switcher.* This segment is similar to the private-label-deal segment, except that the members are not very deal prone and purchase the private labels at their regular price.

Price, product distribution, and promotion also affect the share of market coming from each competing brand. However, a new national brand would expect to gain most of its initial sales from segments 2 and 5, whereas segments 1 and 3 would normally be poor prospects to try a new brand. There are many factors to consider. But remember a camera is not just a camera; markets change with the product, and products change with the market.

---

[13]Robert C. Blattberg, Thomas Buesing, and Subrata K. Sen, "Segmentation strategies for new national brands," *Journal of Marketing,* Fall 1980, 60. (Courtesy: *Journal of Marketing,* a publication of the American Marketing Association.)

What Is a Market?

All advertising and marketing people could easily answer this question, but you might get different answers, depending on their perspectives. For our purposes, a market can be defined as a group of people:

■ who can be identified by some common characteristic, interest, or problem
■ who could use our product to advantage
■ who could afford to buy it
■ who can be reached through some medium

Examples of potential markets are mothers of young children, singles, matures, newly marrieds, skiers, tennis players, Hispanic teens, do-it-yourselfers, runners, and tourists. Gary Knutson's creative team at HM&P used a visual pun to attract people concerned about weeds (Exhibit 4.4) for Pennant for Ciba-Geigy (we'll see more of this campaign in later chapters).

The majority fallacy is a term applied to the assumption, once frequently made, that every product should be aimed at, and acceptable to, a majority of all consumers. Research tells us that brands aimed at the majority of consumers in a given market will tend to have rather similar characteristics and will neglect an opportunity to serve the needs of consumer minorities. Take, for example, chocolate cake mixes. A good-sized group of consumers would prefer a light chocolate cake or a very dark chocolate cake, but the majority choice is a medium chocolate cake. So although several initial cake mix products would do best to market a medium

Exhibit

4.4

Visual puns attract people with lawns that have weeds.
Courtesy: Howard, Merrill & Partners.

chocolate cake to appeal to the broadest group of consumers, later entrants might gain a larger share by supplying the smaller, but significant group with their preference.

What Is Competition?

Have you ever wandered through a drug or grocery store and looked at the toothpaste choices? There were probably a lot of choices—brighteners, abrasives, fresh breath, fluoride, paste, gels, peroxides, and so on. Or in the analgesic section looking for pain killers? You will find many brands competing for your attention: Bayer, Aleve, Advil, Tylenol, Aspirin-Free Anacin, Empirin, Vanquish, Motrin IB, Goody's, BC, Excedrin IB, Cope, and the list goes on. Why does one consumer choose one brand and another consumer something else? How does one even get on the shelf to compete? These are very important questions to the makers of these products.

We speak of competition in the broadest sense to include all the forces that are inhibiting the sales of a product. They may be products in the same subclass as your product, or in the same product class, or forces outside the category of your product. Our list of analgesics included products in different subcategories: Bayer, Tylenol, Aleve, and Advil are each in different analgesic categories, such as aspirin, acetaminophen, naproxen, and ibuprofen. Advil and Nuprin are in the same subcategory. Does that mean they compete with only themselves? The answer is generally no. Many consumers don't even consider the subclasses, they only think in terms of pain relief. If consumers are considering only the benefits of an ibuprofen, then the answer is yes. Advil, Motrin IB, and Excedrin IB would all compete. The point is that advertisers and marketers need to try to find the answers as to which products in what categories compete for the consumer's attention and dollar. It may sound confusing because you don't know the category, but the seasoned marketer for these products knows its category and the products and the reasons people buy.

Marketers for all kinds of products and services must answer: Who are our competitors? What are their brands? What are other product categories? Are there many brands or only a few? Which are strong? Which are vulnerable? What impact, if any, do store brands and generics have? Are there any strong, long-established brands, or is the market volatile? In this context, how would you define the competition for Mountain Dew? Is it Surge? 7-Up? Starbucks' Frappuccino? Colas? Milk? Iced tea? Bottled water? Again, the answer could be all of these. A major purpose of target marketing is to position a brand effectively within a product category (soft drinks) or subcategory (lemon-lime soft drinks).

PLANNING THE ADVERTISING

Market Segmentation

Marketers can't efficiently reach every person who has a dollar to spend. It is just too broad a goal, so in most cases we simply don't and shouldn't try. As a result, most marketers develop target segments or groups. The division of an entire market of consumers into groups whose similarity makes them a market for products servicing their special needs is called **market segmentation.**

This classifying of consumers is generally one of the tasks of a marketing plan's **situation analysis** section. It has been said, "One size does not fit all"—the premise behind segmentation marketing. It's about maximizing your potential in the marketplace by targeting your product to certain segments of the population with similar behaviors, such as people of the same age, gender, ethnic background, or lifestyle. From a communication standpoint, it is more difficult than you may think. You must understand each segment's cultural nuances and choose the right mes-

market segmentation The division of an entire market of consumers into groups whose similarity makes them a market for products serving their special needs.

situation analysis The part of the advertising plan that answers the questions: Where are we today and how did we get here? It deals with the past and present.

sage, so you don't stereotype the service or product you are selling as one designed for only them.

A number of factors must be considered in planning advertising to take advantage of market segmentation. The first step is to determine the variable to use for dividing a market. In addition to demographics, the major means of market segmentation are geographical, product user, and lifestyle segmentation. Bevil Advertising had to target a specialized market for machinery that weighs other people's products. Exhibit 4.5 shows the front of the communication aimed at conveyor needs.

Geographical Segmentation   Geographical segmentation, the oldest form of segmentation, designates customers by geographical area. It dates back to earlier days when distribution was the primary concern of manufacturers. Today geomarketing is of particular importance to media planners in deciding on national, regional, and local ad campaigns. It is only recently that geomarketing has been elevated to a marketing discipline the way demographics was in the 1950s and psychographics was in the 1970s. In this instance, consumers haven't changed but marketers' awareness of regional and global marketing has. Geodemographical marketing is just another way of segmenting the market for companies in search of growth.

Recently, there has been a "data explosion" on local markets. Some of the information comes from an abundant number of research services for use on merchandising and buying decisions. Many retail companies such as supermarkets practice micromarketing—treating each individual store as its own market and trading area. Often this approach translates into different ads for different markets. When thinking about geographic segmentation, advertisers have a number of categories to explore:

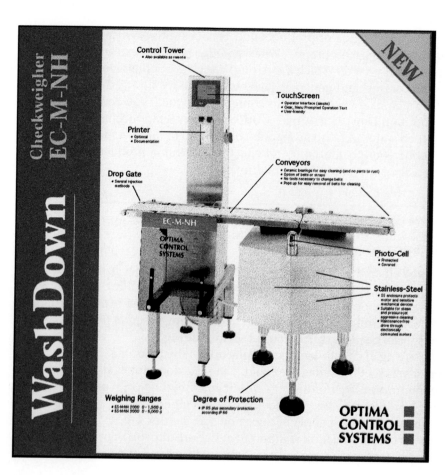

Exhibit

4.5

Not all marketing communication is aimed at consumers. Optima Control Systems sells to companies.

Courtesy: Bevil Advertising.

census trace data	areas of dominant influence (ADI)
zip codes	states
counties	census regions
metropolitan statistical areas	total United States

Companies that lack national distribution may consider geographical segmentation. Pro Balanced dog food is distributed primarily in the South, but has to compete against national brands to survive. There are many local or regional brands that must be successful in their geographical areas to survive. Cheerwine is a cherry cola–like soft drink that is strong in its home area, but would have problems in areas where its history and tradition were unknown. Recently, Cheerwine used a slogan that said, "It's a Carolina Thing." In this example, geographical segmentation is a distribution strategy rather than a promotional one.

It is not unusual for national companies to divide their advertising and marketing efforts into regional units to respond better to the competition. McDonald's uses a major advertising agency to handle its national advertising and numerous (generally smaller) agencies to handle franchise and regional efforts supplementing the national effort. This gives McDonald's the ability to react to the marketplace by cities, regions, or individual stores.

Product User Segmentation   User segmentation is a strategy based on the amount and/or consumption patterns of a brand or category. The advertiser is interested in product usage rather than consumer characteristics. As a practical matter, most user segmentation methods are combined with demographic or lifestyle consumer identification. Here the advertiser is interested in market segments with the highest sales potential. Typically, a market segment is first divided into all users and then subdivided into heavy, medium, and light users. For example, let us look at the frequency of weekly use of fast foods:

product user segmentation Identifying consumers by the amount of product usage.

Frequency	Adults	Men	Women
Heavy (4 plus visits)	11.4%	14.8%	8.3%
Medium (1–3 visits)	44.9	46.5	43.3
Light (less than weekly)	22.8	20.6	24.8

The definition of usage varies with the product category. For example, heavy fast-food use may be defined as 41 times per week; heavy luxury-restaurant use as once a week; and heavy seafood-restaurant use as once a week. As you can see, product user segmentation can get quite complex, but this kind of data allows marketers to use a rifle instead of a shotgun.

Lifestyle Segmentation   **Lifestyle segmentation** makes the assumption that if you live a certain way, so do your neighbors, and therefore any smart marketer would want to target clusters filled with these clones. Lifestyle clusters are more accurate characterizations of people than any single variable would be.

lifestyle segmentation Identifying consumers by combining several demographics and lifestyles.

The concept of lifestyle segmentation is a viable one; however, researchers are having to adjust to a sea of changes taking place among America's shopping public. For example, old attitudes toward work and leisure or fitness don't fit today's realities. As a result, segmentation researchers are changing how they view many of the new lifestyle characteristics driving this new era.[14]

Marketers have used specialized segmentation techniques to find the most fruitful target audiences since PRIZM (Potential Rating Index for ZIP Markets) in 1974 grouped people who had similar demographics and lifestyles into neighbor-

---

[14]Rebecca Piirto Heath, "The frontier of psychographics," *American Demographics,* July 1996, 40.

hood clusters, on the theory that "birds of a feather, flock together." A number of similar programs have popped up since—such as CACI's Acorn and SRI's VALS (**Values and Lifestyle System**)—all based on the premise that people in the same zip code or neighborhood tend to buy the same products. Each research company has its own terminology for the various clusters it identifies. Recently Yankelovich Partners Inc. developed a psychographic segmentation system called Monitor Mindbase. It is premised on the idea of segmenting individuals by values, attitudes, and mindsets, rather than by geography, demographics, and consumption patterns. It segments people into categories of consumers with varying degrees of materialism, ambition, orientation to family life, cynicism, openness to technology, and other elements.[15]

Congoleum says, "Floors for the way you live." The ad in Exhibit 4.6 plays on the fact that women are extremely busy at one or more jobs and don't have time to pamper a kitchen floor. This approach is based upon understanding how people live and think in today's world.

Researchers Kevin Clancy and Robert Shulman argue that "off-the-shelf segmentation studies cannot be as good as customized segmentation done with a spe-

Do You Know Anybody Who Has Time To Pamper A Kitchen Floor? Neither Do We.

Like most women today, you probably have a mountain of details to contend with. Like a full-time job, or being a full-time Mom. Or both.

So the last thing you need is a floor that needs extra attention.

Any vinyl floor that can't take the heat should get out of the kitchen. That's why you'll find Congoleum vinyl floors are designed to stand up to the kind of wear and

tear that your family dishes out.

You'll also find our colors and patterns last over the long haul. (After all, what good is a floor that lasts for years, if it goes out of style in two?)

So for the name of the nearest Congoleum Design Studio retailer call 1-800-934-3567, Ext. 109.

Congoleum
Floors For The Way You Live.

© 1994 Congoleum

[15]David J. Lipke, "Head trips," *American Demographics*, October 2000, 38.

cific product or service in mind. VALS will help break up the world into pieces, but the pieces may or may not have any relevance for any one brand."[16]

One approach to determining lifestyle characteristics is to identify consumers' activities, interests, and opinions (AIO). Typical AIO measures are:

- *Activities:* leisure-time preferences, community involvement, and preferences for social events
- *Interests:* family orientation, sports interest, and media usage
- *Opinions:* political preferences and views on various social issues.

Benefits and Attitude Segmentation   Not everyone wants the same thing from a product. There isn't just a single toothpaste, because some people are interested in taste, or fresh breath, or whiteness of their teeth, or decay prevention, or tartar control for gums, or value, and so on. The basis here is to cluster people into groups based upon what they want in a product.

Segmentation Risks   Although segmentation is very important to successful advertising, it isn't without risks. One problem is that once the outer limits of the niche are reached, sales growth will be limited unless the company can expand beyond its niche. By too narrowly defining your market—that is, by excessive segmenting—you can become inefficient in media buying, creating different ads, and obtaining alternative distribution channels. A few years ago, Taco Bell was the first fast-food chain to target people with their Value Menu. They were so successful that most other fast-food companies followed with their own Value Menus. As a result of this competition, the pool of value-conscious consumers was split among numerous companies, diluting the profit.

Target Market Sacrifice

Consultant Jack Trout says, staying focused on one target segment in a category enables you to be different by becoming the preferred product by the segment: Pepsi for the younger generation, Corvette for the generation that wants to be young, Corona beer for the yuppies on their way up, Porsche for the yuppies who have made it. When you chase after another target segment, chances are you'll chase away your original customer. Whatever you do, you should not get greedy but stay true to your product type, your attribute, or your segment.[17]

Niche marketing can serve at least two purposes. It can gain a product entry into a larger market by attacking a small part of it not being served by the competition. It can also cater to latent needs that existing products do not adequately satisfy.

Niche Marketing

Niches usually are smaller groups of consumers with more narrowly defined needs or unique combinations. But **niche marketing** is not another buzzword for marketing segmentation, says Alvin Achenbaum.[18] It is essentially a flanking strategy, the essence of which is to engage competitors in those product markets where they are weak or, preferably, have little or no presence. The guiding principle of niche marketing is to pit your strength against the competitor's weakness. No-frill motels did not exist for many years, but they were logical means of competing against other

niche marketing   A combination of product and target market strategy. It is a flanking strategy that focuses on niches or comparatively narrow windows of opportunity within a broad product market or industry. Its guiding principle is to pit your strength against their weakness.

[16]Kevin J. Clancy and Robert S. Shulman, *The Marketing Revolution* (New York: Harper Business, 1991), 63.
[17]Jack Trout, *Differentiate or Die* (New York: John Wiley & Sons, 2000), 185.
[18] Alvin Achenbaum, "Understanding niche marketing," *ADWEEK*, 1 December 1986, 62.

motel segments. Red Roof Inn opened their motels with an ad claiming "Sleep Cheap," and positioned themselves to value consumers not wanting to pay high prices for a place to sleep. Later they even made fun of hotels placing a chocolate mint on your pillow for an extra $30 or $40. Today, most major hotel chains have moved into that niche with their own no-frills express motels.

Brand marketers seeking new niche opportunities should pay attention to marketing basics: changing shopping trends, demographics, marketing strategy, and delivery on commitments.[19]

The major growth segments in the United States for the future are in the minority population, as indicated earlier in this chapter. Jack in the Box's fast-food company finds Hispanics make up 20 to 30 percent of its business. Commonalities can be found among the three major ethnic groups—Hispanic, African American, and Asian. Each is also quite diverse and contains many subsets with different buying habits and preferences. African-American consumers differ by age, geographic region, income, and education. Additionally, Caribbean- and African-born Americans have mindsets different from African Americans raised in the United States. Hispanic consumers differ by language preference, birthplace (U.S.-born versus foreign-born), and nationality (Mexican, Puerto Rican, Cuban, or other Latin countries). There is no Asian market per se; Japanese, Chinese, Korean, Filipino, and Vietnamese Americans differ in language, history, and culture. Each factor drives what will be the most effective channel for reaching these consumers.

Ads that address Hispanics in Spanish are more effective according to Hispanic & Asian Marketing Research. Many Hispanic respondents said they bought something they saw on Spanish TV, whereas only one-quarter bought something advertised during English programming. Synergy, however, is a must between general-market and Hispanic advertising "because Hispanics don't live in isolation," says Eduardo del Rivero, CEO at del Rivero Messianu, Coral Gables, which handles McDonald's Hispanic advertising. The increase in the share numbers of Spanish-language media outlets, from television to radio and the Internet is making it easier to reach the target audience.[20]

We must be careful of literal translations. Expressions in one language may be out of context when translated into another language. A ballpoint pen manufacturer once translated the word embarrass to embarazar, a message that suggested the pen wouldn't leak in your pocket and make you pregnant. The word light in English generally connotes something positive. In Spanish, it suggests something insubstantial. The bottom line is to create appropriate messages that will be familiar to the target audience and add value to their lives.

Many marketers think their general-market advertising efforts are effective in reaching ethnic groups; other marketing researchers argue that generic efforts miss the mark. Black people are not dark-skinned white people, says a Burrell Communications Group head. Blacks are significantly different in terms of approach and history. There is a significant difference in behavior, and that manifests itself all the way to the marketplace.[21]

Each niche offers challenges for advertisers. When trying to develop niche marketing to Asians and Latinos, understanding of cultural and language issues is required, as we have indicated. From another perspective, Kraft found that America's Jewish population offers a niche that is mainstream, upscale, educated, and affluent. The purchase patterns of this niche are similar to those of average

[19]Ira P. Scheiderman, "Niche marketers should follow old rules," *BrandMarketing*, August 2000, 6.
[20]Laurie Freeman, "Fast-foods battleground," *Advertising Age*, 18 September 2000, s20.
[21]Christie Fisher, "Ethnics gain market clout," *Advertising Age*, 5 August 1991, 3.

Americans with a little different twist. Traditionally, grocery shopping is heaviest around holiday time. Christmas generates the most volume in the overall food category, but Passover now has become the second most prosperous season in supermarkets, not surprisingly because more than 40 percent of kosher food sales occur during the week prior to the holiday. To top this market, Kraft's Philadelphia brand cream cheese promoted specific Passover ads in Jewish magazines and newspapers throughout the country.

Almost 40 percent of the U.S. Jewish population lives in metro New York, 15 percent in Los Angeles, with other large concentrations in Chicago and southern Florida. Nearly 200 Jewish-targeted publications reach more than 4 million readers monthly. Because the average Orthodox Jewish household has an average of 4.8 children, Beech-Nut baby foods has had kosher certification on their foods for many years. The headline for one of their ads aimed at this niche read, "Feeding your baby kosher is as simple as choosing Beech-Nut."[22]

Companies can build growth out of finding small niches to serve consumers' needs. For example, Kimberly-Clark launched Huggies Pull-Ups training pants in 1989. In 1994, it launched Goodnites for older children who wet the bed. In 1997, it introduced Huggies Little Swimmers designed to survive swimming. The niche for Huggies Little Swimmers is a very narrow category segment. Originally, Procter & Gamble said the training pants niche was too small, but it grew to a $400 million segment within the disposable diaper category.[23]

POSITIONING

Positioning has to be done with a target in mind. You position a product in the mind of a specific prospect. **Positioning** is another term for fitting the product into the lifestyle of the buyer. It refers to segmenting a market by either or both of two ways: (1) creating a product to meet the needs of a specialized group, and/or (2) identifying and advertising a feature of an existing product that meets the needs of a specialized group.

Estrovite vitamins recognized a potential problem among women on birth control pills and created a product positioned to fulfill that need. Their headline read, "Your birth control pills could be robbing you of essential vitamins and minerals." The copy explained why.

The purpose of positioning is giving a product a meaning that distinguishes it from other products and induces people to want to buy it. Positioning is what you do to the mind of the consumer. Specifically, you position the product in the mind of the prospect. You want your positioning to be in harmony with the lifestyles and values we have discussed. It is necessary to understand what motivates people to buy in the product category—what explains their behavior. It is also necessary to understand the degree to which the product satisfies the target's needs.[24] One automobile may be positioned as a sports car, another as a luxury sports car, another as the safest family car, and still another as a high-performance vehicle.

It is possible for some products to successfully hold different positions at the same time. Arm & Hammer baking soda has been positioned as a deodorizer for refrigerators, an antacid, a freezer deodorizer, and a bath skin cleanser without losing its original market as a cooking ingredient.

positioning Segmenting a market by creating a product to meet the needs of a select group or by using a distinctive advertising appeal to meet the needs of a specialized group, without making changes in the physical product.

---

[22]Elie Rosenfeld, "Kosher consumers," *Brandweek*, 19 May 1997, 29–31.
[23]Jeff Neff, "Huggies little swimmers tests out a new niche," *Advertising Age*, 25 August 1997, 8.
[24]Kevin J. Clancy and Robert S. Shulman, *The Marketing Revolution* (New York: Harper Business, 1991), 84–87.

You might try to get the following reactions from consumers to a new line of frozen entrees that are low in calories, sodium, and fat, and have larger servings than the competition's. Before seeing your advertising, the consumer thinks:

> I like the convenience and taste of today's frozen foods but I don't usually get enough of the main course to eat. I would like to try a brand that gives me plenty to eat but is still light and healthy—and, most important, it has to taste great.

After being exposed to your advertising, the consumer thinks:

> I may buy Ru's Frozen Food entrees. They taste great and I get plenty to eat, and they are still low enough in calories that I don't feel I'm overeating. They're better for me because they have less sodium and fat than others. Also, there is enough variety so that I can eat the foods I like without getting bored by the same old thing.

Creating a Product for Selected Markets

One of the ways that marketers attract a focused consumer group is through variations on a conventional product. A new variation looks for a group with needs not fully met by existing products. In addition, marketers or products in the retentive stage may see variations as a means of rejuvenating a product whose sales have gone flat.

Bayer aspirin created an adult low strength for aspirin regimen users. Research indicated that second heart attacks were greatly reduced by simply taking an aspirin daily. The only problem was that regular use of aspirin by some people resulted in stomach problems. A regular aspirin tablet consisted of 325 milligrams. The doctor-recommended daily therapy for patients having suffered an initial heart attack was 81 milligrams. Adults started taking children's aspirin, which was 81 milligrams, to prevent stomach problems and yet get the advantage of heart attack protection. As a result of this consumer action, Bayer introduced Bayer enteric aspirin, which was 81 milligrams and protects the stomach.

Positioning to Expand Brand Share

Positioning—or, more accurately, repositioning—can be an effective method of increasing brand share when a company already has a high percentage of the market for a type of product. Let us assume our company, Acme Widgets, has 80 percent of the widget market. Two strategies that the company might adopt are shown in the following tables.

In Strategy I, Acme, by engaging in direct brand competition, has increased its market share very slightly. However, it is extremely doubtful that further sales can be profitably taken from the competition. Increased advertising expenditures to make inroads into brands A, B, and C will probably cost proportionally more than the revenues realized.

The repositioning strategy depicted in Strategy II has allowed Acme to keep its overwhelming share. At the same time, by spending 40 percent ($4 million of its $10 million advertising allowance) of its budget to position the company in a new market, Acme gained 10 percent of this formerly untapped market segment rather than the 0.1 percent of the primary market it achieved with the first strategy. In this example, no physical changes were made in the product—only different appeals were used. This is the basis for positioning by choice of appeal.

Strategy I: Traditional Brand Promotion
(No Brand Repositioning)

1999 Brand Share (%)		2000 Advertising	2001 Brand Share (%)	
A	10	$10 million spent	A	9.9
B	5	against brands	B	5.0
C	5	A, B, and C	C	5.0
Acme	80		Acme	80.1
Total	100		Total	100.0

Strategy II: Acme Widget's Brand Repositioning

1999 Brand Share (%)		2000 Advertising	2001 Brand Share (%) Primary Market	
A	10	$6 million spent	A	10
B	5	to keep present	B	5
C	5	market share	C	5
Acme	80		Acme	80
Total	100		Total	100
			Alternative Market	
		$4 million spent	Other brands	
		to promote repositioned	and brands already	
		Acme Widget to	in market	85
		new market	A, B, C	5
			Acme	10
			Total	100

HOW TO APPROACH A POSITIONING PROBLEM

As you would expect, not all products lend themselves to the type of positioning discussed here. The advertiser must be careful not to damage current product image by changing appeals and prematurely expanding into new markets. Jack Trout and Al Ries, who have written about positioning for several decades, say that the advertiser who is thinking about positioning should ask the following questions:[25]

■ What position, if any, do we already own in the prospect's mind?

■ What position do we want to own?

■ What companies must be outgunned if we are to establish that position?

■ Do we have enough marketing money to occupy and hold that position?

■ Do we have the guts to stick with one consistent positioning concept?

■ Does our creative approach match our positioning strategy?

David Aaker says the most used positioning strategy is to associate an object with a product attribute or characteristic. Developing such associations is effective because when the attribute is meaningful, the association can directly translate into reasons to buy the brand. Crest toothpaste became the leader by building a strong association with cavity control in part created by an endorsement of the American Dental Association. BMW has talked about performance with its tag line: "The Ultimate Driving Machine." Mercedes, "The Ultimate Engineered Car." Hyundai, "Cars that Make Sense." The positioning problem is usually finding an

[25]Jack Trout and Al Ries, *The Positioning Era* (New York: Ries Cappiello Colwell, 1973), 38–41.

attribute important to a major segment and not already claimed by a competitor.[26] Philip Kotler says many companies advertise a major single benefit position, for example, best quality, best performance, most durable, fastest, least expensive, and so on. In automobiles: Mercedes owns the "most prestigious" position, BMW the "best driving performance," Hyundai owns the "least expensive," and Volvo owns the "safest." They also claim to be one of the most durable.[27]

Positioning Examples

- Dove soap is the moisturizing beauty bar.
- Whirlpool appliances make your world a little easier.
- Cheer is the detergent for all temperatures.
- Intel is the computer inside.
- Saturn is a different kind of company, a different kind of car.
- Milk-Bone dog biscuits clean teeth and freshen breath.

Some marketers frequently alter a brand's positioning for the sake of change. This is especially unfortunate for those brands that are firmly entrenched and successful because their reason for being is widely accepted. In the past, a number of positioning statements were successful, but were dropped; "Good to the Last Drop," "Pepperidge Farm Remembers," and "Two Mints in One" are examples. These campaigns were revised long after they were discontinued because they truly represented the consumer end benefit and character of the brand.[28]

Profile of the Market

market profile A demographic and psychographic description of the people or the households of a product's market. It may also include economic and retailing information about a territory.

Up to this point, we have discussed market segments. Now we examine the overall **market profile** for a product. First, we determine the overall usage of the product type. This is usually defined in terms of dollars, sales, number of units sold, or percentage of households that use such a product. Then we determine if the category is growing, stagnant, or declining. We compare our share of the market to the competition. Next we ask what the share trends have been over the past several years. Finally, we want to know the chief product advantage featured by each brand.

When you look at market share, beware as to whether you are looking at a brand's share (Resolve carpet cleaner, 19.3 percent) or a company's share. (See Exhibit 4.7.) For example, in the hot dog market, Oscar Mayer as a company has a

Exhibit 4.7

Examples of Product Shares

Source: Advertising Age, 25 September 2000.

Liquid laundry detergents		Powdered laundry detergents	
Brand	Share	Brand	Share
Ultra Tide	22.9%	Tide	34.8%
Wisk	7.9	Gain	11.8
Tide	7.6	Cheer	8.4
All Ultra	5.6	Arm & Hammer	3.6
Classic Purex	3.7	Surf	4.3
Arm & Hammer	3.3	Ultra Surf	2.7

[26]David A. Aaker, *Managing Brand Equity* (New York: The Free Press, 1991), 114–115.
[27]Philip Kotler, *Kotler on Marketing* (New York: The Free Press, 1999), 57–58.
[28]Lewis Brosowsky, "Ad themes that last," *Advertising Age*, 28 February 1994, 26.

19 percent share; Sara Lee is second with its Hygrade, Ball Park, Best's, and Bryan Foods brands, which total a 15.2 percent share. Nabisco's Ritz brand is a leader in the cracker category with a 9.6 percent share. In the facial cleanser segment, Andrew Jergens Company's Biore has a 22.5 percent share, Pond's has a 16.7 percent, and Noxzema has a 9.3 percent share. A marketer with a leading share in a product category and a marketer with a very small share will probably approach advertising in very different ways.

If we examine the fast-food restaurants, McDonald's reported a 43.1 percent share in 1999. They were followed by Burger King (21.9%), Wendy's (12.2), Hardee's (5.6), Jack in the Box (4.0), and Sonic Drive-Ins (3.7). McDonald's dominates locations, almost twice as many as its next competitor.

It is important for the advertiser to know not only the characteristics of the product's market, but also similar information about media alternatives. Most major newspapers, magazines, and broadcast media provide demographic and product-user data for numerous product categories. Database marketing is giving the marketer an abundance of information upon which to base integrated promotional decisions.

PROFILE OF THE BUYER

Earlier in this chapter we highlighted ethnic groups (Hispanics, African Americans, and Asians) who were largely ignored by advertisers in the past, but their increasing numbers demand attention in today's marketplace. The Xers, Boomers, teenagers, college students, and the 50-plus markets are all studied by smart advertisers to understand their potential for specific products and services. As indicated, these groups of consumers are not necessarily easy to understand or reach with effective integrated programs. Not all Boomers act the same, and all Gen Yers don't respond to messages in the same manner.

People 50 and older represent 37 percent of the adult U.S. population. More importantly, they control $2 trillion in income and 50 percent of all discretionary income. People over 50 account for 80 percent of leisure travel. They spend more on jewelry, sports cars, and cosmetics than other age groups. Half have PCs at home and 70 percent of those have Internet access. Roper Starch Research found that 22 percent exercise three times a week, an increase of 75 percent in a decade. Women over 55 account for $21 billion in apparel each year.[29] Obviously, they are an important market for some advertisers.

Advertisers have to look at demographics and lifestyles, for starters, to understand any market.

Demography is the study of vital economic and sociological statistics about people. In advertising, demographic reports refer to those facts relevant to a person's use of a product. Exhibit 4.8 presents a snippet of average weekly regular and diet soft-drink demographics.

The selected soft-drink demographics probably offer few surprises to you. However, be sure to examine the differences in regular and diet consumption between males and females, or between age 18 to 24 and older consumers; and compare regional differences for starters. You can begin to understand how demographic differences could be important factors in advertising strategy and expenditure decisions.

---

[29]Chris Kelly, "Active lifestyle central to targeting," *Advertising Age*, 10 July 2000, S8.

Demographic	Regular Cola	Regular Other	Diet Cola	Diet Other
Total 181	60.3	43.3	42.2	29.2
Sex: Male	65.5	46.1	38.6	27.8
Female	55.5	40.5	45.6	30.4
Age: 18–24	72.5	50.4	32.7	24.4
25–34	67.6	48.8	42.5	30.1
35–44	62.6	45.1	45.2	29.3
651	46.3	34.5	41.2	29.2
Region: Northeast	59.8	45.3	37.6	27.7
Midwest	56.6	42.6	46.8	31.6
South	65.0	42.2	41.8	26.9
West	57.2	43.4	42.2	31.5
Race: White	58.9	41.1	43.5	29.1
Black	69.3	55.4	35.7	27.2

Exhibit

4.8

Selected Demographics of Regular and Diet Soft Drink Average Weekly Consumption for Specific Types (in percentages)

Source: Radio Advertising Bureau.

Heavy Users

Take any product category and you will find that a small percentage of users are responsible for a disproportionately large share of sales. The principle of heavy usage is sometimes referred to as the 80/20 rule—that is, 80 percent of the units sold are purchased by only 20 percent of the consumers. Few products meet this exactly, but Kraft's Miracle Whip does. And the most avid Miracle Whip customers live in the Midwest. So Kraft knows who buys the most and where they live. Of course, the exact figure varies with each product and product category, but the 80/20 rule is representative of most product sales. In the case of Diet Coke, 8 percent of the households account for 84 percent of the volume—rather significant information. Keeping that

Users of Brand X

1. Target Audience: Current Consumers

Women	Pop. (%)	Consumption (%)	Index (100 = national average)
18–24	17.5	5.0	29
25–34	21.9	10.1	46
35–54	30.1	24.0	80
551	30.5	61.0	200
Total	100.0	100.0	

2. Geography: Current Sales

Area	Pop. (%)	Consumption (%)	Index
Northeast	24	22	92
East Central	15	18	120
West Central	17	16	94
South	27	24	89
Pacific	17	20	118
Total	100	200	

3. Seasonality

Period	Jan.–Mar.	Apr.–Jun.	Jul.–Sept.	Oct.–Nov.
Consumption (%)	30	36	20	14
Index	120	144	80	

small segment loyal to Diet Coke is smart marketing, pure and simple. Heavy users are identified not only by who they are, but also by when they buy and where they are located. Of course, another issue for marketers is not only how to reach these consumers, but what to say or do once you have made contact.

The following table shows that the heavy users of brand X are women aged 55 and older. In addition, the most effective selling is done from January through June in the East Central and Pacific regions. Obviously, heavy users are an important part of the market; however, they are also the group most advertisers are trying to target, and therefore the competition can be fierce and expensive. Some advertisers find that aiming for a less lucrative segment—medium or light users—may offer more reasonable expectations. A marketer cannot just assume the best prospects are 18- to 49-year-old women, heavy users, or people similar to current customers. Instead, marketers need to carefully study their target audience in great depth. In defining your market, then, you must determine who the heavy users are and identify their similarities, which would define your marketing goal (see Exhibit 4.9).

Data to Be Gathered and Reported (If Possible, to Be Directly Accessible)

Characteristic	Minimum Basic Data to Be Reported	Additional Data— Highly Valued
I. Persons Characteristics		
A. Household Relationship	Principal Wage Earner in HH (defines HH head) Principal Shopper in HH (defines homemaker) Spouse Child Other Relative Partner/Roommate Other Nonrelative	
B. Age	Under 6 6–11 12–15 16–20 18–20 16 or older 18 or older 18–24 25–34 35–44 45–49 50–54 55–64 65–74 75 or older	2–5 6–8 35–49 25–49
C. Sex	Male Female	
D. Education	Last Grade Attended: Grade School or Less (Grade 1–8) Some High School Graduated High School Some College (at least 1 year) Graduated College . . . . If currently attending school. . . . . Full-Time Student Part-Time Student	any postgraduate work —(If pertinent to study)— Live home Live away —Live in student housing —Live off campus

Exhibit

4.9

Segments for Demographic Characteristics for Surveys of Consumer Media Audiences

Exhibit

4.9

(continued)

Data to Be Gathered and Reported (If Possible, to Be Directly Accessible)

Characteristic	Minimum Basic Data to Be Reported	Additional Data— Highly Valued
E. Marital Status	Married	Spouse Present Spouse Absent
	Widowed Divorced or Separated Single (never married)	Spouse working
	Parent Pregnant 'Living together'	Engaged
F. Religion—Political		Protestant ⎤ ⎡ Active (Practicing) Catholic ⎟ ⊢ Inactive Jewish ⎟ ⎣ (Nonpracticing) Other ⎟ None ⎦ Political—Conservative —Liberal —Moderate
G. Race	White Black Other	
H. Principal Language Spoken at Home	English Spanish Other	
H1. Other Languages Spoken at Home	English Spanish Other	
I. Individual Employment Income	Under $10,000 $10,000–14,999 $15,000–19,999 $20,000–24,999 $25,000–29,999 $30,000–39,999 $40,000–49,999 $50,000–74,999 $75,000 and over	$75,000–99,000 $100,000 and over IEI Income by Quintile as Determined by the Survey Ziptiles. Other Income

IEI by Quintile
Income Interval

Quintile	% Adults	Low	High	Median Income
1	20	—	10,156	6,391
2	20	10,757	19,999	13,959
3	20	20,000	29,999	24,953
4	20	30,000	43,243	34,967
5	20	43,244	—	60,150

BEYOND DEMOGRAPHICS: PSYCHOGRAPHICS

When driving through any suburban area past modest-sized yards of middle-class homes, one is struck first by their similarity. But a harder look is more illuminating, for behind the similarities lie differences that reflect the interests, personalities, and family situations of those who live in such homes. One yard has been transformed into a carefully manicured garden. Another includes some shrubs and bushes, but most of the yard serves as a relaxation area, with outdoor barbecue equipment and the like. A third yard is almost entirely a playground, with swings, trapezes, and slides. A swimming pool occupies almost all the space in another yard. A tennis court occupies yet another. Still another has simply been allowed to go to seed and is overgrown and untended by its obviously indoor-oriented owners.

Although the neighborhood consists of homes of similar style, age, and value, the people are not all the same. If you want to advertise to this neighborhood, you would be speaking to people with different interests and different tastes. There may be a big difference in the nature and extent of purchases between any two groups of buyers who have the same demographic characteristics. The attempt to explain the significance of such differences has led to an inquiry beyond demographics into psychographics. **Psychographics**—studying lifestyles—sharpens the search for prospects beyond demographic data. It has been said that lifestyle information gives the soul of the person. Good creative people can devise copy that appeals to a specific segment's lifestyle interest. The media are then selected, and advertising is directed to that special target group or groups. Put very simply, lifestyle information gives the soul of a person; demographics alone gives only a skeleton and not a whole person.

psychographics A description of a market based on factors such as attitudes, opinions, interests, perceptions, and lifestyles of consumers comprising that market.

Target Audience: Beyond Demographics

Let us look at an example of a travel advertiser's defined target. This profile is based upon the advertiser's research that helped define those people most likely to visit the area.

Research indicated that the basic demographic guideline for the consumer target is households with a combined household income of $35,000 or more. Households with less than $35,000 simply do not have the discretionary income necessary for vacation travel.

The other qualifiers in defining a consumer **target audience** are lifestyle and geography:

target audience That group that composes the present and potential prospects for a product or service.

- Primary vacation travelers—vacation travelers who take a one-week plus vacation during the primary season (summer)
- Weekend travelers—those people living in states within close proximity who can be attracted during the fall, winter, and spring seasons
- Mature market (501)—people who have both the discretionary income and available time to travel
- Business travelers—business people coming to an area on business who can be encouraged to either extend their stay for pleasure travel purposes or to bring their spouse and family along
- International travelers—Canada provides an enormous influx of visitors. Also, the increasing number of international flights to and from the area provide increasing opportunities

What is the target for the North Carolina tourism ad in Exhibit 4.10?

Psychographic Research

Today there is much more refined information available. Agency research information includes syndicated research from outside sources, client's research, and the agency's own resources. Syndicated research services specialize in different types of information on what types of products people buy and which brands, who buys them and their demographic and psychographic distinctions, a comparison of heavy and light users, how people react to products and to ads, and people's styles of buying and what media reach them.

Lifestyle categories are numerous. Data categories are available through syndicated research to advertisers and their agencies to help them select the target market. This information is available on a market-by-market basis defining both demographic and lifestyle information. Some of the categories, indicating the percentage of household activities include

■ Credit card usage for travel and entertainment, bank cards, gas and department store usage

■ Good life activities, which include such activities as attending cultural or arts events, foreign travel, gourmet cooking and fine food interests, stock investments, antique interest, wines

■ High-tech activities and usage, which involve home computers, watching cable TV, VCR recording and viewing, photography interests

■ Sports and leisure activities by households, which include bicycling, boating, golf, bowling, tennis, jogging

■ Outdoor activities, which include the number of households in a specific market involved in camping, fishing, motorcycles, environmental interests

■ Domestic activities such as gardening, Bible and devotional reading, coin collecting, pets, sewing, crafts, reading.

Test Marketing

Although extremely helpful, psychographic research cannot replace market testing as the ultimate guide to successful advertising and marketing. Manufacturers seldom introduce new products without doing some prior testing. This kind of testing helps determine if consumers will really purchase a product or react to specific advertising and promotional activities.

It is difficult to say which cities are best for testing. Ira Weinblatt, a Saatchi & Saatchi senior vice president, says, "You can't say one place represents everything because there are so many different lifestyles." Some cities are historically popular for test marketing. The Midwest has been popular because, geographically, it was the heartland of America. Each test market represents a kind of microcosm of America. Saatchi & Saatchi ranks the top performing test markets. To make the list:

■ A city's demographics must fall within 20 percent of the national average

■ The city should be somewhat isolated

■ Local media should be relatively inexpensive

■ Citizens should not be extremely loyal to any particular brand

■ Supermarkets should be impartial enough to give new products good display on their shelves

Milwaukee, one of the test market cities that historically makes the list, is popular because the newspapers offer marketers the flexibility to split production runs.

This allows advertisers to test up to four ads at a time and to experiment with run-of-the-paper color or free-standing inserts. Typically, researchers examine purchases for a number of weeks before ads run, during the period of the test, and afterward.

The perils of introducing a product nationally without test marketing include failure. This can be extremely expensive, and most marketers are not willing to take that risk without some type of testing. In the late nineties Pepsi-Cola took their lemon-lime Storm into 11 test markets over two years without success. Of course, one of their problems was distribution and not necessarily the product since many of their anchor bottlers distribute 7 Up. Pepsi also planned a two-market test of a lemon-lime cola called Pepsi Twist in mid-2000. The test was in Minneapolis and San Antonio using television and FSI (free-standing inserts) support.[30] What makes Twist an interesting product is the fact that it was viewed as a possible in-and-out seasonal product. Pepsi replaced Storm with a new entry, caffeine-free Sierra Mist.

SUMMARY

The accurate identification of current and prospective users of a product will often mean the difference between success and failure. The targeting of advertising to these prospects in an efficient media plan with appropriate creativity is critical.

This chapter has concentrated on fundamentals: Who are the prospects? What is a market? What about competition? Positioning? Numerous methods of examining segmentation and other important considerations in planning integrated marketing programs have been discussed. Understanding these basic concerns through research is part of the process. Research is the key to successful target marketing. Market research to define prime market segments, product research to meet the needs of these segments, and advertising research to devise the most appropriate messages are mandatory for success of a firm in a competitive environment. Also, we need to be familiar with the multitude of research services providing data for aiding our planning.

Ads are aimed at consumers with a rifle instead of a shotgun approach. It is becoming easier to tailor messages through a variety of special-interest media vehicles.

Advertisers place more importance on lifestyle characteristics than on demographic factors. Advertisers recognize that purchase behavior is the result of a number of complex psychological and sociological factors that cannot be explained by a superficial list of age, sex, income, or occupational characteristics.

Finally, we need to keep abreast of changes in population and better understand such important segments as Hispanics, Asians, and African Americans as well as generational groups. This kind of knowledge will lead to better communications and targeting. We need to know more than simply numbers and location. We need to understand consumer lifestyles, identities, and motivations.

REVIEW

1. What is target marketing?
2. What is a market?
3. Name key demographic characteristics used by advertisers.
4. What is positioning?
5. What is the 80/20 rule as it relates to target marketing?

TAKE IT TO THE NET

We invite you to visit the Russell/Lane page on the Prentice Hall Web site at **www.prenhall.com/myphlip** for end-of-chapter exercises and applications.

---

[30]Theresa Howard, "Pepsi plays Misty," *BrandWeek*, 19 June 2000, 4.

PART III

Managing the Advertising

Chapter 5

The Advertising Agency, Media Services, and Other Services

CHAPTER OBJECTIVES

Advertising agencies create most of the national and international advertising. Their role and relationship with marketers is changing. After reading this chapter you will understand:

>> the agency

>> the history of the agency business

>> the full-service agency

>> global advertising agencies

>> agency and client relationships

>> forms of agency compensation

>> other advertising services

All of the turmoil—mergers, partnerships, short-term pressures on the bottom line, employee cutbacks, management reorganizations, and an increasing emphasis on global marketing—have changed the way businesses think and work and are structured. When there is new corporate structure and new managers, you also affect the marketing process and the advertising agencies involved.

The changes in corporations have pressured agencies to become stronger partners in reaching advertisers' marketing and sales goal. Agencies have undergone their own reengineering, adapting to the environment within which they operate and to the clients they serve. Not only have agencies changed their structures, many have gobbled up specialty firms such as health care, on-line, mail-order, and promotion companies, and other units involved in integrated communication. Make no mistake about it, it's not business as usual. Roles and relationships are changing. "We've been here before," says Keith Reinhard, chairman of DDB

Worldwide, of the challenges presented to the ad industry by new technologies like the Internet. "You have to focus on human beings. You can't forget that you're trying to reach someone who has age-old desires to be noticed, admired, and loved."[1]

The agency remains in transition. However, despite all the changes, advertising agencies continue to be the most significant companies in the development of advertising and marketing in the world.

THE AGENCY

An advertising agency, as defined by the American Association of Advertising Agencies, is an independent business, composed of creative and business people, who develop, prepare, and place advertising in advertising media for sellers seeking to find customers for their goods or services. Exhibit 5.1 is an example of an agency's promoting their experience: Gillette/DuPont/Carnation/JVC/Lipton/Dow Brands/Sara Lee/Pinkerton/Johnson & Johnson/Gallo/Warner Lambert, and so on. The Socoh Group's CEO, Brad P. Majors says, "*Know-how* is the result of personal experience applied to scholarly knowledge." Very impressive credentials.

Exhibit

5.1

Some agencies tout their experience level with significant marketers. "We've worked with the best and therefore can share those experiences with your company."

Courtesy: The Socoh Group.

[1]"We've been here before," *Graphic Design:USA*, September 2000, 70.

According to the U.S. Census Bureau, there are more than 10,000 agencies in operation in this country. The Standard Directory of Advertising Agencies (also known as the Agency Red Book) lists 8,700 agency profiles, including full-service agencies, house agencies, media-buying services, sales-promotion agencies, cyber-agencies, and public relations firms. The Adweek Agency Directory lists more than 4,300 agencies and media-buying services. There are about 2,000 agencies listed in the New York Yellow Pages alone. Unfortunately, there isn't a single directory that lists every agency throughout the country.

The majority of agencies are small one- to ten-person shops (we talk about size and services later in this chapter). You will see ads for many specialized products and services throughout this text—from consumer, dot.coms, medical, software, and industrial products, and services to pro-bono causes—in which the agency had to become an expert in marketing as well as writing the ad. Exhibit 5.2 tries to overcome young people's perception of museums as being "old stuff." The North Carolina Museum of History ad talks about the 250,000-plus collection of artifacts, but also *". . . we're making sure these recent achievements get the recognition they deserve. Which would explain why you'll find things as contemporary as military paraphernalia used by North Carolina based troops during Desert Storm. Or the recently retired race car of North Carolina legend, Richard Petty."*

HOW AGENCIES DEVELOPED

Before we discuss present-day agencies further, let us take a look at how advertising agencies got started and how they developed into large worldwide organizations that play such a prominent role in the marketing and advertising process.

The Early Age (Colonial Times to 1917)

It is not generally known that the first Americans to act as advertising agents were colonial postmasters:

In many localities advertisements for Colonial papers might be left at the post offices. William Bradford, publisher of the first Colonial weekly in New York, made an arrangement with Richard Nichols, postmaster in 1727, whereby the latter accepted advertisements for the New York Gazette at regular rates.[2]

Space Salesmen   Volney B. Palmer is the first person known to have worked on a commission basis. In the 1840s, he solicited ads for newspapers that had difficulty getting out-of-town advertising. Palmer contacted publishers and offered to get them business for a 50 percent commission, but he often settled for less. There was no such thing as a rate card in those days. A first demand for $500 by the papers might be reduced, before the bargain was struck, to $50. (Today we call that negotiation.) Palmer opened offices in Philadelphia, New York, and Boston. Soon there were more agents, offering various deals.

Space Wholesalers   During the 1850s in Philadelphia, George P. Rowell bought large blocks of space for cash (most welcome) from publishers at very low rates, less agents' commissions. He would sell the space in small "squares"—one-column wide—at his own retail rate. Rowell next contracted with 100 newspapers to buy one column of space a month and sold the space in his total list at a fixed rate per line for the whole list: "An inch of space a month in one hundred papers for one hundred dollars." Selling by list became widespread. Each wholesaler's list was his private stock in trade. (This was the original media package deal.)

The First Rate Directory   In 1869 Rowell shocked the advertising world by publishing a directory of newspapers with their card rates and his own estimates of their circulation. Other agents accused him of giving away their trade secrets; publishers howled too because his estimates of circulation were lower than their claims. Nevertheless, Rowell persisted in offering advertisers an estimate of space costs based on those published rates for whatever markets they wanted. This was the beginning of the media estimate.

The Agency Becomes a Creative Center   In the early 1870s, Charles Austin Bates, a writer, began writing ads and selling his services to whoever wanted them, whether advertisers or agents. Among his employees were Earnest Elmo Calkins and Ralph Holden, who in the 1890s founded their own agency, famous for 50 years under the name of Calkins and Holden. These men did more than write ads. They brought together planning, copy, and art, showing the way to combine all three into effective advertising. Not only was their agency one of the most successful for half a century, but the influence of their work helped to establish the advertising agency as the creative center for advertising ideas. Many of the names on the list of firms advertising in 1890 (see Chapter 1) are still familiar today; their longevity can be attributed to the effectiveness of that generation of agency people who developed the new power of advertising agency services. The business had changed from one of salesmen going out to sell advertising space to one of agencies that created the plan, the ideas, the copy, and the artwork, produced the plates, and then placed the advertising in publications from which they received a commission.

To this day, the unique contribution to business for which agencies are most respected is their ability to create effective ads.

Agency-Client Relationship Established   In 1875, Francis Ayer established N.W. Ayer & Son (one of the larger advertising agencies today). Ayer proposed to bill advertisers for what he actually paid the publishers (that is, the rate paid the publisher less the commission), adding a fixed charge in lieu of a commission. In

---

[2]James Melvin Lee, *History of American Journalism,* rev. ed. (Boston: Houghton Mifflin, 1933), 74.

exchange, advertisers would agree to place all their advertising through Ayer's agents. This innovation established the relationship of advertisers as clients of agencies rather than as customers who might give their business to various sales-people, never knowing whether they were paying the best price.

The Curtis No-Rebating Rule   In 1891, the Curtis Publishing Company announced that it would pay commissions to agencies only if they agreed to collect the full price from advertisers, a rule later adopted by the Magazine Publishers of America. This was the forerunner of no-rebating agreements, which were an important part of the agency business for more than 50 years. (Agency commissions, however, ranged from 10 to 25 percent in both magazines and newspapers.)

Standard Commissions for Recognized Agencies Established   In 1917, newspaper publishers, through their associations, set 15 percent as the standard agency commission, a percentage that remains in effect for all media to this day (except local advertising, for which the media deal directly with the stores and pay no commission). The commission would be granted, however, only to agencies that the publishers' associations "recognized." One of the important conditions for recognition was an agency's agreement to charge the client the full rate (no rebating). Other criteria for recognition were that the agency must have business to place, must have shown competence in handling advertising, and must be financially sound. These three conditions are still in effect. Anyone may claim to be an agency, but only agencies that are recognized are allowed to charge a commission.

Today's agencies still receive commissions from the media for space they buy for clients. However, artwork and the cost of production are generally billed by the agency to the advertiser, plus a service charge—usually 17.65 percent of the net, which is equivalent to 15 percent of the gross. By preagreement, a charge is made for other services.

The American Association of Advertising Agencies   The most important agency association is the **American Association of Advertising Agencies** (sometimes known as AAAA or 4As), established in 1917. This organization has continuously acted as a great force in improving the standards of agency business and advertising practice. Its members, large and small, place more than 80 percent of all national advertising today.

American Association of Advertising Agencies (AAAA, 4As)   The national organization of advertising agencies.

The No-Rebate Age (1918–1956)

The events of this era that left their mark on today's agency world are summarized here.

Radio   One of the main events of 1925 was the notorious Scopes trial, and the main advent was radio. They did a lot for each other. Radio dramatized evolution-on-trial in Tennessee; it brought the issue of teaching scientific evolution home to Americans and it brought people closer to their radios. Tuning in to radio soon became a major part of American life, especially during the Great Depression and World War II. Radio established itself as a prime news vehicle. It also gave advertising a vital new medium and helped pull agencies through those troubled years. A number of agencies handled the entire production of a radio program as well as its commercials. By 1942, agencies were billing more for radio advertising ($188 million) than they were for newspaper advertising ($144 million). The radio boom lasted until television came along.

Television   Television became popular after 1952, when nationwide network broadcasts began. Between 1950 and 1956, television was the fastest-growing medium. It became the major medium for many agencies. National advertisers spent more on television than they did on any other medium. TV expenditures grew from $171 million in 1950 to $1,225 million in 1956.

Electronic Data Processing   The computer entered advertising through the accounting department. By 1956, it was already changing the lives of the media department, the marketing department, and the research department—all having grown in competence with the increasing number of syndicated research services. Agencies prided themselves on their research knowledge and were spending hundreds of thousands of dollars for research every year to service their clients better.

Business was good, and American consumers were attaining a better standard of living than they had ever enjoyed. The period from 1950 to 1956 proved to be the beginning of the biggest boom advertising ever had. Total expenditures jumped from $4.5 billion in 1950 to $9.9 billion in 1956. More than 60 percent of this spending was national advertising placed by advertising agencies. And the agency business was good, too.

The Age of Negotiation (1956–1990)

Consent Decrees   In 1956, a change occurred in the advertiser-agency relationship. The U.S. Department of Justice held that the no-rebating provision between media associations and agencies limited the ability to negotiate between buyer and seller and therefore was in restraint of trade and a violation of antitrust laws. Consent decrees to stop no-rebating provisions were entered into by all media associations on behalf of their members.

Although the Justice Department's ruling in no way affected the 15 percent that commission agencies were accustomed to getting from the media, it opened the way to review the total compensation an agency should receive for its services, with the 15 percent commission a basic part of the negotiations. Later we look at the effects this has had on the agency-client relationship.

The Reengineering Age

Integrated Services   The 1990s has been about agencies reevaluating how they operate. Integrated services has been a buzzword relating to efforts to coordinate a client's entire marketing mix, including public relations, promotion, direct marketing, package design, and so on. Some agencies have expanded their communication services to clients by expanding departments or buying or creating subsidiary companies that enable them to offer sales promotion, public relations, direct marketing, logo and packaging design, and even television programming. One of the reasons is financial—clients have been moving dollars from advertising to promotion, and clients want their communications integrated. Agencies are trying to change to supply those needs.

Interactive Communications   As cable, computers, satellite communication, video technologies, and the like become global, agencies are having to learn how to use this technology for their clients. This involves understanding the hardware of how interactive services are delivered; the message development, which will be different from traditional advertising; and the interactive consumer. The future will be different.

THE FULL-SERVICE AGENCY

In the simplest terms, the **full-service agency** offers clients all the services necessary to handle the total advertising function—planning, creation, production, placement, and evaluation. Many have expanded this to include the management of all integrated marketing communications. Today, integrated marketing makes it possible to manage the product's message through a variety of disciplines—advertising, promotion, direct marketing, public relations, and so forth—with a tight

full-sevice agency
One that handles planning, creation, production, and placement of advertising for advertising clients. May also handle sales promotion and other related services as needed by client.

strategic marketing focus so that the brand image is reinforced every time the consumer is exposed to a communication.

Many agencies have concluded that the next generation of advertising will require a new concept of the role and responsibilities of an advertising agency. A new mission will demand a different organization. As we have said, many agencies have undergone a restructuring or reengineering in recent years. Most believe that brand building is impossible without creative, persuasive advertising, which is with few exceptions the most potent component in the marketing communication mix. Despite the restructuring, most marketers will find familiar unit names: account management, creative, media, research or account planning, and administration. But many of these agencies have changed how they operationalize the work. It still isn't brain surgery, but it does require a managed process.

First, there isn't a universal model, but let us take a look at the functions full-service agencies perform. When a new account or a new product is assigned to a full-service agency, work on it will generally proceed along the following lines.

Diagnosing the Marketing and Brand Problem

The process begins with the collection of all that you know about the product category, the brand, and its competitors. Research takes the lead, looking at consumer attitudes to develop penetrating insights into the prospects and defining the brand's core: Who are the prime prospects? Where are they? What are their demographics and psychographic characteristics? How does the product fit into their lifestyles? How do they regard this type of product; this particular brand; competitive products? What one benefit do consumers seek from this product; this particular brand? In what distinctive way can the product solve the prime prospects' problems? What media will best reach your market? Some ad agencies sell their research capability to attract clients. Ingalls Advertising's self-ad said, *". . . it's understandable that when you advertise, you tend to do it from your own perspective. . . . we don't promote who you think you want to be. We explore through research who consumers will let you become. Then we apply that knowledge to the most important part of any communication plan, the ad itself."*

The Socoh Group's self-promotion used a quote from David Ogilvy about *". . . most campaigns are too complicated"* (Exhibit 5.3).

Setting Objectives and Developing Strategy

Using the answers to these questions, a strategy is formulated that positions the product in relation to the prime-prospect customer and emphasizes the attribute that will appeal to the prime prospect. Account management is responsible for leading this phase. Here you define what is to be accomplished strategically, such as intensifying brand imagery and recapturing prior users, and plan how to carry it out. These strategic dialogues involve teams of account, creative, media, and research people.

Creating the Communication

Once the overall strategy is determined, you decide on the creative strategy, write copy, and prepare rough layouts and storyboards. In advertising, the creative impulse is always disciplined—an imaginative and persuasive expression of the selling strategy and the character of the brand.

The Media Plan   You define media strategy, checking objectives to ensure that they parallel your marketing objectives. Then you select media. All traditional and nontraditional options are explored, the goal being to avoid mere execution and

Exhibit

5.3

One problem of any campaign is setting objectives that will work.

Courtesy: The Socoh Group.

add value instead. Media schedules are prepared with costs. At this stage, you seek to coordinate all elements of the marketing communication mix to ensure maximum exposure. Media leads the process by developing an environment that multiplies the impact of the creative team. This step may be implemented by the agency or an independent media agency or buying service.

The Total Plan   You present roughs of the copy, layouts, and production costs, along with the media schedules and costs—all leading to the total cost.

Evaluation Plan   The evaluation step in the process is both the end and the beginning. It is the moment of reckoning for the creative work, based on the objectives set in the beginning, and provides the evidence needed to refine and advance future efforts. As such, it is an accountable system.

Notify Trade of Forthcoming Campaign

For many product categories you would inform dealers and retailers of the campaign details early enough so that they can get ready to take advantage of the ad campaign.

Billing and Payments

When ads are run, you take care of the billing to the client and payment of bills to the media and production vendors. As an example of the billing procedure, let us say that through your agency an advertiser has ordered an ad in Leisure Gourmet magazine for one page costing $10,000. When the ad appears, the bill your agency gets from the publisher will read something like this:

1 page, August Leisure Gourmet magazine	$10,000
Agency commission @ 15% (cash discount omitted for convenience)	1,500
Balance Due	$ 8,500

Your agency will then bill the advertiser for $10,000, retain the $1,500 as its compensation, and pay the publisher $8,500.

The agency commission applies only to the cost of space or time. In addition, as mentioned earlier, your agency will send the advertiser a bill for production costs for such items as the following:

finished artwork   reproduction prints/films
typography (typesetting)   recording studios
photography   broadcast production
retouching

The items are billed at actual cost plus a service charge, usually 17.65 percent (which is equivalent to 15 percent of the net).

THE TRADITIONAL AGENCY ORGANIZATION

In this section, we first examine the traditional approach to the full-service agency structure, and then we look at the reengineering of this process.

Advertising agencies come in all sizes and shapes. The largest employ hundreds of people and bill thousands of millions of dollars every year. The smallest are one- or two-person operations (usually a creative person and an account manager). As they grow, they generally must add to their organizational structure to handle all the functions of a full-service agency.

All agencies do not structure themselves in exactly the same manner. For discussion purposes, we have chosen a typical organizational structure under the command of major executives: the vice presidents of (1) the creative department, (2) account services, (3) marketing services, and (4) management and finance (Exhibit 5.4). We discuss briefly how each department is organized.

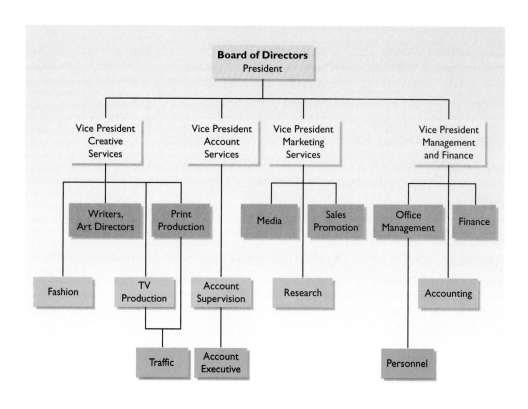

Exhibit

5.4

Organization of a Typical Full-Service Agency

Creative Department

The agency creative director is almost a mythical, often legendary creature positioned near the top of the agency totem pole. The creative director is considered to be responsible for the care and feeding of its most prized possession—the creative product. Today, more than ever before, success is measured by the client's results. The creative director is expected to have an opinion on everything from sales promotion to public relations. In addition to den mother, psychologist, cheerleader, arbiter of taste, basketball coach, team player, historian, jack-of-all-trades, showman, social convener, architect, designer, and Renaissance person, today's more evolved species is also required to be a strategist, businessperson, planner, financier, and new product developer. Bill Westbrook, upon taking over as creative head of Fallon McElligott, stressed the importance of strategy: "If it's not a great strategy, it isn't a great campaign." Lee Chow, chairman and chief creative officer of TBWA/Chiat Day, says, "Managing an integrated campaign is different from doing just ads, as creative directors we've become joined at the hip with account planners."[3]

At first, all writers and artists will work right under one creative director; but as the business grows, various creative directors will take over the writing and art activities of different brands. A traffic department will be set up to keep the work flowing on schedule.

The print production director and the TV manager also report to the creative director, who is ultimately responsible for the finished product—ads and commercials.

Account Services

The vice president in charge of account services is responsible for the relationship between the agency and the client and is indeed a person of two worlds: the client's business and advertising. This vice president must be knowledgeable about the client's business, profit goals, marketing problems, and advertising objectives. He or she is responsible for helping to formulate the basic advertising strategy recommended by the agency, for seeing that the proposed advertising prepared by the agency is on target, and for presenting the total proposal—media schedules, budget, and rough ads or storyboards—to the client for approval. Then comes the task of making sure that the agency produces the work to the client's satisfaction.

As the business grows and takes on many clients, an account supervisor will appoint account executives to serve as the individual contacts with the various accounts. Account executives must be skillful at both communications and follow-up. Their biggest contribution is keeping the agency ahead of its client's needs. But the account supervisor will continue the overall review of account handling, maintaining contacts with a counterpart at the client's office (Exhibit 5.5).

Marketing Services

The vice president in charge of marketing services is responsible for media planning and buying, for research, and for sales promotion. The marketing vice president will appoint a media director, who is responsible for the philosophy and planning of the use of media, for the selection of specific media, and for buying space and time. As the agency grows, there will be a staff of media buyers, grouped according to media (print, TV, or radio), accounts, or territory. The media staff will include an estimating department and an ordering department, as well as a

---

[3]Ann Cooper, "Bernbach's children come of age," *Adweek*, 25 March 1996, 33–36.

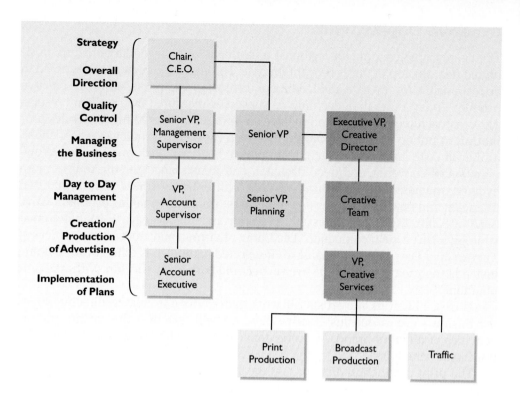

Exhibit

5.5

**Typical Team
Responsibilities**

In some agencies, the account
planner works directly with
creative to provide research
and consumer viewpoints.

department to handle residual payments due performers. The media head may use
independent media services, especially in the purchase of TV and radio time.

The research director will help define marketing and copy goals. Agencies usually use outside research organizations for field work, but in some agencies,
research and media planning are coordinated under one person. The division of
work among the executives may vary with the agency.

The sales-promotion director takes care of premiums, coupons, and other
dealer aids and promotions.

Management and Finance

Like all businesses, an advertising agency needs an administrative head to take
charge of financial and accounting control, office management, and personnel
(including trainees).

THE REENGINEERING OF THE AGENCY

During the past decade a number of attempts have been made to reengineer the
basic agency operations. At this time, there isn't a standard structure brought about
by reengineering or even a desire by most agencies to radically restructure. Some of
the efforts have been successful and others have been questionable. For example,
D'Arcy Masius Benton & Bowles several years ago restructured around brand
teams; although they later decided to return to a more traditional pyramid structure, which better served clients such as Procter & Gamble. However, the driving
force behind any reengineering is the desire to meet the wants and needs of clients
cheaper, faster, and better.

A few years ago, Jay Chiat, a pioneer in agency reengineering, said:

We believe the hierarchical structure [of the traditional agency], if not obsolete at present, is on its way. The traditional pyramid is about personal power and focuses on how to run a business. Therefore most decisions are about the organization's needs, concentrating on fiscal and administrative issues. An agency is a service organization whose sole existence depends on satisfying client needs.[4]

What Reengineering Does

It sets up a process whereby the top management of agencies is in direct contact with clients instead of functioning only as administrators. In traditional agencies, senior managers spend 15 to 20 percent of their time on client business. In reengineered agencies, they spend about 60 percent of their time in the trenches working on client business. Middle managers in reengineered agencies act as coaches, team leaders, and quality control managers. One of the significant changes is that creative staff, account managers, and media planners must work together as a team—a team of people working together to rapidly solve problems. Most agency reengineers say their teams consist of 8 to 12 people, although Sawyer Riley Compton uses teams called account circles of about 20. Most agencies' reengineered structure is somewhat similar to traditional structure. It is how business works that is different. People don't do their thing in isolation; they approach problem solving together. The team concept often helps younger people because it allows them to work side by side with senior people.

In 1997, Leo Burnett announced a reorganization into "miniagencies" built around brand teams. Each miniagency had its own management and was staffed with personnel from client services, planning, creative, and production; it also included specialists from the media division. The groups were no longer housed in their respective departments on different floors, but were grouped together and dedicated to a single piece of business. In the fall of 2000, they abandoned this structure in favor of three or four more traditional account groups.

Changing technology also plays an important part in most restructuring efforts. The linking of teams and clients electronically and the reduction of the time and cost of producing advertising is part of the effort to use technology effectively.

As with any new management trend, traditional agencies will copy and modify those reengineering structures that have been successful to meet their specific needs. There is little doubt that the agency structure in the future will not be a copy of today's.

Reengineering Results

The job function doesn't radically change in the reengineered agency. There is a significant shift, however, in how that job function relates to others in the process. For example, under the traditional structure, an account person may meet regularly with creative people to discuss strategy and ad copy, or with media people to review scheduling, or separately with the public relations person. In some cases, there might be a meeting where specific players in the process meet to discuss a problem or progress. In most reengineered operations, on the other hand, the key people on the team meet on a regular basis so that everyone knows what is going on in every aspect of the account. Richard Riley says the account circle at Sawyer Riley Compton meets every Monday morning to review the week's work—and meets again when necessary. This means the sales promotion person knows about the

---

[4]Jeff Weiner, "Anxious ranks," *Agency,* Spring 1994, 42.

Exhibit
5.6

**Sawyer Riley Compton
Account Circle Approach**

public relations work, and the art director knows about media planning. If necessary, the client participates in the review. Exhibit 5.6 shows the players on a typical account circle team. One of the pluses in this process is that everyone on the team—senior or junior staffer—understands every function in the process and how their work relates to everyone else's work. In theory, a client could call anyone on the team to get an answer.

GLOBAL AGENCIES AND GLOBAL MARKETS

Globalization has become a necessary part of business and advertising. The demands on marketers to survive in a global economy place pressures on large- and medium-sized agencies to become global partners. It is more than simply a language problem. Companies and agencies need to learn cultural and market patterns and understand consumers from a global perspective. Someone trying to sell burgers, fries, and soft drinks outside of the United States may think there is no competition because there are no other burger outlets. The local version of fast food may not include hamburgers at all; the real competition may be a rice shop or a tacqueria.

Unless marketers understand competing sources for that same dollar, they won't be successful.[5] It can be complex. Many small to medium agencies who don't have the resources for international offices have made affiliations with agencies or independent agency networks throughout the world to service clients and give advice. If an agency doesn't have the resources to help clients engage in international marketing, then the client is likely to turn to other agencies that do have the resources and knowledge, or the client may seek a local agency in the country where they are doing business. Major agencies have been global in nature for decades, if not longer, to service their clients' international needs.

J. Walter Thompson opened its first office outside the United States in 1891 in London. It now has 255 offices in 88 countries. They have developed international offices and a system to manage a client's global business that includes the following:

1. *Global teams.* JWT can help clients achieve their communications objectives virtually anywhere in the world.
2. *Director-in-charge system.* JWT uses an account director, who is the director-in-charge (DIC) on a global scale. These people operate as heads of an "agency

---

[5]Jan Larson, "It's a small world, after all," *Marketing Tools,* September 1997, 47–51.

within the agency," working with all offices to service global clients. The DICs work closely with their regional directors, local office CEOs, and account directors in each country to make sure the agency's network comes together seamlessly to execute a multinational advertiser's global communications efforts to build its business.

3. *Regional directors.* The JWT regional directors have the responsibility for a specific group of countries. The CEOs of JWT's offices in that region report to the regional director.

4. *Global directors.* Each worldwide client is represented by a global business director, who sits on the JWT worldwide executive group. The DIC reports to the global business director, whose role is to ensure that the full resources of the JWT global network are brought to bear in servicing multinational accounts.

WWP, the parent of JWT, sponsors BrandZ, a research study that interviews some 70,000 people around the world. This study asks consumers questions in 50 categories to understand and how consumers view 3,500 brands. These insights are available to JWT clients.

In Chapter 24, we deal extensively with international operations.

Global Ad Centers   The leading international advertising centers ranked in terms of local advertising billings are New York and Tokyo—fighting neck and neck for world leadership. Other major advertising centers include: London, Paris, Chicago, Los Angeles, Detroit, San Francisco, Minneapolis, Frankfurt, São Paulo, Düsseldorf, Madrid, and Seoul. Almost every country has an advertising agency center. For U.S. agencies, setting up a foreign office can be very complex. Each country is a different market, with its own language, buying habits, ways of living, mores, business methods, marketing traditions, and laws. So instead of trying to organize new agencies with American personnel, most U.S. agencies purchase a majority or minority interest in a successful foreign agency. They usually have a top management person as head of an overseas office. Key members of the international offices regularly meet for intensive seminars on the philosophy and operation of the agency, and share success stories. Remember, good marketing ideas can come from any place. The United States doesn't have a lock on great ideas.

Global Efficiencies   Cost efficiencies in production of global advertising motivate advertisers to seek a single world execution. A single execution also helps build the same global brand equity. However, "every international brand starts out as a successful local brand . . . reproduced many times."[6] Being a global advertiser and having one global campaign sounds easy. But it is not. Despite being a global advertiser for many decades, it was only in 1992 that Coca-Cola launched its first global advertising campaign—all the ads being similar in each country. Exhibit 5.7 shows an ad developed by Coca-Cola Company–Japan. In 1994, Chanel No. 5 (perfume) was having problems with its global advertising campaign because they were taking a manufacturer approach instead of a consumer approach. A brand and its advertising must be presented in relevant and meaningful ways in the context of local environments, or consumers won't care. As many experienced multinational marketers know, for any given brand, advertising that elicits the same response from consumers across borders matters much more than running the same advertising across borders. That may mean using the same brand concept or advertising concept and similar production format across borders, but the executions need to be customized to local markets so the consumers can relate to and empathize with

---

[6]Ashish Banerjee, "Global campaigns don't work; multinationals do," *Advertising Age*, 18 April 1994, 23.

the advertising. Simply translating American ads into foreign languages has proved dangerous. Perdue's (Chicken) Spanish translation of "It takes a tough man to make a tender chicken," actually said, "It takes a sexually excited man to make a chick affectionate."

Global Marketing Changes   This decade brought reorganization among many major global players as to how they attempted to get their companies even more globally integrated. Such global heavyweights as Coca-Cola, Gillette, Nestlé, Wal-Mart, and Procter & Gamble found a few bumps in the international arena over the past few years. As a result of its problems, Coke's Chairman-CEO Douglas Draft announced a new "Think local, act local" edict for his company early in 2000. For smaller companies, the promise of global branding has been a bumpy road. This includes both old-economy and new-economy players. Global players face a common problem—virtually every global strategy now has a full complement of strong multinational and regional competitors. The promise of managing marketing from a single headquarters hasn't worked the way it was planned. Colgate-Palmolive Co., one of the multinationals in recent years, retains its regional management structure. It was one of the first multinationals to appoint a single ad agency, Young & Rubicam, in 1995.[7]

It is only logical that multinational clients want their agencies to know how to develop great advertising campaigns that can run across all the principal markets of the world. As the chairperson of Leo Burnett International said, "As the world gets smaller, there needs to be brand consistency so people don't get confused as they move from market [country] to market."[8] The result of this need is pressure on U.S. agencies to produce, place, and research global advertising. A sampling of BBDO Worldwide's offices that enable them to service marketers across the globe is shown in the following table.

---

[7]Jack Neff, "Rethinking globalism," *Advertising Age*, 9 October 2000, 1.
[8]"Coke Seeks Ad Formula with Global Appeal," Atlanta Journal-Constitution, 18 November 1991, A5.

United States	Africa	Asia	Europe	Latin America	Canada
Atlanta	Johannesburg	Beijing	Oslo	Buenos Aires	Toronto
Chicago		Sydney	Vienna	Caracas	Calgary
Los Angeles		Hong Kong	Brussels	Santiago	
Miami		Bangkok	Budapest	Bogota	
Minneapolis		Jakarta	Copenhagen	Mexico City	
New York		Kuala Lumpur	Moscow	San Jose	
Southfield, Mich.		Singapore	Prague	Lima	
		Taipei	Stockholm	San Salvador	
			London	San Juan	
			Lisbon	Guatemala City	
			Paris	Managua	

COMPETING ACCOUNTS

The client-agency relationship is a professional one. It may involve new product strategies, new promotions, sales data, profit or loss information, and new marketing strategies—information that is sensitive and confidential. As a result, most clients will not generally approve of an agency's handling companies or products in direct competition; Coca-Cola isn't going to allow their agencies to handle Pepsi products. In some cases, agencies will handle accounts for the same type of product or service if they do not compete directly—for example, banks that do not compete in the same market. Many agency-client conflicts result from mergers in which one merger partner handles an account for a product that competes with a product being handled by the other merger partner. When agencies consider merging, the first question is, "Will any of our accounts conflict?" When True North Communications merged with Bozell, Jacobs, Kenyon & Eckhardt, it forced True North's Foote, Cone & Belding (FCB) agency to resign the $240 million Mazda Motor of North America account. Bozell's key account was Chrysler Corporation (which it has since lost). Chrysler objected to a linkup with an agency holding company involved with Ford Motor Company. Likewise, Ford, which owns 33 percent of Mazda, also raised concerns about seeing FCB even indirectly connected to Chrysler. Sounds complicated and it is. There are a number of large national agencies with independent offices around the country that hope clients will not view the same type of account in another office as a conflict; in the case of Chrysler and Ford, that didn't work.

CLIENT-AGENCY RELATIONSHIP LENGTH

Clients generally keep agencies as long as the relationship seems to be working. However, most contracts allow for a 90-day cancellation by either party if the relationship goes sour. At the same time, agencies can resign an account if they differ with the client's goals and the account isn't profitable. American Association of Advertising Agencies research has indicated that the average tenure of client-agency relationships has declined from 7.2 years to 5.3 years since 1984. Yet in 2000, advertising's oldest continuing client relationships included the following:

Long-Term Client–Agency Relationships (as of 2000)

Marketer	Agency	Duration (years)
Unilever	J. Walter Thompson Co.	98
Sunkist	Foote, Cone & Belding	93
Exxon	McCann-Erickson Worldwide	88
Armstrong World Industries	BBDO Worldwide	83
General Electric	BBDO Worldwide	80
Kellogg	J. Walter Thompson Co.	70
McDonald's	DDB Needham Worldwide	33

AGENCY OF RECORD

In some instances, large advertisers may employ a number of agencies to handle their advertising for various divisions and products. To coordinate the total media buy and the programming of products in a network buy, the advertiser will appoint one agency as the agency of record. This lead agency will make the corporate contracts under which other agencies will issue their orders, keep a record of all the advertising placed, and communicate management's decisions on the allotment of time and space in a schedule. On the McDonald's fast-food account, DDB Needham is the lead agency, with about 66 percent of the business, and Leo Burnett handles about 33 percent. For this service, the other agencies pay a small part of their commissions (usually 15 percent of 15 percent) to the agency of record.

AGENCY MULTIPLE OFFICES

Many major agencies have agency offices in cities throughout the United States. Foote Cone & Belding is typical, with major offices in New York, Chicago, and San Francisco. Ogilvy & Mather has offices in New York, Chicago, Detroit, Atlanta, Houston, and Los Angeles. For the most part, each office functions as an autonomous agency that serves different clients and is able to draw on the talents and services of the other offices. As a rule, these offices don't normally work on the same project for the same client. Whereas the parent organizations are busily marketing themselves as global networks, each local office fiercely tries to protect its unique culture. As Foote, Cone & Belding's CEO puts it, "We have a very New York agency; a very Chicago agency; and a very San Francisco agency. When agencies succeed in putting two or more offices together on a project, a New York office is usually involved." This most commonly occurs on the media side. In fact, some offices will make media buys in their region of the country for all of the agency's offices. BBDO's chairman says, "It's no secret that BBDO in Los Angeles is our best agency in terms of print creative. Why shouldn't we make that expertise available to clients from other offices?"[9] It may be said that because each office handles different kinds of accounts, each office probably has different specialties that could be leveraged on behalf of all clients. But as a general rule, each office works primarily on its own accounts.

A few agencies recently created new West Coast offices to take advantage of the many talents that exist there. These offices are evolving as creative idea centers to help clients in any of the agency brand's offices develop stronger creative products.

---

[9]Mark Gleason, "Agency nets puzzle over brand identity," *Advertising Age,* 6 May 1996, 15.

AGENCY NETWORKS

In general, the agency networks consist primarily of small- and medium-sized agencies that have working agreements with each other to help with information gathering and sharing. Usually there is only one network member in each market or region. The Leading Independent Agency Network is an organization of independent agencies that bills at least $50 million. Only one member is allowed per region of the country. The Mutual Advertising Agency Network provides a way for member agencies to share experience, knowledge, and other ideas with agencies in other parts of the country and the world. They provide a network of information and financial skills used to enhance agency operations.

The Mega-Agency Networks

Mega-agencies have offices or networks of their offices around the world to serve clients. It all started in 1986, when a small London agency, Saatchi & Saatchi PLC, systematically grew over a two-year period to become a mega-agency network with capitalized billings of more than $13.5 billion. This was a significant change in the advertising business as it became the world's largest advertising organization for a brief period and truly changed global advertising. Today, the largest organizations are WWP Group (London), Omnicom Group (New York), and Dentsu (Tokyo). These and other mega-advertising organizations own many advertising agencies throughout the world. Some of the holdings of the Omnicom Group are listed here:

BBDO Worldwide, Inc., New York

TBWA Worldwide, New York

Goodby, Silverstein & Partners, San Francisco

GSD&M, Austin

Martin/Williams Advertising, Minneapolis

Optimum Media Direction, New York

Interbrand (branding & Identity Consultants), New York

Merkley Newman Harty (Corporate/Financial/Business-to-Business), New York

Doremus & Company (corporate/financial, investor public relations) New York

Rapp Collins Worldwide (direct marketing & integrated), New York

Pinhaus (direct marketing), Miami

CPM International (graphic arts & digital imaging), New York

Fleishman-Hillard, Inc. (public relations), St. Louis

Ketchum (public relations), New York

Razorfish (cyber agency), New York

Red Sky Interactive (cyber agency), San Francisco

Mega-agencies offer several advantages to their clients other than sheer size. Among the most important are a greater reservoir of talent and an ability to shift portions of accounts from one agency to another without going through the time-consuming, and often confusing, agency review. (Coca-Cola has switched assignments for its brands among several Interpublic Group of Cos. agencies and given new product assignments to others.) There are also some disadvantages for clients, the most important of which is conflicts with competing accounts.

Size, in itself, doesn't have significant advantages or disadvantages in developing the ads themselves. All agencies—large or small—consist of small units or teams that work on an assigned account or group of accounts. The ability of the team and the dedication to creative and professional excellence are dictated by the talent and innovative abilities of individuals, not the size of their company.

Obviously, size and structure of an agency will attract or repel clients, depending on what level and quality of services they are seeking. The agency business is simply mirroring business in general by diversifying, economizing, and becoming more efficient and profitable.

A tiny communication firm, Latcha & Associates used the Internet and other digital technology to gain Ford Motor Company's $10 million brochure contract previously handled by J. Walter Thompson. The assignment was to produce almost 12-million brochures for five different vehicles. Latcha set up a virtual agency linking freelance designers, photographers, and others. Everything was digital—all the way to the printers, approvals done on-line. Jan Klug, Ford's Division marketing communication manager said, "Had J. Walter Thompson proposed a back-end process like this, we would have gone with them." Most tiny agencies don't try to compete with mega-agencies, but it is a business of ideas and efficiencies.

OTHER ADVERTISING SERVICES

New services are continually springing up in competition with advertising agencies. Each new service is designed to serve clients' needs a little differently. This competition has impacted agency structure and operations.

Talent and Production Agencies Creating Creative

A relatively new resource for clients is the melding of talent sources to develop ad concepts. Creative Artists Agency (CAA), a production and talent agency involving entertainment stars, writers, directors, and others, made inroads with Coca-Cola about a decade ago as a working partner with Coke's advertising agencies, in some cases independently developing advertising concepts and commercials. The 1993 Coke-guzzling polar bears were created by both Coke's agency and CAA. A number of other talent agencies have had working agreements with marketers and their advertising agencies to provide creative and talent services. CAA as it was created does not exist today. Some industry insiders believe such talent agency relationships can add another dimension to the advertising agency and client resources.

Independent Creative Services

Some advertisers seek top creative talent on a freelance, per-job basis. Many creative people do freelance work in their off hours. Some make it a full-time job and open their own creative shop or creative boutique. In general, the creative boutique has no media department, no researchers, and no account executives. The purpose is strictly to develop creative ideas for their clients.

À La Carte Agency

Today, many agencies offer for a fee just the part of their total services that advertisers want. The à la carte arrangement is used mostly for creative services and for media planning and placement. Many agencies are spinning off their media departments into independent divisions to seek clients interested only in media handling. Handling only the media portion of an account typically brings commissions that range from 3 to 5 percent.

In-House Agency

in-house agency
An arrangement whereby the advertiser handles the total agency function by buying individually, on a fee basis, the needed services (for example, creative, media services, and placement) under the direction of an assigned advertising director.

When advertisers found that all the services an agency could offer were purchasable on a piecemeal fee basis, they began setting up their own internal agencies, referred to as in-house agencies. The **in-house agency** can employ a creative service to originate advertising for a fee or markup. They can buy the space or time themselves or employ a media-buying service to buy time or space and place the ads. As a rule, the in-house agency is an administrative center that gathers and directs varying outside services for its operation and has a minimum staff.

Folks, Inc., an Atlanta restaurant company with two different restaurant concepts, had an agency. Then it created an in-house agency, which developed all creative concepts, copy, layout ideas, radio scripts, and so forth. It used art studios and graphic computer services to produce the finished art, and broadcast production companies for its broadcasts. It bought all print media in-house and used a media-buying service to place its broadcast buys. It also developed all direct-mail, store marketing, public relations, and promotion. Recently Folks found a need for strategic marketing services and hired Cole Henderson & Drake advertising to assist in strategic development for one of its restaurant concepts. The agency then created advertisements, produced advertising, and bought media. When the agency contract expired, they turned to their former marketing director's company, Sheri Bevil, now CEO of Bevil Advertising, for their marketing communication. Exhibit 5.8A is a promotional ad for Folks Southern Kitchen and Exhibit 5.8B is an example of collateral later developed by Bevil.

In-house agencies are generally created to save money or give advertisers more control over every aspect of their business. Many industrial companies have highly technical products that constantly undergo technological changes and advances; it may well be more efficient to have in-house technical people prepare ads. This saves endless briefings that would be necessary if outside industrial writers were

Exhibit

5.8b

This is an example of collateral promotion material that agencies produce for clients.

Courtesy: Sheri Bevil, Bevil Advertising.

used. But the companies place their ads through an agency of their choice, at a negotiated commission.

Rolodex Agency

An agency run by several advertising specialists, usually account and/or creative people, that has no basic staff is called a Rolodex agency. It hires specialists—in marketing, media planning, creative strategy, writing, art direction, whatever—who work on a project basis. The concept is similar to hiring freelance creative people to execute ads, except that the experts are hired as needed. The Rolodex agency claims to be able to give advertisers expertise that small full-service agencies cannot match.

Media-Buying Services

The mid-nineties saw major changes in the way advertisers handle their media. Some major advertisers chose to unbundle media or give their media buys to independent media-buying services or other agencies to try to gain buying efficiencies. At the same time, agencies reinvented their media operations to remain competitive with the growing number of media-buying services, and developed it as a stand-alone profit center. Many of the large agencies have made their media services independent of other agency services to better compete.

We've already talked about agencies spinning off their media departments into independent planning and buying companies, which are separate. For example, J. Walter Thompson and Ogilvy, two global agencies owned by the same parent, followed the trend of creating joint media alliances. They formed MindShare, a mega-media planning and buying agency to serve advertisers better. MindShare's Kristen Kyle says, "Technology is opening many doors to reach people through new media. In order to be more efficient and deal with this new terrain, many agencies are spinning off their media departments. There are four main reasons for these newly formed media agencies: First, media agencies are stronger, with better resources to explore new areas within media; second, the fragmentation of target audiences and media vehicles have made media more important than ever before; third, it has the potential to be a major profit center. If the agency loses the creative responsibilities of a client, the media agency could continue serving the client since it is separate. Finally, the reciprocal action allows media agencies to acquire accounts that work with other parent agencies for their creative work.[10] Not all of these relationships have gone smoothly, Zenith Media Worldwide's co-owners Cordiant Communication Group and Saatchi & Saatchi have had legal disagreements about the operation of this combined company. One of the reasons for the consolidation is the fact that mega-advertisers have consolidated their multiple accounts to obtain better rates in their media buying. One example was Kraft trying to create more efficiencies in its marketing by combining its $800 million media account at one company.

In-House Services

A few large advertisers have taken the media-buying function in-house so they will have more control over the buying operation. However, this doesn't appear to be a trend. It is more likely that advertisers will keep a seasoned media consultant on staff to ride herd on their agency or media service's performance.

FORMS OF AGENCY COMPENSATION

Historically, agency compensation has been fairly standardized since the 1930s. An agency received a commission from the media for advertising placed by the agency. The commission would cover the agency's copywriting and account services charges. This method of compensation has been unsatisfactory during recent years due to the changing nature of business. The straight 15 percent remains, but in some instances there are fixed commissions less than 15 percent (some large advertisers have negotiated a rate closer to 10 percent), sliding scales based upon client expenditures, flat-fee arrangements agreed upon by clients and agency, performance-based systems, and labor-based fee-plus-profit arrangements. In other words, compensation arrangements now take many forms. Despite this change, there are only two basic forms of advertising agency compensation: commissions and fees.

■ *Media commissions.* The traditional 15 percent commission remains a form of agency income, especially for modestly budgeted accounts. Clients and agency may agree to a relationship in which the rate is fixed at less than 15 percent. This generally applies to large budget accounts—the larger the budget, the lower the rate for the agency. With a sliding-scale commission agreement, the agency receives a fixed commission based upon a certain expenditure. After

---

[10]Interview with Kristen Kyle, 5 December 2000.

that level of spending, the commission is reduced (there may be a 14 percent commission for the first $20 million spent by the client and a 7 percent commission on the next $15 million). The combinations are endless.

■ *Production commissions or markups.* As indicated earlier, agencies subcontract production work (all outside purchases such as type, photography, illustrators) and charge the client the cost plus a commission—17.65 percent is the norm.

■ *Fee arrangements.* At times, the 15 percent commission is not enough for agencies to make a fair profit. For example, it may cost an agency more to serve a small client than a large one. The agency and client may negotiate a fee arrangement. In some cases it is a commission plus a fee. There are a number of options: A cost-based fee includes the agency's cost for servicing the account plus a markup, a cost-plus fee covers the agency cost and a fixed profit; a fixed fee is an agreed-upon payment based on the type of work being done (for example, copywriting at hourly fixed rates, artwork charges based on the salary of the involved personnel); and a sliding fee is based on a number of agreed-upon parameters. Again, there are many possibilities based on agency and client needs.

■ *Performance fee.* A predetermined performance goal may determine the compensation fee. For example, ad recall scores, unit sales, or market share may determine the level of compensation. If the agency meets the goals, compensation may be at the 15 percent level; if it exceeds them, a bonus could give the agency a 20 percent level; if it fails to meet the goals, compensation could be much less than 15 percent.

Many marketers have replaced the traditional commission system of paying media commissions with performance-based compensation: calculating agency payments on predetermined, measurable goals like growth in sales, increasing awareness of a brand, or gaining broad distribution for a new product. In July 2000, Procter & Gamble, who advertises some 300 brands, stopped paying ad agencies the traditional commissions for placing their ads in media. Compensation, from that point on, was determined by sales objectives, with agencies being paid more of a brand's sales increase and less if sales decline. Nancy Salz, president at Nancy L. Salz Consulting, which conducts annual surveys on advertiser-agency relations, says, "Holding the agency accountable, when it shares the financial risks and the financial rewards, creates a full business partnership that changes attitudes." She also indicated that 35 percent of clients using performance-based compensation said they had more respect for their agency, compared to 12 percent for clients not using it.[11] Agency magazine reported in 1999 that only 9 percent of advertisers paid the full 15 percent commission. It reported that 53 percent of clients said their compensation was labor-based; 12 percent paid a fixed fee.[12] Performance-based compensation plans are described as media neutral—meaning they favor no one medium—and often eschew traditional media for unconventional sales tools.

All Coca-Cola agencies are on fees plus bonuses. This payment system allows the agencies not to worry if Coke cuts their advertising budget; it is designed to give the agency the best return on investment they get. An example of a commission plus a fee is described in the following agency contract copy:

Internal creative services provided by [agency] shall be applied against the monthly agency fee at the prevailing hourly rates [as distinguished from services bought outside our organization]. Such services include prepara-

[11]Stuart Elliott, "P&G to tie agency compensation to sales," nytimes.com, 15 September 1999.
[12]Thom Forbes, "Agency Compensation," *Agency*, Spring 1999, 22–28.

tion of print, radio, television production, storyboards, special comprehensive layouts, booklets, catalogues, direct mail, sales representations, extraordinary research, package design, collateral materials, etc.

Schedule of Agency	Hourly Rates
Creative director	$150
Copywriter	100
Art director	100
Production supervisor	95
Computer design	130
Type and composition	130
Computer artwork	130
Research/planning	130

Most agencies aim for a 20 percent profit on each account to cover personnel and overhead costs plus a profit. The president of Campbell-Mithun-Esty says, "There's a broad acceptance among clients that it's in their best interest that their account be profitable for their agency. The smarter client understands that's what gets it the best people on their account. That's what gets it the best service."[13]

An advertising management consultant suggests the key flaw of compensation based on the price of traditional media is the lack of a consistent relationship between income generated and the cost of providing services required by the clients. This will continue to be a problem as new media techniques are developed. He suggests agencies align their compensation with their roles as salespeople, not buyers of media, and to link agency profit goals to agreed-upon performance standards.[14]

OTHER SERVICES

Barter

One way for an advertiser or agency to buy media below the rate card price, especially in radio or television, is **barter.** For example, a barter company, Media Store, placed all the radio time for Lufthansa Airlines in return for a six-year lease on its Manhattan ticket office. The airline had too many ticket offices, and the original lease was extremely high per square foot. So the Media Store took over the lease on barter and sublet it. They then paid Lufthansa with radio time for the regular schedules they run.

The International Reciprocal Trade Association indicates there is a fast-growing trend among advertisers to barter, particularly through three-way alliances among barter companies, advertisers, and their ad agencies.

Barter houses often become brokers or wholesalers of broadcast time. They build inventories of time accumulated in various barter deals. These inventories are called time banks, which are made available to advertisers or agencies seeking to stretch their broadcast dollars.

One of the drawbacks of barter is that the weaker stations in a market are more apt to use it the most. Some stations will not accept barter business from advertisers already on the air in the market. Generally, the air time is poor time, although it is generally a good value at the low rate paid.

barter Acquisition of broadcast time by an advertiser or an agency in exchange for operating capital or merchandise. No cash is involved.

[13]Terrence Poltrack, "Pay dirt," *Agency,* July/August 1991, 20–25.
[14]Stan Beals, "Fresh approaches to agency compensation," *Advertising Age,* 29 August 1994, 20.

Research Services

The advertiser, the agency, or an independent research firm can conduct any needed original research. Large agencies may have substantial in-house research departments. In some, the research title has been replaced by the account planner. Account planning has a crucial role during strategy development, driving it from the consumer's point of view. The account planners are responsible for all research, including quantitative research (usage and attitude studies, tracking studies, ad testing, and sales data) as well as qualitative research (talking face-to-face to their target). On the other hand, many smaller agencies offer little in-house research staffing, although many agencies have moved to add account planners.

In addition to the syndicated research previously discussed, which regularly reports the latest findings on buyers of a product—who and where they are, how they live and buy, and what media they read, watch, and listen to—these research companies offer many custom-made research reports to advertisers and their agencies, answering their questions about their own products and advertising. Studies cover such subjects as advertising effectiveness, advertising testing, customer satisfaction, concept and product testing, premium or package design testing, image and positioning, brand equity measurement, market segmentation, strategic research, media preferences, purchasing patterns, and similar problems affecting product and advertising decisions.

A fascinating variety of techniques is available to gather such information. They include consumer field surveys (using personal or telephone interviews or self-administered questionnaires), focus groups, consumer panels, continuous tracking studies, cable testing of commercials, image studies, electronic questionnaires, opinion surveys, shopping center intercepts, and media-mix tests. (Research techniques are discussed in Chapter 15.) Regardless of the technique used in collecting data for a research report, its real value lies in the creative interpretation and use made of its findings.

Managing Integrated Brands

A brand needs a single architect, someone who will implement and coordinate a cohesive strategy across multiple media and markets. According to David Aaker, the advertising agency is often a strong candidate for this role.[15] It regularly develops brand strategy and gains insights due to exposure to different brand contexts. An advertising agency inherently provides a strong link between strategy and executions, because both functions are housed under the same roof. Strategy development in an agency is more likely to include issues of implementation. On the down side, many agencies still have a bias toward media advertising, and their experience at managing event sponsorships, direct marketing, or interactive advertising may be limited.

The challenge for today's agency is to be able to develop an integrated program that accesses and employs a wide range of communication vehicles. There are several approaches to managing this.

Agency Conglomerate Many agencies have approached the integrated communication program by acquiring companies with complementary capabilities. The usual mix includes promotions, corporate design, direct marketing, marketing research, package design, public relations, trade shows, and even event marketing. The hope is that advertisers will buy one-stop coordinated communications. The general consensus is that this approach doesn't work well, because the units that make up the conglomerate often don't blend well with each other and are rivals

---

[15]David Aaker, "The agency as brand architect," *American Advertising,* Spring 1996, 18–21.

for the advertiser's budget, and each unit within the conglomerate isn't necessarily best suited to solve the problem at hand.

In-House Generalist Agency   Another option is to expand the agency's capabilities to include such functions as promotions and public relations. Brand teams spanning communication vehicles can then deal with the coordination issue. Hal Riney & Partners exemplified this approach with its set of promotional programs designed for Saturn. Riney was named guardian of the Saturn brand, and created ads, promotions, and a Web site, and even helped design a retail concept. This concept works if the agency has the talent to handle the new services or has the clients or revenues to support such a diverse staff.

Service Cluster   A service cluster team is a group of people drawn together from all the agency affiliate organizations. Strategically, the cluster's purpose is to service client needs, and the cluster has the flexibility to change with the needs of the client. A key characteristic of the service-cluster team is that it focuses on creating ideas rather than ads.

Communication Integrator   In this approach the agency draws from sources outside the agency and integrates these services for the brands.

Brand Strategy In-House

Many advertisers choose not to rely on the agency at all for managing brand strategy. Their view may be that agencies may be great at creating ads, but brand strategy may be better planned by the brand management team. If outside help is needed, their view may be that the agency may not be the best source—particularly if it has limited research resources. Some clients have found it beneficial to employ a team of specialized communication firms that each are the best in what they do. The advertiser may develop specialized expertise—including research, media buying, and strategy consulting.

Here is Brad Majors' (CEO, Socoh Group, Greenville, South Carolina) perspective on large and small agencies of the future. Brad has worked for some the world's largest and also relatively small agencies and promotion agencies.

Large/public agencies will, more than ever, be confined to large, multinational accounts. It will be nearly impossible for them to profitably service smaller clients. And since there will continue to be large multinational clients (with growth primarily from the acquisitions of smaller competitors' brands), there should be room for the larger agencies to profitably handle them.

Medium-sized agencies, which have been the greatest source of creativity historically, will exist but will remain in the state of flux we see today and have seen for 20 years. As they grow, they will have the resources to hire strong talent. Much of this talent, without the cumbrances of public ownership, will continue to produce provocative work. As the work is noticed and clients and prospects become more interested, these medium-sized agencies will become attractive to larger agencies as an acquisition target. As the principals of the agency age, an immediate cash-rich buyout may seem more attractive than a deal with the next generation of the agency's management. Thus, the newly acquired agency will not be medium-sized any longer, but will become only a part of the larger whole. Once acquired, it will be important for them to remain in the niche prescribed for them by the parent agency.

Interestingly, smaller agencies will not only exist, but will thrive, if managed prudently. Historically, small agencies have either fared very well or gone under. To some extent, small agency success has been determined by how strong the agency's financial management was. Managing cash flow and account receivables has been a critical issue for most small agencies and it will continue to be so. But given the instability expected in medium-sized agencies, there should be great opportunities for smaller agencies that combine a marketing-driven creative product with sound financial management.

A small, but growing trend is that of smaller agencies partnering with other agencies (with complementary skills) to handle a single client project that might dwarf the single small agency. However, neither agency has the desire to partner permanently, but only to meet the client need at hand. This allows smaller agencies to "bulk up" and remain competitive without permanently adding overhead that could hinder the agency's profitability at a future point. To some extent this mirrors what some call the "free agent nation" status of a growing number business people in America at the turn of the new century.

SUMMARY

The advertising agency is in a period of transition. It is being reevaluated and reengineered to be more responsive to clients' needs.

A full-service agency works on many aspects of a client's marketing problems: strategy, creative response, media planning, and trade campaigns. Many agencies are organized into four divisions: account services, marketing services, creative services, and management and finance. Some agencies have a domestic network of offices or affiliates to service their large accounts better. The growing importance of global marketing to some clients has led agencies to expand internationally. Clients usually pay agencies by commission, fees, or a combination of the two.

There are other types of advertising services beside the traditional advertising agency: in-house agencies, à la carte agencies, creative boutiques, Rolodex agencies, and media-buying services. Agencies usually cannot and will not handle two accounts that compete in the same market.

REVIEW

1. What is a full-service agency?
2. What is the normal media commission?
3. What is an "agency of record"?

TAKE IT TO THE NET

We invite you to visit the Russell/Lane page on the Prentice Hall Web site at **www.prenhall.com/myphlip** for end-of-chapter exercises and applications.

Chapter 6

The Advertiser's Marketing/Advertising Operation

CHAPTER OBJECTIVES

Marketers have been restructuring their operations to be more competitive. Despite these changes, the goals and functions remain essentially the same. Here we learn about some fundamentals. After reading this chapter you will understand:

>> the marketing service system

>> integrated marketing brand management

>> how advertising budgets are set

>> advertising goals versus marketing goals

>> agency-client relationships

We must always remember that advertising is a business. It is a marketing tool used by marketers. It has a structure and an organization, and must be managed, just like any business. Advertising is a financial investment in the brand or company.

Advertisers have recently been preoccupied with competition, price pressures, and promotion, and have lost touch with consumers. Paul Higham, senior vice president of marketing and communications at Wal-Mart Stores, says, "Perhaps we should think less about our brands and more about our consumers." A Procter & Gamble (P&G) executive has said, "We've become our own worst enemy by creating a system whereby 75 percent of our dollars are trying to win the loyalty of brand switchers." P&G is returning to the tried-and-true practices of hard-sell, demographic advertising, and heavy focus on product innovation.

The 1980s and 1990s brought all kinds of pressures to corporations. Downsizing, cost cutting, mergers, and partnerships, both domestic and foreign, have been common. The same kind of pressures have affected the marketing and advertising departments. Marketers have struggled with price wars, recession, and the growing strength of private labels. It seems no company—successful or not—

has been untouched by these pressures to be more competitive. Companies have restructured and reorganized divisions and departments. Obviously, when restructuring takes place there will be changes in how they manage or handle marketing and advertising.

Today everyone wants to be more efficient and competitive. For some companies it is simply a case of survival. The advertising and marketing departments control the dollars and decide on the need for an advertising agency, or in some case agencies, for different products. At times they may hire an agency to handle only creative or to place the ads in the media. They may choose to use freelancers or creative boutiques or to use a media-buying service or combine their media-buying strength for all their products with one agency. They may decide to staff an in-house agency to develop ads, as discussed in Chapter 5. It is their ball game. They call the shots.

Because companies vary in size and structure, it only makes sense that advertising and marketing staffs also differ from organization to organization. They may have a large department controlling all marketing activities, or they may have limited personnel in marketing, or they may rely on operation managers or the president to make the marketing decisions. Before we complicate the process of integrated marketing structure, let us examine the typical structure.

MARKETING SERVICES SYSTEM

With increasing structural and organizational changes in business, the results are being felt in the advertising and marketing function. The advertising department structure—the traditional system—worked well for most companies. Exhibit 6.1 illustrates this organizational structure.

As companies such as Procter & Gamble grew with a number of brands, this structure needed to change to solve their marketing problems. The result was a new organizational concept called the marketing services system. This concept has been widely adopted, especially in the package goods fields and by a number of service-oriented companies.

Under this concept, developed in 1931, each brand manager is, in essence, president of his or her own corporation-within-the-corporation. The brand manager is charged with developing, manufacturing, marketing, promoting, integrating, and selling the brand.

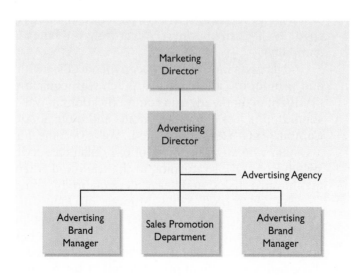

Exhibit

6.1

Simple Organization Chart for Advertising Department

The marketing services system has two parts (Exhibit 6.2). One is the marketing activity, which begins with the product manager assigned to different brands. The other part of the structure is a structure of marketing services, which represents all the technical talent involved in implementing a marketing plan, including creative services, promotion services, media services, advertising controls, and marketing research services. All of these services are available to the product manager, as is

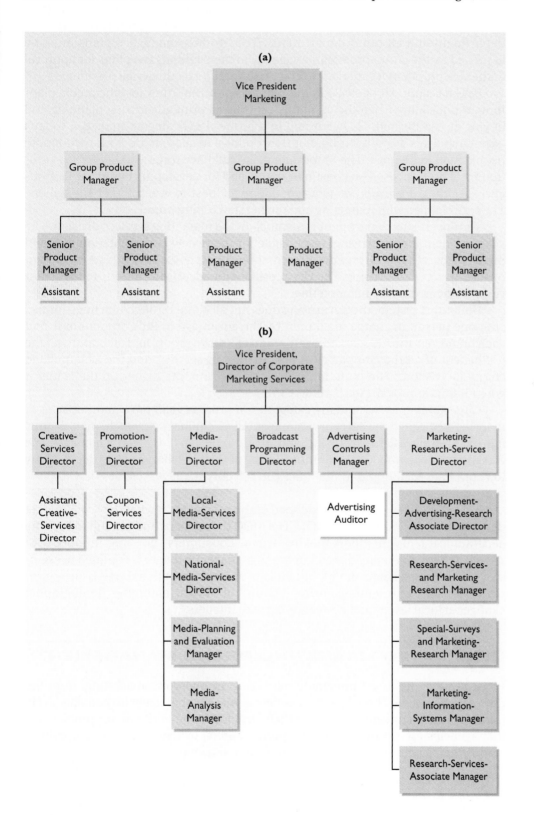

Exhibit

6.2

A large company with a marketing services division may be organized into (a) a marketing department; and (b) a marketing services department, where specialists in creative, media, and research advise product managers and consult with counterparts in the agency.

the help from the advertising agency assigned to that manager's brand. The product manager can bring together the agency personnel and his or her counterpart in the marketing services division, giving the company the benefit of the best thinking of both groups—internal and external. Each group has a group product manager, who supervises the individual product managers.

The **product manager** is responsible for planning strategy and objectives, obtaining relevant brand information, managing budget and controls, and getting agency recommendations, and is the primary liaison between the marketing department and all other departments. The product manager's plans must be approved by the group product manager, who then submits the plans for approval of the vice president for marketing and finally of the executive vice president.

P&G has approximately 80 brand managers. In 1997, they lost the media planning responsibility when the company centralized print advertising planning and buying at Leo Burnett Co. According to a former P&G category manager, today's brand managers are still strong, but they do have to share more power with more people than in the past. The brand managers still have responsibility for the positioning of brands based on consumer needs, and for developing broad media strategy—deciding, for example, what media mix is best to reach target consumers. They are charged with managing and further developing brand equity.[1]

The advertising department is a branch of the marketing services division. The vice president for advertising, responsible for the review and evaluation of brand media plans, attends all creative presentations to act as an adviser and consultant on all aspects of advertising. The vice president for advertising reports to the senior vice president, director of marketing.

Under this system, the advertising does not all come through one huge funnel, with one person in charge of all brands. The advantage to the corporation is that each brand gets the full marketing attention of its own group, and all brands get the full benefit of all the company's special marketing services and the accumulated corporate wisdom. The more important the decision, the higher up the ladder it goes for final approval. (See Exhibit 6.3.)

Large companies with many categories of products can have another layer of management called the **category manager.** All disciplines—research, manufacturing, engineering, sales, advertising, and so on—report to the category manager. The category manager follows the product line he or she is in charge of and decides how to coordinate each brand in that line. The category manager decides how to position brands in each category.

In 1999, Procter & Gamble redefined brand managers in what they call "market development organizations (MDO)." The MDO duties focus and expand to become geographical team members looking at how consumers shop and interact with media. Being a marketing director or brand manager no longer is confined to exclusively managing a single brand, but looking at all kinds of marketing issues—new store formats, redesigning entire sections of stores, emerging demographic changes at local levels, and co-marketing with retailers.[2]

INTEGRATED MARKETING BRAND MANAGEMENT

Previously, we discussed integrated marketing, or one-voice marketing, from the agency perspective. There has been debate about whether agencies can effectively implement this concept because of their structure. One of the major problems is that agencies are set up as separate profit centers, which results in competition among their own units for a strong bottom-line showing.

---

[1]Jack Neff, "P&G redefines the brand manager," *Advertising Age,* 13 October 1997, 1.
[2]Jack Neff, "P&G redefines brand managers for MDO days," *Advertising Age,* 26 April 1999, 4.

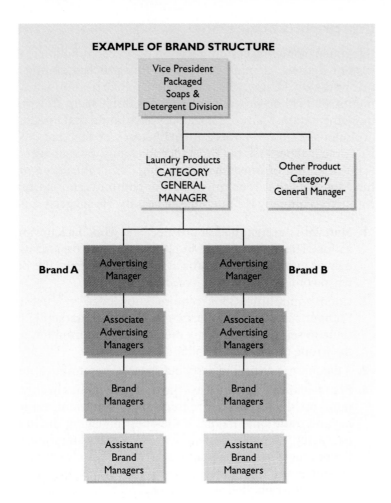

EXAMPLE OF BRAND STRUCTURE

Vice President
Packaged
Soaps &
Detergent Division

Laundry Products
CATEGORY
GENERAL
MANAGER

Other Product
Category
General Manager

Brand A — Advertising Manager

Advertising Manager — Brand B

Associate Advertising Managers

Associate Advertising Managers

Brand Managers

Brand Managers

Assistant Brand Managers

Assistant Brand Managers

Exhibit

6.3

The category manager is responsible for all aspects of the brands in his or her category. Each product's advertising manager reports to the category manager.

Research involving marketing executives indicates that integration of advertising, promotion, public relations, and all other forms of marketing communications is the most important factor influencing how strategies will be set. Larry Light, the former chairman of the international division of Bates Worldwide, says, "The reason integrated marketing is important is consumers integrate your messages whether you like it or not. The messages cannot be kept separate. All marketing is integrated in the mind of consumers. Your only choice is how that message is integrated."[3]

An *Advertising Age* survey found major disagreement between agencies and advertisers in terms of whether integration should be managed inside the corporation or by the agency; 82.9 percent of marketers say integration is their responsibility in terms of setting strategy for and coordination of integration, and 63 percent of agencies said that's their domain.[4] Advertisers feel they can put in place, or already have in place, ad agencies, public relation firms, promotion agencies, direct-marketing companies, and design firms—all outside communication specialists needed to accomplish its integrated goals.

[3]Scott Hume, "Integrated marketing: Who's in charge here?" *Advertising Age,* 23 March 1993, 3.
[4]Adrienne Ward Fawcett, "Marketers convinced: Its time has arrived," *Advertising Age,* 8 November 1993, S-1.

Integrated Functions

Integrated marketing communication (IMC) can function in the marketing services system if there is management of this process among all the departments involved—advertising, sales promotion, public relations, and other existing departments. Radical organizational changes don't seem to work well with regard to implementation. Many organizations have found that integrated functions become evolutionary. However, there are marketers who feel that this kind of management isn't practical because the resistance to change by managers is just too great. Don Schultz, author of *Integrated Marketing Communications* and president of Agora Inc., suggests that reengineering the communications function and structure within the company is sometimes necessary. He suggests the following functions:

1. Start with the customer or prospect and work back toward the brand or organization. That's the outside-in approach. Most organizations are structured to deliver inside-out communications, which allows the budget cycle to dictate when communications can be delivered.

2. Good communications require knowledge of customers and prospects. Without specific customer information, the marketing organization will continue to send out the wrong message and information to the wrong people at the wrong time at an exorbitant cost.

3. A database is critical to carry out the IMC communication task.

4. Brand contacts—all the ways the customer comes in contact with the organization—are the proper way to think about communications programs. This goes beyond traditional media. It includes managing the impact and influence of packaging, employees, in-store displays, sales literature, and even the design of the product so that the brand clearly or concisely communicates with the right person, at the right time, in the right way, with the right message or incentive through the right delivery channel.

There are three forms of adaptation to integrated marketing within corporate structures:[5]

■ *Marcom (marketing communications) manager.* Adapting a business-to-business organizational structure called marcom management centralizes all the communication activities under one person or office (see Exhibit 6.4). Under this structure, all communication is centralized. Product managers request communication programs for their products through a marcom manager. The manager develops the strategy and then directs the communication programs either internally or externally.

■ *Restructured brand management approach.* This approach reduces the layers previously involved in the process. All sales and marketing activities for the brand, category, or organization are reduced to three groups, all reporting to the CEO, and all are on the same organizational level. They are marketing services/communications (MSC), marketing operations, and sales. Marketing operations is responsible for developing and delivering the product to the MSC, which works with sales to develop and implement all sales and marketing programs (including advertising).

■ *Communications manager.* This approach names a communication manager who is responsible for approving or coordinating all communications programs for the entire organization. The various brands develop their own

---

[5]Don E. Schultz, "Managers still face substantial IMC questions," *Marketing News,* 27 September 1993, 10.

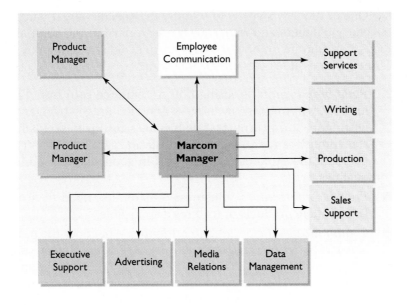

Exhibit

6.4

Marcom management centralizes all the communication activities under one person or office.

communication programs as they have traditionally done. These plans go to the communications manager, who is responsible for coordinating, consolidating, and integrating the programs, messages, and media for the organization (see Exhibit 6.5).

IMC Focus

Using IMC to coordinate all messages a company communicates through advertising, direct marketing, public relations, promotion, and so on helps to create a unified image and support relationship building with customers. The key, however, is to determine exactly what your IMC strategy should achieve.

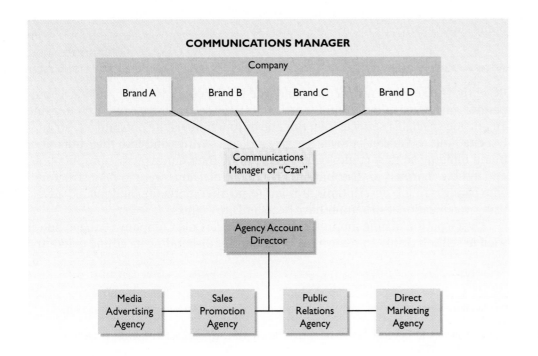

Exhibit

6.5

The communications manager approves or coordinates all communications programs for the entire organization.

One of the first steps is to identify the specific target (such as users or influencers) and understand what each needs from your IMC campaign. To sharpen the focus, concentrate on one or two goals to avoid stretching the strategy or budget. Three such possible goals are the following:[6]

- *Build brand equity.* By using IMC to reinforce your brand's unique value and identity, you increase awareness and encourage stronger preference among customers and prospects. The business-to-business ads for Scotchgard, the stain protector, are aimed at the textile and garment industry, for example, they tell them the product keeps apparel in good shape by adding stain-shedding qualities.
- *Provide information.* Business customers need a lot of information. Differentiate products or features if applicable.
- *Communicate differentiation/positioning.* What does the product stand for and how is it better than the competitors'? IMC helps convey your most significant points. For instance, a UPS ad stressed the range of guaranteed "urgent delivery" choices. These choices differentiated it from its competition while positioning it as able to meet virtually any deadline.

CORPORATE RESTRUCTURING

New Corporate Attitude

There has been a recent trend among leading marketers to dump their marginal brands and focus on the top performers in their portfolios. Many marketers are selling or spinning off divisions or brands that haven't lived up to expectations in their categories. PepsiCo spun off its restaurant operations. Campbell's Soup Company unloaded Swanson frozen foods. This trend is a move by marketers to focus on their core brands and an unwillingness to support those that don't offer large-scale manufacturing, distribution, and advertising synergies. A Reach Marketing executive says, "Retail chains are carrying only the top brands and once you've hit No. 3, media buying efficiency and marketing spending drop." Swanson had dropped to fifth place in its category. Tom Lawson of Arnold Communications says, "Second-tier brands become milked by their owners, then they stop being brands and become products."[7]

Marketing Structure Changes

Recently, Quaker Oats restructured and said if a function does not provide a competitive advantage and does not represent a clear cost savings compared to using an outside specialist service, then the role or function will be outsourced. An analyst cited this as Quaker's movement beyond cost savings and into their pursuit of brand building so they could focus on spreading their equity across product lines and in new channels of distribution. Five major divisions were to be restructured with changes in job descriptions. It is fair to say that marketing and related advertising organizational structures have been and are in flux.

Over a period of nine months in late 1996, Coca-Cola Company changed how it tried to sell soft drinks to minorities by essentially disbanding its ethnic marketing

[6]Marian Burk Wood, "Clear IMC goals build strong relationships," *Marketing News,* 23 June 1997, 11.
[7]Judann Pollack and Jack Neff, "Marketer decree: Be a top brand or begone," *Advertising Age,* 15 September 1997, 1.

department and rolling those responsibilities under the brand managers of its different beverages.

The brand managers and their marketing teams became responsible for developing advertising, promotions, and other marketing tactics to attract all consumers. "Today, each of our brand groups has the responsibility for reaching the Latino consumer," said the late CEO Roberto Goizuita, "Just as each of our brand groups has the responsibility for reaching young consumers, African American consumers, blue-collar consumers." The change in structure was termed a "philosophical change," but under each brand there still is a person whose responsibility is targeting African-American consumers. Coca-Cola realized that some past advertising geared toward ethnic markets appeals to mainstream audiences. One popular television spot called "Pied Piper" depicted young black singer Tyrese Gibson. Domestically, Coke sells about 183 million cases of Coke Classic and 110 million cases of Sprite to African Americans, and 325 million Classic cases and 40 million Sprite cases to Hispanics. The latest independent soft-drink market share figures gave Pepsi a lead among both ethnic groups.[8]

Many other large consumer marketers, such as Anheuser-Busch and Kraft, maintain large ethnic departments. Each marketer perceives the market and how to organize to reach market differently.

SETTING THE BUDGET

We understand advertising is supposed to accomplish some objective. It is a business decision. The three ads in Exhibit 6.6 (a, b and c) are for three totally different kinds of advertisers, each with a different reason for being. What is the ad or campaign supposed to accomplish? Launch a new product? Increase a brand's awareness level? Neutralize the competition's advertising? A key question is how much money is it going to take to accomplish the objective? Even if we have been successful with the product, do we know whether we are spending too much on advertising—or not enough? Despite all the technology available to help us to determine how much should be spent, the final decision is a judgment call by corporate management. The person responsible for the budget decision varies across companies and according to objectives. In general, a Gallagher Report says, the vice president of marketing and the vice president of advertising are the people most responsible for setting the ad budget (see Exhibit 6.7). Two-thirds of advertising budgets are submitted for approval in September or October; almost 80 percent are approved during the period September to November. As you might expect for such an important decision, most presidents or chief operating officers strongly influence the approval process.

Budgets are usually drawn up using one of four approaches: percentage of sales, payout plan, competitive budgeting, and the task method.

Percentage of Sales

The percentage of sales method simply means the advertising budget is based upon a percentage of the company's sales. For instance, a family restaurant chain might budget 5 percent of their sales for advertising. A company using this method to determine their advertising budget will not spend beyond its means because the ad budget will increase only when sales increase. If sales decrease, so will its advertising; however, if competitive pressures are severe, it may have to maintain or increase the budget to retain market share, even though there is no prospect of

---

[8]Chris Roush, "Marketing Shift," *Atlanta Journal-Constitution*, 19 January 1997, D-1.

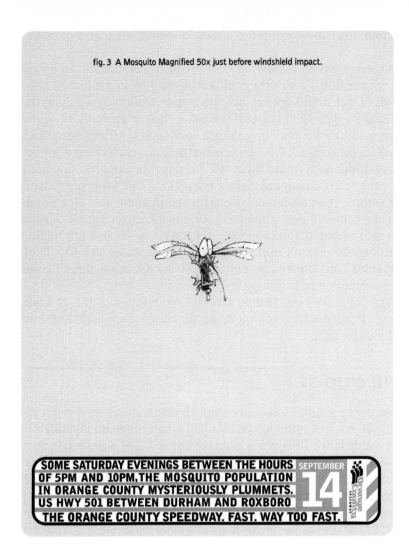

fig. 3 A Mosquito Magnified 50x just before windshield impact.

SOME SATURDAY EVENINGS BETWEEN THE HOURS OF 5PM AND 10PM, THE MOSQUITO POPULATION IN ORANGE COUNTY MYSTERIOUSLY PLUMMETS. US HWY 501 BETWEEN DURHAM AND ROXBORO THE ORANGE COUNTY SPEEDWAY. FAST. WAY TOO FAST. SEPTEMBER 14

increased profit. This method can actually reverse the assumed cause-and-effect relationship between advertising and sales. That is, because the budgeting is based either on the previous year's sales—usually with some percentage of increase added—or next year's anticipated sales, then it can be said that the sales are causing the advertising rather than advertising causing the sales.

A Gallagher Report indicates that about 9 percent of companies surveyed take a percentage of last year's sales.[9] Roughly 35 percent use a percentage of anticipated sales, 30 percent combine needed tasks with percent of anticipated sales, 13 percent outline needed tasks and fund them, 13 percent set arbitrary amounts based on general fiscal outlook of the company, and 9 percent calculate a medium between last year's actual sales and anticipated sales for the coming year. In any method, a change in sales changes the amount of advertising expenditure.

Payout Plan

The payout plan looks at advertising as an investment rather than as an expenditure. It recognizes that it may take several years before the company can recover start-up costs and begin taking profits.

---

[9]26th Gallagher Report Consumer Advertising Survey.

Instead of talking to some automated answering service, you'll speak to one of our pharmaceutical professionals employed specifically to answer your questions about Glaxo products.

These professionals are available by phone Monday through Friday, 8am to 4:30pm EST. And then can be reached any hour of any day in an emergency.

Most information can be provided on the spot. And if requested, we make every effort to send follow-up documentation within ten days.

Just call us toll free at 1-800-334-0089, or write us at **Glaxo** the address below. You'll get a response that's not only fast, but personal.

Glaxo Drug Information Services, 5 Moore Drive, Research Triangle Park, North Carolina 27709

HERE'S WHO YOU WON'T BE TALKING TO WHEN YOU CALL OUR PRODUCT INFORMATION LINE.

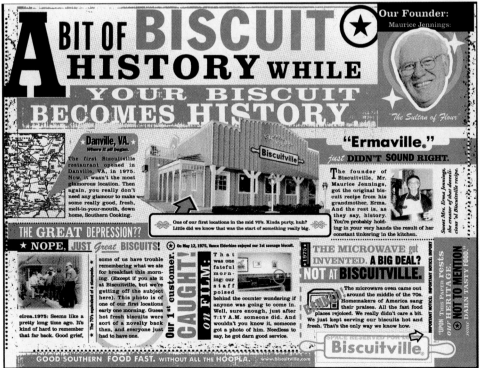

Who Prepares Clients' Ad Budgets[a]		Who Approves Client's Ad Budgets[a]	
VP Marketing	63.2%	President or CEO	68.5%
VP Advertising	31.6	VP Marketing	37.3
Ad manager	22.2	Executive VP	20.9
Brand manager	16.3	Division manager	17.2
Ad agency	21.7	VP Advertising	14.4
Sales promotion	5.6	Treasurer or controller	8.6

Exhibit

6.7

[a]Totals more than 100% due to multiple responses.

Source: 26th Gallagher Report Consumer Advertising Survey.

Exhibits 6.8 and 6.9 are examples of typical payout plans. Let us go briefly through Exhibit 6.8, a payout plan for a new fast-food operation. In the first year of operation, the company spent the entire gross profits ($15,274,000) on advertising. In addition, the company invested $10,300,000 in store development, for a first-year operating loss.

In the second year, the company again invested gross profits ($48,122,000) in advertising and carried over the $10,300,000 debt from the first year. By the third

		Year 1		Year 2		Year 3
Sales		$84,854,000		$218,737,000		$356,248,000
Food cost	34%	28,850,000	34%	74,371,000	34%	121,124,000
Paper cost	5	4,245,000	5	10,937,000	5	17,812,000
Labor	22	18,668,000	20	43,747,000	20	71,250,000
Overhead	21	17,819,000	19	41,560,000	18	64,125,000
Total op. exp.	82	69,580,000	78	170,615,000	77	274,511,000
Gross profit	18	15,274,000	22	48,122,000	25	81,937,000
Advertising/Promo		*$15,274,000*		*$48,122,000*	*13*	*$46,312,000*
Store profit		0		0	10	35,625,000
Corp. invest.		10,300,000		0		0
Corp. profit		(10,300,000)		0		35,625,000
Cumulative		(10,300,000)		(10,300,000)		25,625,000

Exhibit

6.8

Systemwide Payout (Fiscal Years 1, 2, 3)

	Year 1	Year 2	Year 3	3-Year Total	Year 4
Size of market (MM cases)	8	10	11		12
Share goal:					
Average	$12\frac{1}{2}$%	25%	30%		30%
Year end	20	30	30		30
Consumer movement (MM Cases)	1.0	2.5	3.3	6.8	3.6
Pipeline (MM Cases)	.3	.2	.1	.6	—
Total shipments (MM Cases)	1.3	2.7	3.4	7.4	3.6
Factory income (@ $9)	$11.7	$24.3	$30.6	$66.6	$32.4
Less costs (@ $5)	6.5	13.5	17.0	37.0	18.0
Available P/A (@ $4)	$ 5.2	$10.8	$13.6	$29.6	$14.4
Spending (normal $2)	$12.8	$10.0	$ 6.8	$29.6	$7.2
Advertising	10.5	8.5	5.4	24.4	5.7
Promotion	2.3	1.5	1.4	5.2	1.5
Profit (Loss):					
Annual	($ 7.6)	$ 0.8	$ 6.8	—	$ 7.2
Cumulative	($ 7.6)	($ 6.8)	—	—	$ 7.2

Exhibit

6.9

Fast-Food Payout Plan Investment Introduction— 36-Month Payout

year, sales had increased to the point where advertising as a percentage of gross sales had dropped to 13 percent, or $46,312,000, leaving a profit of $35,625,000. After covering the first-year debt of $10,300,000, the payout was $25,625,000.

If the company had demanded a 10 percent profit in the first year (0.10 × $84,854,000 = $8,485,400), it would have had to curtail advertising drastically, reduce corporate store investment, or do some combination of both. In that case, the company would have made a profit the first year but risked future profits and perhaps its own long-term survival.

Competitive Budgeting

Another approach to budgeting is to base it on the competitive spending environment. In competitive budgeting, the level of spending relates to the percentage of sales and other factors: whether the advertiser is on the offensive or defensive, media strategies chosen (for example, desire to dominate a medium), or answers to questions such as, "Is it a new brand or an existing one?" The problem here is that competition dictates the spending allocation (and the competing companies may have different marketing objectives).

The Task Method

The task method of budgeting is possibly the most difficult to implement, but it may also be the most logical budgeting method. The method calls for marketing and advertising managers to determine what task or objective the advertising will fulfill over the budgetary period and then calls for a determination of how much money will be needed to complete the task. Under this method, the company sets a specific sales target for a given time to attain a given goal. Then it decides to spend whatever money is necessary to meet that quota. The task method might be called the "let's spend all we can afford" approach, especially when launching a new product. Many big businesses today started that way. Many businesses that are not here today did too.

The approach can be complex. It involves several important considerations: brand loyalty factors, geographic factors, and product penetration. Advertisers who use this method need accurate and reliable research, experience, and models for setting goals and measuring results.

The task method is used most widely in a highly competitive environment. Budgets are under constant scrutiny in relation to sales and usually are formally reviewed every quarter. Moreover, they are subject to cancellation at any time (except for noncancelable commitments) because sales have not met a minimum quota, money is being shifted to a more promising brand, or management wants to hold back money to make a better showing on its next quarterly statement.

No one approach to budgeting is always best for all companies.

THE CHANGING MARKETING ENVIRONMENT

The changes that have taken place over the past few years in advertiser organizations have not been a result of business cycles. Marketers are in an irreversible restructuring in the way businesses operate—one that may require a major rethinking of the agency-client relationship in today's environment. Some of the factors driving the change at companies include the following:[10]

---

[10]Robert M. Viney, "Solving the agency-client mismatch," *Advertising Age,* 24 May 1993, 20.

- *Fragmented consumer target.* Consumer groups are more fragmented than ever before by demographics, age, ethnicity, family type, geographic location, and media usage.
- *Parity performance.* The importance of value, convenience, and service in influencing preference is increasing, and the impact of low-priced, satisfactorily performing private brands is growing.
- *Cost control.* Marketers must remain price competitive and must develop new strategies for offsetting internal cost increases.
- *Erosion of advertising effectiveness.* Advertisers have settled for advertising that doesn't present a compelling basis for consumer preference and fails to effectively reinforce relevant brand equity in other marketing activities.
- *Strengthened retailer influence.* Retailers are equipped with detailed data on consumer purchase behavior, which gives them leverage against marketers.

MANAGING BRANDS

Efficient Consumer Response

Started in 1993, the grocery industry launched its efficient consumer response (ECR) initiative designed to make the industry more efficient. This initiative included using technology in purchasing, distribution, promotion, reducing inventories, and other aspects of the business, including marketing. It is another attempt by business to prepare for the future by eliminating the inefficient parts of the system of selling grocery products by changing the approach to creating, selling, and distributing those products. In the process, ECR is forcing marketers and retailers to rethink new products, pricing, in-store merchandising, and the division of dollars between trade promotion and consumer marketing.

Slotting Allowances

Every square foot of a supermarket costs money and needs to pay for itself by moving products and brands quickly. There is only so much shelf space for the category manager to obtain from grocers. Because grocers control the space, many charge slotting allowances for shelf space. This admission fee, which comes primarily from the marketer's trade promotion funds, ensures space for a period of about three to six months. Supermarkets use the slotting allowance to pay for slow-moving products and for administrative overhead for placing a new product into their system, including warehouse space, computer input, communications to individual stores about the product's availability, and the redesign of shelf space. The frozen-food section has only a finite amount of space and almost always demands slotting allowances.

Retailer Control

There is no doubt about the control of shelf space and entry into supermarkets, discounters, and mass merchandise stores today. The marketer is at the mercy of the retailer. As a result, category managers must learn the following:[11]

- Marketplace leverage is at the local level. As consumers' tastes, needs, and wants continue to expand and fragment, leverage can be achieved only by

---

[11]Spencer Hapoienu, "Supermarketing's new frontier," *Advertising Age,* 14 April 1988, 18.

delivering relevant products, services, messages, and promotions to consumers as individuals.

- Building brand equity among retailers should become as important as building brands among consumers.
- Marketing decisions must shift to the sales level. Manufacturers' marketing and promotion programs must eventually become store-specific to succeed.
- Information is the most important asset you have. Only the first company to use information wins. As brand building moves from national media to the supermarket shelf, marketing and merchandising executions must be adapted to the needs of each consumer market and store franchise.

Experimentation and Risk

Marketers are forced to find the right formula and be innovative in marketing new products today. Old marketing rules don't necessarily work in today's environment. For example, BellSouth, a telecommunications giant that primarily provides local phone service in the Southeast, tested putting phone service on retail store shelves. The first product, Teen Line Pack, was placed in Kroger, Office Depot, and Target Stores, among others. In addition to a second phone line, the package included a number of services aimed at the demographic group. Although the idea of selling phone services like cereal off the grocery shelf seems odd, it fits with the changes taking place in the telecommunications area. Retail sales are one of the growing ways telecom service providers are trying to grab market share.

Bill Borders, president of Borders, Perrin & Norrander, says, "risk taking is the lifeblood of an agency." However, a former director of creative at Pepsi-Cola says, "the problem with most clients is that they are not willing to join the agency in the risk. Through the years Pepsi-Cola has told BBDO to take the risk. If you miss, we understand that not everything is going to be a home run. But it could be a single. Occasionally, we have burned the film knowing that we tried and it just didn't work."[12] Unfortunately, most clients can't find the courage to join Pepsi in taking chances or risk to seek cutting-edge advertising.

Bob Moore, creative director of Fallon, Minneapolis, says, "I am a believer that you have to do strong ads that stand out. A lot of times that leads you to something that is different. By its very nature, different is going to lead you to something risky. What's risky gets people talking. You can do work that feels good, but no one notices it. It is like wallpaper. That's far riskier."[13]

When meeting with agencies, Paul Michaels, vice president of marketing of M&M/Mars, carries a cardboard contraption that he calls the "Excite-O-Meter," making a point about the candymaker's advertising. Dave Gulick, account director at DMB&B, says Michaels has redefined risk. He wants cutting-edge creative. In the past, many of their ads were described by Michaels as lacking emotional topspin. The ads were wallpaperish and very safe. According to Michaels, the difference in creative came when Mars relaxed its attitude and encouraged its agencies to think creatively. Of course, it has to be on strategy, not just for the sake of being funny.[14]

On-line Experimentation   In the fall of 2000, Volvo launched the S60 completely on-line without any traditional advertising media support for the first three months. They looked to America Online to promote the new vehicle. To entice potential buyers they offered $2,100 worth of free options. It also dispersed banner

---

[12]Joe Mandee, "How far is too far?" *Agency*, May/June 1991, 39.
[13]Eleftheria Parpis, "Moore to come," *ADWEEK*, 18 September 2000, 28.
[14]Judann Pollack, "Engaging creative concept re-emerges as weapon," *Advertising Age*, 20 October 1997, s/4.

ads throughout AOL, particularly in the men's, auto, and map areas. The Web offers marketers personalization, potential for pages of product information, attention-grabbing give-aways, and positive prospects for the future. Some companies are willing to experiment and take risk. "How does the Internet fit into our marketing plan" is a frequent question. Everyone seeks that answer.

AGENCY-CLIENT RELATIONSHIPS

It has been said that agency-client relationships are much like interpersonal relationships: If you don't like each other, you move apart. If you like each other, you gravitate toward each other and great stuff gets produced. The agency should be trusted as an employee—they are in business with the client. The relationship between the agency and the client is a partnership. Yet, some companies view their agency as vendors.

A study conducted by the North American Advertising Agency Network suggests agency professionalism, strategic planning, and cost efficiency beat leading-edge creative and integrated communications capabilities when marketers select an advertising agency. The study suggests that some clients were willing to accept mediocre work delivered on time and on budget. Other factors revealed a degree of importance to integrated communications capabilities: agency experience on a similar account and longevity of client relationships were more important than account rosters with big-name or blue-chip clients.[15] Agencies have always prided themselves on selling the creative product; however, many people feel today's agencies are not producing the strongest creative product.

Why do clients hire agencies? Tom Patty, executive vice president of TBWA/Chiat/Day says, "in essence, clients hire ad agencies because they believe they can help them persuade customers to do or think something." Clients select an agency based on the agency's ability to be persuasive. The real task is to become a persuasion partner. Congoleum needed an agency with the same selling philosophy (Exhibit 6.10).

When advertisers develop a new product or become disenchanted with their existing advertising, they will conduct advertising reviews in which their current agency and others can compete for the account. This review process may take several months. The advertiser will evaluate which agencies it wants to participate in the review. Keep in mind that there are agencies that specialize in certain types of accounts.

With competitive pressures mounting, companies are more enamored with brand strategies and solutions—whether they are "advertising" driven or not—than with creative work. As a result, companies seek solutions from a coterie of other advisers, not exclusively from ad agencies. Today, reengineered agencies are trying to find their place at the table. Many are changing their direction or focus: McCann-Erickson Worldwide is branding itself as a multidisciplined "global-marketing communication" company with distinct "corridors" of specialty services. For Hill, Holliday, Connors, Cosmopilous in Boston, it means developing a consulting specialty from the ground up while using the resources from its parent, the Interpublic Group, to reach into markets overseas. At Leo Burnett, it means playing up the speed of business-to-business "hypermarketing" services via its TFA/Leo Burnett Technology Group. And to TBWA/Chiat/Day's it means trying to be a media artist who can create the right message for any environment—from print and TV campaigns to "wild postings" at construction sites.

---

[15]Melanie Wells, "Many clients prize agency efficiency over creativity," *Advertising Age,* 16 May 1994, 28.

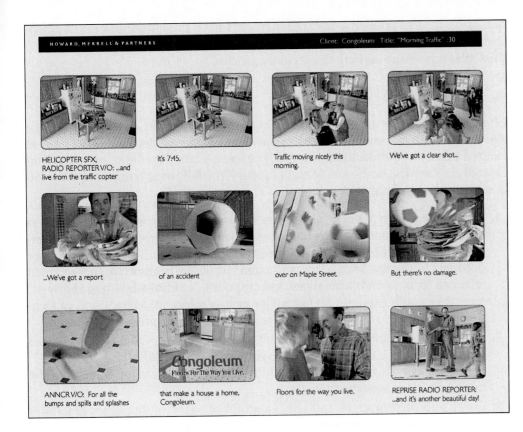

HOWARD, MERRELL & PARTNERS   Client: Congoleum   Title: "Morning Traffic" :30

HELICOPTER SFX,
RADIO REPORTER V/O: ...and
live from the traffic copter

it's 7:45.

Traffic moving nicely this
morning.

We've got a clear shot...

...We've got a report

of an accident

over on Maple Street.

But there's no damage.

ANNCR V/O: For all the
bumps and spills and splashes

that make a house a home,
Congoleum.

Floors for the way you live.

REPRISE RADIO REPORTER:
...and it's another beautiful day!

Congoleum
Floors For The Way You Live.

Exhibit
6.10

Congoleum and its agency
needed to agree on a
strategic selling focus before
establishing a creative
execution.
Courtesy: Howard, Merrell & Partners.

"Clients don't care where good ideas come from," says WPP Group Chief Executive Martin Sorrells. Agencies seek to be full-service partners, as opposed to being vendors, where clients go for any and all business solutions.[16]

Agency Search Consultants

Today more and more clients hire consultants to help them seek out the best agency to handle their accounts. An estimated 60 percent of recent account reviews for major advertisers involved consultants, whose job is to do the initial screening, manage the search process, and in some cases negotiate compensation agreements. This may cost a client between $35,000 and $100,000. In the past, clients relied more heavily on their own marketing departments to conduct searches. Consultants have been hired more in recent years because fewer clients find they are qualified to do it themselves and because there have been so many changes in the agency landscape, according to an agency principal.[17] The consultant has been characterized as a "marriage broker" between client and agency.

Some industry observers believe there are currently more reviews of their agencies by marketers than in recent years. Part of this is a result of the restructuring of businesses. When marketing departments get restructured and people change jobs, there is a tendency to start from scratch and this includes reviewing or changing advertising agencies. In addition, one of the driving forces on account reviews is pressure on advertiser's marketing departments to sell more units and a fixation on quarterly financial results. That position deemphasizes the importance of long-standing relationships and puts the spotlight on how well agencies can deliver

[16]Karen Benezra, "Sea change: Agencies diversify to regain client trust," *ADWEEK,* 19 April 1999, 42–43.
[17]Jennifer Comiteau, "Power play," *ADWEEK,* 10 June 1996, 33–38.

quick fixes to sales problems. Because marketers have already done as much down-sizing as practical, increases now have to be achieved through "real unit growth."[18] This creates pressure on both clients and agencies.

Selecting an Agency

Choosing an agency can be a complicated matter. Do you need a full-service agency, one with integrated services, one with strong media departments, or a specialized agency? After deciding whether you want a large, medium, or small, specialized, full-service, domestic, or global agency, the following points may help you in evaluating specific agencies:

1. Determine what types of service you need from an agency, and then list them in order of their importance to you. For instance: (a) marketing expertise in strategy, planning, and execution; (b) creative performance in TV, print, radio, or outdoor; (c) media knowledge and clout; (d) sales-promotion and/or trade relations help; (e) public relations and corporate- or image-building ability; (f) market research strength; (g) fashion or beauty sense; (h) agency size; (i) location in relation to your office. Your special needs will dictate others.

2. Establish a five-point scale to rate each agency's attributes. A typical five-point scale would be: (1) outstanding, (2) very good, (3) good, (4) satisfactory, (5) unsatisfactory. Of course, you should give different values or weights to the more important agency attributes.

3. Check published sources and select a group of agencies that seem to fit your requirements. Use your own knowledge or the knowledge of your industry peers to find agencies responsible for successful campaigns or products that have most impressed you. Published sources include the annual issue of *Advertising Age,* which lists agencies and their accounts by agency size, and the "Red Book" (*Standard Advertising Register*), which lists agencies and accounts both alphabetically and geographically. In case of further doubt, contact the American Association of Advertising Agencies, New York, for a roster of members. Of course, you can do this on-line.

4. Check whether there are any apparent conflicts with accounts already at the agency. When agencies consider a new account, that is the first question they ask (along with the amount of the potential billings).

5. Now start preliminary discussions with the agencies that rate best on your initial evaluation. This can be started with a letter asking if they are interested or a telephone call to set up an appointment for them to visit you or for you to visit the agency. Start at the top. Call the president or the operating head of the agency or office in your area, who will appoint someone to follow up on the opportunity you are offering.

6. Reduce your original list of potential agencies after the first contact. A manageable number is usually no more than three.

7. Again prepare an evaluation list for rating the agencies on the same five-point scale. This list will be a lot more specific. It should cover personnel. Who will supervise your account and how will the account be staffed? Who are the creative people who will work on your business? Similarly, who will service your needs in media, production (TV) research, and sales promotion, and how will they do it? What is the agency's track record in getting and holding on to business and in keeping personnel teams together? What is the agency's record with media, with payments? Make sure again to assign a weighted value to each ser-

---

[18]Laura Petrecca, "The year in review: Is it a record pace?" *Advertising Age,* 2 June 1997, 1.

vice aspect. If TV is most important to you and public relations aid the least, be sure to reflect this in your evaluation.

8. Discuss financial arrangements. Will your account be a straight 15 percent commission account, a fee account, or a combination of both? What services will the commission or fee cover, and what additional charges will the agency demand? How will new-product work be handled from both a financial and an organizational point of view? What peripheral service does the agency offer, and for how much?

9. Do you feel comfortable with them? As we were introduced to their self-promotion in the last chapter, Exhibit 6.11 appeals to a philosophical and comfort level.

10. If your company is an international one, can the agency handle all of your non-domestic business, and if so, how will they do it?

Client Ad Requirements

Agencies may produce only a few ads for a client during a year, which isn't taxing on their creative and management abilities. At SLRS Advertising, only four print ads were created for Segil Carpets during an entire year. Ogilvy & Mather creates about 6,000 jobs for IBM around the world, creating work for the company's software, services, and systems that requires excellent creative and management skills. Maureen

There is little adversity that cannot be conquered by a good plan implemented decisively.

THE SOCOH GROUP℠

Exhibit 6.11

This self promotion appeals to a corporate philosophy and comfort zone.

Courtesy: The Socoh Group.

McGuire, vice president of IBM worldwide integrated marketing, thinks the creative team at Ogilvy is the best-tested technology creative team in the business. "Some people understand the technology, some people understand marketing. It's very hard to find people who understand both." Television director, Joe Pytka who filmed many IBM commercials says, "We work in a very spontaneous and creative way and the client lets them think on their feet. We may shoot three or four spots in a single day. We change things at the last minute. We come up with new dialogue, we improvise."[19]

Multiple Agency Strategy   Many clients are now hiring several agencies and giving them different assignments for the same product. In some cases, this is changing the agency-client relationship by treating agencies as vendors and not as full marketing partners. One of the reasons for this change is that new marketing executives are under pressures from their CEOs. The message is, "I don't care about your situation. I need an idea and people who are passionate about my business."

In the 1950s, the agency-client relationship was defined in *The Encyclopedia of Advertising*:

> An advertising agency is an organization which provides advertising, merchandising and other services and counsel related to the sale of a client's goods or services. It is understood that the client agrees not to engage a second agency to handle part of the advertising of the product without the consent of the first agency.

Today, many clients are looking for home runs or a bailout to pick up their business fortunes. Many company marketing executives are in power an average of 18 months. They care about what's happening now. According to Larry Light, a marketing consultant, the current brand management system prevents failure by depending totally on research and testing. Brand managers often are promoted if they don't make mistakes as well as if they hit a home run. This creates brand managers who play it safe and won't take risks, according to Light.[20]

About a decade ago, Coca-Cola decided that its agency of many years wasn't creating enough big ideas. As a result, it took the freelance route for a while and then hired about 40 agencies and boutiques over time to create ads. Coke's contention was: We know and understand our strategy better than our agencies do. So their job is to do the best execution of the strategy they can. In 2001, the Coca-Cola Company announced a global alliance with Interpublic Group of Cos., to "develop, refine and focus" strategies to ensure pertinent and consistent messages for the $900-million global advertising for Coke around the world. Interpublic's McCann-Erickson, which has worked on Coke since 1942, is responsible for the brand in 89 countries. Coke is sold in over 200 countries. Coke uses 10 different agencies around the globe, down from more than two dozen a few years ago. "It's a question of efficiency," says a Merrill Lynch analyst. Naming a global partner seems to conflict with Coke's avowed think-local/act-local strategy put in place a few months earlier. But a company spokesperson said it fits because local executives will be involved in local decisions.[21]

What's fueling this boom in clients using more than one agency is the same thing that fostered the recent reverse trends in consolidations: Marketers want a creative edge and are changing the nature of their agency relationships. In the end, successful advertising has more to do with the quality of the advertiser's agency relationship than with the quantity of them. Big advertisers from AT&T to Sears

---

[19]Noreen O'Leary, "Ogilvy & Mather and Big Blue," *Communication Arts*, January/February 2000, 98–103.
[20]Keith Gould, "Limited partners," *ADWEEK*, 22 July 1996, 21–22.
[21]Hillary Chura, "Coke brands IPG as global ad strategist," *Advertising Age*, 4 December 2000.

have trusted their brand images to teams of agencies. "The size of our business is such that it demands the expertise and attention of a number of agencies," said the national director of marketing communications at AT&T. "There are so many projects and assignments to be handled that one agency couldn't do it all. But using multiple agencies puts the onus on us to make sure all the messages are coordinated and represent one consistent voice coming from the company." These needs are different from a client having one agency partner to handle everything.

The ad business is famously cyclical, so it remains to be seen whether this multiple agency trend is a permanent shift or a temporary blip. Right now, advertisers are looking for the best custom-made solutions to their marketing problems.

The Creative Digital Library

McDonald's has created a digital commercial archive holding 15,000 McDonald's commercials from the chain's advertising since 1967 for use by local co-ops and agencies. New work won't be added to the library until it has been in circulation for at least six months to protect current creative from hackers and to avoid anyone from "jumping the gun to reuse creative." It is a password-only system, so consumers or competition can't access the files. For access to new campaigns, agencies can tap a pair of clearinghouse tools—the product Footage Library (which stores current broadcast footage) and Brand Guard (which archives still graphic assets, such as logos, product shots, text custom ads, point-of-purchase displays, and other print material). Over the years, McDonald's has produced between 30,000 and 50,000 commercials on a global basis. The best will be included in the library. Commercial libraries are fairly common among agencies, but rarer among clients and practically unheard of in digital form. In 1987, Leo Burnett created the Great Commercial Library, which contained 7,000 commercials and storyboards for the best work in all categories since the 1960s. An on-line companion has photo pages from the latest two years.[22]

APPRAISING NATIONAL ADVERTISING

The big questions that national advertising and marketing management must answer are: How well is our advertising working? How well is our investment paying off? How do you measure national advertising, whose results cannot be traced as easily as those of direct-response advertising?

Advertising Goals Versus Marketing Goals

The answer is not simple. Much of the discussion on the subject centers around a report Russell H. Colley prepared for the Association of National Advertisers.[23] The thesis of this study is that it is virtually impossible to measure the results of advertising unless and until the specific results sought by advertising have been defined. When asked exactly what their advertising is supposed to do, most companies have a ready answer: increase their dollar sales or increase their share of the market. However, these are not advertising goals, Colley holds; they are total **marketing goals.**

National advertising alone cannot accomplish this task. It should be used as part of the total marketing effort. The first step in appraising the results of advertising, therefore, is to define specifically what the company expects to accomplish

advertising goals
The communication objectives designed to accomplish certain tasks within the total marketing program.

marketing goals
The overall objectives that a company wishes to accomplish through its marketing program.

---

[22]Kate MacArthur, "Fast food meets the internet," *Advertising Age*, 19 June 2000, 28.
[23]Russell H. Colley, *Defining Advertising Goals for Measured Effectiveness* (New York: Association of National Advertisers, 1961).

through advertising. The Colley report defines an advertising goal as "a specific communications task, to be accomplished among a defined audience to a given degree in a given period of time."

As an example, the report cites the case of a branded detergent. The marketing goal is to increase market share from 10 to 15 percent, and the advertising goal is set as increasing, among the 50 million housewives who own automatic washers, the number who identify brand X as a low-sudsing detergent that gets clothes clean. This represents a specific communications task that can be performed by advertising, independent of other marketing forces.

The Colley report speaks of a marketing-communication spectrum ranging from unawareness of the product to comprehension to conviction to action. According to this view, the way to appraise advertising is through its effectiveness in the communication spectrum, leading to sales.

Researchers disagree on whether the effectiveness of national advertising—or, for that matter, of any advertising—should be judged by a communication yardstick rather than by sales. As a matter of fact, in Chapter 15 we discuss whether an ad's effectiveness should be measured by some research testing score.

CHANGES IN MARKETING

Clearly we are in the midst of a revolution. This period of change has been compared to the French and Russian revolutions. The truth is we are in the midst of several revolutions at once, including globalization, technology, management, and economic. We are in competition with everyone, everywhere in the world. Computers and electronics have altered the way we do everything. Word processing replaced the typewriter, ATM machines have replaced bank tellers, and voice mail and e-mail have given us the ability to communicate 24 hours a day. Today's management buzz words are reengineering, downsizing, and eliminating hierarchy. Small flexible organizations have the advantage in today's world. Finally, we are undergoing a revolution in our business structure.

The Traditional Five Ps of Marketing

The traditional five Ps of marketing consist of the elements product, price, place, packaging, and promotion (which includes positioning, advertising, sales promotion, public relations, and so forth). With a strategy in each of these areas, a person can put together an effective marketing plan. In the package goods category, the general belief is that promotion accounts for about 90 percent of the marketing equation. Each product category may be different, as seen with automobiles, where price and product are key, with promotion being a small percentage. So the advertiser must understand what is important.

The New Five Ps of Marketing

Tom Patty of TBWA/Chiat/Day says the old five Ps served us well in a world dominated by stability and a growing economy with much less competitive pressures than we have today. Patty's new five Ps are aimed at helping us succeed in a world where chaos has replaced stability, where the fast-growing economy has slowed, and where global competition demands even greater levels of effectiveness and efficiency. The new five Ps are more abstract and conceptual than the traditional ones. They include paradox, perspective, paradigm, persuasion, and passion.[24]

---

[24]Tom Patty, "Mastering the New Five P's of Marketing," TBWA/Chiat/Day Web site, www.TBWAchiatday. com, 1997.

Paradox A paradox is a statement or proposition that, on the face of it, seems self-contradictory. Example: "All cars are the same; all cars are different." The paradox always contains within it an opportunity. An advertiser must exploit the differentiation. Miller used the paradox of "lite" beer to help them focus on the dual benefits of the lite paradox, "Tastes Great, Less Filling." Everyone knows what a sports car is, but Nissan created a new category of sports cars in which it was first—the four-door sports car. To master the paradox, you first have to find or identify this opportunity and then exploit the changes. One way to create this unique identity is to be the first something. For years, advertising told us that trucks are tough and rugged and durable, whereas cars are comfortable, luxurious, and safe. The new Dodge Ram exploits the paradox of combining many car-type features with the rugged look and performance of a Mack truck.

Perspective Perspective is the ability to see things in relationship to each other. The manufacturer's perspective isn't the proper perspective. Advertisers must look at every issue—whether it's a product issue, a pricing issue, or a distribution issue—from the consumer perspective. The only perspective is the consumer's perspective. Here several questions need answers: What consumer need does my product or service satisfy? How does it satisfy differently and better than competitors? Similarly, as it relates to advertising, are we in the advertising business or are we in the persuasion business? We should be in the business of persuading consumers to think or to do something.

Paradigm Here we need a pattern example, a model way of doing things. We need to understand that we may not need to do business the "old" way. Certainly, the

Exhibit
6.12a

Marketers have to manage many different communications. Ceco Building Systems develops PR publications, targeted trade ads—builder recruitment, architects—direct-mail pieces, sales meeting material, and so on. Each communication must add to the corporate brand equity.

Courtesy: Robinson & Associates, Tupelo.

Exhibit

6.12b

Courtesy: Robinson & Associates, Tupelo.

marketing bundle of Saturn reflects a new automotive paradigm. Instead of believing that product and price are the main ingredients of the marketing equation, Saturn believes that the major components are issues such as the experience of buying and owning a Saturn. They place much less emphasis on the product and much

Exhibit

6.12c

Courtesy: Robinson & Associates, Tupelo.

greater emphasis on the experiential component. There are also different advertising paradigms. In the model advertising paradigm, advertising has a simple task: "Show the product and communicate the product features and benefits." A very different paradigm is called the brand advertising paradigm, for which Saturn again is a good example. In this paradigm the task is to communicate who and what you are.

Persuasion Here we attempt to induce someone to do or think something. All marketing and sales jobs are in the business of persuasion. The advertising agency's role is to help the client persuade potential consumer audiences either to do or to think something. To be persuasive, you have to understand three essential components: the credibility of the speaker, the content of the message, and the involvement of the audience. This is a problem for advertisers. According to Yankelovich Monitor, only 8 percent of people believe advertising. Credibility and trust are emotional, not rational. You can't make someone trust you. You have to earn it over time. The Honda brand has credibility. Consequently, the advertising tends to be simple and sparse. For a brand with less credibility you need to provide more content, more information to be persuasive. The content includes the position of the brand. It needs to address the consumer need or desire this product satisfies. Remember, consumers do not buy products; they buy solutions to their problems. They buy holes, not drill bits; they buy hope, not perfume. The third and final element in any attempt to persuade is that you must understand the motivation of your customer so you can create an emotional connection with them. You also need to select the right persuasion tool. For example, if the brand has a credibility problem, the most persuasive tool might be public relations, although it is more difficult to control the content of the message in public relations. In advertising, you get complete control of content.

Exhibit

6.12d

Passion   Passion is an aim or object pursued with zeal or enthusiasm. We no longer have products for the masses. Instead, products are designed for specific needs and wants. Marketers are moving into a new paradigm in which advertising creates exciting, stimulating dialogues with consumers designed not just to make a sale but to create a relationship. In this new marketing environment, you need passion.

SUMMARY

Procter & Gamble first developed the marketing service system. Today it has two parts: (1) brand management, under a brand manager, who is assigned a brand, and (2) marketing services, comprised of the technical talent involved in implementing the marketing plan, including creative services, promotion services, media services, advertising controls, and marketing research.

As companies consider implementing integrated marketing communications into their firms, there are three basic structures available: a centralized communication function under a marcom manager, a restructured brand manager approach, and the structure involving a communication manager who is responsible for approving and coordinating all communication programs.

Advertising budgets are usually drawn up using the task method, the payout plan, competitive budgeting, and the most commonly used percent-of-sales method.

Advertisers are seeing the advantage of allowing their agencies more creative freedom and encouraging them to take more creative risk as long as it is on strategy. As Bill Borders said, "Risk taking is the lifeblood of an agency."

Exhibit 6.12f

Courtesy: Robinson & Associates, Tupelo.

Agency search consultants are sometimes hired to help find the best agency for their company. The consultant has been characterized as a marriage broker between client and agency. Many clients hire several agencies for multiple products or for the same product. Many senior company marketing executives are in their positions an average of 18 months.

The traditional five Ps of marketing consist of product, price, place, packaging, and promotion. Tom Patty says the new five Ps are paradox, perspective, paradigm, persuasion, and passion.

REVIEW

1. What is the marketing services system?
2. What is a category manager?
3. What are the major methods of developing an advertising budget?
4. Who in the corporation prepares most of the advertising budgets?
5. What is a slotting allowance?

TAKE IT TO THE NET

We invite you to visit the Russell/Lane page on the Prentice Hall Web site at **www.prenhall.com/myphlip** for end-of-chapter exercises and applications.

my **PHLIP**
Prentice Hall's Learning on the Internet Partnership

PART IV

Media

Chapter 7

Basic Media Strategy

The demand for efficiency, expertise, and even creativity in the media-planning process has never been greater. An increasingly competitive marketing environment, unprecedented audience fragmentation, and a steadily increasing number of media and promotional options have combined to create uncertainty for both advertisers and media executives. After reading this chapter you will understand:

» the basic functions of the media planner

» the role of media in the total advertising function

» characteristics of the major media categories

» relationships between media planning and target marketing

The media function, whether executed by an advertising agency, an independent media-buying firm, or a company's in-house media department, is becoming increasingly complex. Let's begin our discussion by examining the primary characteristics of the media function.

ORGANIZATION OF THE MEDIA FUNCTION

media planners
Media planners are responsible for the overall strategy of the media component of an advertising campaign.

1. *Media planner.* The role of the **media planner** is to supervise all areas of the advertising campaign as it relates to the media function. Contemporary media planners have added the role of marketing specialist to their other duties. The media environment is changing so rapidly that it is part of the media planner's job to anticipate future trends in communications and keep agency management and clients abreast of major changes. In such an atmosphere, media planners have come to occupy a pivotal position in the advertising process.

2. *Media research.* The media research department coordinates both primary and secondary research data and functions as a support group for media planners.

Often the media research department is responsible for gauging and anticipating future trends in media.

3. *Media buying*. The media-buying department executes the overall media plan. **Media buyers** select and negotiate specific media placements and they are responsible for monitoring postplacement executions. Depending on the size of a media unit, there may be separate groups for broadcast and print or even local and national broadcast. Recently, some media departments have established units to research and buy Internet advertising or to construct client Web sites.

media buyers Execute and monitor the media schedule developed by media planners.

Few areas of marketing and advertising have experienced the change demonstrated by media planning in the last decade. The media function has been driven by changes in the number of media options as well as by the increasing expenditures in media and the financial risk associated with media-buying mistakes. When a medium-sized dot.com company invests more than $1 million in a single Super Bowl spot, careers ride on the outcome!

In 1999, total advertising expenditures were $185 billion. In 2005, this figure will increase to $264.3 billion (see Exhibit 7.1), an increase of 43 percent. On-line advertising will increase 1,600 percent during the same period while traditional media such as newspapers may experience slight decreases. The media planner of 2010 will be dealing with media outlets that probably don't exist today. Yet, these planners will have to provide clients with buying rationales, budget efficiencies, and measurable audience delivery in this unbelievably complicated environment.

THE NEW MEDIA FUNCTION

As the media adapts to new technology and methods of planning, there are a number of trends that set the tone for these changes and provide an assessment of the future of media planning and buying. Among the most important are convergence, interactivity, creativity, and optimizers.

2005 (in billions)

Media	Spending	% Share	% Growth*
Newspapers	45.8	17.3	(2.8)
Broadcast networks	19.2	7.2	2.8
Spot TV	12.7	4.8	2.0
Syndication	3.8	1.4	3.0
Local broadcast	14.2	5.4	2.0
Radio	23.3	8.8	3.0
Yellow Pages	11.8	4.5	1.5
Magazines	16.0	6.1	4.0
Network Cable TV	23.8	9.0	22.0
Local/regional cable	12.9	4.9	28.0
Online	32.5	12.3	40.0
Outdoor	5.7	2.2	15.0
Other	42.6	16.1	1.0
Total	264.3	100.0	7.7

*Compared to 1999.

Exhibit 7.1

Projected Media Expenditures

Source: Myers Group. *From:* "Media engine gathers head of steam," *Advertising Age,* 14 February 2000, 52.

Convergence

One of the primary trends of the next five years will be media **convergence**. Simply stated, convergence is the blending of distribution, content, and/or hardware from a number of media companies to create a new or significantly expanded communication system. Examples of convergence are numerous—telephone companies offering cable service, cable companies offering Internet connections, or NBC and Microsoft combining to create MSNBC. These types of collaborations are important for the businesses involved and may even expand promotional opportunities for advertisers. However, the audience is more interested in convergences such as WebTV where the home television becomes a computer link or on-line services selling that combines catalog merchandise, TV-like product demonstrations, and immediate buying capabilities.

Consumers will continue to see numerous types of convergence. For example, when ESPN publishes a magazine or CNN (owned by Time Warner) partners with *Sports Illustrated* (another Time Warner property) to create a popular Web site, CNN/SI.com, the media that are created are the result of convergence. Most experts predict that marketing, media content, and technological convergences are in their embryonic state. While we are not certain where it will lead in the next 20 years, convergence is certainly a trend of the present and even more so of the future.

Interactivity

As briefly discussed in Chapter 2, the future of advertising will be controlled to a great extent by the audience. Technology will allow consumers to deal directly with marketers for their entertainment, purchases, and other services, bypassing traditional media and marketing channels. The system will allow buyers and sellers to deal on a one-to-one basis with communication and products tailored to the interests of specific households and individuals.

Companies such as Sony anticipate ". . . being able to use the Web and broadband to sell directly to consumers and supplant broadcasters and cable TV systems and record stores and video-rental outlets as the primary purveyor of Sony's movies and music."[1] In many cases, technological capabilities will probably outpace consumer utilization of these services. However, interactive media are dramatically changing marketing even in their infant stage.

Creativity

Interactivity will not only change the media function, but it will probably have dramatic effects on the creative process. For example, in an era of "permission marketing," the need for attention-getting creative techniques and interest-building advertising formats will be greatly diminished. When a person with an already determined product demand actively seeks out an advertiser, the dynamics of the relationship are dramatically different from mass advertising of past years.

> Media strategists, not art directors, are preparing for the imminent arrival of the ultimate child of technological change: the marriage of TV and the computer. In the very near future, true addressable commercials will be a reality, and the impetus for that advance is coming from media and marketing executives, not creative.[2]

[1]Brent Schlender, "Sony plays to win," *Fortune*, 1 May 2000, 144.
[2]Michael Kassan, "Let's all hail the new star of ad world," *Advertising Age*, 28 September 1998, 38.

Optimizers

In the 1940s, Harry Markowitz developed a mathematical technique (for which he won a Nobel Prize) that showed how to allocate money to various investments in a way that lowered the risk of a financial portfolio. In the late 1990s, the concept of optimization was applied to television spot buys. The rationale was similar to Markowitz's investment allocation strategy, only now media planners were using optimizing computer programs to budget advertising funds to those commercial spots that would deliver the greatest number of prospects at the lowest cost per viewer.

Optimizing models are driven by cost considerations. The job of the media planner is to make a number of qualitative decisions about audience response and demographic value of an audience since common sense tells us that all programs and audiences (even those with similar demographic characteristics) are not the same. Rather than diminishing the role of media planners, the "... job confronting agencies {is} how to prepare program and cost data for optimization. That requires grouping telecasts in an intelligent way for the computer and obtaining accurate cost-estimates for each grouping."[3]

Because of the high levels of investment by major agencies and clients and the fragmentation of the medium, television was the obvious choice for the first attempts at media optimization. However, as the technique becomes more proven, we will see optimizing programs applied to magazines, radio, and other media in the near future.

If there is a commonality in these trends, it is that they clearly demonstrate that media executives must be analytical, creative, and strategic in their approach to the media process. A knowledge of statistics, mathematical skills, and organized thinking are minimum requirements for media planners. For those people with the interest and competency, media planning offers an extremely exciting, lucrative, and challenging career in advertising.

optimizers Computer model and software that allow media buyers to make decisions about the value of various audience segments in a media schedule.

MEDIA UNBUNDLING AND INDEPENDENT MEDIA-BUYING FIRMS

In a media environment characterized by convergence and creativity, one of the new approaches to the media function is known as *unbundling*. Basically, unbundling refers to the establishment of agency media departments as independent units apart from their traditional role as departments in full-service agencies.

The idea of firms established solely to carry out the media function is not new. The first U.S. media-buying company, Time Buying Services (now TBS Media Management), was founded in 1960. During the 1960s a number of other media specialists opened for business, including Western International Media in 1966 and SFM Media in 1969. These early independents concentrated on television, which had the most negotiable rates and was the major medium for most national clients. The obvious premise of these companies was that their media experts could obtain better commercial rates rather than through full-service agencies, which often concentrated on creative services.

While major advertising agencies took exception to this claim, the idea of breaking out the media function as a separate business has become a major trend during the last decade. With the new focus on the media function there are two major areas of disagreement:

---

[3]Erwin Ephron, "Ad world was ripe for its conversion to optimizers," *Advertising Age*, 22 February 1999, S16.

- Where should media planning (as contrasted with media buying) take place? Some independent media firms have control of the overall media function including both negotiation and buying. In other cases, firms only execute the media plan provided by an agency or client. Many argue that by divorcing planning strategy from buying tactics you lose much of the efficiencies promised by the new emphasis on media.

- Degree of coordination between creative and media strategy. A number of media executives argue that, while cooperation and communication is necessary between media and creative departments, they are different functions and can operate well under separate roofs. This view is not shared by other media directors, ". . . the media planning element [is] a very strategic and integral part of the overall communication process. . . . Trying to unbundle that piece and connect with buying is a mistake."[4]

The concept of a totally unbundled media department is a core issue for many agencies. Historically, advertising agencies have promoted themselves to prospective clients on the basis that they could offer a complete menu of advertising services. Creative strategy and execution, account management and interface with a client's marketing department, and media research, planning, and placement could all be handled within a single agency. Up until the late 1980s, most agency reputations were determined by creative expertise and the number of award-winning advertisements and commercials they produced. Media departments (and the few independent media-buying firms that existed) were generally regarded as ancillary functions to the creative departments.

However, a number of factors changed the role of media and eventually led to the era of unbundling.

1. *Integrated marketing.* As clients began to view advertising as only one element in a complex marketing communication program, they began to see that advertising agencies were not the only source of communication expertise. To gain specialization in diverse areas, large companies often hired public relations firms, sales promotion agencies, and direct response companies, in addition to their advertising agencies. As clients became comfortable dealing with a number of communication agencies, it was natural that they would look to specialization within the advertising function—such as unbundled media-buying companies.

2. *Cost factors.* As the cost of media time and space escalated, clients gave more attention to the media-buying function. Clients were demanding greater cost efficiencies, better identification of narrowly defined target markets, and accountability of media expenditures.

    The primary problem of achieving media cost efficiencies is that the goal of low cost is largely contradictory to the current move toward specialized media. Up until a few years ago, advertisers were faced with a limited number of media choices. In an environment controlled by a few mass circulation magazines, dominance by three major networks, and largely monopolistic daily newspapers, advertisers sought to reach as many people as possible, even when the strategy carried high waste circulation. In today's world of fragmented media with much smaller, but homogeneous audiences, advertisers are routinely paying much more for each person reached than only a few years ago.

3. *Globalization.* As clients began to market throughout the world, the expertise and demands on agency media departments grew exponentially. Major clients recognized that without strategic media planning, global brands could not

---

[4]Richard Linnett, "Media planning strives for right fit," *Advertising Age*, 31 July 2000, S4.

achieve worldwide recognition and dominance no matter how well the creative function was executed. For example, "Unilever is in the midst of revamping its global marketing process to make strategic media planning the first order of business in developing brand marketing plans, with creative developed to fit the strategic media plans."[5]

4. *Complexity of the media function.* Media planning has moved light years from the days of dominance by mass circulation media. In the last five years, major businesses such as General Motors and Procter & Gamble have invested advertising dollars in a diversified media schedule including the Internet, numerous niche cable networks, and prototype interactive media on an experimental basis. In addition, companies are demanding that this advertising be monitored and coordinated with event marketing opportunities, sales promotion, and public relations. This type of expertise requires a much greater level of knowledge and specialization than can be provided by a traditional media department.

5. *Profitability.* In addition to the benefits that unbundling accrues to clients, it also has added a profit center for the agencies engaging in it. Now agencies can compete for clients' media accounts even when another agency handles the creative side. As one media executive said, "You need media-only business today to keep you competitive. It costs a lot of money to be in media today." Another pointed out, ". . . there seems to be a lot more profit in specialization than generalization. Usually when you're more focused, you're more profitable."[6] Their observations are borne out by the growth of unbundled companies such as Media Edge, Starcom, and Optimum Media who are playing a significant role in the media plans of major advertisers (see Exhibit 7.2). Only a few years ago, the clients being served by these independent media buyers would have been handled by full-service agencies such as Young & Rubicam, Foote, Cone & Belding, and Leo Burnett, all of whom have unbundled their media department.

Unbundling has given media executives a greater role in the overall planning of advertising strategy. It also has highlighted the importance of media as part of the advertising mix. It is obvious that, in a world of fragmented audiences and niche media, media decisions will continue to occupy a primary position in advertising planning. Advertisers increasingly realize the wasted effort and money in delivering even the most creative messages to the wrong audience.

Top 5 U.S. media specialist companies by 1998 billings (in millions).		Top 5 worldwide media specialist companies by 1998 billings (in millions).	
	Billings		Billings
1 Starcom/MediaVest	$5,430.2	1 McCann-Erickson/Universal McCann	$13,206.4
2 Initiative Media Worldwide	$4,600.0	2 Starcom/MediaVest	$11,700.0
3 McCann-Erickson/Universal McCann	$4,121.5	3 Optimum Medai Directions	$10,564.3
4 Media Edge	$3,494.4	4 Media Edge	$10,277.4
5 Optimum Media	$2,700.0	5 MindShare	$10,079.0

Notes: Starcom/MediaVest is the sum of Starcom ($2,912.5 U.S. billings, $7,300.0 worldwide) and MediaVest ($2,517.7 U.S. billings, $4,400.0 worldwide, a figure estimated by *Ad Age international*, page 25, Dec. 14, 1998: billings in millions). Except for MediaVest Contribution, figures are from *Ad Age's* Agency Report, April 19, 1999.

Exhibit

7.2

The Media Big Guns

From: Hillary Chura, "BDM to create $16.5 bil Goliath in media buying," *Advertising Age,* 21 February 2000, 62.

---

[5]Jack Neff, "Media buying & planning," *Advertising Age*, 2 August 1999, S1.
[6]Chuck Ross, "Media 'stepchild' now moving to head of table," *Advertising Age*, 19 April 1999, S12.

BASIC MEDIA STRATEGY

building block strategy A media concept that buys the medium that reaches the most prospects first and works down to those that reach the smallest number of prospects.

Traditionally, media planners have used a **building block strategy** to develop a media schedule. Keeping in mind cost efficiencies, they start with the medium that reaches the most prospects and works down to those that reach the smallest portion of the audience. In the past, the first or second "blocks" were relatively easy to determine. Most national advertisers used network television or magazines as the dominant medium. The media planner then considered other vehicles to reach smaller audience segments. For example, Campbell Soup Company spends approximately 90 percent of its measured advertising budget on magazines and television, but uses radio and Sunday magazines to cover gaps in its media schedule.

In the last few years, the media options available to supplement an advertiser's primary vehicles have grown dramatically. The introduction of vehicles such as the Internet, video catalogs, and interactive television have brought major changes to the job of the media planner. They also have created new ways to view the media function and media buying. Media planners are forced to go beyond costs in developing plans. When dealing with these specialized media, planners must consider factors such as additional weight against prime prospects, ability to deliver a communication message in a unique manner, and the prestige of a medium that may outweigh low audience delivery. More and more media planners are examining communication interactions between the audience and individual media.

Historically, the advertising process began with development of broad marketing and advertising strategies, moved to creative execution, and finally to media placement, which was often viewed as nothing more than a channel for creative messages. Today, that notion is changing in some fundamental ways:

1. *Core values of media.* Media planners are increasingly working with the creative team to understand the qualitative core values of each medium. These core values interact with advertising messages to enhance or diminish the advertising.

   For example, magazines are about information, television scores better as an emotional medium, and direct mail is about personalization. "If the brand message is in conflict with these values, the advertising won't be credible . . . it simply won't connect to an audience. . . . A thoughtful, introspective-seeming brand . . . might be difficult to sell on a billboard drivers pass going 60 miles an hour, even if they are the right audience for that brand."[7]

   The experienced media buyer must be able to look beyond personal media preferences and determine the media vehicles that will best reach prospects. It may be that a network television spot is needed or the best ad placement may be a stock car carrying a sponsor's logo. In any case, media planners must be able to step away from their personal biases and put themselves in the place of a client's prime prospects.

2. *Fading distinctions among media.* Technology is changing the fundamental relationships among media, audiences, and advertisers and creating an environment where distinctions among media are fading. For example, is the delivery of newspaper content over a computer still a "print" medium? Likewise, are text messages available through television still "broadcast" signals?

   In this new environment, media planners must be creative in the utilization of media vehicles and look less at the distribution system and more at the audiences and communication effectiveness. Even the traditional organiza-

---

[7]Jonathan Bond and Richard Kirshenbaum, "Using media to get under the radar," *Agency*, Winter 1998, 56.

tions of agency media departments will have to be realigned to comply with changing media technology.

3. *Media accountability.* Changes in media buying and scheduling are putting pressure on media planners to become more knowledgeable in areas that were not part of their responsibility only a few years ago. In the near future, job functions such as media planner and media buyer will be replaced by more inclusive terms such as marketing communication specialist. The change in terminology is more than semantic, rather it more accurately reflects both the job function and the expectations for the advertising media executive of the future.

The new approach to media planning also is demanding greater accountability for advertising media planners. A number of research tools are being developed to allow planners to view the media-buying process in unique and creative ways. For example, The Media Edge (TME) has developed software known as TME Television Tree (T3). Basically, it divides the entire network television schedule into program clusters that are most likely to reach particular target audiences.[8]

The clusters are designed to reach demographic audience segments across a number of programs. For example, the Family Cluster includes such shows as *7th Heaven* and *Sabrina, The Teenage Witch.* Understandably, this cluster reaches high levels of teenage girls, but it also has significant viewership among working women and mothers watching with their children. The idea of T3 is to treat programs and program clusters like brands.

Similar research has shown that networks also have distinctive brand identities that appeal to certain demographic and buyer categories. High brand identification for a network does not always translate into short-term viewership. For example, the top two "brands" among television networks are The Discovery Channel and The Weather Channel, but neither averages 1 percent of the viewing audience. However, it bodes well for these networks as audience fragmentation drives more and more viewers to niche vehicles.

Another factor in network branding, just as in the case of products, is that differentiation is not enough. There also is a question of affinity for certain networks. In one study, respondents were asked to identify what types of people are users of certain media. They were then asked about the types of people with whom they wanted to associate. By correlating the two scores, media planners can see which media have the highest affinity and those programs and networks with whom advertisers and consumers would most want to have their products associated.[9]

Ultimately, advertising accountability means that businesses want to be able to link their advertising to specific sales of their brands. As noted earlier, it is difficult to determine exactly what contribution advertising makes to total sales, much less how it influences a single buyer or group of buyers. However, Brandfx, a software program developed by Media Plan, Inc., and Spectra Marketing, attempts to make this link. Using scanner data from the checkout counter, Brandfx relates television viewing and purchase behavior to estimate the sales volume produced by viewers of specific shows. As one media executive said, "We've never had the opportunity to bring sales into the media equation. The point is to go after the best customers, not the most."[10]

The need to find ways to better link advertising and sales becomes even more important as technology continues to change the nature of both mass media and advertising. Many advertisers predict that in the near future we will not be dealing with distinct media vehicles. Rather, through the use of in-home fiber optics, there

---

[8]Cristina Merrill, "Crowd control," *American Demographics*, October 1999, 32.
[9]Joe Mandese, "In the eye of the beholder," *American Demographics*, December 1999, 27.
[10]Cristina Merrill, "Making media sales smart," *American Demographics*, September 1999, 17.

will be a convergence of media into a single multimedia source where telephones, interactive computers, movies-on-demand, and laser printers make obsolete the traditional media categories. Consumers will have much greater control over communication outlets; selecting only those entertainment, information, and advertising messages they want. Waste circulation will be limited, since by definition, self-selected communication will only go to prospects. The organizations we view as media today will be information sources, and the carriers of this information will be limited to a few cable outlets, telephone companies, or other common carriers.

Media Characteristics

Before a media strategy can be planned and implemented, we must have a basic knowledge of the characteristics and functions (both editorial and advertising) of the major media. Faced with a multitude of media choices, one of the most important attributes of a media planner is an open mind. From established media such as network television to the newly emerging Internet, media planners must be able to sort those media that best fit the marketing and promotional goals of individual clients.

We must remember that advertising budgets are not growing as fast as the increase in media options, so hard budget choices are the rule of the day for agencies and their clients. "In broad terms, we cannot sell more cars, sneakers or boxes of cereal to . . . people as a result of new technology. To fund these new media efforts, marketing executives will need to take a fresh look at the macro-level allocation of budgets as new media forms begin to take on some of the blended attributes of traditional advertising media, promotion, and direct marketing."[11] Future chapters will discuss the various strengths and weaknesses of media vehicles from an advertising perspective.

PUTTING IT ALL TOGETHER: THE MEDIA PLAN

Knowing the characteristics of the various media is only a necessary first step. Not having a plan to organize media buys into a meaningful whole is analogous to trying to speak a language knowing many words but without a grammar to make sense of it. Media planners must be able to use the distinctive attributes of each medium as part of a sophisticated analysis that leads to a complete media plan for an advertising campaign. While there is no standard format, we will offer a brief outline of a typical plan and then discuss in detail some of the most important elements:

A TYPICAL MEDIA PLAN

I. Marketing Analysis
   A. Fundamental marketing strategy
      1. Sales, share of market, and profitability goals
      2. Prime prospects identified by:
         a. Demographics characteristics
         b. Lifestyle characteristics
         c. Geographic location
         d. Level of product usage
   B. Product benefits and differentiating characteristics
   C. Pricing strategy
   D. Competitive environment
      1. Number and competitive market share of product category firms
      2. Regulatory and economic situation facing product category

---

[11]Mickey Marks, "Millennial satiation," *Advertising Age*, 14 February 2000, S16.

II. Advertising Analysis
  A. Fundamental advertising strategy
    1. Product awareness goals
    2. Target audience(s) advertising weight
  B. Budget
    1. Allocation to marketing communication mix
    2. Allocation by media category
    3. Allocation by media vehicle
III. Media Strategy
  A. Match media vehicles (*Time,* "Monday Night Football," country music radio, etc.) with target audience media preferences
  B. Creative and communication considerations
    1. Need for product demonstration
    2. Need for complex message
    3. Daypart and/or seasonal requirements
    4. Media compatibility with message themes and competitive considerations
IV. Media Scheduling
  A. Print insertion dates and production requirements
  B. Broadcast allocations and availabilities
  C. Budget allocation each medium (magazines) and media vehicle (*Sports Illustrated*)
  D. CPM estimates (by total audience, prime prospects, etc.)
V. Justification and Summary
  A. Statement of ad goals in terms of measurable results
  B. Research plan to measure achievement of ad goals
  C. Contingencies for media schedule adjustments

No two media plans will have exactly the same components nor will they give the same weight to those media that they include. However, the following section discusses those elements that are found in virtually every plan.

Target Audience

As we have discovered, a **media plan** encompasses a number of factors involving both marketing strategy and advertising tactics. However, none is more crucial to the ultimate success of an advertising campaign than the proper identification of the prime target market(s) for a brand. If errors are made at this stage of the advertising process, it is virtually impossible for the advertising program to be successfully executed. The foundation of media planning is the identification of prime prospect segments within the audience of various media. More often than not, this process is aimed not only at finding demographic niches, but is directed at identifying consumer needs and the product benefits that meet these needs.

Throughout the media-planning operation, buyers and planners must keep their focus on the total picture of consumer, product, and benefit rather than considering only reaching the target market at the lowest cost. In recent years, the process of evaluating media's contribution to the advertising message (in addition to the message itself) has become a major research track. Advertising researchers are constantly seeking more sophisticated tools to get a clear picture of consumers and the ways in which they interact with media and advertising messages.

In viewing these interactions, media planners are looking at cost efficiencies in more sophisticated ways than in previous years. At a minimum, this broader approach to cost efficiency requires that media plans maximize delivery of prospects as opposed to people or households. Until recently, media planners tended to concentrate on overall audience delivery by various media. The hope was

media plan The complete analysis and execution of the media component of a campaign.

cost per thousand (CPM) A method of comparing the cost for media of different circulations. Also weighted or demographic cost per thousand calculates the CPM using only that portion of a medium's audience falling into a prime-prospect category.

that by reaching the greatest audience at the lowest cost, the media schedule would also reach a fair share of prospects. This strategy worked in a day of mass circulation magazines and network television domination of the airwaves. The most common measure of efficiency during that period was the **cost per thousand (CPM).** We will start with a definition of the CPM as we begin our discussion of the relationship between cost and targeting prospects.

The CPM is a means of comparing media costs among vehicles with different circulations. The formula is stated:

$$CPM = \frac{ad\ cost \times 1000}{circulation}$$

Let's assume that *McCall's* magazine has a circulation of 4.2 million and a four-color page rate of $115,000, its CPM is calculated:

$$McCall's\ CPM = \frac{\$115,000 \times 1000}{4,200,000} = \$27.38$$

Obviously, no medium provides an audience where every member is of equal benefit to a specific advertiser, that is, zero waste circulation. Let's assume that our client is a diaper manufacturer and only wants to reach women with children two years old or younger. In order to measure *McCall's* efficiency in reaching this audience, we might use some variation of the *weighted* or *demographic* CPM. Let's look at an example of the weighted CPM.

In this case, we find that of *McCall's* 4.2 million readers, 600,000 have children under two. Now we calculate the CPM weighted to consider only our target audience rather than the total circulation of the magazine.

Therefore:

$$Weighted\ CPM = \frac{\$115,000 \times 1000}{600,000} = \$191.66$$

You will recall that in Chapter 4 we discussed a number of different means of identifying target markets. In the weighted CPM example above, a media planner can substitute any number of lifestyle, product user, or psychographic data for the demographic category we used in the *McCall's* example. It is important to note that CPM figures are important only as comparisons with those of other media. *McCall's* CPM of $27.38 is of interest only to the extent that it might be compared to *Redbook* with a CPM of $36.90.

Media planners are constantly attempting to fine-tune cost efficiencies against more useful and targeted client prospects. An important research focus of recent years involves adding a communication component to the CPM mix. Rather than just measuring the number of prospects that potential readers or viewers of our advertising, we now add some measure of communication impact and audience awareness to the mix.

Among the primary communication considerations that are generally considered by media planners are the following:

1. *Creative predispositions of the audience.* For example, teens are predisposed to radio in a different way than print.
2. *Qualitative environment for the message. Car and Driver* magazine reaches readers who are in the proper frame of mind for advertisements for automobiles and accessories.

synergistic effect In media buying, combining a number of complementary media that create advertising awareness greater than the sum of each.

3. *The **synergistic effect.*** Advertisers seek a combination of media that results in a communicative effect that is greater than the sum of each one. For example, outdoor advertising is used by cell phone manufacturers to gain brand recogni-

tion; magazines for detailed product information; newspapers for dealer location and price; and television for demonstration and image. The net effect is greater than any single medium used alone.

4. *The creative approach.* Does the need for long copy or quality reproduction require print, even if other media might be more cost efficient?

Intuitively, we can understand that these and other communication components should not be ignored in developing a media plan. However, the conversion of intuition into hard data is not an easy process. In recent years, a great deal of attention has been given to quantifying the value of communication in the media plan. Without going into the complex methodology involved, let's examine a few of the possible weighted CPM adjustments that might be made to take into account communication factors:

- *Probability of exposure to a medium.* Should a magazine reader and a person that passes an outdoor sign be given equal exposure weight?
- *Advertising exposure weights to equalize the probability of an ad being seen.* Are the readers of *Time* more likely to see the average message for your product than the viewers of *Friends*?
- *Communication weights to equalize the probability of an advertising message communicating.* What is the communication impact of a four-color magazine advertisement compared to a television commercial or a Web site banner?
- *Frequency of exposure weights in the same medium.* Does the first exposure in a medium have the same or greater value than subsequent exposures?[12]

In some cases, we see the notation CPMI, which refers to Cost Per Thousand *Involved*, which is another way of saying that some measure of audience communication is being used to weight the audience of specific media or media vehicles.

Regardless of how we weight the audience for a medium, the rationale is the same relative to the CPM formula. That is, we are giving the audience greater or lesser value as we plug in the denominator of the CPM formula.

To use a hypothetical example, let's assume that in evaluating the cost efficiency of a media schedule, research shows us that a four-color magazine advertisement should be given a weight of 1.2 (1.0 being the average of all media advertising). Using our earlier *McCall's* example, the CPM for mothers with children under two years old is now:

$$McCall's\ CPM = \frac{\$115,000 \times 1000}{720,000} = \$159.72$$

In this example, we have taken the 600,000 mothers and multiplied them by our magazine weighting factor (1.2) to give this audience more value (and lower CPM, $159.72 versus $191.66) because they are seeing our message in a magazine. Remember that this is only an example. An advertiser wanting to measure cost efficiencies against teenage boys might give radio a weight of 1.5 and magazines a weight of 0.8. However, the point is that advertisers are trying to find some way of factoring in a communication component to their audience delivery measures.

Research has shown that high levels of audience involvement with a medium is positively related to advertising response. These and other methods of audience communication weighting are attempts to address this relationship in the media-planning process as well as to give accurate estimates to the value of the audiences of various media.

---

[12]Erwin Ephron, "A new media-mix strategy," *Advertising Age*, 28 February 2000, S10.

Claritas' Potential Rating Index by Zip Code (PRIZM)

A shortcoming of many audience analysis methods is that they consider only a single variable. In our earlier *McCall's* example we designated women with children under two as our target market for diapers. However, we know that within this broad category there are a number of differences. For example, a working woman might purchase diapers from a day care center without making a brand decision. Some women may use a diaper service rather than purchasing disposable diapers. Likewise, income, education, and other factors might change the purchase behavior of a woman in this general category. Media planners realize that a multivariable approach is often needed to correctly identify a particular target segment.

One of the most innovative methods of segmenting markets on a multivariable basis is the **Potential Rating Index by Zip Market (PRIZM)** system developed by the Claritas Corporation. PRIZM divides the population into 15 social groups (see Exhibit 7.3a) and further subdivides these large segments into 62 subcategories (see Exhibit 7.3b). The primary variables for determining these social groups are urbanization and social class.

The PRIZM categories are arranged in descending order of affluence from the "Blue Blood Estates" who reside in the Elite Suburb social group to "Hard Scrabble" whose residents live in the most rural and lowest social class areas of the country. The value of PRIZM groups is that these general categories can be matched with those products and media that members of a particular group are most likely to use. For example, inhabitants of the "Elite Suburbs" are likely to drive luxury cars and be among the heaviest readers of magazines. By identifying these groups geographically, companies can develop efficient marketing and advertising plans without the waste circulation of a less-targeted campaign.

In the future, the computer and more sophisticated research methodology will make even more finely tuned audience identification possible. In fact, we may be approaching a time when audience segmentation techniques will be able to target prospects more precisely than media vehicles will be able to reach them practically or

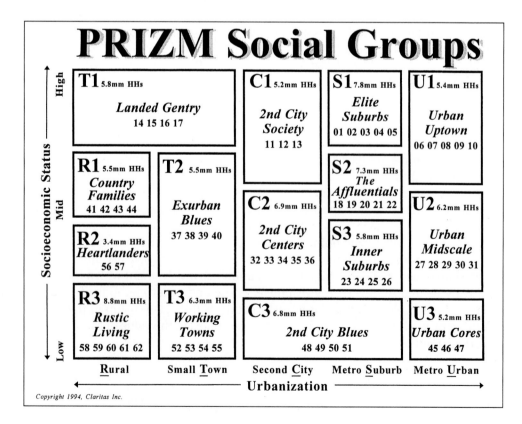

Exhibit

7.3a

PRIZM allows marketers to target customers by geography and lifestyle.

PRIZM by Claritas
Demographic Reference Chart

Race/Ethnicity
W-White, B-Black, A-Asian
H-Hispanic, F-Foreign Born
■ Prevalent • Above Avg

PREDOMINANT CHARACTERISTICS

Grp	Clstr	Nickname	Income Level	Family Type	Age	Education	Occup	Housing	W	B	A	H	F
S1	01	Blue Blood Estates	Elite	Family	35-54	College	Exec	Single	■		•		•
	02	Cashmere & Country Clubs	Wealthy	Family	35-54	College	Exec	Single	■		•		•
	03	Executive Suites	Affluent	Couples	25-34	College	WC/Exec	Single	■		•		•
	04	Pools & Patios	Affluent	Couples	55-64	College	Exec	Single	■		•		
	05	Kids & Cul-de-Sacs	Affluent	Family	35-54	College	WC/Exec	Single	•		•		
U1	06	Urban Gold Coast	Affluent	Singles	25-34	College	Exec	Hi-Rise	■		•		•
	07	Money & Brains	Affluent	Couples	55-64	College	Exec	Single	■		•		•
	08	Young Literati	Upper Mid	Sgl/Cpl	25-34	College	Exec	Hi-Rise	•		•		•
	09	American Dreams	Upper Mid	Family	35-54	College	WC	Single		•	•	•	•
	10	Bohemian Mix	Middle	Singles	< 24	College	WC	Hi-Rise	•	•	•	•	•
C1	11	Second City Elite	Affluent	Couples	35-64	College	WC/Exec	Single	■		•		
	12	Upward Bound	Upper Mid	Family	25-54	College	WC/Exec	Single	■		•		
	13	Gray Power	Middle	Sgl/Cpl	65+	College	WC	Single	■				•
T1	14	Country Squires	Wealthy	Fam/Cpl	35-64	College	Exec	Single	■				
	15	God's Country	Affluent	Family	35-54	College	WC	Single	■				
	16	Big Fish Small Pond	Upper Mid	Family	35-54	HS/College	WC	Single	■				
	17	Greenbelt Families	Upper Mid	Family	25-54	HS/College	WC	Single	■				
S2	18	Young Influentials	Upper Mid	Sgl/Cpl	< 35	College	WC/Exec	Multi	•		•		•
	19	New Empty Nests	Upper Mid	Couples	35-64	College	WC/Exec	Single	■				
	20	Boomers & Babies	Upper Mid	Family	25-54	College	WC/Exec	Single	•		•	•	
	21	Suburban Sprawl	Middle	Fam/Cpl	< 35	College	WC	Mixed	•	•	•	•	•
	22	Blue-Chip Blues	Middle	Family	35-54	HS/College	WC/BC	Single	■				
S3	23	Upstarts & Seniors	Middle	Cpl/Sgl	Mix	College	WC/Exec	Multi	■				
	24	New Beginnings	Middle	Sgl/Cpl	< 35	College	WC/Exec	Multi		•	•	•	•
	25	Mobility Blues	Middle	Fam/Cpl	< 35	HS/College	BC/Serv	Mixed		•		■	•
	26	Gray Collars	Middle	Couples	> 55	HS	BC/Serv	Single	•				
U2	27	Urban Achievers	Middle	Cpl/Sgl	Mix	College	WC/Exec	Hi-Rise	■		•	•	•
	28	Big City Blend	Middle	Family	35-54	HS	WC/BC	Single		•	•	■	•
	29	Old Yankee Rows	Middle	Couples	55+	HS	WC	Multi	•		•	•	•
	30	Middle Minorities	Middle	Fam/Cpl	35-54	HS/College	WC/Serv	Multi		■		•	•
	31	Latino America	Middle	Family	25-34	< HS	BC/Serv	Multi				■	•
C2	32	Middleburg Managers	Middle	Couples	> 55	College	WC/Exec	Single	■				
	33	Boomtown Singles	Middle	Sgl/Cpl	< 34	College	WC/Exec	Multi	■		•		
	34	Starter Families	Middle	Family	25-34	HS	BC	Mixed	■			•	
	35	Sunset City Blues	Lower Mid	Couples	> 55	HS	BC/Serv	Single	■				
	36	Towns & Gowns	Lower Mid	Singles	< 35	College	WC/Serv	Hi-Rise	■				•
T2	37	New Homesteaders	Middle	Family	35-54	College	WC	Single	■				
	38	Middle America	Middle	Family	25-44	HS	BC	Single	■				
	39	Red, White & Blue-Collar	Middle	Family	35-64	HS	BC	Single	■				
	40	Military Quarters	Lower Mid	Family	25-54	College	WC/Serv	Multi	■	•	•		

PRIZM by Claritas
Demographic Reference Chart

Race/Ethnicity
W-White, B-Black, A-Asian
H-Hispanic, F-Foreign Born
■ Prevalent • Above Avg

PREDOMINANT CHARACTERISTICS

Grp	Clstr	Nickname	Income Level	Family Type	Age	Education	Occup	Housing	W	B	A	H	F
R1	41	Big Sky Families	Upper Mid	Family	35-44	HS/College	BC/Farm	Single	■				
	42	New Ecotopia	Middle	Fam/Cpl	35-54	College	WC/BC	Single	■				
	43	River City, USA	Middle	Family	35-64	HS	BC/Farm	Single	■				
	44	Shotguns & Pickups	Middle	Family	35-64	HS	BC/Farm	Single	■				
U3	45	Single City Blues	Lower Mid	Singles	Mix	Mix	WC/Serv	Multi		•	•	•	•
	46	Hispanic Mix	Poor	Family	< 35	< HS	BC	Hi-Rise		•	•	■	•
	47	Inner Cities	Poor	Sgl/Fam	Mix	< HS	BC/Serv	Multi		■		•	•
C3	48	Smalltown Downtown	Lower Mid	Sgl/Fam	< 35	HS/College	BC/Serv	Multi		•		•	
	49	Hometown Retired	Lower Mid	Sgl/Cpl	65+	< HS	Service	Mixed	■			•	•
	50	Family Scramble	Lower Mid	Family	< 35	< HS	BC	Mixed				■	•
	51	Southside City	Poor	Sgl/Fam	Mix	< HS	BC/Serv	Multi		■			
T3	52	Golden Ponds	Lower Mid	Couples	65+	HS	BC/Serv	Single	■				
	53	Rural Industria	Lower Mid	Family	< 35	HS	BC	Single	■			•	
	54	Norma Rae-Ville	Poor	Sgl/Fam	Mix	< HS	BC/Serv	Single		■			
	55	Mines & Mills	Poor	Sgl/Cpl	55+	< HS	BC/Serv	Single	■				
R2	56	Agri-Business	Middle	Family	35+	HS	Farm	Single	■			•	
	57	Grain Belt	Lower Mid	Family	55+	HS	Farm	Single	■			•	
R3	58	Blue Highways	Lower Mid	Family	35-54	HS	BC/Farm	Single	■				
	59	Rustic Elders	Lower Mid	Couples	55+	HS	BC/Serv	Single	■				
	60	Back Country Folks	Lower Mid	Couples	35+	HS	BC/Farm	Single	■				
	61	Scrub Pine Flats	Poor	Family	35+	< HS	BC/Farm	Single	■	■			
	62	Hard Scrabble	Poor	Family	35+	< HS	BC/Farm	Single	■				

Income Level	Avg Annual HH Income
Elite/Wealthy	$65,000 and over
Affluent	$50,000 - $64,500
Upper Mid	$37,000 - $49,500
Middle	$28,000 - $36,500
Lower Mid	$20,000 - $27,500
Poor	under $20,000

Education	
< HS	Grade School
HS	High School / Technical School
HS/College	High School / Some College
College	College Graduates

Family Type	
Family	Married Couples w/Children or, Single Parents w/Children
Couples	Married Couples (few children)
Singles	Singles / Unmarried Couples
Fam/Cpl	Mix of Married Couples with/without Children
Sgl/Cpl	Mix of Married Couples and Singles

Occupation	
Exec	Executive, managerial & professionals (teachers, doctors, etc.)
WC	Other White-Collar (technical, sales, admin/clerical support)
BC	Blue-Collar (assembly, trades & repair, operators, laborers, etc.)
WC/BC	Mix of White-Collar & Upper-Level Blue Collar
Service	Service (hospitality, food prep, protective & health services, etc)
WC/Serv	Mix of Other White-Collar & Service
BC/Serv	Mix of Blue-Collar & Service
Farm	Farming, Mining & Ranching (farm operators, forestry, etc.)
BC/Farm	Mix of Blue-Collar and Farming

Exhibit
7.3b

efficiently. Even the most thoroughly researched media plan will reach some non-buyers. The job of the media planner is to keep waste circulation to a minimum while achieving maximum cost efficiencies. A media schedule with zero nonprospects would not only be theoretically impossible to achieve, but prohibitively expensive.

COMMUNICATION REQUIREMENTS AND CREATIVE ELEMENTS

As discussed earlier, media planners are interested increasingly in the differential value of various media and the value they add or subtract to specific advertising messages. Another dimension of this process is the manner in which art directors, copywriters, and media planners have begun to engage in the process at the strategic level rather than simply seeing their role as executing someone else's advertising plan.

This is not to suggest that it is customary for the media and/or creative team to sit at the table when fundamental decisions are being made about the overall promotion strategy for a brand. However, there is growing recognition by both account supervisors and clients that the earlier in the process these functions are brought on board, the greater the opportunity for creative input into unique ways to position and advertise a brand. This early involvement also allows a more thoughtful approach to the various problems that will have to be addressed inevitably as the campaign goes from strategy to tactics to execution.

As we have discussed, there is a wide gap between advertising exposure and advertising communication. The greater the input from the account team to both media and creative, the better the communication and coordination. Often the creative and media teams must make compromises among those media with the best cost efficiencies and those with the best creative attributes to properly communicate the brand's core message. The earlier that these decisions can be made, the better it is for media buyers who must negotiate prices and determine availabilities of space and time.

In the past, a major criticism of advertising execution was that media and creative functions did not have enough knowledge of what each area was doing within the campaign strategy. The result, according to critics, was advertising that did not fully utilize the communicative strengths of the various media vehicles. Fortunately, the separation between the creative and media functions seems to have diminished in recent years. Among major advertising agencies there seems to be a heightened sensitivity that creative/media cooperation is necessary for effective advertising.

In part, this cooperation has been necessitated by the convergence of media outlets, new media technology, and greater opportunities for interactive approaches to audiences. For example, when businesses experiment with Internet advertising, the integration of message, medium, and audience requires different approaches than in traditional media advertising. The process of planning advertising in new technologies and interactive media demand that all the advertising functions work in concert to make the greatest impact with an audience that is very much in control of the communications process.

GEOGRAPHY—WHERE IS THE PRODUCT DISTRIBUTED?

Geographical considerations are among the oldest factors in buying media. Long before advertisers were knowledgeable about the importance of demographics and target markets, they knew the areas in which their products were distributed and bought those promotional vehicles that best reached those regions. Even in an era of narrowly defined audiences, geography remains a primary consideration of the planner.

Exhibit
7.4

Prime Prospects	Local	Regional	National
Concentrated	1	2	3
	4	5	6
Dispersed	7	8	9

Today, the geographic media-planning boundaries are often much smaller than in previous years. Instead of states or regions, the planner may be dealing in Zip codes and block units or even individuals, especially in direct mail advertising. Geographical considerations also are becoming more important as advertisers find that consumers in different parts of the country demonstrate markedly different attitudes and opinions concerning various product categories. Sometimes these geographic differences are obvious—food preferences in the South are distinctly different from the Northeast, just as the demand for snow tires is different in Los Angeles and Chicago. Other reasons for differences in brand demand are less apparent—why is demand for the Chevrolet Cavalier so much less in Oregon than the rest of the country?

Adding to the complexity of the media planner's job is the fact that media distribution demonstrates some of the same unpredictable distribution patterns as products. For example, according to Nielsen data, *60 Minutes* is the top-rated show in Burlington, Vermont; in Chicago it is not in the top ten. On the other hand, Chicago viewers have *E.R.* at the top of their list, a show that doesn't crack the top ten in Macon, Georgia.

These widely varying patterns of product usage and media preferences must be considered by planners as they develop a media schedule that will reach prime prospects. Planners must begin with the location of buyers and prospective buyers and their concentration in specific areas. Exhibit 7.4 demonstrates the dual nature of geographical areas and the concentration of prospects.

Obviously, Cell 1—with concentrated prospects in a local area—is the easiest to deal with. At the other extreme, an efficient plan for Cell 9 demands a great deal of creativity to appeal to prospects with special interests—say, antiques or fine jewelry—who are not concentrated in any geographical area. These dispersed groups might be reached through specialized magazines, direct mail, or, in coming years, the Internet.

Media planners not only need to know where prospects are located, but also how consumers in different areas rate in terms of current and future sales potential. A common method of relating sales, advertising budgets, and geography is the **brand development index (BDI).** An example of the BDI is shown in Exhibit 7.5.

**brand development
index (BDI)** A method
of allocating advertising budgets
to those geographic areas that
have the greatest sales potential.

Computing the Brand Development Index

ACME Appliance has a media budget of $2 million and sells in 20 markets. The media planner wants to allocate the budget in the 20 markets according to the sales potential of each market.

Market	Population (%)	ACME Sales (%)	Budget by Population (000)	BDI (Sales/ Population)	Budget by BDI
1	8	12	$ 160	150	$ 240,000
2	12	8	240	67	160,800
3	6	6	120	100	120,000
etc.					
20	100%	100%	$2,000	—	$2,000,000

Exhibit
7.5

The brand development index emphasizes prime sales areas.

Example: Market 2, based on its population, should have an advertising allocation of $240,000 (0.12 × $2,000,000). However, the sales potential of market 2 is only 67 percent as great as its population would indicate (sales/population or 8/12). Therefore, the media planner reduces the allocation to market to 2 to $160,800 ($240,000 × 0.67) and reallocates funds to markets with greater potential such as market 1.

Regional differences in product usage require many firms to develop a secondary, localized media plan to supplement their national media schedule. National advertisers are increasingly using regional advertising options such as local cable and specialized product-specific publications such as restaurant guides. As research data allow advertisers to define their markets and media technology more narrowly to reach these segments becomes more readily available, we will see an even greater use of localized media. In some cases, this localization will be a supplement to national campaigns; in other instances, we will see national brands adopt an area-by-area media schedule as their primary strategy.

MEDIA TACTICS: REACH, FREQUENCY, CONTINUITY, AND BUDGET

The media planner deals with four primary elements in developing the final media schedule:

1. *Reach (also called coverage).* The number of different people exposed to a single medium or, in the case of a multimedia campaign, the entire media schedule. It may be expressed as the number of prospects or as a percentage of your target audience, but in either case, it represents a nonduplicated audience. For example, if the target audience is 500,000 housewives and 200,000 are exposed to our advertising, it may be expressed as a reach of 40 percent.

2. *Frequency.* The number of times that each person in the audience is exposed to your media schedule. In our earlier example, if the 200,000 women reached in our campaign generated 1,000,000 exposures, the frequency would be 5.0.

$$1,000,000/200,000 = 5.0$$

3. *Continuity.* The length of time over which a campaign will run or the length of time that reach and frequency will be measured. In other words, our 20 percent reach and 5.0 frequency might be accumulated over one week, one month, or one year. In evaluating reach and frequency, it is important that the continuity over which these elements are measured be clearly stated.

4. *Budget.* The budget is the major constraint of any advertising plan. The core consideration in all media planning is the budget. While the relative weight given reach and frequency can be adjusted, the overriding constraint on the total weight of the advertising schedule is the budget.

As the media-planning process progresses, the planner moves from general strategy considerations to specific tactics. The planner must determine the most efficient media to achieve already determined marketing and advertising objectives.

The value of each media vehicle should be measured according to three criteria:[13]

1. The cost of the vehicle
2. The number of target market members or the weighted target market quality of the audience reached by the vehicle
3. The effectiveness of the advertising exposures the vehicles deliver (e.g., the communications or qualitative component)

These considerations can be combined in a concept known as frequency value planning (FVP). FVP evaluates media vehicles in terms of their frequency distribu-

[13]Hugh Cannon, "Does traditional media planning apply to new media?" in *Proceedings of the 1999 Conference of the American Academy of Advertising,* ed. Marilyn S. Roberts, 279.

frequency   In media exposure the number of times an individual or household is exposed to a medium within a given period of time.

tion—the proportion of the target market that receives different levels of advertising exposure. The important distinction between unweighted frequency and FVP is that FVP estimates the relative value of exposures rather than simply measuring the number of times a person comes into contact with a medium or an advertising message.

From a practical standpoint, the media planner has control over reach and frequency. The budget is a strategic decision largely determined by the client. Likewise, the length of most campaigns is one year, but regardless of the continuity of any campaign, it will not be the decision of the media department.

Reach, frequency, and continuity must be balanced against the demands of a fixed budget. However, the media planner must also consider the balance between the least expensive media (efficiency) and those most able to communicate the core message and reach the best prospects (effectiveness). Exhibit 7.6 shows the relationship among the three elements in some typical media strategies.

The tactics associated with reach and frequency are a direct result of the previously agreed to marketing and advertising objectives and strategies. The decision to emphasize reach or frequency in the communication strategy will most definitely influence the media tactics. A number of tactics can be used when reach or frequency is desired.[14] For example:

Reach Tactics

- Prime-time television reaches a large mass audience, but is very expensive so the budget may be quickly expended.
- Daily newspapers reach 60 million homes and cover from 30 percent to 50 percent of most markets.
- Large circulation magazines such as *TV Guide* or *National Geographic* serve similar functions as network television, but with smaller overall audiences.

Frequency Tactics

- Cable television, particularly specialized outlets such as The History Channel or The Discovery Channel, can be purchased at relatively low cost and tend to build frequency by reaching the same core viewers over a long period.

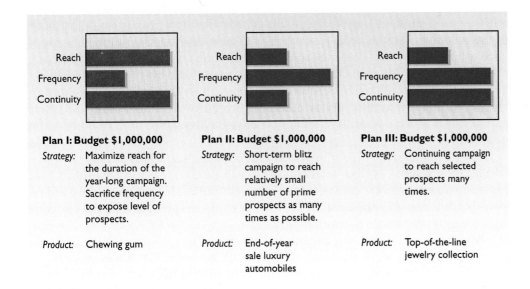

Plan I: Budget $1,000,000

Strategy: Maximize reach for the duration of the year-long campaign. Sacrifice frequency to expose level of prospects.

Product: Chewing gum

Plan II: Budget $1,000,000

Strategy: Short-term blitz campaign to reach relatively small number of prime prospects as many times as possible.

Product: End-of-year sale luxury automobiles

Plan III: Budget $1,000,000

Strategy: Continuing campaign to reach selected prospects many times.

Product: Top-of-the-line jewelry collection

Exhibit 7.6

Reach, Frequency, and Continuity Relationships with a Fixed Budget

---

[14]Allen Brivic, *What Every Account Executive Should Know About Media,* a publication of the American Association of Advertising Agencies, 1989, 14.

- Special interest magazines, as opposed to mass circulation publications, are able to reach the same audience over several issues.
- Radio listeners tend to have one or two favorite stations and listen up to several hours daily.

Regardless of the specific techniques used by media planners to determine proper levels of reach and frequency, the overriding motive remains the same—to achieve cost efficiency with your media dollars. One of the most significant changes in media planning in recent years is a move from the goal of audience accumulation to one of measuring the *effectiveness* of the audience reached. In other words, advertisers realize that every member of a medium is not equal, even those with similar demographic characteristics.

The measurement of effective audiences takes a number of forms. Planners use a number of techniques to exclude waste circulation. For example, they develop estimates of communication impact versus exposure and they add qualitative variables such as media/message compatibility to their equations. Regardless of how they approach the issue, the overriding motive is to more precisely gauge the value of a particular prospect, medium, or message to the overall measure of advertising effectiveness.

THE MEDIA SCHEDULE

media schedule The detailed plan or calendar showing when ads and commercials will be distributed and in what media vehicles they will appear.

One of the final steps in the media-planning process is the development of a detailed **media schedule.** The media schedule is the calendar or blueprint for the media portion of the campaign. It also is the guide for media buyers to execute the media strategy developed by the planner. The schedule must offer in specific detail exactly what media will be bought, when they will be purchased, and how much time or space will be used for each advertisement or commercial. For example, if we decide to purchase *Sports Illustrated*, will we use four-color or black-and-white advertisements; will we use the entire circulation of the publication or one of the numerous geographic editions offered; which weekly editions will we buy?

The advertising schedule for a national brand may entail dozens or even hundreds of similar decisions. If the local broadcast is a primary medium, there may be separate groups of media buyers who negotiate and purchase hundreds of radio and television stations. If cable or broadcast networks are a primary building block of the schedule, senior media executives with extensive television buying experience will negotiate buys that may run into the millions of dollars. Such advertising giants as General Motors and Procter & Gamble may spend over $1 million daily on network television alone. Television media budgets at this level are executed in close coordination among senior marketing executives on the client side, their counterparts at agency or independent media-buying firms, and, of course, the networks.

Another concern at all levels of broadcast buys, but especially among networks and major affiliates, is time availability. As will be discussed in Chapter 8, just because you want to buy spots on *NYPD Blue* or *Frasier* doesn't mean they will be available. It is not unusual for a media-buying group to spend several days negotiating for time on a single network program.

The process of broadcast buying has improved in recent years through the introduction of electronic data interchange (EDI). Basically, EDI is a means of connecting the agencies, clients, and media involved in the buying process in a paperless system that allows the exchange of insertion orders and invoice electronically. Not only is the system more efficient than former approaches to media buying, but it significantly reduces errors by decreasing the number of people involved in the buying and billing process.

Another electronic media-buying process is the Internet. In the last two years, several companies have offered brokering services between advertisers and stations. These services not only list inventories of broadcast spots, but act as a central clearing house where media buyers can bid on available time. To this point, such services are a minor part of the total television time buying process, but they are becoming more important as the process of linking stations with agencies and clients becomes more complex.

Flighting   One of the most used advertising scheduling techniques is **flighting.** Flighting consists of relatively short bursts of advertising followed by periods of total or relative inactivity. For example, a company might run a heavy schedule of advertising for six weeks and then run only an occasional advertisement to its best prospects over the next six weeks. The idea is to build audience perception for the product so that brand awareness carries over those periods of inactivity. Done correctly, the advertiser achieves the same brand awareness at a greatly reduced cost compared to a steady advertising schedule.

The concept is obviously appealing to advertisers who rarely think they have enough funds to reach all their prospects with a consistent advertising program. The problem facing the advertiser is that available research on flighting cannot predict precisely the awareness levels needed to achieve any particular flighting strategy. One thing is certain, advertisers must guard against significant erosion of brand awareness during breaks between flights. Exhibit 7.7 demonstrates the ideal outcome of a properly executed flighting strategy compared to a steady schedule both using the same advertising budget.

In the steady schedule audience awareness peaks fairly quickly (after about 20 weeks) and afterwards shows little if any increase. The flighting schedule grows much more slowly, but because of budget savings it is able to reach more prospects and therefore actually achieve higher levels of brand awareness in the long term. As we cautioned earlier, an advertiser must be careful to consider the communication component of the media plan. Some media planners think that a flighting plan may sacrifice depth of communication even though minimal awareness may be achieved.

Regardless of the flighting schedule used, the following factors should be considered before using the strategy:

1. *Competitive spending.* How does your plan coincide with primary competitors? Are you vulnerable to competition between flights?
2. *Timing of flights.* Does the schedule go contrary to any seasonal features found in the product purchase cycle?

flighting   Flight is the length of time a broadcaster's campaign runs. Can be days, weeks, or months—but does not refer to a year. A flighting schedule alternates periods of activity with periods of inactivity.

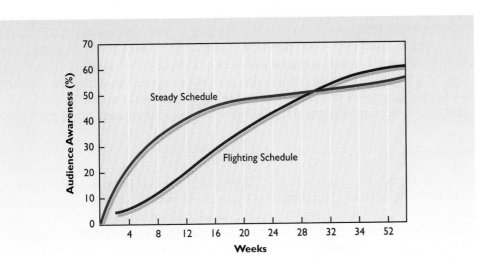

Exhibit

7.7

Steady Versus Flighting Media Schedules

3. *Advertising decay.* Are you spending enough in peak periods to remain visible between flights?

4. *Secondary media.* Should secondary or trade media be used between flights to maintain minimal visibility?

A less extreme form of flighting is called *pulsing.* Pulsing schedules use advertising more or less continuously throughout the year, but with peaks during certain periods. These peaks coincide with primary sales periods or a special promotion during contests or sweepstakes.

The Pressure of Competition

Advertising operates in a competitive environment, usually with a number of companies vying for the same consumers. Advertisers must be constantly aware of competitors' advertising strategy, product development, pricing tactics, and other marketing and promotional maneuvers. The media planner must not only develop an effective campaign for a product, but must do so in a way that distinguishes their client's brand from the competition.

The media planner also must walk a tightrope between a healthy respect for competitors' actions and blindly reacting to every competitive twist and turn. Rather than operating from a defensive mentality, advertisers should take a practical stance in determining what their marketing and advertising plans can reasonably accomplish and how they meet the inroads of competing brands.

Many advertisers find it extremely difficult to analyze the market environment objectively. One of the primary functions of an advertising agency is to bring an objective voice to the table. Companies sometimes unrealistically judge the value and quality of their products. However, a key to successful marketing is an objective appraisal of both your products and those of the competition from the consumer's perspective.

For example, consumers who are aware of your brand, but have never used it, are probably satisfied with the product they are currently buying. Both the creative and media plans will have to work hard to give these consumers a reason to switch. In fact, we may have to recognize that some market segments cannot be captured regardless of the quality of our advertising. In such a case, brand switching would be an inappropriate strategy and instead we might target another market segment with new advertising appeals, creatively positioned products, or both.

A competitive analysis must also consider various media alternatives and how they might be used to accomplish specific marketing goals. For example, a smaller company in a product category may find that television is impractical if it is dominated by advertisers with budgets that are beyond its reach. Likewise, we might find that certain media are so saturated with competitor's advertising that it will be difficult to gain attention for our message in the midst of high levels of competitive advertising. Media buyers must be aware of a number of marketing conditions in preparing the plan. The key point is that advertisers should undertake a thorough and candid appraisal of all aspects of the competitive situation. In doing so, a media buyer becomes an integral member of the campaign team.

The Budget

If there is any advertising axiom, it is that no budget is ever large enough to accomplish the task. With the spiraling cost of media over the last several years, media planners view the budget with a growing sense of frustration. In addition, media planners are constantly caught between large media (especially the major television networks) demanding higher and higher advertising rates and clients demanding more efficiency for their advertising dollars. Since the allocation of dollars to media is by far the largest portion of the advertising budget, it is the media planner who is expected to gain the greatest cost efficiencies.

Advertisers and their agencies have reacted to this cost squeeze by instituting more stringent cost controls and accountability for their advertising dollars. In addition to these stricter controls on media costs, advertisers are constantly looking for alternative methods of promotion and advertising to hold down costs. Already, consumer sales promotion (sweepstakes, coupons, price-off sales, etc.) has passed advertising in terms of total share of promotional dollars. Advertisers also are using media such as cable and first-run syndicated programming to circumvent the high cost of network television. As media continue to fragment, we will see advertisers experiment with nontraditional media vehicles, some that did not exist only a few years ago.

If there is any encouraging sign for advertisers, it is that the increases in media costs of past years seem to have moderated. Instead of double-digit increases, overall media costs are being held to levels more in line with the general rate of inflation. In response to these increases, advertisers are more precisely defining their prospects to cut down on waste circulation and are negotiating more aggressively with media for time and space. With the proliferation of media options and new technology, it is doubtful that we will see significant increases in advertising costs in the near future. However, the fragmentation of media and audiences is driving up the CPM levels to a point that it is costing more and more to reach selected target audiences.

The media schedule is normally summarized in a flowchart that presents the overall media to be included as well as their audience estimates and costs. Exhibit 7.8 presents a media schedule for an Internet company. Notice that the company uses a number of nontraditional media such as bathroom posters and college sampling packs to communicate with an eclectic and often difficult to reach audience. Exhibit 7.9 is a media schedule for a cable television network. From the media buys, it is clear that the Hispanic audience is of primary importance to this network's success.

SUMMARY

The media function is undergoing rapid and significant changes at all levels. The competition for media dollars has never been greater and the growing importance of new media technology promises to add even more options to the media mix. The trend toward localized media strategies accompanied by the expansion of global markets places even greater strains on the research, planning, and execution of media buys. As clients, agencies, and media attempt to make sense out of the mix of traditional and new media opportunities, the role of the media planner takes on even more importance.

While dealing in an unpredictable environment, a number of trends are certain to occupy the media community in coming years:

1. Requirements that media plans achieve high reach levels among prospects as opposed to accumulating total audiences.

2. How to develop media/creative strategies to fully utilize interactive media. After 200 years of the media controlling the communication process, advertisers must quickly adjust to greater audience feedback and control.

3. How to measure media synergism. Research technology must account for a complex mix of communication techniques vying for consumer time. The coming era of fiber optics, the Internet, and on-line versions of traditional media will require creative planning by media planners.

4. Control of media costs and accountability will become driving forces in the media process. As the costs of reaching narrowly defined audience segments or even individual consumers increase so does the demand for accountability from

Independent Media

Major Dotcom
4Q'00 Advertising Campaign

Consumer:	2000 Week of: (9/4 – 12/25)	Total Ins	Circ	Net (M)
Print P4CB				
DC Comics	P4CB / P4CB / P4CB	3	2,500,000	$85.2
Maxim	P4CB / P4CB / P4CB	3	2,000,000	$291.6
FHM	P4CB / P4CB / P4CB	3	400,000	$47.1
Spin	P4CB / P4CB / P4CB	3	525,000	$90.5
Next Gen	P4CB / P4CB / P4CB	3	115,000	$15.7
PSM	P4CB / P4CB / P4CB	3	300,000	$30.1
Tips & Tricks	P4CB / P4CB / P4CB	3	225,000	$12.2
WOW	P4CB / P4CB	2	300,000	$6.9
Shift	P4CB / P4CB / P4CB	3	80,000	$16.1
Vice	P4CB / P4CB / P4CB	3	77,000	$15.2
Total Print		29	6,522,000	$610.6
Bathroom Posters 750 venues in NY, Chicago, SF, and Boston	750/month — Art on disk due by 9/11	750/mo	50,625,000	$273.4
Window Shoppers 140 displays in NY, Chicago, San Francisco, Boston	140/month — Finished posters due in plant by 9/4	140/mo	22,418,340	$66.2
Outdoor (New York) Urban Panels-Manhattan	40/month — Finished panels due in plant by 9/20	40/mo	157,500,000	$324.0
Postcards NY, LA, SF, Boston 120,000 in NY; 80,000 other mkts	360,000/month — Artwork on film due by 9/11	360M/mo	1,325,700	$75.5
College Sampling 550,000 Study Breaker Packs	550,000 samples — Samples due 9/6	N/A	550,000	$48.6
Advertising Trade Cybersweeps-1/2PC plus 4-color Profile	1/2P4C (Aug.) / 1/2P4C / 1/2P4C	3	5,000	$8.5 / $1.6
Grand Total				$1,408.4

Exhibit 7.8

Major Dot.com

Courtesy: Independent Media, prepared by Brian Ludwick.

clients. What were acceptable levels of waste circulation in a period of mass media and low CPMs are no longer tolerable in a stage of individual marketing.

These are only some of the many complex issues facing the media executive of tomorrow. Regardless of what the future brings, it is clear that the media-planning function will occupy an even more important role in an era of targeted advertising. The tension between increased media costs and a search for cost efficiencies by clients will result in planners becoming more willing to try new media or spin-offs of existing media. If there is one sure trend in an otherwise unpredictable area, it is that the advertising media function will continue to look for narrowly defined markets and, with few exceptions, disregard those media vehicles that promise substantial, but largely undefined or unmeasured audiences.

REVIEW

1. How has the fragmentation of media audiences affected media planning?
2. In what significant ways has the responsibility of media planners changed during the last decade?

Independent Media

2000 Week of: 6/26 7/3 7/10 7/17 7/24 7/31 8/7 8/14 8/21 8/28 9/4 9/11 9/18 9/25 10/2 10/9	Total Ins	Net (M)
Spreads and Pages		
Nick Jr. Magazine — S5CB Position: Center Spread $13.0 / P4CB Position: TBD $6.5	2	$19.5
Parenting Category		
Parents (circ: 1,787,321) — S5CB Position: Cvr 2, Page 1 $153.8 / P5CB Position: First half, RHP $77.8	2	$231.6
Parenting (circ: 1,376,928) — S5CB Position: Pre-TOC $100.8 / P5CB Position: RHP, 1st 1/3 of book $52.5	2	$153.3
Child (circ: 923,175) — S5CB Position: Pre-TOC Pg 4-5 $62.1 / P5CB Position: Page 9, opp. Editor's Letter $31.2	2	$93.3
Offspring (circ: 200,000) — P5CB Position: NOW Section (Far Forward) $13.4	1	$13.4
Hispanic Category		
Ser Padres (circ: 407,471) — S5CB Position: Center Spread (saddle stitched) $40.1	1	$40.1
People en Espanol (circ: 292,906) — S5CB Position: 1st 20 pages (Far Forward) $42.0 / P5CB Position: First Half, RHP $21.2	2	$63.2
Latina (circ: 225,000) — S5CB Position: within TOC $27.6 / P5CB Position: Parenting section (last half) $15.2	2	$42.8
Entertainment Category		
People (circ: 3,633,146) — P5CB Position: Pixs & Pans (Far Forward) $125.7	1	$125.7
TV Guide (circ: 9,900,000) — S4CB Position: 2nd Cvr Spread $188.4 / PBW Position: Listings $73.1	2	$261.5
Time ("Flies" Program circ: 38,000) — P4CB Position: Run-of-book $0.0	1	$0.0
Total Print	18	**$1,044.4**
Radio (Target: Hispanic AD18-49)		
New York (Spanish stations only) — 150	150	$20.7
Los Angeles (Spanish stations only) — 150	150	$26.4
Miami (Spanish stations only) — 150	150	$15.3
Radio Total	150	**$62.4**
Grand Total (Print & Radio)		**$1,106.8**

Exhibit

7.9

Cable Network

3. Briefly define reach, frequency, and continuity.
4. Discuss the applications of the Brand Development Index.
5. Discuss the role of the media synergy in advertising planning.
6. What effect has audience fragmentation had on media cost?
7. Discuss cost-media buying from the perspective of the media and the advertiser?
8. Why is direct response growing at its current rate?

TAKE IT TO THE NET

We invite you to visit the Russell/Lane page on the Prentice Hall Web site at **www.prenhall.com/myphlip** for end-of-chapter exercises and applications.

Chapter 8

Using Television

CHAPTER OBJECTIVES

Nowhere is media convergence more apparent than in television. With ownership consolidations, blending of technology, and coproduced programming, television is a multidimensional medium. As the future penetration of digital television makes interactivity a reality, both advertisers and programmers will have to adapt to significant changes in the role of audiences with the medium. From a marketing standpoint, television is not a single medium, rather it is comprised of a number of related broadcast and cable entities that exhibit significant diversity as both advertising and programming sources. From the stars of network prime time to the largely unknown personalities of local cable programs, each of these segments of the television industry have their special characteristics. After reading this chapter you will understand:

>> the diversified nature of the television industry

>> the multiple roles of television as an advertising medium

>> the changing position of network television

>> syndicated rating services and television research methodologies

>> the various segments of television viewing

Pros

1. Television reaches 98 percent of all U.S. households weekly and is particularly popular with 18 to 34-year-olds, a primary market for advertisers.
2. Television's combination of color, sound, and motion offers creative flexibility for virtually any product message.
3. Despite recent audience declines, television remains extremely efficient for large advertisers needing to reach a mass audience. By utilizing selected cable outlets and local broadcast stations, advertisers are able to provide a local or regional component to national television schedules.

4. Government-mandated moves to digital television will open more opportunities for advertising and programming by 2006.

Cons

1. The television message is perishable and easily forgotten without expensive repetition.
2. The television audience is fragmented and skewed toward lower income consumers. Daily viewing time declines significantly as income increases.
3. Shorter spots, some as short as 15 seconds, have contributed to confusing commercial clutter.
4. The introduction of the remote control and channel surfing by viewers have greatly restricted the time spent with commercials by the average television user.

Television, so ubiquitous and pervasive in our everyday lives, had very humble beginnings. In the 1920s when Philo Farnsworth, an Idaho teenager, envisioned the transmission of pictures over radio waves, he could not have imagined the medium that he was helping to launch. Unlike many scientists of the time who were experimenting with spinning disks similar to early film technology, Farnsworth was working on an all-electronic system. On September 7, 1927, Farnsworth and his team transmitted a line from one room to another. In his journal entry for the day, he stated:

> The received line picture was evident this time. Lines of various widths could be transmitted and any movement at right angles to the line was easily recognized. This was experiment #12.[1]

And so the age of television began.

In 1998, television marked its fiftieth anniversary as a major advertising medium. However, at an age when most institutions are maturing, television continues to exhibit dramatic change and innovations. Television-viewing levels and advertising dollars have never been higher and government-mandated introduction of digital technology by 2006 will bring even more innovations in both advertising and programming. Television has long been the most influential medium for most of the population. So much so, that even people who do not watch television are strongly influenced by it. Television news sets the political agenda, entertainment programming creates fads from hairstyles to the end zone antics of professional football players, and TV advertising slogans become part of our everyday vocabulary.

In May 1998, 40 million households tuned in to the final episode of *Seinfeld*. Many of the viewers had come to identify with Jerry, Elaine, George, and Kramer as members of their families and wanted to see what the future held for the group. Such is the power of television. It is more than a simple channel of communication. In a real sense, it connects on an emotional basis with the viewing audience and makes them part of the event they are watching.

The numbers for television are stunning. More than 98 percent of households have at least one set and average daily household viewing is more than seven hours. In fact, Americans spend 50 percent more time with television than with radio, the second most used medium and 10 times more than with newspapers. As

---

[1]David Fisher and Marshall Jon Fisher, *Tube: The Invention of Television* (Washington: Counterpoint, 1996), 22.

impressive as the sheer numbers are, it is the qualitative dimensions of television as a source of news, entertainment, and advertising that are even more significant.

According to the Television Bureau of Advertising (TvB), television is regarded as the primary source of news by 69 percent of respondents, with newspapers second at 37 percent. When respondents were asked which medium has the greatest credibility, television again is tops at 53 percent, with newspapers trailing at 23 percent. Obviously, advertisers want to be associated with a medium that not only reaches all segments of the population, but does so with high believability.

TvB research also found that television's credibility as a news source carries over to positive attitudes toward television advertising. For example, when asked about the image of media advertising, television ranked first as the most authoritative (52%); most exciting (77%); most influential (80%); and most believable (40%). Not only do consumers hold television in high regard as an advertising medium, but 74 percent think that commercials are a fair price to pay for access to free programming.[2]

Over the years, the complexion of television has changed dramatically. Television is moving from a mass medium to a niche medium similar in many respects to radio and magazines. Beginning with the VCR and moving toward the inevitable introduction of a number of interactive formats, the audience has become active participants in the communication process rather than passive receivers. A major catalyst for the introduction of two-way television communication is the Internet. Studies show that viewing levels among households using the Internet demonstrate lower levels of television viewing. Most predictions see Internet household penetration increasing significantly in the next several years. Consequently, it will be imperative for television to continue to move toward interactivity, which can combat the appeal of the Internet. Television's concerns are all the more warranted since research indicates that most adopters of new technology are concentrated among upscale consumers—prime targets for television advertisers.

TELEVISION AS AN ADVERTISING MEDIUM

The business of television, and advertising is a major part of that business, is to function as an audience delivery system. Commercial television programming decisions are rarely made on the basis of aesthetics, entertainment value, or which news personality is most credible. Instead, "These are merely the vehicles for pricing and delivering the real product in the television business: eyeballs. . . . television is a business for the mass manufacture, collection, and distribution of viewers to advertisers. . . . Not stars and stories, eyeballs and households."[3]

With an annual investment of more than $50 million in all forms of television advertising, it is difficult to imagine the medium without commercials. However, in the earliest days of experimental television, commercials were actually illegal. It wasn't until May 2, 1941 that the **Federal Communications Commission (FCC)** granted 10 commercial television licenses and allowed the sale of commercial time. The first commercial aired on July 1, 1941 during a Dodgers-Phillies baseball game. It was sponsored by Bulova watches and cost $4 for air time and $5 for station charges. It is estimated that it was seen by 4,000 people.[4]

For a number of years, television has added program options at a growing rate. In the 1970s, a few independent stations offered sports and off-network reruns as an alternative to network affiliate programming. By the 1980s, cable was extending the number of stations available to the average household and a limited number of

Federal Communications Commission (FCC) The federal authority empowered to license radio and TV stations and to assign wavelengths to stations "in the public interest."

---

[2]"TV basics," a publication of the Television Bureau of Advertising, on-line, www.tvb.org.
[3]Barry L. Sherman, *The Television Standard* (New York: Gerson Lehrman Group, 1999), 2.
[4]Jane Dalzell, "Who's on first," *Advertising Age, 50 Years of TV Advertising*, Spring 1995, 8.

superstations such as TBS and WGN were accessible to most cable homes. However, although the number of channels increased, the variety of programming—most network retreads—remained relatively stagnant except for sports, which proliferated at a quickening pace. However, by the 1990s, this situation took a dramatic turn as cable networks realized that in order to sustain their audiences and compete with the major broadcast networks for advertisers, they had to develop original programming.

Led by premium cable services such as Showtime and HBO, cable began to produce a number of original movies and even an occasional series. During the 1990s, the premium channels were joined by major cable outlets such as TNT and USA in producing a number of made-for-TV films. In addition, basic cable networks were producing highly acclaimed programs such as A&E's *Biography*. More importantly, they were beginning to compete for the prime-time audience long dominated by the broadcast networks. Because both advertisers and audiences were attracted to these new programs, televison fragmentation accelerated and became the order of the day.

In 20 years, television has moved from basically three program and advertising options to a point where the average household receives more than 50 channels. As Clarence Page, noted columnist and television commentator, stated, "In my youth, Americans were united by watching the three network channels. Today, the audience is fragmented over dozens of channels and thousands of other new media choices, including video games, CD-ROMs, and the Internet. With broadcast audiences now fragmenting, we have to ask what happens to that common culture, those common reference points."[5]

The same television fragmentation that creates this lack of a common political culture also is making it more and more difficult for advertisers to reach large audiences with a unified selling message. By the end of the decade, most observers believe that television (or whatever convergence of cable/computer/telephone technology is the standard) will offer tenfold the options we have today.

With digital capabilities, networks can deliver a number of services to a household over the same conduit. Not only will there be more options, but they will be tailored to the entertainment, news, and buying preferences of individual viewers on an interactive basis. In this interactive environment viewers can participate in their favorite game shows and order merchandise directly from commercials. The vertical integration and capital resources of conglomerates such as Disney and AOL Time Warner make this new media landscape closer to a reality than many believe. It also will change the traditional relationships between the television industry and its advertisers.

Another advantage of broadband, digital delivery is that it allows multiple uses (or even versions) of programming; reaching viewers at their convenience and depreciating program costs over multiple cycles. For example, with additional channel capabilities, ". . . CBS could repeat its afternoon soap operas at night for viewers who missed them during the day. NBC could run 'Jay Leno' and 'Conan O'Brien' in the daytime on a second channel in hopes of finding a newer or larger audience. At the local level, TV stations could run their morning, mid-day, and early news programs a second time, perhaps in prime time, when their main digital channel was carrying network programs."[6]

The "new" television will be characterized by a move to the local level. Many predict that the mass era of television is quickly coming to an end. It is being replaced by a localized medium more in touch with its audience and soon will be

---

[5] Clarence Page, "A bridge to the new media century," The Park Distinguished Visitors Series, Ithaca College, 2000, 6.
[6] Sherman, *The Television Standard*, 161.

communicating on a two-way basis. "The broadcast model and the interactive model are converging, creating one of America's most vibrant industries. Within this industry, localism will be at the epicenter of convergence. Those with the best-known and most trusted local television brands and relationships will be best positioned to capitalize on these convergence opportunities."[7] Obviously, the major networks have the brand equity to be future leaders regardless of the method of advertising and programming distribution.

While many of the technological changes are at least a few years in the future, television remains the primary medium for many advertisers. In addition to its high household penetration, television offers creative flexibility not found in any other medium. With its combination of sight, sound, color, and motion, television is equally adept at communicating humorous, serious, or tongue-in-cheek commercials. Television is a 24-hour medium with an ability to reach viewers of every lifestyle from housewives to third-shift workers. Television also offers a number of advertising formats from the 10-second ID to the 30-minute program-length promotion.

Limitations of Television

Cost   Advertising and promotion, regardless of the medium or methods of distribution, are expensive. In recent years, there has been a great deal of publicity about the cost of television and commercials—especially those carried in blockbuster programs such as the Super Bowl, *Friends*, or *E.R.* However, most people would be surprised to learn that even the most costly television commercials are much less expensive on a CPM basis than print media. For example, the average prime-time television commercial has a CPM of $13–15 compared to a typical daily newspaper that delivers 1,000 readers for $50–60 or a national magazine's rate of $25–35. Even with the highest rating series charging $500,000 for a 30-second spot, television is still cost-efficient for businesses needing to reach huge numbers of people.

However, as household viewing hours remain constant, the growing number of options for television audiences has created an extremely fragmented audience and generally lower ratings for all segments of the industry. As discussed earlier, this trend and resulting CPM increases will probably accelerate in future years. Network advertisers, especially products depending on mass marketing such as package goods, automobiles, and fast-food franchises, are particularly concerned about these increases. They know that in spite of high CPM costs and continuing commercial rate increases, there is still no more efficient method of reaching a broadly based consumer market than through television.

However, with the competitive environment for viewer's time and attention, it also is imperative to make attention-getting commercials and they are often the most costly. Consequently, it is important to consider not only the cost of television time, but also the production cost associated with commercials. Chapter 19 discusses in detail the process of commercial production. However, with some network television commercials budgeted for as much as $1,000,000, production expenses are another important cost consideration for any television advertiser.

clutter   Refers to a proliferation of commercials (in a medium) that reduces the impact of any single message.

Clutter   Television **clutter** is defined as any nonprogram material carried during or between shows. Commercials account for more than 80 percent of this material with the other time devoted to public service announcements and program promotional spots. In the last two years, the issue of television commercial clutter has become a major topic among advertisers and their agencies. For example, the 4As has highlighted clutter as one of the primary problems facing advertising.

---

[7]Hearst-Argyle Television, *1999 Annual Report*, 8.

Obviously, as the number of commercials increase, there is an adverse effect on consumer advertising awareness. As one media executive observed, "The combination of demand exceeding supply [of commercial time] and the networks' need to compensate for less revenue due to lower ratings have resulted in the addition of more commercial units."[8]

The clutter controversy has become more heated with reports that 1999 saw a significant jump in commercial time compared to previous years. Studies showed that both ABC and NBC averaged more than 15 minutes of nonprogram content. The rate of prime-time clutter approaches what used to be the norm in daytime—a period where more commercials have traditionally run. One media director pointed out the significance of this prime-time increase, "Certainly one criterion for prime's premium rates has been a substantially less cluttered environment. When you start to see a full 25 percent of an hour made up of nonprogramming minutes you have to say to yourself maybe prime is no longer worth that premium."[9]

Advertisers also point out that not only has the total nonprogram time increased, but the number of commercials has also grown with the use of shorter spots. Prior to the early 1970s, 60-second commercials were the norm. They were replaced by 30-second commercials, but now more than 10 percent of commercials are either 10- or 15-seconds. Research has shown that the number of commercials contributes to the perception of clutter even when overall commercial time remains constant.

The significance of the debate over clutter was summed up by Jon Mandel, chairman of the 4As national TV and radio committee, "It's gotten to the point that a number of us on the advertiser and agency side feel the networks are threatening the very existence of ad-supported, mass-reach broadcast television by adding too many commercial minutes."[10]

THE RATING-POINT SYSTEM

TV advertisers evaluate the medium according to the delivery of certain target audiences. In the case of networks and large affiliates, advertisers tend to look for exposure to fairly broad audience segments, such as women aged 18 to 49. Cable networks and some independent stations are evaluated by their ability to deliver more narrowly defined audiences that are both smaller in size and more expensive to reach on a CPM basis but have less waste circulation.

The basic measure of television is the **rating point**. The rating, expressed as a percentage of some population (usually TV households), gives the advertiser a measure of coverage based on the potential of the market. The rating is usually calculated as follows:

$$\text{Rating} = \text{program audience}/\text{total TV households}$$

When ratings are expressed as percentages of individuals, the same formula is used, but the population is some target segment rather than households. For example, if we are interested only in 18- to 34-year-old males, the formula would be:

$$\text{Rating} = \text{18–34 males viewing program}/\text{total 18–34 males in population}$$

rating point (TV)
The percentage of TV households in a market a TV station reaches with a program. The percentage varies with the time of day. A station may have a 10 rating between 6:00 and 6:30 P.M. and a 20 rating between 9:00 and 9:30.

---

[8]Allen Banks, "Agencies take action on industry's top 12 issues," *Advertising Age*, 28 February 2000, M-2.

[9]Chuck Ross, "TV commercial clutter has ad buyers worried," *Advertising Age*, 6 December 1999, 77.

[10]Chuck Ross and Wayne Friedman, "Big advertisers, shops bristle at net TV ad clutter," *Advertising Age*, 13 September 1999, 2.

Exhibit

8.1

GRPs measure weight of an
advertising broadcast
schedule.

Vehicle	Rating	Cost	Spots	GRPs
All My Children	8.6	$15,950	25	215.0
General Hospital	8.7	15,950	25	217.5
Guiding Light	7.4	15,950	19	140.6
One Life to Live	7.4	15,950	14	103.6
Total GRPs				676.7

Reach = 99.9.
Frequency = 6.77.

A household rating of 12 for a program means that 12 percent of all households in a particular area tuned their sets in to that station. Prime-time network programs usually achieve a rating of between 9 and 25, with the average being around 15.

As we discuss later in this chapter, TV advertising is rarely bought on a program-by-program basis. Instead, advertisers schedule a package of spots that are placed in a number of programs and dayparts. The weight of a schedule is measured in terms of the total ratings for all commercial spots bought (the **gross rating points** or *GRPs*).

**gross rating points
(GRP)** Each rating point
represents 1 percent of the
universe being measured for the
market. In TV it is 1 percent of
the households having TV sets in
that area.

GRPs were calculated by multiplying the insertions times the rating. In the case of *All My Children*, the rating was 8.6 × 25 (the number of insertions) = 215 *GRPs* (see Exhibit 8.1).

Advertisers also use *GRPs* as the basis for examining the relationship between reach and frequency. These relationships can be expressed mathematically:

$$R \times F = GRP$$

$$\frac{GRP}{R} = F \quad \text{and} \quad \frac{GRP}{F} = R$$

where R = reach and F = frequency.

To use these relationships, you must know (or be able to estimate) the unduplicated audience. In the TV schedule in Exhibit 8.1, we estimate that we have reached virtually the entire target market (reach = 99.9 percent) and that the average number of times we reached each person in the audience was 6.77. We can check the formulas using the solutions previously calculated:

$$R \times F = GRP \quad \text{or} \quad 99.9 \times 6.77 = 676$$

$$\frac{GRP}{F} = R \quad \text{or} \quad \frac{676}{6.77} = 99.9$$

$$\frac{GRP}{R} = F \quad \text{or} \quad \frac{676}{99.9} = 6.77$$

One of the principal merits of the *GRP* system is that it provides a common base that proportionately accommodates markets of all sizes. One *GRP* in New York has exactly the same relative weight as one *GRP* in Salt Lake City. *GRPs* cannot be compared from one market to another unless the markets are of identical size. However, Exhibit 8.2 shows that the cost of TV commercial time varies by city size. Here is an idea of the use of *GRPs* in two markets, Los Angeles and Boston:

Exhibit

8.2

Television cost efficiency is
measured on a cost of
audience delivered basis.

Market	TV Homes (Thousands)	Avg. Cost per Spot	Avg. Prime Time Rating
Los Angeles	4,241	$2,800	18
Boston	1,930	2,200	18

The advertiser has to decide how much weight (how many *GRP*s) to place in his or her markets and for how long a period. This is a matter of experience and of watching what the competition is doing. Suppose the advertiser selects 100 to 150 per week as the *GRP* figure (considered a good working base). Within this figure, the advertiser has great discretion in each market. How shall the time be allocated: Put it all on one station? Divide it among all the stations? Use what yardstick to decide? The answers depend on whether the goal is reach or frequency.

Look again at the hypothetical pricing structure in Exhibit 8.2.

If we buy three prime-time spots in these markets, we would expect to receive 54 *GRP*s (3 spots × 18 average rating). However, it would be a serious mistake to equate a 54-*GRP* buy in Los Angeles with the same level in Boston. In Los Angeles, 54 *GRP*s would deliver 2,290,140 household impressions (0.54 × 4,241,000 HH, or households) at a cost of $8,400 (3 spots × $2,800 per spot). On the other hand, a 54-*GRP* buy in Boston would deliver 1,042,200 household impressions at a cost of $6,600. To estimate buys, advertisers often use the **cost per rating point** (*CPP*) calculation:

cost per rating point (CCP) The cost per rating point is used to estimate the cost of TV advertising on several shows.

$$CPP = \frac{\text{cost of schedule}}{\text{GRPs}}$$

In this case:

Boston: $\quad CPP = \dfrac{\$6,600}{54} = \$122.22$

Los Angeles: $\quad CPP = \dfrac{\$8,400}{54} = \$155.55$

If we make the mistake of comparing *GRP*s from markets of different sizes, it would appear that a rating point costs 27 percent more in Los Angeles than in Boston. However, a rating point represents 42,410 households (1 percent of 4,241,000) in Los Angeles versus only 19,300 in Boston. A rating point in Boston costs $33.33 less than in Los Angeles. However, the advertiser is actually getting 219 percent more households for only a 27 percent higher cost in Los Angeles. So Boston is hardly a bargain.

In addition to the problem of intermarket comparisons, the *GRP* has other limitations. It does not tell us the number of *prospects* for the product who are being reached by a program. Still, the *GRP* concept does provide a unified dimension for making scheduling judgments.

It must also be remembered that *GRP*s alone cannot tell how effectively a broadcast schedule is performing. If an advertiser's target audience is women aged 18 to 49, for example, 5 *GRP*s will often deliver more women in that group than 10 *GRP*s will. This, as you would expect, is a function of where the *GRP*s are scheduled. Five *GRP*s during a Sunday night movie will almost always deliver many times more women aged 18 to 49 than will 10 *GRP*s scheduled on a Saturday morning.

SHARE OF AUDIENCE

Although the rating is the basic audience-measurement statistic for TV, another measure, the **share of audience** (or simply, share), is often used to determine the success of a show. The share is defined as the percentage of households using television that are watching a particular show. It is used by advertisers to determine how a show is doing against its direct competition.

share of audience The percentage of households using TV tuned to a particular program.

Let us assume that the *Today Show* has 5,000 households watching it in a market with 50,000 households. In this case we know that the rating for the *Today Show* would be 10.

$$\text{Rating} = \frac{\textit{Today} \text{ viewers}}{\text{total TV households}} \times 100 = \frac{5,000}{50,000} \times 100 = 10$$

The share calculates the percentage of households using television (*HUT*) that are tuned to the program. Let us assume that of the 50,000 households, 25,000 are watching television. In this case, the share for the *Today Show* would be 20:

$$\text{Share} = \frac{\textit{Today} \text{ viewers}}{HUT} \times 100 = \frac{5,000}{25,000} \times 100 = 20$$

It is understood that both the ratings and share of audience are expressed as percentages (hence, the factor of 100 in the equations). Therefore, we do not use decimal points to refer to the measures in the example as "10 percent" and "20 percent." Instead, we say that the rating is 10 and the share is 20.

THE MANY FACES OF TELEVISION

While the average viewer probably makes little distinction among cable, premium cable, broadcast networks, syndicated programs, daytime, or any of the other permutations of television, they are in many respects unique marketing vehicles. Each of the various segments of the medium has its own advertising pricing structure, programming, target audience, and rating expectations.

Except for the fact that they appear on the TV screen, there is little similarity between The Travel Channel and the Cartoon Channel or Home Shopping Network and MTV. Television has become primarily an individual-user medium with the majority of the audience viewing alone during most dayparts. The use of television as a personal medium is further demonstrated by the number of multi-set households.

In the near term, as television technology continues to evolve, the medium will demonstrate even more diverse advertising opportunities. To some viewers, it will be primarily a source of immediate information such as stock quotes, for others it will remain the primary entertainment outlet, and, as we enter a wireless society, for still others, an out-of-home companion serving multiple purposes.

This section examines the many aspects of this extremely complex medium, which occupies so much of our time and advertisers' dollars.

NETWORK TELEVISION

In the 1987–88 television season, *The Bill Cosby Show* was the top-rated program with an average audience share of 44 percent. That same year, *Hunter*, a predictable police drama had a respectable 19 rating with an average share of 34. Now fast-forward 10 years to the top-rated, and award-winning *Seinfeld*, a show that many people would regard as a cult classic. In reality, *Seinfeld* finished behind the largely forgotten *Hunter* in average audience share for almost its entire run. Exhibit 8.3 shows the erosion of the audiences of top network shows over the years.

While much has been written about the decline of network television numbers, why should anyone be surprised? Given the proliferation of television options, it would be an impossible task for **networks** to maintain earlier audience levels. As the television landscape is peppered with competition from The Discovery Channel to The Disney Channel, it is amazing that the Big Three (ABC, CBS, and NBC) have sustained the 45-percent share levels they currently enjoy. Remember, the three networks represent approximately 6 percent of the total viewing options open to the television audience. Rest assured that any of their competitors would trade places with them in a heartbeat!

networks Interconnecting stations for the simultaneous transmission of TV or radio broadcasts.

Networks will continue to prosper, albeit at a lower level of audience and profitability, because they provide the best option for reaching a mass audience for a number of national advertisers. As one media executive pointed out, "... the broadcast networks play a unique, irreplaceable role for advertisers and the agencies that serve them ... as the need to reach both mass and targeted audiences only builds in difficulty and importance."[11]

**TOP RANKED REGULAR PROGRAM SERIES
BASED ON HOUSEHOLD RATINGS**

Year	Program	Network	Household Rating	Share
1950-51	Texaco Star Theatre	NBC	61.6	81
1951-52	Arthur Godfrey's Talent Scouts	CBS	53.8	78
1952-53	I Love Lucy	CBS	67.3	68
1953-54	I Love Lucy	CBS	58.8	67
1954-55	I Love Lucy	CBS	49.3	66
1955-56	$64,000 Question	CBS	47.5	65
1956-57	I Love Lucy	CBS	43.7	58
1957-58	Gunsmoke	CBS	43.1	51
1958-59	Gunsmoke	CBS	39.6	60
1959-60	Gunsmoke	CBS	40.3	65
1960-61	Gunsmoke	CBS	37.3	62
1961-62	Wagon Train	NBC	32.1	53
1962-63	Beverly Hillbillies	CBS	36.0	54
1963-64	Beverly Hillbillies	CBS	39.1	58
1964-65	Bonanza	NBC	36.3	54
1965-66	Bonanza	NBC	31.8	48
1966-67	Bonanza	NBC	29.1	45
1967-68	Andy Griffith	CBS	27.6	42
1968-69	Laugh-In	NBC	31.8	45
1969-70	Laugh-In	NBC	26.3	39
1970-71	Marcus Welby, MD	ABC	29.6	52
1971-72	All in the Family	CBS	34.0	54
1972-73	All in the Family	CBS	33.3	53
1973-74	All in the Family	CBS	31.2	51
1974-75	All in the Family	CBS	30.2	51
1975-76	All in the Family	CBS	30.1	44
1976-77	Happy Days	ABC	31.5	47
1977-78	Laverne & Shirley	ABC	31.6	49
1978-79	Laverne & Shirley	ABC	30.5	48
1979-80	60 Minutes	CBS	28.2	32
1980-81	Dallas	CBS	31.2	52
1981-82	Dallas	CBS	28.4	45
1982-83	60 Minutes	CBS	25.5	40
1983-84	Dallas	CBS	25.7	40
1984-85	Dynasty	ABC	25.0	37
1985-86	The Cosby Show	NBC	33.8	51
1986-87	The Cosby Show	NBC	34.9	53
1987-88	The Cosby Show	NBC	27.8	44
1988-89	The Cosby Show	NBC	25.5	41
1989-90	Roseanne	ABC	23.4	35
1990-91	Cheers	NBC	21.6	34
1991-92	60 Minutes	CBS	21.7	36
1992-93	60 Minutes	CBS	21.6	35
1993-94	Home Improvement	ABC	21.9	33
1994-95	Seinfeld	NBC	20.4	31
1995-96	E.R.	NBC	22.0	36
1996-97	E.R.	NBC	21.2	35
1997-98	Seinfeld	NBC	22.0	33
1998-99	E.R.	NBC	17.8	29

Exhibit

8.3

Historical Ratings

[11]David Poltrack, "In our own defense," *Agency*, Fall 1999, 44.

This section discusses some of the major elements necessary to understand television networks as an advertising medium.

Clearance and Affiliate Compensation   Networks are comprised of local stations that contract to carry network programming. The exceptions are the so-called O&O (owned-and-operated) stations of the networks. These stations (e.g., KABC in Los Angeles and WNBC in New York City) are located in a few major markets and make up a small minority of any network's station line-up. The three major networks have approximately 220 affiliates and FOX about 170. The newest networks, The WB and UPN, have affiliation agreements with smaller stations in most markets. In fact, some of The WB and UPN affiliates are *secondary* affiliates, which means they belong to another network and air WB or UPN shows on a delayed basis, often during non-prime-time hours.

Networks sell national advertising on the basis of station **clearance.** Network clearance is expressed as the percentage of the network's line-up that has agreed to clear their schedules for network programming. In the case of the top four networks, clearances normally run close to 100 percent. The new networks often express their clearance rates as a percentage of the U.S. population that is potentially reached. Clearance rates are crucial to the economics of the smaller networks. For example, if a network fails to get clearance in New York City, it is shut out of 10 percent of the total national audience. Until a network reaches 70-percent potential coverage, it is usually not considered a national program by major advertisers.

Another primary factor in the relationship between networks and affiliates is network **compensation**. Compensation is a system whereby networks share advertising revenues with their affiliates in return for using local station time for its programs. At one time, station compensation was a major profit item for most stations. However, as the cost of network programming has increased and audience levels have fallen, the relationship between networks and stations over compensation has become contentious. Basically, networks have taken the position that the value of a station's local advertising spots are in large measure a result of the audience gained through popular network programming. Consequently, the networks are demanding that their affiliates share in the cost of this programming. For their part, the stations contend that without availability to stations, there would be no networks. In the future, stations may find that rather than a source of profit, affiliation may be an expense. To date, the reduction in station compensation has taken four forms:

1. *Steep reductions in compensation fees paid to stations.* In past years, total network compensation fees have been as much as $200 million annually. However, by 1998, that figure had dropped to $150,000. Television executives think that compensation fees will drop even further, or be eliminated altogether, in the future.

2. *The networks have proposed reducing the number of commercial spots they make available to local stations during network shows.* Instead of returning the time, spots would be sold on a national basis and the money retained by the networks.

3. *Direct payments by stations to networks for special programming.* For example, CBS and FOX assess their affiliates approximately $100 million to help pay for the expensive rights to NFL Football.

4. *Require fees for network affiliation.* This approach turns the traditional network/affiliate relationship on its head by requiring payment from the affiliates to belong to a network. To date, this approach has been confined to The WB Network.

Regardless of the form the compensation debate takes, the root causes of costly programming and falling revenues will make compensation a continuing issue for discussion between networks and their affiliates.

---

clearance   The percentage of network affiliates that carries a particular network program.

compensation   The payment of clearance fees by a TV network to local stations carrying its shows.

Network Ownership   Despite the fact that the major television networks are very large companies with revenues in the billions of dollars, each of them is a relatively small part of a major conglomerate. Not only are the networks part of a larger company, they are not even the most profitable media holding of these corporations. For example, Walt Disney Company owns the ABC Television Network and a number of local affiliated stations. It also owns, among many other holdings, ESPN's four networks and its magazine, Lifetime and A&E Networks, and, of course, The Disney Channel. In addition, the company owns theme parks as well as film studios and production facilities. A similar situation exists for each of the other networks.

The accelerated pace of acquisitions and mergers among media companies has raised some troubling questions in a number of quarters. For example, will the concentration of broadcast and cable ownership restrain the free flow of news and information especially in the case of stories that relate to their parent companies? Will a lack of competition among media affect the economic marketplace in setting advertising rates? Will television content be restricted if networks are pressured to buy programming from production studios owned by the same parent company? Some have argued that Congress should prohibit companies from owning both the means of distribution (a station or network) and the production of content (a program production studio). It is unlikely to happen, but advertisers are very much concerned with the consequences of a marketing environment dominated by a few companies.

Network Commercial Pricing and Declining Audience Shares   As we noted earlier, television is in the business of delivering prospects to advertisers. The networks find themselves in the difficult position of encountering higher and higher program costs at a time when audience levels do not justify significant commercial price increases. Primetime spots vary according to ratings and audience demographics, but an average 30-second commercial will cost approximately $170,000 on the three major networks. At the high side, a spot on a show such as *E.R.* will be in the neighborhood of $500,000, while *Diagnosis Murder* with its lower ratings and older audience will bring something over $100,000.

In the past few seasons, network advertising revenues have grown significantly. However, media buyers complain that these increases are a result of more commercials (the clutter problem) and unjustified rate increases that have resulted in higher CPMs. The networks are often in a dilemma, caught between advertisers clamoring for better cost efficiencies and stars of top-rated series demanding higher salaries. A further complication is that, as shows such as *Frazier*, *Friends*, and *Ally McBeal*, age, there is an inevitable slippage in ratings. However, each year the stars earn higher salaries and networks are reluctant to cancel even their more expensive series, fearing that the odds are slim that potential replacements would fare as well.

Block Programming   Network executives not only have to choose programs that will appeal to a large segment of households and at least a handful of major advertisers, but their work is made even more difficult by the fickle television audience. Research has consistently shown that shows do not stand on their own, but are greatly influenced by the programs directly before, called the *lead-in*, and the total daypart schedule, called a *block*.

The importance of lead-ins can be seen in the investment local stations make to schedule the most popular programming they can buy prior to their early evening news shows. The demand for strong news lead-ins is in large measure responsible for the enormous prices paid for off-network syndicated programs. The same principle is at work in building a network schedule. Programmers strive to make sure that individual programs will attain high ratings, but just as importantly they want to insure that the block will work together to attract consistently high audience levels.

block programming
A series of television shows that appeals to the same general audience.

Network programmers are very aware of the ebb and flow of audiences as they move from one program to another. The pricing of new network shows is dependent in large measure on their placement in the network schedule. Advertisers know that programs that follow proven hits have a high probability of success. An even better situation is the occasional new show that is scheduled between two popular returning programs. This is called a *hammock position*—the analogy being that the new program is placed between two trees (hit shows). Once a new show is on the air, it must hold its own and is judged by how it keeps the audience from its lead-in and sustains the strength of the block.

Network Television Advertising Criteria   Clients and their advertising agencies apply a variety of criteria in determining if, and to what extent, they will use network television spots. However, buying decisions are largely determined by three factors: demos, CPM, and demand.[12]

■ *Demos.* Whereas, at one time households were the unit of measure, today television advertisers place major emphasis on the demographics of television audiences. This change in criteria has altered the manner in which networks choose shows and the pricing structure for advertisers. For most advertisers, the makeup of the audience of potential network buys has become more important than the size of the audience. Of course, both advertisers and the networks demand that a show attain a certain minimum rating, but the price for shows with favorable demographics usually exceeds what their ratings alone would bring.

For example, ABC has always been able to charge higher than normal prices for spots on *Monday Night Football* (MNF). MNF is highly rated, but it has especially strong appeal for younger men, a primary target audience for products such as beer and automobiles.

CPMs   While most advertisers are seeking favorable demographics and are willing to pay a premium to get them, there are other advertisers who are driven primarily by cost considerations. Of course, no advertiser ignores the audience profile of its advertising buys. However, there are a number of advertisers who evaluate cost efficiencies and CPM levels on an equal basis with audience demographics. Advertisers of widely distributed package goods are more likely to take this approach than a product with more limited appeal. These companies take the position that, within certain broad audience criteria, they gain some benefit from virtually any audience since their product usage is so universal.

■ *Demand.* The third criterion that determines the relationship between networks and advertisers is the demand for certain programs. Of course, demand is a function of both demographics and CPMs, but there are also qualitative factors such as association with a special event such as the *Miss America Pageant* or with a star that has unique appeal to a particular target market such as Oprah Winfrey that creates a pricing structure over and above the objective numbers.

Avails   Next Thanksgiving, begin to take note of the number of pages in your favorite magazines. Some November and December issues of popular publications swell to catalog size as advertisers compete for holiday sales. After the first of the year, these same publications will be very thin, with many advertisers standing on the sidelines after spending a sizable percentage of their budgets during the previous two months.

---

[12]"Mil-a-minute TV not all bad," *Advertising Age*, 23 September 1996, 28.

The broadcast media do not have the advantage of flexible advertising inventory. Every day, 365 days a year, each local station and network must sell more than four-hundred 30-second spots. Television advertisers, like their print counterparts, want to heavy-up in peak buying seasons and on the most popular shows. Combined with the problem of high demand and finite network commercial time there is the practical restraint that this amount of time cannot be sold on a spot-by-spot basis.

Networks must ration prime commercial spots among their major advertisers (see yield management in Chapter 2). The availability (called *avails* in network jargon) problem is solved, in part, by combining top-rated avails with less popular ones as advertisers buy packages of commercial time from each network. Whether an advertiser will gain availability to a top-rated show will depend largely on the company's total advertising investment on that network. Package plans allow the networks to work with agencies to place commercials across their entire schedule, with the understanding that each advertiser will have to accept some lower rated (but demographically acceptable) spots in order to obtain some "jewels."

Up-Front and Scatter Buys   Each May major advertisers begin the negotiation process to buy commercials on the network prime-time line-up for the coming fall season. This is the so-called **up-front buying** season in which most prime-time spots are bought. In a period of less than a month, advertisers will purchase prime-time commercials worth more than $8 *billion*. The up-front period opens with each network previewing their shows, followed by the actual negotiation for time.

At one time, the up-front period consisted primarily of negotiation between major agencies and the three major networks. Today, the up-front buying process has become much more complex with a number of new players and different approaches by advertisers. Among the major up-front trends are:

1. *Greater demand for time.* In recent years, two new categories of advertisers, the so-called dot.coms and various telephone services such as 10-10-10, have bought large amounts of television advertising as they compete for consumer attention in a very competitive marketplace. It is estimated that television networks gained more than $500 million from Internet companies in the two years from 1998–2000.

2. *Optimizers.* You will recall in Chapter 7, we discussed the role of computer models called optimizers, which sought to find the most efficient combination of television spots to reach specific target segments. Optimizers have provided additional data to major prime-time advertisers, which gives them confidence to spread their budgets into other dayparts and television sectors such as cable. For example, one agency using optimizer modeling reduced its expenditures in the three major networks by 5 percent and increased cable and syndicated buys by 9 percent. Until recently, neither of these prime-time alternatives would have been considered in the up-front market. As one media planner who relies heavily on optimizers noted, ". . . the old thinking that you had to use network primetime to establish your reach goals is just not true."[13]

3. *Globalization.* If optimizer models began the process of extending the media options considered during up-front selling, globalization has taken it even further. Agencies are having to position their U.S. up-front buys in a context of global media for their multinational clients. In 1999, Turner Broadcasting Sales and McCann-Erickson Worldwide agreed to an up-front deal worth some $50 million. It involved a media package that included a number of Turner networks including CNN, Cartoon Network, TBS, and TNT. The deal was signed on

up-front buying
Purchase of network TV time by national advertisers during the first offering by networks. Most expensive network advertising.

---

[13]Chuck Ross, "Optimizers & TV upfront: How they affect ad buying," *Advertising Age,* 29 June 1999, 16.

behalf of McCann's worldwide accounts such as Coca-Cola, General Motors, and Nestlé.[14] The Turner/McCann buy demonstrates that media companies must structure their deals to meet the demands of global businesses.

4. *Special events.* The up-front market also is affected by time demands made by special events. For example, every four years, demand for political advertising by presidential candidates places an inordinate strain on an already tight commercial inventory. Likewise, when the summer Olympics in Sydney coincided with the Bush/Gore election, advertisers were scrambling for television time, especially during the third and fourth quarters of 2000.

scatter plan The use of announcements, over a variety of network programs and stations, to reach as many people as possible in a market.

The up-front season is followed by a second phase known as **scatter plan** buys.[15] Scatter plans are usually bought on a quarterly basis throughout the year. They are designed for larger advertisers who want to take advantage of changing marketing conditions or, more often, for smaller advertisers who are shut out of up-front buys. Generally, scatter plans will sell at a higher CPM than up-front spots because there is less time inventory and smaller advertisers don't have the leverage to negotiate the CPM levels of huge network advertisers.

There also are up-front markets for other dayparts and prime-time cable. In fact, many media buyers negotiate for cable and over-the-air networks simultaneously. Buyers interested in late night will fight for slots on *The Tonight Show with Jay Leno, The Late Show with David Letterman*, or the upscale audience of Ted Koppel's *Nightline* as well as other after midnight programs. Similarly, early morning and midday programming each have their own up-front seasons, special advertising categories, and pricing structure. It is important to understand that network avails are largely filled through the up-front seasons in each daypart.

Negotiation As mentioned in the last section, negotiation is the key to network buying. Since each advertising package is unique to a particular advertiser, there are no rate cards for network television advertising. Over the last several years, network rate negotiation has undergone a number of changes. First, the decline in network rating and share levels has created a more contentious atmosphere. But the fact is that network television, despite decreasing audiences, remains the best way to reach a mass market.

A second major change in the negotiation process is that advertisers are concurrently negotiating for time across a number of television options. As we mentioned, up-front negotiation still takes place among more or less discrete television formats (e.g., daytime, prime time, broadcast networks, cable networks, etc.). However, a number of media planners are looking to a diversity of options to reach a particular target market. As they negotiate network time, they are considering the cable, syndication, and even Internet markets that will be used as supplements to network or to keep overall costs down. With the billions of dollars at stake, agencies and their clients know that an extremely small difference in the cost of a rating point has great significance when a large national advertiser is involved.

make-goods When a medium falls short of some audience guarantee, advertisers are provided concessions in the form of make-goods. Most commonly used in television and magazines.

Make-Goods One of the major elements of network negotiation concerns **make-goods**. As the name implies, make-goods are concessions to advertisers for a failure to achieve some guaranteed rating level. Make-goods are normally offered on the basis of total GRPs for an advertiser's television advertising schedule. That is, when the advertiser fails to achieve a certain agreed upon cost per point the make-good provisions are initiated. At one time, make-goods were part of most advertis-

---

[14]Chuck Ross, "Turner, McCann ink $50 million global ad pact," *Advertising Age*, 21 June 1999, 2.
[15]The term scatter plan has two definitions. The first refers to buying a group of spots across a number of programs. The second meaning refers to those spots that are still available after the up-front buying season is completed.

ing negotiations—they were always part of the up-front market. Make-goods usually take the form of future commercials to make up for a short fall in ratings. Monetary refunds are virtually never given as part of a make-good plan.

It has only been in the last several years that make-goods have become a major point of contention between networks and agencies. Prior to that time, the networks were so dominant that it was rare for an advertiser to qualify for a make-good. Each network could reasonably expect to get a 25 to 35 share of the total prime-time schedule. Consequently, a make-good was a relatively risk-free incentive offered by networks to agencies and their clients.

The new competitive environment has changed the make-good situation dramatically. With some network shows achieving sub-10 ratings, the make-good has become a major negotiating point with agencies and a high-risk endeavor for networks. If a prime-time network schedule includes a number of low-rated or canceled shows, it may well mean the network will give up a significant portion of its inventory during the winter and spring to accommodate make-goods. In part because of make-goods, networks are very reluctant to support low-rated shows. Each season there are a few shows that are canceled after one or two airings to prevent a significant demand for make-goods.

SPOT TELEVISION

When national advertisers buy from local stations, the practice is known as **spot television** or *spot buys*. The term comes from the fact that advertisers are spotting their advertising in certain markets as contrasted to the blanket coverage offered by network schedules. The primary disadvantages of spot television are that it requires a great deal more planning and paperwork than network since each market must be bought on a one-to-one basis and it is more costly on a CPM basis than network buys.

Spot advertising is an extremely competitive market. Not only are more than 1,000 local stations competing for spot dollars, but the approximately 12,000 local cable outlets are becoming important players with many spot advertisers. In the future, broadcast stations will probably face a number of new competitive options from Internet services and other forms of local, interactive media. Largely as a result of this environment, increases in spot dollars are projected to remain relatively flat for broadcast stations as advertisers divert budgets to other forms of local television.

Today, most spot advertising is placed through station **representatives** or *reps*. The rep is paid a commission by the station based on the time sold. The commission is negotiable, but it usually ranges from 5 to 10 percent depending on the size of the station. A good sales rep is both a salesperson and a marketing specialist for advertisers. The rep must be able to show a national advertiser how a schedule on WAWS-TV in Jacksonville or KDKA-TV in Pittsburgh will meet a national company's advertising objectives.

Rep firms may have 100 or more station clients on a noncompetitive basis. Reps go to agencies and advertisers to convince them that the markets in which their client stations broadcast are prime sales areas for their brands. To make the purchase of spot buys more efficient, a rep will allow advertisers to buy all or any number of stations it represents. Since the idea is to provide one order and one invoice, it offers similar advantages to a network buy. However, the stations sold through a rep are not linked in any way other than being a client of a particular rep. These station groups are called **nonwired networks.** The commercials bought on a nonwired network, unlike a real network, are not necessarily broadcast at the same time or on the same programs. The nonwired concept is simply a means of providing buying efficiency for spot advertisers.

In Chapter 7, we briefly mentioned electronic data interchange (EDI). It is the spot television market where EDI has the greatest short-term potential. EDI,

spot television
Purchase of time from a local station, in contrast to purchasing from a network.

representative (rep) An individual or organization representing a medium selling time or space outside the city of origin.

nonwired networks
Groups of radio and TV stations whose advertising is sold simultaneously by station representatives.

particularly over the Internet, connects the computers of agencies, reps, and media. An EDI system greatly enhances the processing of the thousands of transactions taking place daily in the spot market. Although compatibility among various EDI systems remains a problem, a number of services are being developed that can translate computer codes from otherwise incompatible software to make a universal system more practical in the future.

As in the case of much of the television industry, the rep's role in the spot market will probably undergo significant changes as the move to consolidation in the television industry accelerates. For example, at one time, a single owner could only hold seven television licenses. Today, the rules allow a person or corporation to control stations with total TV household coverage of up to 35 percent of the U.S. population. With this loosening of ownership rules, we have seen a significant growth in the number and size of station groups, some now owning dozens of stations. A number of these groups are large enough to support their own national sales force.

Group owners making direct deals with advertising agencies have created a potential conflict with their reps, since most rep firms have contracts with their station clients calling for a rep commission on all spot sales regardless of how the sale is made. In addition, a few advertising agencies have indicated their intention to deal directly with major stations and groups and bypass reps. These agencies think that they can negotiate more favorable buys direct than through a rep since it eliminates a rep commission. If this trend of direct station deals expands, there is a real question about the future of the station/rep relationship.

Regardless of changes in the manner in which spot advertising is bought and sold, the primary purposes for spot buys will remain the same:

1. To allow network advertisers to provide additional *GRP*s in those markets with the greatest sales potential.

2. To provide businesses with less than national or uneven distribution, a means of avoiding waste circulation incurred by network television.

3. Spot buys allow network advertisers to control for uneven network ratings on a market-by-market basis. For example, a network program with a 15 rating may demonstrate huge rating variances from one market to another. Exhibit 8.4 demonstrates the disparity among local market ratings for the top 10 shows.

Exhibit 8.4

Local Television Viewing

Market	#1	#2	#3	#4	#5	#6	#7	#8	#9	#10
TOTAL U.S.	E.R.	Frasier	Friends	CBS Sunday Movie	Touched by an Angel	Will & Grace	Veronica's Closet	NBC Sunday Night Movie	60 Minutes	Law & Order
SEATTLE TACOMA, WA	Frasier	Friends	E.R.	Home Improvement	Will & Grace	Veronica's Closet	Just Shoot Me	Mad About You	Law & Order	Ally McBeal
SALT LAKE CITY, UT	E.R.	Friends	Will & Grace	Home Improvement	NBC Sunday Night Movie	Frasier	Law & Order	CBS Sunday Movie	Dateline	Veronica's Closet
ORLANDO-DAYTONA BEACH-MELBOURNE, FL	E.R.	Home Improvement	Frasier	Friends	CBS Sunday Movie	Ally McBeal	Touched by an Angel	Jag	Veronica's Closet	NBC Sunday Night Movie
HONOLULU, HI	E.R.	Ally McBeal	Frasier	X-Files	Martial Law	Touched by an Angel	CBS Sunday Movie	20/20-Fri.	Channel 2 News	Law & Order
FARGO VALLEY CITY, ND	E.R.	Home Improvement	60 Minutes	Touched by an Angel	NBC Sunday Night Movie	CBS Sunday Movie	Friends	20/20-Wed.	Walker Texas Ranger	Frasier
ERIE, PA	E.R.	Home Improvement	Frasier	Everybody Loves Raymond	Becker	Friends	Drew Carey	Touched by an Angel	NYPD Blue	Law & Order
DES MOINES AMES, IA	E.R.	Touched by an Angel	News Channel 8 at 6	Home Improvement	60 Minutes	CBS Sunday Movie	Frasier	Friends	NBC Sunday Night Movie	Everybody Loves Raymond
CHATTANOOGA, TN	E.R.	Home Improvement	Touched by an Angel	Frasier	Friends	CBS Sunday Movie	60 Minutes	NBC Sunday Night Movie	Veronica's Closet	Will & Grace
BOSTON, MA	E.R.	Frasier	Friends	Will & Grace	Veronica's Closet	The Practice	Law & Order	Home Improvement	60 Minutes	NYPD Blue

Source: Nielson Cable Activity Report-Primetime 3rd Quarter, 1999 (6/28/99-9/26/99). Note: Data represent primary feed for each cable network within its respective universe. Cable Network Coverage Area Rating % = Average audience in percent of homes are able to receive an individual cable network/superstation. Total U.S. Rating % = Average audience in percent of total U.S. households. <<: Below minimum reporting standards. N/A: Not available.

© 2000 Nielson Media research, 2000 Report on Television

4. National advertisers can use spot to support retailers and provide localization for special marketing circumstances. Automobile companies and restaurant chains, both with extensive local dealer networks, spend almost $5 billion in spot advertising—more than the next 10 product categories combined. In fact, led by DaimlerChrysler, six of the top 10 spot advertisers are automobile advertisers and the other four are major food marketers (see Exhibit 8.5).

Defining the Television Coverage Area

Before the advent of television, companies generally established sales and advertising territories by state boundaries and arbitrary geographical areas within them. However, television transmissions go in many directions for varying distances; they are no respecter of maps. Television research uses three levels of signal coverage to designate potential station coverage of a market area.

1. *Total survey area* is the largest area over which a station's coverage extends.

total survey area
The maximum coverage of a radio or television station's signal.

Rank/Parent company	Jan.–Dec. '98	Jan.–Dec. '97	% change
1. DaimlerChrysler	517.0	433.4	19.3
2. General Motors Corp.	342.6	373.8	−8.4
3. Ford Motor Co.	231.7	183.0	26.7
4. American Honda Motor Co.	228.7	189.9	20.4
5. General Mills	206.4	181.4	13.8
6. Toyota Motor Sales USA	203.6	197.8	2.9
7. Philip Morris USA	189.8	217.0	−12.5
8. Tricon Global Restaurants	186.9	186.4	0.3
9. Nissan North America	177.6	117.0	51.8
10. McDonald's Corp.	165.7	144.5	14.6
11. Procter & Gamble Co.	164.0	197.5	−17.0
12. Viacom	162.6	130.0	25.0
13. Walt Disney Co.	139.0	140.2	−0.9
14. Circuit City Stores	116.4	103.1	12.9
15. Time Warner	105.9	82.4	28.4
16. Bell Atlantic Corp.	97.7	89.7	8.9
17. Sony Corp.	86.6	97.8	−11.5
18. Wal-Mart Stores	85.4	85.2	0.2
19. Best Buy Co.	83.4	70.6	18.2
20. Coca-Cola Co.	79.7	84.6	−5.8
21. Diageo	77.4	64.8	19.3
22. CKE Restaurants	76.9	71.1	8.0
23. Sprint Corp.	75.0	50.7	48.1
24. Dayton Hudson Corp.	71.7	73.4	−2.3
25. Mazda North American Operations	71.0	103.6	−31.5

Exhibit

8.5

Top 25 spot TV advertisers

Automakers dominate local spending.

From: Advertising Age, 10 May 1999, S12.

Sources: Competitive Media Reporting and Publishers Information Bureau. Dollars are in millions.

2. *Designated market area.*[16] A term used by the A. C. Nielsen Company to identify those counties in which home market stations receive a preponderance of viewers.
3. *Metro rating area* corresponds to the standard metropolitan area served by a station.

Local television stations also provide advertisers with signal coverage maps to show the *potential* audience reach of the station. The signal coverage designations have become less important in recent years as cable has greatly extended the area over which a television station can be viewed.

Local Television Advertising

Television advertising is increasingly purchased by local advertisers. Businesses as diverse as record stores and banks place advertising on local stations. However, a significant portion of the approximately $18 billion invested in local television is placed by local franchise outlets of national companies. For example, McDonald's is one of the largest local advertisers.

Currently, local television advertising expenditures are slightly ahead of spot and could challenge network revenues by the end of the decade. Advertisers spend more than $33 billion on spot and local television combined (including cable), compared to $14 billion invested in network (see Exhibit 8.6). The growth in local station advertising is indicative of three factors:

■ The effective marketing promotions by local stations to demonstrate how television can effectively be used by retail outlets.

■ The increased number of local television outlets has created a competitive environment that has kept prices down, bringing the medium within the budget of more local advertisers.

■ The trend by national marketers to move to local strategies. In many cases, this trend has been reflected by greater advertising allowances and control of budgets by local or regional advertisers. Local television advertising is an important

Exhibit 8.6

Television Ad Volume Components

The three original components of television (network, national spot and local spot) grew steadily from 1950 to 1975. By 1980 they were joined by syndication and cable TV. Spot TV (National and Local) accounts for $23.2 billion (45.9%) of the total.

Source: Universal McCann. *Courtesy:* Television Bureau of Advertising.

		(In Millions)			
Year	Network*	Nat'l Spot	Local Spot	Synd*	Cable
1950	$85	$31	$55	$—	$—
1955	550	260	225	—	—
1960	820	527	280	—	—
1965	1,237	892	386	—	—
1970	1,658	1,234	704	—	—
1975	2,306	1,623	1,334	—	—
1980	5,130	3,269	2,967	50	72
1985	8,060	6,004	5,714	520	989
1990	9,863	7,788	7,856	1,109	2,457
1995	11,600	9,119	9,985	2,016	5,108
1996	13,081	9,803	10,944	2,218	6,438
1997	13,020	9,999	11,436	2,438	7,237
1998	13,736	10,659	12,169	2,609	8,547
1999	13,961	10,500	12,680	2,870	10,429

*FOX in syndication prior to 1990, now in network. PAX, UPN, and WB currently in syndication.

[16]The Arbitron Company used a similar designation known as *Area of Dominance Influence.* Even though Arbitron no longer conducts TV ratings the term is still used by many advertisers.

source of revenue for most stations. A decade ago, local advertising accounted for a minor portion of the total revenues of most network affiliates, today it is a growing profit center for most stations.

Buying and Scheduling Spot and Local TV Time   Because advertisers have shifted more of their budgets to local markets, media buyers must be familiar with the specifics of buying spot and local TV time.

The TV Day   Spot and local TV advertising are often purchased by daypart rather than by specific program. Each daypart varies by audience size and demographic profile. Media planners must be familiar with the audience makeup of various dayparts. Some typical daypart designations are

1. morning: 7:00–9:00 A.M. Monday through Friday
2. daytime: 9:00 A.M.–4:30 P.M. Monday through Friday
3. early fringe: 4:30–7:30 P.M. Monday through Friday
4. prime-time access: 7:30–8:00 P.M. Monday through Saturday
5. prime time: 8:00–11:00 P.M. Monday through Saturday and 7:00–11:00 P.M. Sunday. These are East and West Coast Time Zone designations; Central and Mountain Time Zones are 7:00–10:00 P.M. Monday through Saturday and 6:00–10:00 P.M. Sunday.
6. late news: 11:00–11:30 P.M. Monday through Friday
7. late fringe: 11:30 P.M.–1:00 A.M. Monday through Friday

Preemption Rate   A considerable portion of spot TV advertising time is sold on a preemptible (lower-rate) basis, whereby the advertiser gives the station the right to sell a time slot to another advertiser that may pay a better rate for it or that has a package deal for which that particular spot is needed. Whereas some stations offer only two choices, nonpreemptible and preemptible advertising, others allow advertisers to choose between two kinds of preemptible rates. When the station has the right to sell a spot to another advertiser any time up until the time of the telecast, the rate is called the *immediately preemptible* (IP) rate (the lowest rate). When the station can preempt only if it gives the original advertiser two weeks' notice, the rate is designated *preemptible with two weeks' notice* and is sold at a higher rate. The highest rate is charged for a non-preemptible time slot, the two-week preemptible rate is the next highest, and the immediately preemptible rate is the lowest.

The following table is an excerpt from a rate card.

	I	II	III
Tues., 8–9 A.M.	$135	$125	$115

Column I is the nonpreemptible rate; column II, the rate for preemption with two weeks' notice; and column III, the rate for preemption without notice. Notice how the rate goes down.

Special Features   News telecasts, weather reports, sports news and commentary, stock market reports, and similar programming are called *special features*. Time in connection with special features is sold at a premium price.

Run of Schedule (ROS)   An advertiser can earn a lower rate by permitting a station to run commercials at its convenience whenever time is available rather than in a specified position. (This is comparable to run of paper in newspaper advertising; see Chapter 10.)

Package Rates Every station sets up its own assortment of time slots at different periods of the day, which it sells as a package. The station creates its own name for such packages and charges less for them than for the same slots sold individually. The package rate is one of the elements in negotiation for time.

Product Protection Every advertiser wants to keep the advertising of competitive products as far away from its commercials as possible. This brings up the question of what protection against competition an ad will get. Although some stations say that they will try to keep competing commercials 5 to 10 minutes apart, most say that although they will do everything possible to separate competing ads, they guarantee only that they will not run them back to back.

Scheduling Spot and Local Time *Rotation of a schedule* refers to the placement of commercials within a schedule to get the greatest possible showing. If you bought two spots a week for four weeks on a Monday-to-Friday basis, but all the spots were aired only on Monday and Tuesday, your rotation would be poor. You would miss all the people who turn to the station only on Wednesday, Thursday, or Friday. Your *horizontal rotation* should be increased. *Vertical rotation* assures there will be differences in the time at which a commercial is shown within the time bracket purchased. If you bought three spots on the *Tonight Show*, which runs from 11:30 P.M. to 12:30 A.M., but all your spots were shown at 12:15 A.M., you would be missing all the people who go to sleep earlier than that. To avoid this situation, you would schedule one spot in each half hour of the program, vertically rotating your commercial to reach the largest possible audience.

TELEVISION SYNDICATION

Television syndication is the sale of television programming on a station-by-station, market-by-market basis. Syndication companies seek to sell individual programs to one station in every market. Most major syndicated shows are sold on an advertiser-supported or barter basis. **Barter syndication** refers to the practice of offering shows to stations in return for a portion of the commercial time in the show, rather than selling the show to stations for cash. A majority of the commercial time on syndicated shows is packaged into national units and sold to national advertisers. The typical syndicated show comes with spots presold on a national basis and the station sells the remaining time to local and spot advertisers.

barter syndication
Station obtains a program at no charge. The program has presold national commercials and time is available for local station spots.

Syndication began when producers sold their canceled network shows to stations for inexpensive "fillers" during late afternoon or other time periods not programmed by the networks. During the early days of syndication no one thought that it was anything but a method for producers to pick up a few extra dollars by selling programs that had completed their network runs to local stations. During this period, syndication was a minor portion of television advertising.

Currently, syndication accounts for more than $2.5 billion in advertising revenues and major syndicated shows provide coverage comparable to the broadcast networks. For example, leading syndicated shows such as *Wheel of Fortune* and *Home Improvement* have potential coverage in excess of 90 percent of television households, compared to network's 96 percent and significantly greater than the 51 percent provided by the average cable program. In addition, syndication is theoretically available in every television household, while cable programs can come only into the 70 percent of homes wired for cable.

off-network syndication Syndicated programs that previously have been aired by a major network.

Like any television format, the key to syndication's success is quality programming. Syndicated programs are either *first-run*, made for syndication programs such as *Entertainment Tonight* and *The Oprah Winfrey Show*, or **off-network syndication** reruns such as *Seinfeld* and *The Nanny*. Most long-running shows such as *Frasier* and *The X-Files* enter the syndication market during their original network runs. Less than 15 percent of syndicated programs are off-network. However, these shows are consistently the most popular and command the highest advertising rates.

Off-network shows have built-in audiences and reach predictable demographic segments. Advertisers also feel more comfortable with the known content of a high-quality rerun versus the less predictable talk and entertainment first-run product. In fact, advertisers are willing to pay a significant premium for most off-network syndicated programs compared to first-run shows with comparable ratings.

Syndication advertising costs vary much more than other types of television programming. Essentially, there is a three-tier pricing structure for the approximately 150 syndicated shows:[17]

1. The top 10 blockbusters. These include proven off-network reruns such as *Friends* and a handful of proven first-run winners such as *Entertainment Tonight* and *Jeopardy*. These shows will have 30-second spot prices of $80–140,000 with the network reruns invariably getting the top prices.

2. The second tier are a small number of shows that fall short of the top 10, but still have a sizable, loyal audience. *Hollywood Squares* and *Access Hollywood* fall into this category and are priced in the $30–40,000 range for 30-second spots.

3. Finally, there are a large number of talk shows and less-popular reruns that will charge from $7–20,000. Obviously, there is a high level of failure among this group with a few lasting only a few weeks before cancellation.

The demand for syndicated shows is driven by television's insatiable demand for programming—any programming. For local stations and cable networks with 24 hours to fill, there is simply not enough programming for the thousands of hours required to fill their schedules. In addition, as more and more cable networks are added, the demand continues to increase. Nickelodeon, Lifetime, TNT, The Family Channel, and a host of other cable networks are competing with local stations for off-network programs and they are driving up the price of those that remain in the syndication market. Adding to the demand for syndicated time are a number of national advertisers who use syndicated programming as a means of extending reach on a demographic and/or geographic basis. Generally, broadcast syndication will surpass cable networks in achieving significant levels of audience reach since the average over-the-air station has higher audience levels than cable networks.

The demand for syndicated programming has moved some stations to sign long-term contracts with program producers to guarantee continued access to certain shows. For example, in 1988, ABC's O&O stations contracted with *Jeopardy* and *Wheel of Fortune* through 2004 and other stations extended these contracts until 2005.[18] With the relatively few shows that can generate high audience levels, the stations had to make long-term commitments to ensure having them on their schedule in future seasons.

The Audience for Syndicated Television

Syndication has some of the same characteristics as cable. For example, while syndication generates high aggregate audience levels, it does so over multiple programs and showings rather than delivering a mass audience in a single showing as in the case of broadcast networks. In fact, syndicators sell programs on the basis of multiple airings known as *gross average audience ratings*. For example, let's assume that an airing of *Friends* on NBC has a local market affiliate rating of 15.0 and a *Friends* syndicated version has a rating of 5.0. If ACME, Inc. runs one spot on the network version and three spots on the syndicated version, the total rating points

---

[17]Joe Mandese, "'Friends' vaults into top-priced syndie spot," *Advertising Age*, 11 November 1999, S2.
[18]Cynthia Littleton, "ABC inks longterm Wheel/Jeopardy deals," www.tvgen.com, 21 October 1998.

would be 15 for both shows. However, it's very difficult to compare the two because on network, you're achieving your audience all at once. The network audience exposures are unduplicated exposure. In syndication, your ratings are based on spots running within a week.[19]

The future of syndication is extremely bright since local stations find it very lucrative. In the typical network show, stations are allowed to sell one minute of commercial time. In a syndicated show the station can sell from 6 to 12 minutes of commercials depending on how the program was bartered to the station. Consequently, a syndicated program does not have to generate huge ratings to be a financial success for a station.

Since local stations find syndication profitable and the demand for new syndicated programming continues to grow, there is every reason to believe that syndication will be a major advertising vehicle for the foreseeable future. If anything, syndication will be an even stronger competitor to the traditional networks and the relationship between syndicators and stations may become more formal, with long-term contracts and stations buying equity shares in syndicated programs to ensure continued access.

Stripping   Most local stations schedule syndicated shows on a five-night a week basis. That is, they will run "Jeopardy" or "Inside Edition" Monday through Friday in the same time slot. This practice is called **stripping** since the show is stripped across a time period. It is cost efficient to buy fewer shows for multi-showings and allows a station to build a consistent audience for selling commercials to potential advertisers. Since most syndication is used as a lead-in either for early news or prime-time programs, stations don't want huge rating or audience composition swings from one day to another.

Cable Television

Cable television has its roots in the small Pennsylvania town of Mahanoy City. In the 1940s, John Watson, an appliance store owner, was having difficulty selling television sets because of poor reception caused by a mountain range between Philadelphia stations and Mahanoy City. By placing an antenna on a surrounding peak combined with coaxial cable and amplifiers, cable television (then known as Community Antenna Television or CATV) had begun.

Soon cable systems were importing a variety of signals from different cities to rural households. By the 1970s, cable had become attractive to viewers throughout the country and it moved from remote areas to major cities. In 1972, pay television was launched when Home Box Office (HBO) began service. HBO initiated the era of original programming as opposed to simply extending the signals of over-the-air stations. Of equal importance, HBO's programming was delivered by satellite and provided universal availability for cable networks.[20]

From its humble beginnings, cable television has become a major medium in its own right with household penetration of more than 70 percent. In recent years, the cable advertising share of total dollars has shown double-digit increases. Both local and national cable advertising revenues continue to grow at a rate higher than other forms of advertising.

The Contemporary Cable Television Industry

For the first two decades of its existence, cable customers were satisfied to get a wider option of over-the-air broadcast programs and cable operators were making

---

stripping   Scheduling a syndicated program on a five-day-per-week basis.

cable television   TV signals that are carried to households by cable. Programs originate with cable operators through high antennas, satellite disks, or operator-initiated programming.

---

[19]Joe Mandese, "Syndie stars easy to find," *Advertising Age*, 17 January 2000, S4.
[20]"The history of cable," a service of the Pennsylvania Cable & Telecommunication Association, www.pcta.com.

satisfactory profits from cable subscription fees. However, cable industry executives realized that they were missing a major source of revenue by failing to open the medium to advertisers. For the last 20 years, cable has grown as it matured into a medium serving both viewers and advertisers.

The success of cable can be traced to two related elements:

1. Brand identification based on unique and selective networks and programs that appeal to targeted demographic audience segments.
2. The investment by cable networks in first-run programming.

Unlike broadcast networks that reach huge audiences for mass advertisers, cable provides advertisers with much smaller niche audiences who exhibit both common demographic characteristics and interests (see Exhibit 8.7). Advertisers know that Lifetime, MTV, Cartoon Network, and The Discovery Channel will deliver predictable groups of viewers. Cable networks define their brands in the same way as product manufacturers. For both, brand identification and awareness creates an environment of consistent for the users of these brands.

Some cable networks have been so successful that they are actually more valuable on a dollar per rating-point basis than the traditional broadcast networks. For example, ESPN and MTV are the two most valuable networks on a rating-point basis (see Exhibit 8.8). As one cable executive pointed out, ". . . targeted networks like ESPN, MTV, or CNN can deliver large concentrations of men, teens, and influential decision-makers critical for marketers seeking those audiences."[21]

It is favorable brand recognition that is providing the major impetus to cable success in bringing large national advertisers to the medium. Led by companies such as Procter & Gamble, General Motors, and Sony, cable is competing for the same advertisers as the broadcast networks. "Branding also is playing an increasingly important role for cable TV networks in getting the attention of viewers and media buyers, to differentiate individual networks from the growing array of choices on viewers' TV dials."[22]

Cable networks know that it is original programming that will bring both viewers and advertisers to a particular network. Only a few years ago, the majority of cable network programming consisted of off-network reruns and theatrical films that had usually been run several times on both broadcast networks and local stations. Today, cable networks annually invest more than $6 billion in original programming, some of which is among the most popular on television. From the irreverent *South Park* to ESPN's Sunday NFL games and A&E's *Investigative Reports* and *Biography*, cable networks are appealing to a larger share of the total viewing audience. "New development, for the most part, is going into original series, movies and big-event specials that further define a network's particular connection with viewers and sharpen its brand image."[23]

The Future of Cable Advertising

A number of factors make cable television an attractive medium for advertisers.

1. *Ability to target audiences.* When advertisers consider cable television, its ability to reach specific demographic and lifestyle segments is almost always the prime consideration.

---

[21]Joe Mandese, "Matching ratings to ad $$, ESPN comes out tops," *Advertising Age*, 12 April 1999, S2.
[22]Kate Fitzgerald, "Well-oiled cable machine builds fresh fare inventory," *Advertising Age*, 10 May 1999, S28.
[23]Kathy Haley, "Cable networks pump billions into programming for Y2K season blitz," *Advertising Age*, 7 June 1999, A3.

THIRD QUARTER 1999–MON–SUN 8–11PM

Network	Coverage Area Household Rating	Total U.S. Household Rating	Number of Households
Ad-Supported Networks			
A & E NETWORK	1.3	1.0	1,007,000
AMERICAN MOVIE CLASSICS	0.8	0.6	599,000
ANIMAL PLANET	0.5	0.3	251,000
BLACK ENTERTAINMENT TV	0.6	0.3	327,000
BRAVO	0.3	0.1	105,000
CABLE NEWS NETWORK	0.8	0.6	594,000
CMT–COUNTRY MUSIC TV	0.3	0.1	127,000
CNBC	0.4	0.3	300,000
COMEDY CENTRAL	0.7	0.4	391,000
COURT TV	0.4	0.1	137,000
DISNEY CHANNEL	1.9	1.0	1,012,000
E! ENTERTAINMENT TV	0.5	0.3	300,000
ESPN	1.7	1.3	1,319,000
ESPN2	0.5	0.3	340,000
FOOD NETWORK	0.4	0.2	153,000
FOX FAMILY CHANNEL	0.9	0.7	668,000
FOX NEWS CHANNEL	0.5	0.2	189,000
FX	0.7	0.3	292,000
GAME SHOW NETWORK	0.4	0.1	80,000
GOODLIFE TELEVISION NETWORK	0.2	<<	13,000
HEADLINE NEWS	0.2	0.2	167,000
HOME AND GARDEN TV	0.6	0.3	342,000
KNOWLEDGE TV	0.1	<<	N/A
LIFETIME TELEVISION	1.7	1.3	1,268,000
MSNBC	0.4	0.2	213,000
MTV: MUSIC TELEVISION	1.2	0.8	835,000
NICKELODEON/NICK-AT-NITE	1.7	1.3	1,297,000
ODYSSEY	0.2	0.1	59,000
SCI-FI CHANNEL	0.8	0.5	458,000
TBS-SUPERSTATION	1.9	1.5	1,472,000
THE CARTOON NETWORK	1.7	1.0	1,015,000
THE DISCOVERY CHANNEL	1.1	0.8	835,000
THE HISTORY CHANNEL	0.8	0.4	446,000
THE LEARNING CHANNEL	0.8	0.6	578,000
THE TRAVEL CHANNEL	0.2	0.1	71,000
THE WEATHER CHANNEL	0.5	0.3	331,000
TNN	0.7	0.5	532,000
TURNER NETWORK TELEVISION	1.8	1.4	1,358,000
TV GUIDE CHANNEL	0.5	0.3	254,000
TV LAND	0.8	0.3	315,000
USA NETWORK	2.3	1.7	1,718,000
VH1	0.5	0.4	361,000
WGN CABLE	0.8	0.4	395,000
Premium Pay Networks			
CINEMAX	3.2	0.6	586,000
HOME BOX OFFICE	5.6	1.7	1,683,000
SHOWTIME	2.8	0.5	492,000
THE MOVIE CHANNEL	1.3	0.2	157,000

Exhibit

8.7

Cable Network Viewing

©2000 Nielson Media Research, 2000 Report on Television.

2. *Low cost.* The cable industry is faced with a competitive environment that prevents significant increases in CPMs. With an abundance of cable channels, many trying to prove themselves to advertisers, it is very unlikely that we will see the type of advertising increases that have been so prevalent among the major broadcast networks in recent years.

3. *A strong summer season.* In recent years, cable has counterprogrammed the networks by presenting some of their strongest programs opposite network summer reruns. Many advertisers have taken advantage of the audience shifts inherent in this strategy to move dollars into cable during what is typically a down viewing time for networks.

Cable's revenue point			
Network	Ad revenue per rating point	Average rating (total day)	Ad revenue
ESPN	$1,083.3	0.6	$650
MTV	1,037.5	0.4	415
NBC	993.3	4.5	4,470
ABC	962.5	4.0	3,850
CBS	883.3	4.5	3,975
E!	800.0	0.1	80
Comedy Central	725.0	0.2	145
CNN	712.5	0.4	285
CNBC	650.0	0.3	195
Headline News	650.0	0.2	130
USA	642.9	0.7	450
VH1	625.0	0.2	125
TBS	612.5	0.8	490
Discovery	600.0	0.5	300
TNT	571.4	0.7	400
Lifetime	571.4	0.7	400
Weather Channel	550.0	0.2	110
A&E	516.7	0.6	310
Fox	506.4	3.9	1,975
TNN	475.0	0.4	190
Fox Family	475.0	0.4	190
Nickelodeon	458.3	1.2	550
TLC	400.0	0.3	120
ESPN2	400.0	0.2	80
Sci-Fi	375.0	0.2	75
BET	375.0	0.2	75
MSNBC	350.0	0.1	35
CMT	350.0	0.1	35
HGTV	325.0	0.2	65
History Channel	300.0	0.2	60
WB	250.0	1.6	400
Food Network	250.0	0.1	25
Fox News	250.0	0.1	25
Cartoon	230.0	0.5	115
UPN	117.7	1.7	200

Exhibit

8.8

Cable's Revenue Point

From: Advertising Age, 12 April 1999, S2.

Source: Analysis of data from Myers Consulting Group and Nielson Media Research. Insufficient data for TV Land, TV Guide Channel (formerly Prevue), FX, Animal Planet, Court TV, Travel Channel, and Bravo.

4. *Opportunity for local and spot cable advertising.* Approximately 65 percent of cable advertising dollars are spent at the network level. However, local cable advertising is growing at a rate significantly higher than network advertising. Local cable spending comes from national spot buyers looking to enhance advertising weight in specific markets and a wide variety of local firms such as restaurants, video stores, and small retailers. Because of cable's low advertising rates, these retailers now have a chance to use television.

In the future, cable advertisers will have at least three readily available advertising options. The first is traditional advertising spots carried on regular analog cable.

A second option is targeted advertising using digital technology. For example, advertisers will be able to reach cable homes in specific ZIP codes with tailored messages. A third option will be interactive advertising offered through special software added to cable boxes on viewers' television sets.

These interactive systems will allow consumers to shop directly from the screen during commercials. One company, RespondTV, has experimented with banners on commercials such as Domino's pizza. A viewer can click the yes key on a remote pad and order a pizza during the commercial. Television interactive selling (often called *T-commerce*) is already offered in selected homes.[24] Two innovations in local cable advertising have greatly enhanced the importance of this segment—cut-ins and interconnects.

While some of cable advertising options are not readily available, current technology offers advertisers some sophisticated coverage alternatives. The first innovation is the use of *cut-ins* on network cable programs. Cable networks, like their broadcast counterparts, provide some advertising spots to local system operators to sell to local advertisers. Rather than having a spot appear on a largely unwatched local channel, commercials for the local pizza shop now can air on CNN's *Larry King Show* or ESPN's *Sports Center*.

interconnects A joint buying opportunity between two or more cable systems in the same market.

A further strengthening of local cable advertising comes from the use of **interconnects.** "An interconnect exists where two or more cable systems [in the same market] link themselves together to distribute a commercial advertising schedule simultaneously."[25] In Chicago, an advertiser can simultaneously air up to five different commercials in various areas of the city. The agency gets a single bill from all the systems, which facilitates individual client billing. The use of interconnects should greatly enhance the prospects for bringing more spot advertisers to cable.

As cable has garnered more advertising dollars, research has improved to help advertisers measure the cable audience and plan the cable portions of their advertising campaign. In particular, Nielsen Media Research provides a number of services including overnight household ratings and local audience composition data. In addition, Mediamark Research, Inc. (MRI) offers national product and cable media usage information. Advertisers also are able to obtain customized data for local market commercial and information about optimum local commercial efficiencies. As more national advertisers have started to include cable in their spot advertising plans, cable reps have moved to incorporate EDI systems to make the buying of spot cable on an equable basis with broadcast spot buys. Given the number of local cut-in cable options, often running to 20 or more in a local market, the introduction of EDI systems will greatly enhance the selling of local cable to major advertisers and their agencies.

The VCR

Since its introduction in the 1970s, the VCR has become as commonplace as television itself. Approximately 95 percent of American homes have a VCR and the multi-VCR household is growing rapidly. In some sense, the VCR is almost a medium in itself providing access to theatrical movies, made-for-VCR films, promotional and educational tapes, and, of course, recording television shows for later viewing (called **time-shift viewing**).

time-shift viewing Recording programs on a VCR for viewing at a later time.

At one time, it was anticipated that the primary usage of VCRs would be for off-air recording. In the early days of the VCR, advertisers thought that the VCR would

---

[24]Kalpana Srinivasan, "Interactive television allows for shopping by remote," *Athens Daily News*, 13 May 2000, 4B.
[25]"1995 cable TV facts," a publication of the Cable Advertising Bureau, 72.

be a method of increasing the audience of a show for those too busy to watch it during its originally scheduled time. However, studies show that more than half of recorded shows are never watched, the audiences for time-shift viewing tend to be demographically different than original audiences, and the VCR allows viewers to fast-forward through commercials—hardly an advantage for advertisers!

The television industry is well aware that each hour spent watching these prerecorded tapes is time not available for regular television viewing. Of particular concern to both broadcasters and advertisers is the demographic makeup of heavy VCR users. For example, young affluent adults, prime prospects for many television advertisers, are the most likely to rent videotapes. This audience is then unavailable for exposure to traditional broadcast and cable outlets and their advertisers.

Many industry observers think the VCR will soon be an outdated relic, replaced by digital technology that allows much greater flexibility than the VCR. Without going into the technical details of the device, usually called a personal video recorder (PVR), it allows viewers to take control of their viewing in a manner never before possible.

The PVR digitizes all incoming signals and stores up to 30 hours of programs. The viewer can then pause in a program to answer the telephone, provide instant replay or slow motion on demand, and record for later viewing any program just as with a VCR, but it can be done much quicker and easier, and it doesn't require a tape. It also allows advertisers to customize commercials for individual viewers. For example, your favorite show is *Monday Night Football*, but you are not a beer drinker. Therefore, instead of the network Coors commercial, you receive a commercial for Coca-Cola that is digitally stripped in the program. Furthermore, the commercial may be one that fits your age and interests known to Coke from information you previously provided the cable provider.

Obviously, a number of issues among network advertisers, secondary advertisers, program providers, and the networks would have to be addressed before the technology could be used to refit commercials. Advertisers also worry that the technology makes deleting commercials very easy. However, one advantage of the system is that it can measure the households that are zapping commercials. This, in turn, brings up the issue of viewer privacy. Another concern of advertisers is that the technology may make pay-for-view movies a more viable option for viewers, which would further decrease commercial viewing.

It is predicted that 13 percent of U.S. households will have PVR devices by 2004, an adoption rate faster than VCRs when they were introduced. The PVR will provide technical convergence of computers, interactive communication, and multiple options for standard television. If PVRs achieve predicted levels of household penetration, ". . . they will force TV stations and networks to rethink how they schedule and distribute programs. Advertisers will feel added pressure to come up with ads 'sticky' enough to keep viewers from zapping them."[26]

SYNDICATED RATING SERVICES

As mentioned earlier in this chapter, from an advertising perspective television is simply a customer delivery system. Needless to say, it is crucial for advertisers and their agencies to have reliable data on which to make buying decisions and to determine if they are paying a fair price. In recent years, the problems of accurately accounting for the fragmented television audience have become more and more difficult. At the same time, as audiences for each television outlet decrease, the

---

[26]Brent Schlender, "Goodbye to TV as we know it," *Fortune*, 2 August 1999, 219.

magnitude of any error increases as a percentage of the total viewing audience. For example, a 1 rating-point error for a program with a 20 rating is 5 percent; the same error for a program with a 5 rating is 20 percent. Since advertising rates are determined directly by ratings, these errors are a cause for considerable concern among advertisers.

The Nielsen Ratings

The primary supplier of syndicated television ratings is Nielsen Media Research.[27] The company was founded in 1923 by A. C. Nielsen to collect radio audience information and it initiated television ratings in 1950. The Nielsen Television Index (NTI) provides network ratings on a national basis. Data are provided from 5,000 households containing more than 13,000 people. In these households, a *people meter* is attached to each television set. The **people meter** has buttons assigned to each person living in the home and additional buttons for visitors.

people meter Device that measures TV set usage by individuals rather than by households.

Many advertisers are interested in local viewing levels and Nielsen provides ratings for all markets through its Nielsen Station Index (NSI). In the 48 largest markets, Nielsen uses set meters (not people meters) to measure household television set usage on a continuous basis. In each of the more than 200 television markets, Nielsen provides diaries in which individuals record their viewing habits. These diaries are administered four times a year during February, May, July, and November. These four periods are known as *sweeps* and they are used to set the price of local commercials for the coming quarter.

In recent years, the ratings system has come under a great deal of scrutiny by both advertisers and broadcasters. While a number of issues have been raised, we will discuss three major areas of concern:

sweep weeks During these periods, ratings are taken for all television markets.

1. *Sweep weeks.* In theory, **sweep weeks** (or simply sweeps) are an efficient and relatively inexpensive means of estimating quarterly local market ratings. In fact, local market stations have sometimes used the period to artificially distort their ratings by airing sensational news exposés, special promotions, and pressuring networks to program their best miniseries, movies, and specials to support their affiliates during sweeps.

   The result is that the sweep period ratings of local stations may have little relation to the 36 "unrated" weeks. Advertisers are extremely frustrated by what they see as inflated ratings and accompanying higher commercial rates they pay for them. The alleged abuses of sweep week programming has resulted in increasing calls for measuring of local audiences on a continuing basis.

2. *Diaries.* Everyone agrees that in an era of 50 channel household reception and a trend toward individual viewing, the diary is an antiquated measurement tool. A number of major advertisers have called for people meters in at least the top 125 markets, which would include approximately 75 percent of television households. It also would largely eliminate the current sweeps problem by providing ongoing audience measurements for most of the country. The major obstacle to implementing local people meter ratings is cost. It is estimated that each metered market would require a minimum of 300 sampled households or almost 40,000 homes at a cost of several hundred million dollars—much more than either advertisers or broadcasters are currently willing to pay. In 1999, Nielsen did install people meters in Boston as an experiment in collecting local market metered ratings. It remains to be seen if the experiment becomes more than that.

---

[27]Material in this section is from Nielsen Media Research.

3. *Exposure value.* Another area of ratings that has generated great interest is estimating exposure levels versus set usage.

Advertisers want to know who is watching, who is paying attention, and what level of attention is being given any particular show. A number of studies have addressed the question of what programs and commercials create the greatest positive recall among audiences. Nielsen has developed a measure that divides viewers into four groups according to how long and how often they watched a show. The four segments are:

1. *Gold Card* viewers watch most of a show and tune in often.
2. *Occasionally Committed* viewers watch most of a show, but tune in less often.
3. *Silver Sliders* watch only some of a show, but tune in often.
4. *Viewers Lite* watch only some of a show and tune in less often.

Broadcasters contend that if a viewer is watching most of a show, he or she is more interested and so, more likely to be watching the commercial as well. Such data is of particular interest to advertisers, of course, who would like to know how frequently and how attentively viewers watch their ads.[28]

Recently Nielsen and Arbitron announced a joint research effort that holds promise to solve many of the problems facing broadcast audience measurement. They will be engaging in a study using a portable people meter (PPM). The PPM is a device about the size of a pager that measures inaudible signals from the audio portion of television, radio, cable, and the Internet. It eliminates the nuisance of keeping a diary and the PPM is particularly valuable in measuring the out-of-home audience of radio. The major barrier to its use is the cost associated with its introduction.[29]

Regardless of what form changes in syndicated ratings take in the future, it is clear that methods that served the television industry well in a period of three networks and a few stations in each market will not work in the fragmented landscape of the twenty-first century. A primary issue is how much are the major players—stations, networks, and advertisers—willing to pay to gather these elusive data.

Qualitative Ratings

As you will recall in our discussion of cable television, we commented on the need for cable networks to sell the quality and lifestyle of their audiences in contrast to the basic numbers reported by most major rating reports. Another type of qualitative audience measure seeks to offer insight into audience involvement or degree of preference for particular television shows or personalities. These measures can be used to determine if a person can be successfully used as a testimonial spokesperson or to see if a popular show is beginning to wear out.

The best-known qualitative research service is Marketing Evaluations, which compiles a number of "popularity" surveys called "Q" reports. The most familiar of these are **TvQ** and Performer Q.

Let us assume that a TV show, *Big Bob Monday Night Circus*, is familiar to 50 percent of the population, and 30 percent of the people rank it as one of their favorite shows. The *Q* score would be calculated as follows:

TvQ A service of Marketing Evaluations that measures the popularity (opinion of audience rather than size of audience) of shows and personalities.

$$Q = \frac{FAV}{FAM} \quad \text{or} \quad \frac{30}{50} = 60$$

Interestingly enough, the fragmentation of television has taken its toll not only on average program ratings, but also on the TvQ scores. Because the number of

---

[28]Rachel X. Weissman, "Broadcasters mine the gold," *American Demographics*, June 1999, 35.
[29]Katy Bachman, "Nielsen, Arbitron agree to agree," *Mediaweek*, 5 June 2000, 6.

people watching any particular show is so much lower than in recent years, the general recognition level of television personalities has fallen significantly in recent years. A generation ago, Lucille Ball and Jackie Gleason were as well known as the president. Today, stars such as Sarah Michelle Gellar (*Buffy the Vampire Slayer*) and Dennis Franz (*NYPD Blue*) have a loyal following among their fans, but are not necessarily household names. In 1990, the top 25 female television stars had a familiar score of 68 percent, by 1999 the average for the group had fallen to 50 percent.[30]

SUMMARY

The future of television is being written everyday. In the near future, it will become more than a medium of information, entertainment, and advertising. Television, in its various permutations, will be an interactive system that will allow viewers to pay bills, make airline reservations, receive pay-per-view programming on demand, and even play computer games with other viewers. How long it will be before these systems are generally available and what their final form will take are still very much in question. However, programmers, advertisers, and the general public will all be dealing with a dramatically changed television medium in the not too distant future.

In addition to its functional options, television is becoming a gateway to a world of communication never before imagined. Every aspect of the media from audience research to news must be reevaluated in terms of viewer control and a changing economic base. Throughout most of the last century, it was understood that American mass media would be largely financed by advertisers using a business plan of reaching the largest audience possible at the lowest per person cost. The audience fragmentation of the television audience has changed programming, financing, and the criterion of what constitutes a "mass" medium.

While television advertising faces an uncertain future, it is an uncertainty filled with opportunities for those who have the creativity and insight to operate in an era of an audience-driven medium. Nowhere will the customer-oriented notion of the marketing concept be more apparent than in interactive television. It appears certain that both advertisers and viewers will soon pay a higher price for access to the numerous options offered by television. In return, astute advertisers will be reaching customers and prospects on a one-to-one basis with some form of permission marketing being the rule rather than the exception.

REVIEW

1. Discuss major changes in network television advertising during the last 20 years.
2. Define the following terms:
   a. Rating
   b. Share of audience
   c. People ratings
   d. TvQ ratings
   e. Clutter

---

[30]Bill Carter, "Where have television's big stars gone?" www.nytimes.com, 14 June 1999.

3. Compare and contrast syndication and spot television buying.
4. Discuss the relationship between networks and their affiliates.
5. Describe the up-front television buying market for prime time.
6. Compare and contrast cable networks with broadcast networks.

TAKE IT TO THE NET

We invite you to visit the Russell/Lane page on the Prentice Hall Web site at **www.prenhall.com/myphlip** for end-of-chapter exercises and applications.

Chapter 9

Using Radio

In many respects, radio is a medium tailor-made for the segmented marketing of the 2000s. With a host of formats and numerous stations in even the smallest towns, advertisers have options to reach very narrowly defined niche prospects. Radio also is among the most popular media with high levels of listenership throughout the day. After reading this chapter you will understand:

» the role of radio as a selective medium

» radio's strength as a secondary medium

» radio's ability to reach audiences at a low cost

» attempts to overcome radio's lack of a visual dimension

» different roles of AM and FM radio

» the rating systems used in radio

Pros

1. With the exception of direct response, radio is the primary media for targeting narrow audience segments, many of whom are not heavy users of other media. For example, radio is particularly popular with teenagers.

2. Radio is a mobile medium going with listeners into the marketplace and giving advertisers proximity to the sale.

3. Radio, with its relatively low production costs and immediacy, can react quickly to changing market conditions.

4. Radio has a personal relationship with its audience unmatched by other media. This affinity with listeners carries over to the credibility it offers many of the products advertised on radio.

5. Radio, with its low cost and targeted formats, is an excellent supplemental medium for secondary building blocks to increase reach and frequency to specific target markets.

Cons

1. Without a visual component, radio often lacks the impact of other media. Also many listeners use radio as "background" rather than paying full attention.

2. The small audiences of most radio stations require numerous buys to achieve acceptable reach and frequency.

3. Adequate audience research is not always available, especially among many small market stations.

During the week of March 6, 1949, the top-rated radio show was the *Lux Radio Theater*, which reached almost 30 percent of American households.[1] By contrast, the most popular television show of the 2000 season, ABC's *Who Wants to be a Millionaire?*, achieved a 16 rating. Until the 1950s when television became the major broadcast medium, radio was the primary national medium for both advertisers and audiences.

From 1926 when the first network (The National Broadcasting Company) was formed, until the mid-1950s, radio was the most prestigious of the national media. During those golden years of radio, the family gathered around the living room radio set to listen to Jack Benny, Fred Allen, and Bob Hope entertain them while news personalities such as Edward R. Murrow enlightened them. All of this programming was brought to the audience by the major advertisers of the day. By 1951, with the advent of coast-to-coast television broadcasts and the introduction of instant hits such as *I Love Lucy* and *The $64,000 Question*, radio quickly declined as a national medium.

Despite its minor position on the national scene, as a local medium, radio advertising revenues are close to $20 billion and it demonstrates impressive reach to virtually every age group (see Exhibit 9.1). For example, each week radio reaches

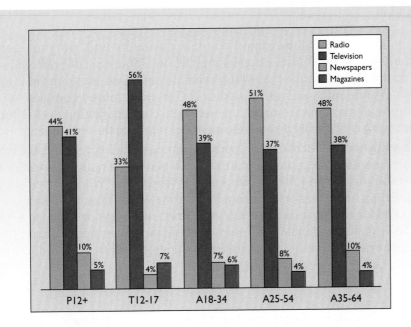

Exhibit

9.1

People Spend More Time with Radio

Average Weekday 6 A.M.–6 P.M.

Source: Media Targeting 2000, conducted by The Arbitron Company in cooperation with The Radio Advertising Bureau.

[1]"Nielsen begins ratings; 'Lux,' 'Lone Ranger' lead," *Advertising Age*, 19 April 1999, 89.

more than 95 percent of all adults and 99 percent of teenagers. By reaching prospects with targeted formats from jazz to all-talk, radio commercials can create an intimate, one-to-one relationship with prospects. In addition, radio can achieve effective creative effects at a lower production cost than virtually any other media.

THE CONTEMPORARY RADIO INDUSTRY

Like most media, radio is having to adapt to a new competitive environment and a very different economic structure. Only a few years ago, the Federal Communications Commission (FCC) limited ownership of radio stations to seven FM and seven AM stations with only one of each in a single market. However, the FCC gradually loosened ownership restrictions and the Telecommunications Act of 1996 allowed corporations or individuals to control as much as 35 percent of the national market (with other rules governing local station ownership determined by the size of a market). The new ownership rules changed the radio industry from one of numerous small groups to one comprised of a few huge conglomerates.

Led by companies such as Clear Channel and AMFM, both with more than 400 stations, more and more radio stations are part of these mega-owners. Accompanying this new movement to large group ownership is a revival of radio as a preferred advertising medium for a number of major businesses. "It seems as if what was once radio's shortcoming vs. television and newspapers—a fragmented audience—is now a strength, as advertisers focus on narrower slices of the population. In short, radio is king of the niche."[2]

Radio and New Technology

Some observers think that the audio platform of the next decade will be computers and satellites, not a radio dial. More and more radio executives see the future of radio as an Internet business with numerous options for reaching niche audiences and eventually individuals with tailored programming, music, and advertising. Web sites have become the new business model for radio.

To predict precisely the future of radio, even in the near term, is difficult. However, we can examine some of the major trends that will drive the medium during the coming years.

1. Radio audiences will be identified more clearly by both programmers and advertisers. In the future, listeners may fill out some type of preference questionnaire and in return they will receive personalized programs and promotions. As one radio executive predicted, "We have moved completely off the platform of mass marketing to targeted media and marketing. Technology will allow us to continually devise new means of reaching the consumer."[3]
2. The audience will increasingly (perhaps someday exclusively) use the Internet to access audio programming. Currently, 60 percent of radio stations have Web sites and more than 1,000 are engaged in Webcasting.[4] While 25 percent of the population has at least sampled audio over the Web, a number of other reasons are cited for visiting a station's Web site. For example, listeners turn to a station's Web site to obtain detailed information about local events and concerts, to read music reviews, to gather more information about advertised products, and to obtain coupons (see Exhibit 9.2).

[2]Roy S. Johnson, "The big buzz behind radio stocks," *Fortune*, 10 January 2000, 208.
[3]Amanda Beeler, "What's that noise," *Advertising Age*, 14 February 2000, S8.
[4]Webcasting is offering all or a portion of a station's programming over the Internet, also known as streaming audio.

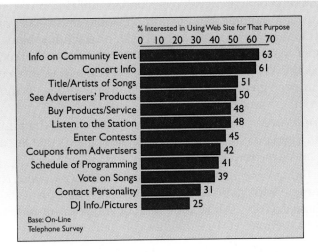

Exhibit

9.2

Interest in Visiting a Radio Station Web Site for . . .

From: "Radio in the new media world."
Courtesy: Radio Advertising Bureau.

3. Webcasting will offer special challenges to local stations particularly those outside the major markets. In a study by the Radio **Advertising Bureau (RAB)**, 17 percent of listeners surveyed indicated that their local market stations did not serve their musical tastes and 33 percent said if they had the option they would listen to out-of-town stations.[5] The fact is that more and more households have this option. Approximately 25 percent of homes have Internet capability and the number is increasing daily. At the same time, companies such as netradio.com and broadcast.com are providing access to either original music or distant broadcast stations. In coming months, similar services will be offered to automobile listeners through satellite. Overnight, radio choices have gone from a relative handful of local stations to thousands of alternatives.

Radio Advertising Bureau (RAB)
Association to promote the use of radio as an advertising medium.

The future of radio as a medium for the delivery of more specialized and personalized programming is very bright. However, the form that this transmission will take, whether local stations can survive satellite and Internet systems, and how advertisers will utilize the new technological options fully is very much up in the air.

FEATURES AND ADVANTAGES OF RADIO

Radio is an ideal medium for the segmented marketing of the twenty-first century. In many respects, radio was the forerunner of many of the localized marketing and advertising strategies so much in use today. As the RAB points out, "Radio gives you the opportunity to take advantage of the most powerful form of communication—the human voice. The right combination of words, voices, music, and effects on radio can help you establish a unique 'one-on-one' connection with your prospects that lets you grab their attention, evoke their emotions and persuade them to respond. All this at a fraction of the production cost of other broadcast media."[6]

According to the Radio Marketing Bureau, radio offers a number of advantages not found in most other media. Some of the primary elements of interest to advertisers are the following:

1. *Radio targets.* One of the greatest strengths of radio is its ability to deliver advertising to a very selective audience. It would be difficult to find a market segment whose needs, tastes, and preferences are not reached by some station's programming.

---

[5]"Radio in the new media world," a publication of the Radio Advertising Bureau.
[6]"How can I stand out from the competition," www.rab.com, 24 May 2000.

Radio's combination of high overall reach and its ability to provide numerous formats, makes it a multifaceted medium. In some sense, each programming category, whether country, classical, all-talk, or rhythm & blues, can be treated as a distinct medium for marketing purposes. From a marketing perspective, radio has the ability to reach prospects by sex, age, or interest with a format that adds an even greater dimension to its already strong personal communication environment (see Exhibit 9.3).

2. *Radio reaches virtually everyone.* Radio reaches a majority of the population, especially those in higher income and educational segments that are of prime importance to many advertisers (see Exhibit 9.4).

3. *Radio advertising influences consumers closest to the time of purchase.* No major medium can compete with radio as a means of reaching prospects as they approach a purchase decision. While both outdoor and point-of-purchase also reach consumers in the marketplace, neither can deliver a sales message the way radio can.

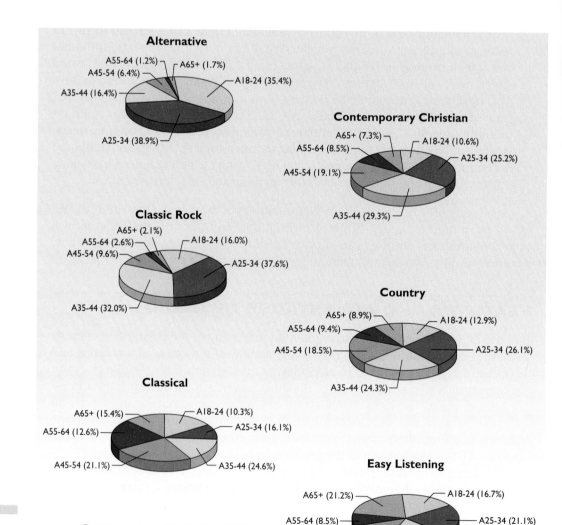

Alternative
A55-64 (1.2%)
A65+ (1.7%)
A45-54 (6.4%)
A18-24 (35.4%)
A35-44 (16.4%)
A25-34 (38.9%)

Contemporary Christian
A65+ (7.3%)
A18-24 (10.6%)
A55-64 (8.5%)
A25-34 (25.2%)
A45-54 (19.1%)
A35-44 (29.3%)

Classic Rock
A65+ (2.1%)
A55-64 (2.6%)
A18-24 (16.0%)
A45-54 (9.6%)
A25-34 (37.6%)
A35-44 (32.0%)

Country
A65+ (8.9%)
A18-24 (12.9%)
A55-64 (9.4%)
A45-54 (18.5%)
A25-34 (26.1%)
A35-44 (24.3%)

Classical
A65+ (15.4%)
A18-24 (10.3%)
A55-64 (12.6%)
A25-34 (16.1%)
A45-54 (21.1%)
A35-44 (24.6%)

Easy Listening
A65+ (21.2%)
A18-24 (16.7%)
A55-64 (8.5%)
A25-34 (21.1%)
A45-54 (13.6%)
A35-44 (19.8%)

Contemporary Hit Radio (CHR)
A55-64 (2.1%)
A65+ (2.5%)
A45-54 (7.6%)
A35-44 (18.9%)
A18-24 (36.1%)
A25-34 (32.8%)

Exhibit

9.3

There's a Radio Format for Everyone

Source: Simmons, fall 1997.
Courtesy: Radio Advertising Bureau.
From: Radio Marketing Guide and Fact Book for Advertisers,
April 1998–March 1999, 38.

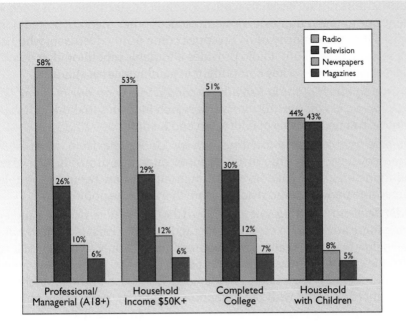

Exhibit

9.4

People Spend More Time with Radio

Average Weekday 6 A.M.–6 P.M.

Source: Media Targeting 2000, conducted by The Arbitron Company in cooperation with The Radio Advertising Bureau.

4. *Radio reaches light users of other media.* Light television viewers spend more than twice as much time with radio as they do with television. In addition, radio can fill in gaps in both newspaper and magazine coverage of prime audiences. Teenagers, in particular, make extensive use of radio. Research indicates that teens are extremely loyal to particular stations. In most markets, ". . . there are typically a few strong teen stations, allowing advertisers to efficiently reach large numbers of teens."[7]

5. *Radio works well with other media.* Exhibit 9.5 demonstrates the way in which radio can reach light users of other media and fill in gaps in a media schedule. For many years, a fundamental marketing strategy for radio has been to pro-

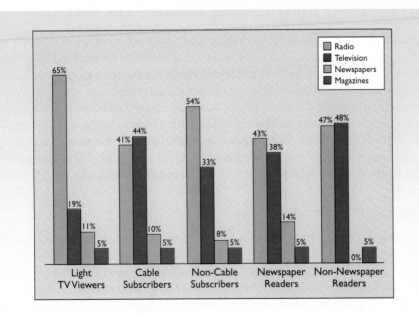

Exhibit

9.5

People Spend More Time with Radio

Average Weekday 6 A.M.–6 P.M.

Source: Media Targeting 2000, conducted by The Arbitron Company in cooperation with The Radio Advertising Bureau.

[7]Peter Zollo, "Not quite the TV generation," *American Demographics*, May 1999, 35.

mote its ability to successfully work with other media to increase reach and frequency or to reach nonusers or light users of other media. The radio industry realizes that the majority of its revenues come from advertisers who use radio as a secondary medium. Radio provides affordable repetition that delivers high levels of awareness—a key component in gaining market share.

6. *Because so much of radio listening is conducted on an out-of-home basis, the medium reaches an upscale market.* Research indicates that the radio audience is above average in terms of education and income.

7. *Radio delivers consistent listening patterns.* Unlike television, radio offers year-round coverage with little or no summer audience drop-off. Likewise, radio maintains high audience levels throughout the day. Even during television prime-time periods, radio reaches more than half the population.

8. *Radio delivers its messages at a very low CPM level.* Advertisers are increasingly giving more attention to cost efficiencies. Radio delivers its audience at a CPM level below that of virtually any other medium. Not only are the CPM levels low, but radio's recent increases also have been below that of its major competitors. For a number of years, radio CPM increases have been approximately half of all media increases and, with the exception of outdoor, radio is the only medium with rate increases lower than the consumer price index (CPI).

9. *Radio provides advertisers with both immediacy and flexibility.* Radio advertising has the ability to react quickly to changing market conditions. With relatively short production deadlines and inexpensive creative techniques, radio is an excellent medium to take advantage of fast-breaking opportunities.

The ability to anticipate or react to changing conditions cannot be underestimated. For example, when the Indianapolis 500 ends on Memorial Day afternoon, radio commercials touting the winner's tire and oil brands begin running that evening. The simplicity of radio can be a major advantage in making tactical marketing decisions. Radio's sense of immediacy and flexibility, all at a cost within the budget of even the smallest advertiser, has made it an important part of the advertising strategy of many advertisers.

LIMITATIONS AND CHALLENGES OF RADIO

No medium is suited for every marketing and advertising situation. Like all media, radio has special strengths and weaknesses that must be considered by advertisers considering placing radio in their media schedule. Radio has a number of characteristics that make it an ideal vehicle for numerous advertisers as either a primary or secondary medium. By the same token, advertisers need to be aware of some of the major disadvantages that must be considered before scheduling a radio buy. Two of the major problems facing advertisers using radio are: (1) the sheer number of stations that creates a very fragmented environment especially for those advertisers needing to reach a general audience and (2) the medium's lack of a visual element.

Audience Fragmentation

audience fragmentation The segmenting of mass-media audiences into smaller groups because of diversity of media outlets.

One of the great strengths of radio is its ability to reach narrowly defined audience niches with formats of particular interest to specific listeners. However, some advertisers wonder if the extent of segmentation has resulted in an overly fragmented medium with audience levels for most stations so small that it is difficult to reach a brand's core prospects. For those product categories with broad appeal, it is difficult to gain effective reach and frequency without buying several radio stations or networks. Radio executives respond that while there are a few major markets where competition has forced stations into continually narrowing their program formats, for the most part, radio remains among the most effective means of achieving the target marketing desired by the majority of advertisers. However, to put the situation in perspective, there are twice as many radio stations as television stations, consumer magazines, and daily newspapers combined!

Clutter

As discussed in Chapter 8, clutter is a major concern to advertisers. The more commercials and other nonprogram content, the less likely listeners will recall any particular advertising message. The number of radio commercials has always been significantly greater than in television. However, with deregulation, the time devoted to commercials has steadily increased. In some cases, radio stations are running as much as 50-percent advertising during peak listening periods.

In yet another use of new technology, some radio stations have resorted to digital editing to add commercial minutes using time compression. For example, one station used sophisticated software known as *Cash* to take out the pauses between words on the *Rush Limbaugh Show*. While these electronic snips were not noticed by the audience, they added as much as four commercial minutes per hour to the show. "While radio executives say the impact of Cash technology is often imperceptible to consumers, advertising executives complain that there is already too much clutter on the dial, making each commercial less effective."[8]

Lack of a Visual Element

A fundamental problem for advertisers is radio's lack of a visual component. At a time when advertisers are attempting to enhance brand image and build consumer awareness, many advertisers find radio's lack of visualization a difficult problem to overcome. With the growth of self-service retailing and competitive brand promotions, package identification is crucial for many advertisers.

Radio has long used a number of creative techniques to substitute the ear for the eye and attempt to overcome the lack of visuals. Sound effects; jingles; short, choppy copy; and vivid descriptions attempt to create a mental picture. In recent years, radio has attempted to show that images familiar to consumers from television commercials can be transferred to consumers through radio.

A major research study by Statistical Research, Inc. (SRI) demonstrated that listeners are able to develop "mental pictures" effectively as a result of radio commercials. Using **imagery transfer research,** SRI showed that a majority of listeners correctly described the prime visual element of television commercials when listening to radio commercials for the same products.

imagery transfer research A technique that measures the ability of radio listeners to correctly describe the primary visual elements of related television commercials.

The study found that imagery transfer is most effective when the same, or similar, audio tracks are used in both television and radio commercials. Data show that 75 percent of all consumers who have seen a television commercial will mentally "replay" the visual images when exposed to a corresponding radio commercial. This research has major implications for both creative approaches to radio and media buying. For example, advertisers who plan for and use radio as an integral part of their television campaigns can do the following:

1. Extend campaign reach
2. Substantially increase message frequency
3. Improve awareness during and between television flights
4. Maximize advertising investments
5. Reach out-of-home consumers

---

[8]Alex Kuczynski, "Radio squeezes empty air space for profit," www.nytimes.com., 6 January 2000.

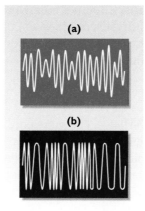

(a)

(b)

Exhibit

9.6

In amplitude modulation (a) waves vary in height (amplitude): frequency is constant. Frequency modulation (b) varies the frequency but keeps the height constant. These drawings, however, are not made to scale, which would reveal that width is the significant difference between AM and FM. The FM wave is 20 times wider than the AM wave. This fact helps to explain how FM captures its fine tones.

The concept of imagery transfer allows television advertisers to enhance their campaigns. "It keeps images fresh in consumers' minds and increases product awareness. It allows advertisers to create a marketing synergy that results in maximum cost efficiency and increased sales."[9] This research reinforces the value of radio as a cost-efficient complement to other media and shows that radio can boost the visual images used in multimedia campaigns.

TECHNICAL ASPECTS OF RADIO

The Signal

The electrical impulses that are broadcast by radio are called the *signal*. If a certain station has a good signal in a given territory, its programs and commercials come over clearly in that area.

Frequency

All signals are transmitted by electromagnetic waves, sometimes called *radio waves*. These waves differ from one another in frequency (the number of waves that pass a given point in a given period of time). Frequencies for AM stations are measured in Kilohertz or KHz and FM stations' frequencies are measured in Megahertz or MHz. The FCC has assigned the following frequencies to all radio stations.

$$AM = 540 \text{ to } 1700 \text{ KHz}$$

$$FM = 88.1 \text{ to } 107.9 \text{ MHz}$$

Amplitude

All electromagnetic waves have height, spoken of as *amplitude*, whose range resembles the difference between an ocean wave and a ripple in a pond, and speed, measured by the frequency with which a succession of waves passes a given point per minute. If, for example, a radio station operates on a frequency of 1,580 KHz, this means that 1,580,000 of its waves pass a given point per second.

On the basis of these two dimensions—amplitude and frequency—two separate systems have been developed for carrying radio waves. The first system carries the variations in a sound wave by corresponding variations in its amplitude; the frequency remains constant. This is the principle of **amplitude modulation** (AM) (Exhibit 9.6a). The second system carries the variation in a sound wave by corre-

amplitude modulation (AM) Method of transmitting electromagnetic signals by varying the *amplitude* (size) of the electromagnetic wave, in contrast to varying its *frequency*. Quality is not as good as frequency modulation, but can be heard farther, especially at night. *See* Frequency modulation (FM).

---

[9]"If you think they're seeing your TV ad now . . . Wait 'til they see it on the radio!" a publication of the Radio Advertising Bureau, 1996.

sponding variations in its frequency; the amplitude remains constant. This is the principle of **frequency modulation** (FM) (Exhibit 9.6b).

The technical structure of AM and FM radio has created, in effect, two distinct media, each offering different values to the listener and the advertiser. AM signals carry farther but are susceptible to interference. FM has a fine tonal quality, but its signal distances are limited. A particular station's quality of reception also is determined by atmospheric conditions and station power (broadcast frequency).

SELLING RADIO COMMERCIAL TIME

Radio advertising dollars are very much concentrated at the local level. Despite significant growth in both radio network and spot advertising, local advertising continues to dominate industry revenues (see Exhibit 9.7).

In recent years, radio has demonstrated more than 10-percent annual growth in advertising dollars. In fact, it trails only cable television among major media in advertising dollar increases. Major advertisers see audience segmentation as a major reason for choosing one medium over another. Advertisers recognize ". . . the ability to target as one of the primary benefits of advertising on radio. In this age of product proliferation, media glut, and ever-changing consumer demands, it is absolutely critical that advertisers focus their advertising on those individuals who are most likely to buy their products and services."[10]

Buying radio can be a difficult task because of the number of stations and formats available to advertisers. For example, there are currently more than 12,000 U.S. radio stations—with 102 stations in New York City alone. In addition, there are 91 distinct formats from which to choose, from Adult Album Alternative to Vietnamese. Even the most sparsely populated state, Wyoming, has 73 commercial stations programming 21 different formats.[11]

Recent consolidation of radio ownership offers the potential for major changes in the radio rate structure and the way radio time is bought. From the outset of the move to group ownership, major radio group executives promised advertisers better service and more efficient buying procedures. Rather than dealing with many individual stations or independent rep companies, a media buyer in a streamlined environment could negotiate time availability and rates for hundreds of stations dealing with a single person and submitting one insertion order.

However, advertisers have feared from the start that the buying efficiency provided by group ownership could come at a steep price. The Television Act of 1996 set substantially more liberal limits on single market ownership than had been previously the case. Exhibit 9.8 shows the number of stations that can be owned per market.

The large group owners have purchased the most profitable, highest rated stations in most major markets—the stations most sought by advertisers. Instead of

frequency modulation (FM) A radio transmission wave that transmits by the variation in the frequency of its wave, rather than its size (as in amplitude modulation [AM]). An FM wave is twenty times the width of an AM wave, which is the source of its fine tone. To transmit such a wave, it has to be placed high on the electromagnetic spectrum, far from AM waves with their interference and static, hence its outstanding tone.

Local	77.6
Spot	18.1
National	4.1

Exhibit
9.7

Sources of Radio Revenues (Percentage of Total)

No. of Stations in a Market	Limit of Ownership by Single Group
45 or more	8
30 to 44	7
15 to 29	6
14 or fewer	5*

*But no more than half the stations in a market.

Exhibit
9.8

Local Market Station Ownership Limits

[10]"Getting results for radio advertisers," a publication of the Radio Advertising Bureau, 2.
[11]Station information from *Broadcast and Cable Yearbook, 1999* (New Providence, NJ: R.R. Bowker Publications, 1999).

independently owned stations competing with each other for advertising dollars, these stations often operate under a senior sales manager whose job is to maximize profits for the group rather than engaging in competitive pricing among group-owned stations. Reacting to the changing local market radio advertising environment, one advertising executive complained, "This is a classic example of what we all feared. It proves that they [local stations] aren't client focused. When consolidation of radio stations was first discussed, the owners said consolidation would give us better service and better ideas. This clearly shows their colors—that for them it's all about price."[12]

While ownership consolidation may have the potential to drive up local radio rates and give stations more leverage with advertisers, it does not eliminate the fierce competition that radio faces for local advertising dollars. Radio advertising continues to operate in a challenging environment as it competes for local advertisers. Radio must compete with traditional selective media such as newspapers, Yellow Pages, and direct response that also reach targeted audiences. In addition, radio is competing with new media such as the Internet and both broadcast and cable television, which see local advertising as major profit centers.

Network Radio

The demise of network radio as a major national medium and the beginning of local radio began in 1948 with the introduction of television. Average ratings for Bob Hope's radio dropped from 23.8 in 1948 to 5.4 in 1953. Soap operas left radio for television throughout the 1950s until *Ma Perkins*, the last survivor, went off the air in 1960. The last major radio dramas, *Suspense* and *Have Gun Will Travel*, ended in 1962 and the era of network radio was essentially over. For the next decade, network programs were largely confined to news and occasional short features.

Network radio, while still a minor source of advertising dollars, has shown a slight comeback in the last decade. Media planners are looking increasingly to network radio as a means of extending reach to light users of other media and building greater brand awareness through inexpensive additional frequency to prime target segments. Despite these gains, network radio advertising only accounts for $1 billion of the $20 billion spent annually in radio, but it is growing at a rate of more than 10 percent per year.

Radio networks are much different from those in television as is the relationship between radio networks and their affiliates. Radio networks are basically program providers, but unlike in television, a single radio station may belong to several radio networks simultaneously. For example, a station might get sports reports from one network, personality profiles and news from another, and entertainment fare from yet another. Whereas in television local stations sell advertising time on the basis of the strength of the network programming, in radio the networks must depend on local ratings to garner national advertising support.

In contrast to television where each network such as NBC provides a single broadcast service (we will not consider cable-distributed services such as MSNBC or CNBC) and has a permanent lineup of affiliates, ABC Radio provides a number of targeted networks. For example, ABC has five full-service networks including the Prime Network directed at adults aged 25–54 with a news/talk format and Galaxy Networks with a number of 24-hour music formats for various demographic markets. In addition, ABC also provides individual programs such as *Paul Harvey News and Comment*, which is broadcast three times daily and news breaks throughout the day.

---

[12]Chuck Ross and Carol Krol, "Chancellor memo raises competition questions," *Advertising Age*, 26 April 1999, 51.

Regardless of the way a radio station uses network programming and the many differences with television, radio networks do offer some of the same advantages as their television counterparts. For example, an advertiser prepares one insertion order for multiple stations, pays one invoice, and is guaranteed uniform production quality for the commercials scheduled on all stations. Radio networks also provide economical reach and, like all radio, target special audience segments who often are light users of other media.

The resurgence of radio networks has been largely a result of satellite technology. The availability of satellite links for national radio programmers offers a number of advantages for their local station affiliates:

1. Stations are guaranteed quality programming based on the latest audience research for a particular format.
2. Radio networks bring celebrities to the medium that local stations could not afford.
3. Even the smallest stations can obtain national advertising dollars as part of a network. Stations that would not be considered by national advertisers as part of a local spot buy may now be included in a network radio schedule.
4. The cost efficiencies of sharing programming with several hundred other affiliates keeps both personnel and programming costs to a minimum.

Network radio will never return to its former status as a primary medium for national advertisers. However, as a source of program services, with its ability to target narrow audience segments, it will continue to play an important role for a number of national advertisers.

Spot Radio

As you will recall from our discussion in Chapter 8, spot advertising is the buying of local stations by national advertisers. Advertisers spend approximately $3.5 billion in spot radio advertising each year. It is almost always a second medium for national companies to build added reach and frequency against selected target markets. Spot radio offers these advertisers an opportunity to react quickly to changing competitive challenges and hit narrowly segmented markets with little waste circulation.

For example, MCI Communications consistently ranks among the top users of spot radio with expenditures of $50 million. However, this expenditure represents only 5 percent of the company's annual advertising budget. Among other leading buyers of spot radio such as General Motors, AT&T, and Time Warner, the percentage of their advertising budget devoted to spot radio is even less.

Despite the relatively low percentage of total advertising dollars, spot radio serves important functions for a number of advertisers. To those companies with a national presence who have widely differentiated market potential it can provide added weight in selected regions or individual markets. A second group of heavy spot radio users are national companies with extensive retail outlets. Spot radio commercials allow these companies to build on their national brand awareness with localized spots directed at the local community. Kmart and Dayton Hudson are advertisers that depend on spot radio to augment their national advertising.[13]

For a number of businesses, spot radio ". . . serves as an excellent partner for advertisers looking to mount a multimedia campaign, combining two or more approaches. Radio fits neatly with other media to extend reach and frequency beyond what either could accomplish alone."[14] Spot radio, as is the case in other

---

[13]"Leading national advertisers," *Advertising Age*, 27 September 1999, S39.
[14]"Media facts," a publication of the Radio Advertising Bureau, 2000, 4.

categories of the medium, will continue to grow as advertisers take advantage of its flexibility and low cost.

As is the case with television, most spot broadcast purchases are made through reps. In principle, radio reps serve the same function as those in TV. The best reps are those that serve as marketing consultants for their client stations. They work with agencies to match target audiences with the appropriate stations in their client list. Sometimes this is done on a market-by-market basis. In other cases buys are made through nonwired networks in the same manner as TV nonwired networks, which we discussed in Chapter 8. It remains to be seen what effect consolidation within the radio industry will have on the relationship between reps and stations. As more and more local stations are bought by major groups, it may mean that a significant amount of spot advertising will be sold directly by group salespersons bypassing rep firms and that reps will be left primarily to sell smaller market stations through their nonwired networks. The rep/station relationship is just one more area of potential change in an industry where reorganization has become the rule.

AM Versus FM as an Advertising Medium

Of the more than 10,000 commercial radio stations about 5,600 are FM and the remainder AM. However, despite the number of stations in each category, FM dominates the overall listening audience and is the clear leader in most formats. In some major markets, as much as 80 percent of the audience is normally listening to FM and, with the exception of several major all-talk stations, most AM stations are far down the list of stations in terms of ratings and audience share. In fact, AM stations tend to reach an older audience with talk, news, and specialty formats such as gospel and nostalgia.

The growth of FM radio audiences and advertising revenues during the last 20 years is the most important trend in the industry in recent years. FM technology was adapted for radio shortly before World War II. During the war all broadcast station construction was halted, but a few stations that had gone on the air prior to the start of the war continued to operate. For almost three decades after the close of the war, FM was largely confined to noncommercial and classical stations with few listeners, and little or no advertising. The exception were the jointly owned AM/FM stations, which usually duplicated programming on both stations. Since AM and FM radio sets were sold separately and there was little original programming, few incentives existed for listeners to purchase the more expensive FM sets.

In 1975, FM independent stations (those without an AM partner) reported a combined loss of almost $10 million. Just three years later, these same stations had profits of slightly less than $25 million. Obviously, this type of economic turnaround did not happen by happenstance. A number of factors have contributed to the vitality of FM with both advertisers and audiences. Among the major elements are the following:

1. In 1972 the Federal Communication Commission ruled that joint owners of both AM and FM stations in the same market had to program different formats. This ruling opened the way for FM as a separate medium.
2. The sound quality of FM is markedly better than AM. Since music formats dominate radio, FM steadily gained audience share at the expense of AM.
3. The decline in the cost of FM sets coincided with the popularity of the medium. Thirty years ago radio sets with an FM band were much more expensive than AM-only sets. Also few cars were equipped with an FM radio. Currently, 88 percent of car radios are AM/FM and virtually all radio sets are equipped with both AM and FM bands.
4. As radio audiences turned to FM for the most popular music formats, AM was left with an audience skewed to older listeners, a less than prime market seg-

ment for most advertisers. Therefore, the switch to FM by audiences was followed quickly by an increase in advertising dollars.

It is clear that FM will continue to be the dominant radio medium as AM stations search for those formats that will attract niche audiences. In fact, many observers say that it was only the emergence of talk radio in the last 10 years that saved AM from economic disaster.

Types of Programming

As we previously discussed, radio is a medium constantly searching for targeted audiences to deliver to advertisers. It also is a medium overwhelmingly devoted to music. The typical radio station depends on a music format and unique talent to appeal to the largest audience in a particular listener demographic. Unlike television, where viewers tune to a certain program for a half-hour or hour and then move to another station for another show, radio audiences tend to demonstrate loyalty to a station because of the *type* of music, sports, or information it programs.

For a number of years, the "country" format has been carried by more stations than any other. Approximately 2,500 stations report that they program some form of country music as their primary format. The number of country music stations can be attributed, in part, to the large quantity of small stations in rural and small-market areas where country music is most popular. Although many of the new country styles (e.g., Faith Hill and Shania Twain) have brought country into the mainstream and larger markets, it has its roots in small town America. The same phenomenon is true in religious radio. Although almost 10 percent of all stations have a religious format, the number of stations in no way equates to the size of the audience. In other words, the number of stations programming a format often has little to do with the size of listenership.

To advertisers, however, it is often the quality of the audience as much as its size that is of most importance. For example, those relatively few stations with "children," "public affairs" or "agriculture and farm" formats might be exactly the advertising vehicle for particular advertisers seeking to reach small, but (for them) profitable prospects.

One of the problems for radio stations is that they function in an environment of economic Darwinism where only the strongest survive. While every station would like to be the leader in a popular format, radio executives know that it is extremely difficult for more than one or two stations in a market to be financially successful in any particular format. Why would an advertiser buy a market's third or fourth rated country station?

Consequently, second- and third-tier stations are constantly searching for niche formats that will allow them to be the leader among some audience segment that is of value to advertisers. Specialty formats, such as classical or jazz, usually depend on an upscale audience that is difficult for advertisers to reach in other media. However, with as many as 50 stations in most large markets, developing niche formats is not only cutthroat, but often it gets a little silly. For instance, stations without impressive total numbers may resort to calling themselves the number one station in a particular daypart (e.g., midnight–6 A.M.) or developing subcategories of a format to differentiate themselves from other stations (easy listening country).

Radio should be considered a quasi-mass medium. Despite its high aggregate audiences, the number of people listening to any particular station at a given time is very small. Even the top stations in a market will be lucky to achieve ratings of 8 or 10, and a rating of 1 to 3 is more common. Consequently, an audience increase that would be insignificant in other media might make a major difference in the financial health of a radio station. For example, a change of one rating point for a station with an average rating of 3 is an increase of 33 percent, a figure that often will move a station significantly up the rankings among stations in a market.

RADIO RATINGS SERVICES

As discussed in Chapter 8, the growth of television has created some significant problems in determining accurate audience-rating data. However, the problems in television research pale in comparison to those facing radio. Not only are there more than 10 times the number of radio stations compared to television, but the lack of specific programming on most stations makes respondent recall much more difficult than in television. As we have discussed, television recall is not a problem for the majority of viewers where meters are used. In addition, much of the radio audience listens out-of-home where it is impractical to keep a diary or reach respondents by telephone.

Dozens of companies provide research services for radio. However, most of these firms are engaged in program consulting or custom research for individual stations and advertisers. The major source of local syndicated radio ratings and the dominant company in radio research is **The Arbitron Company**, which provides audience data through its Arbitron Radio division.

Arbitron measures radio audiences in 268 local markets through the use of listener diaries. All members of sampled households over the age of 12 have a personal diary in which they record listening behavior over a seven-day period. Rating periods in a specific market last for 12 weeks. The number of weeks that a market is sampled is determined by its size, with the largest metropolitan areas sampled on a continuous basis for 48 weeks of the year. The smallest markets will be sampled for only one 12-week period and the ratings will be published in a condensed version of the larger ratings books. Overall, Arbitron collects and analyzes more than one million diaries each year.

In 1999, Arbitron began to collect Webcast audience information through a service called InfoStream. Preliminary data for 290 radio stations demonstrated that the audience for Webcast is already larger than many broadcasters and advertisers may have anticipated. For example, ". . . Arbitron research reported that 34 percent of the online population has listened to or watched streamed media at least once."[15]

The study showed that some top-rated audio services have monthly audiences of almost 60,000 listeners with many listening as much as seven hours per month. Clearly, streamed audio has already become a major factor in radio and it only increases the complexity of collecting accurate rating information.

Because of the local nature of radio, station ratings are much more critical to most advertisers than those for networks. However, as we have discussed earlier, network radio is becoming increasingly important to a number of advertisers. As major businesses move into network radio advertising the demand for accurate ratings will become even more important. The primary source of radio network ratings is the **Radio All Dimension Audience Research (RADAR)** reports, a service of Statistical Research, Inc. Research data for RADAR reports are collected through telephone recall interviews. Currently, approximately 40 networks are surveyed for RADAR reports.

An overriding problem in dealing with radio ratings is money. The funds available to solve an advertising research problem are directly related to the level of advertising expenditures by major advertisers. For example, when General Motors and Procter & Gamble invest $1 billion annually in television there is a major incen-

---
[15]John Gaffney, "Arbitron to rate streamed media by end of year," *Revolution*, May 2000, 60.

The Arbitron Company Syndicated radio ratings company.

Radio All Dimension Audience Research (RADAR) Service of Statistical Research, Inc., major source of network radio ratings.

tive to invest millions of dollars in research. On the other hand, even though the problems may be more difficult in media such as radio and outdoor, the overall advertising investment will simply not support a research expenditure comparable to television.

BUYING RADIO

Radio demonstrates a number of characteristics as an advertising medium:

- Advertising inventory is inflexible and when a spot goes unsold, revenue is permanently lost.
- Radio is normally used as a supplement to other media. Therefore, coordination with the total advertising plan is crucial for most radio sales.
- Every radio buy is unique. Almost all radio advertising is sold in packages of spots that are tailored, to some degree, to each advertiser.
- Because of the unique nature of each buy, a fixed rate card rarely exists for radio advertising. Pricing is largely the result of negotiation between media buyers and radio salespersons.

Despite the complexity of buying radio advertising, the fundamentals of buying radio are very similar to those of other media. For example, as with most advertising plans, we must examine a number of elements before we proceed to an advertising execution:

1. Review product characteristics and benefits and decide whether these benefits can be effectively communicated through radio.
2. Who is the target market and can they be reached effectively with radio and, if so, what formats, what dayparts? For example, Exhibit 9.9 shows the concentration of the African American audience in five formats and the contrast among these audiences with white listeners. The ability to reach audience segments with this type of pinpoint precision remains radio's major strength.
3. Who is our competition? How are they using radio and other media? Will radio provide a unique differentiation for our product or will we be up against strong competing messages?
4. What is our basic advertising and marketing strategy and can it be effectively carried out with radio?

In virtually all advertising situations, we start with a clear delineation of our target market. This audience definition is particularly important in buying radio because of the narrowly defined formats that are offered by the medium. We then must look at the cost of alternative radio outlets and must compare the options available against the CPM/prospects or some other method of evaluating value per advertising dollar.

Format	African-American	White
R&B	59%	17%
Christian/religious	48%	18%
Rap/hip-hop	44%	11%
Oldies	41%	43%
Jazz	39%	13%
Country	7%	43%
Classic	9%	35%
Rock	7%	31%

Exhibit
9.9

Format Preferences

On a typical day, African-Americans listen to about four hours of radio.

Source: Yankelovich African-American Monitor.
From: Advertising Age, 31 July 2000, 26.

Radio, from both a marketing and creative standpoint, must be considered in terms of the advertising objectives we have set out for our advertising. For example, radio in general or a specific station may meet our objectives for reach and cost, but fail in terms of the creative strategy. Since radio advertising is often used as a secondary medium, it may be the case that we will evaluate radio in terms of how it complements other more primary media in our advertising schedule and what proportion of our budget should be devoted to radio in this complementary role.

Once we have decided that radio can play a role in our advertising plan, we must begin the task of selecting particular stations that both reach our target audience and also provide a program environment that fits our product image. As we have discussed, the number of radio stations provide advertisers, particularly those with national distribution, with many options from which to choose. For some advertisers, network radio is a better option, in terms of cost and guaranteed quality of editorial, than a spot or local schedule. Nevertheless, radio is one of the most challenging aspects of media planning.

The final step in radio buying is the actual scheduling of the spots. Because most advertisers use a great number of spots to achieve reach and/or frequency, the scheduling process can be difficult. While most radio spots are 60-seconds, some advertisers use shorter messages to gain frequency while a few opt for longer form commercials to achieve greater impact. In addition, decisions such as whether to use specific dayparts or use a combination of time periods and, in a few instances, whether to take advantage of program sponsorship or on-site event promotions must be considered. Regardless of the final determinations of these and other questions, radio can provide great flexibility and fit into the plans of virtually every advertiser.

Because of the complicated nature of radio, buyers must often rely on the expertise of radio sales personnel—at the station, network, or rep level. Given the nature of radio buys, it is imperative that both buyers and sellers understand the relationship involved in the process. This starts with credibility. One of the primary ways a radio salesperson gains trust is to position radio as a part of the marketing plan. This entails walking a fine line between aggressively selling the medium and your station, but, at the same time, acknowledging the strengths and contributions of other media.

Rather than trying to convince heavy newspaper advertisers to move out of the medium, it is more reasonable to show how radio can make newspaper advertising more effective. The key to successful selling is identifying with the problems of the clients. To do this, the salesperson needs to show advertisers that radio can solve their specific marketing problem. Remember, advertisers are not interested in buying time, they are interested in finding prospects and demonstrating major product benefits to these prospects.

USING RADIO RATINGS

We defined both television ratings and share of audience in Chapter 8. Radio rating and share figures are calculated in the same way. However, the size of the radio audience and the highly fragmented nature of programming and formats has created a system where ratings are used differently than in television. This section discusses some uses of ratings that are unique to radio.

Among the primary differences between the use of ratings in television and radio are the following:

1. Radio advertisers are interested in broad formats rather than programs or more narrowly defined television scatter plans.

2. Radio ratings tend to measure audience accumulation over relatively long periods of time or several dayparts. Most television ratings are calculated for individual programs.

3. The audiences for individual radio stations are much smaller than television, making radio ratings less reliable.

4. Since most radio stations reach only a small segment of the market at a given time, there is a need for much higher levels of advertising frequency compared to other media. Consequently, it is extremely difficult to track ratings information accurately for national radio plans that include a large number of stations.

Let's begin our discussion by examining several definitions used in radio-rating analyses.

Geographical Patterns of Radio Ratings

Radio audience ratings use two geographical boundaries to report audiences: Metro Survey Area (MSA) and Total Survey Area (TSA). Typically the majority of a station's audience comes from within the MSA.

Metro Survey Area An MSA always includes a city or cities whose population is specified as that of the central city together with the county (or counties) in which it is located.

Total Survey Area The TSA is a geographic area that encompasses the MSA and certain counties located outside the MSA, but meet certain minimum listening criteria.

Definitions of the Radio Audience

The basic audience measures for television are the rating and share of audience for a particular show. It would be a serious mistake to buy radio and television on the same basis without considering major differences in the way audience figures are considered between the two media. In radio, audience estimates are usually presented as either Average Quarter Hour (AQH) audiences or the cumulative or unduplicated audience (Cume) listening to a station over several quarter hours or dayparts.

Average Quarter Hour Estimates (AQHE)

1. *Average Quarter Hour Persons*. The AQH persons are the estimated number of people listening to a station for at least five minutes during a 15-minute period.

2. *Average Quarter Hour Rating*. Here we calculate the AQH persons as a percentage of the population being measured:

$$\text{AQH persons}/\text{population} \times 100 = \text{AQH rating}$$

3. *Average Quarter Hour Share*. The AQH Share determines what portion of the average radio audience is listening to our station:

$$\text{AQH persons to a station}/\text{AQH persons to all stations} \times 100 = \text{Share}$$

average quarter-hour estimates (AQHE) Manner in which ratio ratings are presented. Estimates include average number of people listening, rating, and metro share of audience.

Cume Estimates

Cume estimates are used to determine the number or percentage of different people who listen to a station during several quarter hours or dayparts.

1. *Cume persons*. The number of *different* people who tuned to a radio station for at least five minutes.

2. *Cume rating.* The percentage of different people listening to a station during several quarter hours or dayparts.

$$\text{Cume persons/Population} \times 100 = \text{Cume rating}$$

Let's look at a typical station's audience and calculate these formulas.

Station XYYY, −F 10 A.M.–3 P.M., Adults 12+

AQH persons = 20,000

Cume persons = 60,000

Metro Survey Area population = 500,000

Metro Survey Area AQH persons = 200,000

For station XYYY:

The AQH rating = 4 (20,000/500,000)[16]

The Cume rating = 12 (60,000/500,000)

The AQH share = 10 (20,000/200,000)

Using our XYYY example, we can also calculate the following:

1. Gross Impressions (GI) = AQH persons × No. of commercials
   If we buy six commercials on XYYY we have purchased 120,000 impressions (20,000 AQH persons × 6 spots). Remember these are *impressions* not people.
2. Gross Rating Points = AQH rating × No. of commercials
   Again, six commercials would deliver 24 GRPs (4 AQH rating × 6 spots).
3. Listeners per Dollar (LPD) = AQH persons/spot cost
   If a spot on XYYY costs $500 then the LPD is 40 (20,000 AQH persons/$500).

The media planner must be able to manipulate the various radio data to develop a plan most suited to a particular client. While the computer makes these manipulations quickly, it doesn't substitute for a basic understanding of the process. The same budget, and even the same number of spots, used in different dayparts and across multiple stations, can deliver vastly different levels of cumes, reach, frequency, and demographics.

SUMMARY

Radio has never been more popular in terms of advertising revenues and listenership. Every day more Americans use radio than any other medium and only newspapers can challenge radio in terms of the number of advertisers who make use of the medium. With thousands of stations, multiple formats, inexpensive production, and low commercial cost, it can provide effective reach and frequency for a number of product categories.

Technology promises to take the already impressive immediacy and person-to-person nature of radio to another level. With satellite transmission and out-of-home capability, radio can reach individual customers with programs and commercials tailored to their demographics and lifestyle. However, this same technology, particularly computer-delivered programming and music services, represents a challenge to radio, especially small market stations.

---

[16]It is understood that decimals are not used in reporting rating and share figures.

Radio has a significant advantage in achieving high penetration among light or nonusers of other media. For example, many teens use radio almost exclusively as a means of entertainment and information. Given the current demand by advertisers for narrowly defined audience segments, radio is increasingly becoming at least a secondary option in more and more media plans.

Despite the opportunities for radio to become more important in the advertising plans of both large and small advertisers, the medium faces two major problems. First, the medium lacks the type of research data enjoyed by most other media. A mobile, out-of-home audience makes it very difficult to reach a large majority of radio listeners. In addition, the lack of traditional programming makes recall more complicated than similar audience research in television.

A second major problem with radio is the lack of a visual element. Many advertisers think that without strong visual brand identification the medium can play little or no role in their advertising plans. The industry has sponsored a number of research studies to show that radio can work effectively with television to remind consumers of the commercials they have seen previously. This concept, known as imagery transfer, offers radio advertisers a strong selling point to national advertisers seeking an inexpensive supplement to their television schedules. However, it fails to fully compensate for a lack of visuals.

Radio also is providing national advertisers with a number of opportunities through satellite-distributed, syndicated programming. Technological advances and decreases in the cost of satellite time and equipment have made it easier, cheaper, and less risky to launch national syndicated shows. Shows such as Rush Limbaugh demonstrate that properly packaged, syndicated radio can deliver significant advertising impact to advertisers on both a local and national basis.

There is an irony that radio, once the major national medium, may be returning to its roots. Obviously, national syndication alone cannot bring radio back into the media spotlight. However, its new found success coupled with advanced technology and radio's inherent strengths as a vehicle to deliver narrowly targeted audiences bode well for the future.

REVIEW

1. What has been the major contributing factor to the lack of rate increases in radio during the last decade?
2. What is the major disadvantage of radio for most advertisers?
3. What are the primary advantages of radio to advertisers?
   a. low cost—cost of commercials, commercial production, and CPM
   b. ability to target narrowly identified target markets
   c. proximity to purchase and its ability to reach a mobile population
4. How do most national advertisers use radio?
5. What is the role of radio networks?
6. Who are the listeners of AM radio? What do they listen to?
7. Where do most advertisers obtain radio audience information?
8. Define the following:
   a. Drivetime
   b. Run-of-station
   c. Total audience plans

TAKE IT TO THE NET

We invite you to visit the Russell/Lane page on the Prentice Hall Web site at **www.prenhall.com/myphlip** for end-of-chapter exercises and applications.

Chapter 10

Using Newspapers

Newspapers trail only television in terms of total advertising revenues and they are the leader by a significant margin among local businesses. Each day approximately 60 million newspapers are distributed, providing a large segment of the population with news, entertainment, and advertising. Newspapers also enjoy a reputation for credibility that creates a positive advertising environment. After reading this chapter you will understand:

>> the changing character and role of newspapers in the marketing mix

>> challenges to newspaper advertising from other media options

>> the marketing of newspapers to readers and advertisers

>> the many categories of newspaper advertising

>> the newspaper advertising planning and buying process

>> the role of weeklies and ethnic-oriented newspapers

Pros

1. Newspapers appeal primarily to an upscale audience, especially those adults 35 and older.
2. Newspaper advertising is extremely flexible with opportunities for color, large and small space ads, timely insertion schedules, coupons, and some selectivity through special sections and targeted editions.
3. With coupons and sophisticated tracking methodology, it is much easier to measure newspaper response rates than with most other media.
4. Newspapers have high credibility with their readers, which creates a positive environment for advertisers.

Cons

1. Most newspapers have about 60-percent advertising content. This high ratio of advertising, combined with average reading time of less than 30 minutes, means few ads are read.
2. Overall newspaper circulation has fallen far behind population and household growth. In many markets total newspaper penetration is below 30 percent. In addition, readership among a number of key demographics such as teens and young adults has not kept pace with population growth.
3. Advertising costs have risen much more sharply than circulation in recent years.

Each day some 56 million newspapers are distributed in large cities and small towns. These papers are read by almost 60 percent of the population and an even greater percentage of readers from households with higher than average income and education levels. Annual advertising revenues in these newspapers is almost $50 billion with approximately 87 percent coming from local and classified advertisers. In addition, national advertisers are looking increasingly to local and regional advertising strategies to communicate with consumers in the most effective manner.

Newspaper advertising offers a number of advantages to businesses from large national corporations to the smallest retailer. Among the most important features of newspaper advertising are the following:

■ Flexibility of advertising formats and audience coverage. Advertisers can buy space ranging from a full-page, four-color advertisement to a small classified notice. In addition, virtually every newspaper offers a variety of specialized advertising plans, including on-line options, to allow advertisers to reach selected portions of newspaper's total circulation.

■ Newspapers are especially useful in reaching upscale households and opinion leaders. However, compared to most other media, newspapers have significant reach in all major demographic segments.

■ Newspapers offer advertisers a number of creative options including outstanding color reproduction and preprinted inserts.

■ Finally, newspapers provide an environment of credibility and immediacy unmatched by most media. A number of surveys have shown that consumers regard newspaper advertising as an important and reliable source of both information and advertising—just the type of medium with which advertisers want to be associated.

With so much to offer both advertisers and readers why is the newspaper industry so concerned about its future? The fact of the matter is that a number of trends cause concern for newspapers. Let's examine four areas that are keeping newspaper publishers awake at night.

1. *Circulation.* According to the Newspaper Association of America, in 1976 newspaper circulation was 77 million; by 2000 this figure was approximately 56 million in spite of significant increases in both population and households during that period. Throughout the 1990s, newspaper circulation dropped about 1 percent each year.

   The reasons given for the decline in newspaper circulation vary from not enough time in single-parent and two-income families to devote to newspaper reading; younger demographic segments don't like to read or they never developed the habit of reading newspapers; and other media, especially television, have encroached on the newspaper's position as the preferred method of getting news and information. All of these factors have probably played a role in the decline of newspaper readership.

Different newspapers have attacked the readership problem with diverse approaches. In some cases, newspapers engage in aggressive subscription sales campaigns including telemarketing and setting up booths on college campuses. Other newspapers such as *The New York Times* have accepted the inevitability of circulation decreases, but point to its upscale readership. For example, a *Times* executive said, "The quality of our journalism demands a premium price from readers. That, in turn, attracts the kind of audience that is very, very appealing to advertisers."[1] Of course, a formula that works for *The New York Times* is transportable to few other papers.

2. *Advertising revenues.* Obviously, newspaper circulation problems have not been ignored by the advertising community. As recently as 1980, newspapers' share of total advertising revenue was 28 percent. Currently, the figure is 22 percent. Some observers are predicting that newspaper share of advertising will drop below 20 percent before the end of the decade. In fact, newspapers may be the only medium to show a drop in advertising dollars in coming years.

Several problems have beleaguered newspapers in maintaining their share of advertising dollars. A number of retail chains have turned to direct mail and inserts to reach customers. Even the inserts that are distributed through newspapers provide lower profits for newspapers than traditional advertising. Second, newspapers have been unable to increase support from national advertisers. Even as national advertisers look to regional and local strategies, newspapers have had a difficult time gaining significant support from major national advertisers. Despite a number of newspaper initiatives to overcome national advertisers' reluctance to use the medium, dollars in the sector remain stagnant.

While newspapers have never enjoyed a large amount of revenue from national advertisers, currently their franchise with local advertisers is being threatened from a number of quarters. Local television; local cable cut-ins; free niche advertising books featuring real estate, automobiles, and so forth; regional and city editions of magazines; and, of course, radio continue to fight for local advertising dollars that 20 years ago would have gone automatically to newspapers. Later in this chapter we will discuss some of the ways in which newspapers are countering these problems.

3. *Changing technology.* Newspapers, like all media, face challenges from new media technology. In fact, many believe that the newspaper as we know it will be dramatically changed by this technology—not the many functions it serves but the method of distribution. The argument is that the cost of paper, ink, postage, and physical distribution is simply not going to be viable in a world of electronic communication. Going back no further than 1990, virtually no one outside the scientific community had ever heard of the Internet.

Today, for many people it is an indispensable, and preferred, form of communication. Research indicates that in 2000, 24 percent of adults used the Internet during the past 24 hours for news and information. Among 18- to 24-year-olds, the Internet and newspapers are used equally as a source of information with Internet usage growing.[2]

In light of the foothold already enjoyed by the Internet, imagine the improvements in instantaneous delivery, clarity and reliability of content, and portability of technology over the next 20 years—it is hard to imagine thick wads of paper being thrown in the driveways of the 2025 household! As one print executive predicted, "I believe that they [newspapers], and all forms of

---

[1]Marc Gunther, "Publish or perish?," *Fortune*, 10 January 2000, 148.
[2]Rebecca Ross Albers, "Study reveals Internet gains," *Presstime*, November 2000, 25.

print, are dead. Finished. Over. Twenty, thirty, at the outside forty years from now, we will look back on the print media the way we look back on travel by horse and carriage, or by wind-powered ship."[3]

This gloomy prediction for newspapers does not mean the functions of newspapers will be dead or even the companies that provide these services will be gone. It certainly does not mean that there will not be reporters, advertising salespeople, and most of all businesses with dollars to spend to reach a literate audience. It does mean that the methods of reaching these customers and "readers" will change dramatically.

Currently, some 1,200 newspapers provide Web sites for their readers and/or advertisers. But as we will discuss later in this chapter, the immediacy of newspapers is being replaced by electronic formats—many developed by newspapers themselves. In addition, newspaper classified advertising, which provides more than 40 percent of total revenues for the newspaper industry, is being challenged by dozens of on-line Web sites seeking a share of the lucrative employment (see monster.com) and real estate (see realtor.com) dollars.

The continuing challenge for both newspaper publishers and newspaper advertising executives is to provide the audience with readers to look to the daily paper as a primary source of information, advertising, and entertainment. The task is becoming more difficult as newspapers try to serve a diverse audience of young and old, affluent and middle-class, and numerous ethnic cultures. It is clear that newspapers will face growing competition from other media and information sources as they attempt to retain their position as a leading medium. The newspaper industry faces both problems and opportunities as we approach the next century. However, it is obvious that long-term trends will continue to endanger the basic foundation of newspaper readership and advertising. In the meantime, newspapers, despite declines in readership, remain one of the most effective means of reaching a broad, heterogeneous audience (see Exhibit 10.1).

As we will see throughout the remainder of this chapter, newspapers are more than up to the task of meeting these challenges as they take innovative initiatives to function successfully in a competitive environment. As we discuss major aspects of contemporary newspaper advertising, we must keep in mind the evolving and dynamic nature of the industry.

THE NATIONAL NEWSPAPER

Historically, the United States, unlike most other developed countries, did not have a national newspaper. When the first newspapers were founded, distances were too great and unique regional concerns made nationally distributed newspapers impractical. However, a number of newspapers now have national circulation, national stature, or both.

Competitive Media Report, a company that compiles data on advertising expenditures, defines a national newspaper as having the following characteristics:

- It publishes at least five days per week.
- It has no more than 67 percent of its circulation in a single area.
- More than 50 percent of its advertising revenue must come from national advertising (compared to 13 percent for all newspapers).

Based on these criteria, there are three national newspapers: *The Wall Street Journal*, *USA Today*, and *The New York Times*. *The Wall Street Journal* is an upscale,

---

[3]Dan Okrent, "The Death of Print?" Hearst New Media Lecture, Columbia University, December 14, 1999.

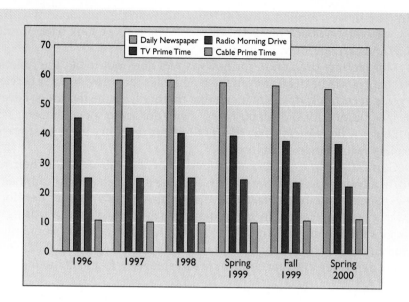

Exhibit

10.1

Competitive Media Index

From: NAA Facts About Newspapers 2000, 14.

Source: Scarborough Research 1999. Release 2. Top 50 Market Report Prepared by NAA Research Department.

Note: Radio drive times reflect Monday-Friday average quarter hour

	Percent of Adults Reached			
Year	Daily Newspaper[1]	Prime Time TV[2]	Morning Drive Radio[3]	Prime Time Cable[4]
1996	58.8	45.3	25.5	11.0
1997	58.7	42.4	25.4	10.4
1998	58.6	40.8	25.7	10.3
Spring 1999	57.9	39.6	25.5	10.5
Fall 1999	56.9	38.5	24.5	11.3
Spring 2000	56.2	37.8	23.4	12.0

[1]Average day readership; [2]Average half hour; [3]Average quarter hour; [4]Average half hour

specialized paper with an emphasis on financial news, but with great influence in politics and public policy issues. In fact, with a circulation of more than 1.7 million it is the highest circulation newspaper in the country. It also is among the most respected newspapers in the world and it reaches readers with the most elite audience demographics of any U.S. newspapers.

In 1998, *The Wall Street Journal* began a "Weekend Journal" lifestyle section in its Friday edition. The section allowed the newspaper to tap into advertising categories such as wine and liquor, entertainment, and other upscale brands that had never used the publication. The section proved so popular that on-line spin-offs such as wine.wsj.com have proved very popular.

All three of the leading national publications have extensive Web sites. However, *The Wall Street Journal* has one of the few profitable sites among all newspapers. Because of its reputation and specialized business content, it is able to charge an annual subscription fee of $59 (or $29 if a person subscribes to the print edition). The on-line edition currently has almost 500,000 subscribers.[4] By comparison most other newspaper sites are free, advertising supported, and, at best, only marginally profitable.

In 1982, the Gannett Company made a commitment to develop *USA Today* as a general readership national newspaper. While newspaper purists often criticized the paper's lack of depth, *USA Today* was popular with readers from the beginning with a mix of bright colors, short articles, and extensive business and sports cover-

---

[4]Jon Fine, "New Web site in WSJ's plans for 'Weekend'," *Advertising Age,* 14 August 2000, 1.

age. In a short time it gained wide distribution, especially bulk sales to hotels and airlines. After years of financial losses, Gannett has made *USA Today* profitable. However, few corporations would have had either the resources or management support to invest in such an endeavor. It is estimated that before *USA Today* had its first profitable year in 1993, it had lost over $250 million. This loss was not the result of a lack of readers. The paper averages 1.6 million readers and generally passes the two million mark on Friday with its weekend edition.

The problem facing all newspapers that aspire to national circulation is finding a profitable advertising niche. A national newspaper is a hybrid vehicle for most advertisers. Unlike other newspapers, national papers are unlikely to gain advertising from grocery stores, department stores, and other local product categories that have been traditionally major profit centers for newspapers. Instead, *USA Today* and other national newspapers depend on national automotive, computer, and communication companies and financial services for much of their revenue.

The New York Times has been classified only recently as a national newspaper. In addition, the *Los Angeles Times* has a national edition with limited circulation in selective East and West Coast markets. However, most large metropolitan newspapers such as *The Washington Post* and the *Chicago Tribune* are considered regional advertising media. They are bought much like spot broadcast to reach specific high-potential markets as a supplement to other primary media. Despite attempts by some newspapers to broaden their coverage, most advertisers classify all newspapers other than *The Wall Street Journal* and *USA Today* as regional. Exhibit 10.2 shows the largest U.S. newspapers.

Newspapers will probably continue to have a difficult time reaching out to national advertising as a primary medium. Newspapers have a long tradition as a local vehicle, which is a difficult perception to change. As one media buyer commented, "*The New York Times* is clearly prestigious, and there is certainly no drawback to using it for national exposure. But on an emotional level, it still has 'New York' in its title, which makes you think of them as more of a regional [newspaper]."[5]

The key to a move toward national newspapers is not how papers define themselves, but how they are defined by readers and advertisers. Until a number of newspapers achieve widely dispersed, upscale audiences (not likely for any but a handful of papers), advertisers will continue to regard the medium as a local vehicle with occasional national advertising opportunities.

MARKETING THE NEWSPAPER

It is obvious from our discussion thus far that newspapers are a product in need of extensive marketing to both readers and advertisers. Like any product with declin-

Average Daily Circulation[1]

The Wall Street Journal	1,752,693	(m)	Chicago Sun-Times	468.170	(m)
USA Today	1,671,539	(m)	The Boston Globe	462,850	(m)
The New York Times	1,086,293	(m)	San Francisco Chronicle	456,742	(m)
Los Angeles Times	1,078,186	(m)	New York Post	438,158	(m)
The Washington Post	763,305	(m)	The Arizona Republic	433,296	(m)
Daily News, New York	701,831	(m)	The Star-Ledger, Newark	407,129	(m)
Chicago Tribune	657,690	(m)	The Philadelphia Inquirer	399,339	(m)
Newsday	574,941	(m)	Denver Rocky Mountain News	396,114	(m)
Houston Chronicle	542,414	(m)	The Plain Dealer, Cleveland	386,312	(m)
The Dallas Morning News	490,249	(m)	The San Diego Union-Tribune	376,604	(m)

[1]Average for six months ended Sept. 30, 1999.

Exhibit
10.2

Top 20 U.S. Daily Newspapers by Circulation
Source: Audit Bureau of Circulation; Editor & Publisher.
From: NAA Facts About Newspapers 2000, 18.

---

[5]Ann Marie Kerwin, "Big city dailies eye national stage," *Advertising Age*, 22 February 1999, 24.

ing sales, newspapers must make a number of strategic and tactical decisions to reverse the trends they are seeing. Despite being the second leading source of advertising dollars, the traditional retail base of newspaper revenues is being challenged by a number of new and traditional media competitors. At the same time, newspapers are finding it more difficult to maintain the broad base of readership that has made them such a powerful medium for more than 200 years.

A positive trend among newspapers is the quality, as contrasted to the quantity, of readership enjoyed by newspapers. Newspapers are very strong among college graduates and households with incomes in excess of $100,000. Unfortunately, newspaper circulation also skews toward the oldest portion of the population. Newspaper readership is inversely related to age with those in the 18–34 age group (prime prospects for the majority of advertisers) the least likely to read newspapers on a regular basis. Newspapers must take strong steps to develop marketing strategies that will reverse the trend of declining readership and share of advertising revenues.

In the last 20 years newspapers have taken a number of steps to identify their customers, advertisers, and preferences of both. This process starts with marketing research. It is rare for any newspaper not to conduct at least one readership or market survey each year. Large newspapers annually sponsor several studies of their markets. A number of concerns have become apparent as a result of these studies.

Among the most important is the fact that readers are obtaining their information from a number of sources including television, the Internet, and so forth. They no longer see the newspaper as an indispensable source of information. While many advertisers regard newspapers as the most economical means of reaching a mass audience especially at the local level, many are adopting strategies that replace newspaper advertising with direct mail and other forms of promotion such as product sampling. On the plus side, these same studies demonstrate that newspapers maintain their reputation for integrity and prestige as sources of both advertising and editorial information.

While newspapers face some formidable challenges, there is no question that they will remain a major advertising medium in the foreseeable future as newspapers continue to offer unique advantages to both readers and advertisers. However, since newspapers dominated the local market for so long, they did not develop a marketing mentality. Unfortunately, the industry is now playing catch-up with its more aggressive media competitors. The next sections will discuss how newspaper publishers are marketing the medium to both readers and advertisers. We will examine some of the approaches that newspaper publishers are using to protect and extend their franchise with both readers and advertisers.

Marketing to Readers

Newspapers are fully aware that they cannot reverse the decline in advertising share unless they first address the problem of falling readership. Advertisers will only buy newspaper space when they are convinced that the medium will deliver prospects for their brands. Some elite newspapers may be able to survive decreasing readership by marketing the quality of their audience. However, most newspapers will continue to depend on a broadly based audience and high household penetration for their financial success.

It is obvious that the current problems facing newspaper advertising are caused by a number of factors. Consequently, publishers must address several issues if they are to compete with other media in the future. Among the primary steps that newspapers should take are the following:[6]

---

[6]Adapted from Leo Bogart, "Newspapers," *Media Studies Journal*, Spring/Summer 1999, 68.

1. Make circulation growth the highest priority with constant tests of pricing, promotional and sales techniques, and new distribution methods. Newspapers should place renewed emphasis on getting newspapers into the hands of younger readers.

2. Editors and reporters should be free of control by marketing departments. The news staff should understand that the newspaper is a business enterprise and even they can make use of market research in the development of a more reader-friendly newspaper, but this does not mean that the editorial product should be directed by advertising or business concerns. To do so will undermine the newspaper's editorial credibility, which is one of its major strengths.

3. Go after the opportunities in national advertising. Newspapers should move aggressively to gain new national advertising dollars. Newspaper advertising departments must undertake creative approaches to demonstrate that newspapers can provide national advertisers with audiences that cannot be reached effectively with other media. Too many newspapers simply accept the status quo that national advertising dollars cannot be diverted to newspapers, thus making it a self-fulfilling prophesy.

4. Newspapers should consider their Web sites as a distinctive product rather than a mere spin-off from the printed paper. The Internet can offer profitable opportunities to exploit a fuller range of information than what is printed in the paper. The Internet can reach specific readers (and non-newspaper readers) with selective news and advertising and, properly marketed, make it a profit center rather than a value-added to both readers and advertisers.

5. Give readers a choice and market to new audience segments. For example, some newspapers have developed youth-oriented sections within the general newspaper. The marginal costs are often worth the expense, even if only a relatively few new readers are added.

6. Take a long view toward profitability. Invest in research and new sections that will allow the newspaper to remain competitive over the long term even though it may not contribute to short-term profits.

These and many other areas are being considered as newspapers attempt to adapt to a changing media environment. To meet these changes, publishers are designing the newspaper with various sections that cater to a host of different tastes. The modern newspaper is more a cafeteria than a set meal. Most of the audience reads only certain sections of a paper and spends different amounts of time with those sections that they do read. For example, while the classified advertising and the main news sections are read almost equally by men and women; only 48 percent of women read the sport pages, compared to 77 percent of men. Conversely, women are 17 percent more likely to read the entertainment page and 40 percent more likely to look at the food pages.[7] Knowing readers' preferences among the different sections of a newspaper is a great advantage in selling advertisers who wish to reach specific prospects.

One of the most serious problems facing publishers is the claim by many former readers that they are simply too busy to read a newspaper. For example, in a *Washington Post* survey, 47 percent of former subscribers said that they dropped their subscription because of a lack of time and the majority could offer no suggestions as to how the paper could win them back.[8]

Finally, newspapers must face the problem of gaining young readers. While maintaining overall readership remains the most important challenge for newspapers, publishers are particularly concerned about gaining younger readers.

---

[7]"Facts about newspapers," a publication of the Newspaper Association of America, 1999, 8.
[8]Barbara Z. Gyles, "Time on their minds," *Presstime*, July/August 1999, 23.

Newspaper publishers fear that once media habits that exclude newspapers are established, it will be very difficult to reach these people as older adults. Newspaper reading habits are formed by about age 30, and tend to change very little after that.

An encouraging trend shown in recent research is that young people do read newspapers, just not on a regular basis. Approximately 70 percent of 12- to 17-year-olds report reading a newspaper in the last week. The key for publishers is to provide content that will turn these occasional readers into regular readers. Of course, newspaper executives realize that young readership is not divorced from household newspaper reading. It would be a rare teen who subscribes to a newspaper that only he or she reads.

Despite the medium's many strengths, newspapers will continue to see a need to aggressively market the medium to readers. Most newspaper readers and potential readers see the value of a newspaper in local news and information with relevance to their lives. Readers want information about things to do and places to go, self-help articles, local news of personal interest, and national and international news that has an effect on their lives. In a diverse, multicultural society, appealing to diverse reader interests is extremely difficult. But newspapers will have to find ways to address this heterogeneous population if they are to maintain their position as a primary source of news and advertising.

Marketing to Advertisers

Advertising constitutes more than 70 percent of all newspaper revenues and more than 50 percent of total newspaper space is devoted to advertising. Clearly, newspapers must continue to attract a number of business categories if they are to remain financially viable. In a fragmented media market, newspapers are finding it more difficult to maintain their share of advertising. In fact, among major media categories, only cable television has increased its advertising share and that was from a relatively small revenue base (see Exhibit 10.3).

While newspapers may take some solace in the fact that other media face similar problems, it does not stop the decline in advertising share. As one newspaper publisher lamented, "Television and radio already have taken a huge chunk of the

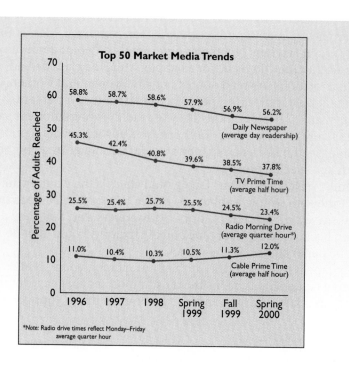

Exhibit

10.3

The Competitive Media Index

Courtesy: Newspaper Association of America.

Source: Scarborough Research 2. Top 50 Market Report.

Prepared by NAA Research Department.

advertising budget, Yellow Pages and direct mail have grown into formidable foes, niche product target our automotive and real-estate base, and alternate delivery and baggie operations go after our pre-prints. Now the Internet and e-commerce threaten our local-news and local-ad franchise."[9]

One of the problems facing newspapers is the dramatic increase in advertising rates and CPM caused by rising fixed costs. According to the **Newspaper Association of America (NAA)**, in 1965, if an advertiser bought a half-page advertisement in every daily newspaper, it would have cost $312,112 for a combined circulation of 60.3 million or a CPM of about $5.20. By 1997, this same half-page advertisement purchased for all newspapers would deliver 56.7 million circulation at a cost of $2,993,000 or a CPM of $52.77. Obviously, other media also showed significant advertising cost increases during this same period, but few were higher on a percentage basis than newspapers.

In order to justify this growth, it is imperative that newspapers continue to convince advertisers that they are an efficient means of meeting a variety of marketing and advertising objectives. In order to accomplish this goal, newspapers must develop a plan that shows a diverse group of current and potential advertisers that newspapers should be a part of their media plans.

The marketing task for newspapers is a twofold undertaking: (1) to deliver the audience and (2) to compete for advertisers. The newspaper industry must convince advertisers that it represents the best local medium and at the same time demonstrate to national advertisers that it should constitute an important element of their advertising strategy. To accomplish these goals, newspapers must retain local retailers who have traditionally comprised the bulk of newspaper revenues and must gain more support from national advertisers who have not used newspapers to any great extent. In the current media climate neither job will be easy. However, newspapers have a tremendous advantage in providing readers with localized, in-depth information concerning products and services in their community.

Newspapers have taken a number of steps to position themselves more favorably to advertisers. One approach has been to provide readership as well as paid circulation data. Virtually all media report readership or total viewers, while newspapers have traditionally reported only the number of newspapers distributed. Obviously, this difference in reporting standards relative to other media places newspapers at a significant disadvantage. For example, in 1999, daily newspaper circulation was approximately 57 million. However, when including pass-along readers the newspaper audience was more than 136 million in the top 50 markets alone. Newspaper executives have long advocated readership as the circulation standard of the medium.

Newspapers also have found that their marketing efforts are most successful when they develop a client-oriented perspective with their advertisers. Rather than attempting to sell an array of advertising options to their clients, many newspapers are training their salespeople in *consumer relationship management,* which is also known as **relationship marketing.** This concept, which has its root in direct-response advertising, attempts to develop a team approach between the newspaper and its advertisers to work with them as partners to solve problems rather than operating on a salesperson/customer basis.

Newspapers also are approaching major advertising agency media buyers on a personal basis to demonstrate the utility of newspaper advertising in national media schedules. Many of the complaints of media buyers center around the difficulty of making multi-paper buys across a number of markets. This is a particular problem for media buyers who are accustomed to the relative ease of buying national broadcast spots and magazines.

Newspaper Association of America (NAA) The marketing and trade organization for the newspaper industry.

relationship marketing A strategy that develops marketing plans from a consumer perspective.

---

[9]Andrew B. Kniceley, "You can take back market share," *Presstime,* November 1999, 72.

To address the buying problem, newspapers are developing information centers to make it easier for national and regional advertisers to know what services and products are available from advertisers. The NAA in cooperation with *Editor & Publisher* magazine provide advertisers with a database of which newspapers provide special editions, targeted inserts, and other advertising options to make it easier to plan multi-newspaper media buys.

Despite the difficult competitive environment in which newspapers operate, there is little question that they are adapting quickly to this changing marketplace. As we will discuss in later sections, newspapers are developing advertising strategies that meet the demands of the smallest retailer as well as the largest national firms.

NEWSPAPER INSERTS, ZONING, AND TOTAL MARKET COVERAGE

Newspaper advertising executives must provide service to a number of advertisers, many with distinctly different marketing and advertising problems. While there are a number of variations of newspaper advertising strategy, we will discuss four approaches here:

1. *Full coverage of a newspaper's circulation.* In the past, most newspapers simply sold advertising space in their pages and advertisers received whatever circulation the paper provided. Large department stores, grocery stores with a number of locations, and national businesses with widely distributed products could take advantage of the majority of a newspaper's readers while other advertisers had to accept some level of waste circulation.

2. *Zoned preprints.* By the early 1980s, targeted direct mail began to offer advertisers a viable alternative to newspaper advertising without its inherent waste circulation. Newspapers countered by offering advertisers the opportunity to have advertising circulars and preprinted inserts delivered with the paper. The first businesses to make significant use of inserts were grocery stores and major retailers. In recent years, newspaper preprints have become the major vehicle for the distribution of coupons for businesses such as fast-food franchises.

The next step in the evolution of newspaper preprints, again in reaction to direct-mail competition, was the zoned distribution preprints. Rather than simply being inserted in every issue of the newspaper, zoned preprints could be delivered to specific ZIP codes within a metropolitan area. Initially, most papers offered these so-called *zoned preprints* only in upscale ZIP codes, but in recent years advertisers have been able to buy any ZIP code within a newspaper's primary circulation area. In some instances, newspapers have begun to distribute preprints to even smaller, sub-ZIP-code circulation clusters called *microzones*.

Preprints have become so popular that they have replaced traditional advertising as the primary revenue source for newspapers. In 1997, preprinted inserts surpassed traditional advertising (or run-of-paper, ROP) as a source of newspaper revenue (see Exhibit 10.4). Today, more than 70 percent of newspapers provide ZIP-code zoning for advertising inserts.

While preprinted inserts allow newspapers to compete with direct mail, they also create problems for the newspaper industry. Among the major issues are the following:

- Inserts are less profitable than ROP advertising.
- Although surveys show that newspaper inserts attain higher reach and they are preferable to direct mail, the newspaper is no more than an advertising delivery system for these inserts.

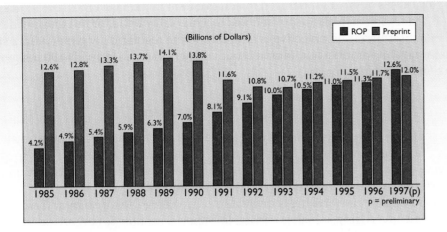

Exhibit

10.4

Preprints Now Outsell ROP

From: Presstime, October 1998, 46.

Source: NAA Market & Business Analysis Department.

■ As ROP advertising decreases, the space for news and editorial matter (the so-called *news hole*) shrinks and ultimately it may change the character of newspapers as both an advertising and information medium.

Despite any associated problems, **zoning** has offered newspapers a compelling weapon against direct mail and other forms of targeted media. It also holds the potential for bringing an increased number of national advertisers to newspapers. "National marketers from Microsoft and IBM to Cuisinart and Bacardi are turning to custom inserts as the ideal way to communicate complex ideas to their target audience, with high impact and surprisingly low CPM."[10]

zoning Newspaper practice of offering advertisers partial coverage of a market, often accomplished with weekly inserts distributed to certain sections of that market.

3. *The zoned newspaper.* In addition to preprint zoning, many metropolitan newspapers are providing suburban weekly or even daily sections in the newspaper to serve both the reader and advertiser demand for information about particular suburbs of a city. In the past, many newspapers devoted limited resources to these sections. Today, most newspapers are making meaningful investments in their zoned editions and, in many cities, publishers have been rewarded with significant readership and advertising increases.

The zoned newspaper has major advantages for both advertisers and publishers. Advertisers can gain the advantages of zoning, but still run ROP advertising, which has greater prestige and credibility. The zoned newspaper also overcomes the problem of insert clutter. Some major newspapers, especially their Sunday editions, carry as many as 40 inserts, which drastically decreases their readership and impact.

4. *Total market coverage.* Ironically, while newspapers seek to serve those advertisers who are interested in a narrowly defined group of readers, they also find that a number of advertisers are seeking total penetration of a market. Since no newspaper has complete coverage of its market (in many markets it is as low as 30 percent), other means must be used to augment regular circulation and achieve **total market coverage** (TMC). Total market coverage may be accomplished in a number of ways:

Total Market Coverage (TMC) Where newspapers augment their circulation with direct mail or shoppers to deliver all households in a market.

■ Weekly delivery of a nonsubscriber supplement carrying mostly advertisements

■ Using newspaper-supported direct mail to nonsubscribers

■ Delivering the newspaper free to all households once a week

---

[10]"The newest brand-building power tool: Targeted newspaper inserts," *Promo,* November 1999, 49.

Regardless of the method used to achieve total market coverage, the aim is the same, that is, to reach all the households in a market whether or not they are newspaper subscribers. The objective is to combine the regular daily paper with a supplemental TMC product and thus allow advertisers to reach virtually 100 percent of the households in a market.

Categories of Newspaper Advertising

Newspapers derive approximately 70 percent of their revenues from advertising with the remainder coming from subscription and newsstand sales. Newspapers provide a number of categories and subcategories of advertising. This section discusses some of the primary types of newspaper advertising.

All newspaper advertising is divided into two categories: *display* and *classified*. **Classified advertising**, which is carried in a special section, is comprised of a variety of advertisements from a small notice announcing a yard sale to those for the largest automobile dealers and real estate firms. Display is all the nonclassified advertising in a newspaper. Within the display category, advertising is considered either *local* (also called *retail*) or *national*. Newspaper advertising revenues amount to more than $45 billion and come from the following sources:

	% of Total
Classified	40
Local	46
National	14

As we mentioned earlier, marketing research is an important element of newspaper advertising. Newspaper executives have sponsored a number of research studies showing that newspapers are equal to or better than their media competitors on a number of measures. Much of this research has been oriented toward audience delivery data, demonstrating the quality and/or the size of newspaper readership. However, advertisers also are interested in communication effectiveness and the **Newspaper Association of America** (NAA) has examined newspaper advertising from this perspective. Among the major findings were the following:

- ■ Color works. Newspaper color advertising works. It increases both attention and readership significantly compared to black-and-white advertisements. Furthermore, the more color the better as four-color advertising gains higher readership than two-color advertising.
- ■ Use pictures. Illustrations scored better than all text and photographs are better than line art. Inclusion of a model also increases readership.
- ■ Showing the product in use will increase the reader's attention by as much as 25 percent.
- ■ Newspaper readers are price-driven and the prominent display of prices will increase readership.
- ■ Size is an important element in newspaper advertising. Full-page advertisements were noticed 39 percent more often than quarter-page advertisements.
- ■ Location is not important. The study showed that location of a newspaper advertisement had no effect on readership. Advertisements on the left-hand versus the right-hand page, below or above the fold, and placement within a section of the paper had the same level of readership.
- ■ Page clutter had no effect on readership. Advertisements on pages with as few as three advertisements scored the same as pages with as many as nine advertisements.

classified advertising Found in columns so labeled, published in sections of a newspaper or magazine set aside for certain classes of goods or services—for example, Help Wanted, Positions Wanted, Houses for Sale, Cars for Sale. The ads are limited in size and generally are without illustration.

Newspaper Association of America (NAA) The marketing and trade organization for the newspaper industry.

Classified Advertising

Classified advertising (the common "want ads") is often ignored unless you are looking for a car, house, or job. Newspapers also carry advertisements with illustrations in the classified section. These are known as *classified display* advertisements, and normally are run in the automotive and real-estate sections. All these notices are included under the heading of classified advertising, which has its own rate card and it is usually operated as a separate department within the newspaper. Classified revenues account for more than $20 billion annually and they are the most profitable department of most newspapers.

In recent years, classified advertising has become a major competitive battleground for newspapers. Competition for classified advertising constitutes one of the most serious financial threats to the newspaper industry. The maintenance of classified advertising revenue is so important to newspapers that it has become a major preoccupation with most publishers. For example, Anthony Ridder, chairman and CEO of Knight-Ridder Newspapers, commenting on the competition for classified advertising, said, ". . . nothing is more critical to the newspaper industry's future."[11] Newspaper executives acknowledge that traditional classified revenues will sharply decline in the next five years. Some estimates predict a loss of as much as $4 billion annually.

To understand the problem facing newspapers, we have to examine a number of factors that are rapidly changing the face of classified advertising. First, the classified advertising sector is very concentrated in three areas: employment, real estate, and automotive. These three categories account for about 75 percent of all classified dollars. This concentration among so few advertisers has allowed specialized on-line services to gain a foothold in competition with newspapers' more broadly defined classified sections. That is, a person wanting a car can look at Web sites that are dedicated to only automobiles.

The initial competition for newspaper classified advertising came from on-line services that introduced two concepts to the world of classifieds: *aggregation* and *vertical sites*. Newspapers regarded classified as local advertising and catered more or less exclusively to the local employment, real-estate markets, and so forth. However, new Web competitors offered vertical services, that is, a single category of classified advertising such as jobs and, perhaps more importantly, they compiled (or aggregated) classified advertising from across the country.

Prospective job seekers, particularly those looking to relocate from other areas, now could look at a single site and see employment opportunities anywhere in the country (or even internationally) on one site without going to the trouble of subscribing to a number of out-of-town newspapers.

Newspapers have countered these incursions from independent on-line classified sites in two ways. First, the vast majority of newspapers have created their own Web sites, most with classified sections. Second, newspapers have established a number of aggregate sites such as www.careerpath.com, a consortium of six of the leading newspaper chains. In addition, the NAA has created www.bonafideclassified.com, an aggregate Web site that links consumers to individual newspapers' online advertising for real estate, employment, and automotive on a national basis.[12]

In spite of the competitive marketplace for classified advertising, surveys offer newspapers both encouragement and a clear mandate for change. The good news is that ". . . newspapers remain far and away the chief source of classified advertising for adults of all ages. No other medium even comes close to the reliability,

---

[11]Rebecca Ross Albers, "No rest in battle for classified," *Presstime*, July/August 1999, 13.
[12]Jake Finch, "Online classified ads: Branded for success," *Presstime*, May 1999, 32.

trustworthiness and efficiency of newspapers. . . . Newspapers have tremendous opportunities to build on their strong print franchises as electronic classifieds grow."[13]

Newspaper advertising executives know that significant dollars are going to be shifted to on-line classified services. For them, the key is to use their strong franchise in the classified market to capture the lion's share of the dollars being diverted from print classified advertising. As one newspaper consultant pointed out, "By now it's evident that classifieds work better online than they do in print—they are searchable, deep, interactive, and up to date, when done right. Help-wanted ads link job hunters with company Websites. Car ads include photos and detailed specs. Homes for sale offer virtual tours. Best of all, classifieds can be distributed far more efficiently online than in print; no wonder it costs less to place classifieds on the Web than in a big-city paper."[14]

It is important to emphasize that despite the recent challenges to newspaper classified advertising, newspapers remain far and away the most used source of such notices. Nevertheless, in less than five years, the World Wide Web has brought dramatic changes to classified advertising. Some predict that in the near future, and we are already seeing this on a limited basis, print classified advertising will be devoted largely to a directory of Web sites—a starting place for further shopping and gathering detailed information. Regardless of where classified advertising moves, it seems that newspapers have positioned themselves to take advantage of future changes.

Display Advertising

Virtually, all nonclassified newspaper advertising falls into the category display advertising. The general segment of display advertising is divided into two subgroups: local and national.

Local Advertising Newspaper advertising has an overwhelming local focus. The financial structure of the newspaper industry is built on retailer support and, by any measure, newspapers are the most popular local advertising medium with both readers and advertisers. Local advertising refers to all nonclassified advertising placed by local businesses, organizations, and individuals. Traditionally, newspaper advertising revenues have been provided by major retailers and that continues to this day. In fact, the top seven newspaper advertisers, led by Federated Department Store and May Department Stores, are all major retailers. These companies spend from 40 to 60 percent of their advertising budgets in newspapers. There is no question that for the foreseeable future newspapers will dominate retail advertising.

Because of their dependence on retail advertising, newspapers are acutely aware of any changes in the local advertising landscape that might impact advertising dollars. Some of the major retailing trends and the potential impact on newspaper advertising are the following:

- Consolidation of general merchandising and discount retailers will reduce the number of retail advertisers and it has the potential to reduce the amount of total retail advertising dollars. In recent years, mergers and acquisitions have resulted in a greater concentration of sales among leading retailers. For example, the top 10 discount retailers accounted for 88 percent of all category sales in 1990; by 2000 it was 96 percent. Likewise, the top 10 specialty retailers held a 30-percent share of sales in 2000, up from 17 percent in 1990. Fewer retail out-

---

[13]"Newspapers are leading source for classified advertising, survey shows," *The SNPA Bulletin,* 15 November 1999, 6.
[14]Marc Gunther, "Publish or perish?," *Fortune,* 10 January 2000, 152.

lets present two problems for newspapers. First, consolidation of retail ownership can result in a decrease in total retail advertising dollars. Second, since each of these retail conglomerates account for a greater share of dollars, the risk associated with the loss of any account is much greater than in past years when the number of retailers spread total newspaper advertising revenues among numerous businesses.

- In addition to a concentration of traditional retail outlets, they also have created a concentration of services not usually associated with these type of outlets. For example, rather than having separate outlets for automotive repairs, banking, home decorating, and eye care, many of the new mega-stores are housing all these services under one roof.

- Retailers are moving to promote their store names as brands. Since price has traditionally been a key ingredient in newspaper advertising, this shift may have a significant effect on newspapers. As image, rather than price, becomes a core retail strategy for many of these chain retailers, we may see a diversion of dollars from newspapers to television or even upscale magazines.

- Retailers will continue to add shopping options to cater to the changing preferences of consumers. Catalogs, on-line marketing, and other options will augment in-store selling and may result in a shift of advertising dollars to other media.

- As retailers move to promote themselves as brands, we will see more emphasis on store brand and private-label merchandising. Traditionally, a private brand marketing strategy has resulted in a reduction in advertising budgets and newspaper fear that this might happen if there is significant movement to house brands among national retailers.

While predicting the future of retail advertising is difficult, newspaper advertising directors can anticipate continuing changes in the near term. As one newspaper marketing executive observed, "Newspaper marketers must keep up with changes taking place inside and outside markets. Reading trade publications, surfing retail World Wide Web sites and keeping close to local retailers can help publishers formulate strategies for future profitability."[15] Nowhere in advertising and marketing is the concept of relationship marketing more important than in the alliance between newspapers and their retail advertising customers.

National Advertising   One of the recent success stories in newspaper advertising is the increase in national advertising. In 1999, the 17 percent increase in national advertising was surpassed only by cable television networks among all major media. "For newspapers, national's performance in 1999 was the largest percentage increase since 1976. The gains were broad, across most categories. . . . Automobile manufacturers doubled newspaper spending. . . . Other categories with significant gains included household furnishing and appliances, medical product and drugs, alcoholic beverages, and apparel among others."[16]

Despite these increases, national newspaper advertising remains a relatively small contributor to overall revenues. National advertising accounts for less than 15 percent of total newspaper dollars and only 2 percent of overall advertising expenditures. Nevertheless, it is heartening to newspaper executives that national advertising has demonstrated significant growth.

Two elements have fueled the resurgence in national newspaper dollars. First, many national advertisers, particularly newer categories such as Internet services and telecommunications, are relying on newspapers to target high potential

---

[15]James Conaghan, "What's roiling retail," *Presstime*, January 2000, 20.
[16]James Conaghan, "National ads ride through time," *Presstime*, May 2000, 17.

markets. Many of these hi-tech companies also see newspapers as a highly credible source, just the environment needed for a new business with little consumer brand recognition.

A second factor in the growth of national newspaper advertising is the success of the Newspaper National Network (NNN). The NNN was formed in 1994 when 23 major U.S. newspaper chains provided funds to the NAA to provide an avenue for national advertisers to gain easy access to national newspaper buys. The NNN provides a network of participating newspapers, which could be bought using one insertion order and one invoice.

The intent of the NNN was to duplicate for national media buyers the convenience they experience in buying network television. "Targeting seven categories of advertisers that had virtually abandoned [national] newspapers—automotive, cosmetics and toiletries, drugs and remedies, food, household products, liquor and beverages, and small computers and software—NNN racked up $30 million in its first year and forced newspaper executives to listen more to advertisers and make appropriate changes in the way they do business."[17]

In only five years, NNN revenues have grown to $130 million. All the more impressive, since NNN only sells advertising in seven product categories and, even in these seven, not all national advertising is placed through the NNN. Clearly, the NNN has been instrumental in gaining greater recognition for the advantages of newspapers among national advertisers. While the rate of increase may not be sustained in future years, there is every reason to think that more and more national media buyers will at least test newspapers as an option.

The idea that national advertisers do not consider newspapers equal to other media was addressed by a former media buyer. "We generally have a national box full of network broadcast and cable TV and magazines, and a local or regional box that holds spot TV, radio, newspapers, and out-of-home. . . . The problem is that the world has changed. Today we are faced with more and smarter competition, and many more mature brands."[18] If the NNN and other industry-wide efforts do no more than create a higher profile and greater consideration of newspapers among national advertisers, it will have served an important purpose.

The NNN also provides national advertisers with **Standard Advertising Units** (SAU) from one newspaper to another (Exhibit 10.5). Standardization allows national advertisers to purchase space in virtually every major U.S. newspaper and prepare one advertisement that will be accepted by each of them. As you can see, NNN formats are flexible enough to provide virtually every advertiser a design that will fit any creative execution.

Overcoming some of the more cumbersome buying procedures has helped newspapers to market the medium more effectively on a national basis. However, these procedural changes have not addressed one of the most serious points of disagreement between national advertisers and newspapers—the continuing debate over the so-called local/national rate differential. Most newspapers charge a substantial premium to national advertisers. As shown in Exhibit 10.6, this differential ranges from 58 percent to more than 100 percent, with the average of all newspapers being 89 percent. Newspapers defend the difference on the basis that they must pay an agency commission for national advertising and many of these advertisers are only occasional users of their papers unlike retailers from whom they enjoy continuing support.

In summary, newspapers must overcome several obstacles if they are to increase their national advertising share. Given the tight retail market and the potential for growth in the national sector, newspapers must continue to make it

Newspaper networks Groups of newspapers that allow advertisers to buy several papers simultaneously with one insertion order and one invoice.

Standard Advertising Unit (SAU) Allows national advertisers to purchase newspaper advertising in standard units from one paper to another.

---

[17]Barbara Z. Gyles, "Newspaper National Network, thriving at five," *Presstime*, January 2000, 55.
[18]Bob Watson, "Newspaper myth-busting," *Agency*, Fall 1998, 60.

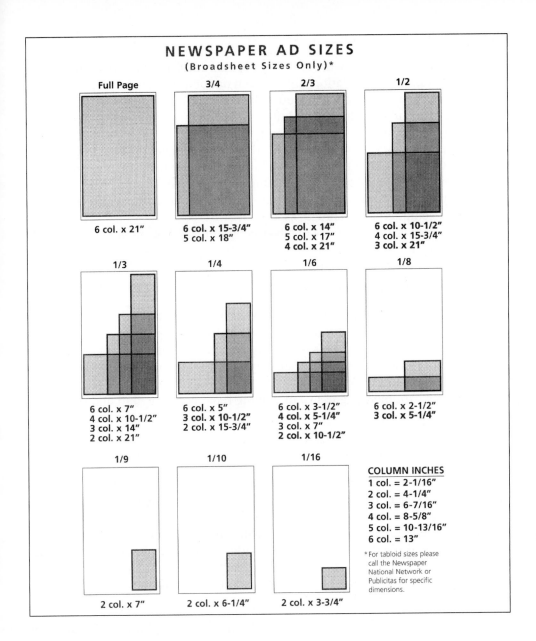

NEWSPAPER AD SIZES
(Broadsheet Sizes Only)*

Full Page	**3/4**	**2/3**	**1/2**
6 col. x 21"	6 col. x 15-3/4" 5 col. x 18"	6 col. x 14" 5 col. x 17" 4 col. x 21"	6 col. x 10-1/2" 4 col. x 15-3/4" 3 col. x 21"
1/3	**1/4**	**1/6**	**1/8**
6 col. x 7" 4 col. x 10-1/2" 3 col. x 14" 2 col. x 21"	6 col. x 5" 3 col. x 10-1/2" 2 col. x 15-3/4"	6 col. x 3-1/2" 4 col. x 5-1/4" 3 col. x 7" 2 col. x 10-1/2"	6 col. x 2-1/2" 3 col. x 5-1/4"
1/9	**1/10**	**1/16**	
2 col. x 7"	2 col. x 6-1/4"	2 col. x 3-3/4"	

COLUMN INCHES
1 col. = 2-1/16"
2 col. = 4-1/4"
3 col. = 6-7/16"
4 col. = 8-5/8"
5 col. = 10-13/16"
6 col. = 13"

* For tabloid sizes please call the Newspaper National Network or Publicitas for specific dimensions.

Exhibit

10.5

Standardized ad formats are crucial to national newspaper advertisers.
Courtesy: Newspaper National Network.

easier for national advertisers to buy the medium. An effective system of national newspaper advertising will take time. In addition, it seems clear that some accommodation must be made concerning the national/local rate issue. Perhaps the ultimate catalyst for finding solutions to the problems of national advertisers will be the mutual self-interest of both groups.

ABC Circulations	Numbers of Papers		Rate Differential		% Increase/ Decrease
	1995	1997	1995	1997	
More than 250,000	44	42	103%	104%	+1%
100,000–249,999	70	64	86	81	−6
50,000–99,999	113	119	60	62	+3
25,000–49,999	227	201	52	58	+12
Total	454	426	77%	89%	+16%

Exhibit

10.6

Average National-Local Rate Differential By Circulation Size

Source: American Association of Advertising Agencies, 1997 study of national and local advertising rates.

Cooperative Advertising

One of the historical outgrowths of the newspaper local/national rate differential
was the development of a relationship between national advertisers and their retail
distributors called **cooperative (co-op) advertising**. We will discuss cooperative
advertising more fully in Chapter 14, but it is such an important part of newspaper
advertising that we need to mention it here.

Co-op advertising is placed by a local advertiser, but paid for, all or in part, by a
national advertiser. The national manufacturer usually provides the advertisements, allowing space for each participating retailer's logo. The original reason for
the development of co-op advertising was that it allowed national advertisers to
place advertisements at local rates.

Today, co-op is a huge source of advertising funds. It is estimated that $24 bil-
lion are available for co-op in virtually all media including television, radio, outdoor, and direct mail. Co-op also is a source of building goodwill with distributors
and retailers and exercising some creative control over local advertising as well as
saving money for national advertisers.

Since national advertisers pay anywhere from 50 to 100 percent of the cost of
locally placed co-op, it extends the budgets of local advertisers as it saves money for
national firms. It is ironic that a system that was developed largely to circumvent
the national/local newspaper rate differential is strongly supported by the newspaper industry. Since newspapers receive over half of all co-op dollars placed, their
sales staffs are extremely aggressive in helping retail accounts find and use co-op
money.

The Rate Structure

The local advertiser, dealing with one or two newspapers, has a fairly easy job buying newspaper space. The rate structure and discounts for any one newspaper are
usually straightforward. However, as we have seen, the national advertiser has a
much more difficult time. An advertiser buying space in a number of newspapers
confronts an unlimited set of options and price structures, including discounts,
premium charges for color, special sections, preferred positions, and zoned editions. In the following discussion, we look at some of the primary options and rate
decisions that an advertiser must make.

Discounts   Newspapers are divided into two categories: those with a uniform
flat rate that offers no discounts, and those with an **open rate** that provides some
discount structure. The open rate also refers to the highest rate against which all
discounts are applied. The most common discounts are based on *frequency* or *bulk*
purchases of space. A bulk discount means there is a sliding scale so that the advertiser is charged proportionally less as more advertising is purchased. A frequency
discount usually requires some unit or pattern of purchase in addition to total
amount of space.

Frequency Within 52-Week Contract Period Full-Page Contract		Bulk Within 52-Week Contract Period	
Open Rate	$2.50/Column Inch	No. of Column Inches	Rate
10 insertions	2.20	500	2.40
15 insertions	2.20	1,500	2.30
20 insertions	2.10	3,000	2.20
30 insertions	2.00	5,000	2.10
40 insertions	1.90	10,000	2.00
50 insertions	1.80	15,000	1.90

ROP and Preferred-Position Rates The basic rates quoted by a newspaper entitle the ad to a run-of-paper (abbreviated ROP) position anywhere in the paper that the publisher chooses to place it, although the paper will be mindful of the advertiser's request and interest in getting a good position. An advertiser may buy a choice position by paying a higher, preferred-position rate, which is similar to paying for a box seat in a stadium instead of general admission. A cigar advertiser, for example, may elect to pay a preferred-position rate to ensure getting on the sports page. A cosmetic advertiser may buy a preferred position on the women's page. There are also preferred positions on individual pages. An advertiser may pay for the top of a column or the top of a column next to news reading matter (called *full position*).

Each newspaper specifies its preferred-position rates; there is no consistency in this practice. Preferred-position rates are not as common as they once were. Now many papers simply attempt to accommodate advertisers that request a position, such as "above fold urgently requested."

Combination Rates A number of combinations are available to advertisers. What they all have in common is the advantage of greatly reduced rates for purchasing several papers as a group. The most frequently seen combination rate occurs when the same publisher issues both a morning and an evening paper. By buying both papers, the advertiser can pay as little as one-third to one-half for the second paper. This type of combination may involve as few as two papers in a single metropolitan market or many papers bought on a national basis. In either case, the advertiser has to deal with only one group and pays a single bill.

The Rate Card

For most media, the advertising rate card, if it exists at all, is simply a starting point for negotiation. As discussed earlier, most radio and television stations don't publish formal rate cards since rates are determined by negotiated scatter plans that are unique to each advertiser. During the 1980s many consumer magazines also initiated a system of rate negotiation. Today, newspapers are one of the few media to maintain rate integrity by offering all advertisers the same rates and discounts.

Unlike broadcast media with their fixed time inventory and magazines with their lengthy advertising production cycles, newspapers can adjust quickly to whatever advertising space is needed. We only have to look at the typical newspaper's bulky Sunday and Wednesday (best grocery day) editions compared to the lightweight Saturday edition to see the flexibility enjoyed by newspapers.

Despite a traditional rate card, we should not leave the impression that newspapers do not accommodate advertisers with flexible rates in the face of competitive pressure. For example:

- ■ *Multiple rate cards.* Many newspapers offer a number of rate cards for different categories of advertisers. For example, package goods, travel, business, and retail stores may all qualify for different rates. Even the NNN provides buying opportunities for only seven categories of products such as automotive, drugs, and beverages. Some advertisers think that the array of different rates makes the buying process unnecessarily complex and, for national advertisers and other multiple paper advertisers, it has the same effect as individual rate negotiation. Newspapers see the process as a type of yield management (see Chapter 2) where a premium is charged for high demand space.
- ■ *Newspaper merchandising programs.* Many newspapers, while refusing to negotiate rates directly, are willing to make other types of merchandising concessions. These programs, also known as *value-added programs,* may include sharing of detailed audience research and providing free creative or copy assistance to advertisers.

■ *Offer pick-up rates.* An advertiser who agrees to re-run an ad may receive a lower rate. This encourages return business and passes along some of the savings that the newspaper enjoys from not having to deal with the production process involved with a new advertisement.

Because of the tradition of the newspaper rate card, it is unlikely that we will see the type of rate negotiation that has become so prevalent in other media. However, newspapers recognize that they will have to meet new competitive pressure. Consequently, we will see even more creative value-added programs offered by newspapers in the future.

Comparing Newspaper Advertising Costs

National advertisers, many of whom consider hundreds of newspapers in a single media plan, want to make cost comparisons among their potential newspaper buys. For many years, the standard measure for comparing the cost of newspaper space was the milline rate.[19] The milline rate has been replaced in recent years by the CPM comparison discussed earlier.

Using the CPM for newspaper rate comparisons has two advantages:

1. It reflects the move to page and fractional-page space buys. Media planners are much more comfortable using the standardized space units of the NNN than lines or column inches in space buys.

2. Comparisons among media are more easily calculated using a standard benchmark such as the CPM. Although qualitative differences among newspapers and other media must still be considered, the CPM does offer a consistent means of comparison:

Newspaper	Open-Rate Page Cost	Circulation	*CPM*
A	$5,400	165,000	$32.72
B	3,300	116,000	28.45

Example: $\dfrac{\$5,400 \times 1000}{165,000} = \$32.72$

The Space Contract, the Short Rate

If a paper has a flat rate, obviously there is no problem with calculating costs—all space is billed at the same price regardless of how much is used. However, space contracts in open-rate papers must have flexibility to allow advertisers to use more or less space than originally contracted. Normally, an advertiser will sign a *space contract* estimating the amount of space to be used during the next 12 months. Such a space contract is not a guarantee of the amount of space an advertiser will run, but rather an agreement on the rate the advertiser will pay for any space run during the year in question.

The space contract involves two steps: First, advertisers estimate the amount of space they think they will run and agree with the newspaper on how to handle any

---

[19]The milline rate is a hypothetical figure that measures what it would cost per agate line to reach a million circulation of a paper, based on the actual line rate and circulation. The formula is:

$$\text{Milline} = \frac{1,000,000 \times \text{rate per line}}{\text{circulation}}$$

(There are 14 agate lines per column inch.)

rate adjustments needed at the end of the year; they are then billed during the year at the selected rate. Second, at the end of the year, the total linage is added, and if advertisers ran the amount of space they had estimated, no adjustment is necessary; but if they failed to run enough space to earn that rate, they have to pay at the higher rate charged for the number of lines they actually ran. That amount is called the **short rate.**

The Newsplan contract outlines the arrangement as follows:

> Advertiser will be billed monthly at applicable contract rate for entire contract year. At end of contract year advertiser will be refunded if a lower rate is earned or rebilled at a higher applicable rate if contract is not fulfilled.

As an example, let us assume that a national advertiser plans to run advertising in a paper with the following rates:

- Open rate, $5.00 per column inch
- 1,000 column inches, $4.50/column inch
- 5,000 column inches, $4.00/column inch
- 10,000 column inches, $3.50/column inch

The advertiser expects to run at least 5,000 column inches and signs the contract at the $4.00 (5,000 column-inch) rate (subject to end-of-year adjustment). At the end of 12 months, however, only 4,100 column inches have been run; therefore, the bill at the end of the contract year is as follows:

Earned rate: 4,100 column inches @ $4.50 per column inch = $18,450

Paid rate: 4,100 column inches @ $4.00 per column inch =   16,400

Short rate due = $ 2,050

or

$$\text{Column inches run} \times \text{difference in earned and billed rates}$$
$$= 4,100 \text{ column inches} \times 0.50$$
$$= \$2,050$$

If the space purchased had qualified for the 10,000 column-inch rate ($3.50), the advertiser would have received a **rebate** of $5,000. The calculation then would be:

Paid rate: 10,000 column inches @ $4.00 per column inch = $40,000

Earned rate: 10,000 column inches @ $3.50 per column inch = $35,000

Rebate due = $ 5,000

Newspapers will credit a rebate against future advertising rather than actually paying the advertiser. Some papers charge the full rate and allow credit for a better rate when earned.

CIRCULATION ANALYSIS

The Audit Bureau of Circulations

Prior to the founding of the **Audit Bureau of Circulations** (ABC) in 1914, those newspaper publishers that bothered at all provided advertisers with self-reported circulation figures. Obviously, many publishers grossly inflated their circulation

short rate The balance advertisers have to pay if they estimated that they would run more ads in a year than they did and entered a contract to pay at a favorable rate. The short rate is figured at the end of the year or sooner if advertisers fall behind schedule. It is calculated at a higher rate for the fewer insertions.

rebate The amount owed to an advertiser by a medium when the advertiser qualifies for a higher space discount.

Audit Bureau of Circulations (ABC) The organization sponsored by publishers, agencies, and advertisers for securing accurate circulation statements.

and created an adversarial relationship among newspapers, advertising agencies, and clients.[20]

The ABC serves advertisers, agencies, and publishers. It is a self-regulating and self-supporting cooperative body. Revenues for the ABC come from annual dues paid by all members and auditing fees paid by publishers.

The verification process involves three reports: two publisher's statements and the ABC audit. The publisher's statements are issued for six-month periods ending March 31 and September 30. The ABC audit is conducted annually for 12-month periods ending either March 31 or September 30. Advertisers can also get summary information in reports called FAS-FAX, which are available more quickly than the full reports. Exhibits 10.7 and 10.8 are portions of an ABC audit report. It should be noted that the information in ABC reports is constantly changing in response to subscribers' needs.

The ABC report includes the following primary information:

1. Total paid circulation.
2. Amount of circulation in the city zone, retail trading zone, and all other areas. (*Note:* The city zone is a market made up of the city of publication and contiguous built-up areas similar in character to the central city. The retail trading zone is a market area outside the city zone whose residents regularly trade with merchants doing business within the city zone.)
3. The number of papers sold at newsstands.

The ABC reports have nothing to do with a newspaper's rates. They deal with circulation statistics only. Publishers have always been glad to supply demographic data on their readers, but the ABC now has its own division for gathering demographic data for many of the markets in the United States. All data are computerized and quickly available.

While the verification of newspaper circulation seems to be a relatively straightforward process, it has been surrounded by controversy in recent years. In particular, two areas are of primary concern to the newspaper industry:

1. *Discounted circulation and bulk sales.* ABC rules require that to qualify as paid circulation, copies must be sold for 50 percent or more of the standard subscription price. The rule was initiated to prevent newspapers from simply giving away unsold papers and counting them as normal circulation in determining advertising rates.

   Newspaper publishers, while admitting that strict controls must be applied to deep-discounted or free circulation, argue for greater flexibility. They point out that newspapers delivered free to rooms in upscale hotels, made available on airplanes or at special events such as trade shows, or sold at greatly discounted prices to college students are reaching prime advertising prospects. Many advertisers take the position that the liberal interpretation of circulation advocated by some publishers would take the industry back to pre-ABC days when newspapers counted any distribution as quality circulation.

   Ultimately, the debate will be settled by advertisers, not newspaper publishers. The basic ABC auditing process is the standard by which most media buyers judge newspapers. Advertisers may accept some changes in the requirements for audited circulation. However, it is doubtful that they will agree to the most liberal changes in bulk and discount circulation advocated by some in the industry.

---

[20]*Academic Casebook,* a publication of the Audit Bureau of Circulations.

Audit Bureau of Circulations

AUDIT REPORT:

THE TRIBUNE (Evening)
Anytown (Red County), Illinois

TOTAL AVERAGE PAID CIRCULATION FOR 12 MONTHS ENDED SEPTEMBER 30, 19--:

	Evening
1A. TOTAL AVERAGE PAID CIRCULATION (BY INDIVIDUALS AND FOR DESIGNATED RECIPIENTS):	41,315

1B. TOTAL AVERAGE PAID CIRCULATION (BY INDIVIDUALS AND FOR DESIGNATED RECIPIENTS) BY ZONES:
(See Par. 1E for description of area)

CITY ZONE

	Population	Occupied Households
1980 Census:	80,109	29,143
#12-31-87 Estimate:	80,500	30,000

Carrier Delivery office collect system, See Pars. 11(b) & (c).....	1,875
Carriers not filing lists with publisher........................	18,649
Single Copy Sales...	2,168
Mail Subscriptions	47
School-Single Copy/Subscriptions, See Par. 11(d)	50
Employee Copies, See Par. 11(e)	100
Group (Subscriptions by Businesses for Designated Employees), See Par. 11(f)	50
TOTAL CITY ZONE	**22,939**

RETAIL TRADING ZONE

	Population	Occupied Households
1980 Census:	268,491	75,140
#12-31-87 Estimate	272,000	79,000

Carriers not filing lists with publisher	15,138
Single Copy Sales...	1,549
Mail Subscriptions	908
School-Single Copy/Subscriptions, See Par. 11(d)	25
Employee Copies, See Par. 11(e)	25
Group (Subscriptions by Businesses for Designated Employees), See Par. 11(f)	50
TOTAL RETAIL TRADING ZONE	**17,695**
TOTAL CITY & RETAIL TRADING ZONES	**40,634**

	Population	Occupied Households
1980 Census:	348,600	104,283
#12-31-87 Estimate:	352,500	109,000

ALL OTHER

Single Copy Sales & Carriers not filing lists with publisher	256
Mail Subscriptions	375
School-Single Copy/Subscriptions, See Par. 11(d)	20
Employee Copies, See Par. 11(e)	20
Group (Subscriptions by Businesses for Designated Employees), See Par. 11(f)	10
TOTAL ALL OTHER	**681**
TOTAL PAID CIRCULATION (BY INDIVIDUALS AND FOR DESIGNATED RECIPIENTS)	**41,315**

1C. THIRD PARTY (BULK) SALES:

Airlines — Available for passengers	1,000
Hotels, Motels — Available for guests	500
Restaurants — Available for patrons	500
Businesses — Available for employees.......................	50
Other	600
TOTAL THIRD PARTY (BULK) SALES.....................	**2,650**

#S&MM Estimate. See Par. 11(a).

Exhibit

10.7

ABC reports provide valuable information concerning the distribution patterns of newspapers and type of purchase.

Courtesy: Audit Bureau of Circulations.

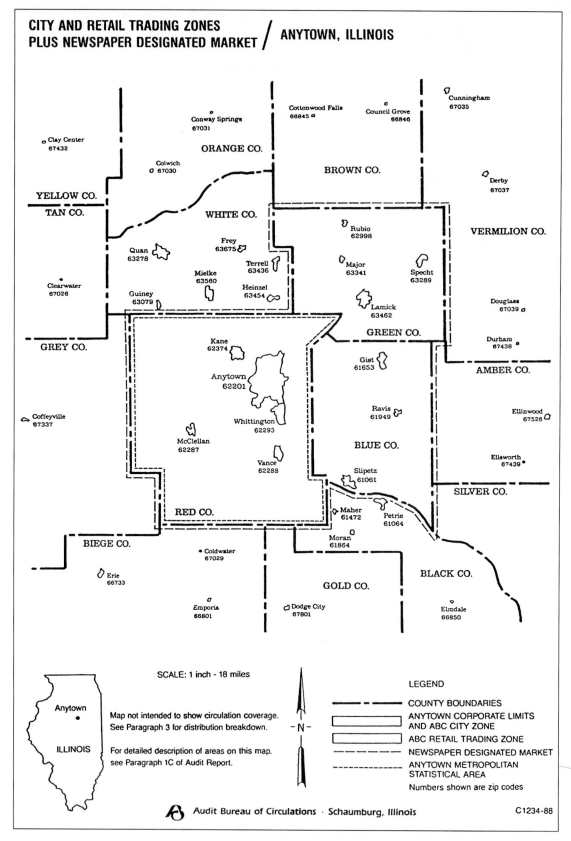

CITY AND RETAIL TRADING ZONES PLUS NEWSPAPER DESIGNATED MARKET / ANYTOWN, ILLINOIS

Cunningham
67035

Cottonwood Falls
66845

Council Grove
66846

Conway Springs
67031

ORANGE CO.

BROWN CO.

Derby
67037

Clay Center
67432

Colwich
67030

YELLOW CO.

TAN CO.

WHITE CO.

VERMILION CO.

Rubio
62998

Quan
63278

Frey
63675

Terrell
63436

Major
63341

Specht
63289

Mielke
63560

Clearwater
67026

Guiney
63079

Heinzel
63454

Lamick
63462

Douglass
67039

GREY CO.

Kane
62374

GREEN CO.

Durham
67438

AMBER CO.

Gist
61653

Anytown
62201

Ravis
61949

Ellinwood
67526

Coffeyville
67337

Whittington
62293

McClellan
62287

BLUE CO.

Ellsworth
67439

Vance
62288

Slipetz
61061

SILVER CO.

RED CO.

Maher
61472

Petrie
61064

BIEGE CO.

Moran
61864

Coldwater
67029

BLACK CO.

Erie
66733

Emporia
66801

Dodge City
67801

GOLD CO.

Elmdale
66850

SCALE: 1 inch - 18 miles

Anytown

ILLINOIS

Map not intended to show circulation coverage.
See Paragraph 3 for distribution breakdown.

For detailed description of areas on this map,
see Paragraph 1C of Audit Report.

- N -

LEGEND

— · — COUNTY BOUNDARIES

ANYTOWN CORPORATE LIMITS
AND ABC CITY ZONE

ABC RETAIL TRADING ZONE

NEWSPAPER DESIGNATED MARKET

ANYTOWN METROPOLITAN
STATISTICAL AREA

Numbers shown are zip codes

Audit Bureau of Circulations · Schaumburg, Illinois

C1234-88

Exhibit

10.8

Geographical newspaper coverage is important to advertisers.

Courtesy: Audit Bureau of Circulations.

2. *Readership versus paid circulation.* Newspapers are at a significant disadvantage in that they measure audiences by circulation or newspapers distributed rather than the total readers of these newspapers. While magazine circulation is audited by ABC, media buyers put great stock in readership of these publications. In 1998, the NAA enlisted the Competitive Media Index (CMI) to measure newspaper readership in the top-50 markets. That same year, the ABC agreed to a pilot study to audit readership studies conducted by independent research firms. Called the "Reader Profile Survey," the ABC certifies that a particular newspaper readership study was conducted according to accepted research methodology.

Most major papers routinely commission readership and market research from a number of companies. The Reader Profile Survey offers outside confirmation that these surveys have been done according to traditional research standards. Again, whether readership replaces or supplements circulation will be up to advertisers. Given the long history of circulation as the norm for measuring newspaper audiences, it may be a hard sell. As one retail advertising executive commented, "A paid-circulation paper is always where I prefer to be. Readership numbers get varied quite a bit, anywhere from four readers per copy to 10 readers per copy. I think it will be very difficult to prove readership is the better way."[21]

The ongoing debate over circulation simply emphasizes the competitive environment in which newspapers are operating. Regardless of how these issues are settled, the decline in paid circulation, the loss of household penetration, and the decrease in newspapers' share of total advertising dollars are all concerns that must be addressed by the industry.

Technology and the Future of Newspapers

As we discussed in an earlier section, the Internet has the potential to significantly change the way in which readers search and respond to classified advertising. While we are still some years away from the fulfillment of the most optimistic predictions of the electronic super highway, it is clear that new technology must be a factor in the marketing plans of any media company.

In the future, newspaper executives may come to view themselves as information providers not newspaper editors and publishers. This distinction is not one of simple semantics. Rather, it allows people to think beyond the newspaper as a print-on-paper product, and consider alternative delivery systems as well as the type of information that is provided.

More than two-thirds of daily newspapers have some Internet presence. Soon that figure will be over 90 percent. Surveys by the NAA show that users of newspaper-sponsored Web sites read the print version with the same regularity as they did prior to introduction of the on-line version. Complementary usage of on-line and print versions is encouraged by many newspapers that offer Web addresses at the end of some stories where readers can obtain more in-depth information than what is included in the printed newspaper.

Despite the relatively modest inroads into newspaper readership by the Internet, newspapers have reason for concern. Not only is serious erosion beginning to be seen in classified revenues, but the newspaper's role as a news medium is being affected by the Web. Research shows that among people using the Internet for breaking news and current information, newspaper Web sites are far down their preference list. The only top-20 Web site among news, information, and

---

[21]Ann Marie Kerwin, "Changing the numbers game," *Advertising Age,* 29 November 1999, 32.

entertainment sites that is sponsored by a newspaper is the *USA Today*, which ranks nineteenth.

Of more concern is the fact that one study found that the majority of readers don't see current news as newspapers' major role. For most readers, newspapers are a source of sports, entertainment, arts, money matters, and relationships. Not coincidentally, these are many of the areas where specialized services and other media have developed Web sites (e.g., www.espn.com and www.morningstar.com).

Not only do these topical Web sites offer a broader range of information on specific subjects, they also have brand recognition that most local newspaper sites lack. As one technology executive commented, "[Newspapers] are under attack from both sides. On the advertising side from companies such as Internet auction houses, which are usurping the classified business, and on the editorial side from online news services."[22]

Despite its potential threat, it will be some time before the Internet is a viable competitor to the daily newspaper. The convenience, portability, and lack of Internet household penetration all will work against the so-called "electronic newspaper" as a substitute for traditional print. However, as technology and reading habits of younger generations become more mainstream, it may make some form of new media a decided threat to traditional newspapers. The fact that newspapers are moving aggressively into the world of new media is testimony to the changing world of both advertising and communication.

NEWSPAPER-DISTRIBUTED MAGAZINE SUPPLEMENTS

One of the most enduring newspaper traditions is the Sunday magazine supplement. For years, most major dailies published a Sunday magazine with features on gardening, local lifestyles and fashion, and personalities. Today, only 26 independent Sunday magazines survive. Most of these are concentrated in major newspaper markets such as New York City, Los Angeles, and Chicago where they attract national advertisers and the newspapers are large enough to invest millions of dollars annually in these upscale publications. From a marketing perspective, national supplements appeal to advertisers who gain network buying efficiency, a broad based newspaper circulation, a magazine format, consistent quality reproduction, and a CPM lower than both newspapers and most magazines.

Individual newspapers view the expense of production combined with declining advertising support as the primary reasons to move to syndicated national publications. The two leaders in the category are *USA Today* and *Parade*. Both magazines deliver huge readership (at a cost to both newspapers and advertisers that is less than most independent supplements.) *Parade* tends to be more popular at larger newspapers, with a circulation of 37.3 million in 327 papers. On the other hand, *USA Today* is distributed by more than 500 newspapers, but has a lower circulation of 21.2 million.

In fact, *Parade* is the largest circulation consumer magazine by a wide margin. As is the case with most consumer magazines, both publications offer numerous opportunities for regional buys. While a number of advertisers such as the Franklin Mint advertise on a national basis, some form of less-than-full-run buy is very common in Sunday supplements.

While there is little question that *USA Today* and *Parade* will continue to dominate the market, there are several other specialized supplements serving the news-

---

[22]"Caught in the web," *The Economist*, 17 July 1999, 17.

paper industry. The newest publications, both launched in 2000, are *American Profile* and *Cachet*. *American Profile* began in April 2000 to reach readers in D (less than 20,000 population) and C (20,000 to 85,000 population) counties where the larger supplements are usually not distributed. It has approximately one million circulation, mostly in the Midwest and Southeast. Since many of the newspapers carrying *American Profile* are weekly or small dailies without Sunday editions, the day of distribution varies. *Cachet* was first published in August 2000 and is intended to reach suburban communities adjacent to metropolitan markets.

A number of other supplements reach ethnic markets in newspapers directed toward these readers. Among the most well known is *Vista*, a magazine carried in 36 newspapers with primarily Hispanic audiences. It is published on a monthly basis and has a circulation of 1.1 million. Other targeted magazines include the *National Black Monitor*, a monthly publication distributed by more than 120 African-American newspapers with combined circulation of 1.15 million.

In addition to these newspaper-distributed magazines, a number of newspapers have special sections that are carried throughout the week to reach a number of different prospects. These special issues cover topics as diverse as agriculture, boating, health, and senior citizen issues. The NAA provides a "Newspaper Advertising Capabilities Database," which allows advertisers to know which papers are offering particular special sections.

Comics

Any discussion of newspaper special features would have to include a mention of the comics. The newspaper comic traces its origins to 1889 when the New York *World* used newly installed color presses to build circulation with a comic section. The importance of comic strips became obvious in 1895 when two titans of journalism, Joseph Pulitzer and William Randolph Hearst, waged a fierce battle over ownership of the most popular cartoon of the day, "The Yellow Kid."

In 1897, "The Katenjammer Kids" was introduced as the first modern comic strip with separate panels and speech balloons. In 1912 Hearst's *New York Evening Journal* published the first full page of comics. From the 1920s on, comics became a major source of readership with the introduction of "Blondie," "The Phantom," "Beetle Bailey," and the only recently concluded 50-year run of "Peanuts."

While not a major advertising vehicle, comics are used by a number of advertisers to reach millions of readers. Editors constantly evaluate comics as they choose among the hundreds of available strips. Recent research indicates that approximately 113 million readers see the comics on Sunday alone. For those advertisers who want to use the comic sections, there are networks that sell the comic sections in a variety of combinations so that advertisers can place advertisement simultaneously in a number of papers.

THE ETHNIC AND FOREIGN LANGUAGE PRESS

We are all aware of the growing diversity of the U.S. population (see Exhibit 10.9).

Race	Percent of U.S.		
	2000	2010	2050
White	72	67	53
African-American	12	13	14
Hispanic	12	15	25
Asian	4	5	8

Exhibit

10.9

Projections of U.S. Diversity

In this changing, multicultural environment it is not surprising that a number of media are being introduced to reach this audience with information, entertainment, and advertising. Newspapers play a different role among the three major ethnic markets. The largest and fastest growing group are Spanish language newspapers. This growth coincides with a Hispanic population is outpacing all other segments in the United States. In 2000, there were approximately 515 Hispanic newspapers with a combined circulation of 12.7 million and advertising revenues approaching $500 million. Unlike other members of the ethnic press, many Hispanic-oriented newspapers are dailies (see Exhibit 10.10).

The best evidence of the importance of the Hispanic press is the support and investment in these publications by major newspaper companies. For example, the *Los Angeles Times* is part owner of *La Opinion, The Dallas Morning News* publishes a free weekly magazine *La Fuenta,* and the *Miami Herald* began publishing *El Nuevo Herald* in 1976 as an insert, but it has been a stand-alone publication since 1998.

Despite healthy circulation growth, Hispanic newspapers face a number of problems reaching a very fragmented Spanish language population with roots in a number of countries with different cultures and product preferences. In addition, surveys show a wide disparity in language preferences. Some would like their information in Spanish, some in English, and still others prefer a bilingual publication. Despite these problems, the Hispanic press is among the fastest growing sectors of the newspaper industry in both readers and advertising revenues.

The African-American press has not shown the same economic vitality as its Hispanic counterpart. The black press was at its height from the 1930s to the early 1960s with almost 300 papers and total circulation of four million. These newspapers were sources of news, political agitation, and advertising. They contributed to much of the social progress made during this period. Among their significant legacies was the drive for passage of the Voting Rights Act and other civil rights legislation during the term of President Lyndon Johnson.

Ironically, the black press has suffered financially as opportunities have opened to African-American citizens. During the 1960s and 1970s, the majority press began to incorporate coverage of black readers into their papers. As time went on, it was less important to have separate newspapers to cover news of African-American readers.

Newspaper	Circulation	City
*El Nuevo Herald	102,000	Miami
*La Opinion	102,000	Los Angeles
Diario las Americas	72,000	Miami
*El Diario La Prensa	68,000	New York
*El Vocero de Puerto Rico	45,000	New York
Noticias Del Mundo	25,000	New York
Laredo Morning Times	23,000	Laredo, Texas
El Diario	20,000	McAllen, Texas
El Heraldo de Brownsville	20,000	Brownsville, Texas
El Nacional	20,000	New York
*Imperial Valley Press	16,000	Imperial Valley, Texas
El Dia	13,300	Houston
El Diario de Juarez	10,000	El Paso
Norte de Cuidad Juarez	10,000	El Paso
El Imparcial	3,000	Tucson, AZ
El Mexicano	3,000	San Diego
El Sol de Tijuana	3,000	San Diego
Espo	3,000	San Diego
El Financiero	2,000	Los Angeles
Hoy	NA	New York

*Audit Bureau of Circulations figures.

Exhibit

10.10

Spanish-Language Dailies

These 20 newspapers provide marketers daily access to Hispanic consumers.

Source: Western Publication Research.

From: Advertising Age, 26 April 1999, S20.

Today, there are still a number of newspapers directed primarily to the African-American audience. Virtually every major metropolitan center has at least one newspaper published for these readers. With a few exceptions such as the *Atlanta Daily World* and the *Chicago Daily Defender*, virtually all are weeklies or biweeklies. During the last two decades most black-oriented newspapers have lost both circulation and advertising revenue. However, several newspapers directed to the black community still maintain significant levels of circulation and advertising support. Among these are the *New York Beacon*, the *Washington Afro-American*, and the *New York Amsterdam News*, all with circulations of more than 40,000.

The mergers and consolidations, so common in the media industry, have also influenced the black press. For example, in 2000 PublicMedia Works, Inc., a black-owned multimedia group bought Sengstacke Enterprises, which published the *Chicago Defender*, the *Michigan Courier, New Pittsburgh Courier*, and the *Memphis Tri-State Defender*. With stronger financial backing and synergism from a more broadly based media company, it may be that these African-American newspapers can be restored to their former vigor.

A continuing problem for traditionally black newspapers is the preference among African Americans for television and a few selected magazines. For example, "Cable TV's Black Entertainment Television (BET) network has an 89 percent black viewership and reaches 55 percent of black households."[23] In light of these data, it is not surprising that advertisers, particularly major national companies, have shifted significant dollars from newspapers to television, radio, and magazines with high African-American audiences. For example, *Soul Train, Jet, Black Enterprise*, and *Essence*, have all enjoyed notable support from corporations seeking to reach the lucrative African-American market.

One development that should help both Hispanic and African-American newspapers is the NNN's recently announced efforts to provide national insertion services for them. Working through Latino Print Network and the Amalgamated Publishers, advertisers will be able to engage in one-order, one-bill services with more than 120 Hispanic and some 200 African-American newspapers.

The Asian press faces many of the problems of both the Hispanic and African-American press—only more so. Like the Hispanic population, Asians come from dozens of different cultures from China to Korea. Lumping them into a single category makes the same mistake as considering all Hispanics to be alike. Added to the problem is that the Asian population is not nearly as large as the Hispanic population so the large population centers to support a national Asian press system are not as readily available.

Still, there are a number of newspapers that serve the Asian population. New York City's Chinese language *Sing Tao Daily* and Japanese language *The Yomiuri Shimbun* and San Jose's *Viet Mercury* all have circulations of between 25–50,000. Interestingly enough, the foreign language press in the United States is not a new phenomenon. Beginning in 1732 when Benjamin Franklin published Philadephische Zeitung (The Philadelphia Newspaper), the foreign language press has played a major role in this country. The increasingly multicultural nature of the United States is reflected in a growing number of newspapers available in more than 40 languages. Virtually every language is represented by at least one newspaper. From French, Italian, and Czech to Vietnamese, Chinese, and Arabic, every part of the world is represented by a publication unique to an ethnic group.

Ultimately, the success of the ethnic press is largely determined by the same formula used by mainstream media—advertising support. As population diversity increases along with growing economic power among these groups, we should expect to see a growth in advertising-supported media directed at these cultural

[23]Rachel McLaughlin, "Market focus," *Target Marketing*, March 1999, 101.

and ethnic members. The degree to which newspapers will fill this communication gap remains to be seen.

WEEKLY NEWSPAPERS

Weekly newspapers fall into a number of categories: suburban papers covering events within some portion of a larger metropolitan area, traditional rural weeklies providing local coverage, specialty weeklies covering politics or the arts, and free shoppers with little editorial content (see Exhibit 10.11). During the last 30 years, the complexion of the weekly newspaper field has changed dramatically. Far from its rural, small town roots, the typical weekly is more likely to be located in a growing suburb and rather than covering weddings and family reunions, its major topics are probably zoning disputes, overcrowded schools, crime, and how to control future growth while increasing the county's tax base.

As important as their content is the marketing strategy employed by many weeklies. More and more weeklies are part of networks. These networks are sometimes owned by a single company including the major local daily newspaper or they may be independent weeklies that joined a consortium to sell their space through a single rep. These groups recognize that the core city trade zone is no longer as economically viable as in previous years. Today, many cities exist only as suburban clusters with one or two large malls anchoring the advertising base. Retailers in these malls depend on a narrowly defined suburban area or neighborhood for their customers rather than an entire metropolitan area.

In some cases, these suburban newspaper groups exist as a supplement to the daily metropolitan newspaper. "Suburban presses thrive on copy that metros can't squeeze in—crimes and fires, real-estate transactions, school news, township meetings. Many weekly publishers have tapped the efficiencies earned by technology to add newsroom slots, improving the quality of their local, local, local coverage and expanding news holes."[24]

From an advertising standpoint, the strength of suburban weekly newspaper networks is that they can serve equally well small, local advertisers who may buy a single member of the group and national advertisers or major retailers who want high penetration into most of the suburban market. Weekly growth will be concentrated in suburban and urban areas for the foreseeable future. Weeklies, once rarely considered by large metro retailers or national advertisers, will play a more important role in the localized marketing strategies of many advertisers.

Topic	Number of Publications	Number of Editions	Paid Circulation	Free Circulation	Total Circulation
Alternative	125	128	170,800	7,164,888	7,335,688
Black	196	226	3,538,232	2,175,277	5,713,509
Community	6,646	7,187	20,600,518	28,569,970	49,170,488
Ethnic	167	231	2,723,190	1,040,764	3,763,954
Gay and Lesbian	47	49	25,497	740,805	766,302
Hispanic	146	211	1,209,396	5,079,930	6,289,326
Jewish	111	114	1,259,087	717,740	1,976,827
Military	130	131	116,793	1,542,931	1,659,724
Parenting	148	160	155,652	6,499,108	6,654,760
Real Estate	91	100	104,819	2,649,000	2,753,819
Religious	128	297	4,740,612	337,905	5,078,517
Senior	129	199	20,743,294	5,044,586	25,787,880
Shoppers	1,413	3,608	666,099	60,430,181	61,096,280
Total	9,477	12,641	56,053,989	121,993,085	178,047,074

Exhibit

10.11

Free Publications Fill Many Niches in the United States

Source: 2000 Editor & Publisher International Year Book, Volume 2, New York City.

From: Presstime, May 2000, 53.

---

[24]Nancy M. David, "Ring around the metros," *Presstime,* September 1999, 54.

SUMMARY

With almost $50 billion in annual advertising revenues, almost 60 million daily circulation, and more than 130 million daily readers, it is hard to view the future of newspapers as anything but bright. However, newspaper publishers recognize that they face a number of challenges if they are to maintain their historical position as a major source of news and advertising.

Despite a number of industry-wide efforts, newspapers have had little success in convincing national advertisers that newspapers should be a major part of their marketing plans. Newspapers must standardize all aspects of the buying and placing of ads. The NNN's attempt to build a national newspaper network is the latest hope for a move in that direction.

However, no amount of standardization will outweigh the perception by national advertisers that newspapers are unfairly priced. The huge local/national rate differentials are a primary impediment to increased national advertising investment. In addition, newspapers must be prepared to offer national discounts and value-added programs on an equal basis with their retail clients.

As newspapers attempt to increase national advertising, their local advertising franchise is coming under increasing attack from a number of quarters. For example, local cable companies provide advertisers opportunities to cut-in to major cable networks that provide targeted opportunities to reach viewers interested in news, music, or sports, often at a CPM less than that of the newspaper. Metropolitan newspapers are competing with suburban weeklies' and shoppers' intent on exploiting the move to the suburbs by both consumers and retailers.

Added to the traditional advertising competitors is the potential for Internet and other new digital-based media formats to take away both readers and the lucrative classified advertising market. Finally, newspapers are continuing to deal with a declining reader base as younger market segments are increasingly finding alternative sources for information and entertainment.

Newspapers have a major advantage over most of their competitors in that they are perceived as among the most influential and credible communication vehicles. They have an established brand that most competitors look upon with envy. As we discussed in this chapter, newspapers must continue to experiment with alternative methods of reaching audiences to prepare for the electronic super highway of the future. Larger newspapers have already made a number of strides in the area of technology. However, the major challenge for the future is how to make these alternative delivery systems widely accepted and profitable.

REVIEW

1. What are some of the factors that have eroded the local newspaper advertising base?
2. What has been the major hurdle *USA Today* faced in becoming an effective national newspaper?
3. Many newspapers are offering "value-added" merchandising to advertisers. Explain.
4. What does the term relationship marketing mean in newspaper advertsing?
5. Contrast zoned editions and total market coverage programs.
6. What are three major categories of newspaper advertising and how much advertising revenue does each account for?
7. What are the two major problems in newspapers gaining national advertising?
8. In what area have newspapers been most successful in achieving standardization?

9. What is the difference between the short rate and rebate?

10. What are the primary advantages of newspaper magazine supplements?

TAKE IT TO THE NET

We invite you to visit the Russell/Lane page on the Prentice Hall Web site at **www.prenhall.com/myphlip** for end-of-chapter exercises and applications.

chapter 11

Using Magazines

Virtually all magazines are targeted to special interests, businesses, demographics, or lifestyles of their readers. The era of the mass circulation publication is long past and the successful magazines of today are those that appeal to niche readers especially those in categories with special value to advertisers. Magazines have adopted Internet technology to provide Web versions of their publications as value-added resources for both readers and advertisers. After reading this chapter you will understand:

>> the history and development of the American magazine

>> the financial support of the modern magazine

>> characteristics of consumer and trade publications

>> magazines as a targeted advertising medium

>> the role of magazines in national media plans

>> the effect of new communications technology on magazines

Pros

1. The number and range of specialized magazines provide advertisers with an opportunity for narrowly targeted audiences.

2. Magazines provide strong visuals to enhance brand awareness and they have the ability to deliver a memorable message to their niche audiences.

3. Most magazines offer some form of regional and/or demographic editions to provide even greater targeting and opportunities for less-than-national advertisers to use magazines.

4. Magazines are portable, they have a long life, and they are often passed along to several readers. Business publications are especially useful as reference tools and leading publications within various industries offer advertisers an important forum for their messages.

Cons

1. In recent years, magazine audience growth has not kept up with increases in advertising rates. Magazines are among the most expensive media on a per prospect basis.

2. Advertising clutter has become a concern of many magazine advertisers. Many magazines approach 50-percent advertising content and consequently time spent with any single advertisement is often minimal.

3. Most magazines have relatively long advertising deadlines, reducing flexibility and the ability of advertisers to react to fast-changing market conditions.

4. Despite the obvious advantages of magazine specialization, it means that a single magazine rarely reaches the majority of a market segment. Therefore, several magazines must be used or alternative media must supplement magazine buys. With more than 1,000 consumer magazines, advertisers have difficulty in choosing the correct vehicle.

ADVERTISING AND CONSUMER MAGAZINES

With the introduction of television as a national advertising medium in the 1950s, magazines began to market themselves as a specialized medium to reach targeted prospects within the more general population. Fueled by economic necessity and unable to duplicate the huge numbers that the then three television networks could deliver, magazines based their economic future on the quality of audience they could deliver rather than the quantity. The modern niche magazine evolved in much the same way as narrowly formatted radio stations and both did so as a reaction to the ultimate mass medium, television.[1]

Today, magazines find that they must continue to change and adapt to a marketplace that exhibits competitive pressures every bit as daunting as those encountered by the magazines of 50 years ago. Consequently, the magazine industry is undergoing dramatic changes in all aspects of the way it does business. In fact, there is little in the way of magazine production, distribution, circulation, or advertising that is not undergoing some type of transition.

In many respects, the contemporary magazine is enjoying unprecedented success. However, magazines also face problems in common with both radio and newspapers. The segmented and fragmented nature of magazine publishing means that publications are constantly seeking to define their audiences in narrower ways. Like the radio industry, magazines find that marketers invest an overwhelming percentage of their advertising dollars in the two or three leaders in a category, leaving a small share of advertising dollars to the also rans. This has led to magazines attempting to create editorial differentiation directed to interest groups that are often too small to support them financially.

If magazines are similar in some respects to radio, they also have common characteristics with newspapers. The costs of paper, delivery, and marketing to readers and advertisers are creating profitability problems even as gross revenues increase. Standard Rates & Data list more than 2,700 consumer magazines. In such a competitive marketplace, gaining and maintaining readership is a constant headache for publishers. One only has to look at the number of discounted subscriptions for even the most popular magazines to see the extent of the problem.

---

[1]Unless otherwise noted, the source of information in this chapter is the Magazine Publishers of America.

On average, 10 magazines are introduced each week covering topics as diverse as sex and religion. While consumer magazines has a number of attributes in common, in many respects each magazine or category of magazines has unique problems and opportunities. In this atmosphere there are simultaneous successes and failures among different categories of publications. The women's magazine category is an example of the feast-or-famine nature of magazine publishing. In recent years, the number of women reading these magazines and the advertising dollars invested in them have been relatively flat.

With a number of new titles entering the women's market, there has been fierce competition within the category. As *Martha Stewart Living* and *O: The Oprah Magazine* entered the market with great success, titles such as *Marbella* and *New Woman* ceased publication. A former editor of *New Woman* summed up the dilemma facing virtually all magazines, "Distinctiveness is more important than ever. When I was at *New Woman*, I knew we had to be distinctive and we were creating a new identity, but in retrospect we probably weren't different enough. And in the current marketplace, we couldn't do it fast enough."[2] In the current marketplace, those comments could be made by most magazine publishers and, in the fragmented world of media, also by a number of broadcast station managers, especially in radio.

In order to understand the contemporary consumer magazine industry, we have to examine two primary factors: (1) selectivity and (2) cost versus revenue considerations.

SELECTIVITY

While magazines represent an eclectic continuum of titles and interests, the success stories are almost universally confined to narrow editorial interests and audience segments. A sampling of the top magazines in terms of revenues and advertising pages demonstrates this range of interests. For example, *Maxim, Harvard Business Review, Jane, ESPN the Magazine*, and *This Old House* are among the leaders in advertising revenue growth in recent years. Virtually the only thing these publications have in common is that they were able to find a distinctive niche among both readers and advertisers.

Magazines are searching for the right editorial formula in a market that is increasingly fragmented. There are very few large homogeneous groups, but there are homogeneous segments within more general groups. For example, publishers have long tried to reach the valuable teen market effectively. However, they find that no market as such exists. First, boys and girls differ markedly not only in what they read, but the amount of reading, with teen girls reading significantly more than boys.

Even among boys who do read, reaching them is a challenge. If there is anything approaching a "must read" for teen girls, it is *Seventeen* (with slightly more than half reading one of the last four issues). On the other hand, the most popular magazine with boys is *Sports Illustrated* (with 32 percent reading one of the last four issues). The only publication that ranks in the top five with both boys and girls is *TV Guide*. Obviously, advertisers seeking to reach the teenage market cannot afford the waste circulation of these adult-targeted publications.

Consequently, advertisers must be content to reach narrow slivers of the teen market one publication at a time. *Jump, Transworld Skateboarding, Latingirl,* and *YM* all reach small but important parts of the teen segment, but none give the type of coverage needed by businesses trying to reach the broad teen market. At the same time, publishers continue to try to develop magazines that will bridge the

[2]Lisa Granatstein, "Darwin's law: Women's books evolve," *Adweekonline*, 28 May 2000.

elusive gender gap. For example, *Teen People*, launched in 1997, now has almost 20-percent male readership among its 1.3 million readers—hardly a huge number, but still encouraging given the lack of past success in developing a general teen publication.[3]

The Evolution of the Modern Magazine

Although selectivity is one of the keys to contemporary magazine success, audience and editorial selectivity is actually rooted in the historical development of magazines. The magazines of the mid-nineteenth century were targeted to audiences of special interests, sold at a high cost, and carried little advertising. Most magazines were literary, political, or religious in content and depended on readers or special-interest groups to provide most of their financial support.

In the latter years of the nineteenth century a rising middle class, mass production, and national transportation combined to provide the opportunity for nationally distributed branded goods. The opportunities offered by national brands could be exploited only with the efficiencies of mass promotion. During the 1890s a number of publishers provided the foundation for today's ad-supported, mass circulation magazine. Frank Munsey (*Munsey's*) and S. S. McClure (*McClure's*) were among the most successful publishers of the period. However, it was Cyrus H. Curtis who, "developed the magical possibilities of national advertising, and demonstrated more clearly than anyone else that you could lose millions of dollars on your circulation by selling at a low price yet make more millions out of your advertising. . . ."[4] The formula was so successful that by 1900 his *Ladies Home Journal*, under the editorship of Edward Bok, was the first magazine to achieve a circulation of one million.

Until the advent of radio in the 1920s, magazines remained the only national advertising medium. With the introduction of radio, they had to share the national advertising dollar. Still, magazines were the only *visual* medium available to national manufacturers. However, when television came on the scene in the 1950s, people's reading habits became viewing habits, and national magazines had to change to survive.

The change from a mass to a class medium, which began in the competitive turmoil of the 1950s, continues up to the present. Perhaps the most dramatic indication of the demise of the mass magazine was the March 2000 demise of the monthly version of *Life* after 64 years of publication.

Today, even the largest circulation publications tend to appeal to a fairly narrowly defined market segment. For example, *Sports Illustrated*, *Time*, *Consumer Reports*, and *Modern Maturity*, all among the circulation leaders, would not be classified as general editorial magazines. Only newspaper-distributed *Parade* and *USA Weekend* have both huge circulations and general appeal. However, as we discussed in Chapter 10, they are hybrid publications that many advertisers consider more newspapers than magazines.

Costs and Revenues   Consumer magazine revenues are huge and the publication is largely dependent on advertising for their existence. Typical consumer magazine content consists of slightly more than 48-percent advertising pages. Led by Time, Inc. (publisher of *Time*, *Sports Illustrated*, *People*), four publishers have total advertising revenues of more than $1 billion and 23 others have space sales of more than $100 million. However, even with magazine advertising revenues booming and circulation figures for many magazines at an all-time high, publishers are concerned about profitability.

---

[3]Cristina Merrill, "Keeping up with teens," *American Demographics*, October 1999, 29.
[4]James Playsted Wood, *Magazines in the United States* (New York: The Ronald Press Company, 1949), 104.

Magazine cost concerns can be summarized largely in four primary categories:

1. *Marketing costs.* With the number of publications and a sometimes fickle readership, publishers are seeing significant increases in the cost of gaining and maintaining readers. Approximately 80 percent of all consumer magazines are sold through subscriptions as opposed to newsstand sales. Consequently, it is imperative for publishers to invest huge sums of money in gaining new readers and keeping current ones.

   Unfortunately, the major means of subscription sales are either less viable than in the past or are becoming increasingly expensive. The traditional sweepstake sellers such as Publishers Clearing House and American Family Publishers have been hit with a number of federal regulations that have greatly restricted their activities and have hurt the circulation of several major magazines. Likewise, increased cost of printing and postage have made direct-mail campaigns increasingly expensive.

   Added to these problems is the competitive environment of magazine publishing, which prevents publishers from raising the cost of subscriptions to cover higher expenses. According to the Magazine Publishers of America (MPA), since 1990 the average cost of a one-year subscription has fallen 16 percent. Overall, publishers are losing almost $15 on every new subscription they sell and are depending on advertising to make up the deficit.

2. *Postage and distribution costs.* Since 1995, the U.S. Postal Service has imposed three rate increases on magazine publishers. These increases have been far greater than the rate of inflation and they have caused a major rift between publishers and the Postal Service. As the president of the MPA, the leading industry trade association, pointed out, "There is no doubt that increases of this magnitude are a significant bottom-line issue for publishers, and . . . they will have to be reflected in increased costs for readers and advertisers over the next few years."[5]

   At the same time publishers are facing hefty increases in postal charges, they are witnessing similar boosts in the cost of newsstand distribution. Consolidation at both the retail and wholesale levels have created a more streamlined, and limited, distribution channel. Retailers, concerned with profit margins, are insisting that wholesalers limit the number of titles they send to them. "As a result, magazines seem to be losing the distribution levels they once took for granted. More outlets are being controlled by a smaller group of companies, making it harder for new titles to get to the newsstand."[6] The result has been an even greater reliance on subscription sales and a continuing upward cost spiral for publishers.

3. *Concentration of advertisers.* While a primary strength of magazines is their selectivity, it works against them in terms of broadly based advertising appeal. Magazines receive a disproportionate percentage of their advertising revenues from a very few product categories. Thirteen categories account for 88 percent of all magazine advertising (see Exhibit 11.1). In fact, just 10 companies, led by General Motors, provide almost one-third of all magazine revenues.

   If even one of these major advertisers decreases its magazine spending, it can have a significant impact on a number of publications. Advertising cutbacks are even more damaging to magazines geared to a very narrow interest such as computing or golf. In these cases, a magazine has few practical alternatives to make up for the loss of even one large advertising client. In light of the

[5]Nina Link, "Postal rate plan is indefensible, must be fought," *Advertising Age*, 24 April 2000, 68.
[6]"High circulation costs stymie magazine growth opportunities," *Advertising Age*, 14 February 2000, S14.

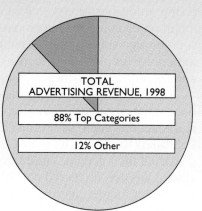

TOP CATEGORIES ACCOUNT FOR 88% OF ALL SPENDING

The top advertising categories account for 88% of total magazine spending, according to the Publishers Information Bureau. For example, the automotive category accounts for more than 10% of all advertising.

TOTAL ADVERTISING REVENUE, 1998

88% Top Categories

12% Other

Exhibit

11.1

Top Magazine Advertising Categories

Source: Publishers Information Bureau. Sunday supplements excluded.

Courtesy: Magazine Publishers of America.

recent agreement between major tobacco companies and state attorneys general, magazines also are preparing to deal with the potential loss of cigarette advertising, especially among publications with a large proportion of younger readers, which are prohibited from carrying tobacco advertising.

Over the past 20 years magazines have tried to insulate themselves from their dependence on advertising by shifting a disproportionate percentage of the cost of magazines to readers. Magazines passed a major milestone in 1985 when, for the first time, advertisers contributed less than half of total magazine revenues; that percentage is now about 70 percent. Of course, with the increase in reader marketing costs, magazines have simply substituted one problem for another.

4. *Increases in CPM.* The continued increase in cost and difficulty of attracting new readers are, of course, reflected in advertising rates. Despite shifting more of the expense burden to readers, magazine advertising rates have risen significantly. Exhibit 11.2 shows the upward CPM trend.[7]

Cross-Media Buys

As we enter the twenty-first century, there are few magazine, television, or newspaper companies. They have been replaced by multimedia companies with interests in all traditional media as well as the Internet, interactive media, and various forms of direct response. Magazines are major players in many of these huge conglomerates and they form a symbiotic relationship with their media partners. From an advertising standpoint, it can be of great benefit for a magazine to be sold as part of a multimedia package—known as a **cross-media buy.**

cross-media buys
Several media or vehicles that are packaged to be sold to advertisers to gain a synergistic communication effect and efficiencies in purchasing time or space.

	CPM	% increase over previous period
1965	$5.53	—
1975	6.62	19.7
1985	14.30	116.0
1990	19.62	37.1
1997	34.23	74.4
2000 (est.)	41.00	19.4

Exhibit

11.2

Magazine CPM Trends (4-color, full-page)

[7]"Magazine advertising cost analysis," www.tvb.org, 11 May 2000.

Since magazines reach niche audiences, they can often reach prime prospects who are light users of other media. Companies such as Time Warner, Disney, and News Corp. can offer advertisers hundreds of options for their advertising messages—often at a significant discount compared to buying the same properties on an individual basis. One of the most creative cross-media sellers is Disney, especially with its sports-oriented programming.

Since Disney is typical of many of the major media companies, let's look at how they handle some of their cross-media sales. One of Disney's most profitable franchises is *Monday Night Football* (MNF) through its ownership of the ABC Television Network. In order to gain synergism with some of its other media properties, Disney sold MNF as a package with ESPN's *Sunday Night Football* and the ESPN lead-in show to MNF. Since Disney is a major owner of ESPN, it was able to combine its ABC and ESPN football capital with both ABC and ESPN Web sites, *ESPN the Magazine*, and the ESPN radio show.

By combining the various Disney sports media and programs, an advertiser is able to reach a broad audience (e.g., the ESPN Web site audience is significantly younger than the audience of MNF), yet do so with only two basic media identities (ABC and ESPN). As the editor of *ESPN the Magazine* pointed out, "We (Disney) use all our brands to reinforce all the other brands. Personalities from the network write columns in the magazine. Linda Cohn is doing Linda Cohn's Hotline. At the end of an article we may say: 'For more on this, chat with the writer Wednesday at ESPN.com.'"[8]

One of the appealing features of cross-media buys for national advertisers is the complementary nature of magazines and television in reaching different segments of the general population. As Exhibit 11.3 demonstrates, television simply does not reach those prospects who are the heaviest users of magazines. There is such a strong inverse relationship between magazine readership and television viewing that mass advertisers are almost compelled to use both media. Not only does the combination of magazines and television extend reach, but it also provides a welcomed diversity of advertising themes and creative executions.

Despite some obvious advantages to advertisers in terms of lower media costs, they should be careful in analyzing cross-media buys. Marketers have to realize that a package of media owned by a single company is not necessarily the best

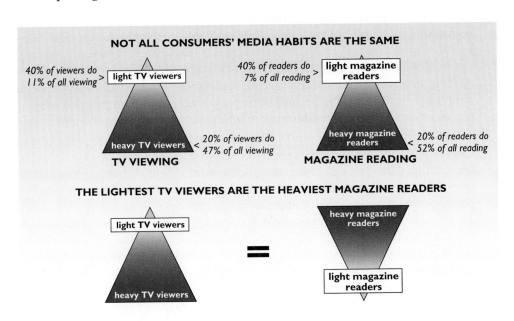

NOT ALL CONSUMERS' MEDIA HABITS ARE THE SAME

40% of viewers do 11% of all viewing > light TV viewers

40% of readers do 7% of all reading > light magazine readers

heavy TV viewers < 20% of viewers do 47% of all viewing

TV VIEWING

heavy magazine readers < 20% of readers do 52% of all reading

MAGAZINE READING

THE LIGHTEST TV VIEWERS ARE THE HEAVIEST MAGAZINE READERS

light TV viewers

heavy TV viewers

=

heavy magazine readers

light magazine readers

Exhibit

11.3

Magazines Role in the Media Mix

Source: MRI Media Quintiles.

Courtesy: Magazine Publishers of America.

[8]Karla Nagy, "Print scores big for ESPN," *Media & Brand Marketing*, May 2000, 31.

choice in each category. For instance, even though we buy spots on MNF, are we sure that *ESPN the Magazine* is a better fit for our target audience than *Sports Illustrated* or is ESPN.com a better Web choice than CNN/SI.com? There is nothing inherently wrong with cross-media buys as long as advertisers realize that they are put together largely for the benefit of the media companies. As single media companies come to control more and more media properties the possibilities of building tailored media packages for individual advertisers increase.

MAGAZINES AS A NATIONAL ADVERTISING MEDIUM

Advantages of Magazines

Among national advertisers, magazines trail only television with 33 percent of all advertising dollars—three times more than newspapers and radio combined. Depending on the product and advertising objectives, magazines may offer a number of advantages as a primary or secondary media vehicle. This section will examine the primary considerations that determine whether or not magazines in general, or a particular title, will be included in a media plan.

1. *Does it work?* An advertiser is interested in the various advantages and characteristics of a medium only to the extent that these elements allow the medium to contribute to sales and profits. Over the last three years, the MPA has commissioned a series of studies conducted by independent research firms to determine the value of magazines as an advertising tool.

   In one study, results showed that for nine out of ten package-goods measured, consumers exposed to magazine advertisements were more likely to purchase an advertised product than those who did not. In one case, the difference was 35 percent.[9] In another study, researchers found that magazines created high levels of brand awareness, especially when used in tandem with television. Advertising awareness increased 19 percent with magazines alone, compared to 16 percent with only television. However, when both magazines and television were used, advertising awareness was up 65 percent (see Exhibit 11.4).

2. *Audience selectivity.* Assuming that magazines can accomplish the required communication task, the next question is can they reach a specific target market? It is here that magazines excel. There is a magazine targeted for virtually every market segment and essentially everyone reads a magazine during a given month. It is estimated that magazines are read by almost 90 percent of all adults in a typical 30-day period. With magazines, total readership is often a secondary advertising consideration to how they reach target audiences.

3. *Long life and creative options.* Unlike a perishable broadcast message or the daily newspaper, many magazines are kept and referred to over a long period of time, others are passed along to other readers. MRI, a leading magazine research firm, suggests that the average magazine has more than four readers per copy and is assessable for approximately 28 weeks. In addition, magazines are portable with readers reporting that approximately 60 percent of their reading is done out of home. In this disposable media world, magazines are almost alone as a long-term medium. Magazines are often used as reference sources—articles are clipped, back issues are filed, and readers may go back to a favorite magazine numerous times before finally discarding it. Advertisers potentially benefit from each of these exposures.

---

[9]Lorraine Calvacca, "Making a case for the glossies," *American Demographics*, July 1999, 36.

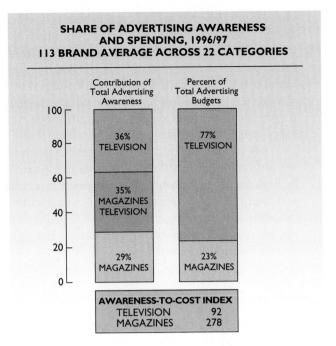

100 — 80 — 60 — 40 — 20 — 0

36% TELEVISION

77% TELEVISION

35% MAGAZINES TELEVISION

29% MAGAZINES

23% MAGAZINES

AWARENESS-TO-COST INDEX
TELEVISION   92
MAGAZINES   278

The magazine is also a visual medium with a number of creative options. Magazines offer advertisers a wide range of flexible formats such as double-page spreads, bright colors, even product sampling. Magazines are particularly suited to long copy. Discussions of detailed product attributes for automobiles and appliances as well as advertising for financial services all lend themselves to magazines.

4. *Availability of demographic and geographic editions.* In Chapter 10, we discussed newspaper zoning as a reaction to advertiser demand for selected segments of a publication's circulation. On a national scale, magazine demographic and geographic editions meet the same demands of large advertisers. It is very rare that a national magazine does not offer some type of regional or demographic breakout of its total circulation. These special editions are called **partial runs** and are so common and important to magazine advertising that they will be discussed separately in a later section of this chapter.

5. *Qualitative factors.* Advertisers are interested in the demographics of the audience, but they are also interested in how the audience thinks of themselves when they read a particular publication. The *Playboy* man and the *Cosmopolitan* woman are as much a matter of readers' perception as reality. Unlike many other media, magazines offer advertisers relatively high levels of audience involvement. Consequently, magazine advertisers are more apt to use understated creative approaches as contrasted to the hard-sell advertising found in so many other media. Few media connect with their audiences to the degree that magazines do.

In Chapter 7 we discussed the PRIZM system of categorizing people by their lifestyle characteristics. Increasingly, magazines use psychographic and lifestyle research to sell advertisers on the qualitative aspects of their audiences. Take a moment to review the various PRIZM categories in Exhibit 7.3a and try to match these audiences with the primary readers of some major magazines. Research indicates that magazines are preferred by a wide margin as a source of ideas and information on topics as diverse as automobiles, fashion, and fitness. This editorial connection with readers should carry over to a

partial runs When magazines offer less than their entire circulation to advertisers. Partial runs include demographic, geographic, and split-run editions.

connection between readers and advertisers. When readers pick up *Golf Digest, Money, Organic Gardening,* or *PC Computing,* there is little doubt about their interests. These same readers also watch prime-time television, listen to the radio on the way home from work, and see numerous billboards each day. However, it is difficult to anticipate what they are thinking about at these moments. On the other hand, specialized magazines can practically guarantee a synergism between reader and editorial content, which in many cases will carry over to advertising content.

Despite the recent attention given to the qualitative nature of magazines, the ultimate measure of magazines as an advertising vehicle will be determined by their ability to deliver prime prospects at a competitive cost. Media planners will continue to judge magazines on a cost-efficiency basis using criteria such as CPMs, and reach and frequency. The final evaluation of magazines, as with any medium, is whether they can deliver the right audience, at the right price, and in the right environment.

Disadvantages of Magazine Advertising

Despite the many advantages that magazines offer advertisers, there are some important considerations for advertisers contemplating buying magazines.

1. *High cost.* As we have discussed, magazines generally are the most expensive media on a CPM basis. It is not unusual for specialized magazines to have CPM levels of over $100 compared to $10–20 for even relatively low-rated television shows. However, in an era of niche marketing, the CPM is important only in relation to the prospects reached and the waste circulation of a medium. A related problem to overall cost is the fact that, as magazines have refined their audiences, many advertisers need to use several publications to achieve acceptable reach levels. As the number of magazines in a media schedule increases, so does the risk of duplicated audience levels, which often results in an unacceptable overlap in readership.

   closing date Date when all advertising material must be submitted to a publication.

2. *Long **closing dates**.* Because of the printing process, most magazine advertisements must be prepared well ahead of publication. Unlike the spontaneity of radio and newspapers, magazines tend to be inflexible in reacting to changing market conditions. For example, a magazine advertisement may run eight to ten weeks after an advertiser submits it. This long lead time makes it difficult for advertisers to react to current marketing conditions either in scheduling space or developing competitive copy. The long closing dates are one reason why most magazine copy is very general.

   Many magazines have one date for space reservations and a later date for when material must be submitted. Normally, the space contract is noncancellable. It is not unusual for a magazine to require that space be reserved two months prior to publication and material sent six weeks before publication. Some publications require that material be submitted with the order.

   fast-close advertising Some magazines offer short-notice ad deadlines, sometimes at a premium cost.

   Many magazines have sought to overcome the competitive disadvantage of long closing dates by providing **fast-close advertising.** As the name implies, fast-close allows advertisers to submit ads much closer to publication dates than standard closing dates allow. At one time, fast-close was very expensive, carrying a significant premium compared to other advertising. However, competitive pressure and improvements in print technology have seen many publications offer fast-close at little or no extra expense.

The remaining sections of this chapter will examine some specific features and techniques involved in buying advertising in magazines.

FEATURES OF MAGAZINE ADVERTISING

Partial-Run Magazine Editions

Partial-run editions refer to any magazine space buy that involves purchasing less than the entire circulation of a publication. The oldest and most common partial-run edition is the geographic edition, followed by demographic and vocational/special interest editions. Basically, the partial-run edition allows relatively large circulation magazines to compete with smaller niche publications for specialized advertisers.

As advertiser demand for more and more narrowly defined audiences has increased in recent years, magazines with fairly small circulations and/or specialized editorial formats have begun to offer some form of partial-run edition. Again, the smaller the circulation and the more specialized the content of a magazine, the more likely that the geographical edition will be the only partial-run offered.

Of the more than 250 magazines that offer partial-run editions almost half offer only geographic ones. On the other hand, major publications, especially large circulation weeklies such as *Time, Newsweek*, and *People*, offer dozens of options to advertisers. These publications combine both geographic and demographic editions so that an advertiser can reach *Time* readers who occupy positions in top management throughout the country or in selected locations.

About 10 percent of all magazine advertising is bought on a partial-run basis. As advertisers continue to demand that all media deliver narrowly targeted audiences and the techniques honed by direct mail and other direct marketing media become more prevalent, we will see the majority of magazines offering some form of partial-run circulation. Computer technology and advances in high-speed printing also are allowing magazines to meet these advertiser requirements.

Split-Run Editions A special form of the partial-run edition is the split-run. Whereas most partial-run editions are intended to meet special marketing requirements of advertisers, split-run editions normally are used by both advertisers and publishers for testing purposes. The simplest form of split-run test is where an advertiser buys a regional edition (a full-run is usually not bought because of the expense) and runs different advertisements in every other issue.

Each advertisement is the same size and runs in the same position in the publication. The only difference between the advertisements is the element being tested. It may be a different headline, illustration, product benefit, or even price. A coupon is normally included and the advertiser, based on coupon response, can then determine the most productive version of the advertisement. This split-run technique is called an A/B split. Half of the audience gets version A and half version B.

As the competition for readers has grown, so has the use of split-run tests by magazines themselves. Magazines occasionally experiment with different covers for the same issue—either for testing purposes or to take advantage of some story of regional interest. The split-run technique has been instrumental in providing both publishers and advertisers with insight into how magazine advertising can be most effective. Partial-run and split-run editions offer a number of benefits to advertisers (and in some cases publishers).

1. Geographic editions allow advertisers to offer products only in areas where they are sold. For example, snow tires can be promoted in one area, regular tires in another.

2. Partial-runs can localize advertising and support dealers or special offers from one region to another. As advertisers increasingly adopt local and regional strategies, the partial-run advantages will become even more apparent.

3. Split-run advertising allows advertisers to test various elements of a campaign in a realistic environment before embarking on a national rollout.

4. Regional editions allow national advertisers to develop closer ties with their retailers by listing regional outlets. This strategy also provides helpful information to consumers for products that lack widespread distribution.

Partial-run editions also have some disadvantages that make them less than ideal for all advertising situations.

1. CPM levels are usually much more expensive than full-run advertising in the same publication and close dates can be as much as a month earlier than other advertising.

2. In the case of demographic editions, the lack of newsstand distribution for these advertisements can be a major disadvantage if single-copy sales are significant for the publication.

3. Some publications bank their partial-run advertising in a special section set aside for such material. There also may be special restrictions placed on partial-run advertising. For example, such advertising often must be full-page and only four-color will be accepted by some publications.

selective binding
Binding different material directed to various reader segments in a single issue of a magazine.

Selective Binding   **Selective binding** makes the customization of partial-run editions even more sophisticated. While the concept of selective binding is essentially the same as that of partial-run advertising, it refers to different editorial material or large advertising sections that are placed in less than the full-run of a publication. Using computer technology and sophisticated printing techniques, advertisers and publishers can develop advertising and editorial material specifically for one group or even individual readers.

Selective binding first gained popularity among major farm publications. Articles and advertisements were published only in editions delivered to farmers who raised certain types of crops or livestock. In recent years, selective binding has been offered to advertisers by consumer magazines on a limited basis.

Selective binding is most useful when there are significant subcategories of larger target markets within a publication's audience. Occasionally, a magazine will offer selective binding that is fully integrated into the editorial format of a magazine. More commonly, the technique is used with multi-page advertising inserts distributed to a select audience segment identified by age, income, and so forth.

Selective binding is an example of a technology that, in order for it to be successful, must be advertiser driven. That is, advertisers must be convinced that it offers enough value to justify the additional expense. Many advertising executives think that the practical applications of selective binding are more apparent for business and farm publications than for consumer magazines where there are a number of selective publications. Like interactive television, selective binding is a technology that is readily available, but where widespread demand by either advertisers or consumers is not yet apparent.

Obviously, the widespread use of selective binding has major implications for direct-mail. If the technique becomes widely used, advertisers could combine the individual characteristics of direct-mail with the high prestige environment of the magazine. Just as importantly, selective binding costs the advertiser about double what a normal magazine ad costs, but direct-mail CPMs generally run five times that of consumer magazines. Like most partial-run techniques, a major drawback of selective binding is that it can only be used for subscribers.

Since selective binding adopts some of the techniques of direct response, it also raises the same questions of readers' concerns with invasion of privacy. If subscribers are targeted by anything more than name and address, they may regard selective binding as inappropriate, with negative consequences to both the advertiser and magazine. Still, the idea that each reader can have a custom-made magazine, including both editorial and advertising material of specific interest to that individual, is an intriguing concept.

City Magazines   Magazines directed to readers within a particular city are not a new idea. *Town Topics* was published in New York City in the late nineteenth century, but most observers credit *San Diego* magazine, first published in the 1940s, as the forerunner of the modern city magazine. Today, city magazines are available in virtually every major city.

At one time, city magazines were often regarded as nothing more than booster publications for a city. Many of them were published by a local business or tourism organization and they offered little in terms of hard news or in-depth reporting. While most city magazines continue to feature lifestyle and entertainment stories, a growing number of publications report on local business, technology, and medical issues. Many publishers are combining the traditional strengths of the city magazines with specialized publication content and initiating such titles as *Chicago Bride, Atlanta Business Chronicle,* or the *Fulton County Reporter,* a publication devoted to the Atlanta legal scene.

Because of the generally upscale readership of city magazines, they are popular with upscale local and regional firms, and even some national advertisers who want to target individual markets. Advertising revenues are very cyclical. During the economic downturn of the early 1990s, many city magazines experienced significant decreases in advertising pages. A soft economy tends to be seen first in areas such as retailing and automobile sales, two prime categories of city magazine advertising. In addition, city magazines are normally a supplement to mainline advertising for many of these magazines' clients. Consequently, when the advertising market goes soft, they are often among the first media to be dropped.

Today, with a strong economy city magazines are prospering with strong advertising and circulation gains. One of the signs of the health of the city magazine category is the number of magazines that have been introduced into smaller communities. Whereas the city magazine was formerly a domain of large metropolitan centers, we now find successful publication in cities with populations of less than 100,000 (e.g., Macon, Georgia).

City publications are in some ways a hybrid between small circulation specialty publications and the partial-run editions of national magazines. However, they have an advantage over both in reaching upscale local audiences with editorial and advertising content specifically directed to the special, local interests of their prime prospects.

Custom Publishing

Another growing and specialized area of magazine publishing is custom publishing. It is one of the fastest growing sectors of the magazine business and consists of advertiser-produced publications intended to reach prospects or current customers in a communication environment totally controlled by the marketer. These publications are a cross between direct-mail and traditional magazine publishing. "Once a niche business dominated by specialty publishing houses with limited—if any—editorial credentials, custom publishing is now a mainstream discipline crowded with big-name publishers in search of new profit engines."[10]

Custom publishing is not a new concept. In 1949, General Motors commissioned its agency, Campbell-Ewald, to publish *Friends,* a magazine sent to Chevrolet car and truck owners. However, since those early days, customer

---

[10]Ann Marie Kerwin, "Are tailor-made publications the right fit for advertisers?," *Advertising Age,* 5 October 1998, 3.

magazines account for expenditures of $700 million with more and more companies seeing it as an extension of their direct-response marketing. Most mainline magazine publishers such as Time Inc., Meredith, and Hearst have customized publishing divisions.

The objectives of custom publishing vary from company to company. For Lincoln, *CitySource* was a way of introducing its Lincoln LS sport sedan. *Tomorrow* is published by DaimlerChrysler to reach its more than 75,000 United Auto Workers (UAW) employees. Sabre Group uses *VirtuallyThere* as a value-added guidebook for customers booking trips through its affiliated travel agencies.

Regardless of the specific use of custom publishing, to be successful it needs to function as part of a planned and integrated marketing program. Custom magazines can be a valuable tool for companies to speak directly to their customers and prospects. The current status of custom publishing is made possible by market research. ". . . people and their buying patterns have never been segmented so precisely before. Most marketers today know a lot about the individual man, woman, or child buying their products, and custom media is considered the best way to talk to them."[11]

Some custom-published magazines are evolving to look much like traditional publications. One of the most obvious features of this transition is the acceptance of outside (albeit noncompetitive) advertising by some publications. For example, a recent issue of *Corvette Quarterly*, published by GM for Corvette owners, carried advertisements for Rolex, Goodyear Tires, and 3M. As one custom publishing executive commented, "In the past few years, custom publishing has grown more and more like the traditional publishing industry. Many custom magazines are audited members of Audit Bureau of Circulations and Business Publications Audit and hold themselves to stringent editorial and design standards to attain equal footing with paid and non-paid titles in the magazine world."[12]

MAGAZINE ELEMENTS

Once an advertiser has made the hard choice of which magazine to select among the hundreds of options, the job is not over. Now the media planner must decide the size, color, placement, and format that will best serve the advertiser's marketing goals and the creative message.

Sizes

The page size of a magazine is the type area, not the size of the actual page. For convenience, the size of most magazines is characterized as *standard size* (about 8 by 10 inches, like *Time*) or *small* (about 4 3/8 by 6 1/2 inches, like *Reader's Digest*). There also are a few oversized publications such as *Rolling Stone*, but they are the exception. When you are ready to order printing plates, you must get the exact sizes from the publication, because sizes may change.

Position, Color, and Size of Magazine Advertising

Space in magazines is generally sold in terms of full pages and fractions thereof (half pages, quarter pages, three columns or one column; see Exhibit 11.5). The small advertisements in the classified pages of many magazines are generally sold by the line. Magazine covers are the most expensive positions in most magazines, although some magazines offer deep discounts for large advertisers. The front

[11]Verne Gay, "Milk, the magazine," *American Demographics*, February 2000, 32.
[12]Chris McMurry, "Outside ads offset production costs; Give custom magazines credibility," *Advertising Age*, 12 October 1998, A-6.

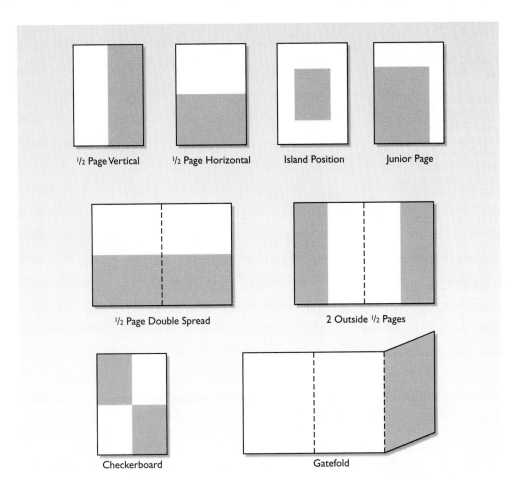

Exhibit

11.5

Various ways of using
magazine space.

cover of a magazine is called the *first cover*, which is seldom, if ever, sold in American consumer magazines (although it is sold in business publications). The inside of the front cover is called the *second cover*, the inside of the back cover is the *third cover*, and the back cover the *fourth cover*.

Advertisers are trying constantly to determine the optimum combination of color, size, and placement that will achieve the highest readership. Exhibit 11.6 shows 22 different combinations of elements and the effect that they have on recall compared to a standard four-color advertisement. These findings are consistent with most research that has determined that four-color advertising is worth the additional cost in terms of added attention and readership. By the same token, this same research indicates that two-color fails to add to reader attention levels and is usually not worth the additional expense.

Another concern of many advertisers is the placement of an advertisement within a magazine. Traditionally, many advertisers have regarded right-hand pages at the front-of-the-book, preferably near related editorial matter, as the ideal ad placement. "FFRHPOE" or "far forward, right-hand page opposite editorial" is routinely stamped on many insertion orders delivered to magazines in spite of no evidence that these positions add any value to an advertisement.

As the size of an advertisement increases, the audience does not grow proportionately (nor does the cost). For example, in Exhibit 11.6, note that a one-half page, four-color advertisement achieves 72 percent of the impact of a full-page unit. If we run a two-page spread, we increase readership by 30 percent (even though we have increased the space by 100 percent). The reason, of course, is that as size increases there are not enough nonexposed readers remaining to continue to increase readership at the same rate.

Ad Type	Recall Index
Page 4C Ad	**100%**
4th Cover (4C)	120
2nd Cover (4C)	112
3rd Cover (4C)	90
2nd Cover Gatefold (4C)	145
Inside Spread (4C)	130
Inside Spread (2C)	110
Inside Spread (B&W)	95
Vertical 2/3 Page (4C)	81
Horizontal 1/2 Page (4C)	72
Vertical 1/3 Page (4C)	60
Horizontal 1/3 Page (4C)	60
Vertical 2/3 Page (2C)	60
Vertical 2/3 Page (B&W)	60
Horizontal 1/2 Page (2C)	56
Horizontal 1/2 Page (B&W)	56
Horizontal 1/3 Page (2C)	47
Horizontal 1/3 Page (B&W)	47
Vertical 1/3 Page (2C)	42
Vertical 1/3 Page (B&W)	42
Page 2C	78
Page (B&W)	74

Exhibit

11.6

Readership by Advertising Unit Type

Source: Magazine Dimensions, 1999 Media Dynamics, Inc., based on Burke, Starch and Gallup & Robinson.

Although the increase in audience exposures is not proportionate to increases in magazine ad size, larger space allows more creative flexibility. Advertising objectives that require long copy can be much more effectively presented in a larger space. Larger advertisements have greater impact and recall over time, even though in the short term they don't score significantly higher than smaller space advertisements. It is important to remember that these studies held creative content constant while in reality the quality of the message is perhaps the most important variable in advertising readership and recall. These findings point out again that the specific objectives and creative approach must be considered in designing magazine advertising.

Bleed Pages

Magazine advertising is able to use a number of formats and designs unavailable or impractical in other media. A common technique is bleed advertising where the ad runs all the way to the edge of the page with no border. **Bleed** ads are used to gain attention and use all the space available. Without a border, the advertisement does not have the appearance of being confined to a particular space. Typically, bleed advertising will be seen by 10 to 15 percent more readers than nonbleed advertising.

There is no standardization for premium charges for bleed advertising. In the competitive marketplace for magazine advertising, a number of publications offer bleed advertising at no charge as a value-added or extra incentive for advertisers. Even when a magazine has a standard charge for bleed advertising, large advertisers often make these charges a point of negotiation with publishers. With modern printing equipment, most advertisers contend that bleed charges are an unjustified anachronism and many resent even minimal charges for bleed.

Inserts and Multiple-Page Units

Multiple-page advertising covers a broad spectrum of insertions. The most common form of multi-page advertising are facing, two-page spreads. Among the most frequent users of multi-page inserts and spreads are automobile manufacturers.

bleed Printed matter that runs over the edges of an outdoor board or of a page, leaving no margin.

They face an extremely competitive environment, they need to show their cars in the most favorable, bigger-than-life fashion, and they often have an in-depth story to tell about the features of their brands—all reasons to use large space advertising. A spread increases the impact of the message and eliminates any competition for the consumer's attention. As we showed in Exhibit 11.4, gatefold spreads come off the front cover and normally are either two or three pages.

Cost is a major consideration when planning inserts. While the insert will be less expensive on a per-page basis than run-of-publication advertising, the advertiser is still concentrating significant dollars in the publications that carry the inserts. This expense will reduce the number of media vehicles that can be included in a media schedule. Since an advertiser is putting a disproportionate share of advertising into one or a few vehicles, the likely result is a reduction in reach and frequency compared to a more traditional media plan.

Finally, one of the problems with the growing use of multiple-page advertising is that it has lost much of its novelty to consumers. When a reader can turn to practically any consumer magazine and find numerous examples of such advertising, they come to be taken for granted, even by serious prospects. It is important to work closely with the creative team to make sure that such expensive space is going to be fully utilized with a meaningful message. The most effective multiple-page units are for advertisers with an interesting product, a new story to tell, and an interested and involved group of prospects.

HOW SPACE IS SOLD

Advertising Rates, Negotiation, and Merchandising

In the competitive world of magazine advertising, it is not surprising that publishers are constantly seeking merchandising and value-added programs to differentiate their titles from others in a particular category. Unfortunately, many publishers find themselves in a situation where advertising rates are the primary consideration for most advertisers.

Scheduling and buying full-run magazine advertising was at one time the easiest function for a media planner. Clients usually bought full-page advertisements, circulations were audited, discounts for frequent usage were obtainable from straightforward rate cards, and rates were consistent for every advertiser who qualified for available discounts. In addition, most advertisers would buy only a few, high-circulation publications.

The rate situation underwent fundamental changes when magazine advertising experienced a downturn in revenues during the 1980s. Faced with flat advertising revenues and new publications continually coming into the market, magazines began to negotiate with individual advertisers for special rates. This practice of one-to-one negotiation is called *going-off-the-card*. Starting as a short-term fix during a period of weak advertising spending, negotiation has become a common practice among magazines with many advertisers regarding the rate card as simply a point at which to start negotiation. In a survey of media buyers, one expressed an opinion held by many in the advertising industry, ". . . magazines are becoming much more like conventionally negotiated media, such as TV. . . . within several years, the magazine industry will convert to negotiated rates as the basis of page costs."[13]

Obviously, publishers would like to maintain rate integrity and attempt to do so with a number of merchandising and value-added plans. One of the most common means of magazine merchandising is through brand extensions. The *Good Housekeeping* Seal is one of the oldest and most recognized merchandising tools.

---

[13]Joe Mandese, "Survey reveals extent of rate card flexibility," *Advertising Age*, 19 October 1998, S30.

The publication sponsors test laboratories through which readers are offered a guarantee of the quality of the products and services advertised in the publication. The program is almost 100 years old and still going strong.

Magazine merchandising services take numerous forms and they are used by virtually every major magazine. *Better Homes and Gardens* produces greeting cards, provides real-estate services, and franchises garden centers. Meanwhile, consumers can buy *Family Circle* classical CDs, *Field & Stream* bass lures, and *Popular Mechanics* work boots. In order to promote its *Parenting* magazine, Time Inc. bought a product sampling company, First Moments, that delivers products to new mothers in hospitals. Ownership of First Moments will allow the delivery of its magazine, subscription offers, and related samples to build relationships with both readers and advertisers.[14]

The key to merchandising programs is to coordinate a magazine's reputation and expertise with marketing techniques that help advertisers sell their products. Among the more traditional merchandising programs are trade shows, conferences, newsletters, database services, and copromotions such as point-of-purchase that highlights certain advertisers who are using a publication. For example, a women's magazine may cosponsor a fashion show with an advertiser or promote a recipe contest where ingredients from an advertiser must be used. All of these techniques allow advertisers to extend the message of their advertising into related areas.

Magazine Merchandising and the Internet

Magazines were among the earliest media to utilize the Internet as part of their overall marketing and merchandising plans and they remain heavily involved in on-line endeavors. The most common use of the Internet by publishers is the on-line version of print publications. Hundreds of publications offer full or edited on-line versions of their magazines. These on-line vehicles may be advertiser supported, used as a value-added for readers and advertisers, and/or intended to extend the audience reach of the core magazine to on-line users.

Magazines also have entered into numerous joint ventures with other businesses for various on-line objectives. Many of the on-line sites are established as part of cross-media programs as in the earlier mentioned CNN/SI. In other cases, magazines have co-ventured with established sites to create a synergy between the expertise of an on-line company and the visibility of a magazine. Hearst's purchase of an interest in Women.com allowed the company to promote its women's books (e.g., *Redbook, Country Living*, and *Good Housekeeping*) in a compatible environment. Interestingly, the relationship between magazines and on-line interests has moved in both directions. For example, Krause Publications published *eBay Magazine* and Ziff-Davis introduced *Yahoo! Internet Life* magazine.

In addition, a number of titles have begun to use the Internet as a traditional e-commerce business. For example, Meredith offers its *Better Homes & Gardens*'s books and a select group of other products on its Web site. Regardless of the objectives of a magazine's on-line presence, the selective, targeted audiences of magazines offer an ideal marriage for the one-to-one marketing of the Internet. While this relationship will continue to take many forms, "... publishers are realizing they can leverage their magazine brands not only to get people to read their content, but also to shop."[15]

---

[14]Ann Marie Kerwin, "Time Inc. buys sampling biz to help bolster 'Parenting'," *Advertising Age*, 2 November 1998, 6.

[15]Jennifer Gilbert and Ann Marie Kerwin, "E-commerce: Magazines' new darling," *Advertising Age*, 17 May 1999, 46.

Magazine Rate Structure

In the examples that follow, we will assume the advertiser is making a full-run magazine buy. That is, the entire circulation of the publication is being purchased. An advertiser buying a partial-run edition will consider a number of other options. A typical rate card for a weekly publication might look like this:

Space	1 ti	6 ti	12 ti	26 ti
Living World Bulletin Color Rates (4-color)				
1 page	32,800	29,750	28,150	26,675
2/3 page	24,210	22,950	21,740	20,630
1/2 page	22,880	18,430	20,615	19,510
1/4 page	11,800	11,050	10,550	9,860

An advertiser buying this publication will pay $32,800 for a one-time, four-color, full-page insert. The advertiser who buys at least 26 inserts in the publication will pay only $26,675 per ad for the same space.

Before placing a magazine on its advertising schedule, the advertiser will compute the cost efficiency of that publication against others being considered. Let's assume that *Living World Bulletin (LWB)* has an average circulation of 660,132. Using the CPM formula discussed earlier, we can calculate the efficiency of the publication as follows:

$$\text{CPM} = \frac{\text{cost/page}}{\text{circulation (000)}} = \frac{\$32{,}800}{660} = \$49.69$$

Discounts

Frequency and Volume Discounts   The one-time, full-page rate of a publication is referred to as its *basic*, or *open, rate*. In the case of *LWB*, its open rate is $32,800. All discounts are computed from that rate. Most publications present their discounts on a per-page basis in which rates vary according to frequency of insertion during a 12-month period, as we have done here. However, some publications use either **frequency** or volume **discounts** based on the number of pages run. For instance:

Frequency, Pages	Discount, %
13 or more	7
26 or more	12
39 or more	16
52 or more	20

frequency discounts   Discounts based on total time or space bought, usually within a year. Also called *bulk discounts*.

In a similar fashion, the volume discount gives a larger percentage discount based on the total dollar volume spent for advertising during a year. The volume discount is convenient for advertisers that are combining a number of insertions of different space units or that are using a number of partial-run insertions. A volume discount might be offered as follows:

Volume, $	Discount, %
83,000 or more	8
125,000 or more	11
180,000 or more	17
260,000 or more	20

Other Discounts   In addition to discounts for volume and frequency, individual magazines offer a number of specialized discounts, usually for their largest advertisers. Among the more common discounts in this category is a lower per page price for advertisers who combine buys with other publications or media owned by the same magazine group. We previously discussed these arrangements in the section on cross-media buys. As media companies become larger, the opportunities for these buys will be more numerous. Cross-media discounts operate similarly to volume discounts except advertisers accumulate credit across a number of media vehicles.

In addition, some magazines offer discounts called continuity discounts for advertisers who agree to advertise at a certain rate over a period of time, usually two years. These discounts are sometimes designed to guarantee the magazine a certain level of advertising pages even in normally slack months such as January and July in exchange for a lower cost to the advertiser. Continuity discounts might be compared to scatter plans in network television advertising where advertisers buy lower rated shows in order to gain commercials on the most popular programs. In magazine continuity discounts, advertisers accept "off periods" to get lower rates during peak advertising seasons. In both cases, the media are offering the discount to manage their time and space inventory.

Remnant Space   A number of publishers, especially those with geographic or demographic editions, often have unsold space in one or more editions. This **remnant space,** also called *standby space*, is sold at a deep discount. For advertisers whose products or advertising messages are not time or location sensitive, remnant space can be a great bargain. However, it is strictly a take-it-or-leave-it proposition. Magazines will not allow any position requests and normally advertisers must take whatever partial-run editions are available.

In the past, it has been difficult to match publications with excess space with advertisers willing to buy on a remnant basis. However, as we see throughout this text, the Internet is changing the traditional practices for most media. Today, Web sites such as MagazineRemnants.com and Adoutlet.com provide on-line auctions for advertisers to bid on remnant space from hundreds of publications.

remnant space
Unsold advertising space in geographic or demographic editions. It is offered to advertisers at a significant discount.

The Magazine Short Rate

As we have seen, most magazine discounts are based on the amount of space bought within a year. However, the publisher normally requires that payment be made within 30 days of billing. Therefore, an advertiser and a publisher sign a space contract at the beginning of the year and agree to make adjustments at the end of the year if the space usage estimates are incorrect. If the advertiser uses less space than estimated, the publisher adjusts using a higher-than-contracted rate. If more space is used, the publisher adjusts using a lower rate.

Let's look at a typical short rate, using the rate card for *Living World Bulletin*. Acme Widgets contracted with *LWB* to run eight pages of advertising during the coming year. At the end of the year, Acme had only run five pages. Therefore, it was short the rate for which it had contracted and an adjustment has to be made, as follows:

$$\text{Ran 5 times. Paid the 6-time rate of } \$29{,}750 \text{ per page} = (5 \times 29{,}750)$$
$$\$148{,}750$$

$$\text{Earned only the 1-time rate of } \$32{,}800 \text{ per page} = (5 \times 32{,}800)$$
$$\$164{,}000$$

$$\text{Short rate due } (\$164{,}000 - 148{,}750) = \$15{,}250$$

Some publishers charge the top (basic) rate throughout the year but state in the contract, "Rate credit when earned." If the advertiser earns a better rate, the publisher gives a refund. If the publisher sees that an advertiser is not running sufficient pages during the year to earn the low rate on which the contract was based, the publisher sends a bill at the short rate for space already used and bills further ads at the higher rate earned. Failure to keep short rates in mind when you are reducing your original schedule can lead to unwelcome surprises.

Placing the Order

Placing magazine advertising is a two-step process. The first step is the *space contract*, which tells the magazine the total number of pages that an advertiser will use during the coming year. It enables the publisher and advertiser to establish a rate level for billing and is considered a binding contract. However, the space contract does not deal with the specific issues in which the advertising will run, but it allows both parties to agree on the cost of future advertising.

The second step is the *space order* (also called an insertion order). The space order commits the advertiser to a particular issue and is usually accompanied by production materials for the ad. Exhibit 11.7 shows an example of the 4A publication order blank. Note that the form can include both the space contract and insertion order, depending on which box is checked. In fact, an advertiser can also use the form to cancel or change ad requirements, if such changes are permitted by the magazine.

Exhibit
11.7

An example of a space contract and insertion order.

Courtesy: American Association of Advertising Agencies.

Magazine Dates

There are three sets of dates to be aware of in planning and buying magazine space:

1. *Cover date:* the date appearing on the cover
2. *On-sale date:* the date on which the magazine is issued (the January issue of a magazine may come out on December 5, which is important to know if you are planning a Christmas ad)
3. *Closing date:* the date when the print or plates needed to print the ad must be in the publisher's hands in order to make a particular issue

Dates are figured from the cover date and are expressed in terms of "days or weeks preceding," as in the following example:

New Yorker

- Published weekly, dated Monday
- Issued Wednesday preceding
- Closes 25th of 3rd month preceding

Magazine Networks

The term network, of course, comes from broadcast where affiliated stations cooperated to bring audiences national programming as early as the 1920s. In recent years, a special adaptation of the network concept has been employed by virtually every medium as a means of offering advertisers a convenient and efficient means of buying multiple vehicles. There are newspaper networks, outdoor networks, and even networks for direct-mail inserts and comic strips. Magazines are no exception.

As we mentioned earlier, one of the problems of the growing specialization in magazines is that advertisers increasingly need to buy a number of titles to achieve reach and frequency goals. Another consequence of smaller circulations is that magazine CPM levels have increased. Many large national advertisers have complained about both the difficulty of buying numerous magazines and the higher CPMs. In order to accommodate these advertisers, a number of publishers have established **magazine networks.** As with networks in other media, their intent is to make it possible for an advertiser to purchase several publications simultaneously with one insertion order, one bill, and, often, significant savings compared to buying the same magazines individually.

magazine networks Groups of magazines that can be purchased together using one insertion order and paying a single invoice.

Currently, there are more than 100 magazine networks, some representing dozens of different titles. The network concept allows several magazines to compete for advertisers by offering lower CPMs and delivering a larger audience than any single publication. Networks must be carefully tailored to reach a particular audience segment with as little waste circulation or audience duplication as possible. While there are a number of magazine networks, they generally fall into two categories.

1. *Single publisher networks.* Here a network is offered by a single publisher who owns several magazines and will allow advertisers to buy all or any number of these publications as a group. For example, Hearst Magazine Group publishes 15 magazines and allows advertisers who use at least three titles to build network discounts.

   The publisher network can be especially effective in encouraging a media buyer to choose among similar magazines. For example, let's assume a media buyer has decided to purchase space in *Cosmopolitan* and *Town and Country*, both Hearst magazines. A third option is to purchase either *Redbook*, another

Hearst magazine, or *Ladies Home Journal.* Assuming both magazines meet the advertising criteria of a particular client, the discounts available from buying *Redbook* as part of the Hearst network may well sway the media buyer in that direction.

To a degree, the single publisher network is being replaced by cross-media buying. As more and more magazines become part of media conglomerates, they no longer confine a "network" buy to magazines, but broaden the concept to all media vehicles owned by a particular company.

2. *Independent networks.* The second type of magazine network is made up of different publishers who market magazines with similar audience appeals. These networks are usually offered by a rep firm that contracts individually with each publisher and then sells advertising for magazines within the group. The concept is similar to the space wholesaling that George Rowell began in the 1850s, discussed in Chapter 5. Media Networks, Inc., the largest independent network firm, offers six networks, each geared to a specific audience. For example, the Media Networks Business Network consists of seven magazines including *Financial World* and *Time.* Even though these magazines are owned by different publishers, they know that there are advantages to cooperating in selling space to large advertisers.

MAGAZINE CIRCULATION

As with any medium, accurate magazine readership measurement of magazines is extremely important to advertisers. Media planners don't buy magazines, television spots, or outdoor signs; they buy people. More specifically, they buy certain groups of people who are customers or prospects for their products. In the magazine industry there are two distinct methods of determining their audiences: *paid circulation and the rate base.*

The most commonly used and reliable method of audience measurement is paid circulation. Most major consumer magazines have their circulations audited by an outside company. Magazine rates are based on the circulation that a publisher promises to deliver to advertisers, referred to as the *guaranteed circulation.* Since the guaranteed circulation is the number of readers advertisers purchase, it also is referred to as the **rate base,** or the circulation on which advertising rates for a specific magazine are based.

rate base The circulation that magazines guarantee advertisers in computing advertising costs.

You will recall from our earlier discussion that magazine publishers are finding it increasingly expensive to maintain high readership levels. As circulation for a magazine rises, the increases are sometimes created by marginally interested readers who subscribed because of special introductory deals, among other things. Publishers usually find it very expensive to keep these fringe readers when it is time to renew subscriptions. Added to the problem is the fact that major auditing organizations such as the Audit Bureau of Circulations (ABC) require that a subscriber must pay at least 50 percent of the full subscription price to be counted as a reader. Consequently, magazines are limited in the marketing promotions they can use and still count readers as paid for auditing purposes.

In the last few years, a number of major magazines including *TV Guide* and *Reader's Digest* have lowered their rate bases substantially. Rate base management is fundamentally a financial consideration. As circulation rises, advertising rates also will increase. However, if publishers are spending more on marketing to keep circulation figures artificially higher than they can gain in increased advertising revenue, it doesn't make economic sense to continue to do it. ". . . publishers often may find that the money spent to produce and deliver more copies to subscribers lured into short term subscriptions with introductory prices can quickly dissipate any gains made from new ad revenue."[16]

While some publishers are cutting their rate base, others are asking audit companies to review the rules that require at least 50-percent subscription payments in order to count readers. A number of publishers want to count any circulation that is paid, regardless of the price of a subscription. A number of advertisers think that removing requirements for the amount that must be paid for a subscription opens the door to serious abuses. Advertisers ask, "If not 50 percent, then what? A dime, a nickel, a penny—where does it end?"

In an editorial addressing the circulation rate base "mess," *Advertising Age* commented, "Advertisers are as much to blame as publishers for putting magazines in this situation. Although they talk about circulation quality, advertisers still interpret rate base reductions as signs of weakness. Instead they should encourage magazines to charge a fair price for their products and let circulation settle at natural levels. . . . One reader willing to pay full freight and re-up is worth 10 sweepstakes subscribers."[17]

There will not be an end to the debate soon. However, it is clear that advertisers would rather buy space in magazines with a quality readership, that is, those readers who are interested in both the magazine and its advertising. By the same token, advertisers generally will gravitate to those publications with the largest number of readers within their target audience. Common sense tells us that publishers, particularly of second-tier magazines, will continue to explore whatever steps necessary to keep circulation levels as high as possible within their profit constraints.

A magazine does not necessarily offer a rate base to advertisers. In fact, a number of audited publications do not make a specific guaranteed circulation claim. These publishers provide advertisers with accurate circulation for past issues, but they don't take any risk for circulation shortfalls in the future. In the volatile world of magazine advertising, many smaller magazines do not want to deal with the financial problems of make-goods related to audience decreases.

Readership In magazine terminology "readership" usually combines paid circulation (subscribers and newsstand purchasers) with pass-along readers. For example, according to Mediamark Research, Inc., *Family Circle* has a paid circulation of 4.97 million, but with 4.85 readers per copy (RPC), more than 20 million people see each issue. The more general the publication's editorial, the more likely it is to have significant pass-along readership.

Many advertisers and even magazine publishers are concerned about the use of readership as a substitute for paid circulation. Historically, the use of readership is rooted in the magazine industry's competition with television. As we discussed in the last section, magazines are retrenching somewhat from a "numbers at any cost" circulation mentality and again selling quality of readership. Nevertheless, publishers want to keep readership surveys to take into account fairly their total readers.

It would seem that total readership, accurately measured, would be a reasonable approach to measuring magazine audiences. The problem arises from the fact that many media buyers regard pass-along readers of consumer magazines as inherently inferior to paid circulation. Between those advertisers who see no value in readership and those who view it as equal to paid circulation, there is probably a middle ground. As in most marketing and advertising questions, the real answer is determined by the specific objectives of the publication and its readers. However, regardless of the value that one places on readership, most acknowledge that it is different from paid circulation.

---

[16]Steve Wilson, "Fine-tuning of rate bases changes advertisers' take," *Advertising Age*, 19 October 1998, S26.
[17]"No dodging circ issues," *Advertising Age*, 12 June 2000, 34.

MEASURING MAGAZINE AUDIENCES

We now turn to the issue of how publishers verify the circulation and readership of their magazines. Advertisers normally will not purchase a magazine unless its publisher can provide independent verification of the magazine's readership. In magazine terminology, *readership* has two distinct meanings. One refers to the time spent with a publication. The other, and the one we will discuss here, includes all readers of a magazine as contrasted to only those who buy a publication.

The Audit Bureau of Circulations The Audit Bureau of Circulations (ABC) is the largest of several auditing organizations that verify magazine circulation. The ABC provides two basic services: the Publisher's Statements, which report six-month periods ending June 30 and December 31; and the ABC Audit, which annually audits the data provided in the Publisher's Statements. The ABC reports total circulation, as well as circulation figures by state, by county size, and per issue during each six-month period. ABC reports also state the manner in which circulation was obtained—for example, by subscription, by newsstand sales—and any discounts or premiums provided to subscribers. Exhibit 11.8 is a sample of the ABC Publisher's Statement.

The ABC reports are very matter-of-fact documents that deal only with primary readers. They do not offer information about product usage, demographic characteristics of readers, or pass-along readership. As we discussed in the previous section, the ABC continues to be embroiled in the debate over how to define paid

PROTOTYPE

CLASS, INDUSTRY OR FIELD SERVED: Travel, customs of people, products and related human interest, subject to geographical and sociological nature.

1. AVERAGE PAID CIRCULATION FOR 6 MONTHS ENDED DECEMBER 31, (YEAR)

Subscriptions:	295,069
Single Copy Sales:	109,721
AVERAGE TOTAL PAID CIRCULATION	404,790

Advertising Rate Base and/or Circulation Guarantee
Paid Circulation:

Average Total Analyzed Non-Paid Circulation	10,000
Average Total Non-Analyzed Non-Paid Circulation	2,050

NOTE: THIS PUBLICATION ALSO PROVIDES AN ABC PUBLISHER'S STATEMENT ANALYZING ITS NON-PAID CIRCULATION

1a. AVERAGE PAID CIRCULATION of Regional, Metro and Demographic Editions

Edition & number of issues		Edition & number of issues		Edition & number of issues	
Eastern (6)	149,772	Central (6)	161,916	Western (6)	93,102

2. PAID CIRCULATION by Issues

Issue	Subscriptions	Single Copy Sales	Total Paid	Issue	Subscriptions	Single Copy Sales	Total Paid
July	285,960	116,637	402,597	Oct.	301,738	105,764	407,502
Aug.	297,181	107,749	404,930	Nov.	290,590	109,495	400,085
Sept.	300,315	102,700	403,015	Dec.	294,630	115,979	410,609

ANALYSIS OF TOTAL NEW AND RENEWAL SUBSCRIPTIONS

Sold during 6 Month Period Ended December 31, (Year)

3. AUTHORIZED PRICES

(a) Basic Prices: Single Copy: $1.50.	
Subscriptions: 1 yr. $12.00; 2 yrs. $22.00; 3 yrs. $30.00	19,431
(b) Higher than basic prices:	None
(c) Lower than basic prices: 1 yr. $7.00, $8.00, $8.99; 2 yrs. $13.99	78,924
(d) Association subscription prices	None
Total Subscriptions Sold in Period.	98,355

4. DURATION OF SUBSCRIPTIONS SOLD:

(a) One to six months (1 to 6 issues)	660
(b) Seven to twelve months (7 to 12 issues)	85,669
(c) Thirteen to twenty-four months	1,021
(d) Twenty-five to thirty-six months	143
(e) Thirty-seven to forty-eight months	9,100
(f) Forty-nine months and more	1,822
Total Subscriptions Sold in Period.	98,355

5. CHANNELS OF SUBSCRIPTION SALES:

(a) Ordered by mail and/or direct request	68,501
(b) Ordered through salespeople:	
1. Catalog agencies and individual agents	8,644
2. Publisher's own and other publisher's salespeople	590
3. Independent agencies' salespeople	14,100
4. Newspaper agencies	None
5. Members of schools, churches, fraternal and similar organizations	6,317
(c) Association memberships	None
(d) All other channels, See Par. 11(a)	203
Total Subscriptions Sold in Period.	98,355

Exhibit 11.8

ABC offers total circulation analyses for publications.
Courtesy: Audit Bureau of Circulations.

circulation. The controversy is yet another indication of the importance that both publishers and advertisers place on the accuracy of audience data.

Syndicated Magazine Readership Research   Advertisers are, of course, interested in the primary readers of magazines. But they are also interested in who these readers are and what they buy, as well as pass-along readers who are given the publications. Currently, there are two principal sources of syndicated magazine readership research: A&S/Simmons Magazine Metrics, and Mediamark Research, Inc. (MRI).

MRI methodology consists of selecting a sample of approximately 20,000 households and eliciting media usage, demographic characteristics, and product purchase information. Using personal interviews, respondents are then prompted by logo cards of the various magazines being tested and they are asked how recently they read a particular publication. This technique is called the *recent reading method*. The recent reading method provides estimates of readership and product usage.

A&S/Simmons is a joint venture between Audit and Surveys Worldwide and Kantar Media Research, parent company of **Simmons Market Research Bureau** (SMRB). Its study uses mailed questionnaires and measures some 600 magazines with an emphasis on audience information.[18]

Simmons Market Research Bureau (SMRB) Firm that provides audience data for several media. Best known for magazine research.

CONSUMER MAGAZINES—SUMMING UP

The challenges and opportunities facing consumer magazines cover a wide range of concerns. From practical considerations of cost management in distribution and printing to the ways in which the Internet can be integrated into traditional magazine practices, publishers must deal with an ever-changing marketplace.

In spite of these challenges, magazines are well positioned to deal with the communication issues of the twenty-first century. As demonstrated in Exhibit 11.9, magazine readers are among the most upscale of any media audience. Ironically, they show great strength among Internet users that, combined with the selective nature of most publications, may offer a profitable convergence for many publishers. New technology aside, magazines are well positioned as a major marketing and advertising tool.

Exhibit 11.9

The "Average" Magazine Reader

Base: Individuals reading 5+ magazine issues in the past month.

Percentages add up to more than 100% due to multiple responses.

Source: MRI, Spring 1999.

Magazine Readers Index vs. Total Population (Index = 100)	
Graduated College+	114
Household Income $75,000+	117
Employed Full-time	106
Home Value $150,000+	111
Primary Wage Earner	107
Executive/Managerial/Administrative/Professional	114
Top Management Decision Makers	108
Surf the Net 3+ times per week	122

Magazine Reading By Place	
In own home	91%
Out-of-home	68%

Average time spent reading:
46 minutes per issue

---

[18]Ann Marie Kerwin, "Joint venture to expand A&S study," *Advertising Age,* 26 January 1998, 51.

300   PART IV   Media

Magazines can play a role as either the primary medium for a national advertiser or as a niche medium to reach prime prospects. Magazines will continue to be a major source of news, information, and entertainment for millions of prime prospects. It is this combination of prestige and segmentation that gives magazines a major qualitative advantage over most other media. The fact that magazines are asking readers to carry a major share of the financial support of magazines also has enhanced their value to advertisers.

The combination of upscale readers, opportunities for targeted advertising, editorial involvement, and both reach and frequency among a number of qualitative and quantitative audience segments of importance to advertisers will work to the advantage of magazines in the future. Despite these positive characteristics, magazines will continue to face a number of economic problems. Some, like postage increases and newsstand distribution concerns, are beyond their immediate control. In the long term, it may be that financial elements will determine the future of the medium as much as readership.

THE BUSINESS PRESS AND BUSINESS-TO-BUSINESS ADVERTISING

Professional Candy Buyer, National Hog Farmer, Modern Tire Dealer, Pizza Today, and *National Jeweler* are only a handful of the more than 3,600 publications that make up the business press. In Chapter 2, we briefly discussed the business-to-business (B2B) media. It is a marketplace where million dollar deals are commonplace and the methods for sales, marketing, and advertising are markedly different from those in consumer advertising. A number of media and promotions are used to reach business buyers. We will discuss them in this chapter since business magazines constitute the primary source of B2B expenditures.

Prospects for most business advertisers are fewer and more concentrated, they tend to be experts concerning the products they purchase, and audience selectivity is much more important than the CPMs or reach measures used in consumer media. Another feature of business publications is their efficient reach of major decision makers (see Exhibit 11.10). Given the specialized audience of these publications combined with moderate cost, the business magazine continues to be a bargain.

Both the tone and advertising of business publications differ significantly from consumer magazines. The business press is a medium of reference and commerce,

business-to-business advertising Advertising that promotes goods through trade and industrial journals that are used in the manufacturing, distributing, or marketing of goods to the public.

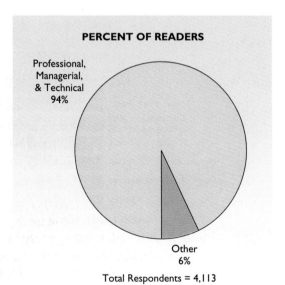

PERCENT OF READERS

Professional, Managerial, & Technical 94%

Other 6%

Total Respondents = 4,113

whereas consumer magazines are vehicles of entertainment, news, and leisure reading. Many business publications are used on a regular basis to keep up with the latest industry trends, competitive activity, and product category marketing strategy.

Communicating the Business-to-Business Message

B2B advertising has to consider a number of factors in addressing its specialized audiences. First and foremost, the message must be directed at the profitability of the customer. Exhibit 11.11 shows the type of product information that most business prospects are looking for in business advertising. Whereas few consumer advertisements contain technical product specifications and details about equipment compatibility and delivery terms, these are the types of information commonly contained in business publications.

In communicating with the business community, there are a number of considerations. For example:

1. Appeal to prospects in terms of specific job interests and demands. The advertisement should address how a product or service can increase the productivity and enhance the job performance of a particular function.

2. Sell the benefits to the buyer not the features of the product. Again, these benefits need to be couched in terms of sales and productivity. It is rare that cute or humorous business advertising is successful.

3. The job of business advertising, particularly for high-end products, is to support and facilitate the sales function. Business transactions, unlike their consumer counterparts, are rarely completed with a single advertisement or even solely through advertising. Most business advertising is a means of moving prospects into the personal sales channel. That is, advertising should function to make the job of personal selling or prospect follow-up easier.

4. Avoid product puffery. Remember the readers of your advertising are trained professionals with high levels of expertise in their fields. They expect to see product information, often with detailed diagrams, charts, and technical specifications. The type of appeals common in consumer media will not work in the business and trade press.

5. Business advertising, even more so than consumer advertising, needs to have clear objectives and these objectives need to be measurable in terms of the specific publics that the message is directed toward.

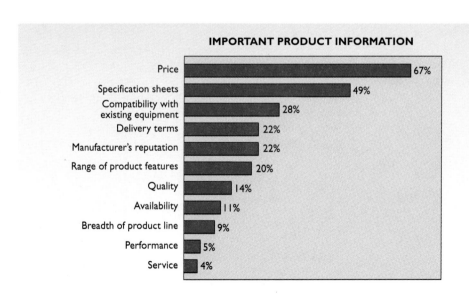

Exhibit

11.11

What are the Most Important Product Information Needs of a Specialized Business Publication Reader?

The most important product information needs are for price, specification sheets, compatibility with existing equipment, delivery terms, and manufacturer's reputation.

Source: Cahners Advertising Research Report.

IMPORTANT PRODUCT INFORMATION

Price	67%
Specification sheets	49%
Compatibility with existing equipment	28%
Delivery terms	22%
Manufacturer's reputation	22%
Range of product features	20%
Quality	14%
Availability	11%
Breadth of product line	9%
Performance	5%
Service	4%

Corporate Branding

Business-to-business selling is about buying products, but it also is about buying the reputation of the companies with whom other companies do business. A general consumer may take a chance with an unknown company even for a product costing several hundred dollars. The same is rarely true in the world of business marketing where the future of a business can be at stake when major purchases are made.

In recent years, more and more emphasis has been placed on *corporate branding* by companies. As companies grow and become more complex in terms of different divisions, products, and distribution channels, it becomes difficult to approach customers with a single message. Corporate branding attempts to integrate a company's total image through a coordinated marketing communications process.

Ideally, corporate branding allows a company to speak with its various customers through advertising, public relations, the Internet, even product design and other identity programs such as logos and product trademarks. Effective corporate branding allows a company to establish its reputation and set brands apart from the competition. It also allows a company to provide a consistent message to prospects, customers, stockholders, and employees.[19]

The remainder of this section will examine some of the special features of the business-to-business sector and the differences and similarities with consumer advertising.

Audiences of the Business Press   There are both important qualitative and quantitative differences between readers of business publications and the typical audiences of consumer magazines. Most importantly trade publications are for most readers part of the job. They are not read for entertainment but rather will be judged on the basis of how well they improve the readers' ability to do their jobs, market their products, and improve their profits. Consequently, business magazines must develop a depth of understanding of their readers that is not required typically in the consumer press.

In addition to the approach that readers take to the business press, there also are significant differences in the audience composition of business versus consumer magazines. In terms of age, income, job categories, education (see Exhibit 11.12), and other basic demographic data, business publications skew far higher than typical consumer magazines. Basically, the tone of a business magazine, both in editorial and advertising, is one of a problem solver. There is a special relationship between business magazines and the industries they serve.

Competition for Business-to-Business Advertising   Television, newspapers, radio, and consumer magazines are the core of consumer advertising. On a national basis television is in fierce competition for consumer dollars, while radio and newspapers serve local retailers in reaching these same buyers. However, business selling and marketing have devoted most of their dollars to personal sales, trade and business publications, direct-mail, and telemarketing.

As discussed earlier, for most major accounts, marketing communication is used as a means of providing entry for personal selling. Studies show that, by an overwhelming margin, executives with purchasing authority will not make appointments with salespersons unless they have a thorough knowledge of the companies and products they represent. In many respects, the environment of business marketing was unchanged for the 50 years from the end of World War II

---

[19]"The value and role of corporate advertising for business-to-business marketers," *Cahners Advertising Research Report*, #2000.15.

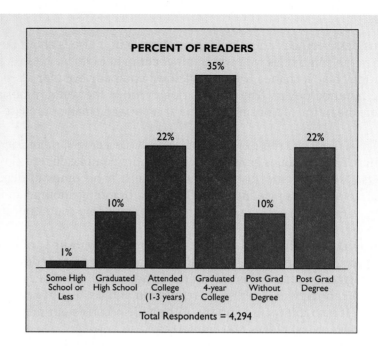
to the mid-1990s. Then, you guessed it, the Internet became a major force in business marketing.

The Internet and Business-to-Business Marketing

The Internet gained acceptance faster in B2B marketing than on the consumer side. For one thing, businesses were mostly computer savvy long before the Internet came along, so it represented just another phase in the development of computer integration into the business world. Exhibit 11.13 demonstrates the acceptance of the Internet as a form of marketing and product information. The Internet also was more functional for B2B marketing since the number of cus-

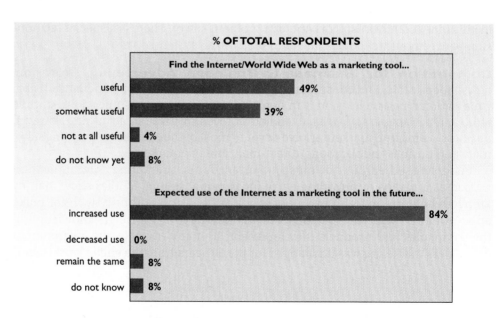

tomers was infinitesimal compared to most consumer products. Both customers and their e-mail addresses could be identified easily and the Internet quickly became part of the integrated marketing communication plans of most companies.

Despite the greater utility of the Internet B2B marketing, it was used in relatively traditional ways of reaching customers, providing Web sites with product information, and for less-expensive products or regular customers a method of order-taking. However, the use of the Internet in B2B marketing and potentially the practices of business selling changed dramatically in the late 1990s with the introduction of the Internet auction.

The Internet Auction and Business-to-Business Marketing

When Ford Motor Company wants to purchase several million dollars' worth of rubber hoses or General Mills wants to buy ten million cereal boxes, the procedure has been to send out product specifications to a network of suppliers or their wholesalers and typically after a round of questions and negotiations accept bids from qualified companies. In this process sometimes suppliers got the word about a buy and purchasing agents were never sure that they were getting the best deal.

The coming of the Internet auction promises to change many of the methods of marketing and selling goods in the business-to-business world. Basically, it allows buyers and sellers to make a connection, bid on parts and supplies, and make the final deal all through a direct-marketing channel between buyer and seller. This process has even greater potential for change given the emphasis placed on price in the business-to-business environment. Once a supplier meets buyer specifications for steel, packaging cartons, or electrical wiring, it becomes a generic commodity.

It is a marketplace that closely resembles those envisioned in many economic models where advertising, brand reputation, and company name have little relevance to how a product is purchased. These Internet auctions also provide a true global economy to the process. Sellers from around the world—even those where buyers and sellers have never heard of each other—theoretically have an equal chance to make a sale if the price is right.

The largest Internet auction company is FreeMarkets, but a number of other specialized auctions have been established such as e-Steel, MetalSite, and PlasticsNet.com. In some cases, large companies such as General Motors and Sears have set up their own in-house auctions to network with present suppliers. Rather than a lengthy process of negotiation, the bidding process is over in as little as 20 minutes with sellers besting competitors' offers until one—the low bidder—is left standing.[20]

While a change of this magnitude in the business marketplace is no doubt interesting, why should advertisers care? If manufacturers have immediate and full communication with all potential suppliers and products become generic commodities with sales almost totally dependent on price, what role is there for advertising and promotion? If we review the section on corporate branding, we see that many of the advantages of such promotions assume the need for enhanced company reputation and product identity—roles largely unnecessary in a virtual auction marketplace.

Whether it is a household buying an airplane ticket from priceline.com or DuPont buying a million dollars' worth of chemicals from i2i.com, the concept is the same and that is that price, not advertising and promotion, sells. "... the Internet is altering the rules on how companies manage their sales, service, and distribution operations. It is providing new opportunities for businesses of all stripes to reach new customers, as well as forge closer ties with existing customers. ... [The Internet] enables companies that once relied on middlemen to begin

---

[20]Shawn Tully, "The B2B tool that really is changing the world," *Fortune*, 20 March 2000, 132.

selling directly to its retail customers. As a result, e-commerce can pit manufacturers against their wholesalers, retailers, and other traditional partners."[21]

Business Publication Expansion of Services   You will recall that we discussed the fact that many consumer magazines have introduced a number of merchandising and ancillary services. Because of the specialized nature of business-to-business publications, they are even better positioned to engage in ancillary services than their consumer counterparts. As the competition for B2B advertising and promotional dollars increases, business publications have increasingly engaged in a number of ventures to reach their core readers and at the same time increase the profitability of their companies.

1. Subscriber list rentals. Major business publications find that their subscriber list is one of the most valuable commodities they own. In fact, depending on the degree of specialization and the business they service, business publications make as much as 10 percent of their total revenue from list rentals.
2. Event-related publications. Golf tournaments, car shows, and conventions from religious denominations to service organizations often provide an advertiser-supported program with the schedule of the event as well as information about the group. These publications are usually published by an independent trade publisher.
3. Custom publications. As we discussed in an earlier section, custom publishing is a very lucrative business. These custom magazines are a major source of revenue for many trade publishers.
4. Trade shows. In Chapter 14, we will discuss in detail the role of trade shows in the marketing channel. Major trade shows bring buyers and sellers from an entire industry together to view new products and methods of doing business. In some cases, business publications organize and sell sponsorship to these usually under the name of the publication. A named trade show demonstrates leadership in the field and can also be a profitable enterprise for the publication.

Entry into ancillary services usually is more successful for established magazines than their smaller less well-known competitors. Magazines provide credibility and high visibility to these ancillary events, which would be lacking without the tie-in to a major publication. Seeing the growth of promotional techniques in business-to-business advertising, many magazine publishers employ ancillary vehicles to add to their overall profitability and decrease their dependence on advertising from their publications.

Regardless of their format, ancillary activities offer a number of advantages to a publisher. First, they utilize the publisher's knowledge of a particular industry to help clients develop a coordinated promotional and advertising campaign. Second, they gain revenue from companies who do not use advertising as a primary business-to-business marketing tool. Finally, they increase a magazine's credibility by demonstrating far-reaching expertise in a number of promotional areas. In the future, we will see publishers developing a variety of information services and promotional techniques in addition to their basic magazines.

Some Special Features of Business Publication Advertising

Business publications exhibit several differences from consumer magazines. This section briefly discusses the more important ones.

---

[21]"Setting up shop," *Fortune Tech Guide, 2000,* 44.

Pass-along Readership   A significant number of readers of business publications receive their magazines on a pass-along basis. We earlier noted that such readership among consumer magazines is generally regarded as inferior to paid circulation. However, one of the notable differences between business and consumer publications is the way advertisers view pass-along readership. The typical consumer medium has a relatively short life and low pass-along readership. Occasionally, a recipe will be clipped or a magazine will be passed on to a neighbor, but consumer magazines are read largely for pleasure and tossed aside. In any case, advertisers view pass-along readership of consumer magazines as vastly inferior to primary readership.

Business publication advertisers, in contrast, view pass-along readership as quite valuable. For one thing, readers don't normally browse through *Electronic Design* or *Concrete Construction*; they pay close attention to the copy. For another, some business publications limit their circulation in a way that forces pass-along readership.

Types of Business-to-Business Publications

Despite the wide array of business publications, they can generally be placed in one of four categories:

- Distributive trades (trade)
- Manufacturers and builders (industrial)
- Top officers of other corporations (management)
- Physicians, dentists, architects, and other professional people (professional)

Trade Papers   Because most nationally advertised products depend upon dealers for their sales, we discuss advertising in **trade papers** first. Usually, this advertising is prepared by the agency that handles the consumer advertising, and in any new campaign both are prepared at the same time. The term *trade papers* is applied particularly to business publications directed at those who buy products for resale, such as wholesalers, jobbers, and retailers. Typical trade papers are *American Druggist, Supermarket News, Chain Store Age, Hardware Retailer, Modern Tire Dealer, Women's Wear Daily,* and *Home Furnishings.*

Almost every business engaged in distributing goods has a trade paper to discuss its problems. Trade papers are a great medium for reporting merchandising news about the products, packaging, prices, deals, and promotions of the manufacturers that cater to the particular industry. The chain-store field alone has more than 20 such publications. Druggists have a choice of over 30, and more than 60 different publications are issued for grocers. There are many localized journals, such as *Texas Food Merchant, Michigan Beverage News, Southern Hardware, California Apparel News,* and *Illinois Building News.*

Industrial Publications   As we move into the world where a company in one industry sells its materials, machinery, tools, parts, and equipment to another company for use in making a product or conducting operations, we are in an altogether different ballpark—the industrial-marketing arena.

There are fewer customers in this arena than in the consumer market, and they can be more easily identified. The amount of money involved in a sale may be large—hundreds of thousands of dollars, perhaps even millions—and nothing is bought on impulse. Many knowledgeable executives with technical skills often share in the buying decision. The sales representative has to have a high degree of professional competence to deal with the industrial market, in which personal selling is the biggest factor in making a sale. Advertising is only a collateral aid used to pave the way for or support the salesperson; hence, it receives a smaller share of the marketplace budget.

trade paper   A business publication directed to those who buy products for resale (wholesalers, jobbers, retailers).

Advertising addressed to people responsible for buying goods needed to make products is called **industrial advertising**. It is designed to reach purchasing agents, plant managers, engineers, controllers, and others who have a voice in spending the firm's money.

Management Publications   The most difficult group for a publication to reach is managers. After all, even the largest companies have only a relatively few decision makers. When these decision makers are widely dispersed across a number of industries and job descriptions, publications find they must be extremely creative to reach them.

The management category is one that straddles a gray area between consumer and business-to-business publications. Magazines such as *Business Week, Fortune*, and *Nation's Business* have characteristics that would place them in either the business or the consumer category. Even magazines such as *Time* have at least some of their partial-run editions listed in the *Business Publications SRDS*.

Professional Publications   The **Standard Rate and Data Service**, in its special business publication edition, includes journals addressed to physicians, surgeons, dentists, lawyers, architects, and other professionals who depend upon these publications to keep abreast of their professions. The editorial content of such journals ranges from reportage about new technical developments to discussions on how to meet client or patient problems better and how to conduct offices more efficiently and profitably. Professional people often recommend or specify the products their patients or clients should order. Therefore, much advertising of a high technical caliber is addressed to them.

Controlled Circulation   Magazines are sometimes distributed free to selective readers. Free circulation is known as **controlled circulation.** The term controlled refers to the fact that publishers distribute only to a carefully selected list of people who are influential in making purchase decisions for their industry. They use the same database techniques that direct mailers use in building their mailing lists. Controlled circulation makes sense when you are dealing with an easily defined audience of decision makers. To some media planners, the logic of controlled circulation is little different than that of direct-mail except the ad is delivered in an editorial environment. Despite the fact that controlled circulation is widely used in the trade press, it is not universally embraced. In the past, most research has indicated that a high percentage of both clients and media directors prefer the reader commitment inherent in paid circulation.

The number of controlled publications in the business field plays a major role in their share of advertising-to-circulation revenues compared to consumer magazines. On average, approximately two-thirds of trade publication circulation is controlled. A number of publications use a mix of controlled and paid circulations where qualified readers receive the magazine free and others can buy it if they wish.

Controlled circulation creates a significant dependence on advertising support. Unlike consumer magazines, business publications have been largely unsuccessful in shifting to a reader-driven revenue stream. This dependency on advertising is another reason why business publications suffer so much during economic downturns.

Vertical and Horizontal Publications   Industrial publications are usually considered either *horizontal* or *vertical*. A **vertical publication** is one that covers an entire industry. An example is *Baking Industry*, which contains information concerning product quality, marketing, plant efficiency, and packaging.

Horizontal publications are edited for people who are engaged in a single function that cuts across many industries. An example is *Purchasing* magazine, which is circulated to purchasing managers. It discusses trends and forecasts applicable to all industries.

North American Industrial Classification System For many years, U.S. businesses were defined according to a federal designation known as the Standard Industrial Classification (SIC). The SIC also was a standard method for business magazines to define the segmentation of their audiences. With the coming of a global economy, there was a need for a standardized system that could be used on a multinational basis. In 1999, a new system, the **North American Industrial Classification System** (NAICS) was implemented to deal with comparisons between the three members of the North American Free Trade Association (NAFTA), but it also can be used for comparisons with the United Nations' International Standard Industrial Classification System, which is used worldwide.

The NAICS (pronounced nakes) defines with descending specificity. For example:[22]

North American Industrial Classification System System that uses six-digit identification numbers for classifying manufacturing firms.

NAICS Code	Description
51	Information
513	Broadcasting and telecommunications
5133	Telecommunications
51332	Wireless telecommunications, carriers, except satellites
513321	Paging

While the applications of the NAICS go far beyond advertising, it is extremely useful in determining how a particular publication reaches an industry and specific segments of an industry of interest to a marketer.

Circulation Audits Business-to-business advertisers are keenly interested in the circulation of the publications in which they advertise. In some respects, the readership numbers are more important than those in general consumer magazines. The total audience is smaller, the CPM for most publications is significantly higher than consumer magazines, and the competition makes it imperative that business-to-business marketers reach their target audience in a timely fashion.

Because of the number and diversity of audiences contacted by the trade and business press, a number of auditing organization are used by business publishers and advertisers. More than 1,000 trade and industrial magazines are audited by the Business Publications Audit of Circulation International (BPA), the leading business auditor. Since many business publications are circulated to a general business audience, the ABC is used for publications such as *Business Week*, and a few publications use both auditing firms.

A third auditing organization is the Verified Audit Circulation (VAC). Founded in 1951, VAC provides circulation audits for a wide variety of newspapers, shoppers, magazines, and even Yellow Pages directories. There are a number of publications in the business area that are not audited. While an unaudited publication can survive, there are a number of business-to-business advertisers and agencies that, as a matter of policy, will not consider an unaudited publication.

Agribusiness Advertising

At one time farm media, both print and broadcast, was geared largely to the millions of families who lived and worked on small farms. In recent years, the farm press has had to adapt to dramatic changes in the way agriculture is conducted in this country. Between 1940 and 1991, the number of farm workers declined by

---

[22]"Classified information," *American Demographics*, July 1999, 16.

almost 70 percent. During that same period, the number of farm residents dropped from 31 million to five million.[23]

Contemporary agribusiness media and advertisers are tailoring their messages to a concentrated industry of huge farm cooperatives and farm managers with income and educational levels that rival those of the CEOs of any major business. While weather and crop prices are still major topics of the farm press, these publications are just as likely to be discussing the weather in Russia and price controls and export policies as opposed to what is happening in a local community.

The farm press is facing many of the problems of the business press in general. A number of media competitors have come on the scene in recent years to take advertising dollars from the print media. Unlike business-to-business advertising where television and radio have only recently been used by advertisers, farm broadcasting has a long history of serving the farm community.

There are a number of local and regional farm broadcasters, but on a national level the primary sources of agribusiness news and advertising are:

- *AgDay*, a daily syndicated television show that reaches 130 markets and is supported by a number of national advertisers such as DuPont and Chevrolet.
- The weekly *U.S. Farm Report*, which is syndicated to approximately 93 percent of the nation's television households.
- *National Farm Report*, which is syndicated to some 350 radio stations.
- The *Agri-Voice Network*, a network of 90 smaller Midwestern radio stations broadcasting daily farm reports.

In addition, a number of Web sites have been established by the farm media and agribusiness advertisers. It is estimated that some 33 percent of farmers are actively using the Internet for information and exchanging views on farm issues.[24]

Advertising products to the agribusiness community uses many of the same techniques demonstrated by other sectors of business marketing. However, agribusiness promotional techniques are even more specialized than those of traditional business-to-business selling. The relatively small agribusiness population makes sophisticated information readily available. Agribusiness advertising can target audiences and deliver a message that solves specific problems of the farm industry.

The business of farming has been hit hard during recent years with an uncertain farm economy, high prices for feed and other supplies, and the ravages of the great Midwestern flood of 1993. These factors have combined to make it very difficult for farm magazines and agribusiness advertising in general. A continuing consolidation of farms has reduced the number of farmers and companies involved in agribusiness. This trend toward consolidation has been reflected in the farm press by lower circulation and fewer advertising dollars during the last two decades.

Ironically, as the number of farms and major agribusiness suppliers have decreased, the number and diversity of media competing for advertising dollars in the sector has grown dramatically. In order to compete in this environment, farm publications have utilized many of the techniques of the business press in expanding the means they use to reach their audiences. For example, these magazines have accumulated sophisticated databases to develop subscriber list rentals, do their own direct-mail to nonsubscribers, and publish special catalogs and other material. Like the business press, farm magazines will probably see more revenue coming from nonpublishing sources as they become more successful in promoting these ventures.

---

[23]Marc Spiegler, "Hot media buy: The farm report," *American Demographics*, October 1995, 18.
[24]Barnaby J. Feder, "Getting personal and global in farm broadcasting," *The New York Times*, 18 December 1995, C5.

THE ORGANIZATION OF THE FARM PRESS

Farm magazines fall into three classifications: general farm magazines, regional farm magazines, and vocational farm magazines.

General Farm Magazines

The three major publications in the category are: *Farm Journal, Successful Farming,* and *Progressive Farmer*. In recent years, each of these publications have experienced circulation decreases reflecting the consolidation of the farming industry. The general farm publications are designed to address all aspects of farm life, but with a clear emphasis on business. For instance, the SRDS Publisher's Editorial Profile for *Successful Farming* reads as follows:

> *Successful Farming* editorial is designed as management guidance for business farmers and their families. Articles are written as practical help in making those decisions which directly affect the profitability of the business, and the welfare of the family. Editors seek their information from those in the forefront of farm change, and much editorial is case history reporting of successful innovation. There are also monthly reports on developments in government, finance, equipment, etc. Editorial is 100% business of farming and farm family management.

Regional Farm Magazines A number of farm publications are directed to farmers in a particular region. These publications tend to be general in nature, but they contain little of the family-oriented topics found in the large-circulation farm magazines. They address issues of crops, livestock, and government farm policy unique to a particular region. Among the publications in this category are the *Prairie Farmer,* the majority of whose readers live in Indiana and Illinois; the *Oregon Farmer-Stockman,* and the *Nebraska Farmer.*

Vocational Farm Magazines The last category of farm publications comprises those devoted to certain types of farming or livestock raising. Typical of these publications are *Soybean Digest, The Dairyman, American Fruit Grower,* and *Tobacco*. Many of the vocational magazines combine elements of both regional and vocational publications—for instance, *The Kansas Stockman* and *Missouri Pork Producer.*

Whatever a farmer's interests may be, a number of publications are edited to cater to them. Many farm homes take several publications.

SUMMARY

Summing Up—The Business Press

Business-to-business publications are facing a number of challenges in the future. Among the most obvious are the consolidation of many industries into fewer and fewer firms. This merging of firms has resulted in a decrease in both the number of potential advertisers to support the business press and the number of companies that are being reached with advertising.

A second major trend in the business press has been the growth of competition for advertising dollars. At one time trade and business publications had a virtual monopoly in the business sector and the farm press had only radio as a major competitor. Today, that situation has changed dramatically. Business advertisers are putting their marketing communication dollars in numerous vehicles and utilizing sophisticated database technology to demand immediate and measurable results from their advertising.

Because of the relatively low price of trade magazine advertising, it is possible to appeal to specialized job interests with different messages in a variety of publications. The messages of these publications are also specialized. Factual copy with product information is presented to a knowledgeable audience in a manner that would be impractical in most consumer magazines.

Business-to-business publications are an ideal medium for reaching the targeted audience segments that advertisers seek, in an environment suited to the mood of that audience. Business magazines also provide audience involvement to a degree impossible in most of other media and the affinity for these magazines carries over to the advertising messages.

With the ability of computers to track employment demographics and new technology to reach them through partial-run editions and selected binding, business magazines can compete in an increasingly competitive media environment. On the negative side, business magazines face the same problems of rising costs of postage, printing, and marketing as their consumer counterparts. Quality, credibility, believability, and audience selectivity are the elements that will continue to make the business press a primary choice of business-to-business advertisers.

REVIEW

1. The two major concerns of the magazine industry are costs and selectivity. Explain.
2. What is meant by the term "magazine imperative"?
3. What are some qualitative features of importance to magazine advertisers?
4. Contrast full-run and partial-run magazine editions.
5. What is selective binding?
6. What is the role of negotiation in setting magazine advertising rates?
7. Contrast circulation and readership in magazines.
8. What are the major competitors for business magazines?
9. What has been a primary method for business magazines to extend their services and increase profits?
10. What are vertical and horizontal publications?

TAKE IT TO THE NET

We invite you to visit the Russell/Lane page on the Prentice Hall Web site at **www.prenhall.com/myphlip** for end-of-chapter exercises and applications.

chapter 12

Out-of-Home Advertising

Outdoor advertising, with its bold colors, catchy phrases, and imposing size, is an attention-getting medium without equal. With the current move to targeted formats in most advertising vehicles, outdoor is fast becoming the last of the truly mass media. As the American public becomes more mobile, the highway billboard is being joined by a host of innovative out-of-home approaches. After reading this chapter you will understand:

CHAPTER OBJECTIVES

>> basic marketing strategy of out-of-home advertising

>> the various types of out-of-home media

>> the legislative environment of outdoor advertising

>> out-of-home advertising's role in brand building

>> the complementary function of out-of-home media

>> measurement of the outdoor audience

Pros

1. Outdoor can provide advertising exposure to virtually every adult in a geographic market with high frequency and at a very low cost per exposure.

2. With 24-hour exposure, outdoor is an excellent means of supplementing other media advertising for product introduction or building brand-name recognition.

3. With the use of color and lighting, outdoor is a medium that gains immediate audience attention and can provide reminder messages in proximity to retail outlets such as fast-food franchises.

4. The outdoor industry has diversified the product categories using out-of-home in an attempt to lose its image as a "beer and cigarette" medium.

Cons

1. With a typical audience of high-speed drivers, outdoor is unable to communicate detailed sales messages. Copy is usually limited to headline length—seven to ten words.

2. Outdoor advertising is extremely difficult to measure, making audience comparisons with other media almost impossible.

3. Outdoor has been attacked in many communities as a visual pollutant, which has made it the topic of some controversy. It also faces a number of additional legal restrictions in selected jurisdictions. A few state and local governments have banned the medium altogether. This negative image may discourage some advertisers from using outdoor.

Outdoor is the oldest form of promotion. Evidence of outdoor messages can be found in prehistoric carvings on bronze and stone tablets in the Middle East. In ancient Egypt, outdoor was a popular means of posting public notices as well as sales messages. These were placed on well-traveled roads and they are the forerunner of the modern highway billboard. Painted advertising dates to Pompeii where elaborately decorated walls promoted local businesses.

In this country, outdoor "broadsides" announced the Boston Tea Party and reported the Boston Massacre and posters publicized the presidential campaign of Andrew Jackson. The first American commercial billboard was a poster by Jared Bell for the 1835 circus season. Throughout the 1800s posters promoted a number of products and political causes. In 1850, signs were first used on streetcars in major cities and by 1870 some 300 bill-posting firms served advertisers throughout the East and Midwest.

In 1900, the first standardized outdoor sign format was introduced, and national advertisers such as Kellogg and Coca-Cola began to share the outdoor market with local advertisers. The modern era of outdoor advertising was introduced when the automobile created a mobile society early in this century. In addition to a population on the move, outdoor benefitted from new printing techniques and a growing advertising industry that was always looking for effective means of reaching prospective customers. During this period, the industry adopted standardized signs; formed the forerunner of its national trade association, the **Outdoor Advertising Association of America (OAAA)**; established what is now the **Traffic Audit Bureau for Media Measurement (TAB)** to authenticate audience data; and initiated a national marketing organization, OAAA Marketing.[1]

To most people, the contemporary image of the outdoor industry is far from the reality. An industry once known primarily as a medium for beer and cigarettes, outdoor is used increasingly by major advertisers. "Image-conscious marketers like Gap, Calvin Klein, Apple, and Disney are paying $100,000 a month or more for attention-getting displays in New York's Times Square and along Sunset Strip in Los Angeles. Even Internet trend setters like HotBot and Excite rely on billboards to stay visible in the real world."[2]

Fueled by advertisers' need to gain brand awareness and a number of new outdoor formats, the industry is growing at a rate surpassed by only cable television and Internet advertising (see Exhibit 12.1). The variety of outdoor advertising vehicles has even resulted in the term out-of-home advertising replacing the more familiar outdoor advertising in recent years to more fully reflect the scope of this

Outdoor Advertising Association of America (OAAA) Primary trade and lobbying organization for the outdoor industry.

Traffic Audit Bureau for Media Measurement (TAB) An organization designed to investigate how many people pass and may see a given outdoor sign, to establish a method of evaluating traffic measuring a market.

---

[1]Unless otherwise noted, material for this section was provided by the Outdoor Advertising Association of America.

[2]Marc Gunther, "The great outdoors," *Fortune*, 1 March 1999, 152.

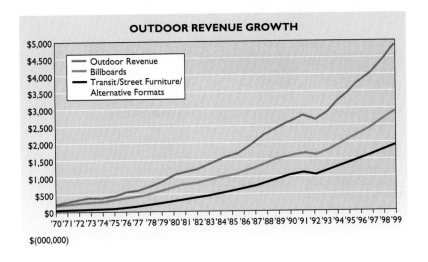

OUTDOOR REVENUE GROWTH

Legend:
— Outdoor Revenue
— Billboards
— Transit/Street Furniture/ Alternative Formats

$(000,000)

Exhibit

12.1

Source: CMR and OAAA.
Courtesy: Outdoor Advertising Association of America.

industry. Today, outdoor normally has a more narrow meaning, referring only to highway posters and large signs. The change is more than just semantic since it reflects the diversity of the industry and its marketing strategy.

While traditional billboards are still the primary source of industry revenues, they constitute only 60 percent of the industry's total income (see Exhibit 12.2). The growth of alternative advertising options offered by out-of-home is a major reason for the growth of the industry. Overall, the OAAA estimates that there are more than 30 types of out-of-home media including everything from the largest outdoor signs, airport and shopping mall kiosks, stadium signs, and airplanes towing banners (see Exhibit 12.3).

Media executives predict that the future of the out-of-home industry will continue to be one of consistent growth. Among the contributing factors to out-of-home's popularity are the following:

1. *An increasingly mobile population.* Americans rarely stay in one place for long. Approximately 125 million people commute to work each day, placing them in the out-of-home market for a variety of messages. Since 1970, automobile ownership has increased by 147 percent and annual miles driven has doubled in the last 20 years.

2. *Cost of out-of-home advertising.* No major medium comes close to matching the inexpensive CPM levels of out-of-home advertising (see Exhibit 12.4). The relatively low cost of out-of-home means that advertisers can generate extremely high levels of both reach and frequency at inexpensive levels. These affordable CPM figures mean that out-of-home is an ideal medium to fill in gaps among target segments missed or underexposed by other media.

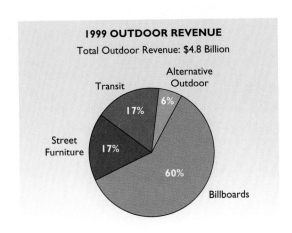

1999 OUTDOOR REVENUE

Total Outdoor Revenue: $4.8 Billion

Alternative Outdoor 6%
Transit 17%
Street Furniture 17%
Billboards 60%

Exhibit

12.2

Source: OAAA.

Exhibit

12.3

Source: 1998, Outdoor Services.

Courtesy: Outdoor Advertising Association of America.

NUMBER OF OUTDOOR DISPLAYS/VEHICLES

Billboards	Street Furniture	Transit
30-Sheet Posters 210,000	Shelters 34,000	Buses 37,600
8-Sheet Posters 140,000	Shopping Malls 1,200 Malls	Commuter Rail /Subways 13,000 Cars
Bulletins 56,000	C-Stores 10,000 Stores	Airports 100+
	In-Stores 34,000 Stores	

Alternative Outdoor

Sports Stadiums/Arenas
77 Facilities

3. *Media fragmentation.* Outdoor advertising is benefitting from the growing audience fragmentation witnessed in other media. In the last 30 years, the number of television channels per household has increased 800 percent and the number of magazines and radio stations has grown by some 200 percent during the same period. The result of this growth is a fragmented audience for most media. While the ability to target prospects is a major benefit for many advertisers, widely distributed package goods and other mass-appeal brands need high levels of exposure to virtually everyone. Outdoor can inexpensively deliver massive audience exposures.

4. *Advertiser diversification.* The old saying, "we are known by the company we keep," is very appropriate for outdoor. Even before the recent prohibition against outdoor tobacco advertising, the outdoor industry was appealing to a more diversified roster of advertisers. When major companies such as General Motors, Walt Disney, McDonald's, Procter & Gamble, and Time Warner made major investments in outdoor, it encouraged other mainstream businesses to add outdoor to their media schedules. The result has been increased revenues and an improved public image for the outdoor industry.

Exhibit

12.4

Courtesy: Outdoor Advertising Association of America.

AVERAGE CPM
ADULTS 18+ (CALENDAR YEAR 2000)

Outdoor (Top 100 Markets)	
8-Sheet posters #50 showing	$0.85
30-sheet posters #50 showing	$1.78
Rotary Bulletins #10 showing	$3.90
Radio (Top 100 Markets)	
:60 drive-time	$5.92
Magazines	
4-color page	$9.62
Television	
:30 prime-time spot	$20.54
:30 prime-time network	$11.31
Newspapers	
Half page black & white	$23.32
Quarter page black & white	$11.66

STRATEGIC ADVERTISING AND OUT-OF-HOME

Out-of-home advertising is one of the most flexible and adaptive of all media. Outdoor is one of the last opportunities to reach consumers prior to purchase. In this regard, it combines the best features of radio and point-of-purchase. Outdoor advertising has many characteristics that set it apart from other media vehicles. With its ability to command attention, outdoor also is well suited to enhance the effectiveness of other advertising media. It can function as an economical supplement to a media plan or it can stand alone as a primary medium. While there are some opportunities to reach particular portions of a geographic or demographic market with outdoor, its major strength is its ability to reach broad population centers quickly and cheaply.

As is the case with other media, individual advertisers have specific marketing objectives when they select out-of-home. However, there are a number of primary marketing advantages that are common to most out-of-home buys. Among these are the following:

- Quickly builds awareness for new brands and maintains and reinforces brand identity for established products
- Creates continuity for a brand or message by extending basic advertising themes beyond traditional media
- Offers a localized approach for national advertising campaigns
- Is adaptable to virtually any advertising message or brand with multiple formats
- Provides local support by offering directions to retail outlets
- Serves as a point-of-purchase reminder to customers in the shopping and buying process
- Can enhance direct-response offers by providing Web addresses and telephone numbers

Despite the fact that a number of high-profile national advertisers are using out-of-home currently, the medium remains an essentially local vehicle. Even in the largest markets, only about 50 percent of out-of-home advertising is placed by national advertising. Outside the top 50 markets, about 80 percent of all out-of-home is local. However, in recent years, a number of changes in the out-of-home industry have taken place that make it likely that more national advertisers will consider out-of-home as part of their future advertising schedule. For example:

1. *Consolidation of ownership.* Only a few years ago, the outdoor business was made up primarily of local companies that provided little audience research, had no national force, or had limited funds to upgrade their facilities. Today, the industry is dominated by large conglomerates that control hundreds of sites throughout the country. These companies are in a position to deal effectively with large national and regional advertisers to gain a larger share of their advertising budgets.

2. *Research.* National advertisers routinely expect sophisticated audience and creative effectiveness research to justify their expenditures. In past years, out-of-home research fell far short of other major media. Even basic demographic data were unavailable in some markets. In recent years, the out-of-home industry has made major strides in providing meaningful research to prospective advertisers. As we will discuss later in this chapter, the industry provides audited audience information as well as eye movement research and demographic segmentation information in areas as small as ZIP codes. Obviously,

the outdoor research investment does not compare to that of media with 10 times its advertising revenues, but marketers are being given reasonable information on which to base their media decisions.

3. *Creative improvements.* The quantity and quality of out-of-home production has improved dramatically in the last decade. Rather than simply printed or painted signs, advertisers have the choice of options such as backlit dioramas, vinyl surfaces for outdoor and transit, and a number of building-sized signs.

4. *Terminology.* Over the years, outdoor developed a terminology that was unique to the industry. Not only did media buyers feel uncomfortable dealing in a "foreign" language when buying outdoor, but, more importantly, it made intermedia comparisons difficult. With the adoption of the gross rating point as the basic measure of outdoor audience reach, the industry has taken steps to address this issue.[3]

While outdoor can achieve a number of advertising goals, it is not suitable for every advertiser or every advertising or marketing situation. Like other advertising medium, outdoor is most successful when it is used in accordance with narrowly defined marketing objectives that utilize the strengths of the medium. In some respects, outdoor presents special challenges since in almost every case it is used as a supplemental media in a more general campaign.

Since outdoor is rarely a primary campaign building block, it must be coordinated, both creatively and in terms of audience reach, with other media. It is important that the main advertising themes be translated properly to outdoor, so that the target audience is exposed to a seamless message. Outdoor is rarely effective as a stand-alone medium. Its major strength is the extension and reinforcement of the more detailed advertising messages carried in other media.

Of course, no amount of planning can overcome some of the inherent weakness in a medium. While analyzing the strengths of out-of-home, advertisers also must consider its shortcomings and how these may influence a particular marketing, media, or creative strategy. Since exposure to outdoor is both involuntary and brief, there is little depth of communication, even among a product's most loyal customers. It is estimated that the average person sees most signs for less than 10 seconds. In addition, the average outdoor "copy" is seven to ten words or about the length of a headline.

In addition, most out-of-home vehicles provide little audience selectivity. The major advantage of most out-of-home advertising is that it is more a shotgun than a rifle. Even though advertisers can tailor their messages to reach specific audiences by pinpointing certain neighborhoods or specific streets such as roads that lead to stadiums or shopping malls, targeting specific audiences is not considered a primary attribute of the medium.

Finally, as the popularity of out-of-home advertising has grown, it has encountered availability problems. In major markets, demand for premium outdoor sites means some advertisers cannot have access to choice locations. Despite these disadvantages, properly executed outdoor advertising can be an inexpensive method of gaining immediate product visibility.

OUTDOOR REGULATION AND PUBLIC OPINION

Outdoor advertising's major advantage—its size—is also a significant public relations problem. For years, a vocal minority of environmentalists and public activists have argued for strict limits or complete removal of all outdoor signs. However, a number of research studies conducted during the last decade indicate that approx-

---

[3]Eugene Morris, "O-O-H—Media's plain Jane sister," *Inside Out of Home,* January 2000, 7.

imately 70 percent of the public sees value in outdoor advertising and by the same majority think that its positive aspects outweigh any negatives. Given the controversies that surround outdoor, it might be well to examine some of the primary areas of criticisms and the reaction of the outdoor industry to them.

Federal Legislation

The most comprehensive attempt at regulating outdoor advertising dates to The **Highway Beautification Act of 1965** (known as the "Lady Bird Bill" since Mrs. Lyndon Johnson lobbied for the legislation). The Act restricted the placement of outdoor signs along interstate highways and provided stiff penalties for states that failed to control signs within 660 feet of interstates. Since passage of the legislation, the number of signs has been reduced from 1.2 million to less than 400,000. Most of the remaining signs are concentrated in commercially zoned areas. Exhibit 12.5 outlines some of the major provisions of the Act.

Highway Beautification Act of 1965
Federal law that controls outdoor signs in noncommercial, nonindustrial areas.

Tobacco Advertising

Historically, one of the most criticized aspects of outdoor advertising was the promotion of tobacco. Critics charged that the uncontrolled exposure of cigarette messages encouraged usage by underaged smokers. In April 1999, the issue became moot when outdoor advertising of tobacco was banned as part of an agreement with 46 state attorneys general and the major tobacco companies.

In the 1980s, one-third of all billboards promoted tobacco products. This concentration of dollars not only made the outdoor industry too dependent on one product category, the controversy surrounding outdoor also discouraged other product categories from buying the medium. "Conventional wisdom once dictated that the outdoor industry couldn't survive without the . . . dollars from U.S. tobacco marketers. Now it seems not only can the industry survive the loss of that revenue,

---

Summary of Existing Outdoor Advertising Control Programs

- Billboards are allowed, by statute, in commercial and industrial areas consistent with size, lighting and spacing provisions as agreed to by the state and federal governments.
- Billboard controls apply to Federal-Aid Primaries (FAP's) as of June 1, 1991. Interstates and other highways that are part of the National Highway System (NHS). The FAP routes were highways noted by state DOTs to be of significant service value and importance. Approximately 260,800 FAP Miles existed as of June 1, 1991 (226,440 rural miles and 34,360 urban miles). These roads have full HBA protections and controls are very important. Maps can be obtained from your state DOT or FHWA Division office or from the OAAA in Washington, D.C.
- States have the discretion to remove legal nonconforming signs along highways; however, the payment of just (monetary) compensation is required for the removal of any lawfully erected billboard along the Federal-Aid Primary, Interstate and National Highway System roads.
- States not complying with the provisions of the HBA are subject to a 10% reduction in their highway allocations.
- States and localities may enact stricter laws than stipulated in the HBA.
- No new signs can be erected along the scenic portions of state designated scenic byways of the Interstate and federal-aid primary highways.

Exhibit
12.5

Federal & State Controls
The Highway Beautification Act of 1965 (23 USC 131)

it can thrive in a nicotine-free world . . . outdoor's day of reckoning is fast becoming its day in the sun."[4]

The OAAA Code of Advertising Practices for Children

The industry has moved on a number of fronts to improve its image and create positive public relations in the communities it serves. One step to counteract negative publicity toward the industry has been the enactment of a voluntary Code of Advertising Practice by the OAAA. As part of this code, outdoor companies are asked to limit the number of billboards in a market that carry messages about products that cannot be sold to minors. Specifically, the code asks that member companies "establish **exclusionary zones** which prohibit advertisements of all products illegal for sale to minors which are either intended to be read from, or within 500 feet of, established places of worship, primary and secondary schools and hospitals." Furthermore, such "off-limit" boards will carry a decal featuring the symbol of a child (see Exhibit 12.6 for a copy of the code and decal).

exclusionary zones (outdoor) Industry code of conduct that prohibits the advertising of products within 500 feet of churches, schools, or hospitals of any products that cannot be used legally by children.

Outdoor Industry Public Service

Each year the outdoor industry contributes almost $300 million in donated space to a number of charities and public service campaigns. Many of these messages are posted in connection with local service projects. However, the OAAA has formed a

---

The OAAA Endorses this Code and Encourages its members to cooperate in conformance with the following principles.

The outdoor advertising medium delivers advertisers' messages to the consumer in a public arena necessitating a high sensitivity to community standards as well as a vigilant defense of commercial free speech.

We, the members of the Outdoor Advertising Association of America (OAAA), are careful to place outdoor advertisements for products illegal for sale to minors on advertising displays that are a reasonable distance from the public places where children most frequently congregate.

In our vigilant support of children and free speech, we recommend that each OAAA member company adopt standards that include the following code of advertising practices.

1. Establish exclusionary zones that prohibit outdoor advertisements of products illegal for sale to minors that are intended to be read from, or within 500 feet of, elementary and secondary schools, public playgrounds, and established places of worship.
2. Identify all outdoor advertising displays within the exclusionary zone(s) by attaching the international children's symbol in a clearly visible location.
3. Establish reasonable limits on the total number of outdoor displays in a market that may carry messages about products that are illegal for sale to minors.
4. Maintain broad diversification of customers that advertise in the outdoor medium.

Exhibit

12.6

Code of Advertising Practices for Children

---

[4]Carol Krol, "Life after tobacco," *Advertising Age*, 19 April 1999, 48.

number of partnerships to coordinate national projects with organizations such as the Advertising Council, the National Center for Missing and Exploited Children, and the American Red Cross.

The Outdoor Advertising Plan

Successful outdoor advertising depends on both a strategic marketing plan and effective execution of the creative, media, and research elements of this strategy. A number of strategic issues should be considered before we move ahead with the creation of outdoor messages. Among the most important are the following:

1. *Clearly stated objectives.* As we discussed earlier, most outdoor advertising is used as either an introduction for a new product or event (such as a sale) or as a reminder to keep consumers continually aware of a brand. With its headline format, outdoor is rarely suited to offer a complete sales message. Furthermore, national advertisers rarely use outdoor as their primary medium. Consequently, it is extremely important to plan the outdoor portion of the total advertising campaign in a manner that will assure maximum efficiency and support to other advertising and promotional vehicles.

2. *Define the target market.* Generally, outdoor media has broad coverage throughout a market. However, outdoor does offer some opportunities for geographic targeting. "Most products and brands have distinct regional and local-market purchase patterns. It is common to find that a large group of local markets [or areas within a single market] will index at or above 130 in per-capita brand purchases. Geo-targeting with outdoor is a fine complement to demo-targeting with television or print."[5]

3. *Specify measurable goals.* An outdoor plan needs to specify what objectives it hopes to accomplish and how these goals will be measured. For example, do we want outdoor to contribute to increases in brand awareness, increases in sales, or higher market share? Finally, what research methodology will be used to determine if these goals were met and what was the contribution of outdoor?

4. *Coordinating the buy.* Outdoor advertising is purchased from local outdoor companies known as **plants.** Increasingly, most local plants are part of large national outdoor companies that provide network buying options to national and regional advertisers. With today's tight marketplace, it is more important than ever for agencies and advertisers to work with plants well ahead of the starting date for a showing. Ideally, space should be purchased at least four months in advance; some markets require even more time. Like spot television and radio, out-of-home is a supply-and-demand business with site availability a recurring problem.

5. *Post-buy inspection (called riding-the-boards).* After the posters are up, an in-market check of poster locations should be made. This inspection determines if proper locations were used and that the signs were posted or painted properly.

plant In outdoor advertising the local company that arranges to lease, erect, and maintain the outdoor sign and to sell the advertising space on it.

All this only emphasizes that successful outdoor advertising demands the use of the same fundamental principles of advertising planning that apply to other media. In some respects, planning in outdoor is even more complex than in other media. As a supplement to other media, planners must make certain that the characteristics and objectives of outdoor mesh properly with those of more dominant media. The complementary nature of outdoor is an overriding concern in most outdoor schedules. The planner must be certain that outdoor can, in fact, reinforce the media schedule in a cost-efficient manner.

---

[5]Erwin Ephron, "About the medium," Outdoor Advertising Association of America, www.oaaa.org.

FORMS OF OUTDOOR ADVERTISING

As we mentioned at the outset of this chapter, outdoor is only one of several categories of out-of-home advertising. However, in terms of revenues, public familiarity, and long-term usage, the two basic forms of outdoor are posters and painted bulletins (see Exhibit 12.7). In either case, the message is designed by the advertising agency. The creative design is then reproduced on paper or vinyl and posted on panels. The larger painted bulletins are prepared by outdoor company artists either in a studio or on-site. Even large posters that once were painted are now being reproduced in vinyl.

Poster Panels

poster panel A standard surface on which outdoor posters are placed. The posting surface is of sheet metal. An ornamental molding of standard green forms the frame. The standard poster panel is 12 feet high and 25 feet long (outside dimensions).

The 30-sheet poster is the most widely used form of outdoor advertising. The most common type of poster is really two posters in one. Bleed and 30-sheet posters, which use the same frame, constitute the typical highway billboard with which we are so familiar. These posters are available in some 9,000 communities. Poster buys can be made for a single location or total national coverage.

The primary use of most posters is to reach the majority of a market quickly and inexpensively. However, with geo-marketing, posters also can be used to reach more targeted prospects. For example, posters placed in financial districts or on routes to and from upscale residential neighborhoods reach more affluent customers and those near colleges communicate with a younger audience.[6]

The standard poster panel measures 12 by 25 feet. The bleed poster either prints to the edge of the frame or uses blanking paper matching the background of the poster. The term "bleed" is, of course, borrowed from the bleed magazine advertisement that has no border. The term *sheet* originated in the days when presses were much smaller and it took many sheets to cover a poster panel.

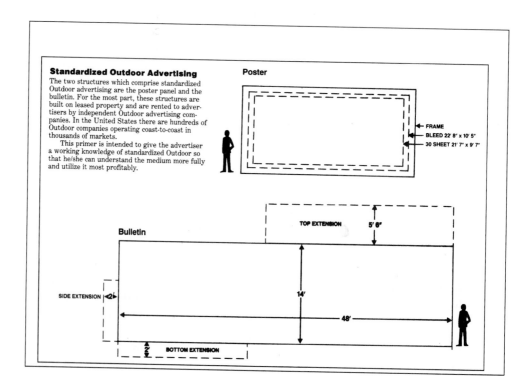

Exhibit 12.7

Posters and bulletins make up the standardized outdoor industry.

Courtesy: Outdoor Advertising Association of America.

---

[6]"30-Sheet Poster Buyers Guide, 1997," a publication of Waggener & Associates, Inc., p. 19.

Today, posters are often printed on vinyl instead of paper. The *vinyl-wrapped poster* uses the standard 30-sheet board, but by "wrapping" or covering the entire board, it expands the coverage area. Wrapped posters are usually available at any 30-sheet location. Although it lasts longer and retains color better than paper, vinyl is more expensive to produce so it is used at high traffic locations and for longer contract periods than paper posters.

Poster displays are sold on the basis of **illuminated** and *nonilluminated* panels. Normally, poster contracts are for 30 days with discounts for longer periods. Those panels in locations with high-traffic volume are illuminated normally for 24-hour exposure. A typical poster showing will consist of 70 to 80 percent illuminated posters, but major advertisers often request full-illuminated postings. When buying an outdoor showing, the advertiser is provided information about the number of displays, the number that are illuminated and nonilluminated, the monthly and per-panel cost, and total circulation or exposure.

illuminated posters
Seventy to 80% of all outdoor posters are illuminated for 24-hour exposure.

The Eight-Sheet Poster

One of the fastest growing types of outdoor advertising is the eight-sheet poster.[7] **Eight-sheet posters** measure 5 feet by 11 feet, slightly less than one-third the size of 30-sheet posters. Eight-sheet posters are bought by small, local businesses as well as by national companies (see Exhibit 12.8). Often they are placed immediately adjacent to the point of sale as the last customer contact before a purchase decision. These compact posters add enormous reach and frequency to advertising plans at a modest cost.

Eight-sheet posters rapidly build brand awareness, announce new products and services, and provide reminder messages for a brand. In addition, eight-sheet space costs are much lower than traditional billboards and, because of their smaller size, production costs are significantly lower as well. The average CPM of eight-sheet posters is approximately half that of 30-sheets.

In most markets, zoning regulations are more favorable for the smaller eight-sheet posters than traditional billboards. Therefore, they can be used in a cost-effective way to reach various target audiences without expensive waste circulation. Like billboards, eight-sheet posters generally are bought to support a larger

eight-sheet poster
Outdoor poster used in urban areas, about one-fourth the size of the standard 30-sheet poster. Also called *junior poster.*

Exhibit
12.8

Eight-sheet posters promote a diverse group of products and brands.
Courtesy: Jacobs Billboard Company.

---

[7]Unless otherwise noted, material in this section is provided by the Eight-Sheet Outdoor Advertising Association, Inc.

advertising campaign. Eight-sheet can enhance television by adding frequency and recall; it adds a visual element to radio messages. It also can offer reminder messages to print media (see Exhibit 12.9).

Eight-sheet posters are handled by special poster plants, but frequently appear concurrently with 30-sheet showings in a market. The Eight-Sheet Outdoor Advertising Association (ESOAA) was founded to promote the interests of the eight-sheet poster medium. Currently they are available in some 2,500 markets.

Painted Bulletins

Painted bulletins are the largest and most prominent type of outdoor advertising. Painted bulletins are of two types: *permanent* and the more popular *rotary*. The permanent bulletin remains at a fixed location and can vary in size since it is never moved. The **rotary bulletin** is a standardized sign that is three times larger (14 feet by 48 feet) than the standard poster and it is placed at high-traffic locations for maximum visibility. Rotary bulletins can be moved from site to site to insure maximum coverage of a market over a period of months. Both types of bulletins are almost always illuminated.

Bulletins are approximately four times more expensive than posters. In recent years, the basic bulletin has been augmented with special embellishments, such as cutouts, freestanding letters, special lighting effects, fiber optics, and inflatables. Painted bulletin contracts usually are for a minimum of one year; however, short-term contracts are available at a higher monthly rate.

Rotary bulletins offer advertisers the advantages of the greater impact of the painted bulletin combined with more coverage and penetration than a single site could deliver. A rotary bulletin can be moved every 30, 60, or 90 days, so that during a 12-month period consumers throughout the market will have seen the advertiser's message.

rotary bulletins (outdoor) Movable painted bulletins that are moved from one fixed location to another one in the market at regular intervals. The locations are viewed and approved in advance by the advertiser.

Exhibit
12.9

Spectaculars

As the name implies, outdoor spectaculars are large one-of-a-kind displays designed for maximum attention in urban centers. They may consist of special lighting or other types of ingenious material and innovations. In some cases they utilize a building as the canvas for the message. Spectaculars are very expensive and both production and space rentals are negotiated normally on a one-time basis with the minimum contract for most spectaculars being a year.

With the advent of new technology in outdoor advertising what was once a spectacular may soon be the norm. Currently the outdoor industry is using a variety of digital and laser technology for computerized painting/printing systems. More and more outdoor is being printed on flexible vinyl, which provides consistent, magazine-quality reproduction in all markets. In the future, outdoor planners envision the ability to provide satellite-distributed video images similar to giant television screens where computerized messages can be changed immediately. Regardless of what new technology comes to outdoor, it is obvious that the traditional paper poster soon may be history.

A growing segment of the spectacular category is the *wall mural* (also called wallscapes). Actually, it was ancient Roman wall painting that gave outdoor advertising its start. Wall murals, done properly and in selected areas, can add a sense of urban art to an area. One of the largest examples of a wallscape was a series of four ads for Samsung electronics. The messages covered four New York City buildings and ranged in size from five to 12 stories. Most wall murals are printed on vinyl, which holds down production cost and makes installation much easier. Many building surfaces will not hold paint well and, from a practical standpoint, most building owners will not allow someone to paint their building.[8]

THE ELEMENTS OF OUTDOOR

Outdoor advertising is a visual medium with creative elements playing a much greater role than in most other advertising vehicles. The creative options available for outdoor and out-of-home advertisers are almost limitless with dozens of shapes and sizes offered to carry persuasive messages. As the OAAA points out, "Outdoor advertising is visual storytelling. The expression of an idea can surprise viewers with words or excite them with pictures. . . . designing for the outdoor medium is a challenging communication task that requires the expression of a concept with clarity and focus."[9]

Outdoor Design

Designing an outdoor display is among the most difficult tasks for a creative team. Creating a picture and a few words to be seen by fast-moving traffic at distances of up to 500 feet is hard enough—to do so in a manner that moves customers to buy a product adds an obstacle not found in other media. However, outdoor also is one of the most enjoyable media to work with from a creative standpoint. Its size and color allow maximum creativity without the space constraints of other advertising vehicles.

---

[8]"Wall to wall walls," *Inside Out of Home*, April 1999, 1.
[9]"Creative points: The creative challenge," www.oaaa.org, 9 June 2000.

Copy   Outdoor only allows a headline, usually no more than seven words. Unlike copy in traditional media, there is no theme development and copy amplification. Conciseness is not only a virtue, it is a necessity. Advertisers have learned to work with these constraints to provide not only interesting but motivating sales messages.

Color   Color is one of the primary advantages of outdoor. However, colors must be chosen carefully to insure readability. Outdoor designers use those colors that create high contrast in both *hue* (red, green, etc.) and *value* (a measure of lightness or darkness). For example, Exhibit 12.10 demonstrates 18 combinations of colors with one being the most visible and 18 the least visible.

Type   Typefaces in outdoor should be simple, clear, and easy to read. Some of the basic rules of outdoor type and lettering include the following:

- The use of capitals should be kept to a minimum.
- Considerable care should be given to spacing between letters and between words.
- Whatever typeface is selected, the ultra-bold or ultra-thin version should be avoided.
- A simple typeface is best for most creative designs.

Outdoor Advertising and the Internet

One of the difficulties facing outdoor is developing a way to have clients visualize creative concepts in a realistic environment. Most other media can demonstrate how a finished advertisement or commercial will look or sound in finished form. Translating an 8 1/2" × 11" piece of paper to a 300-square-foot billboard is more difficult. However, a growing number of outdoor plants are providing Internet systems that allow advertisers and media planners to see how their posters will appear in actual locations. Exhibits 12.11a and 12.11b demonstrate ways that the Internet can promote outdoor advertising. Exhibit 12.11a offers a driver's view of a poster location. Through computer scanning, any creative execution can be superimposed on the board. The system also can be used to make riding-the-boards a thing of the past as advertisers can see posters from their office computers. Exhibit 12.11b offers a potential advertiser the address of the plant's Web site for further information and contacts about placing advertising.

Exhibit

12.10

Some color combinations are much more effective than others for outdoor advertising.

Courtesy: Outdoor Advertising Association of America.

Exhibit

12.11a

Potential clients can do a
video ride from the
convenience of their office
computer.

Courtesy: The Billboard Connection.

Computer technology also offers the potential for a number of creative innovations in outdoor. Computers for some time have directed the design and painting process on vinyl, which is used in 70 percent of the larger bulletin displays. In addition, individual advertisers and plants are beginning to experiment with digital technology on billboards that offer changing messages such as days-to-Christmas and other current text. As we mentioned earlier, some outdoor executives envision a day when most high-traffic signs will consist of digital displays that are similar to large television screens and programmed from a central location.

Exhibit

12.11b

Note the Web address for
prospective clients to contact
the plant.

Courtesy: The Billboard Connection.

BUYING OUTDOOR

Both the methods and terminology used in buying outdoor advertising are different in a number of ways from those used in other media. Poster advertising is purchased on the basis of *gross rating points* (GRPs). You will recall from our earlier discussion of television that one GRP is equal to 1 percent of the population. Similarly, GRPs normally are bought in units of 50 or 100 and measure the *duplicated* audience reached by a poster *allotment*. An allotment is the number of posters used in an individual buy. To achieve a showing of 50 GRPs in a market means that an advertiser will have daily exposures to outdoor messages *equivalent to* 50 percent of the adult population of the market.

The audience for outdoor is called the *daily effective circulation* (DEC) and is calculated by using the following formula:

24-hour traffic count = 36,000

For nonilluminated posters the traffic count is multiplied by .45, therefore .45 × 36,000 = 16,200 adult DEC

For illuminated posters the traffic count is multiplied by .64, therefore .65 × 36,000 = 23,040

Let's examine a market and work through these calculations:

Market: Metropolis

Population: 800,000

Audience level purchased: 50 GRPs

Allotment: 26 posters (20 illuminated; 6 nonilluminated)

Explanation:

Our 26 poster allotment generated a DEC of 400,000. We calculate this by the following formula:

$$\text{GRPs} = \frac{\text{Daily effective circulation}}{\text{Market population}}$$

$$50 \text{ GRP} = \frac{400,000}{800,000}$$

You may not compare GRP levels in markets of different size, except as a measure of advertising weight and intensity. For example, a 50 GRP might require an allotment of 50 or 100 posters in a large market. Whereas in a very small market 50 GPRs might be achieved with one or two posters. By the same token, in a market of 2,000,000 population, a 50 GRP buy would generate a DEC of 1,000,000, while the same weight in a market of 50,000 would show a DEC of only 25,000.

VERIFYING

The success of outdoor advertising is dependent on providing advertisers and agencies with reliable research data on which they can base their media-buying decisions. The outdoor industry, dealing with an audience that is entirely out-of-home and on the move, faces significant challenges in developing audience research.

The Traffic Audit Bureau for Media Measurement (TAB)

The primary source of out-of-home audience information is the TAB. Founded in 1933, the organization audits the circulation of 30-sheet posters, bulletins, eight-sheet posters, shelter advertising displays, and, most recently, truck advertising. The TAB provides field auditors to check plant operators' adherence to TAB auditing standards and they also check visibility of signs as well as traffic flow. A plant is audited every three years and a TAB Audit Circulation Report is issued after each audit (see Exhibit 12.12).

Communication Effectiveness

In addition to traffic audits, which are primarily measures of potential audiences, advertisers are interested in the communication effectiveness of outdoor advertising. In order to address this issue, Perception Research Services (PRS) was engaged by the OAAA to conduct eye tracking studies to determine the levels of outdoor visibility and the impact of this visibility. Using a technique that recorded drivers' and passengers' eye movements, PRS found that 74 percent of subjects noticed outdoor signs and 73 percent of those read the copy. Results also showed that the size of boards and creative enhancements such as three-dimensional figures and board

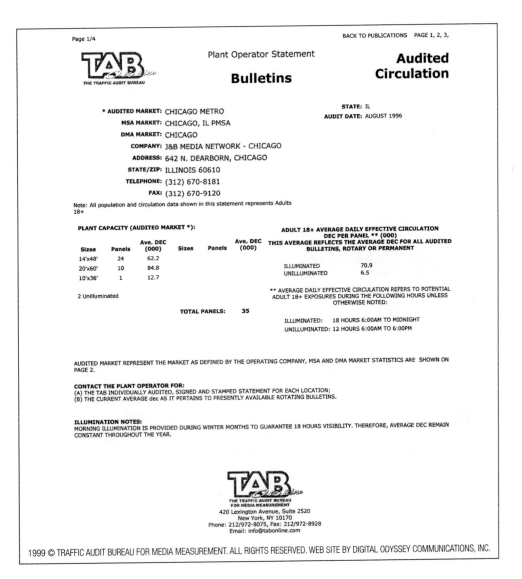

Exhibit

12.12

extensions increased attention levels. Overall the study showed that outdoor can be effective in building brand recognition and it is able to draw attention from all target groups.

Another approach to measuring outdoor communication is the Harris Donovan Model for Outdoor Planning. It is another example of computer technology being adapted to media planning in outdoor. Available for personal computers, the Harris Donovan Model measures the potential audience exposed to an outdoor campaign. The model combines cost and audience information in order to determine if specific campaign objectives have been met with a particular outdoor campaign.

Marketing and Rate Data

■ The Simmons Market Research Bureau (SMRB) is a national consumer study conducted annually with over 19,000 respondents. SMRB reports the reach of target audiences, media usage habits, and outdoor delivery for 750 consumer products and services.

■ Waggener & Associates, Inc. publishes a number of rate guides for 30- and 8-sheet posters and bulletins. The *Buyers Guide* provides information concerning costs, number of panels in a showing, and market population (see Exhibit 12.13 for an example of an eight-sheet rate card).

As the outdoor industry seeks to encourage more advertising from package goods and retail advertisers, it is adopting many of the buying practices used by other media. One of the potential benefits of consolidation within the outdoor industry is a movement toward more industry-wide support for a number of

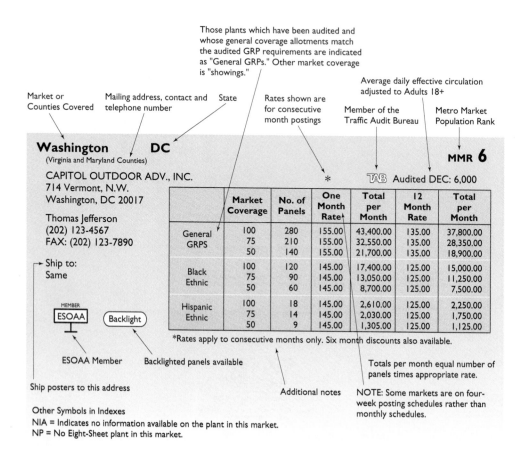

Exhibit 12.13

research and audience measurement studies. As outdoor continues to appeal to major national advertisers, it will become necessary to provide standardized audience data and research.

Trends in Outdoor Advertising

Outdoor advertising is becoming a popular choice with a number of advertisers seeking increased brand awareness and a means of differentiating themselves from traditional media messages. In an environment where people are bombarded by hundreds of messages everyday, outdoor is a means of gaining high attention levels to a mass audience.

Outdoor complements and enhances other media advertising by providing high levels of reach and frequency at a lower cost than other media. Research shows that outdoor creates a synergistic effect when combined with most other media. In particular, out-of-home offers advertisers a last chance to create brand awareness among potential prospects. The influx of product categories such as package goods, dot.coms, retailers, and high profile fashion brands have given the outdoor industry much needed diversification.

Research and reliable audience measurements continue to be a challenge to the industry. In recent years, outdoor has sponsored a number of new and innovative approaches to verifying the reach and communication effectiveness of the medium. Computer technology has permitted researchers to undertake a number of studies that would have been impossible only a few years ago.

Finally, the industry is able to provide even better creative approaches for advertisers. The use of computer design, vinyl and other new materials, and on-line visualization of final creative products combine to make outdoor even more appealing to advertisers. The many formats of out-of-home are motivating a number of advertisers to use the medium—even those who resist traditional outdoor posters. The remainder of this chapter will discuss some of the out-of-home formats beyond billboards.

TRANSIT ADVERTISING

Transit advertising is designed to accomplish many of the same tasks as traditional outdoor messages. It builds brand awareness and provides reminder messages to a mobile population. Transit provides extensive reach and high repetition at a fraction of the cost of other media. Because transit audiences demonstrate repetitive travel patterns, it provides extremely high levels of frequency and consistent reach year-round. For example, in New York City, the largest transit market, ridership varies less than 3 percent from the highest to the lowest month.

Transit advertising offers a variety of formats for advertisers. The basic marketing strategy of transit advertising is that it reaches a mobile urban population on an out-of-home basis. Unlike outdoor media, exposure is more likely to take place in an environment where there is more time to read a message and, in the case of interior displays, where the audience is exposed over a relatively long period of time during the average commute. Transit advertising is available in three basic categories:

Exterior Displays   The majority of revenues for the transit industry come from exterior displays. These messages are carried on the outside of buses and subway cars, and, increasingly, on the sides of trucks. While exterior signs are generally available on all sides of a bus, the basic units are the *king-size bus posters* and the *queen-size posters* (see Exhibit 12.14).

Exhibit

12.14

Two of the most popular
exterior transit formats.

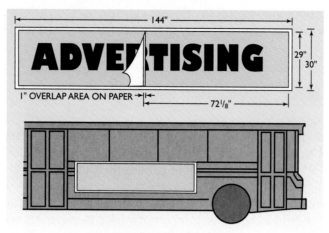

KING-SIZE BUS POSTERS

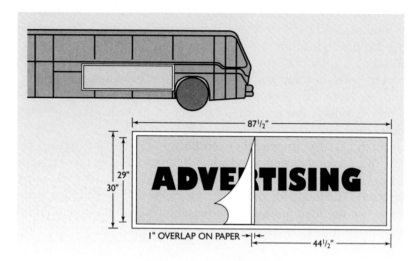

QUEEN-SIZE BUS POSTERS

King-size posters are carried on both the curb and street sides of buses while queen-size posters are displayed on the curb. A relatively recent innovation is the *full bus wrap* where an entire bus is covered by a single advertising display. Material is used to cover the windows so that passengers can see from the inside, but it maintains a continuous design when viewed from the outside. All exterior signs are printed on vinyl and either placed in frames or, more often, affixed with adhesive. In most markets, advertisers can choose from a number of bus routes to create all or only a portion of a market. The intent of exterior signs are to reach both pedestrian and vehicular traffic primarily during daylight hours.

Interior Displays

Interior signs, often referred to as *car-cards*, come in a number of sizes and they are fitted into racks inside buses and subway cars. The advantage of interior signs is that they can be seen over a relatively long period of time, especially compared to most other forms of outdoor. Interior signs are ideal for building high levels of frequency since most commuters travel the same routes on a daily basis. Occasionally, interior signs include cards or tear-off slips that can be taken by riders—thus combining features of both transit and direct-response advertising.

Station Posters and Airport Panels

Station posters and other forms of station signage include clocks, panels on platforms, entry turnstiles, airport boarding areas, and so forth. While these messages are not "transit" in terms of being included in or on vehicles, they are classified as transit category since they reach the same audience as traditional transit advertising. Among familiar station formats are one-sheet posters (see Exhibit 12.15). Regardless of the specific format, station posters are intended to reach pedestrian traffic in a captive environment.

Transit costs are generally below $1 CPM. Its ability to generate significant audience levels and reach an upscale audience has resulted in a number of advertisers moving into the medium. A major growth area for transit, like their outdoor counterparts, has been e-commerce businesses. For example, Lands' End promoted the company's on-line shopping service (www.landsend.com) using transit signs on Manhattan buses. The company used the theme "Shopping online beats standing in line" to remind harried New Yorkers of a convenient way to do their buying.[10]

SHELTER ADVERTISING

A specialized sector of the transit medium is shelter advertising. Shelter posters are a fast-growing medium in major metropolitan areas. In the last 20 years, the number of shelter displays has increased from 6,000 to more than 30,000, accounting for total revenues of some $220 million. Shelter displays are approximately 4 feet by 6 feet and provide attention-getting messages for both commuters and pedestrian traffic. The back-lit panels provide 24-hour exposure with no clutter from competing media. Shelter operators offer full market coverage or geographic targeting in selected sections of a metropolitan area.

Like station posters and interior transit, shelter advertising generates extremely high frequency among commuters. The cost of individual panels varies with the population, the number of displays purchased, and the length of contracts (space contracts run from one to 12 months). The CPM for shelter is comparable to other forms of transit with CPMs running only a few cents. Even though the posters are

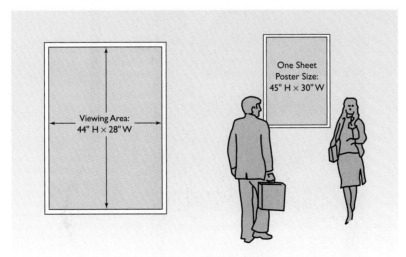

ONE SHEET POSTERS

[10]Grant Lukenbill, "Bus ads move in-line shoppers online," *DMNews*, 12 July 1999, 4.

Exhibit

12.15

A typical station poster.

small by outdoor standards, "... when you take into account that they're seen at eye level, they have every bit as much ... impact as the big boards which obviously are viewed from a much greater distance."[11]

Shelter advertising is used by a number of major advertisers and it has been a leader in developing the type of diverse advertising support sought by other forms of out-of-home (see Exhibits 12.16a and 12.16b). Shelter advertising, although accounting for a small portion of total advertising, will continue to grow at a faster rate than overall advertising expenditures. Finally, rather than facing the regulatory problems of outdoor, the revenues generated by shelter posters are often shared with municipal transit companies, making the medium a welcome revenue producer to many cities facing tight budgets.

SUMMARY

Outdoor and out-of-home advertising is fast becoming part of mainstream media. While it currently comprises only 3 percent of total advertising revenues, it is predicted that this figure will grow to 5 percent by the end of the decade. Outdoor

Exhibit
12.16a

Shelter advertising is used to promote a number of products and organizations.
Courtesy: Transtop.

[11]"Eller goes whole hog to promote transit shelter O-O-H," *Inside Out of Home*, April 1998, 4.

Exhibit

12.16b

offers an opportunity for advertisers to provide brand reminders to current customers and introduce brands to prospective customers at a cost less than virtually any other medium.

In many respects, out-of-home functions in the same way as point-of-purchase advertising to reach consumers immediately before purchase. With the many options available in out-of-home, there is a format for almost every advertising objective. As traditional media become more fragmented, outdoor remains a medium that can provide both reach and frequency to a mass audience. At a time when outdoor is appealing to national advertisers, industry consolidation is creating efficient means of buying multiple markets.

Out-of-home media also are enjoying the benefits of more sophisticated research addressing both audience measurement and communication effects of the medium. As more national advertisers begin to consider out-of-home advertising, it will be necessary for the industry to provide research similar to what is available from other media competitors.

REVIEW

1. Why is a diversity of product categories important to the outdoor industry?
2. Why has the term out-of-home replaced outdoor?
3. What are the primary categories of outdoor posters?
4. What is the function of the Traffic Audit Bureau for Media Measurement (TAB)?
5. Why has transit advertising grown significantly in recent years?

6. What are the primary uses of outdoor for most advertisers?
7. What are the major advantages of the 8-sheet posters?
8. What are the major disadvantages of outdoor posters?

TAKE IT TO THE NET

We invite you to visit the Russell/Lane page on the Prentice Hall Web site at **www.prenhall.com/myphlip** for end-of-chapter exercises and applications.

Chapter 13

Direct-Response and Internet Advertising

No area of marketing and advertising has been changed more significantly by new technology than direct response. The techniques of direct response have become increasingly sophisticated in the last 25 years with the introduction of computer technology. However, since the mid-1990s, every aspect of direct response from selling techniques to consumer information acquisition has undergone dramatic change. Today, virtually every advertiser is using the techniques of direct response as a key ingredient of their marketing strategies. After reading this chapter you will understand:

>> effects of new technology on direct-response advertising

>> the concept of consumer relationship management

>> the principles of integrated marketing and direct response

>> major components of direct-response marketing

>> the future growth of new technology and direct response

>> planning for marketing on the Internet

Direct Response—Pros

1. Direct response has the potential to reach virtually any prospect on a geographical, product usage, or demographic basis.
2. Direct response is a measurable medium with opportunities for short-term, sales-related response.
3. Direct response allows advertisers to personalize their messages and build an ongoing relationship with prime target audiences that is often impossible in traditional mass media vehicles.

Direct Response—Cons

1. High-cost-per contact is a major problem with many forms of direct response, especially direct mail. Expenses for printing, production, and postage have all increased significantly in recent years.

2. To keep up with an increasingly mobile population, prospect lists must be updated constantly at considerable expense to the advertiser.

3. Public and government concerns with privacy issues have become a major problem for the direct-response industry. Telemarketers and Internet marketers, in particular, are facing a number of threats of restrictive legislation and regulations at both the state and federal levels.

4. Couponing, long one of the fundamental techniques of direct response, is demonstrating a significant decrease in redemption levels reducing the impact and tracking of many direct-response campaigns.

The Internet—Pros

1. The Internet offers an inexpensive, quick, and easily available interactive medium especially among niche markets such as business-to-business.

2. The Internet is the ultimate research tool with its ability to measure exactly how many people used the medium and/or purchased a product.

3. The Internet is among the most flexible media with an ability to change messages immediately in reaction to market and competitive conditions.

The Internet—Cons

1. To this point, the Internet is more promise than performance. It is difficult to determine the effectiveness of the service since it is still looking for profitable executions.

2. Despite the growing popularity of the Internet as a means of informal communication, many consumers are still reluctant to use the service for purchasing products and services. In particular, consumers are reluctant to give their credit card numbers over the Internet even though secure sites are available.

3. The sheer number of commercial and noncommercial Web sites makes it difficult for consumers to know what is available or, once known, to have much time to spend with any single site.

There is nothing new about the concept of selling directly to consumers. Benjamin Franklin sold scientific books by mail in the 1740s and more than 100 years ago, Montgomery Ward had a thriving mail-order business through his catalog. For the last twenty years, marketers have moved toward a more personal relationship with their customers. They have progressed steadily:

- From mass marketing where prospects were reached relatively indiscriminately at the lowest possible cost per impression.
- To category marketing where prospects who belong to some broad demographic category such as women age 18 to 34 were targeted.
- To niche marketing where these broad categories were more narrowly defined (e.g., women age 18 to 34 with children).
- To group (or community) marketing where prospects who regard themselves as part of a group with common interests (e.g., tennis players, opera lovers, antique collectors) are reached with messages and product benefits that acknowledge these interests.

■ To one-to-one marketing where products and messages are tailored to the expressed interest of the individual (e.g., Dell computers where every machine is made to order).

From the first direct-mail research of the 1920s to computer-driven technology of the Internet, direct-response marketers have been able to refine their identification and outreach more precisely to various customer groups. It was not that many years ago that people were amazed when direct-mail offers addressed customers by name in the body of letters.

At the same time this technological renaissance was taking place, the competitive environment was lessening the distinction among brands and resulting in (1) price competition with shrinking profit margins for sellers and/or (2) a reliance on trusted brands to provide customers with a perception of consistent quality. For example, the local Ford dealer faced with an informed customer armed with the latest dealer invoice information from edmunds.com is faced with a choice of lowering the profit margin or increasing after-sale service. In fact, the dealer probably will have to do some of both.

Marketers are increasingly asking their marketing communication programs to blend old and new communication strategies. On the one hand, television commercials and other traditional media messages are establishing or maintaining brand visibility and positioning. On the other hand, high brand identity makes contact through e-mail and Web sites much more effective. New technology can rarely create brand image; it can reach consumers with interactive media at a time of the prospect's choosing and with messages crafted to meet the needs of each individual.[1]

DIRECT RESPONSE AND THE INTERNET

Throughout this text we will offer examples of ways in which the Internet has dramatically changed the way marketers and the media do business. In this section, we will not only discuss how the Internet is being used directly by direct response firms, but how the blending of the Internet and direct response is being used in both competitive and complementary ways to promote products and services. We also will examine some of the primary concerns facing direct response and its use of new technology.

Customer Relationship Management

Customer relationship management or **customer relationship marketing** (CRM) is a core principle of both direct response and Internet marketing. The concept of CRM should be viewed from both the customer and marketer perspective. From the standpoint of the consumer, it is clear that the audience feels empowered by interactive media and they use this empowerment in a proactive manner. From a lifestyle standpoint, research shows that the on-line audience uses traditional media less than they did before gaining Internet capability and less than those who are not on-line.

In addition to media usage, consumers also are embracing on-line couponing, entering sweepstakes on-line, and participating in other targeted sales promotion activities. It is not surprising that consumers would respond to targeted promotions tailored to their interests. Likewise, businesses are happy to avoid the expense of waste circulation by reaching this selective audience. Research also indicates that the Internet audience is receptive to the advertising carried on the Web. A

customer relationship marketing
A management concept that organizes a business according to the needs of the consumer.

---

[1]Robert McKim, "Strengthen affinities with spiral branding," *DMNews*, 19 June 2000, 32.

study by Arbitron New Media indicated that nearly 70 percent of people who tune in to audio or video broadcasts on the Web clicked on advertisements carried on these shows. In addition, 49 percent of these respondents said they buy products they see advertised on Web sites.[2]

The CRM concept offers several other advantages to businesses. While sacrificing some control to consumers, marketers are dealing with a much higher percentage of prospects than in mass advertising or even in the direct-response methods used only a few years ago. For example, the combination of sophisticated software and the Internet allows companies to achieve the following:

- More effective cross-selling and up-selling from current customers
- Higher customer retention and loyalty
- Higher customer profitability
- Higher response to marketing campaigns
- More effective investment of resources[3]

None of these benefits should be surprising. As a company develops a closer relationship with each of its customers, we would expect that it would use the greater understanding to approach consumers with offers that fit their interests and tastes. The use of interactive technology allows businesses to deal with the unique purchasing, lifestyle, and behavioral histories of each customer. Rather than dealing with statistical aggregations of groups of customer data, a business now has the capability of one-to-one marketing. Communication and product offers can be based on predetermined consumer needs and can be differentiated from similar competitive offers. The end result is that the consumer gains better value and the company engenders continued customer loyalty.[4]

THE INTERNET AND MARKETING RESEARCH

Clearly one of the primary benefits of Internet marketing is the ability to gain information about individual buying habits and product preferences. These data are, of course, collected as part of the consumer transaction process. However, one of the emerging advantages of Internet technology is the ability to collect market research quickly and inexpensively from a larger respondent base than might be possible with conventional research methodology. The Internet allows marketers to reach samples of specific consumers to determine a number of product, marketing, or advertising responses. Instead of being confined to a few locales, a marketer can now sample on a global basis. Even something as relatively simple as getting response data back from product testing is faster and demonstrates higher levels of cooperation than other methods.

General Mills is one of the major users of on-line research. The company has found that it gains higher response rates and more in-depth information with on-line testing. As one company research executive pointed out, "We've found Internet research to be faster, less expensive and able to provide a greater depth of insight and understanding than the traditional forms of consumer research."[5]

The dangers of on-line testing involve a possible loss of competitive advantage by testing on the Web. In addition, there are questions about samples and perceptions in on-line testing. Marketers are concerned that on-line respondents may be

[2]Lisa Napoli, "Webcast audiences aren't just sitting there, survey finds," www.nytimes.com, 29 June 1999.
[3]Bill Hopkins and Britton Manasco, "The new technologies of marketing," *DMNews*, 22 May 2000, 51.
[4]Steve Diller, "Direct marketing's role in a new society," *DMNews*, 1 May 2000, 22.
[5]Jack Neff, "Researchers attract untraditional buyers," *Advertising Age*, 26 June 2000, 19.

■ *The two- or three-minute commercial.* This longer spot usually has problems gaining clearance during peak periods and consequently most often is scheduled in fringe time programming such as late night movies. The format has the advantage of allowing more sales time and an opportunity for information about ordering the product. As a major retail executive commented, "What distinguishes short-form advertising from Madison Avenue advertising is its direct response component which means that it's accountability advertising."[25]

■ *The infomercial.* In the last decade, the **infomercial** has become a multi-billion dollar advertising format. Utilizing well-known personalities, slick production techniques, and blanket coverage during certain dayparts, the infomercial has created a number of legendary product success stories. However, with the advent of various forms of interactive and convergent technology, it remains to be seen whether infomercials will continue to be as prevalent in the future.

infomercial Long form television advertising that promotes products within the context of a program-length commercial.

Regardless of its format, DRTV has certain inherent advantages as an advertising tool:[26]

1. It shows the product in use and provides opportunities for product demonstrations in realistic circumstances.

2. DRTV can create excitement for a product. For example, *Sports Illustrated* uses sport clips for what would otherwise be an advertisement for a static magazine.

3. DRTV offers immediate results. Within 15 minutes of a commercial spot, you will receive 75 percent of your orders.

4. Because most DRTV spots are not time sensitive, they can be scheduled in fringe dayparts for significant discounts. In addition, production costs of most DRTV are less than traditional television commercials.

5. DRTV complements retail sales. For generally distributed products, businesses find that they sell as many as eight units at retail for every one ordered through direct response.

6. DRTV is a great technique for testing various product benefits and measuring sales response.

Direct-response advertising is sold both on a paid and **per inquiry** (PI) basis. In fact, with the competitive environment so prevalent in the broadcast area, PI is relatively common in television especially in fringe time. Basically, PI advertisers share their risk with a television station or cable channel. There are no initial costs for time, but the television outlet will divide the profits (if any) when the orders come in. PI advertising can be very beneficial, especially to companies with good products, but little capital.

per inquiry (PI) Advertising time or space where medium is paid on a per response received basis.

TV Shopping Networks

The logical extension of long-form infomercials is an entire network devoted to selling. Home shopping channels have been a major source of product sales for the past decade. It is not unusual to see name brand merchandise being sold on QVC or the Home Shopping Network and celebrities as diverse as Marie Osmond, Pete Rose, or Joan Rivers appearing to sell products such as dolls, sports memorabilia, and jewelry. A number of major retailers and designers use home shopping networks to sell their products to this niche consumer market.

While home shopping has grown significantly in recent years, the executives involved in these ventures see the full potential for home shopping being in interactive systems. The most optimistic proponents of shopping networks predict that

[25]Kelly J. Andrews, "Selling short," *Target Marketing*, March 1999, 56.
[26]Denny Hatch, "Making DRTV work for you," *Target Marketing*, September 1999, 76.

they will change retailing fundamentally in the next two decades. Some experts estimate that sometime in the next 20 years traditional retailing will all but be replaced by interactive home shopping. Of course, we have seen similar predictions for the Internet in recent years. Nevertheless, there is little question that these networks will continue to grow and occupy a larger place in general retailing.

Radio and Direct Response

Radio, despite its targeted audiences and niche programming, has not been a major player in direct-response marketing. Traditional radio has suffered from its lack of visualization. Radio is deficient in many of the elements so familiar to direct response in other media. Radio cannot show a product, no coupons can be provided, and a toll-free number cannot be flashed on a screen.

As discussed in Chapter 9, all of this may change if so-called streaming audio becomes a major medium. With the introduction of computer-based audio programming, an advertiser can incorporate all the missing elements of traditional radio in this new convergent medium. As in the case with interactive television, electronic coupons can pop on the screen, offers can not only be seen along with the music, but downloaded at the request of the listener, and, with database technology, listeners can be prompted about products that fit their consumer profiles.

While the economic promise of "visual" radio is in the near future, for the present, radio can serve as a valuable supplement for a variety of direct-response marketers. The combination of low commercial rates and tightly targeted audience composition makes possible high frequency to saturate prime prospects. Even with the competition from other forms of direct response, radio can continue as a niche medium for direct-response marketing.

Per-inquiry also makes radio a bargain for many direct-response advertisers. Radio stations often find that PI advertising is a means of moving unsold commercial inventory. With the number of stations and commercial spots available, it is almost impossible for even the most prosperous station to sell all of its time. Unsold inventory can be especially acute during certain months such as the after-Christmas period. Rather than using this time for public service announcements or station promotions, the sales manager may be willing to run PI spots at significant discounts.

Magazines and Direct Response

Magazines provide a targeted medium for a number of direct-response advertisers. As discussed in Chapter 11, the success of most magazines depends on their ability to reach a targeted group of readers with common interests, demographics, or vocations. It is in the area of business and trade publications that direct response is especially important. Magazines with editorial objectives geared specifically toward some particular business or profession can be extremely beneficial for direct-response marketers. In the business press, the majority of direct-response messages are attempting to gain leads for personal salespersons, telemarketers, or means of follow-up.

Despite the importance placed on business-to-business magazine direct response, consumer magazines also can provide an important means of reaching prospects. You only have to look in the back of many major publications to find lengthy classified sections offering a number of direct-response products. In addition, the majority of regular magazine advertisements carry some form of direct response either to provide additional information to consumers or to provide opportunities for direct orders (see Exhibit 13.1).

Many of the magazine characteristics we discussed in Chapter 11 are of primary importance to direct-response advertisers. Audience selectivity combined with high reach among prospects who are not heavy users of other media (especially television) make it ideal for many direct marketers. Magazines also appeal to a number of major advertisers because of the prestige associated with national publications. Magazine direct response provides the intimacy of direct response with the traditional advertising virtues of magazines.

Catalogs

One of the oldest and one of the most popular forms of direct-response selling is the catalog. The use of catalogs dates at least to 1498 when Aldus Manutius published his book catalog containing 15 titles. Since its humble beginnings, the catalog has become a keystone of direct marketing. As early as 1830 New England companies were selling fishing and camping supplies by mail. By the end of the 1800s both Sears Roebuck & Co. and Montgomery Ward brought retail merchandise to every household in the country through their catalogs. However, it was the 1970s that marked the major growth period of catalog selling.

Today, the catalog industry is facing many of the uncertainties and challenges of other forms of marketing and advertising. The role of the Internet has huge potential for the industry, and many in the industry see the need to make important long-term decisions regarding how interactive media will fit into their future. Whether the Internet is a curse or an opportunity is in the eye of the beholder. As one marketing executive predicted, "The time for theorizing is over. It's either catalog.com or die."[27] Another direct-response vice president noted, ". . . catalogers have little to fear, and much to gain, from the Internet."[28]

The role of the Internet is a major question for catalogers who mail almost 15 billion books each year. However, it is only one of the several challenges facing traditional catalog sales companies. First, the number of companies, including mainline retailers such as Macy's and The Gap, are going into either catalog sales, Internet sales, or, in many cases, both. The growing number of catalogs has significantly increased the players in an already crowded field. Some like L.L. Bean, the long-time marketer of outdoor gear and clothing, have reacted to competition from mainline retailers by opening new retail stores themselves. Since 1998, Bean has expanded from one headquarters outlet in Freeport, Maine, to a number of retail sites mostly in the East.

At the same time, virtually every cataloger has gone into Internet selling. Lands' End is among the most aggressive, spending more than $10 million annually in advertising to promote its Web site. Lands' End, like other catalogers, sees a number of benefits in e-commerce. First, its online system is able to adjust to changing trends in merchandising or weather. When the winter of 1999 proved milder than usual, the company changed its focus to lighter weight outerwear. The company also hopes that eventually the Internet will offer relief from catalog-related production and postage costs that account for more than 40 percent of total operating costs.[29]

Catalog companies realize that the Internet, traditional brand advertising, and the core catalog are all part of multiple channels that must work together to reach consumers. Different customers prefer different channels and the same customers will use various channels at different times. Earlier we discussed data warehouses. Catalogers must embrace the concept of the data warehouse as they integrate information into a single transaction history regardless of what channels a customer uses.

[27]Brett Shevack, "Catalogers have a choice: Catalog.com or death," *DMNews*, 28 June 1999, 26.
[28]Steve Tamke, "How will the Internet affect catalogers?" *DMNews*, 19 July 1999, 24.
[29]Alice Z. Cuneo, "Lands' End ads pitch 'ultimate direct merchant,'" *Advertising Age*, 19 April 1999, 85.

As catalogers move into on-line options, they are finding that their basic marketing techniques must adapt to these new channels. One of the primary challenges is to deal with the customer-controlled on-line environment and to find ways to encourage prospect visits to a cataloger's Web site. Catalog companies find that there are fundamental differences between on-line and off-line selling. For example, ". . . paper catalogs are intrusive by nature, online catalogs are passive by nature. Once businesses understand this fundamental limitation of e-cataloging, they can become creative in the ways that generate more traffic and, importantly, more sales, through the Web."[30]

Neither bricks-and-mortar retailers nor paper catalogs are going away anytime soon. However, surveys show that businesses that ignore e-commerce do so at their own peril. One study indicated that 19 percent of consumers and 16 percent of businesses reported that they were buying less from catalogs as a result of Web shopping. The respondents who were regular on-line users, reported three primary benefits for on-line buying:

- Convenience was the primary benefit cited by 92 percent of respondents.
- Time savings was reported by 83 percent as a reason for on-line purchases.
- Finally, 69 percent said that detailed product information was a benefit of on-line buying.[31]

Regardless of the channel(s) used by a catalog seller to reach prospects and customers, there are a number of keys to the successful process of moving a person from a prospect to a buyer:

1. *The right product.* As with any product or service, the selling process must begin with merchandise that appeals to consumers. Quality, price, consumer benefits, and range of merchandise are all elements in successful selling. However, catalogers often find that an added consideration is uniqueness of products. Generally, catalog sellers have a difficult time moving merchandise that is easily obtainable at retail outlets. Product differentiation is always important, but doubly so for catalog products.

2. *Exciting creative execution.* Remember that the customer can't try on clothes, handle camping gear, or sample a food item. The sales story has to be conveyed in attention-getting messages that grab the imagination of the reader.

3. *Reach a targeted group of prospects.* No element of direct selling is more important than the prospect list. Waste circulation is even more expensive in direct marketing than in other forms of promotion and every effort has to be made to keep it to a minimum.

4. *Fulfillment and customer service.* Nothing will kill a catalog company faster than a reputation for faulty customer service. The process begins with knowledgeable customer representatives, then the right merchandise must be shipped promptly, and finally, when mistakes are made, they need to be dealt with fairly and quickly.

5. *The process of successful selling doesn't end with a single purchase.* Catalogers must establish a means of database management that will allow product inventory management as well as a means of determining the quality of customers on a lifetime value basis.

---

[30]Jack Schmid and Steve Trollinger, "Who's making the net work?" *Target Marketing*, June 1999, 73.
[31]Ken Magill, "Survey: Net eating into offline sales," *DMNews*, 19 July 1999, 6.

Negative Option Direct Response

Continuing relationships with loyal customers is a key to successful and efficient marketing. The negative option technique is designed to initiate and maintain just such an association. Rather than selling a single item, it provides consumers with an open-ended invitation for the purchase of future merchandise.

The Book-of-the-Month Club is credited with introducing this method of "one-package-a-month" selling. Today we see records, CDs, as well as miniature cars, porcelain figurines, and a host of other merchandise offered on a **negative option** basis. The idea is that the buyers must notify the company in order *not* to have an item sent.

The consumer benefit of negative options is that companies make the initial offer ridiculously inexpensive in order to encourage consumers to sign up. For example, music distributors will offer 10 CDs for a dollar as an introductory offer. The advantage to sellers is that once customers join the plan, the company hopes to maintain them for some period of time. It is another example of the lifetime value concept we discussed earlier. Under negative option plans, sale costs are virtually nonexistent for continuing customers.

negative option direct response Technique used by record and book clubs whereby a customer receives merchandise unless the seller is notified not to send it.

Fulfillment

One of the most important elements in the direct-marketing environment is the **fulfillment** function, that is, getting merchandise to customers after the order. Unfortunately too many businesses view fulfillment as nothing more than a shipping service. In fact, the functions of a well-planned fulfillment operation include "... telemarketing, order management, information management, order fulfillment, parcel distribution, returns processing, customer service, merchandise procurement, payment processing, and data mining."[32] If there is a breakdown in any of these functions, it affects the rest of the system.

fulfillment The tasks of filling orders, shipping merchandise, and back in marketing.

In recent years, the fulfillment function has become extremely complex and many companies are finding it difficult to maintain a smooth fulfillment operation in the face of multi-channel order processing. As one fulfillment manager pointed out, "Combining multi-channel order processing systems into one working multi-channel customer service database has proven to be a big challenge to fulfillment systems. While fulfillment houses have spent years developing an infrastructure to handle certain kinds of order processing, Web orders entail a greater degree of complexity."[33]

Problems in fulfillment were especially acute during the Christmas seasons of 1998 and 1999 among Web-based retailers. After repeated customer complaints and news reports of poor service, the FTC announced that it was undertaking an investigation of a number of major on-line retailers to see if they were complying with federal mail-order rules. These rules require that merchandise be shipped within the time frame promised by sellers or that consumers be notified if the delivery date cannot be met. The FTC has levied fines of up to $900,000 for failure to comply with these rules.

The failure of so many businesses to manage their fulfillment operation has made it a major focus for companies seeking a competitive advantage. Customers are sensitive to the problems that a number of companies are having with fulfillment. Those companies that maintain a reputation for effective customer service have gained a significant competitive advantage in the race for on-line sales.

---

[32]John Buck, "What to look for in a fulfillment partner," *iMarketing News*, 24 September 1999, 22.
[33]Steven Konstantino, "Web fulfillment presents challenges," *DMNews*, 6 December 1999, 64.

DIRECT-MAIL ADVERTISING

Despite recent competition from e-mail, telemarketing, and other direct-marketing options, direct-mail remains a primary advertising vehicle. More than $40 billion is spent on direct-mail advertising or approximately 25 percent of all direct-response expenditures. Because of the rising expenses associated with direct-mail, it is anticipated that direct-mail's share of direct-response advertising will decrease in the future. However, with direct-mail accounting for almost $450 billion, it remains second only to telemarketing in terms of sales produced.

One of the problems facing direct-mail is the sheer volume of mail coming to households makes gaining a competitive advantage very difficult. Without question, Americans are the champion direct-mailers of the world. Exhibit 13.2 shows a sampling of countries and the annual pieces of mail they receive.[34]

Clearly, the number of mailing pieces combined with the "junk mail" perception held by many people is a challenge for direct-mailers. This challenge is all the more reason that direct-mailers must take steps to reach targeted prospects with an interesting message and a worthwhile product. Assuming that a business has a quality product and a competitive offer, the success of direct-mail usually hinges on the mailing list.

In direct-mail, the advertiser determines the circulation. The list is the media plan of direct-mail. Just as the media planner must carefully analyze the audiences of the various vehicles that will make up the final media schedule, the advertiser must carefully choose the list(s) that will provide the greatest number of prospects at the lowest cost. Most lists are *compiled lists*, that is, they are developed from a number of existing sources. The problem for the direct-mail advertiser is developing these names into a single list and then fine-tuning it for accuracy, nonduplication, and so forth.

There are a number of organizations that are involved in the direct-mail list process:

list broker In direct-mail advertising an agent who rents the prospect lists of one advertiser to another advertiser. The broker receives a commission from the seller for this service.

■ *List brokers.* One of the key figures in direct-mail are **list brokers.** Brokers function as liaisons between mailers who need lists of particular target prospects and those with lists to rent. The primary functions of list brokers include determining the availability of appropriate lists, negotiating with list owners on behalf of their clients, and offering general marketing advice. The list broker is generally paid a commission of approximately 20 percent by list owners. This commission is similar to the media commission paid to an advertising agency.

■ *List compilers.* The list compiler is usually a broker who obtains a number of lists from published sources and combines them into a single list and then rents them to advertisers. The first format list compiler is considered to be Charles Groves, superintendent of Michigan City schools. In the late 1800s, he compiled lists of teachers by writing other school superintendents around the country. He then sold the lists to textbook publishers and other companies wanting to reach teachers.[35] Compilers tend to specialize in either consumer or business lists although a few do both.

Exhibit

13.2

Annual Pieces of Direct Mail

United States	350+
Switzerland	107
Germany	68
England	40
Ireland	20[34]

---

[34]"Deutsche delivers," *American Demographics*, February 2000, 20.
[35]Lewis Rashmir, "The first compiler was Charles Groves," *DMNews*, 15 February 1993, 35.

- *List managers.* The **list manager** represents the *list owner* just as the broker is the agency for the mailer. The primary job of the list manager is to maximize income for the list owner by promoting the list to as many advertisers as possible. List managers are usually outside consultants, but some large companies have in-house list managers. Most national magazines, record clubs, and other direct marketers offer their lists for rent. These lists are ideal direct-response vehicles since most have been accumulated through sales to a narrowly defined, specialized audiences. They also have the benefit of providing prospects who are proven direct-mail buyers.

list manager Promotes client's lists to potential renters and buyers.

- *Service bureaus.* Service bureaus engage in a number of functions. One of the primary jobs of the service bureau is to improve the quality of lists. This function is called *list enhancement*, which includes a number of steps. One of the most important is known as **merge/purge.** Basically merge/purge systems eliminate duplicate names from a list. Such duplication is costly to the advertiser and annoying to the customer. For example, duplication mailings offset any personal contact with the customer by portraying the message as a mass mailing—and one done with little care. Merge/purge is accomplished by computers that are so sophisticated that names are cross-checked against the same addresses and similar spellings.

merge/purge (merge & purge) A system used to eliminate duplication by direct-response advertisers who use different mailing lists for the same mailing. Mailing lists are sent to a central merge/purge office that electronically picks out duplicate names. Saves mailing costs, especially important to firms that send out a million pieces in one mailing. Also avoids damage to the goodwill of the public.

- *Lettershop.* The **lettershop** is in reality a mailing house. These companies coordinate the job of mailing millions of pieces of mail from printing labels to keeping abreast of the latest postal regulations. Large lettershops even have a representative of the USPS on the premise to work with every aspect of the delivery of mail in a timely fashion.

lettershop A firm that not only addresses the mailing envelope but also is mechanically equipped to insert material, seal and stamp envelopes, and deliver them to the post office according to mailing requirements.

- *Response lists.* The majority of mailings are sent to people on existing lists. However, a number of mailing-list houses sell or rent lists of people who have responded previously to a direct-mail offer or demonstrated some interest in doing so. People on **response lists** are those who are prone to order by mail; therefore, these lists are more productive than compiled lists and the rental charges are higher than for compiled lists. By combining response and compiled lists, a mailer can reach both previous customers and a larger pool of prospective customers.

response lists Prospects who have previously responded to direct mail offers.

Response lists are often obtained from previous customers of a company. These are called *house lists* and are among the most valuable commodities of a direct-mailer. Owners of house lists rent their lists to noncompeting companies and they are often a major source of revenue. Advertisers can find an endless number of response lists of people who have gone on cruises, hunted specific animals, or have bought books on psychoanalysis in the past six months.

List Protection

Since mailing lists are so valuable, companies go to great lengths to protect them from misuse. The most common list abuse is multi-mailings beyond an agreed upon limit. For example, one direct-mailer reported that a company rented his list on a one-time basis and used it 13 times.

The traditional protection for such misuse is to include a number of fictitious names so that the list owner can trace the number of mailings. This is known as *list decoying*. In addition, to protecting the list itself, list renters should also ask for a sample of the mailing material. Occasionally, a mailing may be in bad taste or contain a deceptive offer. However, the much greater problem is that the mailing may be too closely competitive with the list owner's products. Renting a list should provide additional profit, not additional competition!

Testing Direct-Mail Advertising

In 1926 Claude Hopkins published *Scientific Advertising,* which many advertisers credit with providing the foundation of formal advertising research. Hopkins based his findings on the results of direct-mail and direct-response offers and testing and research remain a core element of modern direct-mail advertising. The key elements in testing direct-mail are the list, the offer (or featured consumer benefit), and the creative presentation.

Let's look at some examples of the type of elements most commonly tested in direct-mail:

1. List tests:
   Various list sources including response lists
   Demographic segments
   Geographic segments

2. Offer tests:
   Guarantee wording
   Free-trial, send-no-money-now offers
   Use of incentives

3. Format tests:
   Single mailing versus series
   Window versus closed envelope
   Live postage versus meter
   Envelope size

4. Copy tests:
   Personalization
   Letter length
   Use of testimonial
   Various opening paragraphs

5. Layout and design tests:
   Photographs versus line art
   Four-color versus one- or two-color
   Type size and font
   Product alone or with models[36]

Direct-mail testing can be expensive so it is important to concentrate on major elements that normally determine the success or failure of a mail campaign. It is extremely crucial to research validity to test only one element at a time. Too many mailers try to cut corners by testing several items in a single mailing. Obviously, if you change the format, the mailing list, and the offer, it is impossible to determine what factor created any changes in test results.

Other Direct-Mail Techniques

Because of the expense of stand-alone direct-mail, many advertisers are looking at alternative means of distribution of their sales pieces. Some of the primary print alternatives are the following:

---

[36]Pat Friesen, "Direct response creative: What to test first," *Target Marketing,* May 1999, 50.

- *Package inserts.* A number of companies will allow the insertion of sales messages when they ship merchandise. These messages called bounce-back circulars are delivered to customers who are proven direct-marketing users. In addition, the cost is much less than solo mailings since your message is being delivered as part of another package. Generally, package inserts are limited to five offers.

- *Ride-alongs.* A form of package inserts are ride-alongs, which are included in a company's own packages. **Ride-alongs** have many of the same advantages of package inserts except they are going to a company's loyal customers with whom a company has a proven and recent sales relationship. Depending on the product, ride-alongs can be extremely profitable since the overhead is so low.

ride-alongs Direct-mail pieces that are sent with other mailings, such as bills.

- *Statement stuffers.* Few companies miss an opportunity to include a message with your monthly bill. The idea behind statement stuffers is the same as ride-alongs and they have several advantages. First, they cost nothing to deliver since the mailing expense is going to be incurred in any case. Second, they are at least seen, since everyone eventually gets around to opening their bills. Finally, most recipients are credit qualified and have already dealt with the company before or they would not be getting a statement.

- *Ticket jackets.* A popular form of ride-alongs are promotions on airline, bus line, or train ticket jackets. Companies such as car rental firms find that they are ideal to reach their prime target audiences.

- *Cooperative (joint) mail advertising.* With the cost of postage continuing to increase, direct-mailers often attempt to share expenses through cooperative mailings. A number of firms specialize in joint mailings. These mailings may include as many as 20 different advertising offers in one envelope. Each advertiser provides a coupon or other short message and the joint mailer handles the mailing and divides the cost among the advertisers.

Cooperative mailings have two major drawbacks. First, they are extremely impersonal since each advertiser's message must be very short. Second, it is difficult to reach your specific customers through joint mailings with the precision you would have with your own list. The dilemma of joint mailings is that as the number of participating advertisers increase, the cost per advertiser goes down, but, likewise, the unique feature of the mailing decreases.

The use of inserts is big business and is growing as the cost of postage increases. It is estimated that as many as 25 billion inserts are distributed in various venues. Its position as an alternative "medium" can be demonstrated in the number of sources that are seeking to track the advertising options available to advertisers. For example, both SRDS and the DMA's Alternative Response Media Council have devoted resources to tracking the choices open to advertisers in placing inserts.

SUMMARY

Direct-response marketing is targeted, personal, and measurable. In an era of increasing accountability, these traits have moved it center stage as a means of reaching and selling a diverse universe of consumers. In terms of sales produced and expenditures, it represents more dollars than all other forms of advertising combined. It is rare for a company not to include direct marketing and direct-response advertising as a major element in its marketing mix. Companies have come to realize that the ability to combine personal messages with highly selective audience segmentation gives direct response advantages seen in few other media.

The tremendous strides in computer technology has made the future of direct response both exciting and uncertain.

The emergence of the Internet has given a new focus to many of the practices of direct marketing. While the Internet and other forms of interactive media have not fulfilled their promise as the primary means of reaching prospects and achieving sales, they have changed the landscape of direct marketing dramatically. The challenge is to make the obvious advantages of e-commerce profitable for general selling.

To date companies have been successful in gaining on-line traffic, but not necessarily in producing revenue. For example, all the major cereal makers have an on-line presence for kids, many for specific brands. Kellogg has a number of sites (e.g., www.tonythetiger.com), and Quaker Oats' (www.capncrunch.com) recently had more than 100,000 children register to solve a "Where's the Cap'n?" promotion. Unfortunately, interest in the mystery was much greater than interest in the cereal. As one on-line executive commented, "The challenge that awaits the industry is how to translate all the great opportunities to build relationships and talk to kids for prolonged periods of time into sales."[37] Even though he was talking about the children's cereal market, his remarks could be applied to virtually any area of e-commerce.

Regardless of the channel that direct response uses, its flexibility makes it practical for virtually every advertiser. In addition, the ability to test and verify direct marketing is vitally important in the current era of accountability and measured results. Not only does measurement of direct response provide a major advantage to advertisers, but it also creates the type of audience databases so valuable to companies in all their advertising, marketing, and promotion endeavors.

There is little question that direct response will continue to outpace most other forms of media advertising. Not only will direct response become more important in the marketing plans of many companies, but because of its influence even more sophisticated forms of audience segmentation than at present. History will probably mark the 1990s as the end of the era of mass media and mass audience delivery. In the future, even the one-to-one communication of today will slowly give way to some form of interactive media. There is little question that direct response will play a major role in this transition.

In addition to the technological advances of direct-response advertising, societal changes also are working in its favor. For example, the two-income family, working mothers, an aging population, and less leisure time are only a few of the factors leading people to favor in-home buying. Greater demand and customer acceptability of direct response are pushing more companies to enter the field.

Perhaps the greatest challenge facing direct marketing is public skepticism, especially concerns over privacy issues. However, industry-wide efforts sponsored by the Direct Marketing Association and other organizations have made great strides in improving the industry's image. The fact that most Fortune 500 companies routinely include some form of direct marketing in their promotional plans is testimony to its growing respectability among advertisers and improved credibility among consumers. Nevertheless, the industry is aware that legislation affecting its operation is constantly being introduced and presents a threat to future growth.

REVIEW

1. What have been some of the major factors causing the growth of direct-response advertising?

---

[37]Stephanie Thompson, "Cereal makers entice online kids," *Advertising Age*, 3 July 2000, 20.

2. What is direct marketing?

3. What steps have been taken to improve the image of direct-response advertising?

4. What role does database marketing play in direct-response advertising?

5. What is the inbound telemarketing?

6. What is the key element in direct-mail?

7. What is the Telephone Consumer Protection Act?

8. What is per inquiry?

9. What is the function of a list compiler?

10. What is the difference between a list broker and a list manager?

TAKE IT TO THE NET

We invite you to visit the Russell/Lane page on the Prentice Hall Web site at **www.prenhall.com/myphlip** for end-of-chapter exercises and applications.

Chapter 14

Sales Promotion

When strategically planned and implemented, sales promotion and advertising should interact in a complementary fashion. In recent years, total investment in all forms of sales promotion has significantly outpaced spending in advertising. In particular promotions directed to the trade channel have become extremely important as manufacturers compete for retail distribution for their products. The major challenge facing many sales promotion plans is achieving short-term sales motivation without diminishing brand equity. After reading this chapter you will understand:

>> The complementary roles of sales promotion and advertising

>> The various formats and executions of sales promotion

>> Uses of sales promotion as consumer and trade incentives

>> Current trends in sales promotion

>> The major reasons for the growth of sales promotion

Pros

1. Sales promotion provides a means of encouraging consumer sales response.
2. Sales promotion is extremely flexible with a number of techniques to reach consumers across demographic and lifestyle categories. There are few product categories that cannot benefit from some form of sales promotion.
3. Promotion functions at both the consumer and trade levels to encourage high levels of distribution and goodwill with the distribution channel.

Cons

1. If not executed properly, sales promotion can damage brand equity by replacing the image of a product with price competition.

2. Because of the variety of formats and techniques of promotion, care must be taken to coordinate the various messages of advertising and sales promotion. High levels of promotion demand some form of integrated marketing communication if the company is to speak with a single "voice."

3. Some forms of promotion such as couponing have become so prevalent that they no longer provide a competitive differentiation for a brand and, in fact, may become a consumer expectation rather than a temporary sales boost.

We all come into contact with numerous examples of **sales promotion** each day. The various forms of sales promotion remind us of brands and persuade us to make purchases in subtle ways that often make little or no conscious impression. When you turn the page on the calendar from your insurance agent, the agency name is reinforced. When technical support managers tee up their golf balls given to them by their computer vendor, they are reminded of its services. And when doctors write prescriptions with the pen left behind by the pharmaceutical rep, a particular drug is being promoted. All of these items and thousands more are examples of sales promotion.

Many sales promotion techniques were well established by 1900, but they often consisted of gimmicks and trinket give-aways rather than the well-planned promotional campaigns we see today. However, many modern methods of sales promotion were initiated by retailers and manufacturers of the nineteenth century. In 1895, both Asa Candler and C.W. Post were offering coupons for free Coca-Colas and reduced prices on boxes of Grape Nuts cereal. At the same time, Adolphus Busch was promoting his beer with free samples, lithographs of "Custer's Last Stand," and red, blue, and gold pocket knives. By 1912, Kellogg was including rag dolls, cartoons, and spoons in its cereal boxes.

These and the other forerunners of modern sales promotion recognized that brands need attention and differentiation to gain sales and that customers react positively to extra incentives when making purchase decisions. Sales promotion provided both. What most sales promotion of the period failed to do was complement a company's overall marketing program and provide long-term strategies for brand building. In fact, on occasion the give-aways and promotions overshadowed the product. A classic example is Topps bubble gum baseball cards. After years of promoting the cards as an incentive to buy gum, in 1990 the company dropped the gum and simply began marketing the baseball cards as collectibles.

By the 1960s, promotion firms were offering marketing advice to complement their promotional programs. Promotion firms, in response to client demand, were transformed from companies developing stand-alone incentive programs to full-service marketing consultants. They began to offer expertise in consumer marketing, merchandising, and branding. During this period the full-service promotion shop took root and integration with advertising and marketing became the norm.[1]

To provide better balance between advertising and sales promotion we are finding that a number of companies are consolidating overall responsibility for both under a single corporate executive. Despite the fact that advertising and sales promotion are different in many respects, coordination between them is imperative. More and more sales promotion and advertising agencies are consolidating, at the very least, coordinating their efforts to retain clients who demand a synergistic approach to their total advertising and promotional programs. "Ad agencies, promo shops, and even premium suppliers are feverishly buying or cultivating disciplines to complement their core expertise. Promo execs sitting at the pitch table with their sister ad agencies find themselves more central to the conversation as ad shops

sales promotion
(1) Sales activities that supplement both personal selling and marketing, coordinate the two, and help to make them effective. For example, displays are sales promotions. (2) More loosely, the combination of personal selling, advertising, and all supplementary selling activities.

---

[1]David Vacek and Richard Sale, "100 years of promotion," *Promo*, August 1998, 142.

Chapter 14   Sales Promotion   **365**

turn to promo types for their expertise at retail."[2] Despite the merging of advertising and sales promotion in terms of both management responsibility and creative execution, we should be aware that they differ in both execution and objectives. Yet, it is impossible to be successful as an advertiser, marketing executive, or promotion manager without a knowledge of the broad concepts involved in the total system of **marketing communication.**

marketing communication The communication components of marketing, which include public relations, advertising, personal selling, and sales promotion.

This chapter discusses the primary types of sales promotion and how they complement media advertising. As with advertising, the opportunities for successful execution of sales promotion programs depend on an understanding of the marketing objectives of a particular firm or individual brand. Both advertising and sales promotion failures are most often a direct result of poor planning and a lack of integration with the elements of the marketing mix.

PROMOTION AND ADVERTISING

Effective sales promotion has two basic functions: (1) to inform and (2) to motivate. Normally, sales promotion is most effective when its message is closely related to advertising themes. Point-of-purchase displays may feature a testimonial spokesperson who is simultaneously appearing in television commercials, counter displays often use the same headlines and copy style as print advertisements, and product sampling will offer miniature packages to enhance brand identification promoted in the company's advertising. While the means of communication may be different than in advertising, consistent information and formats are a key ingredient in successful promotions.

The second aspect of promotions—motivation—differs in some major respects to advertising. Motivation, in a marketing sense, is the means used to move a customer to purchase a brand. This process usually moves across a continuum from awareness (initially hearing about a product) to purchase. In Exhibit 14.1 we can see that advertising and sales promotion have markedly different responsibilities in the communication and purchase process.

The key to successful marketing communication is determining the purposes and objectives of advertising, sales promotion and other components and how best to coordinate and integrate these objectives. In the past, a major distinction between advertising and sales promotion was that sales promotion was viewed as a short-term sales incentive and advertising was intended to build brand equity over time. Today, most marketers recognize that it is counterproductive for sales promotion to gain short-term sales at the expense of long-term brand equity. One only has to look at a number of package good categories that have used coupons and other price-oriented deals to the point that consumers see little inherent value in the brands and simply purchase the one with the lowest cost at any moment.

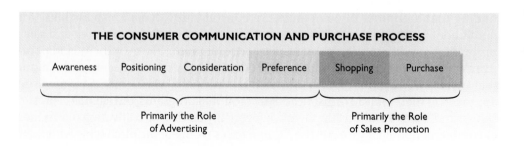

Exhibit

14.1

Advertising and sales promotion should function in a complementary fashion.

THE CONSUMER COMMUNICATION AND PURCHASE PROCESS

Awareness	Positioning	Consideration	Preference	Shopping	Purchase

Primarily the Role of Advertising

Primarily the Role of Sales Promotion

[2]Betsy Spethmann, "Is advertising dead," *Promo*, September 1998, 32.

As one promotion executive observed, "Increasingly, the gimmicks are gone. We must all step up to the challenge of adding real, brand-building value with promotion—the kind that sparks genuine consumer, retailer, and client interest."[3] In this environment where promotion must work with advertising and contribute to the overall marketing goals, objectives for promotion might include:

- To gain trial among nonusers of a brand or service
- To increase repeat purchase and/or multiple purchases
- To expand brand usage by encouraging product uses in addition to usual use
- To defend share against competitors
- To support and reinforce an advertising campaign/theme or specific image
- To increase distribution and/or retailer/dealer cooperation[4]

Note that none of these objectives advocate short-term sales increases except when these sales are part of a larger marketing strategy. For example, when we encourage product trial by nonusers or expansion of uses by present customers, the implication is that these trials will lead to long-term consumer relationships. In turn, consumer relationships, initially gained through promotion, will be reinforced over time by advertising.

Promotional expenditures are directed at a wide range of programs. Exhibit 14.2 shows some of the major categories of trade and sales promotions and the investment in each. It is interesting to note that the largest percentage increase is in the area of interactive promotions. Like their advertising counterparts, promotion executives are experimenting with various means of using new technology in the marketing process.

Total promotion budgets are generally divided into three categories: consumer advertising, consumer promotion (usually referred to as either sales promotion or simply promotion), and trade promotion (known as dealer promotion or merchandising). While coordination among these promotional classifications is important,

PROMOTION INDUSTRY GROSS REVENUES
(in millions)

SEGMENT	1999 REVS	INCREASE	% OF TOTAL
Premium Incentives	$26,300	5.2%	28.1%
Ad Specialties	14,800	12.1	15.8
P-O-P	14,400	5.1	15.4
Sponsorships	7,600	11.8	8.1
Coupons	6,980	8.2	7.5
Printing	6,200	10.7	6.6
Licensing	5,500	5.0	5.9
Fulfillment	3,297	20.1	3.5
Agency	2,178	49.2	2.3
Interactive	1,471	44.2	1.6
Sweeps	1,380	15.0	1.5
Research	1,340	8.9	1.4
Sampling	1,120	10.9	1.2
In-store	870	8.7	0.9
Total	$93,436	9.4%	

Exhibit

14.2

Promotion Industry Gross Revenues

From: Promo, May 2000, A5.

[3]Peter Breen, "Seeds of change," *Promo*, May 2000, A5.
[4]Russell Bowman and Paul Theroux, "By the book," *Promo*, March 2000, 95.

they each serve a distinct purpose. Let's examine the role of each in the marketing mix and the share of promotional budgets spent in these promotional categories.

1. ***Consumer advertising.*** The role of measured media advertising is to build long-term brand equity and promote basic product attributes, location of dealers, and/or comparisons with other products. The percentage of total promotional budgets spent on advertising has declined steadily over the last decade. Approximately 25 percent of promotional dollars are currently spent in advertising.

2. *Consumer sales promotion.* These are sales-promotional incentives directed to the consumer. Cents-off coupons are the most common consumer promotion, but premiums, rebates, and sweepstakes also are frequently used. Driven primarily by a decrease in the use of coupons, consumer sales promotion has fallen slightly to 25 percent of spending.

3. *Trade promotions.* Accounting for about half of the promotional budget, trade incentives are designed to encourage a company's sales force or retail outlets to push its products more aggressively. These are the most expensive types of promotion on a per-person basis. Winning dealers or retailers may get a trip to Hawaii, a new car, or a cash bonus. Behind the significant increase in trade promotions is the fact that companies think they get more immediate payout for their spending in this sector and that they have more control over expenditures than in other forms of promotion.

Despite some movement of dollars among the three categories, the long-term trend seems to be a ratio of 75 percent of promotional dollars in trade and sales promotion and 25 percent in advertising. The relatively low figure for advertising might be even further depressed if we had an accurate measure of the advertising dollars that are allocated to support major promotions such as sweepstakes, rebates, or sales. For example, it is estimated that as much as 20 percent of total advertising expenditures are devoted to supporting some form of promotion. Most marketing executives predict minimal future increases in advertising's share of total promotion budgets.

FORMS OF SALES PROMOTION

The remainder of this chapter will discuss the primary types of sales promotion. Priority will be given to those techniques most associated with advertising, especially at the consumer level. However, we also will briefly discuss trade-oriented promotions. In all cases, we need to keep in mind the complementary purposes of advertising and promotion. The most frequently used forms of sales promotion are:

- Point-of-purchase advertising
- Premiums
- Specialty advertising
- Coupons
- Sampling
- Deals
- Event marketing
- Sweepstakes and contests
- Cooperative advertising
- Trade shows and exhibits
- Directories and Yellow Pages
- Trade incentives

POINT-OF-PURCHASE ADVERTISING

With annual expenditures of almost $14 billion, **point-of-purchase** (P-O-P) displays are among the most prevalent and fastest growing segments of sales promotion. P-O-P is tailor-made for a retail environment where almost 60 percent of consumer purchases are unplanned. In recent years, the industry has sponsored a number of studies to help retailers and manufacturers better utilize P-O-P. Findings of these studies demonstrate that P-O-P has several primary advantages as a sales promotion technique:

point-of-purchase advertising Displays prepared by the manufacturer for use where the product is sold.

1. *Motivate unplanned shopping.* One major study indicated that displays at the end of aisles and at the checkout counter were most conducive to promoting sales. The same study also found that factors such as the age of the shopper, predilection to influence by in-store deals, and time pressure all played a role in the influence of P-O-P. It also showed that retailers could influence impulse buying by encouraging shoppers to go down as many aisles as possible.[5]

2. *Brand and product reminders.* One of the major roles of P-O-P is to remind consumers about product categories and brands that they might overlook. The P-O-P industry is upgrading the creative options available for in-store selling. In addition to the familiar cardboard signage, more and more displays are utilizing computer technology to change messages electronically and target selective demographic shopper segments. For example, AdMedia, Inc. is experimenting with in-store electronic billboards where sound and images are rotated on one-minute intervals. Different messages can be downloaded from remote locations to respond to changing marketing conditions, different audiences in various dayparts, or in-store promotions.[6]

3. *Influence brand switching.* Consumers show remarkably low levels of brand loyalty in food categories. In a study by the Meyers Research Center, ". . . more than half of grocery shoppers would switch brands if their preferred items were not available, compared to only a third of shoppers who would do the same if their favorite non-food items were unavailable."[7] This research not only shows the need for P-O-P, but indicates that the use of such displays will be an ongoing necessity to motivate unpredictable consumers.

The major industry trade association, the Point of Purchase Advertising International (POPAI), in cooperation with the Advertising Research Foundation (ARF), is currently engaged in a multi-year study to provide reliable audience measures and place P-O-P on a level with other measured media such as print and broadcast. According to the POPAI, the study seeks to measure:

1. *The amount of P-O-P advertising erected in stores.* The industry knows that all the signage that is purchased and distributed is not displayed.

2. *The estimated number of consumer impressions generated.* The study seeks to gather data concerning reach, frequency, and CPM in order to allow intermedia comparisons.

3. *The effectiveness of P-O-P advertising.* Ultimately, the industry hopes to provide information on sales increases that are attributable to P-O-P.

---

[5]J. Jeffrey Inman and Russell S. Winer, "Where the rubber meets the road: A model of in-store consumer decision making," Working Paper, Marketing Science Institute, October 1998, 25.
[6]"E-gads," *Promo*, August 1999, 59.
[7]"Out of sight, out of mind," *Promo*, March 1996, 16.

One of the historical problems facing P-O-P advertising has been guaranteeing that the displays were properly displayed or displayed at all. In the past, manufacturers' salespersons were largely responsible for maintaining in-store displays. Particularly among small companies, signs were simply placed by manufacturers' reps in those stores that would give them space. Now, marketing in-store displays is a much more sophisticated process and highly coordinated at both the local and national levels. For huge retailers such as Home Depot and Walmart, some P-O-P signs are made exclusively for their outlets.

To insure better usage of in-store displays, a number of companies have hired independent firms called *retail merchandising service* companies to work with retailers to gain maximum P-O-P coverage on an outsource basis. Many companies find that ". . . hiring merchandising companies may mean extra costs, but the expense is offset by the fact that crack sales forces don't need to waste valuable selling time setting up displays, doing store sets and out-of-stock correction, or updating merchandise."[8]

In the future, we will see even more innovations in the uses of P-O-P. The P-O-P industry will provide better research as well as utilizing a number of electronic, interactive, and broadcast media. For example, the growing use of grocery store checkout computers will allow more accurate identification of local store customers, which, in turn, will allow targeted in-store messages. Video and audio displays will increase and provide immediacy to react to changing marketing conditions in local areas. In addition, new technology such as holograms will soon provide even more eye-catching store displays.

Increasingly, P-O-P will be dominated by retailers, and manufacturers will be required to meet rigid requirements to gain retail shelf and floor space. Retail space is the most valuable commodity that local merchants have, and they will allocate P-O-P spots only to those companies and brands that provide the highest quality displays, greatest merchandising and advertising support, and, most importantly, the most significant profit potential.

Not only are these innovations in point-of-purchase interesting in themselves, they point up once again that advertising, promotion, and marketing are increasingly becoming interrelated to the point that it is difficult to tell when one stops and the other begins. Rather than trying to decide in what category a promotion element belongs, managers are becoming more concerned with using whatever techniques work.

Premiums

premium An item, other than the product itself, given to purchasers of a product as an inducement to buy. Can be free with a purchase (for example, on the package, in the package, or the container itself) or available upon proof of purchase and a payment (self-liquidating premium).

Premiums are items given to customers in exchange for a purchase or some other action such as a store visit or test drive. In other words, they are rewards given with strings attached. Premiums are among the most common sales incentives, accounting for approximately $5 billion at the consumer level. Premium incentives also are popular trade promotions. Each year more than $22 billion in travel, cash bonuses, and merchandise are awarded to retailers, wholesalers, and company sale reps for meeting various sales goals.

Premiums are not only one of the largest categories of sales promotion, they also are among the oldest. Premiums date to the mid-1700s when calendars, wooden specialty items, and other promotional products were quite common. According to the industry's major trade association, the Promotional Products Association International (PPAI), by the 1850s specialty printers had established a relatively formal business for premium items.

---

[8]Richard Sele, "The display police," *Promo*, March 1999, 80.

Premiums are comprised of a number of types of merchandise with writing instruments, calendars, and clothing being the most popular. The key to successful premium promotions is that the merchandise has some logical connection to the product and the target market. Remember that premiums are not traditional gifts, they are *marketing* gifts. Premium offers are generally categorized by either the purpose or the method of distribution. Among the major sectors of the premium industry are the following:

1. ***Traffic-building premiums.*** Most premiums are offered at the time of purchase. However, other premiums, particularly those associated with high-cost products and services, are given for merely visiting a retailer, real-estate development, or automobile dealer. For example, Cadillac dealers offered Greg Norman video golf lessons to prospects visiting their showrooms. In an interesting twist on the usual traffic-building premium, customers had to return a second time to pick up the tape—thus, increasing sales opportunities for dealers.[9]

2. *Continuity premiums.* Continuity premiums build in value as a consumer continues to buy a product. Slim Jims meat snacks awards points with each purchase for redemption in one of three catalogs. Developed in response to their target market demographics, the company provides wrestling, in-line skate, and stock car related merchandise. The key to successful continuity premiums is that "... programs shouldn't neglect the brand. Points games are a great chance to build brand image by getting consumers actively involved with them for months, or even years. If prizes, too, are related to the brand, so much the better."[10]

   In recent years, continuity premium programs have been widely adopted by e-commerce companies. Various Web sites use continuity programs to encourage return visits and brand awareness. The continuity concept "... is the essence of incentive-oriented Web sites such as MyRewards.com, MyPoints.com, and FreeRide.com. Consumers who visit these sites are offered points toward rewards for clicking on sponsoring merchant sites, searching for information, or making purchases."[11]

3. *In- or on-pack premiums.* Also called **direct premiums,** these are among the most popular items with both advertisers and customers since they offer an immediate incentive and instant reward in return for a purchase. The direct premium has become so popular that advertisers are constantly searching for ways to differentiate their offers. When Lucky Charms and Honey Nut Cheerios offered four plastic characters from *Toy Story 2*, they provided viewing windows so children could pick the premium they wanted and not duplicate earlier purchases—a much appreciated bonus for parents.[12]

   Many direct premiums are offered as a copromotion so that compatible brands can cooperate and extend promotional opportunities and at the same time reduce costs to the participating companies. General Mills' Cinnamon Graham cereal cosponsored a promotion with Old Navy. Cereal boxes included coupons for Old Navy stores and the stores provided samples of the cereal. Likewise, Diet Coke packs carried samples of excerpts from upcoming novels by major publishers such as Doubleday. The Diet Coke Story promotion was in response to research that showed Diet Coke drinkers were greater than average book readers.[13]

traffic-building premium A sales incentive to encourage customers to come to a store where a sale can be closed.

direct premium A sales incentive given to customers at the time of purchase.

[9]Kate Bertrand, "Premiums prime the market," *Advertising Age*, May 1998, S6.
[10]David Vacek, "Getting in gear," *Promo*, May 1998, S5.
[11]"Motivating matters," *Promo*, May 2000, A14.
[12]Betsy Spethmann, "Wrapped attention," *Promo*, January 2000, 25.
[13]David Vaczek, "The company they keep," *Promo*, January 1999, 86.

self-liquidating premium A premium offered to consumers for a fee that covers its cost plus handling.

4. *Self-liquidating premiums.* Regardless of the method of distributing the premium, the most popular type of premium is self-liquidating offers (SLO). As the name implies, these premiums are designed to require that customers pay all or a major portion of their cost. On average, customers are required to pay approximately 75 percent of the premium. It is not surprising in this era of tight budgets, self-liquidating premiums are the most popular and the fastest growing category. During the last decade, SLO have increased by more than 30 percent and the average cost to consumers has risen sharply.

At one time, it was thought that SLO could only be marketed successfully for low-end merchandise, usually under five dollars. However, marketers are finding that consumers will pay considerably more for items that have high perceived value or interest. Old Style beer offered an inflatable "Goat Boat" for just under $40. The boat promoted the legend of an irate goat owner placing a hex on the Chicago Cubs baseball team when his goat was denied entry to Wrigley Field. The promotion proved successful because it was funny, included functional merchandise, and hit the right chord with Cub fans.[14]

In some cases, the premiums have become so popular that they have actually become major profit centers for a company. Coca-Cola and Harley Davidson are but two of the many examples where branded merchandise is so popular that it is sold as "stand-alone" stock. This merchandise is no longer a premium, but it shows the popularity that some brands (and their premiums) have achieved.

With the thousands of available items for premium markets, it is extremely important that great care be given to the selection of this merchandise. The primary concern is that any premium promotion is complementary to the overall marketing goals of a firm and that the relatively high investment in such an endeavor can be justified. Among the primary consideration that a marketer would want to contemplate before moving to a premium campaign are the following:

1. *Exclusivity.* Make sure that your premium will be unique in its product category. Survey the competition and determine what premiums they are using.

2. *Quality.* If you can't afford quality merchandise, don't bother. Remember your brand is associated with the quality of the premium.

3. *Popularity.* What is hot now may be passe in a few months. Trying to relate your premium with a fad can be risky unless you have a short time line for execution.

4. *Research.* Match the premium with your customer's demographic profile. It is not uncommon for premium companies to offer clients general advice on the best products to meet the preferences of various market segments.

5. *Fit the customer.* Make sure you are rewarding the decision maker rather than the purchaser. Cereal makers have long directed their premiums to children who decide which cereal brands are purchased in most families.

6. *Price.* If at all possible, you need to test to see what the optimum premium cost should be. Remember quality counts, but you don't want to overspend if a less-expensive premium will do the job. On the other hand, you need to be aware of the general level of premiums that are offered by competitors.

7. *Profits.* While profits from a self-liquidating offer should be secondary to marketing considerations, don't overlook the potential for money-making offers.

8. *Premiums,* like other sales promotions, are most effective when supported and coordinated with a strong advertising campaign. Most research shows that premiums almost always do better when combined with advertising.[15]

---

[14]"Liquid assets," *Promo,* May 1998, 31.
[15]"Key to premium marketing," *Promo,* May 1996, P6.

Fulfillment

As we discussed in Chapter 13, the physical work of handling, organizing, and responding to requests for merchandise is normally managed by **fulfillment firms.** The fulfillment function is extremely important to companies using mail-in premiums, especially self-liquidators. Fulfillment firms usually operate on a fee basis according to the number of requests. Their work is crucial to the success of any mail-in promotion. Sloppy fulfillment services can virtually guarantee an unsuccessful promotion as well as long-term damage to customer goodwill. Before contracting with a fulfillment firm, it is important to determine if the company is experienced in handling the type of promotion you are planning. Fulfillment is an extension of customer service and it is your company, not the fulfillment firm, that will be blamed if something goes wrong.

fulfillment firm
Company that handles the couponing process including receiving, verification, and payment. It also handles contests and sweepstake responses.

SPECIALTY ADVERTISING

The same items used in premium promotions—clothing, writing instruments, calendars—are among the most popular with specialty advertisers.[16] However, there are two major differences between premiums and specialties:

specialty advertising A gift given to a consumer to encourage a purchase.

1. Advertising specialties are imprinted with the advertiser's name, logo, or short advertising message. Premiums are normally not imprinted since the customer is being given a reward for purchasing a product.
2. Unlike premiums, specialties are given with no obligation on the part of the recipient.

The uses and formats of advertising specialties are almost limitless with more than 15,000 items available to carry out virtually any marketing objective. Specialties also complement other media and can be targeted to prime prospects with little waste circulation. The ideal specialty is one that is used on a regular basis, thereby creating continuing frequency with no additional cost.

The disadvantages of specialties include their significant expense on a CPM basis and, like outdoor, they offer little opportunity for a sales message. In addition, there is no natural distribution system for specialties and, depending on the item selected, production time may take up to six weeks.

Specialty advertising has experienced significant growth in recent years as businesses attempt to establish brand identities in an increasingly competitive environment. Like so many areas of advertising, specialties have been influenced by e-commerce and the Internet. As one specialty executive pointed out, "With all the dot-com companies and e-commerce companies racing to create brands, people are looking for better, higher-end [specialty] products. Dot-coms are spending lavishly on promotional products to help their brand names stand out in the minds of consumers."[17]

The Web also has the potential to change many traditional sales approaches within the industry. Instead of carrying bulky catalogs from client to client, reps can show an array of targeted merchandise using portable computers. For low-end merchandise and small clients who don't warrant a personal sales call, the Web is a way for specialty suppliers to reach this market. In the future, direct selling by specialty manufacturers may become more important or even in some cases replace independent reps who have traditionally been the primary sales force in the industry.

---

[16]Unless otherwise noted, material in this section was provided by the Promotional Products Association International.
[17]"The digital sales pitch," *Promo*, May 2000, A19.

Since a major role of specialty advertising is to provide long-term brand awareness, it is not surprising to find the heaviest users in markets with little perceived product differentiation and a number of competitive brands. Financial institutions such as banks and stockbrokers, hospitals and health care providers, and telecommunication and Internet companies are examples of categories that spend heavily on specialty advertising.

Specialty advertising, like all forms of promotion, should be planned in terms of specific marketing goals and objectives. One survey of advertisers found that some of the primary reasons for using specialties were:[18]

1. Customer retention and appreciation
2. In connection with trade shows
3. To build goodwill and enhance company image
4. Create awareness for new products and services
5. Generate sales leads and responses

In choosing specialty items it is important to determine that the item has some logical relationship to both the target market and the product or service being promoted. The items need to have some useful function if the specialty is going to be kept as a reminder of a brand. Since the advertising message can be no more than a few words, a specialty needs to adapt the theme of a company's overall advertising campaign to offer an integrated communications approach to consumers.

Business Gifts A separate category of specialty advertising is business gifts. Business gifts serve the same role as specialties, but they are given in a business-to-business setting. Since business gifts are usually given to a relatively small group of recipients, they can be more individualized than consumer items. Approximately half of businesses give gifts to either customers or employees and they cite the following as primary reasons for offering gifts:

■ To thank customers	83 percent
■ To develop future business	56 percent
■ To recognize employee performance and longevity	25 percent
■ Customers expect them	10 percent

From a marketing perspective, specialties and business gifts serve many of the same functions; however, there are notable differences. The most significant contrast between business gifts and specialties is that business gifts often do not carry the advertiser's logo, although sometimes the items will be imprinted with the logo of the firm to whom the gift is given.

Business gifts must be chosen with a great deal of care. For one thing they are costly compared to specialties. However, most marketers advise against very expensive gifts. In fact, Internal Revenue Service regulations limit deductibility of business gifts to $25. An overly generous gift may offend some recipients who might view it as an obligation. In some cases, businesses with relatively few clients select individual gifts such as books on a topic of interest to the person. This personal touch will probably mean more than a more expensive gift chosen with little thought for the recipient.

There are other factors that should be considered before a gift is given. For example, does the client company have policies that would prevent a person from accepting the gift? Normally, companies will allow executives to accept relatively inexpensive gifts—another reason to keep the price low. Be very careful to consider cultural, gender, and religious etiquette in choosing a gift. Finally, since the major-

---

[18]Research by Louisiana State University and Glenrich Business Studies reported in www.ppai.org.

ity of business gifts are given at the end of the year, some companies choose other times for gift giving to gain a degree of exclusivity. The Fourth of July, Halloween, or some date of significance to the recipient such as the date of the founding of the company are typical alternatives to end-of-year giving.

COUPONS

Coupon promotions are among the oldest forms of sales promotion, and they are without question the most pervasive category within the promotion industry. Each year, more than 250 billion coupons are distributed—almost 2,500 per household—at a cost of more than $7 billion. The overall redemption rate is less than 2 percent, although targeted coupon distribution sometimes achieves levels of as much as 30 percent. Despite the generally low rates of redemption, more than 80 percent of customers use at least one coupon annually.

There are two basic approaches to coupon marketing and distribution. Traditionally, the primary marketing objectives for distributing coupons are to encourage product trial by prospective customers and to combat competitive encroachments against present customers. Both of these goals were normally addressed through mass coupon distribution. By far the most preferred method of coupon distribution is the **free-standing insert** (FSI) usually included in Sunday newspapers. FSIs are responsible for more than 80 percent of total coupon distribution. Exhibit 14.3 gives a breakdown of other methods of coupon circulation.

One of the recurring complaints about the number of coupon promotions is that they create price competition at the expense of building brand loyalty. In recent years, a number of major advertisers such as Kraft and Nestlé have taken steps to include coupon promotions within a traditional advertising environment. Such an approach serves to encourage both product trial *and* build brand equity. Kraft distributed its coupons in an eight-page newspaper insert entitled *food & family*, which included traditional advertisements, articles on food-related topics, as well as coupons for six of its brands including Tombstone pizza and Minute Rice.[19]

In addition to FSI and other blanket coupon distribution methods, we are starting to see a number of more targeted efforts. These more narrowly defined approaches to coupon promotions have one of two goals:

1. To reach targeted prospects based on lifestyle and demographic information
2. To build loyalty among current customers

coupon Most popular type of sales-promotion technique.

free-standing inserts (FSI) Preprinted inserts distributed to newspaper publishers, where they are inserted and delivered with the newspaper.

BESIDES FSIs
Breakdown of Distribution by Non-FSI Media
FSIs account for 81.3 percent of all coupon distribution. Here's how the remaining 18.7 percent breaks out:

Other <0.5%
Newspaper 1.4%
Direct Mail 2.1%
Electronic <0.5%
Magazine 3.0%
Handouts 8.7%
In-/On-Pack 3.0%

Exhibit

14.3

Besides FSIs

From: Promo, April 2000, 70.

---

[19]Betsy Spethmann, "So much for targeting," *Promo,* April 2000, 69.

In both cases, scanning checkout data and other computer-based data retrieval systems give manufacturers insight into past purchase behavior of individual buyers. Using this information retailers and manufacturers can provide offers that reflect this specific consumer behavior and their brand preferences. For example, CVS Pharmacy tracks purchases and, by using past transaction data, can customize future coupon offers to maintain or increase specific pharmaceutical purchases.[20]

Coupons and the Internet

Less than 5 percent of consumers currently obtain coupons on-line. However, the combination of consumer convenience and manufacturer's ability to build customer databases make the growth of Web couponing inevitable. A growing number of package goods manufacturers have their own Web sites with coupon offers and even more use independent Web sites to offer access to hundreds of different coupon offers.

On-line services such as Catalina Marketing's valupage.com and Val Pak Direct Marketing's valpak.com offer coupons in exchange for some consumer information. As on-line services continue to develop consumer databases, we will see a number providing services such as e-mail offers tailored to a person's past buying behavior. While Internet-distributed coupons constitute a small percentage of total coupons, it is growing rapidly. With household Internet penetration predicted to be 70 to 80 percent by the end of this decade, on-line couponing offers significant potential for inexpensive, targeted coupon promotions.

Coupon Redemption Fraud

When we redeem our 50-cent coupons, we give little thought to the significant investment for manufacturers offering them. Unfortunately, those interested in defrauding manufacturers through the illegal redemption of coupons are very much aware of their value. The most common type of fraud occurs when a person sends in coupons for which no product purchase has been made. There have been instances where criminals have obtained thousands of coupons and sent them to manufacturers using the name of supermarkets and other retailers. In some cases, manufacturers have spent millions of dollars on redemptions for fraudulent claims.

In recent years, the U.S. Postal Service has made a number of arrests for mail fraud in connection with coupon misredemption (the mails are generally used to send coupons to fulfillment houses). Postal authorities have had some success in stopping this type of coupon fraud by publishing coupons for nonexistent products. Since no product could have been purchased, any coupon redemption request constitutes fraud. This approach has been tried a number of times and has led to the successful prosecution of many retailers and coupon thieves.

In addition to fraud, significant funds are lost each year in misredemption errors. With an estimated 150,000 retailers accepting coupons by as many as 350,000 checkout personnel, it is no wonder that errors are routinely made. Mistakes such as accepting outdated coupons or coupons for the wrong items are just two of the most widely seen problems with coupon redemption.

With the introduction of home computer-generated coupons, the potential for fraud entered a new arena. Manufacturers and retailers worry that altered coupons that change the amount or other redemption requirements will become more prevalent with scanning and graphic capabilities common on many computers. The industry is working with bar code technology and other techniques to address the problem. However, regardless of the distribution method, coupon fraud and misredemption remain a problem.

---

[20]Richard Sale, "Not your mother's coupon," *Promo*, April 1999, 56.

SAMPLING

We have emphasized throughout the text that, regardless of the quality of the advertising and promotion, ultimately the product must sell itself. This is the philosophy behind product **sampling.** Sampling is the free distribution of a product to a prospect. In recent years, product sampling has grown significantly and in many cases it has replaced coupons as a manufacturer's primary method of gaining product trial. The total cost of sampling, including products and distribution, is approximately $1.3 billion.

sampling The method of introducing and promoting merchandise by distributing a miniature or full-size trial package of the product free or at a reduced price.

Direct-mail is the most popular method of sample distribution. However, advertisers are increasingly utilizing creative approaches to getting samples in the hand of prospective buyers. One of the significant changes in sampling is the move away from mass distribution campaigns and toward narrowly targeted dissemination. Targeting of prospects allows manufacturers to drastically decrease waste and obtain more accurate results from sampling tests. Some of the growing areas of sampling include the following:

1. *Newspaper distribution.* As newspapers begin to define their delivery areas in smaller geographic areas (e.g., ZIP codes and block units), the medium has gained a share of sampling expenditures. In 1991, Vidal Sassoon shampoo was the first product sampled through newspapers. Since then, numerous businesses and product categories from coffee to salad dressing have used newspapers. In addition to the ability of newspapers to target prospects, many advertisers think they offer a conducive environment for product trials.

2. *Event/venues marketing.* Since events such as rock concerts and sporting events tend to appeal to specific demographic and/or lifestyle segments, they offer ideal venues for sampling. In many cases, venue sampling—suntan lotion at the beach—gives an immediate opportunity for product usage.

3. *In-store sampling.* Usually, in-store sampling is combined with a coupon incentive to encourage immediate purchases of the product. It is rare that a trip to the grocery store doesn't include at least one opportunity to sample some food product and receive a coupon.

4. *In-pack/co-op programs.* On-pack and in-pack distribution is popular when one product has a natural affinity to another. Washing machines often are delivered with a box of detergent, or shaving cream might come with a razor attached. In other cases, a multi-brand manufacturer might want to inexpensively sample a new product by including it with one of its established brands.

5. *Internet sampling.* Many of the same characteristics that offer substantial advantages for Internet coupon distribution apply to sampling over the Internet. In the future, manufacturers will probably make much greater use of the Internet and permission marketing to reach narrowly defined prospects. A major advantage of this approach is that by sending samples only on request, manufacturers drastically decrease waste distribution.

As is the case with any marketing strategy, sampling must be planned with a specific objective in mind. Because of its expense, it is imperative that sampling be conducted only after it is determined that it can add significantly to the promotional mix. Among the most cited reasons for companies using sampling are the following:

- Introducing new products
- Gaining trial for product line extensions
- Building consumer goodwill
- Demonstrating retail merchandising support

Like most marketers, those engaged in sampling are demanding more accountability for their expenditures. At a minimum they are asking:

1. The extent to which the program has reached the intended audience
2. The extent to which the samples were tried and who tried them
3. The level to which the free samples inspired consumer purchase and repeat purchase of the brand[21]

In the past, answers to these questions were either not known or could be determined only at great expense. With a greater knowledge of consumer purchasing behavior combined with targeted distribution, research is able to provide much more reliable information about the role of sampling in gaining consumer trials and, more importantly, establishing long-term consumer preferences for brands.

EVENT MARKETING/PRODUCT LICENSING

What do Tide detergent, Home Depot, Hot Wheels, Coca-Cola, and DuPont have in common? Besides being among the largest and most sophisticated marketers in the world, they are primary sponsors of NASCAR racing teams. Executives at these businesses aren't necessarily racing fans, but they know what sells and racing fans have tremendous loyalty to the brands that sponsor the various cars. ". . . these folks spend freely to support the companies and brands that back their favorite drivers. Slap your logo on a stock-car product and race fans will embrace you. Coke has filled orders for 20,000 new NASCAR-themed vending machines. Visa says it's running to keep up with demand for its new NASCAR affinity cards. Sales of Hot Wheels cars jumped 30% last year after the brand became Kyle Petty's primary sponsor."[22]

One of the oldest types of advertising is the testimonial by which a brand gains from an association with a celebrity through a product endorsement. The idea, of course, is that the star power of famous sports or entertainment figures will rub off on the brand. It is this idea of benefit-by-association that has driven event market and product licensing deals to a multi-billion dollar level.

There are three basic approaches to product association and tie-ins:

event marketing A promotion sponsored in connection with some special event such as a sports contest or musical concert.

1. *Event marketing.* There is hardly a sporting event, musical concert, or art exhibit that does not enjoy some form of corporate sponsorship. From sponsored scoreboards at football stadiums to the Nike swoosh on players' uniforms, every aspect of public events is open to purchase by a business. We have even divided up parts of events for sponsorship. When a relief pitcher comes in from the Atlanta Braves bullpen, he gets a BellSouth call from the manager and each year the outstanding relief pitcher in major league baseball receives the Rolaids Award. The Olympics is among the most high-profile event marketing venues with companies making multi-million dollar investments in return for being named an official sponsor.

   Advertisers understand that sports fans and patrons of the arts are extremely loyal to their special favorites. Sponsors hope that an association with these events will increase brand visibility and foster goodwill for their products. Event marketing is most effective when it involves a long-term relationship that offers advertisers a chance to develop a continuing connection with a loyal audience.

---

[21]"Where marketing starts," a publication of the Promotion Marketing Association/Product Sampling Council, T9.
[22]Roy S. Johnson, "Speed sells," *Fortune*, 12 April 1999, 59.

2. *Staged promotions.* A staged promotional event differs from event marketing in that the sponsor(s) not only sponsors an event, but initiates it. For example, both *Mademoiselle* and *Glamour* magazines have for years sponsored college tours as an extension of the publications' efforts to reach young women and to enhance their image with this prime target market.

   Among the most sponsored events of this type are concerts. Each summer, companies with youth-oriented brands such as Coca-Cola, PepsiCo, and Levi Strauss hit the road with the band du jour for a cross-country tour. These events combine product sampling, couponing, interviews with local media, and in-store publicity to maximize brand identification with the band.

3. *Product licensing.* Related to event marketing is the concept of commercial relationships with movies, television shows, cartoon characters, and so forth to gain recognition for a brand. Examples of licensing agreements cover numerous opportunities. Sometimes it involves product placement in a film. Some of the best-known instances are when BMW introduced its roadster in a James Bond film and when Reeses's Pieces sales spiked after being showcased in *E.T.*, as did sales for Ray-Ban sunglasses when they were seen in Tom Cruise's *Risky Business* and *Top Gun* and later in *Men in Black*.

Movie licensing often involves a marketing tie-in between a fast-food company, a toy manufacturer, or some other children-related item. For example, McDonald's included replicates from *Tarzan* and *A Bug's Life* in its children's meals, while Burger King did likewise with its tie-ins with *Small Soldiers*, *The Rugrats Movie*, and *Teletubbies*. Other examples include J. Crew clothing being featured on television's *Dawson's Creek* and Levi's 12-piece clothing line based on what characters wore in *The Mod Squad* movie.

The biggest beneficiaries of licensing agreements are toy manufacturers. It is estimated that nearly half of toy revenues come from licensed figures. From *Charlie's Angels* to the World Wrestling Federation, action toys have become a core income source for most toy manufacturers. These companies invest millions in these agreements and their success is largely dependent on the popularity of a particular entertainment project. However, hit movies like *Toy Story* can produce millions for both the licensee and the manufacturer for many years to come.

Not all licensing agreements involve entertainment and some involve cross-licensing contracts between two brands. For example, the Lincoln Town Car Cartier model combines two prestige brands and offers a number of cross-promotions. Another example of co-branding involves one brand buying a license from another more well-known brand. Procter & Gamble granted a license to Marine Optical, which allowed them to sell a line of P&G's Cover Girl brand glasses frames.[23]

As you can see from our discussion, the opportunities for event sponsorship and licensing agreements are endless. However, their success depends on a positive connection with a brand's target market. In order to accomplish this goal, it is imperative that the image of the event and that of the product are compatible and that there is a logical relationship between the product and the event.

Virtual Advertising

Throughout the text, we have discussed the changes in advertising and marketing created by the Internet and computer-based technology. Among the most interesting innovations are so-called virtual ads. These are computer-inserted brand messages that are not seen and, in fact, don't exist at the actual event. The San Diego

---

[23]"Evergreen appeal," *Promo*, May 2000, A24.

Padres baseball team started using them in 1997. Today, sponsors such as Home Depot, Toyota, and Pacific Bell are regular advertisers.[24]

In addition to virtual advertising at sporting events and other venues, the technique has been adapted for product placement in movies and television shows. UPN's Series *Seven Days* was the first television series to use virtual placement. Products such as Coca-Cola and Evian were edited into the shows.[25] The long-term marketing adaptations are endless. For example, older network reruns can edit in products that fit current demographics—Oreo cookies in *Leave it to Beaver* reruns. Producers will be able to insert local or regional brands in films and television shows. As you might imagine, purists are not particularly happy about the intrusion of product promotions into entertainment content, but virtual advertising does open interesting possibilities to reach target audiences.

Deals

Deals are a catch-all category of promotional techniques designed to save the customer money. The most common deal is a temporary price reduction or "sale." The cents-off coupon is also a consumer deal because it lowers the price during some limited period. A deal also may involve merchandising. For example, a manufacturer may offer three bars of soap wrapped together and sold at a reduced price. Another deal possibility is attaching a new product to a package of another established product at little or no extra cost—an effective way of new product sampling.

Among the most familiar deals are rebates toward the purchase of a product. Among the most frequent rebates are those for automobiles. Rebates gained popularity during the oil embargo of the early 1970s, but trace their roots to 1914 when Henry Ford offered a rebate of $40–60 toward the purchase of a Model T.[26] Sometimes a deal lets the consumer save money on another product or an additional purchase of the same product. A two-for-one sale offers a free product after the consumer buys the first one. Mail-in rebates are among the most common deals offered by manufacturers.

The down side of offering frequent deals is that a promotion may start off as a temporary incentive and become, to some buyers, an expectation. The automotive rebate is an excellent example of such an expectation. These promotions have worked so well and have become so popular with buyers that many potential car purchasers simply wait for the next rebate plan before purchasing a car that they might have bought for full price without the probability of a rebate. Deals can be extremely effective in building sales at the trade level. Trade deals offered to retailers and wholesalers and others in the trade channel will be discussed later in the chapter as a type of trade incentive.

SWEEPSTAKES AND CONTESTS

The primary goal of most promotions is to gain immediate sales and consumer involvement. A technique often used to accomplish both of these goals are sweepstakes and contests. While the strategies of both are similar, there are significant differences in the two types of promotions. **Sweepstakes** are much more popular than contests and are based solely on chance. **Contests,** on the other hand, must contain some element of skill, for example, writing a jingle or completing a puzzle. Annual expenditures for sweepstakes and contests are approximately $1.5 billion.

sweepstakes A promotion in which prize winners are determined on the basis of chance alone. Not legal if purchaser must risk money to enter.

contest A promotion in which consumers compete for prizes and the winners are selected strictly on the basis of skill.

---

[24]Amanda Beeler, "Virtual ads grab more attention from marketers," *Advertising Age*, 29 May 2000, 93.
[25]Eric Effron, "Ad ventures," *Brill's Content*, June 2000, 50.
[26]"100 years of auto ads," *Advertising Age*, 8 January 1996, S6.

Each year more than 70 percent of American businesses sponsor a game of some kind and it is estimated that almost 30 percent of the population will enter a commercially sponsored contest or sweepstakes. The major marketers of these games are soft drink companies, fast-food franchises, and movie studios. In the last few years, these traditional sponsors have been joined by the dot-com companies looking for new customers. A contest or sweepstakes is an ideal marketing strategy for these companies. They can involve customers with their Web sites at the same time they are entering the game.

Other company Web sites are established specifically for a particular game or contest. "Promotion agencies are finding the number of Web sweepstakes entries are routinely eclipsing the number of mail-in entries for certain promotional campaigns. As a result, the Web site must be seamlessly integrated into the overall sweepstakes campaign [for] marketing efforts, random drawings, and database collection."[27] Some of the more creative Web games incorporate traditional gaming tactics such as scratch-and-win, only they use the mouse to "rub-off" a game piece.

Since contests call for some element of skill, there must be a plan for judging and making certain all legal requirements have been met. The typical contest is much more expensive than a sweepstakes. When millions of entries are anticipated, even the smallest overlooked detail can be a nightmare for the contest sponsor. It is estimated that almost 30 percent of the public enters either a sweepstakes or contest each year. A major contest can place a tremendous burden on a company to properly administer and judge a contest. Most games are handled by outside firms specializing in these promotions.

Another limitation of contests is the time (and skill) required of participants. The majority of consumers are not going to devote the time necessary to complete a contest. Therefore, if the intent of the promotion is to gain maximum interest and participation, a sweepstakes will probably be better suited to the objective. On the other hand, a cleverly devised contest that complements the product and appeals to the skills of prime prospects can be extremely beneficial and encourage greater involvement than a sweepstakes.

The Deceptive Mail Prevention & Enforcement Act

Sweepstakes that require a purchase (known as consideration) by an entrant are considered lotteries and, with the exception of state-sponsored lotteries, are usually illegal. The next time you receive a sweepstakes offer, notice that there is some language indicating that no purchase is necessary to enter. Despite these disclaimers, it has been alleged that a number of people, especially the elderly, have assumed that a purchase would enhance their chances of winning. In some cases, people bought thousands of dollars worth of merchandise as they entered one sweepstakes after another.

In 1999, Congress passed the Deceptive Mail Prevention & Enforcement Act, which addressed a number of these issues. Exhibit 14.4 outlines the basic provisions of the act. Industry criticism of the bill has been directed largely at the provision for a national opt-out list where recipients can remove their name from all sweepstakes solicitations. As one promotion executive commented, "It [the legislation] will have a chilling effect. . . . Some marketers who make occasional use of sweepstakes may not use them. I don't think you will see marketers abandoning sweepstakes, but they may proceed more cautiously."[28]

---

[27]"Net games," *Promo*, May 2000, A34.
[28]Ira Teinowitz, "Marketers yield to sweepstakes curbs," *Advertising Age*, 24 May 1999, 61.

COOPERATIVE ADVERTISING

You will recall in Chapter 10, we briefly discussed co-op advertising in the context of the local/national rate differential. Historically, co-op was initiated primarily as a means of overcoming the significant rate premiums charged national advertisers by newspapers. While that is still a purpose of co-op, it has become a major category of trade promotion with annual expenditures in the $30 billion range. The marketing goals and objectives differ from one manufacturer or retailer to another, but some of the primary purposes of co-op include the following:

1. It benefits retailers by allowing them to stretch their advertising budgets. Most co-op is offered on a 50-percent basis; that is, the national firm pays half of the local advertising costs. However, a number of co-op plans will reimburse retailers at a rate of 100 percent. In other cases, a manufacturer will place some limit on the amount of reimbursement according to a formula based on sales of the product by the retailer. As we will discuss in Chapter 25, federal law requires that regardless of the formula of reimbursement, manufacturers must treat all retailers proportionately the same.

2. National manufacturers build goodwill with retailers, encourage local support of their brands, and, by having the retailer place the advertising, qualify for lower local rates, especially in newspapers. Manufacturers also gain a positive association between local retailers and their products thus enhancing the brand equity among customers of specific retailers. Many co-op advertisements are prepared by national advertisers and require only that retailers add their logo.

3. The media are among the strongest supporters of co-op. Co-op allows current advertisers to place more advertising and at the same time brings new advertisers into the marketplace. Since co-op involves local advertising, it is not surprising that the majority of co-op dollars are spent in newspapers. However, in recent years co-op has reflected the diversity of local media. Currently over 60 percent of co-op budgets are spent in newspapers, followed by direct-mail, television, and radio, each with approximately 10 percent. In the future, we will see significant dollars going into local cable co-op programs and this will increase the share of television co-op.

One of the surprising aspects of co-op advertising are the dollars that are available, but go unspent. It is estimated that as much as one-fourth of co-op dollars go unspent. The primary reasons for the failure to fully use co-op are primarily a result of a lack of knowledge on the part of retailers as to how to use co-op or an unwillingness to meet the restrictions placed on their expenditure by manufacturers.

Special Forms of Co-op

Vendor Programs   A special form of co-op normally used by large retailers is the **vendor program.** The primary difference between vendor programs and other forms of co-op is that they are initiated by retailers. Vendor programs are custom programs designed by retailers (often in cooperation with local media). In vendor programs, manufacturers are approached by retailers to pay all or a share of the program.

vendor program
Special form of co-op advertising in which a retailer designs the program and approaches advertisers for support.

For example, a department store might plan a summer "Beach Party" promotion. The store would then approach manufacturers of swim wear, sunglasses, suntan preparations, and so forth and request funds to support the advertising and promotion of the event. Often manufacturers fund vendor programs from their unspent co-op money.

Ingredient Manufacturer Co-op   Most co-op programs are set up between manufacturers and retailers. However, as discussed in Chapter 2, many companies make ingredients that they sell to other manufacturers for inclusion in finished products. This strategy is called end-product advertising and represents another opportunity for co-op. Often the ingredient manufacturer will contract with finished product manufacturers to co-op with retail outlets or even to co-op in the manufacturer's national advertising to promote the ingredient.

Manufacturer to Wholesaler Co-op   Occasionally, distribution in an industry is dominated by a relatively few wholesale outlets and manufacturers have little direct relationship with retailers. In this situation, it often is more worthwhile for manufacturers to allocate co-op dollars to wholesalers who then make co-op arrangements with individual retailers. Most manufacturers avoid going through wholesalers since they lose both the goodwill and control achieved by direct allocation of co-op dollars by the national company.

CONTROLLING CO-OP DOLLARS

Retailers are paid for advertising when they submit documentation or proof of performance. For print inserts, the validation process involves having newspapers send tear sheets[29] giving the name of the publication and the date an advertisement ran. These advertisements can be matched with the media invoice. For radio and television cooperative ads, proof of performance was once a perennial problem until the Association of National Advertisers, the RAB, and the TvB developed an affidavit of performance that documents in detail the content, cost, and timing of commercials. The adoption of stricter controls in broadcast co-op has been a contributing factor in the growth of co-op dollars for both radio and television. In the near future, CD-ROM technology will probably be commonplace for broadcast co-op verification. Stations will be able to provide manufacturers with the actual on-air commercial and the context in which it ran.

Despite attempts to improve the process, expenditures of co-op dollars still are allocated improperly out of neglect or inexperience by retailers. In a few cases, there is evidence of outright fraud. Co-op fraud usually takes one of two forms. In the first, retailers bill manufacturers for ads that never ran, using fake invoices and

---

[29]The term tear sheet comes from the practice of newspaper ad manager tearing a page from the paper and sending it to a manufacturer.

tear sheets. The second type of fraud, called *double billing*, occurs when manufacturers are overcharged for the cost of advertising. Basically, retailers pay one price to the medium and bill the manufacturer for a higher price by using a phony (double) bill. It should be noted that double billing is regarded as an unethical (in most circumstances illegal) practice, and only a small minority of retailers and media engage in it.

Trade Shows and Exhibits

It is estimated that almost 100 million people will attend more than 5,000 trade and consumer shows this year. Products as diverse as boats and cosmetics will be promoted through these shows. In some cases, a show will be open to both the trade and the public and might be visited by 100,000 prospects. In other cases, the shows are extremely selective and open by invitation only to a few dozen prospects.

Trade shows are one of the best examples of integrated promotion. They combine a number of media and other forms of marketing communication. Trade show sponsorship is almost never used as a stand-alone marketing tool. A trade show can fulfill a number of objectives including product introduction, lead-getting, and direct selling. Research shows that trade shows are most successful for those sponsors with high brand recognition. Specialized trade publications are the most popular form of trade advertising (see Exhibit 14.5). However, trade magazines and other forms of promotion and communication, including e-commerce, work both before and after the show to encourage the final sale.

The higher the level of brand recognition created before a show, the less time sales reps have to spend creating a product image and the more time they can devote to selling. By the same token, trade shows create opportunities for on-site market research as well as follow-ups by personal or on-line selling.

Successful trade shows are strategically planned and customer-oriented. Trade shows are an excellent venue for addressing customer concerns and gaining valuable product feedback from primary users and prospects. "Customers want solutions; and by understanding their problems, needs and wants, you can tailor your program to showcase how your company can meet those needs."[30]

Overall, trade shows are a major component in the marketing strategy of many firms. However, trade shows are normally only one piece in a total marketing program, rather than an end in themselves. Trade shows provide a number of advan-

Exhibit 14.5

What Percentage of Business Marketing Budgets Is Spent on Specialized Business Publications?

Percentage of Business Marketing Budgets

From: *Cahners Advertising Research Report*, No. 510. 1E.

Allocated for:	1999	1996	1993	1991	1989	1988	1987
Specialized Business Publication Advertising	23%	27%	22%	23%	23%	22%	21%
Trade Shows	18%	22%	18%	18%	18%	16%	16%
Direct Mail	10%	10%	11%	12%	12%	9%	8%
Promotion/Market Support	9%	7%	10%	9%	10%	12%	12%
Dealer/Distributor Materials	5%	6%	13%	11%	9%	9%	9%
General Magazine Advertising	6%	6%	2%	5%	6%	7%	8%
Internet/Electronic Media	9%	6%	N/A	N/A	N/A	N/A	N/A
Directories	5%	4%	6%	5%	5%	3%	4%
Telemarketing/Telecommunications	3%	4%	6%	7%	6%	9%	9%
Publicity/Public Relations	7%	5%	5%	5%	7%	7%	7%
Market Research	4%	3%	5%	4%	4%	5%	5%
Other	1%	*	2%	1%	2%	1%	1%

*Less than 0.5%.

---

[30]LaNay Kitzing, "Keep your eyes on the prize," *Trade Show Marketing*, May 2000, 59.

tages for both buyers and sellers. They allow face-to-face selling at a cost much lower than traditional personal sales calls. In addition, trade shows are a self-selecting process with only serious prospects attending. While some sales take place at these exhibits, they are more likely to provide leads for future sales calls or introduce new product lines to prospective customers.

Directories and Yellow Pages

Although often given little attention, one of the most important advertising vehicles for local businesses is the Yellow Pages and other business and consumer directories. Directories are a cost-efficient medium that reaches serious prospects who are in the mood to purchase. It is estimated that there are more than 10,000 directories aimed at both consumers and trade buyers. Since directory advertising is available when the purchase decision is being made, there are few companies that do not include at least some directory advertising in their marketing plans. Many retailers, particularly service businesses such as plumbers, rely on directories as their only type of promotion.

The evolution of the marketplace can be witnessed through Yellow Pages subject headings that trace changes in consumer lifestyles. For instance, the increase in listings for day care centers, elderly care, divorce lawyers, moving companies, and truck rentals indicate a society that is increasingly mobile while we pursue careers and end marriages.[31] Without much thought, we make tremendous use of the Yellow Pages on a daily basis.

Directory advertising has many of the characteristics of the more expensive direct-response media with none of their obtrusiveness. It also offers advertisers a continuing presence and high frequency without continuing advertising expenditures. Specialized directories are a major medium for business-to-business advertising and frequent references sources for business buyers.

Yellow Pages   Since its beginning in New Haven, Connecticut, in 1878, Yellow Pages have become a major advertising medium. Today, it is estimated that more than 19 billion annual references are made to The Yellow Pages with 60 percent of the population referring to them on a weekly basis. Many Yellow Pages directories offer a number of advertising formats from simple one-line listings to four-color ads.

The Yellow Pages Industry   There are two types of Yellow Pages publishers: utility publishers and independent publishers. Utility publishers provide a directory in connection with their telephone service while independent publishers are not associated with a telephone company. In both categories, consumers might be provided with a number of directories from a core directory with general reach throughout the market to foreign language, special interest and age groups, or specialized business directories.

The Yellow Pages industry is not a unified medium. Instead it is comprised of some 250 publishers who produce more than 6,000 separate directories. Annual expenditures for Yellow Pages are almost $13 billion and ranks the medium as a major source of advertising dollars. Approximately 86 percent of these dollars are placed by local advertisers with the remaining 14 percent in the national category, a figure larger than expenditures for all consumer magazines (see Exhibit 14.6). The Yellow Pages are an important complement to other forms of advertising and promotion. In many cases, the medium is the last chance to reach the prospect at the time a purchase decision is being made. In fact, more than half of Yellow Pages

---

[31]John Hess, "Yellow Pages offer insight into trends," *Advertising Age*, 18 November 1996, 38.

Exhibit

14.6

**Total Yellow Pages
Revenues**

Courtesy: Yellow Pages Publishers
Association.

TOTAL YELLOW PAGES REVENUES (BILLIONS $)

Year	Revenue
'80	$2.9
'84	$4.9
'88	$7.8
'92	$9.3
'96	$10.8
'97	$11.5
'98	$12.0
'99	$12.7

users have not made a purchase decision when they turn to the Yellow Pages. More importantly, research shows that 84 percent of Yellow Pages references result in a contact and more than half of those result in a sale.

Consumer usage of the Yellow Pages varies significantly from one product or service category to another. For many business categories, Yellow Pages are a prime source of communication with prospects. For categories such as "Auto Repair," "Attorneys," and "Florists," Yellow Pages are the leading medium used by purchasers. However, in other categories such as "Banks" and "Furniture," Yellow Pages are secondary to traditional advertising (see Exhibit 14.7).

More important than the size of the Yellow Pages audience is the quality. Research shows that heaviest users of Yellow Pages are concentrated among higher income and educational groups. More importantly, since Yellow Pages users are already in the market for the products and services advertised, this finding is of particular significance. Yellow Pages are rarely intended to work alone. Rather than a competitor to traditional advertising media, Yellow Pages are *designed* to increase the effectiveness of other advertising vehicles. Research shows that by combining Yellow Pages with other media, the proportion of purchasers influenced increases significantly compared to using these media alone. It also is true that the stronger the brand equity and awareness of a product, the more likely the customer will associate the Yellow Pages listing with positive images of the product.

Yellow Pages and New Technology   Like most promotion and advertising, the Yellow Pages face the potential of new technology as both a complement and competitor to traditional Yellow Pages. For example, we are starting to see more and more directory advertising that includes a Web address so that customers can obtain detailed information that would be impractical to include in a directory listing. On the other hand, the Web presents a competitor if it is used instead of Yellow Pages and other directories. For some time publishers have made available

Exhibit

14.7

**Percentage of Consumers
Using Media in Purchase**

Source: Mediamark Research (MRI).

Courtesy: Yellow Pages Publishers
Association.

Category/Heading	Yellow Pages	Newspaper	Television	Radio
Auto Body Repair or Painting	32%	16%	5%	3%
Attorney/Lawyer	36	5	4	1
Florists	37	12	4	3
Building/General Contractor	38	16	3	1
Rental Services	44	18	9	2
Banks	13	16	8	5
Furniture	11	49	18	8
Sporting Goods	14	46	13	7

Internet-based Electronic Yellow Pages, which provide information such as directions to a business, restaurant menus, and even the capability of making on-line reservations. In addition, these electronic directories provide businesses with the option of making copy changes and promoting specific merchandise on a seasonal basis.

In a number of locations, customers have access to interactive voice services called "audiotex." Telephone numbers included in directory listings allow callers to access prerecorded information about a specific business. Sometimes, audiotex services provide information such as local weather reports or information about upcoming civic events. These services are usually free to callers and sponsored by local businesses. Both on-line and audiotex services provide similar advantages to both customers and advertisers and they show the way in which new technology is continuing to change the advertising and promotion environment. In the near future, we will see more integration of directory advertising and on-line services.

Trade Incentives

While the average consumer is not familiar with trade promotion, businesses will spend some $25 billion in promotions to reach wholesalers, retailers, and company sales personnel. These promotions are referred to as sales incentives or simply **incentives.** Incentives include everything from cash bonuses to travel, with various types of merchandise (clothing leads the list) being the most popular type of incentive.

Sales promotions directed to the trade channel are called incentives. There are two types of incentives: *dealer incentives*, which are directed to retailers and wholesalers; and *sales incentives*, which are directed to a company's sales force. Almost 80 percent of incentives are offered to direct salespeople. The most common incentives to wholesalers or retailers are price reductions in the form of promotional allowances. In effect, these incentives are comparable to cents-off promotions at the consumer level. In addition, sweepstakes, contests, and continuity promotions (some with prize catalogs) based on sales volume are all used at the trade level.

Regardless of the type of incentive used, primary objectives are to motivate either members of the distribution channel or company reps to achieve higher sales and profitability. Exhibit 14.8 demonstrates the importance of sales as an incentive goal. In addition, most of the other objectives on the list are also intended to achieve an increase in sales.

Dealer and trade incentives are becoming more and more crucial as retailers take greater control of the distribution channel. Most dealers have the option of selling a number of brands from different manufacturers. Manufacturers have to compete for retail distribution and, once achieved, for dealer support for their

incentives Sales promotion directed at wholesalers, retailers, or a company's salesforce.

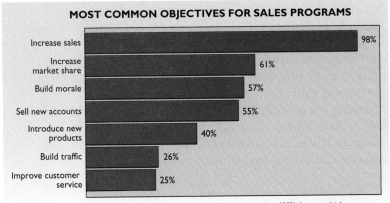

MOST COMMON OBJECTIVES FOR SALES PROGRAMS

Increase sales	98%
Increase market share	61%
Build morale	57%
Sell new accounts	55%
Introduce new products	40%
Build traffic	26%
Improve customer service	25%

Figure adds up to more than 100% due to multiple responses.

Exhibit

14.8

Most Common Objectives for Sales Programs

From: Incentive, April 2000, 29.

brand (e.g., premium shelf space, co-op advertising agreements, and in-store recommendations to customers). As one incentive consultant pointed out, the relationship between a manufacturer and a dealer is similar to that of a tenant and a landlord. "The dealer actually owns the distribution channel. The manufacturer is really just a tenant in the channel. Just like anything else in life, the power lies with the owner."[32]

The key to successful incentive programs is to have them complement overall business strategy. The goals that the incentive program are intended to address should be very specific. For example, a company may use incentives to gain support for a new product line, to motivate salespersons to increase sales to current retailers, or to expand distribution to new retailers or in new territories.

There is no question that trade incentives can be extremely effective in increasing sales, productivity, and morale. However, increasingly regulatory agencies are questioning the ethics of some trade incentives that do not provide full disclosure to customers. For example, in a retail store consumers may seek objective information from a salesperson about one brand over another. How objective can retailers be if they are receiving significant rewards for promoting a particular brand? Currently, there is no effective system of providing consumer disclosure for trade incentives. However, as competition in many industries grows more intense and the financial value of incentives increase, we may see both state and federal regulators take a new look at the entire system of trade incentives.

SUMMARY

It is clear that distinctions between the various elements of marketing communication are becoming less clear and less important to both marketers and their customers. Businesses are increasingly demanding accountability for the dollars invested in promotion. Whether a customer is reached through traditional media, e-commerce, or one-to-one selling is less important than the contribution to profits that these elements contribute.

Another notable change in recent years in sales promotion is the concept that promotion, like advertising, must contribute to brand image and brand equity. Astute marketers reject the idea that sales promotion is intended only for a quick fix, immediate sale at any cost. Today, promotion and advertising have a complementary relationship that works to develop a seamless relationship with consumers. Not only must advertising and promotion be coordinated, but it also is crucial that promotion is used in a manner that will enhance, rather than erode, brand equity.

In addition to consumer sales promotion, companies normally use some combination of trade and retail promotions to carry out overall marketing objectives. In fact, by far the largest segment of marketing communication involves trade promotions. To a significant degree, the increase in trade promotions reflects the growth of large retail chains that require national manufacturers to compete for shelf space and divert funds from promotions and advertising that encourage consumer loyalty. The consequence of this emphasis on trade promotion is an erosion of brand equity in some product categories and an emphasis on price as the primary factor in consumer purchases.

Finally, we are only beginning to see the impact of the Internet on sales promotion. Technological convergence has created new ways to reach and cultivate prospects. It also has created concerns about privacy, the practicality of permission marketing, and how to deal with growing trends toward consumer opt-out pro-

[32]Paul Nolan and Vincent Alonzo, "Making the mark," *Incentive*, August 1999, 30.

grams. We may not be able to predict the twists and turns of new and old media, but as we see the growth in on-line couponing, sweepstakes and games accessed through the computer, and electronic versions of the Yellow Pages, it is certain that advertising and promotion will never be the same.

REVIEW

1. Contrast sales promotion and advertising.
2. What is the primary disadvantage of sales promotion?
3. What is the difference between premiums and specialties?
4. What are the major advantages and disadvantages of event marketing?
5. What are the primary purposes of co-op advertising?
6. What is the primary regulation of co-op?
7. Why is point-of-purchase so important to many advertisers?

TAKE IT TO THE NET

We invite you to visit the Russell/Lane page on the Prentice Hall Web site at **www.prenhall.com/myphlip** for end-of-chapter exercises and applications.

PART V

Creating the Advertising

Chapter 15

Research in Advertising

Advertisers need to understand what motivates consumers in the marketplace. Research helps them accomplish that. Research is a critical informational tool that can help the advertiser understand how consumers react to their messages. After reading this chapter you will understand:

>> how advertisers use research

>> the role of the account planner

>> anthropology, sociology, and psychology, in relation to advertising

>> values and lifestyle and life-stage research

>> research steps in advertising

>> types of advertising research

As we discussed in earlier chapters, there are many questions to be answered. What consumer need does my product or service satisfy? How does it satisfy differently and better than competitors? How can I reach consumers? Here, we look at various types of research available—product, market, consumer, advertising strategy, and message research—to answer the advertiser's questions. We also examine ways to judge whether an ad will communicate effectively before we spend the money to run it in the media.

You cannot build strong campaigns without knowing the motivations, attitudes, and perceptions behind consumers' choices. The failure for not understanding the consumer may be failure for the product or service. Remember Howard Johnson's restaurants—with their orange roofs, they dominated the restaurant business for about 20 years. In fact, in the mid-1960s, their sales were more than McDonald's, Burger King, and KFC combined. But what about Howard Johnson's restaurants today? If it were so easy to be successful, new products wouldn't have such a high failure rate, and established brands might not get into trouble. Advertisers would simply plug in the magic formulas. But there are no formulas to guarantee success. Was the failure of the many upstart dot.coms a lack of money, or strategy, or understanding of how consumers used (or would use) the Internet? Or, was it so new that even consumers didn't understand it? Did their pioneering advertising not work?

Think about how you buy products or services. Why do you choose your toothpaste or laundry brand? Why do you buy the products you put in your shopping cart—either in the store or on-line? Was it the brand? Was it the price? Quality? Package? Do you really know? It is not always rational. It is like asking someone, "Why did you fall in love with him?" They likely would respond, "I just did." Could you explain your reasons for your preferences to a marketing researcher? Use the same thought pattern to items you buy at the supermarket or drugstore. For that matter, why do you choose the supermarket where you usually shop? Location? Image? Prices? Service? Fresh vegetables? Chances are you may consider as many as three options. Those options make up your *competitive set*. These brands immediately come to mind when you think about buying a product or service. How did they get to be the top-of-mind brands in your brain? Marketing guru, Sergio Zyman, says, "In marketing, understanding the why is the crucial step, because when you understand *why*, it's a lot easier to figure out *how* to produce and *what* that you want."[1]

What kind of advertising motivates you to buy something? As a marketer, how do I reach you? What was the last ad that made you go out and buy anything? And what message do we take away from viewing, hearing, or reading an ad message? (see Exhibit 15.1)

RESEARCH IS AN INFORMATIONAL TOOL

Research is and should be used to help improve an advertiser's effectiveness and profitability by staying in touch with the consumer. More specifically, research is used most often in the following ways:

■ to help identify consumers

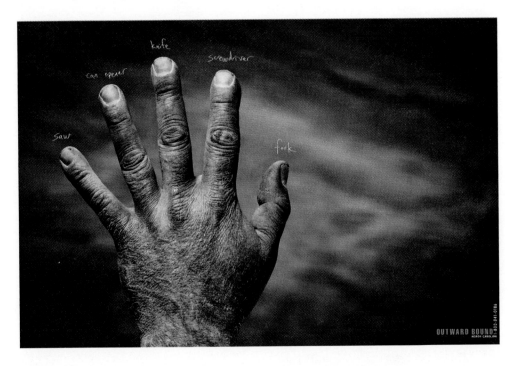

Sergio Zyman, The End of Marketing As We Know It (New York: HarperCollins, 1999), 62.

Exhibit 15.1

What a great visual and related head. What is your take away of the message?
Courtesy: North Carolina Outward Bound.

- to help look for new ideas in products or services
- to help improve what is offered in product or services
- to help pinpoint causes of special problems
- to monitor activities
- to help in communications development
- to study promotional tools

THE RIGHT KIND OF RESEARCH

What kind of research and how much research are always legitimate questions. And there are dangers. Former chairman of Roper Starch Worldwide's Roper division commented on a classic failure—Ford's Edsel—and the misuse of research. In the case of the Edsel automobile, the research was used to make people believe something that wasn't true, not to design a product to meet consumers' tastes. Ford designed a powerful, flashy car with a horse-collar grille before doing any consumer research. After the car was designed, research found consumers wanted a quietly styled, conservative, American-made, Mercedes-Benz–like vehicle. Ford then tried to make consumers fit the car by marketing Edsel as a conservatively styled automobile. It generated interest, but when consumers saw the car they were disappointed.

On the other hand, Roper cited new Coke as an example of research overkill and overreliance. In several taste tests, new Coke beat Pepsi. But other studies have shown that sweeter products often are preferred initially. In-house and outside research for Coca-Cola failed because it didn't run normal usage taste tests on consumers. If Coke had given consumers a case of new Coke and came back in two or three weeks and asked them what they thought, a more accurate response would have been generated. Roper's conclusions are that people shouldn't always follow the findings of a research study, whether it be a consumer products study or a political campaign. There are dangers as well as potential rewards.

PUBLIC ATTITUDE TOWARD SURVEY RESEARCH

Research on research shows that although refusals to cooperate in survey research are on the rise, respondents believe that research surveys serve a useful purpose. The Council for Marketing and Opinion Research (CMOR) Respondent Cooperative Study clearly shows that respondents think surveys provide an opportunity for feedback on products and services. In four years the refusal rate increased by 5 percent. Some 37 percent of the CMOR survey indicated that they had refused to participate in at least one study during the past year. The study confirmed that shorter interviews are better and that incentives possibly help. Eighty percent of those who were given an incentive said they would be willing to participate again, compared with 70 percent who received no incentive. Disclosing the length of the survey up front actually hurts and has no effect on future willingness to participate.

According to CMOR, 80 percent reported receiving telemarketing calls in the past year, which competes for time with research calls. One study found an average of 28.3 telemarketing calls and 4.2 marketing calls per year. Some 56 percent said they screen calls on answering machines because they get too many telemarketing calls, and another 36 percent screen because they get too many market research calls. Refusal rates are higher among African Americans and Hispanics.[2]

---

[2]"Public Believes Research Is Useful," The Frame, a publication of Survey Sampling, Inc., June 1996.

ADVANCED ANALYTICS

Some researchers can now study the impact of advertising by directly measuring sales tied to each available element of the marketing mix through what is called advanced analytics, a mathematical modeling system. Joe Plummer, noted researcher at McCann-Erickson, says, "With larger data sets and analytic software, the modeling can deliver." Advanced analytics isn't new; its principle began with retail scanner data. Advances in computer technology and software now allow researchers to manipulate large amounts of data, and they have refined the modeling and research process. "It will definitely change the way we do business," says Lewis Cashman, vice president of global research at Campbell Soup Co. "We have more insight into how our dollars are being spent."

At present, only a small portion of advertisers is measured this way. Advanced analytics isn't considered a breakthrough, but its use is expanding among research firms, clients, and agencies. The 1980s saw dollars shift from advertising to promotions. In the companies that use advanced analytics, and use it well, the emphasis on advertising is much stronger than it has been in years, according to Simon Dratfield, ASI Market Research.

STRATEGIC OR ACCOUNT PLANNERS

A British concept of research has become fundamental for many worldwide agencies. In the 1980s, some U.S. agencies moved toward copying the British restructuring of the research department. British agencies found clients doing much of their own research, yet the agency research function remained necessary to understand the information on consumers and the marketplace. The agencies restructured their research departments by adding **account planners,** sometimes called strategic or marketing planners. Their task was to discern not just who buys specific brands but why. The account planners are usually responsible for all research including quantitative research (usage and attitude studies, tracking studies, ad testing, and sales data) as well as quantitative research (talking face-to-face to their targets).

Account planning is based on a simple premise. A client hires an advertising agency to interpret its brand to its target audience. The account planner is charged with understanding the target audience and then representing it throughout the entire advertising development process, thereby ensuring that the advertising is both strategically and executionally relevant to the defined target. Planners provide insight and clarity that move discussion from I think to I know. It sorts through the multilayers that develop around marketing a brand, eliminating the irrelevant and highlighting the relevant. It is more productive and more focused than traditional research, according to Jane Newman, partner of Merkley Newman Harty.[3]

Jon Steel says, "If the agency has a true planning philosophy, it is interested in only one thing, and that is getting it right for its clients."[4] Account planning has a crucial role during strategy development, driving it from the consumer's point of view. During creative development, account planners act as sounding boards for the creative team. They are responsible for researching the advertising before production to make sure it is as relevant as it can be, and finally, once the work runs, they monitor its effect in depth with a view to improving it the next time around.

The key benefit to the creative teams is usable research—someone who explains and communicates, giving them useful insights.

account planner An outgrowth of British agency structure where a planner initiates and reviews research and participates in the creative process. In some agencies, the planner is considered a spokesperson for the consumer.

---

[3]Jane Newman, "What Is the Client Relationship to Account Planning?" Essays on Account Planning, World Wide Web (www.apgus.org/2_2a.html), 1997.
[4]Jon Steel, *Truth Lies & Advertising* (New York: John Wiley & Sons, 1998), 43.

Because many marketers direct much of the needed research themselves, the agency is not necessarily a partner in planning the type and direction of research studies conducted for a specific brand or company, but the agency researchers or planners are available to the account groups to help them get the needed information and may be involved in all kinds of advertising research.

The planner works with both account management and creative, covering most research functions. The planner is more a partner to the account team than a traditional researcher, who would basically supply information. The planner is considered the team's spokesperson for the consumer and an interpreter of available research (see Exhibit 15.2). To work, advertising must deeply understand, empathize with, and speak the same language as the consumer.

AGENCY FUTURIST DEPARTMENTS VERSUS ACCOUNT PLANNERS

Clients are saying to agencies, "Tell me something I don't already know." More than ever before marketers want to know what comes next in trends, consumers, the market, and so forth. As a result many agencies are hiring futurists to help them think out of the box and bring a new perspective to marketing. Young & Rubicam recently launched its Brand Futures Group as the Intelligence Factory with its horizon-gazing services for clients. GSD&M established its Futures Lab to help clients with "brand visioning, repositioning and future mapping." OgilvyOne has a director of scenario planning as its internal forecaster. Saatchi & Saatchi has a director of knowledge management as its visionary. DDW Worldwide employs a cultural anthropologist as its resident prognosticator. The boom in forecasting has several antecedents, but experts agree that one overriding force has been today's fast-paced environment.

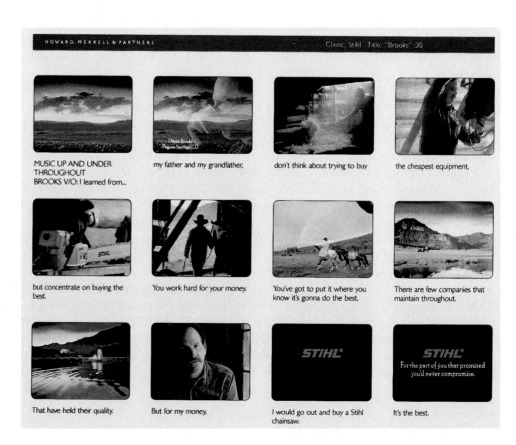

Exhibit

15.2

The planner's job is to understand how consumers view a product and the context of the message. Here buying the best equipment is a crucial theme.

Courtesy: Howard, Merrell & Partners.

A futurist function at the agency appears similar to that of an account planner. Faith Popcorn, author of EVEolution, says, "Unfortunately, strategic planners don't do enough looking forward."[5]

WHAT KIND OF RESEARCH IS NEEDED?

Now that we have a better understanding of the research structure, let us look at the kinds of research available and some specific examples. Keep in mind that marketing has become far more complex than in the past because of the tremendous increase in new products, the high cost of shelf space, the expansion of retailer control over the distribution system, changing media habits, overload of information, and the bewildering array of communication choices.

Marketing research—up-front research—tells us about the product, the market, the consumer, and the competition. There are four basic considerations in any market research undertaking: (1) maintaining a consumer-behavior perspective, (2) being sure the right questions are being asked, (3) using appropriate research techniques and controls, and (4) presenting the research findings in a clear, comprehensible format that leads to action. After completing market research, we do advertising research—principally pretesting of ads and campaign evaluation—to get the data we need to develop and refine an advertising strategy and message.

The behavioral sciences—anthropology, sociology, and psychology—have had a strong influence on up-front research.

Anthropology and Advertising

Today, marketers employ anthropologists who use direct observation to understand consumer behavior. They study the emotional connection between products and consumer values. When Warner-Lambert wanted to find out what consumers thought of Fresh Burst Listerine, a mint-flavored product designed to compete with Scope, they paid families to set up cameras in their bathrooms and film their routines around the sink. Users of both brands said they used mouthwash to make their breath smell good, but they treated their products differently. Users of Scope typically swished and spat it out. Devotees of the new Listerine felt obliged to keep the mouthwash in their mouths longer; one went so far as to keep it in his mouth until he got to his car.

Ogilvy & Mather's Discovery Group also uses cameras. They send researchers into homes with hand-held cameras to get an up-close picture of how people live various aspects of their lives. Hours of footage then are condensed into a documentary-like 30-minute video that gives marketers and agency staff the chance to see how people really communicate and interact in certain situations. The videos may give marketers a clearer sense of how people use their products and their motivation, which can influence marketing decisions and help craft creative strategy.[6]

Whirlpool appliances enlisted an anthropologist to tap into consumer's feelings about, and interactions with, their appliances. They visited people's homes to observe how they used their appliances and talked to all the household members. Usage patterns and behavior emerged that helped Whirlpool gain insight into the flow of household activities and how tasks got accomplished. For instance, after finding that in busy families women aren't the only ones doing the laundry, Whirlpool came up with color-coded laundry controls that children and husbands can understand.[7]

---

[5]Laura Petrecca, "The oracle workers," *Advertising Age*, 12 June 2000, 20.
[6]David Goetzl, "O&M turns reality TV into research tool," *Advertising Age*, 10 July 2000, 6.
[7]Tobi Elkin, "Product Pampering," *BrandWeek*, 16 June 1997, 28–40.

Anthropologists have found that certain needs and activities are common to people the world over. Bodily adornment, cooking, courtship, food taboos, gift giving, language, marriage, status, sex, and superstition are present in all societies, although each society attaches its own values and traditions to them. Anthropologists see the United States as a pluralistic society made up of an array of subcultures. In each subculture lives a different group of people who share its values, customs, and traditions. Think about the cultural differences among Italians, Poles, African Americans, and Hispanics, as a starting point.

We are all aware of regional differences in the American language. For example, a sandwich made of several ingredients in a small loaf of bread is a "poor boy" in New Orleans, a "submarine" in Boston, a "hoagie" in Philadelphia, and a "grinder" in upstate New York. Geomarketing allows advertisers to use these cultural differences in food preferences, terminology, and subgroup identities when they advertise their products.

Sociology and Advertising

Sociology examines the structure and function of organized behavior systems. The sociologist studies groups and their influence on, and interaction with, the individual. Advertisers recognize group influences on the adoption of new ideas, media use, and consumer purchase behavior. They use sociological research to predict the profitability of a product purchase by various consumer groups.

Social Class and Stratification   We are a society that is clustered into classes determined by such criteria as wealth, income, occupation, education, achievement, and seniority. We sense where we fit into this pattern. We identify with others in our class ("these are my kind of people"), and we generally conform to the standards of our class. Experienced advertisers have recognized that people's aspirations usually take on the flavor of the social class immediately above their own.

Social-class structure helps explain why demographic categories sometimes fail to provide helpful information about consumers. A professional person and a factory worker may have the same income, but that doesn't mean their interests in products will coincide. In today's marketing environment, research has shown that no single variable, such as age, income, or sex, will accurately predict consumer purchases. We have discovered that using several variables gives a more accurate prediction of consumer behavior. Think of the differences between homemakers and working women of the same age, income, and education in their food preferences for themselves and their families, usage of convenience goods, child care, and media habits.

Trend Watching   Quantitative research is as important as ever, but there seems to be a new premium on nuggets of more attitudinal, psychographic market smarts with which marketers hope to base the creative approach to their communication.

Trends come from all forms of media and advertising. They come from music, from politics, from travel, and from the Internet. They develop everywhere. Fads, on the other hand, are like crushes; they burn fast and hot, but die quickly and often leave a bitter taste. The macarena and platform shoes came and went quickly. Trends are a product of society. They reflect our changing attitudes, behaviors, and values. They are the most obvious and most concrete signs of the times. Trends can be two sizes: macro and micro.

Macro trends are about the "big issues"—our definitions of happiness, success, fulfillment. Macro trends come from the way people think. They emerge when people feel a dissatisfaction with the status quo, in their own lives and in society. They announce our new definitions of happiness. Some of the neotraditionalism is reflected in the return to traditions—people setting new priorities in the balance among work, family, and friends.

Micro trends are the detail in the bigger picture. They are the tangible manifestations of the macro trends in fashion, music, and sports activities. For example, the macro trend of neotraditionalism will foster micro trends such as cooking schools cropping up as the microwave generation tries to behave like their grandparents and throw dinner parties. In 2001, retro nostalgia was big. Chrysler's PT Cruiser became Motor Trend's Car of the Year replacing the Lincoln LS.

Generally, young people set trends, but not every young person is a trendsetter. Those most comfortable on the cutting edge are the ones called early adopters, alphas, trendsetters, leading edgers, innovators—all these terms mean the same thing. These are the people who are willing to experiment. Not all trends will work for a brand. Yet, look at what Mountain Dew did by using extreme sports and over-the-top imagery to become the extreme brand despite being around for over 30 years. Many companies spend much money trying to track trends. Coffeehouses and teahouses—are they fads or trends?

Cohort Analysis   Using a research technique called cohort analysis, marketers can access consumers' lifelong values and preferences, and develop strategies now for products they will use later in life. Cohorts are generations of people with the same birth years and core values. According to Natalie Perkins of Trone Advertising, these values are formed by significant events between the ages of 13 and 20 and endure throughout one's life. For example, such events as the Great Depression, the Korean War, McCarthyism, the Vietnam War, the sexual revolution, and the Gulf War, or the influence of Martin Luther King, television, computers, divorced and single families, and environmental crisis can form a value system.

Generally, we study consumers using demographics, psychographics, lifestyles, and behaviors. Cohort analysis combines these data and adds to the consumer profile by examining the past as well as the present. Four cohort groups exist: traditionalists, transitioners, challengers, and space-agers. Each group is unique, evolving, and maturing. The following is an example of challengers: In their thirties and forties, many challengers are in unconventional households: single parents, working women. They have high incomes, high debt, and have started later than their cohorts before them to raise a family. They idolize youth but are becoming middle-aged, and they don't like it. Highly educated, they are concerned about retirement but are financially unable to plan for it. They are obsessed with reducing stress and guilt. They still believe in having it all. They seek information before they buy. They are caught between reality and their black-and-white morality and have difficulty dealing with the world of gray. They are still concerned with what others think, but they haven't abandoned the self-indulgent lifestyle.

By identifying a generation's collective hot buttons, mores, and memories, advertisers can hone messages and create persuasive icons to better attract them.[8] This kind of research can aid in developing a product marketing plan that follows the lifetime of a consumer.

Life-Stage Research   Advertisers have traditionally considered the family as the basic unit of buying behavior. Most traditional households pass through an orderly progression of stages, and each stage has special significance for buying behavior.

Knowledge of the **family life cycle** allows a company to segment the market and the advertising appeal according to specific consumption patterns and groups. Of course, the concept of the family has significantly changed over the past decades. Yet there are still crucial points in the lives of consumers—they leave

family life cycle Concept that demonstrates changing purchasing behavior as a person or a family matures.

---

[8]Natalie Perkins, "Zeroing in on consumer values," *Advertising Age,* 22 March 1993, 23.

home, get married or stay unmarried, bear children, raise children, and send adult children into lives of their own. As a result of these life transitions, people suddenly or gradually go from one stage of life to another.

According to census data, the nature of the traditional family life cycle has changed in the past 30 years. For example, people are waiting longer to get married, women are postponing childbearing, the incidence of divorce has almost tripled, the proportion of single-parent households has significantly increased, and more young adults are living with their parents than in the past. As a result, some advertisers have reevaluated the way they look at the family life cycle. By examining these segments' subgroups, advertisers begin to get a clearer picture of buying behavior and lifestyles. Researchers refer to these subgroup studies as life-stage research. As with the family life cycle, life-stage research looks at the crucial points in consumers' lives. Advertisers can find syndicated research services that analyze young singles, newlyweds, young couples, mature couples, and teenage households. As we approach the millennium, advertisers need knowledge of the life stages to help them develop and understand the changes taking place so they can create more effective integrated marketing communications.

Psychology and Advertising

Psychology is the study of human behavior and its causes. Three psychological concepts of importance to consumer behavior are motivation, cognition, and learning. Motivation refers to the drives, urges, wishes, or desires that initiate the sequence of events known as "behavior." Cognition is the area in which all the mental phenomena (perception, memory, judging, thinking, and so on) are grouped. Learning refers to those changes in behavior relative to external stimulus conditions that occur over time.[9] These three factors, working within the framework of the societal environment, create the psychological basis for consumer behavior. Advertising research is interested in cognitive elements to learn how consumers react to different stimuli, and research finds learning especially important in determining factors such as advertising frequency. However, in recent years, the major application of psychology to advertising has been the attempt to understand the underlying motives that initiate consumer behavior.

Values and Lifestyles   The research company that popularized the lifestyle approach to psychographic segmentation developed Values and Life Style (VALS 2). SRI International's VALS 2 is designed to predict consumer behavior by profiling attitudes of American consumers. It segments respondents into eight clusters of consumers, each with distinct behavioral and decision-making patterns that reflect different self-orientations and available psychological and material resources (see Exhibit 15.3).

VALS classifies consumers along two key dimensions: self-orientation—the fundamental human need to define a social self-image and create a world in which it can thrive—and resources—the range of psychological and material resources available to sustain that self-concept.

This concept takes into account personal or psychological orientations such as principle, status, and action. Consumers with the principle orientation look inside themselves to make choices, rather than to physical experience or social pressure. Those with status orientation make choices in relation to the anticipated reactions and concerns of others in the group to which they belong or aspire to belong. Action-oriented consumers base their choices on consideration related to activity. They value feelings only when they result from action.

---

[9]James A. Bayton, "Motivation, cognition, learning—Basic factors in consumer behavior," *Journal of Marketing*, January 1958, 282.

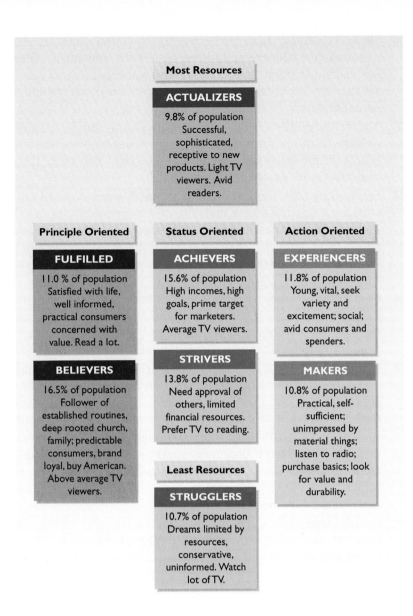

Most Resources

ACTUALIZERS

9.8% of population Successful, sophisticated, receptive to new products. Light TV viewers. Avid readers.

Principle Oriented

FULFILLED

11.0 % of population Satisfied with life, well informed, practical consumers concerned with value. Read a lot.

BELIEVERS

16.5% of population Follower of established routines, deep rooted church, family; predictable consumers, brand loyal, buy American. Above average TV viewers.

Status Oriented

ACHIEVERS

15.6% of population High incomes, high goals, prime target for marketers. Average TV viewers.

STRIVERS

13.8% of population Need approval of others, limited financial resources. Prefer TV to reading.

Least Resources

STRUGGLERS

10.7% of population Dreams limited by resources, conservative, uninformed. Watch lot of TV.

Action Oriented

EXPERIENCERS

11.8% of population Young, vital, seek variety and excitement; social; avid consumers and spenders.

MAKERS

10.8% of population Practical, self-sufficient; unimpressed by material things; listen to radio; purchase basics; look for value and durability.

Exhibit

15.3

VALS 2 American Lifestyle Categories

Source: Compiled from data from SRI International, Menlo Park, California.

Resources, on the other hand, include both material and acquired attributes (e.g., money, position, education) and psychological qualities (e.g., inventiveness, interpersonal skills, intelligence, energy).

According to VALS, an individual purchases certain products and services because he or she is a specific type of person. The purchase is related to lifestyle, which in turn is a function of self-orientation and available resources. VALS is a network of interconnected segments. Neighboring types have similar characteristics and can be combined in varying ways to suit particular marketing purposes.

Advertisers can use the VALS typology to segment particular markets, develop marketing strategies, refine product concepts, position products and services, develop advertising and media campaigns, and guide long-range planning.

In the targeting chapter, Yankelovich's Mindbase was mentioned as a segmenting tool. They identified eight major consumer groups with shared life attitudes and motivations. These eight groups were further divided into 32 distinct subsegments for greater differentiation and clarification. Here is a brief summary of the eight major Mindbase segments.[10]

---

[10]David J. Lipke, "Head trips," *American Demographics*, October 2000, 38–39.

- **Up and Comers.** These are Generation X, young single, no children with average incomes, who are ambitious, optimistic, and social. They think of themselves as intelligent and creative and are receptive to new technology, not neighborly or old-fashioned. Ideal targets for products and services offering something new.

- **Young Materialists.** Gen Xers who are young, single, with no children; have average incomes, primarily males, who believe money and success equal happiness. Prime targets for products and services that make them feel important and successful, as well as fun and stylish.

- **Stressed by Life.** These Gen Xers, primarily women, often unmarried, parents with lower incomes have a strong desire for novelty to help escape stress of daily life. Enjoy spending time with family and friends, watching movies and games. They think of themselves as family-oriented, but not practical or old-fashioned. Good targets for products or services that reduce stress and escape from reality.

- **New Traditionalists.** Married Boomers, with high incomes but reduced levels of materialism. They are conservative, family- and community-oriented. Perceive themselves as neighborly, old-fashioned, and responsible. Excellent target for products/services that help them maintain control of their well-ordered lives.

- **Family Limited.** These Boomers are married with children, have high incomes, and an intense focus on family life. This impedes their social and community consciousness and they become cynical. They aren't into technology and are disinterested in style. Self-perception is noncreative, not ambitious or adventurous. They respond to messages with family focus, in family programming.

- **Detached Introverts.** Boomers, usually male, with no children, with average incomes, inactive, not social, are not concerned with style. Not socially conscious, self-focussed, spiritual, nor self-confident, but somewhat cynical. They are considered a less desirable target.

- **Renaissance Elders.** These are older, active, with average but comfortable incomes for whom family and community are important. They are socially conscious and old-fashioned, who are spiritual, self-confident, open to new technology and outside interest. Ideal target for products and services that help them maintain their health, financial security, and family ties.

- **Retired from Life.** Older, highly cynical, not concerned about style or material goods. They think of themselves as neighborly and old-fashioned, but not intelligent, creative, or spiritual. Enjoy game shows and gardening. Hold little appeal as a target.

Personal Drive Analysis

personal drive analysis (PDA) A technique used to uncover a consumer's individual psychological drives.

BBDO has used the **personal drive analysis** (PDA) technique to uncover a consumer's individual psychological drives toward indulgence, ambition, or individuality, which play a role in his or her brand choices. BBDO found that people are often attracted to brands because of their psychological reward. It is important for marketers to identify this reward if they are to understand the equity of their brands and successfully sell their products. When the agency applied PDA to athletic shoes, Nike emerged as the brand a person would buy if motivated by such drives as status or winning. Reebok was the brand for those who desired comfort and stability. Results indicated that Reebok represents the athletic shoe you can count on; Nike represents the athlete you want to be.[11]

---

[11]Cyndee Miller, "Spaghetti sauce preference based on whether you're in the mood for love," *Marketing News,* 31 August 1992, 5.

Value Segments of Global Youth

"Global youth are notorious for challenging norms and defying labels, teenagers can be identified, marketed to and reached," argues Elissa Moses, senior vice president of global consumer for Royal Philips Electronics.[12] After studying 27,000 teenagers in 44 countries, Moses gives insights into what motivates them in life and what drives their decisions in the marketplace. One of the findings from the New World Teen Study is the existence of six distinct value segments for global youth. Of course, you must remember that marketers cannot assume teens are alike worldwide, except for the common cultural unifiers. Moreover, within a specific country, teens are not homogeneous. Within countries their preferences depend largely on their classification within six value segments:

- **Thrills and Chills** (18%). Driving principles: *fun, excitement, irreverence, and friends*. They expect everything in life and make it a goal to get as much of the good times as they can. They have ample money and like to spend it. They develop loyalties to brands that speak their language. They are constantly seeking the new, and experimenting is second nature. They are the popular kids in high school, the trendsetters that the other kids try to copy. They reside mostly in Europe: Germany, England, Lithuania, Greece, Netherlands, South Africa, United States, Belgium, and Canada.

- **Resigned** (14%). Driving principles: *fun, friends, low expectations*. There are huge numbers of teens in this segment. They do not have as much discretionary income as teens in other segments. They are drawn to advertising using irony and ads making fun of the pompousness of society. They tend to be cynical about overly happy communications that portray an optimistic world. They reside mostly in Denmark, Sweden, Korea, Japan, Norway, Germany, Belgium, Netherlands, Argentina, Canada, and Turkey.

- **World Savers** (12%). Defining principles: *environment, humanism, fun, and friends*. The world savers are the models of what gives hope to the next generation. These are the "good kids," who really care. These are the class and club leaders who join many organizations. They are technologically advanced. They attend the same parties as the thrills-and-chills kids, but they are not motivated by the new and exciting. They will be attracted by honest and sincere messages that tell the truth. They are offended by any ad that puts people down or makes fun of another group. They are sophisticated and have a sense of humor, but do not want to laugh at others' foibles. They respond to promotions that piggyback a good cause. Key countries include Hungary, Philippines, Venezuela, Brazil, Spain, Columbia, Belgium, Argentina, Russia, Singapore, France, Poland, and Ukraine.

- **Quiet Achievers** (15%). Defining principles: *success, anonymity, anti-individualism, and social optimism*. These teens go through their lives with determination and restraint. Their purpose is to study hard and do well in school. This preoccupation with studies limits involvement in other activities. This group lives primarily in Thailand, China, Hong Kong, Ukraine, Korea, Lithuania, Russia, and Peru.

- **Bootstrappers** (14%). Key definers include: *achievement, individualism, optimism, determination, and power*. These are kids who make their parents proud, or at least try hard to please. They are determined to succeed and are teen leaders. In the United States, bootstrappers represent one in every four teens. They represent 40 percent of young African Americans. Brands that convincingly

---

[12]"The six value segments of global youth," *BrandWeek*, 22 May 2000, 38–50.

connect to the positive values of the good life will do well with these teens. Key countries include: Nigeria, Mexico, United States, India, Chile, Puerto Rico, Peru, and Venezuela.

■ **Upholders** (16%). Defining principles: *family, custom, tradition, and respect for individuals.* The upholders are the most dreamy and childlike of the six segments. They are the quiet good teen citizens of the world. They plan to follow in their parents' footsteps. They do not like to take consumer risks and use products with proven track records. Once they choose a product it may be for a lifetime. Key countries include: Vietnam, Indonesia, Taiwan, China, Italy, Peru, Venezuela, India, and Philippines.

Marketing Environment

Companies and agencies want to accumulate as much information about their markets as possible before making crucial integrated marketing decisions. Technology has been assisting marketers in getting more information faster. What did Cybertunes.org know about their marketing before creating the ad in Exhibit 15.4?

Universal Product Code   Universal product code (UPC) information has greatly enhanced the process of tracking product sales. When the grocer scans a price into the register at checkout, that information is instantly available to the retailer. Scanner reporting systems have allowed marketers to track their performance quickly, rather than monthly or bimonthly, and at local levels. UPC informa-

tion allows marketers to determine what their share of market is, if one kind of packaging sells better, and which retailers sell the most units. Cash-checking cards can be scanned into the system to keep a record of what kind of products consumers buy. This offers the retailer and manufacturer the opportunity to target promotions directly to people who have used the product in the past. This information can contribute to any database marketing effort by the retailer.

Single-Source Data   For single-source data, retail tracking scanner data are integrated with household panel data on purchase patterns and ad exposure. The information comes from one supplier and is extracted from a single group of consumers. These data can be combined with other research sources to supply micromarketers with a wealth of information on who, what, and how. Despite these new micromarketing capabilities, research firms are far more adept at generating data than most clients are at using the information.

Database Marketers   Database marketers use sweepstakes entries, rebate information, merchandise orders, free product offers, requests for new-product information, and purchase information to build consumer databases telling them a great deal about how consumers live. This information offers many opportunities for database marketing.

Internet Data   Many major advertisers and research companies have embraced the Internet for on-line focus groups and other marketing research, despite its flaws and problems (i.e., how representative are Web users of the overall population). On-line research shouldn't replace traditional marketing research, but harnessing the Internet improves the research process. Web-based research should be part of the mix.

General Motors Corp. recently started real-time, on-line clinics to gather consumer reaction to upcoming products. Mark Hogan, president of GM's e-commerce unit, said, "The days when we brought 1,000 people over a weekend to look at our products will soon be a thing of the past." Nissan's development of Xterra sport utility stemmed partly from cybersurfer input. After winning Motor Trend magazine's SUV of the year (1999), Nissan sent 1,500 e-mails to targeted buyers to find out the credibility of the awards among consumers.[13]

THE SERIES OF RESEARCH STEPS IN ADVERTISING

The term "advertising research" is broadly defined. It includes research that contributes to all four stages of the advertising process:

1. *Advertising strategy development.* Research tries to answer many questions: Who is the market and what do they want? What is the competition we are specifying? What communication do we want our selected market to get from our advertising? How will we reach the persons selected as our market?
2. *Advertising execution development.* There are two kinds of research used at the execution stage of advertising. The first is exploratory research to stimulate the creative people and to help them know and understand the language used by consumers. The other is research to study proposed creative concepts, ideas, roughs, visuals, headlines, words, presenters, and so forth, to see whether they can do what the creative strategy expects of them.
3. *Evaluating pretesting executions.* Pretesting is the stage of advertising research at which advertising ideas are tested. Partly because of the finality of much pretesting, it is the most controversial kind of advertising research.

---

[13]Jean Halliday, "Automakers involve consumers," *Advertising Age*, 31 January 2000, 82.

4. *Campaign evaluation.* Campaign evaluation usually involves a tracking study to measure the performance of a campaign.

The primary goal of advertising research is to help in the process of creative development. Before we examine the research process advertisers would use in developing advertising strategy for campaigns, let us get a better perspective on using research information.

Translating Information into Strategy

Information isn't enough by itself to answer marketing problems. A few years ago the brilliant McCann-Erickson researcher, Jack Dempsey, said, "By itself information has no value." It acquires value only when the strategist takes "a point of view" about what the information means—a point of view that is relevant to the marketing and advertising issues. You have to get involved in all the data at your disposal and, if necessary, fill in some gaps by acquiring more information. But then you have to step back from it. The secret of effective strategy formation lies in deciding which data are important and which are not. It is a process of organizing simplicity out of complexity, for the best strategic insights are usually the very simple ones.

Take the consumer's point of view. Ask yourself what the consumer is really buying. Is he or she buying the product because of its functional benefits? How important are the psychological benefits? The corporate landscape is littered with examples of companies and industries that failed to appreciate what their consumers were really purchasing. Because of this, they defined their markets inappropriately and often disastrously. Begin with an analysis of how people behave rather than an analysis of how they feel or what they believe. You will probably get into these issues, but behavior is the foundation from which you build. And above all, try to see the world with the consumers' eyes.

Think about the question, "How many pairs of shoes do you buy in a year?" Now, if you disregard such factors as style and fashion, the number of shoes bought in a year depends largely on how much walking is done, not on age, sex, or social class. These may be associated variables, but less determinant than the amount of walking the individual does. You see, information by itself has no value.

Market, Product, Competitive, and Consumer Research

Basic information is gathered and analyzed to determine the marketing strategy for a product or service, projected sales, the source of business, pricing and distribution factors, geographic information, and how to develop data to identify the size and nature of the product category. This kind of research includes data on competitors, sales trends, packaging, advertising expenditures, and future trends. Situation analysis helps to define clearly the market in which the product or service competes (see Exhibit 15.5).

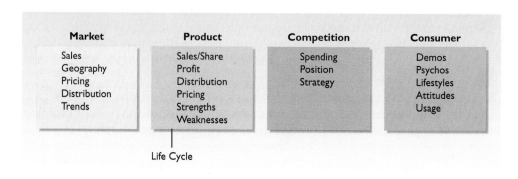

Exhibit

15.5

Situation Analysis

Prospect research is critical to define clearly who is expected to buy the product or service. Studies may identify users, attitudes, lifestyles, and consumption patterns—all of which identify the prime project.

The amounts and kinds of information required will vary according to the product category and marketing situation. Exhibit 15.6 outlines strategy choices indicated by different levels of brand trial and awareness. It is difficult to talk about strategy until you have information on awareness levels for each brand in the market. "Brand trial" will occur if what consumers know about the brand fits in with their needs and is sufficiently important or motivating. The relationship between a brand's level of awareness and its trials may be expressed as a ratio. A high ratio will suggest one strategy option, a low ratio another. For example, high awareness and low trial (lower left-hand box of Exhibit 10.3) clearly indicates that what people know about the brand is not sufficiently motivating or relevant, and the brand may need repositioning.

Research does not always tell us what we want to hear, which can create problems if we think an advertising idea is really strong. Take the classic, "Avis. We try harder," campaign. It tested poorly in research. Consumers said the "We're number two" concept meant Avis was second rate. Research was against running it, but creative genious Bill Bernbach fervently believed in the idea and convinced Avis to take a chance with it. Today, the Avis campaign is considered one of the most powerful, memorable ad campaigns in history.

Advertising Strategy or Message Research

Message research is used to identify the most relevant and competitive advertising sales message. It may take many forms: focus groups, brand mapping, usage studies, motivation studies, or benefit segmentation.

Focus Group Research   **Focus groups** became fashionable in the late 1960s as a **qualitative research** tool. They have become most marketers' main method of qualitative research to find out why consumers behave as they do. The focus group offers a means of obtaining in-depth information through a discussion-group atmosphere. This process is designed to probe into the behavior and thinking of individual group members. The focus group can elicit spontaneous reactions to products or ads. A trained moderator leads a group of 8 to 12 consumers, usually prime prospects. The typical focus group interviews last one-and-a-half to two

focus group   A qualitative research interviewing method using in-depth interviews with a group rather than with an individual.

qualitative research   This involves finding out what people say they think or feel. It is usually exploratory or diagnostic in nature.

	Awareness—High	Awareness—Low	
Trial—High	• Increase Frequency of Purchase • Expand Number of Product Uses	• Increase Awareness so as to Broaden Trial Base	**Trial—High**
Trial—Low	• Reposition Brand	• Increase Awareness • Make Sure Positioning Is Sound	**Trial—Low**
	Awareness—High	Awareness—Low	

Exhibit

15.6

Brand Trial/Awareness Ratios: Strategic Options

hours. The number of different group sessions vary from advertiser to advertiser based somewhat on expense, topic being discussed, and time considerations. Most clients conduct five or six focus groups around the country. The client usually watches the interview from behind a one-way mirror so as not to disrupt the normal function of the group.

As we indicated earlier, researchers are using more on-line focus groups to gather consumer's responses to questions and products.

Videoconferencing links, television monitors, remote-control cameras, and digital transmission technology allow focus group research to be accomplished over long-distance lines. Many advertising agencies believe videoconferencing enriches the creative process because it gives more people input. This technique allows more agency and client people to watch groups from all over the country without having to travel.

There are critics of the overemphasis on focus groups. They point to the fact that many good ideas—whether a 30-second commercial or a new product or concept—often get killed prematurely because they did not do well with a focus group. One increasing criticism is the growing number of "professional" respondents who are savvy enough to go from focus group to focus group speaking the marketers' language picking up as easy forty or fifty dollars each time. Most account planners agree that focus groups should never be used as a replacement for quantitative research. But these groups are useful to determine consumer reaction to certain language in a TV commercial or in the development process for creative.

Pretest Research   The client wants assurances that the advertising proposed will be effective. In pretesting, a particular ad passes or fails, or selects one offering as better than all the others. The only alternative is for the client to depend solely on the judgment of the agency or their own personnel.

In general, there are two levels of research aimed at helping advertisers determine how well an ad will perform. **Copy testing** is done in two stages:

1. Rough copy research is needed to determine if the copy is effectively achieving its goals in terms of both message communication and attitude effects.

2. Finished copy research is done on the final form of the copy to evaluate how well the production process has achieved communication and attitude effects (see Exhibit 15.7).

Pretesting is the stage of advertising research in which a complete ad or commercial is tested. It is important that the objectives of pretesting research relate back to the agreed advertising strategy. It would be wasted effort to test for some characteristic not related to the goal of the advertising.

A number of variables can be evaluated in pretesting, including the ability of the ad to attract attention, comprehension by the reader/viewer, playback of copy points (recall), persuasion (the probability that the consumer will buy the brand), attitude toward the brand, credibility, and irritation level.

Pretests should be used as guides and not as absolute predictors of winners or losers. In copy testing, a higher score for one ad over another does not guarantee a better ad. As Bill Bernbach once said, "Research is very important, but I think it is the beginning of the ad." Norm Grey, former creative director and now head of the Creative Circus, once commented on creative testing, "If you don't like the score an ad gets, demand another test. The only thing that's certain is that you'll get another score." These comments do not imply that creative testing is bad. They simply point to the fact that it is controversial and simply another tool for the advertiser.

There have been arguments about the value of testing ads for years. In general, clients demand them and agency creatives are suspect of the process. Australian social researcher Hugh Mackay says, "The best advertising research never, at any stage, mentions advertising. The pre-testing of rough executions puts a fence

"They've walked around our muddy scrap yard in
three-piece suits and wing tips. They take care of us."

It takes a lot to surprise a guy like
Bernard Steinberg. But just leave it to
his bankers at BB&T. To them, it's all in
a day's work.

"Without their backing and blessing,
we probably wouldn't be here
today. They're fast, they're
responsive, and they understand
what you need."

We appreciate the high praise,
Bernard. Next time you see us, you
can bet we'll all be wearing boots.

BB&T
You can tell we want your business.
www.bbandt.com. Member FDIC. ©1998 BB&T

around what you can talk about with consumers. The real challenge is to establish
what concepts exist in the consumer's mind."[14] Ed McCabe, chairman of McCabe &
Company, makes a distinction between research and testing: "Without great
research, you can't make great advertising. However, testing is the idiocy that keeps
greatness from happening. Testing is a crutch the one-eyed use to beat up the
blind." He points to his Hebrew National hot dog campaign in which an actor portraying Uncle Sam is brought up short by the company's insistence on exceeding
federal regulations because its products are kosher and must "answer to a higher
authority." The ads did not test well, and the client was reluctant to run them. After
much discussion, the ads ran. Some 20 years later, the ads are still running. The
point is that testing can be useful, but it is not a foolproof science. If you were
spending millions of dollars on a creative idea, wouldn't you do everything possible
to reduce the risk—or, to put it another way, "to better guarantee" a chance for
success?

Campaign Evaluation Research   In evaluating advertising, within the
total marketing effort, an advertiser should analyze the market and competitive
activity and look at advertising as a campaign—not as individual ads. This informa-

---

[14]Jim Aitchison, *Cutting Edge Advertising* (Singapore:Prentice-Hall: 1999), 28–29.

tion can help determine whether changes in the advertising strategy are needed to accomplish the objectives established for the campaign or to deal with a changed situation (Exhibit 15.8).

Advertisers frequently conduct tracking studies to measure trends, brand awareness, and interest in purchasing, as well as advertising factors. The research at the end of one campaign becomes part of the background research for selecting the next campaign strategy.

TESTING CREATIVE RESEARCH

Creative research takes place within the context of the preceding research stages. This kind of research aids in the development of what to say to the target audience and how to say it. Copy development research attempts to help advertisers decide how to execute approaches and elements. Copy testing is undertaken to aid them in determining whether to run the advertising in the marketplace.

1. A good copy-testing system provides measurements that are relevant to the objectives of the advertising. Of course, different advertisements have different objectives (for example, encouraging trial of a product).

2. A primary purpose of copy testing is to help advertisers decide whether to run the advertising in the marketplace. A useful approach is to specify action standards before the results are in. Examples of action standards are the following:
   - Significantly improves perceptions of the brands as measured by _____.
   - Achieves an attention level no lower than _____ percent as measured by _____.

3. A good copy-testing system is based on the following model of human response to communications; the reception of a stimulus, the comprehension of the stimulus, and the response to the stimulus. In short, to succeed, an ad must have an effect.
   - On the eye and the ear—that is, it must be received (reception)
   - On the mind—that is, it must be understood (comprehension)
   - On the heart—that is, it must make an impression (response)

4. Experience has shown that test results often vary according to the degree of finish of the test. Thus, careful judgment should be exercised when using a less-than-finished version of a test. Sometimes what is lost is inconsequential, at other times it is critical.[15]

Exhibit

15.8

Effectiveness Measures by Type of Consumer Response for Copy Research

Adapted from John Leckency, "Current Issues in the Measurement of Advertising."

Response Criterion	Measurement
Cognitive (Think)	
Attention	Eye camera
Awareness	Day-after recall
Affective (Feel)	
Attitude	Persuasion
Feelings	Physiological response
Conative (Do)	
Purchase intent	Simulated shopping
Sales	Split cable/scanner

[15]PACT—Positioning Advertising Copy Testing, *The PACT Agencies Report 1982*, 6–25.

Forms of Testing

Each advertiser and agency uses similar but modified steps in the testing of creative research. The following are examples of this process.

Concept Testing   Concept testing may be an integral part of creative planning and is undertaken for most clients as a matter of course. Creative concept testing can be defined as the target audience evaluation of (alternative) creative strategy. Specifically, concept testing attempts to separate the "good" ideas from the "bad," to indicate differing degrees of acceptance, and to provide insight into factors motivating acceptance or rejection.

There are a number of possible concept tests:

1. *Card concept test.* Creative strategies are presented to respondents in the form of a headline, followed by a paragraph of body copy, on a plain white card. Each concept is on a separate card. Some concepts cannot be tested in card form (for example, those requiring a high degree of mood, such as concepts based on humor or personalities).

2. *Poster test.* This is similar to a card test except that small posters containing simplified illustrations and short copy are used rather than plain cards without illustrations.

3. *Layout test.* A layout test involves showing a rough copy of a print ad (or artwork of a TV commercial with accompanying copy) to respondents. Layout tests are more finished than poster tests in that they use the total copy and illustration as they will appear in the finished ad. Additionally, whereas a card or poster test measures the appeal of the basic concept, the purpose of the layout test may be to measure more subtle effects such as communication, understanding, and confusion.

Finished Print Tests   This testing procedure can take many forms of measuring the finished ad as it would appear in print.

Print Testing Example   The video storyboard test tests television and print ads. Its ad promoting the testing of rough print ads says "develop testing procedures which allow you to compare alternative executions without spending the time and money to finish an ad." Its procedure goes something like this: Test ads, finished or unfinished, are inserted into a 20-page magazine-in-a-folder containing both editorial and control ads. Prospects preview the magazine in one-on-one interviews in high-traffic malls. Respondents are questioned regarding unaided, aided, and related recall of the test ad. Next they are asked to focus on the test ad only and are probed for reactions. Agencies are furnished with diagnostic data to improve the ad. The ads are measured for stopping power, communication, relevance, and persuasion. They also provide likes and dislikes about the ad. All of this costs about $3,500 for each test execution per 100 respondents. Results take about 12 days.

Test Commercials   Generally, commercial testing on film or videotape falls into one of four categories:

1. *Animatics.* This is artwork, either cartoons or realistic drawings. Some animatics show limited movement; those that do not are usually called video storyboards. Animatics cost from about $1,500 to $4,000 plus artists' fees, although the simplest nonmovement video storyboard may cost as little as $750.

2. *Photomatics.* These are photographs shot in sequence on film. The photos may be stock (from a photo library) or shot on location. Photomatics cost about $10,000 to produce.

3. *Liveamatics.* This involves filming or taping live talent and is very close to the finished commercial. A liveamatic commercial test costs $10,000 to $20,000 to produce.

4. *Ripamatics.* The commercial is made of footage from other commercials, often taken from ad agency promotion reels. Ripamatics are used many times for experimentation on visual techniques.

Finished Commercial Testing   TV testing techniques can generally be classified into two categories:

1. Those that attempt to evaluate a commercial's effectiveness in terms of viewers' recall of a certain aspect of the commercial

2. Those that attempt to evaluate a commercial's effectiveness in terms of what it motivates a viewer to say or do

Recent advances in production technology are helping the testing process. The more closely the test spot resembles the finished commercial, the more accurate the test results will be. Computer animation has become less expensive, and so there is more computer-generated artwork in commercial testing.

BBDO's Emotional Testing   According to BBDO, traditional copy tests have failed to measure emotional response accurately. The techniques tend to measure thoughts rather than feelings. Instead of asking consumers to choose from a list or write in their own words, the agency has devised a deck of 53 photos representing the universe of emotion. Each features one of six photos with different expressions ranging from happy/playful to disgusted/revolted. There are a total of 26 categories of emotions expressed. Here is how it works:

- As with most copy testing, consumers are shown a single commercial or group of spots. Then they are given a questionnaire to test whether brand names and copy points are remembered.

- Photos are given to the participants. They are asked to sort through the photos quickly, setting aside any or all that reflect how they feel after viewing the commercial.

- A researcher tabulates how often a particular photo is chosen by the 150 to 600 participating consumers. In the system, the expressions are plotted on a "perceptual map" to determine whether the response is positive or negative, active or passive.

Agency researchers can compare a spot's effect on different groups: women versus men, teenagers versus adults. They cannot tell whether consumers will buy one brand or another, but they can say whether the ad has generated the intended emotion.

According to BBDO, the main advantage to this system is that it can be used to validate creative approaches and ensure that "we're punching the right buttons." When testing Gillette's Atra Plus razor campaign, "The best a man can get," the agency wanted to know whether the male-targeted campaign would alienate women. Men were more likely than women to feel "proud and confident" after watching the spot, but more women than men felt "happy and joyful." The vice president of marketing for Wm. Wrigley Jr. Co. put it this way, "We've always known there's been an emotional component to advertising, but when you try to put it into measurable terms, it goes touchy-feely." This system is one of the first to test feedback on whether a commercial did elicit a response on the emotional level. However, there is a great distance between measuring emotional response and manipulating it.[16]

---

[16]Rebecca Piirto, "Future focus groups," *American Demographics,* January 1994, 6.

Readership

Advertisers face mounting competition both in the market and on the printed page. It is important to have the ability to determine if an advertisement is being seen. One such readership service that supplies this kind of information is the Starch Readership Service from Roper Starch.

The Starch Readership Service is designed to measure the extent to which advertisements are being seen and read and the level of interest they arouse. Starch interviews more than 75,000 consumers each year to determine their responses to more than 50,000 print ads. Starch uses the recognition method of interviewing. With the publication open, the respondent explains the extent to which he or she had read each ad prior to the interview. For each ad, respondents are asked, "Did you see or read any part of this ad?" If yes, a prescribed questioning procedure is followed to determine the observation and reading of each component part of each ad—illustration, headline, signature, and copy blocks. After these questions are asked, each respondent is classified as follows:

■ *Noted reader.* A person who remembers having previously seen the advertisement in the issue being studied. (See Exhibit 15.9.)

■ *Associated reader.* A reader who not only noted the advertisement, but also saw or read some part of it that clearly indicated the brand or advertiser.

■ *Read most.* A person who read half or more of the written material in the ad.

Clients receive Adnorm data with the Starch Readership Reports. Adnorms enable advertisers to compare readership data of their ad in a given magazine issue to the norm for ads of the same size and color in the same product category. These data can help advertisers identify the types of layouts that attract and retain the highest readership. They can also compare current ads against those of competitors, compare the current campaign against previous campaigns, compare the current campaign against a competitor's previous campaign, and compare current ads against the Adnorm tables.

Consumer Outdoor Recognition Study (CORS)

To conduct CORS research, interviewers visit three or four locations, mostly malls, in designated markets for person-to-person interviews. Participants are asked if

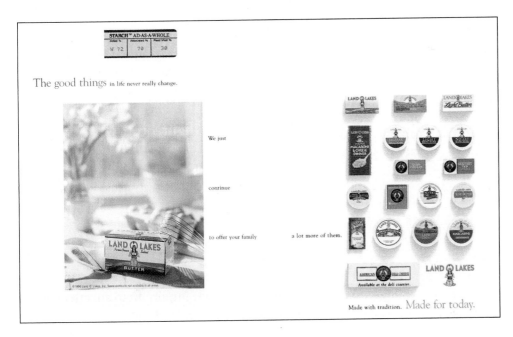

Exhibit

15.9

The label represents the Starch scores for this ad.

Courtesy: Land O' Lakes.

Exhibit

15.10

Courtesy: Robinson & Associates, Inc.

they can remember particular outdoor campaigns. Then they are shown 30 to 50 different recent advertising campaigns run in the area and are quizzed about those that they recall. Besides demographics, the survey is tracking other variables, including text size and picture placement, that make outdoor advertising effective. The average recognition score is 30 and the range of scores is between 5 percent and 75 percent. (See Exhibit 15.10.)

SUMMARY

Advertising is a people business. Successful advertisers know who their prospects are and—to whatever extent is practical—their needs and motives, which result in the purchase of one product or service and the rejection of another. Consumer behavior is usually the result of a complex network of influences based upon the psychological, sociological, and anthropological makeup of the individual.

Advertising rarely, if ever, changes these influences, but rather channels needs and wants of consumers toward specific products and brands. Advertising is a mirror of society. The advertiser influences people by offering solutions to their needs and problems, not by creating these needs. The role of the advertiser is to act as a monitor of the changing face of society.

Advertisers pay special attention to what we call up-front research or market research that reflects the market, the consumer, and the competition. Such information as cohort analysis, VALS, and Mindbase can help us understand consumer lifestyles and values, which aids in developing strategies.

Once all of this information is digested, it is used in the four stages of advertising development: strategy development, execution development, pretesting of executions, and campaign evaluation. By itself, information has no value. It aquires value only when we take a point of view about what the information means.

There are a number of stages of testing available in creative research ranging from concept testing and commercial testing techniques to finished print and commercial tests. It is much less expensive to test concepts and ads prior to buying expensive media schedules.

REVIEW

1. Why are sociology, psychology, and anthropology important to advertising?

2. What kind of research is used in advertising execution development?

3. What is the role of the animatic commercial?

4. What is qualitative research?

TAKE IT TO THE NET

We invite you to visit the Russell/Lane page on the Prentice Hall Web site at **www.prenhall.com/myphlip** for end-of-chapter exercises and applications.

Chapter 16

Creating the Copy

Great advertising copy is essential to great advertising. Understanding consumers and what appeals to them is part of the developmental process needed to create great copy. After reading this chapter you will understand:

>> the nature and the use of appeals

>> elements of an ad

>> structure of an ad

>> copy styles

>> slogans

>> the creative work plan

Earlier we discussed developing integrated marketing communication strategic plans. It has been said that strategy is everything. British creative director, Tony Cox likened creative development to a dance: "Sometimes creative leads, sometimes strategy leads, but both have to remain close and in harmony for a great ending."[1] So don't forget the importance of being on strategy as you read about "how to create. Often there are dangers in our decision process." Frederick Smith, founder of Federal Express, said, "We thought we were selling the transportation of goods; in fact, we were selling peace of mind. When we finally figured that out, we pursued our goal with vengeance".

Before we get to details about developing ads, let us put today's and tomorrow's advertising in perspective. Let us see what challenge lies ahead for us in creating effective concepts and ads.

---

[1]John Hegarty, "My apologies for this letter being so long. Had I more time it would have been shorter," *Creativity*, March 1997, 12.

A CHALLENGE AND CREATIVE VISION

We know we are living in an explosive information age. It is also true to say that knowledge is power, and the speed with which marketers utilize that knowledge in the future will determine success or failure. Because advertising is, in its most basic form, a conveyor of information, it will be at the center of this revolution. But there are a number of factors working against that happening.

According to global creative director John Hegarty, we are already having to deal with a major communication problem. It's called time famine. How do consumers assimilate this ever-growing mass of messages that is being directed at them? How do they cope with the volume of traffic going through their brains? How do they process this valuable information as opposed to allowing it to pass straight through unnoticed? Another related issue that has been debated for years is media clutter. Are consumers reaching the point of "overchoice," as futurist Alvin Toffler predicted? "We are racing against overchoice—the point at which the advantages of choice and individualization are canceled by the complexity of the buyer's decision-making process."[2]

Yet another issue is our audience's ability to turn us off. Advertisers interrupt viewing and listening, or we sit alongside printed material shouting for attention. As electronic media take a greater hold on the distribution of information, our audience will have great control over turning us off, unless we are compelling and necessary. This is totally true with the Internet—the user controls the information. Unless we recognize the change in the balance of power and take into account our consumers' aspirations, we will be cut out of the loop and become irrelevant. What can we do as communicators?

Strategy and Great Writing

Creative director, Scott Ballew, created a simple little ad for Ciba-Geigy Turf and Ornamental Product's Subdue for weeds. The Exhibit 16.1 ad said:

IT WORKS BETTER.

IT COSTS LESS.

END OF AD.

This ad idea has been ripped off by a number of agencies since. There probably was a reason.

Another brilliant simple idea was created for the Economist. The typical ad for *The Economist* (a British publication read in more than 140 countries) has been three columns of copy. The ads talked about the benefits of reading the publication—much information aimed at a sophisticated, well-educated target. Yet a simple poster says,

I've never read *The Economist.*

SIGNED, MANAGEMENT TRAINEE, AGED 42

There is a valuable message in these examples for those creating advertising. The lesson is, the faster ideas get across, the more powerful they become. As you reduce the idea down, as you hone it to its essential structure, its power increases. The faster it penetrates the thinking the longer it stays there. You aren't trying to buy newspaper or magazine or Web space or time in a commercial break. The space you

---

[2]"DDB—The creative springboard," 1997, 18.

It Works Better.
It Costs Less.
End Of Ad.

Exhibit

16.1

Simple. Simple. Simple.

Courtesy: Howard, Merrell & Partners.

are trying to buy is in the consumer's head. That is the most valuable space. That is what you are trying to influence.

WestWayne's chief creative officer, Luke Sullivan, speaking of ad ideas: simplicity, simplicity, simplicity. Tony Cox says, "Inside every fat ad is a thinner and better one trying to get out." Maurice Saatchi on simplicity says: "Simplicity is all. Simple logic, simple arguments, simple visual images. If you can't reduce your arguments to a few crisp words and phrases, there's something wrong with your argument."[3]

Was it Oscar Wilde—it doesn't really matter—who understood that an idea got better as it got faster? How do we do that? The brilliance of our craft is to reduce, to distill messages down, not to elongate. Remember Abraham Lincoln's quote, "You can fool all the people some of the time, and some of the people all the time, but you cannot fool all the people all of the time." He captured the essence of modern politics in one sentence, and most of us remember it. Great writing is about using fewer words to be more compelling. When you do that, you liberate your ideas to become more powerful, more involving, and hopefully more memorable. Brevity not only allows us to become more powerful, it allows us to become more stimulating. If you are more stimulating, there is a good chance you are becoming more relevant. We have to change because our audience is demanding it.

The Greeks said that information is taken through the heart. As we have moved from the unique selling proposition (USP) to the *emotional selling proposition*, we need to understand that the way we talk to consumers must also change. Advertising still needs to be based upon the foundation of product or corporate attributes. But we must remember that it may no longer be unique, nor will it necessarily be obvious.

---

[3]Luke Sullivan, *Hey. Whipple, Squeeze This: A Guide To Creating Great Ads* (New York: John Wiley & Sons, 1998), 60–65.

Creative Vision

Creativity isn't just about putting a strategy down on a piece of paper but about capturing the essence of that strategy and giving it a creative vision. That is both compelling and competitive. What worked yesterday isn't necessarily going to work today or tomorrow. The consumer has not only less time to listen to us, but also less inclination.[4]

HOW DO WE CREATE GREAT ADVERTISING?

We've already heard this, but we need to hear another viewpoint. Ron Huey, award-winning creative director of Huey/Paprocki, says, "Simplicity is the key to great advertising. Take the single most salient feature of your product or service and communicate that in a simple, thought provoking or entertaining way. Good copy speaks to the common man. It should be smart, entertaining and conversational, not fancy or frilly. Today's best creative people are resilient. Great ideas are killed every day for sometimes stupid reasons. The best creatives accept that and come back with something even better." (See Exhibit 16.2.) Huey's thoughts on advertising through the years: "The great ads from Bernbach in the '60s, Fallon McElligott in the '80s, Wieden [Wieden & Kennedy], Goodby [Goodby, Silverstein & Partners] and

NAME THAT WEED

Goosegrass is just one of many weeds that Pennant® prevents. So now you can choke out your worst weeds without beating up on ornamentals and warm-season turf.

P E N N A N T

©1992 CIBA-GEIGY Corporation. Always read and follow label directions.

Exhibit

16.2

Another simple visual and verbal idea.
Courtesy: Howard, Merrell & Partners.

[4] John Hegarty, "My apologies for this letter being so long. Had I had more time it would have been shorter," *Creativity*, March 1997, 14.

The Martin Agency today, all have a common thread—The headline, visual and logo communicate the idea immediately." He also believes, "Three quarters of today's best ads use humor. But it's wry humor. Not a bathroom joke or humor that's intended to shock people."[5]

Into Consumer's Hearts

Lou Centlivre, formerly of Foote, Cone & Belding, said: "The days are gone of left-brained reason-why messages; so insignificant and strained and boring and unbelievable they fall on deaf ears. The creative people who can get into the heart—not just the brain—and make people cry or laugh or silently say, 'Yeah, that's how I really feel' will be the superstars."

Procter & Gamble's president said, "I have seen through 25 years that the correlation between profitable business growth on our brands and having great copy on our brands isn't 25 percent, it's not 50 percent. It is 100 percent. I have not seen a single P&G brand sustain profitable volume growth for more than a couple of years without having great advertising."

THE NATURE AND USE OF APPEALS

appeal The motive to which an ad is directed, it is designed to stir a person toward a goal the advertiser has set.

Advertising motivates people by appealing to their problems, desires, and goals, and by offering a means of solving their problems. Let us look at the value of using a psychological **appeal** in advertising. David Martin, founder of The Martin Agency, points to decades of research indicating the relative strengths of motives and appeals in advertising. He believes human desires are woven into our basic nature. They do not change with lifestyles or external environmental stimuli. Consumers will always have a desire for food and drink; for rest, comfort, and security; and for a sense of social worth, independence, power, and success. Parental feelings to protect and provide are basic. Human nature is a constant. Humans are born with certain instincts: fear (self-preservation), hunger (need for food and drink), sex (love), and rage (anger). People also have five senses: sight, touch, smell, hearing, and taste. The instincts and senses are often a starting point for advertising appeals.[6]

The creative genius of the late 1960s, the late Bill Bernbach, put it this way:

> There may be changes in our society. But learning about those changes is not the answer. For you are not appealing to society. You are appealing to individuals, each with an ego, each with the dignity of his or her being, each like no one else in the world, each a separate miracle. The societal appeals are merely fashionable, current, cultural appeals which make nice garments for the real motivations that stem from the unchanging instincts, and emotions of people—from nature's indomitable programming in their genes. It is unchanging person that is the proper study of the communicator.[7]

John Hegarty says,

> there was always one word that came through [when defining great advertising]: irreverence. Because what you are doing is changing the rules. You are trying to do something in an incredibly different way which captures the imagination.

[5] Ron Huey, interviews by W. Ronald Lane, September 1994 and September 1997.
[6] David Martin, *Romancing the Brand* (New York: Amacom, 1989), 134–136.
[7] From an American Association of Advertising Agencies speech, 17 May 1980.

Jeff Goodby of Goodby, Silverstein & Partners adds, "Great advertising scrabbles logic a little bit, it jumps beyond that by being likable and watchable and captivating. It surprises you." Someone once said that great advertising is great ideas simply executed.[8]

Glaxo, a pharmaceutical research company, needed an image ad for Duke Medical Centers Children's Classic Program. HM&P created an ad that used a strong illustration and head to appeal to anyone having spent time with children, especially parents (see Exhibit 16.3). The head read: "Nobody can watch a child and not believe in magic."

Selecting the Appeal

Most products have a number of positive appeals that could be successfully promoted, so how do we go about making the decision as to which direction to go with an ad or appeal? The idea is to choose the one that is most important to the majority of our target. Because selecting the primary appeal is the key to any advertising campaign, many research techniques have been developed to find which appeal to use. In Chapter 15, we discussed some of the aspects of advertising research that help us make strategic and creative decisions. Here we limit the discussion to three

NOBODY CAN WATCH A CHILD AND NOT BELIEVE IN MAGIC.

Glaxo

Glaxo Inc. A Pharmaceutical
Research Company

Exhibit

16.3

The illustration and head appeal to parental feelings.

Courtesy: Howard, Merrell & Partners.

[8]Dick Costello, "The big picture," *Adweek*, 29 March 1999, 25.

techniques that may help us decide on appeals: concept testing, focus groups, and motivational research.

Concept Testing   Concept testing is a method to determine the best of a number of possible appeals to use in your advertising. A creative concept is defined as a simple explanation or description of the advertising idea behind the product.

A tourism association developed several appeals that might motivate prime prospects to drive two hours to the mountains from a large metro area in another state:

1. Only two hours to relaxation
2. Mountain fun in your own backyard
3. The family playground in the mountains
4. Escape to white water rafting, fishing, and the great outdoors
5. Weekend vacation planner package

By using cards with the theme statement and/or rough layouts, the advertiser tries to obtain a rank order of consumer appeal of the various concepts and diagnostic data explaining why the concepts were ranked as they were.

The tourism group found that targets had not realized they were so close to these mountain areas. As a result, mountain areas had not been considered in their vacation or recreation plans.

In the case of a car rental company, a test of vacation travelers found that one benefit stood out: the lowest-priced full-size car. The second most important benefit was no hidden extras.

One drawback of concept testing is that consumers can react only to the themes presented to them. You may find that they have chosen the best of several bad concepts.

Focus Groups   In Chapter 15, we discussed the nature, cost, and typical procedure of focus group research. Here we examine the role of focus groups in selecting the primary appeal. Generally, the interviewer starts by discussing the product category, then proceeds to products within the category, and finally brings up past or current ads for a product or products. And, of course, the focus group can be used to test several new ad concepts of the appeal of print, storyboard, or more finished ad forms. The creative team watching from behind the one-way mirror has the opportunity to hear how participants perceive its products, ads, and ideas.

The leader of the group directs the conversation to determine what problems or "hang-ups" the prime prospects associate with the product. Thus, the answers are not predetermined by the advertiser or the researcher. Rather, they are direct responses to the product and the benefits and problems these prime prospects see in it. Further, because the research is done in a group, people feel less inhibited than they do in one-on-one interviews. The result is usually a good evaluation of the problems, attributes, and particular strengths and weaknesses of the product from the consumer's point of view.

When qualitative research became fashionable in the late 1960s, ad agencies adopted the focus group as a more enlightened way to expose rough creative ideas than rigid quantitative tests. Account planners saw it as a way of getting early consumer feedback to an idea without putting it through the artificiality of a formal test. Today the focus group is often qualitative in name only and has become a weak and invalid shadow of the mechanism and behaviorist thinking it was meant to challenge in the first place, according to Hy Mariampolski of Qualidata Research.

One example of this type of research was conducted by the Atlanta Symphony Orchestra. Its agency interviewed two groups of prime prospects: attendees at regular-season symphony concerts and pop concert goers. The symphony's management wanted to discover prospects' attitudes about programming, length of concerts, and types of soloists. In this case, the results were not surprising. They confirmed management's original perceptions but provided a more tangible basis for arriving at strategic marketing decisions.

Alternative Testing   Account planner, Justin Holloway at Hill, Holliday, Connors, Cosmopulos, Boston says, "There are a few quantitative tests that are very good. In fact, mold-breaking creative today stands a better chance in well-thought-through quantitative pre-tests than in badly conceived focus groups. He offers some alternative. One-on-one in-home interviewing, or mailing of an animatic commercial to a respondent's home followed by an interviewer's phone call, are other alternatives to the focus group."[9]

Motivational Research   Motivational research has its foundation in the psychoanalytic techniques of Sigmund Freud. Popularized by Ernst Dichter during the 1950s as a marketing tool, this type of research seeks to find the underlying reasons for consumer behavior. Its value rests on the premise that consumers are motivated by emotions they may not be aware of consciously.

Motivational research uses unstructured techniques to elicit open-ended responses that are recorded verbatim. The idea is that among these responses there will be the kernel of an unanticipated consumer motivation that can be translated into a unique advertising appeal. Although motivational research has lost some of its glamour, it still has its advocates in the advertising community.

All research data must be interpreted. In fact, data interpretation may be the most critical step in effective advertising research. It requires insight and skill. We also must remember that many advertising appeals result from intuition and personal observation.

Whether created by research or in other ways, the appeal provides the basis of the advertising structure. This appeal can be expressed in many ways. Here we discuss how to make use of words, called copy, in presenting the appeal.[10]

GREAT ADVERTISING ELEMENTS

The Creative Council of Ogilvy & Mather Worldwide found that examples of great advertising have certain elements in common (the same fundamental principles apply to direct-response and sales promotion):[11]

- *Potent strategy.* The strategy is the heart of advertising. It is impossible to do great advertising if the strategy is weak or does not exist at all.
- *A strong selling idea.* Great advertising promises a benefit to the consumer. The idea must be simple, and it must be clear. The brand must be integrated into the selling idea.
- *Stands out.* A great ad is memorable, even when competing for attention with news and entertainment.
- *Always relevant.* Prospects can easily relate the advertising to their experience and to the role of the product in their lives.
- *Can be built into campaigns.* No matter how clever one idea may be, if you cannot make it into a campaign, it is not a great idea.

---

[9]Justin Holloway, "Focus groups: Are they stacking up?" *Agency*, Winter 2000, 38–41.

[10]The term *copy* is a carryover from the days in printing when a compositor, given a manuscript to set in type, was told to copy it. Before long, the manuscript itself became known as copy. In the creation of a printed ad, copy refers to all the reading matter in the ad. However, in the production of print ads, copy refers to the entire subject being reproduced—words and pictures alike. This is one of those instances in advertising when the same word is used in different senses, a practice that all professions and crafts seem to enjoy because it bewilders the uninitiated.

[11]Luis Bassar, "Creative paths to great advertising," *Viewpoint*, September/October 1991, 23–24.

Advertising's Nonrules Rules

This probably is going to sound like a contradiction, but it really isn't. There are no rules in developing ads. That said, we need to understand there are nonrules or guidelines that are generally accepted and sometimes draw on years of research results or accumulated wisdom of creative communicators. You might say they are similar to fashion rules—some things just work better. And it's your job to figure out which. Over the next pages we'll discuss "how to. . . " and the words will form what appears to be rules. It is a means of sharing and analyzing. The real challenge is to use this knowledge in the context of your specific communication problem. Remember earlier in this text we talked about creative risk. Look at taking smart risk, where you know what the norm of thinking is and go from there—with caution. The goal is to communicate.

STRUCTURE OF AN ADVERTISEMENT

In some instances, the promise is the whole advertisement.

Surf Removes Dirt and Odor

Usually, however, a fuller exposition is required, in which case the promise can act as the headline—the first step in the structure of the advertisement. Most ads are presented in this order:

- Promise of benefit (the headline)
- Spelling out of promise (the subheadline, optional)
- Amplification of story (as needed)
- Proof of claim (as needed)
- Action to take (if not obvious)

People tend to scan print ads in the following manner: illustration first, followed by the headline, first line of the body copy, and then the logo. If they are still interested, they will go back and read the rest of the copy. Yes, you can get people to read the copy, but the first sentence and first paragraph are extremely important in keeping readers. As a matter of fact, the drop-off rate of readers is pretty significant during the first 50 words, but not so great between 50 and 500 words.

The Headline

The headline is the most important part of an ad. It is the first thing read, and it should arouse interest so the consumer wants to keep on reading and get to know more about the product being sold. If the headline does not excite the interest of the particular group of prime prospects the advertiser wants to reach, the rest of the ad will probably go unread.

Gary Knutson's creative team at HM&P repositioned a typical weight-reducing spa as a world-class spa brand for stressed-out female executives. The series of ads increased inquiries 350 percent, no small feat, and sales increased 25 percent (Exhibit 16.4). The head reads: "The spa for those who place more value on what they gain than what they lose." The body copy says, "Mind you, there's nothing inherently wrong with visiting a spa in hopes of returning home a few pounds lighter. We merely suggest that with the right spa you have so much more to gain. At Palm-Aire, you will enter a sanctuary in which the greatest ambition of those surrounding you is to provide a respite from the pressures of everyday life. . . . What you gain in self-awareness simply can't be measured on any scale."

No formula can be given for writing a good headline. However, several factors should be considered in evaluating an effective headline:

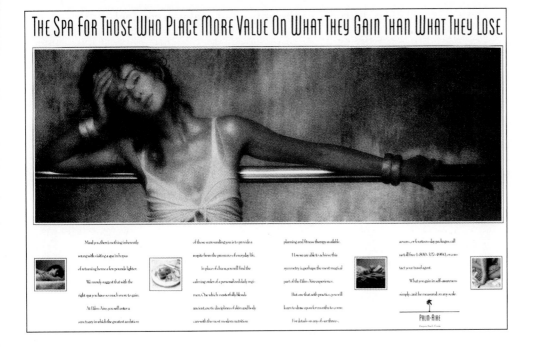

- It should use short, simple words, *usually* no more than 10.
- It should include an invitation to the prospect, primary product benefits, name of the brand, and an interest-provoking idea to gain readership of the rest of the ad.
- The words should be selective, appealing only to prime prospects.
- It should contain an action verb.
- It should give enough information so that the consumer who reads only the headline learns something about the product and its benefit.

Not every headline is going to adhere to these guidelines. However, when you write a headline that excludes any of these points, ask yourself: Would this headline be more effective if it did adhere to the guidelines? You want to be sure you have thought through the process.

Many headlines fall into one of four categories:

1. *Headlines that present a new benefit.* The moment of peak interest in a product is when it offers a new benefit. That is why, in our innovative society, you often see headlines such as these:

Re-define your profile. It's the new way to a younger look.
L'OREAL REVITALIFT SLIM

My mom said your new rooms are so beautiful, she never wants to leave. She's kidding, right?
SHERATON

Hershey's introduces cinnamon like you've never seen before.
HERSHEY'S

Introducing the world's first all-optical network. Not the promise of one. The one.
BROADWING

ZIPLOC introduces the only color seal you can feel.

The best SUV we've ever tested.

Now, getting on the Internet is so easy, even an adult can do it.

A revolution in purity.

Designed by women for women to help even more women.

2. *Headlines that directly promise an existing benefit.* Products cannot be offering new benefits all the time, of course, so headlines often remind consumers of a product's existing features:

Food can't help your body if it can't get past your taste buds.

Easy to clean grout lines.

Heavy isn't healthy.

Take clear control. Take Claritin.

The National Osteoporosis Foundation recommends a diet rich in calcium from broccoli, salmon, milk and Tums.

Sweet. Decadent.

3. *Curiosity-invoking and provocative headlines.* By invoking curiosity, an advertiser may grab attention from an otherwise disinterested audience by challenging the curiosity of the readers, thereby prompting them to read further and leading them into the key message. David Ogilvy warned against using heads that don't communicate the benefits because of the large numbers of readers that don't read the body copy. It can work, but the writer must be careful to build a strong relationship between the curiosity point and the brand. Palm-Aire says, "For two glorious weeks a year, we'll make you forget the other fifty ever existed." That's quite a promise. The readers want to find out how this will happen! (See Exhibit 16.5.) Here are some more curiosity-invoking headlines:

Not that you would. But you could.

The greatest risk is not taking one.

FOR TWO GLORIOUS WEEKS A YEAR, WE'LL MAKE YOU FORGET THE OTHER FIFTY EVER EXISTED.

Exhibit 16.5

Courtesy: Howard, Merrell & Partners.

15 seconds to heaven.

COOL WHIP

Here I shall stay.

MONSTER.COM

The gift that improves complexions, promotes weight loss, helps fight disease, and sustains life itself. . .

BRITA WATER FILTER

Don't forget to blink.

JVC

What the best dressed chickens will be wearing this year.

KRAFT FARM PLUS HERBS

The question headline that works best is the kind that arouses curiosity so the reader will read the body copy to find the answer. Readers do not like being tricked. They want a strong relationship between the curiosity and the product.

4. *Selective headlines.* Readers looking through a magazine or newspaper are more likely to read an ad they think concerns them personally than one that aims at a broad audience. The selective headline aimed at a particular prime prospect who would be more interested in the product is often used. If the head says "to condominium owners," and you don't own a condominium, you probably don't pay attention; conversely, if you do own a condo, you might read it. A Pampers ad headline reads, "Babies absorb everything around them. Wetness doesn't have to be one of them." Obviously, if you don't have a baby in your life, you probably aren't going to read this ad. However, if you do have a baby, you may be attracted to the copy. Four such headlines that specifically reach out to special groups are the following:

- To All Men and Women
- To All Young Men and Women
- To All College Men and Women
- To All College Seniors

The first headline is addressed to the greatest number of readers, but it would be of the least interest to any one of them. Each succeeding headline reduces the size of the audience it addresses and improves the chances of attracting that particular group. What about "All College Seniors Who Need Jobs"? You get the idea!

Besides addressing a particular group directly, headlines can appeal to people by mentioning a problem they have in common:

Most baby bottoms stink. (And their tops aren't great, either.)

HEALTHTEX

Urinary discomfort shouldn't be a burning issue.

AZO-STANDARD

Another vital quality in headlines is specificity. Remember, consumers are more interested in the specific than the general. Therefore, the more specific you can be in the headline, the better: "A Peppermint Peroxide Toothpaste That Will Help Kill Bacteria and Keep Tartar From Your Teeth" is better than "A Nice Tasting Toothpaste That Cleans Your Teeth."

Headline

A headline must say something important to the reader. The actual number of words is not the deciding factor; long or short headlines may work well. But say what you need to say in as few words as possible (see Exhibit 16.6). Remember, simple is better.

Imagine "Intelligent" drugs that could tell sick cells from healthy ones, and then selectively destroy the targeted ones.

MIRAVANT MEDICAL TECHNOLOGIES

Exhibit
16.6

This provocative head has 18 words. A headline may be as short as one word, or as many as it takes to get an idea across.
Courtesy: Howard, Merrell & Partners.

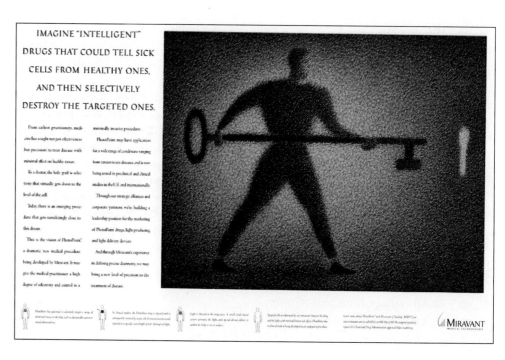

A headline sometimes can be more than one sentence.

Commuting, every month:
$82
Health club, every month:
$54
Insurance, every month:
$62
Trading a checkbook for a storybook:
Priceless

MASTERCARD

The Subheadline

If the message is long, it can be conveyed with a main headline (with large type) and a subheadline (with smaller type but larger than the body copy). The subheadline can spell out the promise presented in the headline. It can be longer than the headline; it can invite further reading; and it serves as a transition to the opening paragraph of the copy.

Headline   **Baby Gap is expecting**
Subhead   **Clothes for mothers-to-be are coming soon to babygap.com.**

BABY GAP

Headline   **New Breathe Right strips for colds.**
Subhead   **(The idea was right under our nose.)**

CNS, INC.

Headline   **The world's leading imaging products.**
Subhead   **NEC's expertise in multiple technologies opens new worlds.**

NEC

Amplification

The headline and, if used, the subheadline are followed by the body copy of the ad. It is here that you present your case for the product and explain how the promise in the headline will be fulfilled. In other words, the body copy amplifies what was hinted in the headline or subheadline. What you say and how deep you go depend on the amount of information your prime prospect needs at this point in the buying process. A high-cost 50-inch high-definition digital projection television probably calls for more explanation than a low-cost product, such as a barbecue sauce with a new flavor. If a product has many technical advances there probably is not sufficient room to detail all the features. In this case, the objective is to create enough interest to get the prime prospect to the store for a demonstration and more information.

Amplification should emphasize those product or service features that are of primary importance but cannot be included in the headline. Take, for example, the spa resort positioned for women executives (Exhibit 16.5, p. 427):

For two glorious weeks a year, we'll make you forget the other fifty ever existed.

and then the amplification:

Your body will be massaged with fragrant oils of avocado and almond.
Bathed in a whirlpool cascading with fresh flower petals or sweet nectars.
And cleansed to a silken softness by the hand-rubbed salts of a loofa scrub.
You will discover a sanctuary in which your every need and desire are met
by a staff of people wholly immersed in their work (which is you) and thus

refreshingly compliant. We will pamper you with gourmet meals so rich in flavor and so artful in their presentation as to belie any sense of diet whatsoever. And we'll show you how to lastingly embrace improved nutrition in your own everyday life. . . . whether it's a few days, a week, or—the ultimate—two weeks, what you will remember the most about your time at Palm-Aire Spa Resort is how much you were able to simply forget.

Proof

The body copy does amplify what the headline promised. At times the process acts to reassure the consumer that the product will perform as promised. Consumers may look for proof in an ad, and proof is particularly important for high-priced products, health, and new products with special features. Here are a few ways in which proof can be offered to the reader.

Seals of Approval Seals of approval from such accredited sources as *Good Housekeeping* and *Parents* magazines, the American Dental Association, the American Medical Association, and Underwriter's Laboratories allay consumers' fears about product quality. An Ayer senior vice president of planning says that it gives a product a difference and that the seal can give a new product an edge of credibility in the market. Niagara spray starch advertises the *Good Housekeeping* seal.

Guarantees Wendy's, Arby's, and Mrs. Winner's have offered consumers money-back guarantees for trying specific products to reduce the risk and get trial by consumers. Products such as Silent Floor systems guarantee their floors will be free from warping or defects. Hartz Control Pet Care System will refund your money if you don't see an improvement in 30 days. Pacific Coast Down Comforters suggests you "try one for 30 nights. If you're not completely comfortable, we'll give you a full refund."

Trial Offers and Samples BMG Music offers any eight CDs for the price of one with their 10-day risk-free trial. Proctor & Gamble offered free industrial-strength Spic and Span liquid samples to consumers who called a toll-free telephone number, to reduce the risk, and to get trial.

Warranties Pacific Coast Down Comforters also has a "100% allergy-free warranty." Sherwin-Williams SuperPaint is advertised with a 20-year warranty against peeling. James Hardie Building Products touts its 50-year warranty for its siding. Maytag water heating appliances are covered by a 10-year tank warranty.

Reputation Copy for Woolite says, "It's recommended by the makers of more than 350 million garments."

Demonstrations "Before" and "after" demonstrations are used to show how a product works. Starch Research says showing models to demonstrate cosmetic products is powerful. In one ad, Almay showed a supermodel from the neck up, making it easy to see her facial imperfections—or lack thereof after using Almay's line of hypoallergenic cosmetics. Find a way to tell consumers a benefit, and you will do well; find a way to show them, and you will fare even better.

Testimonials The ability to attract attention to ads and offer a credible source has made testimonials a popular device. Testimonials should come from persons viewed by consumers as competent to make judgments on the products they are endorsing. BB&T bank used a campaign of business customer's stories to attract more business customers. One ad read: "As far as I'm concerned, if your word's no good, nothing else about you is good. . . . they're in the bank ready to answer our needs. That sets them apart." (See Exhibit 16.7.)

Exhibit

16.7

This ad relies on a customer's own words to add credibility.

Courtesy: Howard, Merrell & Partners.

Dean Rieck, president of Direct Creative, promotes the use of testimonials and suggests that companies actively collect testimonials and success stories. He says they support your claims and build confidence. He also suggests:[12]

■ Use testimonials from people similar and relevant to prospects. A teacher will believe other teachers, a business owner will believe other business owners, seniors will believe seniors. They are more effective if they are from experts or people with relevant experience.

■ Don't try to rewrite or fabricate testimonials. The real words of real people are always more believable than anything a writer can come up with. Besides, making them up isn't ethical.

■ Testimonials are a form of proof, so whenever you have a chance to increase the credibility of that proof. Use full names when possible. Appropriate titles may be an indication of a person's experience or expertise.

---

[12]Dean Rieck, "Build consumer confidence with testimonials," *DM News,* 8 February 1999, 12.

COPY STYLE

As with a novel or a play, good ad copy has a beginning, a middle, and an ending. And, like a novel, the transition must be smooth from one part to another. Up to this point, we have discussed how the building blocks of copy are put together. Now we need to think about what it takes to create special attention and persuasion. It takes style—the ability to create fresh, charming, witty, human advertising that compels people to read. Remember what Ron Huey said: "Take the single most salient feature of your product or service and communicate it in a simple, thought provoking or entertaining way." See the product in a fresh way, explore its possible effects on the reader, or explain the product's advantages in a manner that causes the reader to view the product with a new understanding and appreciation.

Most ads end with a close by asking or suggesting that the reader buy the product. The difference between a lively ad and a dull one lies in the approach to the message at the outset.

The lens through which a writer sees a product may be the magnifying glass of the technician, who perceives every nut and bolt and can explain why each is important, or it may be the rose-colored glasses of the romanticist, who sees how a person's life may be affected by the product. That is why we speak of **copy approaches** rather than types of ads. The chief approaches in describing a product are the factual, the imaginative, and the emotional.

copy approach The method of opening the text of an ad. Chief forms; factual approach, imaginative approach, emotional approach.

Factual Approach

In the factual approach, we deal with reality—that which actually exists. We talk about the product or service—what it is, how it is made, and what it does. Focusing on the facts about the product that are most important to the reader, we explain the product's advantages.

One of the interesting things about a fact, however, is that it can be interpreted in different ways, each accurate but each launching different lines of thinking. Remember the classic example of an eight-ounce glass holding four ounces of water, of which can be said: "This glass is half full" or "This glass is half empty." As you know, both are correct and factual. The difference is in the interpretation of reality, as the Mitsui O.S.K. ad headline for shipping seafood says, "We cater to the best schools." Their copy talks facts: "MOL takes a great deal of pride in catering to the needs of the world's most discriminating shippers. Salmon, shrimp, crabs, mussels and other gourmet seafood, for example, are delivered in 409 high-cube reefer containers so that they arrive fresh and delectable in Asian and American markets." Skill in presenting a fact consists of projecting it in a way that means the most to the reader.

The factual approach can be used to sell more than products or services. Facts about ideas, places—anything for which an ad can be written—can be presented with a fresh point of view.

Imaginative Approach

There is nothing wrong with presenting a fact imaginatively. The art of creating copy lies in saying a familiar thing in an unexpected way. Kimberly-Clark B2B ads were selling to lab technicians a line of contamination control solutions. They could have simply said, "We can help you clean with Kimwipes." How much more interesting the approach in Exhibit 16.8 is. "It seems we've always been obsessed with lint." The illustration and head work together. The copy says, "When you're a baby, finding a piece of lint can be like discovering a new toy. But when you're a lab technician, it can mean contamination, tainted results, and ruined work in the process. Which explains why scientists all over the world trust Kimwipes low-lint, high purity wipers. . . ."

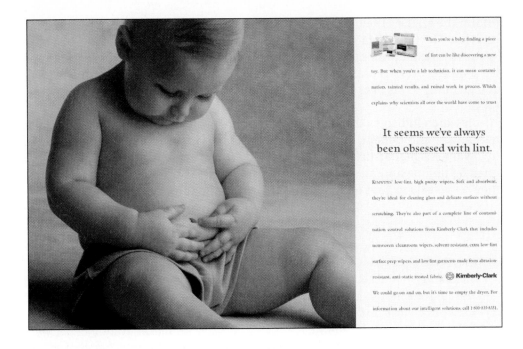

Emotional Approach

Emotion can be a powerful communicator. The feelings about your product or company can be an important plus or minus. Copy using psychological appeals to love, hate, or fear has great impact. The illustration and headline in Exhibit 16.9 show not only sensitivity, warmth, maternal instincts, but also emotion—every parent can identify with the feeling. "If Just Looking At This Has A Profound Effect On You, Imagine What It's Doing For This Three Pound Baby." Often the copy will continue the emotional appeal, although at times it will take a factual direction to

inform the reader about specific features of the product to convince the reader of its value. The Columbia Hospital copy starts: "What it's doing is giving a baby who spends his first few months in an incubator a chance to bond with his parents. And it's soothing every muscle in his little body, allowing him to tolerate his feedings and go home to his own bed sooner. This program is called skin-to-skin, Kangaroo Care."

Research indicates that emotion can create positive feelings, such as warmth, happiness, and delight, which work best for low-involvement goods. For high-involvement, higher-ticket items, such as CD players or automobiles, emotions must be unique and mesh with the brand. Kodak has produced ads so emotional they bring tears to your eyes.

Learning About Emotion

Kevin Roberts, former CEO Worldwide of Saatchi & Saatchi, talks about the use of "emotion." What science can tell us about the brain and about "emotion" has grown exponentially over the last 20 years.

Research tells us that human beings THINK with feeling and emotion. We just can't help it. Emotion is the KEY to every decision we make, every thought we have, whether it's to click on an attached file or reach for our usual brand of soap powder. Human beings tend to take everything personally and respond with feeling. Joseph Ledoux, one of the world's leading researchers into the emotional brain, had this to say: "Emotions are mostly processes at an unconscious level."

They are quick and focused on what really matters. They acknowledge that intuition, loyalty, and emotion can't be quantified, and then move on.

All the stuff we've been told about "think before you act" and "think it through"—rubbish. It doesn't happen. Rational man is a myth. Women, of course, have always been too smart to have gotten into the rationality arena because in reality it doesn't work.

Humans have the ability to focus. People focus on new events, on changes in their environment. They disregard the everyday and the routine. They pay attention until a need is satisfied and then they move on. How do we attract attention? Kevin Roberts believes we can only do this with emotion.

Put emotion first. Pull them with emotion, touch them with emotion, compel them with emotion. It may make them laugh, make them cry, make them jump.[13]

Comparative Advertising

Comparing your product directly with one or more competitors is called **comparative advertising**. It is actually encouraged by the Federal Trade Commission, but it has risks. Some advertisers think it isn't smart to spend money to publicize your competition. Others think it creates a bad atmosphere for the company that demeans all advertising. Pepsi has frequently run ads in Nation's Restaurant News featuring "Coke and Pepsi View Your Business Two Different Ways," and the copy talks about how they do business differently.

Despite each comparative ad being different, there are certain rules of thumb that can be applied: (1) The leader in the field never starts a comparative campaign. (2) The most successful comparison ads are those comparing the product with products identical in every respect except for the special differential featured in the ad. The stronger the proof that the products are identical, the better. (3) The different features should be of importance to the consumer.

---

[13]Kevin Roberts, "Emotional rescue," speech, The AdTech Conference, San Francisco, May 2000.

SLOGANS

Originally derived from the Gaelic slugh gairm, meaning "battle cry," the word slogan has an appropriate background. A slogan sums up the theme for a product's benefits to deliver an easily remembered message in a few words—"It's the Real Thing."

There have been many very memorable slogans in advertising over the years. Yet, not all effective slogans are etched in every consumer's mind. Many slogans, however, do help communicate the essence of the product position. For example, "Pawleys Island. Arrogantly Shabby."

Used even more often on television and radio than in print, slogans may be combined with a catchy tune to make a jingle. Slogans are broadly classified as either institutional or hard-sell.

Institutional Slogans

Institutional slogans are created to establish a prestigious image for a company. Relying on this image to enhance their products and services, many firms insist that their slogans appear in all of their advertising and on their letterheads. An entire ad may feature the slogan. Some institutional slogans are familiar:

The Document Company

XEROX

The Power of Intelligent E-Business

MICROSTRATEGY

The Possibilities Are Infinite

FUJITSU

You're in Good Hands With Allstate

ALLSTATE INSURANCE

Inspiration Technology

COMPAQ

The Power to Change

NOVELL

Hard-Sell Slogans

These capsules of advertising change with campaigns. They epitomize the special significant features of the product or service being advertised, and their claims are strongly competitive.

The Fastest Way to B2B Integration

NETFISH TECHNOLOGIES

Do More

AMERICAN EXPRESS

Get Met. It Pays.

METLIFE

Breakfast Made Right.

POST

A Different Kind of Company. A Different Kind of Car.

SATURN

M&M's. The Milk Chocolate Melts In Your Mouth—Not In Your Hands.

M&M'S

Slogans are widely used to advertise groceries, drugs, beauty aids, and liquor. These are products that are bought repeatedly at a comparatively low price. They are sold to consumers in direct competition on the shelves of supermarkets, drugstores, and department stores. If a slogan can remind a shopper in one of those stores of a special feature of the product, it certainly has served its purpose. Slogans can also remind shoppers of the name of a product from a company they respect. Not all advertising needs slogans. One-shot announcements—sale ads for which price is the overriding consideration—usually do not use slogans. Creating a slogan is one of the fine arts of copywriting.

Elements of a Good Slogan

A slogan differs from most other forms of writing because it is designed to be remembered and repeated word for word to impress a brand and its message on the consumer. Ideally, the slogan should be short, clear, and easy to remember.

Nobody Can Eat Just One.

LAY'S BAKED POTATO CHIPS

Nationwide Is On Your Side.

NATIONWIDE INSURANCE

Where Shopping Is a Pleasure

PUBLIX SUPERMARKET

Just Slightly Ahead of Our Time

PANASONIC

The Rules Are Changing

DATEK ONLINE

Aptness helps:

Feel the Hyatt Touch.

HYATT HOTELS

Trusted By More Women Than Any Other Brand.

MASSENGILL

Be Absolutely Sure.

FEDEX

It is an advantage to have the name of the product in the slogan:

Kroger. For Goodness Sake.

KROGER

THE CREATIVE WORK PLAN

Before most agencies start creating an ad, they develop a creative work plan to guide them in the right direction. The brief is the starting point for the creative process. You will recall from Chapter 3, the creative brief consists of the following elements:

- Key observation
- Communication objective
- Consumer insight
- Promise
- Support
- Audience
- Mandatories

What does a brief accomplish? In simple factual terms, a good brief should accomplish three main objectives. First, it should give the creative team a realistic view of what the advertising really needs to do, and is likely to achieve. Second, it should provide a clear understanding of the people that their advertising must address, and finally, it needs to give clear direction on the message to which the target audience seems most likely to be susceptible. In some agencies there is a creative briefing where an account planner will outline the nature of the advertising problem for the creative team, and suggest ways of solving it.[14]

The purpose of the work plan is to provide proper direction for the creative team prior to developing ideas, heads, and copy. Exhibit 16.10 shows a work plan format originally developed by Young & Rubicam that is widely used by a number of agencies and is different from the Lintas approach. Note that the work plan emphasizes factual information and research data. The creative process is not a "shot in the dark" but rather depends on knowing as much as possible about the product, the consumer, and the expected benefits. The advertising professional is able to channel objective information into a creative and attention-getting sales message. Many agencies and clients have their own format and style for specific information they think necessary for creative strategy development.

GUIDELINES FOR CREATING AN AD

The following was written by Philip W. Sawyer, editor, Starch Tested Copy, after years of studying Starch Advertisement Readership Studies. Here he offers some specific rules and thoughts on developing effective advertising:[15]

What follows are 10 guidelines that we believe advertisers should keep in mind whenever they sit down to create an ad. As we offer these, we are well aware that any number of ads ignore these guidelines yet are very successful. That's fine. Mark Twain broke almost every rule of grammar when he wrote *The Adventures of Huckleberry Finn*. But he had to know the rules before he could break them effectively.

1. *Keep It Simple, Stupid* The KISS principle, as this is called, has no better application than in advertising, yet it is probably the most abused principle of all. Here is the best argument for simplicity: A great many magazine readers do not read magazines to look at the ads. Therefore, advertising needs to catch the eye quickly, deliver its message quickly, and allow the reader to leave as quickly as possible. Ads that clutter the page with multiple illustrations and varied sizes and styles of type offer no central focus for the eye, no resting place. Because of these visual disincentives for staying with "busy" ads, readers naturally move on, having spent little or no time with them.

---

[14]Jon Steel, *Truth, Lies, and Advertising* (New York: John Wiley & Sons, 1998), 141.
[15]Starch Tested Copy, a publication of Roper Starch Worldwide.

Exhibit

16.10

A Creative Work Plan

2. *You're Not Selling the Product; You're Selling the Benefits of the Product* An old New Yorker cartoon depicts a pompous-looking young man at a party, talking to a young woman. "Well, that's enough about me," he says. "Now, what do you think about me?" Most advertisements suffer from the same kind of egotism. They assume that the reader is as interested in the product as is the advertiser. In reality, most readers do not enter the advertiser's realm readily. They do so only when convinced that the product will do something for them. If an advertiser does not answer the reader's implicit question—What's in it for me?—the ad is unlikely to attract any real interest.

   Hangers Cleaners use new technology, but who cares? They tried to use heads and main visuals followed by feature article writing to explain the benefits that couldn't be told in a few words (see Exhibit 16.11).

   Most ads are simply descriptive; they explain what the product or service is. The worst ads give you a long history about the company, its values, commitments, and size—as if anyone really cares. But the best ads directly address the problems that the product or service solves and suggest how that solution makes life better for the potential consumer.

3. *When Appropriate, Spice It Up with Sex* Psychologist Joyce Brothers once predicted that "the days of sexy advertising are numbered. The reason is that within five years, the number of marriageable women will be greater than the number of marriageable men. This will be the beginning of the 'she' generation, which will be a generation unimpressed with sex as a selling point."

Exhibit 16.11

The variety of illustrations and captions help this ad to be inviting. You say to yourself, "Maybe I'll learn something."
Courtesy: Howard, Merrell & Partners.

Dr. Brothers makes the common (and, it could be argued, sexist) mistake of assuming that men are interested in sex and women are not. In truth, the publications that carry the sexiest advertising today are women's publications. And that kind of advertising attracts considerable notice and readership and will continue to do so until human beings reproduce exclusively by parthenogenesis.

At the same time, it should be emphasized that sexy ads tend to be simple ads—perfectly reasonable because clutter and salaciousness are not really compatible. The best ads of this type may feature nudity, but are not explicitly erotic.

To the politically correct, we say: Sex sells. Get used to it.

4. *Use Celebrities*   Opinion surveys indicate that Americans do not believe an ad simply because it features a well-known person hawking the product. However, according to our data, ads with celebrities earn "noted" scores that are 13 percent higher than average. They are particularly effective with women readers, scoring 15 percent higher than average, compared with 10 percent higher for men. Overall, ads with testimonials from celebrities score 11 percent above the average, whereas testimonials from noncelebrities actually earn below-average scores. Celebrities may not be believable, but they are very effective at attracting reader attention, the first job of any advertisement.

5. *Exploit the Potential of Color*   Print advertising has the potential to contend with television. The moving image is a profoundly effective means of communication, and anyone who has ever tried to amuse a baby knows that the eye has an inherent attraction to motion. At the same time, the eye is also attracted to bold, bright, and beautiful color. Our data indicate that one-page color ads earn "noted" scores that are 45 percent higher on average than comparable black-and-white ads; two-page color ads earn scores that are 53 percent higher than similar black-and-white ads. Generally, the more colorful, the better (as long as the advertiser keeps in mind the other nine principles).

Television has a lock on the moving image, but print's ability to generate astonishing, eye-catching colors is substantial, and publications should do everything possible to stay current with new advances in color technology.

6. *Go with the Flow*   Every ad has flow to it, and the flow is determined by the positioning of the various creative elements. Ads with good flow send the reader's eye around the page to take in all the important elements: the illustration, headline, body copy, and brand name. Ads with bad flow may attract a fair amount of attention at first, but send the reader off the page. For example, a number of advertisers make the mistake of placing a flashy illustration toward the bottom of the page and the copy and headline at the top. In such cases, the most powerful element of an ad can turn out to be the most detrimental, because that alluring illustration steals attention away from the copy.

For another example, consider the automobile industry and the way some advertisers position the automobile on the page. The eye, our data indicate, tends to follow the car from back to front. Thus, if the car is facing to the right on the page and is positioned above the body copy, the eye, moving back to front, ends up over the beginning of the copy, exactly the right place if you want to have your copy read. But consider how many advertisers position their cars facing left to right, thus "leading" the reader to the right side of the page, the point at which the reader is most likely to continue on to the next page without studying the rest of the ad.

7. *Avoid Ambiguity*   Although it appears that Europeans accept, if not welcome, ambiguous themes and symbols, we have found that Americans have little tolerance for advertising that does not offer a clear and distinct message. Several years ago, Benson & Hedges attracted a great deal of attention with an ad featuring a man clad only in pajama bottoms and a bewildered expression, standing in a dining room in the middle of what appears to be a brunch party. The trade press evidently was far more attracted to the ad than were readers, who, our data indicated, were as nonplused by the ad as its star was by his predicament, and reacted with considerable hostility to the advertiser who dared to confuse them.

Americans like it straight. They choose not to spend a great deal of time thinking about the messages in their advertising. If the point of the ad is not clear, the typical American reader will move on to the next page.

8. *Heighten the Contrast*   We live in a visual culture, and one thing that delights the eye is contrast. So advertisers would do well to employ what might be called "visual irony" in their advertising. One suggestion: contrast the content of the ads.

American Express produced one of the best ads of 1988 by featuring the diminutive Willie Shoemaker standing back to back with the altitudinous Wilt Chamberlain. The contrast was humorous and eye-catching. Another way to fullfill this principle is to contrast the elements constituting the form of the ad—color, for example. Our data indicate that using black as a background makes elements in the foreground pop off the page. Stolichnaya earned average scores with a horizontal shot of the product against a white background. When the same layout was produced with a change only in the background, from white to black, the scores increased by 50 percent, on average.

9. *Use Children and Animals* Almost any advertising can succeed with an appeal to the emotions, and children and animals appeal to all but the most hard-hearted. It is logical, of course, to use a close-up of a child when selling toys. (Yet flip through an issue of a magazine for parents and notice how many products for children's clothing, for example, do not use children—a missed opportunity if there ever was one.) And pets, of course, are naturals for pet food.

The trick is to find an excuse to use a child or furry little beast when your product is not even remotely connected to those models. Hewlett-Packard pulled this off beautifully by featuring a Dalmatian and the headline, "Now the HP LaserJet IIP is even more irresistible." The ad won the highest scores in the computer and data equipment product category for the 1990 Starch Readership Award. Hitachi has used the double lure of celebrity Jamie Lee Curtis and various animals—cats and parrots primarily—to hawk the company's televisions in a campaign that has consistently garnered the highest "noted" scores for the category.

10. *When an Ad Has a Good Deal of Copy, Make It as Inviting as Possible* A source of never-ending astonishment to us is the advertiser who insists on shrinking and squeezing copy into a tight corner of an ad in order to maximize "white space"—a triumph of style over common sense. Others present copy over a mottled background, making it almost impossible to read easily. Two other common problems are reverse print over a light background, offering too little contrast, and centered copy (i.e., unjustified right and left margins), which forces the reader to work too hard to find the beginning of each line. An advertiser who includes a fair amount of copy obviously hopes that it will be read. Relatively few readers choose to spend the time to read most of the copy of any advertisement; if you get 20 percent of magazine readers to delve into your copy, you are doing very well. So the challenge is to make the whole process as easy for the reader as possible. Good content alone will not attract readers. The best-written, wittiest, and most powerful copy will be overlooked unless it is well spaced and sufficiently large and clear to invite the reader.

Thoughts on Outdoor

The new production technologies offer the opportunity to create something bigger than life. Here you can create disruption from the ordinary. A giant peach sitting in a field will attract attention because it is a thousand times larger than a peach should be. The Richards Group in Dallas had cows painting an outdoor poster for their client Chick-Fil-A. We all know that cows don't paint or climb, but when they do, we look.

Just a few thoughts on outdoor. First, you have a responsibility to create something wonderful, because most people dislike them cluttering up the environment. You should ask, as with any medium, how the ad will be integrated into the other kinds of communications. In Chapter 12, an overview of creative was given. Generally, there should no more than seven words in the main head. No, we're not saying it won't communicate with more than seven, but the more you have the harder it is to grasp quickly. This is truly a medium where simple is better. Reduce all the elements, if possible. If you have a bottle of Sobe energy drink as your illustration, do you need to also have a logo? Maybe, but if the bottle is large enough you'll easily see the logo on it. The point is to reduce the visual and verbal elements down to their simplest form. But that offers a challenge to be creative (Exhibit 16.12). The art director, Scott Ballew designed fiberglass pigeons and had them manufactured (about 3X normal size) to put on top of this outdoor board. That should not only attract attention, but entertain and be memorable.

Exhibit

16.12

This creative not only included the message but the pigeons.

Courtesy: Howard, Merrell & Partners.

SUMMARY

Simplicity is the key to great advertising. Good copy speaks to the common man. The great creative shops of today have a common thread running through their advertising—the headline, visual, and logo communicate the idea immediately.

Advertising motivates people by appealing to their problems, desires, and goals, and offering them a solution to their problems, satisfactions of their desires, and a means of achieving their goals.

In general, ads have a definite structure consisting of a promise of benefit in the headline (and maybe the spelling out of the promise in a subheadline), amplification of the story or facts, proof of claim, and action to take. Effective heads can be long or short, but they need to clearly communicate the message. The subheadline can expand on the promise presented in the headline and can provide transition between the headline and the first sentence of the body copy. The body copy is where you build your case with consumers for the product and support the promise in the head or subhead. The details about the product or service are presented here, along with support for your claim.

The creative essence of copywriting is to see a product in a fresh unique way. The chief approaches used to describe products are the factual, the imaginative, and the emotional. A slogan sums up the theme for a product's benefits. It needs to be a memorable message with few words.

Slogans can be developed from several points of view; the institutional and hard-sell viewpoints are the most common.

The place to start planning an ad is the creative work plan or the creative brief. If written properly, the creative work plan will tell you what the message should be in the ad and what the ad is to accomplish. It tells you the ad's specific purpose. However, no work plan will tell you how to execute the copy—that's part of the creative process.

REVIEW

1. What is time famine?
2. How can advertisers use psychological appeals?
3. What are Ogilvy's great advertising elements?
4. What's the purpose of the headline?
5. What is the purpose of amplification?
6. What is meant by "copy style"?
7. What are the characteristics of an effective slogan?

TAKE IT TO THE NET

We invite you to visit the Russell/Lane page on the Prentice Hall Web site at **www.prenhall.com/myphlip** for end-of-chapter exercises and applications.

Creative Directors try to inspire their creative staff to produce better ads. One way of doing this is to try and foster thinking about the process and execution. Below are two thought-provoking memos sent to the staff at Howard, Merrell & Partners, by Gary H. Knutson, Vice Chairman/Chief Creative Officer.

> **memo # 1**
> **to**   *The creative department*
> **from**   *Knutson*
> **re**   *Wordplay*
> **date**   *15 May*

Now that you've got all those puns out of your system, show me the real headlines.

Writing provocative, memorable, compelling headlines is the most rigorous test of a copywriter.

Indulging in puns and wordplay will retard your professional development, leaving you unfit for anything but a job at a huge agency where they mistake that sort of vapidity for wit.

When was the last time you saw a pun in an Ed McCabe headline? Or one by Julian Koenig? Or one by David Ogilvy?

Never, that's when.

But every would-be copywriter's portfolio is full of the stuff.

Now, I will confess that I have also sinned.

A dozen years ago, I worked at BBDO on the first campaign wherein the phone company announced that consumers could buy their phones instead of leasing them. Featured were decorator-style phones.

What do you suppose one of my first headlines was?

Class rings.

I loved it. The art director loved it. We did more of the same.

I took the campaign to the creative director in New York for approval and practically got thrown out on my ear.

And on the plane ride back, what do you suppose was the first headline I came across in an inflight-magazine ad from *another* telephone company?

Class rings.

So not only was I subjected to calumny from my boss because my headline failed to communicate the essential information (now you can buy your phone from Ma Bell instead of paying rent forever), but it was the ultimate *generic* headline for *any* telephone ad featuring good-looking phones, new or old, bought or leased.

That's the main problem with wordplay. It creates a false sense of accomplishment, keeping you from digging deeper for the real "killer" headlines.

Make no mistake, writing great headlines is hard. Wordplay is easy. That's why puns are used so much in magazine-article titles, morning-tv billboards, retail ads, and every other job where some poor schlub has to write twenty quick blurbs with a superficial gloss.

Do most agencies indulge in wordplay? Absolutely. Can you win awards with it? Absolutely. But it's still ten-minute advertising.

I won't say show me no puns, no-how, no-time, but they'd better be both relevant and very, *very* good.

Gary H. Knutson

memo # 2
to   *The creative department*
from *Knutson*
re   *wordplay*
date *15 May*

**If this is what we want to say,
why can't we just say it?**

How many times have you heard this from a client?

The answer is that if that was all there was to this business, we wouldn't need all you high-paid employees. It would be more like a civil service job, sort of like working at the post office.

You'd do what you're told, do it on time, and everyone would be happy. We wouldn't need fancy writers or art directors, certainly not for those clients who know exactly what they want to say and probably have a pretty good idea of how the ad should be laid out, too.

Imagine that Don Solomon's goal is to get all the single women in the agency to think that he's a wonderful, bright, handsome guy.

Now suppose that Don goes up to a girl and says, "I'm a wonderful, bright, handsome guy."

He has said what he wanted to say. Why wouldn't it work?

The reason, of course, is that there is a big difference between persuasion and flatulent braggadocio, and we're being paid to create the former.

Q: Who decides what is a good ad?

A: I do. There has to be a final say, one.

ghk

The Total Concept: Words and Visuals

Ideas and ads. How does a creative team get from an idea to a finished ad? What kind of visuals are best? How do we generate fresh ideas? After reading this chapter you will understand:

>> concepts and executional ideas

>> left- and right-brain ideas

>> how a creative team works

>> visualizing the idea

>> principles of design

>> kinds of visuals

The advertising industry has long debated between advertising that engages consumers in an entertaining way and creates an emotional bond and advertising that features fact-fueled messages and USP promises to differentiate the product. Jeff Goldsmithof Lowe Lintas & Partners says, "More and more clients are realizing creative ads work better, are more memorable and make their point effectively in the marketplace. You can run a good creative ad fewer times. People can remember it after seeing it three times rather than 30 times. Any USP advantage is gone in 15-minutes if you don't create an emotional bond with consumers." Grey Worldwide's chief creative officer: "You should bring together art and commerce. But you can do some of the most engaging funny work in the world and if it doesn't motivate the consumer to do something or stimulate some part of their brain, then it doesn't work."[1] So again we find that there isn't a simple set of rules that works for creating strong ads or other marketing communications. But all agree that strategic concepts and ideas are the foundation.

---

[1]Noreen O'Leary, "Does creative count," *AdWeek*, 11 December 2000, 32.

Create Relevant Ideas

What are some of the great ads you remember from your growing-up years? Why do you remember them? There probably was an idea that was relevant or entertaining to you. Our minds work in mysterious ways. We have to learn to take the reader or viewer beyond the strategy. We also need to go beyond style into a magical dimension. Classic campaigns did this: Brylcream's Greasy Kid Stuff, Avis's We're Only No. 2, Volkswagen's Lemon, Wendy's Where's the Beef, and AT&T's Reach Out and Touch Someone. Before we can create this kind of advertising, we have to learn to develop the idea behind the strategy.

George Lois, the outrageous art director, was once asked, "What is advertising?" He answered, "Advertising is poison gas. It should bring tears to your eyes, and it should unhinge your nervous system. It should knock you out." He admitted that his description is probably excessive but regards it as a forgivable hyperbole because it certainly describes the powerful possibilities of advertising. Great advertising should have the impact of a punch in the mouth. Great advertising should ask, without asking literally, "Do you get the message?" And the reader(viewer) should answer, without literally answering, "Yeah, I got it!" Lois says all of this can be accomplished with the "big idea." Robert Shaw West took a simplistic approach to sell candles—a light bulb. Using simple white space, a lightbulb and a logo. On the end of the lightbulb where the wattage number reads, "How romantic can a 60 watt dinner be?"(see Exhibit 17.1).

The creative process can be broken down into four basic areas: concepts, words, pictures, and the medium or vehicle used to present them. The dictionary defines a concept as a general notion or idea, an idea of something formed by mentally combining all its characteristics or particulars. In advertising, the **total concept** is a fresh way of looking at something—a novel way of talking about a product or service, a dramatic new dimension that gives the observer a new perspective. A concept is an idea. Many in advertising, including Lois, call it the big idea—one that is expressed clearly and combines words and visuals. The words describe what the

total concept The combining of all elements of an ad—copy, headline, and illustrations—into a single idea.

Exhibit 17.1

The headline is written on the lightbulb, "How romantic can a 60 watt dinner be?" The visual and words work together as one.

Courtesy: West & Vaughan.

basic idea is, and the visuals repeat what the words say or, even better, reinforce what the words say or provide a setting that makes the words more powerful.

Your creative concept must not only grab attention, it must also get across the main selling point and the brand name. How often has someone seen a compelling ad only to later say, "I don't remember the brand name or product."

IDEAS COME FROM THE LEFT AND RIGHT BRAIN

The left hemisphere of the brain provides reasoning, controls verbal skills, and processes information (characteristics of copywriters). The right side provides intuition, processes information, controls the creative process, thinks nonverbally, responds to color, and is artistic (characteristics of art directors). So we are talking about a left-brain person and a right-brain person working together to develop a concept. Each comes to the table with a different point of view.

Having created a host of memorable campaigns—"Millertime," "Soup Is Good Food," "Things Go Better With Coke," "Tastes Great, Less Filling"—Bill Backer, in his *The Care and Feeding of Ideas*, defines a basic idea or concept as an abstract answer to a perceived desire or need. And an **executional idea** is a rendering in words, symbols, sounds, colors, shapes, forms, or any combination thereof, of an abstract answer to a perceived desire or need. We use the word *execute* in ad development. It is a schizophrenic verb. It means to complete or put into effect or to use according to a pattern—as a work of art. Of course, it also means "to put to death."

John Hegarty believes it is the idea that drives things. He has a quote blown up on his wall from a dictionary and it says, "An idea is a thought or plan formed by mental effort." In other words the color blue is not an idea. It's a means of making your idea more profound.

executional idea It is a rendering in words, symbols, sounds, colors, shapes, forms, or any combination thereof, of an abstract answer to a perceived desire or need.

THE CREATIVE TEAM

In general, the responsibility for the visual, layout, and graphics is that of the art director. The copywriter has the job of creating the words for the ad, and maybe the ad concept. We say "maybe" because where creative teams are used it is the responsibility of the team to develop a concept. The copywriter needs to understand art direction and the art director needs to appreciate the impact of words. Together they need to have a rapport to be successful. Both are concept thinkers. Both think in terms of words and pictures, after the team arms themselves with all the information they need. When they have settled on a target audience and a creative strategy, these left- and right-brain people begin to create.

This relationship between copywriter and art director is almost like a marriage. You spend an average of 8 hours a day with your partner—that's 40 hours a week, or 2,080 hours a year. The truth is, that better teams feed off each other. Each has their own method of developing big ideas. But there probably isn't a single method. Dick Lord, chairman of The Lord Group, says, "I get my biggest drawing pad and I'll draw little thumbnails and I'll just do headlines or visual ideas. I'll brainstorm myself. I'll sit by myself and do 60, 70—I don't edit them. And then you go over them a little later and you find that maybe 10 or 12 that you could look at again. Then, you get with your art director partner, and say, 'Well, what have you got? I have this.'" Some art directors and copywriters like to work by themselves first.

The tag reads, "If your store doesn't carry them, patronize better stores." Costa Del Mar sunglasses uses a quality for your money approach as it educates you to the basics of buying sunglasses (Exhibit 17.2). Could you have written 60 heads for this ad?

How to tell a pair of quality sunglasses from high-priced junk.

When you pay a premium price for an automobile, you quite rightly expect superior workmanship. We regret to inform you that this logic does not hold with sunglasses.

The kind of flimflam artists who got rich making "designer" jeans have also inflicted themselves on our industry.

Examples of their incompetence abound. Consider *lenses*, for example:

Many sunglass makers offer lightly-tinted lenses, in every conceivable hue, with seeming disregard for their effectiveness.

You won't find any such glasses with our name on them.

We are not in business to make fashion glasses to wear in restaurants. *Our glasses are designed to provide eye protection from the sun.*

All our lenses are either Polycarbonate or Polarized CR-39, the materials that opticians specify. Our lenses are optically perfect, hard-coated to resist scratches, and provide 100% ultraviolet protection.

Compared to glass, they are both stronger and lighter.

There is no finer example than in our official *America's Cup* models. These lenses are *ultra dark* Polarized, with a unique double-gradient tint for superior glare protection.

But as stringent as we are about lenses, we are equally demanding of our frames. Cheap sunglasses — and an appalling number of expensive ones — are made with nylon frames. The nature of this material is that it has a "memory."

This might be of benefit if you routinely sit on your glasses.

Unfortunately, it also makes it impossible to *adjust* them.

By contrast, Costa Del Mar frames are individually hand-cut from top quality *Zyl* (cellulose acetate) material. It is both durable *and* thoroughly adjustable.

And where our competitors' frames may be painted, ours are *polished* to a natural sheen by tumbling them in *teakwood chips* for six full days.

Our metal-frame models receive equally meticulous attention.

And every pair comes with the assurance of American-made quality, backed by a *lifetime warranty.*

Costa Del Mar sunglasses range from $40 to $100 in price. Not enough money to gratify every purchaser's ego, perhaps, but enough to ensure that these are very simply the best sunglasses made.

Costa Del Mar

If your store doesn't carry them, patronize better stores.

Exhibit 17.2

The art direction and head work hard to communicate the ad's basic idea.
Courtesy: Howard, Merrell & Partners.

THE IDEA

Strong ideas may be difficult to develop but are worth fighting for when you find one. Strong ideas are simple ideas. People do not remember details as clearly as they recall concepts. In advertising, simple concepts become great ads through attention to detail—the words, typestyle, photography, and layout. A great advertising concept might survive poor execution, but the better crafted the ad, the better the chances that prospects will become customers.

We are not necessarily talking about hitting home runs with breakthrough advertising. We are not talking about Nike, Coke, or Pepsi, or glamorous products. We are talking about ideas that solve problems and communicate to consumers. Ogilvy & Mather took the declining Lever Brothers' Surf detergent brand and increased their sales by more than 20 percent by telling it like it is—doing laundry is a drag and there's no point in trying to deny it. Research showed that 45 percent of all laundry-doers do laundry only as a last resort. Lever's even has a name for them—the un-laundry people. The campaign's idea was to accentuate the negative by playing up the drudgery of doing laundry in a light-hearted way.

The idea must come alive, leap off the page, or grab your senses while you watch television. In addition, creative ideas do two important things: (1) They make the prime prospect consider your product first. (2) They implant your brand name indelibly in the prospect's mind and connect it to the positive attributes of your products.

Visualizing the Idea

It is time to execute the big idea. At this stage of the process, the creative team forms mental pictures of how the basic appeal can be translated into a selling message. Just as a good novel has various subplots that are brought together in a creative and interesting, cohesive story line, a good ad has a well-coordinated layout that flows well to create a compelling message about the product and its benefits.[2] You might

---

[2]Roper Starch Worldwide, Inc., *Starch Tested Copy,* Vol. 5, No. 3, 4.

visualize a sports car as speeding on a mountain road and around hairpin curves. You might see a sedan of understated luxury in front of a country club.

These mental pictures can be shown in words or in the crudest sketches. The crucial thing is to imagine the kind of mental picture that best expresses your idea. While thinking in the visual form (remember a picture is worth a thousand words), find the words that work with the visual for the most powerful effect. Show, if you can. Make as many versions of the basic idea as you can. Stretch your idea to the limit. Remember, Dick Lord said he sketched 70 rough ideas with heads. And yes, they could be done on the computer, but most seasoned art directors believe it should be sketched first. There is no magic number, some creative teams may do twice that number of sketches. Try every possibility, but remember your end result must deliver the basic message and the brand name. Does the illustration and copy deliver the creative work plan promise?

Marketing Approach to Visualization

We know that ads are not created for the sake of creativity. Each ad is created for a specific marketing purpose. All ads for a product should conform to the same set of objectives, even though some ads may not appear to be related, and usually they use the same theme or slogan in each ad.

Using all the information you have about the product or service, write a statement of the one thing you need to say about the product to the prime prospect. This is your promise, or the basic theme. A family restaurant might shift to low-fat menu items and promise, "We offer you all the things you like about family-style restaurants—convenience, great tasting foods, and reasonable prices, with the added benefit of fitting into your lifestyle since you want food that is nutritious and good for you." The illustrations must reflect these marketing concepts.

The promise is a consumer benefit statement that tells the prospect what the product will do for them.

THE CREATIVE LEAP

Are we about ready to begin to create an ad? Yes, if we have done our homework. Joseph Wallas, a creative theorist, said creativity is the product of four developmental stages: preparation, incubation, illumination, and verification or evaluation. A Leo Burnett creative director has said, "The best creative comes from an understanding of what people are thinking and feeling. Creativity is a sensitivity to human nature and the ability to communicate it." Starch Research suggests that we have to evaluate the consumer, address the consumer's needs, and suggest the clear benefit of using the product: "Tell her how her life will change for the better if she uses the product, and she'll pay close attention."

Where does the inspiration come from? Some think brainstorming or free association is the answer to creative inspiration, but others say very few ideas come from these techniques. A crazy idea may be the spark for a great campaign. The idea usually comes when you are not looking.

Jim Aitchison gives a few suggestions for the source of inspiration for an idea:

- Is there an idea in the packaging? Shape. Color. Label. Material the product is made of.
- How the product is made? Where it is made?
- In the product's history
- Showing what happens with the product
- Product's old advertising

The process is one part reason, one part heart, and one big part simple intuition, say others. So the creative leap is not necessarily the same for everyone. There may be truth that you spend more time on the logical process, and then the emotional part comes easier. Once you get the idea—the concept and visual and words that work together—you've made the creative leap. Leonard Monahan developed a visual idea for North protective work gloves that got right to the point of product advantage by using a wet sponge cut out in the shape of a hand as the illustration. The headline read, "This is what your hand looks like to most toxic chemicals." The headline and visual spoke to the reader as one. A mundane product became the most talked-about ad in its industry.

Have you ever thought about going to the hospital for a lobster dinner? Probably not, but in Raleigh Community Hospital it may be ordered from the Gourmet Room service Menu. They hired Culinary Institute chefs to teach their chefs how to create a gourmet menu worthy of fine restaurants. This ad doesn't look like a hospital ad (see Exhibit 17.3). It also uses a different approach to branding a hospital and developing a point of difference.

Layout

The creative leap is only the first step in ad making. The ad itself has a variety of elements: headlines, illustration, copy, logotype, maybe a subheadline, several other illustrations of varying importance, a coupon—the number of components varies tremendously from ad to ad. Putting them all together in an orderly form is called making up the layout of the ad. **Layout** is another of those advertising terms that is used in two senses: It means the total appearance of the ad—its overall design, the composition of its elements; it also means the physical rendering of the design of the ad—a blueprint for production purposes. You will hear some say: "Here's the layout," while handing another person a typed or keyboarded copy and a drawing. Right now, we are talking about the layout as the overall design of the ad.

layout A working drawing (may be computer developed) showing how an ad is to look. A printer's layout is a set of instructions accompanying a piece of copy showing how it is to be set up. There are also rough layouts, finished layouts, and mechanical layouts, representing various degrees of finish. The term *layout* is used also for the total design of an ad.

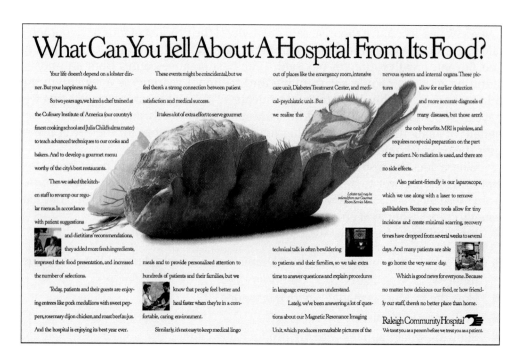

Layout Person as Editor

Although the person who creates the visual idea may be the same as the one who makes the layout, the two functions are different. The visualizer translates an idea into visual form; a layout person uses that illustration and all the other elements to make an orderly, attractive arrangement.

Before putting pencil to paper, however, the layout person—usually an art director—and the writer review all of the elements. The first task is to decide what is most important. Is it the headline? The picture? The copy? How important is the package? Should the product itself be shown, and if so, should it be shown in some special environment or in use? Is this ad to tell a fast story with a picture and headline, or is it a long-copy ad in which illustration is only an incidental feature? The importance of the element determines its size and placement within the ad.

The Need to Attract Attention

Attracting attention. Getting noticed. High visibility. No matter how you say it, this is the primary creative objective of an ad. Today's advertising has to work very hard to get noticed. You cannot rely on strategy alone—the positioning, the product appeals, the demographic and psychographic data that tell you what wavelength the consumer is on—to sell the consumer. Obvious as it sounds, you cannot sell people until you attract their attention. Put another way, people are not going to read the ad if they do not see it. Remember, your ad is competing with all the advertising clutter and editorial matter in a publication. Unfortunately, most ads in most publications are invisible.

Strong art and design are taking a front seat as companies try to cut through media clutter. A properly designed visual can provide an instantaneous message and feeling. And it can capture the attention of consumers quickly. But it has to be more than simply attracting attention. It must communicate the strategy. Good art direction can offer a fast, deep, and emotional connection. Alison Burns, president of Fallon McElligott, New York, says, "Using design to help solve the brand problem seems to me a no-brainer—it's where the whole thing starts." It is about things around the product that engage you, almost like guerrilla marketing. The product is noticed after the feeling, says the executive director of the Art Director's Club in New York.[3]

All the creative elements—the visual, the headline, the copy—must be strongly executed if the ad is to succeed. Research cannot tell us which creative techniques will work best because creative is not that scientific. Research generally tells us what has been successful, but there are no yardsticks to measure breakthrough advertising ideas. The basic guidelines for writing and designing ads are helpful, but there are not really any rules. How do you get an ad to stand out? The illustration is usually the key. Either an ad grabs people or it does not, and most often it is the illustration that gets them. Of course, many illustrations cannot tell the story alone—they require a headline to complete the communication. So the headline is extremely important to keep people's interest.

A picture is worth a thousand words, but we do not use illustrations solely to attract attention. They must have a strong relationship to the selling concept. Using a shock visual merely to gain attention is generally a mistake. If you are selling a hammer and your dominant visual is a woman in a bikini, you are using sexist imagery that has no relationship to the product. You are duping people. Now that we have your attention, buy our hammer. And because most people dislike being

---

[3]Patricia Winters Lauro, "Delivering a message before the consumer sees it," www.nytimes.com, 9 July 1999.

Exhibit
17.4

The beautiful illustration, head
brings you into a testimonial
for the product.

duped, they will resent your ad—and often your product as well. Yet, powerful images can demand your attention. The breathtaking scenic photo used by Stihl meshed with the head, "Out here, there's no bad news. There's no news at all," leads into a testimonial from a person from Pagosa Springs, Colorado (Exhibit 17.4).

There are three basic means of attracting attention:

1. Using the visual alone
2. Using the headline alone
3. Using a combination of the visual and headline

Do not assume that because we listed the visual first that the art director is more important than the copywriter. Remember, they are a team working together on both visual and language ideas.

Basic Design Principles

There are some general principles that guide the design of advertising and promotional layouts. Some art directors may use different terminology from that used here, but the basic assumptions are the same.

The following design principles, properly employed, will attract the reader and enhance the chances that the message is read.

Unity   All creative advertising has a unified design. The layout must be conceived in its entirety, with all its parts (copy, art, head, logo, and so forth) related to one another to give one overall, unified effect. If the ad does not have unity, it falls apart and becomes visual confusion. Perhaps unity is the most important design principle, but they are all necessary for an effective ad.

Harmony   Closely related to unity is the idea that all elements of the layout must be compatible. The art director achieves harmony by choosing elements that go together. This process is similar to dressing in the morning. Some items of clothing go together better than others—for example, stripes, plaids, or paisleys with solid colors. The layout needs harmonious elements to be effective; there should not be too many different type faces or sizes, illustrations, and so on.

Sequence   The ad should be arranged in an orderly manner so it can be read from left to right and top to bottom. The sequence of elements can help direct the eye in a structural or gaze motion. Place the elements so that the eye starts where you want it to start and travels a desired path throughout the ad. "Z" and "S" arrangements are common.

Emphasis   Emphasis is accenting or focusing on an element (or group of elements) to make it stand out. Decide whether you want to stress the illustration, the headline, the logo, or the copy. If you give all of these elements equal emphasis, your ad will end up with no emphasis at all.

Contrast   You need differences in sizes, shapes, and tones to add sparkle so the ad will not be visually dull. Altering type to bold or italic or using extended typefaces brings attention to a word or phrase and creates contrast between type elements. Contrast makes the layout more interesting.

Balance   By balance, we mean controlling the size, tone, weight, and position of the elements in the ad. Balanced elements look secure and natural to the eye. You test for balance by examining the relationship between the right and left halves of the ad. There are basically two forms of balance: formal and informal.

Formal Balance   The Subdue ad (Exhibit 17.5) signals sophistication and has elements of equal weights, sizes, and shapes on the left and right sides of an

A CAT WILL ALWAYS LAND ON ITS FEET.

IF YOU WASH YOUR CAR, IT WILL RAIN.

TOAST WILL ALWAYS FALL BUTTERED-SIDE DOWN.

Subdue

USE SUBDUE AND YOU'LL ELIMINATE PYTHIUM.

Exhibit

17.5

Clearly this fits our definition of a formal layout. If we were to draw a line down the center, you have equal weights on both sides.

Courtesy: Howard, Merrell & Partners

It's in May. It's in a field.
And there's no shade.
But every thirty minutes you
get a really good breeze.

Saturday, May 3, come to a sport where the athletes provide the air conditioning:
Brookhill. Aside from having to touch up your exquisitely coifed hairdo every
half hour, it's a social outing you'll find refreshing. To RSVP, just call 510-7915.

BROOKHILL ⸺ THE STEEPLECHASE

imaginary vertical line drawn down the center of the ad. Such symmetrical ads give an impression of stability and conservatism. Exhibit 17.6 has a few more ad elements to incorporate but also fits the description of formal balance above. Keep in mind that not all formal layouts will have exact equal weights. For instance, a logo may be on the lower right-hand corner and not have an equal element on the opposite side, but if all other elements are symmetrical, we would consider it a formal layout.

Informal Balance   The optical center of a page, measured from top to bottom, is five-eighths of the way up the page; thus, it differs from the mathematical center. (To test this, take a blank piece of paper, close your eyes, then open them, and quickly place a dot at what you think is the center of the page. The chances are that it will be above the mathematical center.) Imagine that a seesaw is balanced on the optical center. We know that a lighter weight on the seesaw can easily balance a heavier one by being farther away from the fulcrum. (The "weight" of an element in an ad may be gauged by its size, its degree of blackness, its color, or its shape.) In informal balance, objects are placed seemingly at random on the page, but in such relation to one another that the page as a whole seems in balance. This type of arrangement requires more thought than the simple bisymmetric formal balance, but the effects can be imaginative and distinctive, as illustrated by Exhibit 17.7. Yes, that's an ad for *cmyk* magazine, for those interested in color.

we
are
the
only
project
we
will
never
finish

we
are
all
students

cmyk magazine

subscribe
800 784 0745

Exhibit
17.7

This is an informal balanced
layout for CMYK magazine.
Courtesy: West & Vaughan.

Other Composing Elements

Color   One of the most versatile elements of an ad is color. It can attract attention
and help create a mood. Depending on the product and the advertising appeal,
color can be used for a number of reasons. Exhibit 17.8a and b is a two-part business-to-business ad that uses color to attract attention to a mundane product, a
conveyor washdown. It may not be interesting to you, but it would be beautiful if
your livelihood depended on selling it. Sheri Bevil Advertising focused on a color
water photo to add some interest.

A classic example of a product using color to differentiate itself was Nuprin
analgesic tablets. It increased its share of the ibuprofen market by using a superficial product difference—the yellow tablet. Nuprin's ads that simply said research
showed two Nuprins gave more headache relief than Extra Strength Tylenol did not
advance its share. Grey Advertising's Herb Lieberman said, "You have to convince
consumers that your product is different before they will believe the product is better." The color idea happened when their group creative director emptied a whole
bunch of pain relievers on his desk and found Nuprin was the only yellow tablet
there. Color was a way to dramatically and graphically show that Nuprin was different. Thus, the yellow-tablet campaign was born, showing a black-and-white photo
of hands holding two yellow tablets. The tagline explained that Nuprin is for your
worst pain.

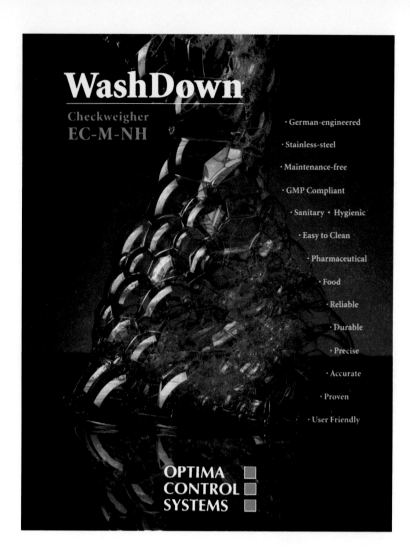

WashDown

Checkweigher
EC-M-NH

· German-engineered

· Stainless-steel

· Maintenance-free

· GMP Compliant

· Sanitary · Hygienic

· Easy to Clean

· Pharmaceutical

· Food

· Reliable

· Durable

· Precise

· Accurate

· Proven

· User Friendly

OPTIMA ■
CONTROL ■
SYSTEMS ■

Color can be extremely important in everything from ad layouts, products, and packaging to the psychological messages consumers perceive. Starch Advertisement Readership Service has over the years consistently found that color—bold colors and contrast—adds to an ad's pulling power.

Color Is an Attention-Getting Device   With few exceptions, people notice a color ad more readily than one in black and white. Exhibit 17.9 illustrates that the addition of four colors (using color photographs, for example) significantly increases the average advertising readership score beyond both two-color and black-and-white ads.

Some products can be presented realistically only in color. Household furnishings, food, many clothing and fashion accessories, and cosmetics would lose most of their appeal if advertised in black and white. Studies have been done to find the best consumer color or colors. For instance, the Pantone Color Institute asked consumers to select their current and future color preferences in specific product categories. In addition, a questionnaire collected data on demographics and placed the respondents into five lifestyle categories: prudent, impulsive, pessimistic, traditional, and confident. Advertisers found significant differences for such products as luxury cars versus economy cars. Leatrice Eisman, executive director of the Pantone Color Institute, says, "The impact of color can be used to gain attention to

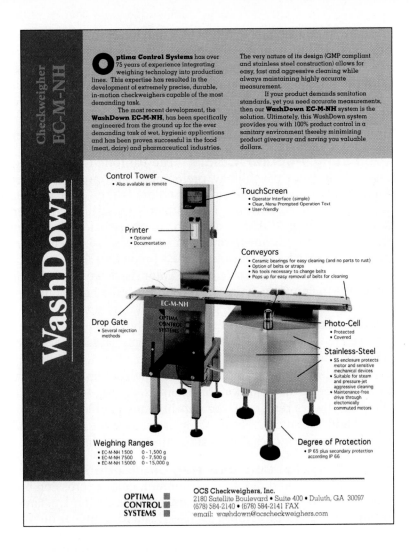

an ad or product. If used out of context, colors can get enormous attention on the printed page."[4]

Color for the Web and Products In creating for the Web, according to Barry Ridge, Color Marketing Group chairholder, designers must deal with a smaller color palette than what is available in print. Clients that have traditionally been conservative in their graphics are using bright yellows, bright lime greens,

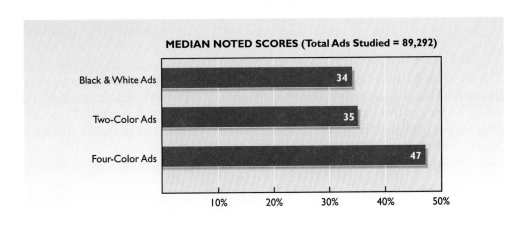

---

[4]Anne Telford, *Communication Arts,* January/February 1977, 84–89.

orange to grab attention on the screen, but never would use these in print. The Web is opening up the range of acceptable color to bright hues in our daily lives.

People involved in product design are trying to develop new colors to make their products look new. Among the developments and applications are layering of colors, new vapor colors that change as they are viewed from different angles. Ridge says, metallic silver and variations are very hot.[5] Purple is becoming the new blue. As it becomes more accepted, it's not seen as a radical color or feminine color.

Predicting Popular Colors The Pantone Color Institute conducts color research on color psychology, preferences, and professional color applications. Another organization that predicts colors is the Color Association of America, which forecasts color trends for products and fashion. Another group, the Color Marketing Group (CMG), is a not-for-profit association of some 1,500 designers that forecasts trends one to three years in advance for all industries, manufactured products, and services. Obviously, these predictions have an impact on advertisers.

Margaret Walch, director of the Color Association of the United States, says, "since the millennium, we're shaking off the influences of heaven, water and spirituality as expressed by blues, green and yellow tones." This is giving way to emerging reds and "aristocratic" scarlet and mahogany hues as well as re-browns and rich-yellow-browns. Designer Stephen Loges says, "color ought to enhance and reinforce the design concept rather than be an arbitrary choice." Color has always been a key component of branding. Unquestionably some brands are so strong they supercede the need for consistent color use. IBM comes to mind, although IBM may always remain as *Big Blue* in many people's mind. Most brands, on the other hand, are so connected to one or two colors that the brand is evoked just by looking at two swatches side by side. Purple and Orange? FedEx, of course."[6]

Color Globalization and Regionalization With the global aspects of today's business and design environment, color is crossing borders and boundaries. Still, strong regional and cultural preferences remain. For example, the bright sunny colors of tropical areas such as Costa Rica appear out of place and context when applied to a setting like New York City, and people in Seattle where the weather is primarily gray all winter, people choose brighter colors such as yellow.

White Space Some layout people and designers become so preoccupied with the illustration that they forget that white space or blank space is a very significant design tool. The basic rule for using white space is to keep it to the outside of the ad. Too much white space in the middle of an ad can destroy unity by pushing the eye in several directions and confusing the reader. Obviously, the *CMYK* magazine is an extreme case of using white space (Exhibit 17.6). VisArt uses a color headline, a small illustration, and a lot of white space to make their ad distinctive (Exhibit 17.10).

Preparing the Layout

The layout is the orderly arrangement of all the copy elements in a print ad. It is basically a blueprint that the production people will follow to complete the finished ad. An ad may go through different levels of roughness as it is developed. These different types of layouts represent different stages of conventional, that is, not electronic, development of the ad.

[5]"Color forecast," *Graphic Design:USA*, June 2000, 78–82.
[6]Stephen Loges, "Graphic designers on color," *Graphic Design:USA*, June 2000, 97.

EVEN OUR AMERICAN FILMS ARE FOREIGN TO MOST PEOPLE.

VisArt Video

The locally-owned video alternative, with six area locations. Call 683-2795 for the store nearest you.

- *Thumbnail sketches*: miniature drawings trying out different arrangements of the layout elements. The best of these will be selected for the next step.
- *Rough layouts*: drawings that are equivalent to the actual size of the ad. All elements are presented more clearly to simulate the way the ad is to look. The best of these will be chosen for the next step.
- *The **comprehensive,** or mechanical, layout (often just called the comp or the mechanical)*: all the type set and placed exactly as it is to appear in the printed ad. Artwork is drawn one and a half times the actual size it will be in the ad (to be reduced by one-third for sharper reproduction) and is prepared separately; therefore, it is precisely indicated on the comprehensive by blank boxes or electronically scanned into position for a computer comp. This layout will be used for client approval.

comprehensive A layout accurate in size, color, scheme, and other necessary details to show how a final ad will look. For presentation only, never for reproduction.

The rough layout in Exhibit 17.11 uses markers, whereas the comprehensive (Exhibit 17.12) uses computer-generated type and illustration. Exhibit 17.13 is the finished color ad as it appeared in the publications.

Once the basic ad for a campaign has been approved, layouts for subsequent ads usually consist of just a rough and finished layout.

Computer Design

Today most agency ad layouts are created in-house on their own computers. However, there are independent graphic computer service houses that are specialists and have the expertise to operate their expensive and highly sophisticated hardware and software for a reasonable fee.

We define computer graphics as the ability to draw or display visual information on a video terminal. Raster scan graphics is the most common computer display. Each spot on the screen, called a **pixel,** represents a location in the computer's memory. The number of individual pixels will determine the resolution of the image—this is the difference between poor-quality computer-set type or visuals and good reproduction-quality images. The more pixels, the higher the resolution and the smoother the image. The resolution of a screen controls its clarity and sharpness.

In the past, the creation and production processes have been separate and distinct. Because of the advances in computer hardware and software, it is possible for one person to do both layout and production, although software expertise may continue to keep these functions specialized. Today, mastery of layout demands a knowledge of art, type, design, and also photography, computers, and electronic imaging.

pixel The smaller element of a computer image that can be separately addressed. It is an individual picture element.

The Visual

Research indicates that 98 percent of the top-scoring ads contain a photograph or illustration, proving that human beings are highly visual creatures, according to Cahners Advertising Performance Studies. In most ads, the photograph or illustration takes between 25 and 67 percent of the layout space (see Exhibit 17.14).[7]

Art Directing and Photography

Art directing and photography are twin disciplines—each, in theory, raises the other up a notch. Having a great photo in the wrong layout makes for bad advertising. Betsy Zimmerman, art director at Goodby, Silverstein & Partners, says, "The layout's gotta come first. I'll bring a photocopy of the layout to the shoot, and we try to do Polaroids to size, so I can put the two together. The key is to shoot a million Polaroids so I can iron out all the idiosyncrasies rather than be surprised on film." It might look great as a photo, but once you put it in its environment, it is totally different. Jeff Weiss of Margeotes/Fertitta & Weiss says every ad contains two things: what you want to say and how you want to say it. What art directing can do is deliver things emotionally, not intellectually. Great art direction takes the selling idea and furthers it without your even knowing it. Take Saks, for example. Their ads cannot just say Saks is glamorous in words—it has to feel glamorous and sophisticated.[8]

Photography can be very expensive. A photo for use in an ad may cost between $700 and $10,000, depending on the photographer's reputation and the advertiser's willingness to pay.

The Artist's Medium

The tool or material used to render an illustration is called the artist's medium, the term medium being used in a different sense than it is in the phrase advertising medium (for example, television or magazines). The most popular artist's medium in advertising is photography. Britain's award-winning art director, Neil Godfrey says, "I like to use something people can believe in. I rarely use illustration. Nine-tenths of the time, it just doesn't have the impact of photography."[9] The Smoky Mountain photo of North Carolina has much more impact than an illustration of the same scenery (Exhibit 17.15). Other popular ones are pen and ink, pencil, and

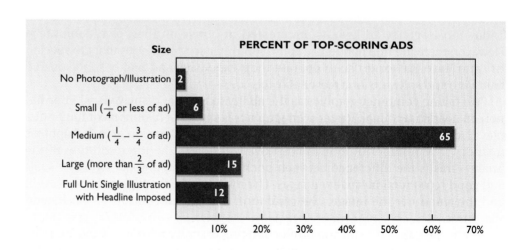

Exhibit

17.14

The majority of top-scoring ads contain a photograph or illustration.

---

[7]Cahners Publishing Co., *CARR Report* No. 118.5, 4.
[8]"Art directing photography," *Art Direction*, March 1993, 42–54.
[9]Jim Aitchison, *Cutting Edge Advertising* (Singapore: Prentice-Hall, 1999), 243.

crayon. Perhaps a photograph will be used as the main illustration for an ad, but pen and ink will be used for the smaller, secondary illustration. The choice of the artist's medium depends on the effect desired, the paper on which the ad is to be printed, the printing process to be used, and, most important, the availability of an artist who is effective in the desired medium.

Trade Practice in Buying Commercial Art

Creating an ad usually requires two types of artistic talent: the imaginative person, who thinks up the visual idea with a copywriter or alone and makes the master layout; and an artist, who does the finished art of the illustrations. Large agencies have staff art directors and layout people to visualize and create original layouts, as well as studios and artists to handle routine work.

In the largest advertising centers, a host of freelance artists and photographers specialize in certain fields for preparing the final art. In fact, agencies in some cities go to one of the major art centers to buy their graphic artwork for special assignments.

There are two important points to observe in buying artwork, especially photographs. First, you must have written permission or a legal release (Exhibit 17.16) from anyone whose picture you will use, whether you took the picture or got it from a publication or an art file. (In the case of a child's picture, you must obtain a release from the parent or guardian.) Second, you should arrange all terms in advance. A photographer may take a number of pictures, from which you select one. What will be the price if you wish to use more than one shot? What will be the price if you use the picture in several publications?

Freelance artists' and photographers' charges vary greatly, depending on their reputation, the nature of the work, in what medium the work is being used, and whether the ad is to run locally, regionally, or nationally. An art illustration for a magazine may cost $200 if by an unknown artist and up to about $5,000 if by an established artist. A photography session may cost $200 a day for an unknown photo 7 graphs to about $2,500 for an established photographer. People charge what they think the art or photography is worth or what the client can or is willing to pay. As a result, the better the reputation of the artist or photographer, the more expensive the final product will likely be.

Exhibit
17.16

Typical Model Release Used by Agencies

Other Sources of Art and Photography

Clients will not always be able to afford the money or time for original advertising art or photography. There are three basic sources of ready-made images: clip art, computer clip art, and stock photos.

Clip Art and Computer Clip Art   Ready-to-use copyright-free images are available from clip-art services. The art may be available on CD-ROM or from printed services in which the illustrations are in black and white on glossy paper, ready to use. All you have to do is cut it out or print it off your computer. Almost any kind of image is available from clip-art services: families, men, women, children, business scenes, locations (e.g., farm, beach), and special events. The disadvantage to using clip art is that you have to match your idea to available images, and many of the illustrations are rather average. The advantages are the very reasonable costs and extensive choice of images. Some clip-art services offer a monthly book or computer disk (or on-line service) with a wide variety of images; others offer specialized volumes—restaurant art, supermarket art, or medical art, for example. Once you purchase the clip-art service, the art is yours to use as you see fit.

Stock Photos   There are hundreds of stock-photo libraries available to art directors and advertisers. Each maintains thousands of photographs classified according to the subject categories, including children, animals, lifestyle situations, city landscapes, sports, and models. A photographer submits photos to the stock company, which will publish some photos in their catalog (or on a CD-ROM). The photographer pays for the space occupied by the photos. Clients then browse through the stock company's catalog to research its files for a suitable photo. The art director or advertiser then leases or contracts for use of the selected photo to use in an ad. The fee is based on the intended use of the photo.

More than 80 percent of graphic design professionals use stock imagery in their work when the situation calls for it. *Graphic Design:USA* found a number of reasons for deciding to use stock images. They include:[10]

- Time pressure: deadlines and fast turnarounds
- Budget restraints: stock is less expensive than assignment photography offering clients cost-savings
- Quality, choice, variety: stock collections have grown in quality, sophistication and quantity
- Ease of accessibility: lots of resources, royalty-free options, digital delivery, e-commerce sites for easy access.

Masterfile, a stock photo company, enables an agency to clear Global Rights Protection for a specific photograph within minutes. Their proprietary computer network can determine any potential conflicts, locally or around the world. It operates on-line 24 hours a day. Another company, Comstock's Encyclopedia of Stock Photography has an on-line access service, which is a computer bulletin board that lets you access and preview your images from one of their catalogs 24 hours a day. They add new images daily. Comstock says, "Stock photo pricing isn't based on the known cost of producing the photo: It's based on exactly how you will use it. The more modest your project, the less an image will cost." Their on-line service is described as: "Your selection, hand picked from our library of more than 5 million images, will be fully digitized and accessible via modem for you to download and review in 4 hours." In the past, the delivered image was in the form of a transparency or chrome image. Many on-line capabilities have been around since 1994, featuring stock-photo agencies that allow ad agencies to select images from an on-line network from numerous stock-photo sources. The agency can select images and then instantly download low-resolution thumbnail images for inspection. The image may also be marketed and delivered by means of CD-ROM. Images are scanned, stored, digitized, and reproduced on a CD-ROM.

Other companies offer a whole disc of images—ranging from about 300 to 500 digitized picture files—on a CD-ROM for a single purchase price. The CD technology offers individual photographers the opportunity to market their images on their own CDs. When a user decides to order an image, the computer will notify the company and negotiate fees.

SUMMARY

We have now made the transition from thinking of ideas to making ads. We have started with the primary consumer benefit, the most important thing we can say about the product.

In advertising, the total concept is a fresh way of looking at something. A concept is an idea. A big idea is one that expresses clearly and combines words and visuals. Another way of looking at it is that a basic idea is an abstract answer to a perceived desire or need.

The creative team—an art director and a copywriter—next develops the best approach to presenting the executional idea—a rendering in words, symbols, sounds, shapes, and so forth, of an abstract answer to a perceived desire or need. Then comes layout preparation (usually done by an art director), in which the various elements of the ad are composed into a unified whole. Creating an ad that will attract attention is one of the art director's primary concerns. When arranging the

---

[10]"Stock visual decisions," *Graphic Design:USA*, 128.

elements of an ad, the layout artist has to consider the principles of design: unity, harmony, sequence, emphasis, contrast, and balance.

Ads usually begin as thumbnail sketches. Subsequent steps are rough layout, the finished layout, and the comps. The computer simplifies this process: In computer design, the roughs are no longer rough, and the comprehensives are better because the layout and typography are exact.

In most cases, art and photography are original executions of the art director's ideas, illustrated or shot according to his or her specifications by freelance artists or photographers. When time or money is short, clip-art or computer-art services or stock photography may be used.

REVIEW

1. What is the big idea?
2. What is the executional idea?
3. What do art directors and copywriters do?
4. What are the basic means of attracting attention?
5. What is the difference between a thumbnail and a rough layout?
6. What are stock photos?

TAKE IT TO THE NET

We invite you to visit the Russell/Lane page on the Prentice Hall Web site at **www.prenhall.com/myphlip** for end-of-chapter exercises and applications.

Print Production

CHAPTER OBJECTIVES

The age of digital production is almost complete. Many publications and printers have instituted computer-to-plate production systems over the past few years; however, advertising production has been behind the curve. Today, both traditional and digital production exist. After reading this chapter you will understand:

>> production department

>> digital and traditional production processes

>> mechanical and artwork

>> proofing

Advertisers need to understand what happens after a print ad, collateral, or promotion has been written, the layout prepared, and the illustrations completed. What do we need to send to the publication so they can print the piece? What are the preparation steps and printing procedures for the brochure or insert? Is it to be traditional or digital methods of production? How long will this take?

Advertising and marketing people need to have a working knowledge of production because it involves quality, cost, and time issues. This conversion process, going from the original layout to a finished piece (see Exhibit 18.1), is the responsibility of the advertiser or agency, and is called print production. Production requirements differ from ad to ad. Advertising and marketing staff may be producing magazine or newspaper ads, collateral brochures, direct response, outdoor, and transit. They need a working knowledge of all these production processes, as well as publication mechanical specifications. The planning process may involve a great deal of money and people. Before we get into the organization, let us look at some important issues.

DIGITAL ADVERTISING AND PRODUCTION

Most ads are created on a computer, but much of the production still involves converting the ad from the computer screen to film for the publication or printer. To some extent, the advertising industry controls only a portion of their production efforts. If you have a print ad going into a publication, the publication sets its own specifications standards of how ads are to be produced and presented. Traditional production requires converting all of the ad elements to film and then to plates. Total digital production is converting the computer images directly to plates, bypassing any film. The ad created digitally on your computer may have to be converted to a piece of film so that printing plates can be made. You have to understand the requirements.

In this chapter we are forced to think in terms of both—digital production and traditional printing. It may be some time before all ads and printing are produced totally in digital formats in all publications.

The creation of an ad is primarily digital. A printer's or publication's prepress operations may be a combination of digital and traditional. Once the press has a plate made from either technology, the printing process is generally traditional.

Technical Considerations

Problems with digital advertising are often attributed to technology issues, and there can be many of these. The printer is not the only person having to be computer proficient. The computer artists must be knowledgeable in preparing files so they can output properly. The computer artist must have font and photo files in the proper resolution.

Compatibility   File compatibility can also be an issue. The files should be saved in a version common to all parties involved in the process. Today's computer artists, writers, prepress service providers, and publishers work in a variety of computer environments that can lead to file compatibility problems. Often agencies will send a test file to determine whether or not their electronic files can be read correctly. This may avoid unnecessary lost time, frustration, and film costs.

Industry Standards   It appears that digital file transmission formats such as TIFF/IT and Adobe's PDF (portable document format) are close to becoming industry standards, and proofing devices such as Kodak Approval, the Iris, and the Rainbow are becoming more acceptable. Many believe that the real issues aren't technological, but rather financial. The investment can be huge.

Preflighting   Agency production managers have to check who is responsible for preflighting, the prepress service provider/printer or the agency. Preflighting, a term borrowed from the checklist procedures airplane pilots use before taking off, is used to make sure digital files will image correctly. This process thoroughly analyzes a design or electronic mechanical for output readiness, regardless of the intended output device. It is a way to discover incomplete or missing digital files or fonts.

Color Calibration   This is another issue of concern to everyone in the process. All monitors, proofing devices, and printers must be calibrated so that images and hard copy look the same no matter where the files are viewed. Otherwise, a client may output a digital proof on the other side of the country that doesn't match what the prepress or printer is producing.

Bidding   When the advertiser/agency is producing collateral material, the advertiser or agency finds a printer who can efficiently produce the job at a reasonable price. There are on-line services, such as printbid.com, who assist in getting the best cost. It should be remembered that not every printer can efficiently produce every job—or at the same quality. It becomes the production manager's job to ensure that the "right" printer is chosen. Usually, the advertiser or agency requests three bids from comparable printers.

PREPRESS PROCESS

What has to be done to the layout design before it can be printed involves the preparation for the act of printing. Here we outline the major steps for the traditional and digital methods.

Traditional:	Ad concept: copy, layout, and approvals
	Typesetting
	Electronic color separations
	Layout
	Film preparation
	Platemaking
	Printing
Digital:	Ad concept: copy, layout, and approvals
	Scanning
	Layout
	Proofing
	Preflight
	Proofing
	Film preparation (if not CTP)
	Platemaking
	Printing

Change to Digital

Here are a few of the changes that digital production has made to the production process:

Comprehensives, or Comps   In the initial stages, a comp is created digitally by an art director or designer. Today there are very few "loose" comps (hand- or marker-drawn). The comp presented to the client appears to be finished. Costs for type, cellos, paper, and studio labor have all been eliminated, leaving only color-output charges for presentation comps.

Type   Typography, photostats, and mechanicals rarely exist. These are subsumed in the digital studio, under the heading of electronic type/mechanical. The material costs for typesetting, film, stats, mechanical boards, and studio labor have basically vanished.

Artwork   Art in various forms, such as dye-sublimation prints, is no longer submitted for reproduction. These prints, too, are being replaced by digital processes. The turnaround time for production has significantly decreased. For example, to produce a rush newspaper ad, once the idea is created, the agency sets it in the desktop (several hours), pulls stock photos off the Internet (several hours), then digitally transmits the execution to six daily newspapers (one hour). The total cost of materials to the client is the stock-photo charge plus digital transmission: $550 to $1,200. The material costs are a fraction of what they were 10 years ago, and the turnaround time is slashed from days to hours.

Publication Material   Material for publication used to be manufactured in the photoengraving process. Now, photoengraving charges have been replaced by separation/composition, and the average turnaround time has been reduced from eight to one or two working days for the first submission. In addition, the average cost for separations and composition has been cut in half. The cost reductions are due to the advances in desktop publishing and telecommunications, which allow agencies to produce work more efficiently at a fraction of the cost.[1]

PRINT PRODUCTION

The agency's print production group performs that transformation process from the original creative concept to the client's printed communication; this may include magazines, newspapers, outdoor and transit, point-of-purchase, collateral brochures (see Exhibit 18.2), and direct response. This group must have a working knowledge of all these production processes, as well as publication mechanical specifications, budgetary considerations, and quality requirements. Last but not least, they must understand the time span available for the execution. All of these factors may be interrelated in a complicated manner.

These print production people are not merely technical people who are knowledgeable. They are graphic arts consultants, production planners, and production liaison people. They function both internally, with the creative, traffic, media, and account management areas, and externally, with graphic arts vendors and the print media.

The size of a print production group is related to the billing size of the agency. A very small agency may employ a single print production expert. In a very large agency, the print production staff, headed by a print production manager, may consist of a considerable number of people with very specialized expertise.

---

[1] Robert Hannan, "Better, faster, cheaper," *Agency,* Fall 1997, 42–43.

The print operations area encompasses the following:

■ Illustration buyers are versed in various forms of photographic and illustrative techniques. They know the available talent and make all contracts with photographers, illustrators, digital artists, and others, in coordination with art directors (see Exhibit 18.3).

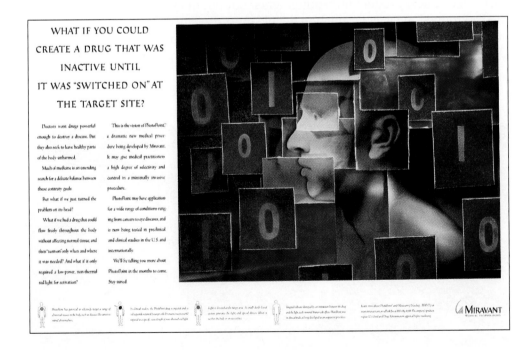

- Typography experts are trained in the creative as well as technical aspects of typography. They select and specify type, working with the art directors. Of course, in some agencies the art director may create the final type on his or her computer. Or the type director may send the disk to a supplier for final output.
- Print producers coordinate all print production activities with the traffic, account management, and creative groups.
- Printing buyers specialize in the production planning and buying of outdoor and transit advertising, newspaper and magazine inserts, as well as collateral printed material from brochures to elaborately die-cut direct-mail pieces. A printing buyer's knowledge reaches into properties of paper and ink, and into the capabilities of printing, binding, and finishing equipment (see Exhibit 18.4).

In addition to those functions already mentioned, a large production department may include estimators and proofreaders. Generally, clients require an agency to submit a production budget on work to be done. As a rule, a total yearly campaign production budget is estimated to give the client an understanding of approximately how much ads and/or collateral will cost to produce. Clients must sign off on each project's production cost in advance of the work being prepared. It is important for the production department to supply accurate production cost estimates.

The production department works closely with the traffic department, which sets and monitors schedules of the operation from creative through final production.

PRODUCTION DATA

Production people need to be well versed in the technical aspects of art and type processes, printing methods, and duplicate plates, which we discuss later in the chapter. Let us look first at sources of information for print media. The production person will usually reach for the Standard Rate and Data Service (SRDS) production source—SRDS Print Media Production Data—which carries essential production information for major national and regional publications. The SRDS publications for other media (e.g., newspapers, consumer, business) carry closing dates and basic mechanical production requirements, but not in as complete detail as Print Media Production Data. Production people must directly contact publications that are not included in the SRDS publications to obtain their production requirements. Of course, each publication determines its own advertising due dates and mechan-

Exhibit
18.4

This outdoor ad required the print buyer to be knowledgeable about the printing process.
Courtesy: Robinson & Associates.

Mechanical Specification

All national editions are printed offset. The SWOP standards for proofing should be followed

Proofs

Black and white—10 complete proofs.
2-color and 4-color—10 complete proofs and 10 sets of progressives.

Bleed Sizes

Page 8-1/4″ × 11-1/8″

2 pages facing—16-1/2″ × 11-1/8″

For bleed pages keep the essential matter 1/2″ from top, bottom, and sides of all film, and at least 11/16″ from front bleed edge on both pages of facing page spread.

Live matter in facing pages should not be closer than 1/8″ to center fold.

Publication reserves the right to crop up to 3/16″ from either side of full page film to compensate for variations in trim page size.

Columns	Column Width in Picas	Minimum Depth in Agate Lines
1	13 picas and 9 points	14
2	28 picas and 2 points	28
6	85 picas and 10 points	148

Due Dates

Issue	Color	Black & White
August 9	June 19	July 3
August 23	July 4	July 11
September 6	July 25	August 7
September 20	August 8	August 21
October 10	August 15	August 28
October 24	September 4	September 18
November 8	September 18	October 2
November 21	October 2	October 16
December 6	October 16	October 30
December 27	October 30	November 12

Page Makeup

All run-of-paper advertising units are measured in terms of agate lines and number of columns. The width of a single column is 13 picas and 9 points (2 9/32″). Each additional column is 14 picas and 5 points (2 3/8″).

Advertisements exceeding 270 agate lines line depth must occupy full columns (296 agate lines).

Exhibit 18.5

Mechanical and Due Dates Requirements

ical specifications based upon printing requirements. Exhibit 18.5 shows some of the specifications for a typical publication.

PRODUCTION PLANNING AND SCHEDULING

To ensure that the creative and production work moves along with the necessary precision, a time schedule is planned at the outset. The closing date is the date or time when all material must arrive at the publication. Once this is known, the advertiser works backward along the calendar to determine when work must begin to meet the date.

Now that we better understand the production environment, let us take a look at the key considerations in a number of production steps.

Digital Studios

Before desktop computers became the staple for creating ads or promotional printed materials, most art directors had only to design, create accurate mechanicals, and specify color breaks or other information on tissues. The production managers were responsible for the remaining production steps and procedures. Today, many art directors and/or studio designers working on their computers perform many production steps.

Some agencies call their computer area an image studio or digital imaging studio, where art directors work on computers to develop the visuals and layout. In some agencies (especially in small- or medium-sized shops) art directors take on part of the production. They can design, typeset, do layouts, create tints, scan, separate, produce final film, and in some cases, transmit the job directly to the press or service bureau. In general, most production jobs will require the services of outside vendors or service providers. Most agencies rely on outside services for imagesetting, high-resolution scanning, and printing. There are output service bureaus that offer high-quality PostScript imagesetter output and scanning primarily for those companies or agencies. Then there are electronic prepress shops that offer imagesetting for computer-generated files. If asked to do so, they will use their expertise in taking care of trapping and other operations necessary to prepare the files for film output. Suppliers can be found for almost every stage of the prepress operation.

Computer-to-Plate

Print production has been going digital—either partial or total. The same can be said about the printing process. There has been a growing use of computer-to-plate printing, which eliminates the film traditionally required to make plates for the press. Again, it should be remembered that the advertiser or agency controls only part of the process. If it is an ad for a magazine, the magazine controls how the publication will be printed—digital or traditional. However, digital design is controlled by agency. If the agency is producing collateral material (brochures, inserts, etc.), the agency controls the entire process.

Producing plates directly from computer files rather than film has its advantages. It may provide better registration and a crisper dot, which results in a sharper image on press. The digital workflow cuts both design and printing schedules.

Another advantage of computer-to-plate technology is the proofing and approval process. In traditional printing, if a problem was detected on the job, it could take as long as 16 hours to make corrections, shoot and strip new film, remake plates, and restart the presses. Digital technology allows a printer to pull the plate, correct the digital files, prepare a new plate, and mount the plate in approximately 30 minutes. Now let's look at the printing options.

SELECTING THE PRINTING PROCESS

In most cases, the printing process used depends on the medium in which the ad is running, not on the advertiser or the agency. However, in some areas, such as sales promotion, ad inserts, direct mail, and point-of-sale, the advertiser must make the final decision regarding print production. To deal effectively with printers, the advertiser must have some knowledge of the basic production techniques and which one is the most appropriate for the job at hand.

If the printing process is not predetermined, the first step in production is to decide which process is most suitable. There are three major printing processes:

- Letterpress printing (from a raised surface)
- Offset lithography (from a flat surface)
- Rotogravure (from an etched surface)

Each of these printing processes has certain advantages and disadvantages, and one process may be more efficient than another for a particular job. Once the printing process has been established, the production process has been dictated, for all production work depends on the type of printing used.

As we have indicated, the prepress operation is in transition from traditional to digital operations. Once the ad, collateral advertising, or promotion has been created and converted to a printing plate, the printing process is very similar to what it has been for many decades. The presses are more efficient now than ever before, but the printing concept is not new.

Letterpress Printing

Letterpress printing isn't as popular as it once was in printing publications; however, advertisers have many uses for this printing process, and you should know the basics. In its simplest form, think of the concept of **letterpress** as follows: If you have ever used a rubber ink stamp (with name, address, etc.), you've applied the principle of letterpress printing. You press the rubber stamp against an ink pad. Then, as you press the stamp against paper, the ink is transferred from the stamp to the paper, and the message is reproduced.

In letterpress printing, the area to be printed is raised and inked. The inked plate is pressed against the paper and the result is a printed impression (see Exhibit 18.6).

Your artwork, photographs, type, and so forth must be converted to a photoengraving (a process of making the plate a raised surface) before printing can occur. The advertiser or agency must supply the photoengraving or duplicates of such plates to the newspaper, magazine, or letterpress printer. In general, this process doesn't reproduce photos as well as offset or gravure. Each of the printing processes has advantages and disadvantages that the advertising person needs to learn over time.

Offset Lithography

In its basic description, **offset lithography** is a photochemical process based upon the principle that grease and water will not mix. In theory, offset can print anything that can be photographed. In reality, there are some things that will not print very well by offset.

Offset lithography is a planographic (flat-surface) process using a thin, flat aluminum plate that is wrapped around a cylinder on a rotary press. The plate is

letterpress Printing from a relief, or raised, surface. The raised surface is inked and comes in direct contact with the paper, like a rubber stamp.

offset lithography A printing process by which originally an image was formed on special stone by a greasy material, the design then being transferred to the printing paper. Today the more frequently used process is *offset* lithography, in which a thin and flexible metal sheet replaces the stone. In this process the design is "offset" from the metal sheet to a rubber blanket, which then transfers the image to the printing paper.

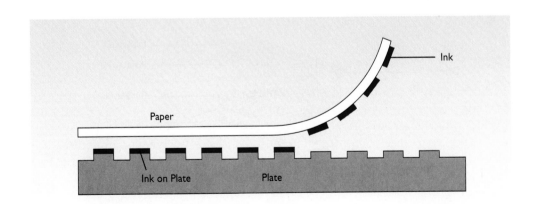

Exhibit
18.6

Letterpress Printing

The letterpress printing process involves a plate with a raised surface.

Chapter 18   Print Production   475

coated with a continuous flow of liquid solution from dampening rollers that repel ink. The inked plate comes in contact with a rubber blanket on another cylinder. The inked impression goes from the plate to the rubber blanket. The inked blanket then transfers or offsets the inked image to the paper, which is on a delivery cylinder. The plate does not come in direct contact with the paper (Exhibit 18.7).

Because offset is a photographic process, it is very efficient and is the most popular printing process in this country. It is used to reproduce books (including this text), catalogs, periodicals, direct-mail pieces, outdoor and transit posters, point-of-sale, and most newspapers.

Advertisers or their agencies must supply the artwork and electronic mechanicals or films from which offset plates can be made.

Rotogravure

rotogravure The method of printing in which the impression is produced by chemically etched cylinders and run on a rotary press; useful in long runs of pictorial effects.

The image in **rotogravure** printing is etched below the surface of the copper printing plate—the direct opposite from letterpress printing—creating tiny ink wells (tiny depressed printing areas made by means of a screen). The gravure plate is inked on the press and wiped so that only the tiny ink wells contain ink. The plate is then pressed against the paper, causing suction that pulls the ink out of the wells and onto the paper (see Exhibit 18.8).

Gravure is used to print all or parts of many publications, including national and local Sunday newspaper supplements, mail-order catalogs, packaging, and newspaper inserts. The gravure plate is capable of printing millions of copies very efficiently; however, it is not economical for short-run printing. Rotogravure becomes competitive with offset when printing exceeds about 100,000 copies. When printing exceeds a million copies, gravure tends to be more efficient than offset.

Rotogravure prints excellent color quality on relatively inexpensive paper, but the preparatory costs are comparatively high, and it is expensive to make major corrections on the press.

Sheet-Fed Versus Web-Fed Presses

Letterpress, offset, and gravure printing processes can all utilize sheet-fed or web-fed presses.

- Sheet-fed presses feed sheets of paper through the press one at a time. The conventional sheet-fed press prints about 6,000 to 7,000 "sheets" per hour.
- Web-fed presses feed paper from a continuous roll, and the printing is rapid—about 1,000 feet per minute. Most major promotional printing utilizes web-fed presses.

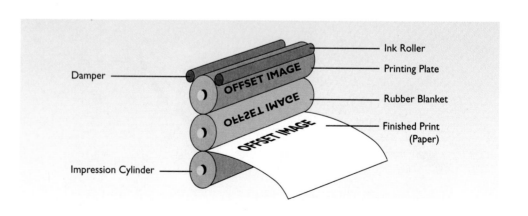

Ink Roller
Printing Plate
Rubber Blanket
Finished Print (Paper)
Damper
Impression Cylinder

Exhibit

18.7

Offset printing press system, showing image coming off plate, onto rubber blanket, and offsetting to paper.

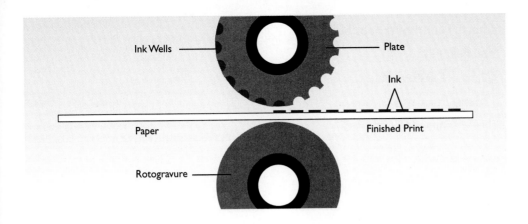

Exhibit

18.8

Rotogravure
In the rotogravure process, ink wells fill with ink.

Screen Printing

Another printing process, **screen printing,** which is based on a different principle than letterpress, offset, and rotogravure, is especially good for short runs. This simple process uses a stencil. The stencil of a design (art, type, photograph) can be manually or photographically produced and then placed over a textile (usually silk) or metallic-mesh screen (it actually looks like a window screen). Ink or paint is spread over the stencil and, by means of a squeegee, is pushed through the stencil and screen onto the paper (or other surface), as illustrated in Exhibit 18.9.

Screen printing is economical, especially for work in broad, flat colors, as in car cards, posters, and point-of-sale displays. It can be done on almost any surface: wallpaper, bricks, bottles, T-shirts, and so on. Basically, screen printing is a slow short-run process (from one copy to 100 or 1,000 or so copies), although sophisticated presses can print about 6,000 impressions per hour. This expanding printing process is becoming more useful to advertisers.

screen printing A simple printing process that uses a stencil. It is economical but is limited in reproduction quality.

New Ways to Interact

Digital technology is also changing how suppliers and advertisers/agencies interact. The digital environment has changed the way artwork is prepared; now it is changing the way jobs are designed. To speed communication, many computer artists post files on FTP (file transfer protocol) servers, which eliminates any incompatibility between designer-favored Macintoshes and client-favored PCs. While some FTP servers are Web-based, many are part of an Intranet or Extranet and may not require a Web browser for access. Some production houses have interactive Web sites, which allow the computer artist at the agency to access the job in progress. As a virtual job jacket, it serves as a repository for all project-related correspondence and art files. Once everyone is satisfied with the artwork, the printer can

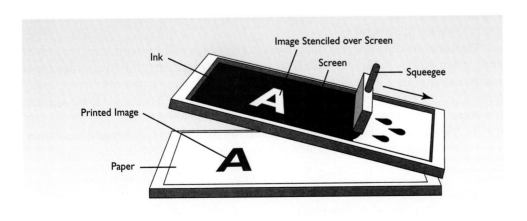

Exhibit

18.9

Screen Printing

Exhibit

18.10

These are examples of
different typefaces in the
same size, each presenting a
different feeling or look.

This is Garamond Semibold

This is Impact

This is Arial Black

This is Palatino

This is Garamond Condensed

use security codes to access and download files with all the specifications needed to print the job.[2]

UNDERSTANDING TYPOGRAPHY

Type has always been an important part of ad design. It creates moods, enhances or retards readability, and gives your communication an image (Exhibit 18.10). It is now more important than ever before for advertising people to understand how to use type because so much of it is being created in-house on the agency or client computer. Before the computer explosion, art directors would use specialists—typesetters or typographers—for type. Most agree that few art directors or designers have as good an understanding of type use as the typesetters or typographers. Getting type up on the screen does not mean that it is typeset effectively. We talk about this again after we learn some of the fundamentals.

typography The art of
using type effectively.

The art of using type effectively is called **typography**. It entails a number of issues: choosing the typeface and size of type; deciding on the amount of space between letters, words, and lines; determining hyphenation use; and preparing type specifications for all the ad copy. The Pennant ad in Exhibit 18.11 separates copy elements by using a different typeface.

TYPE AND READING

The objective of text typography is to provide quick and easy communication. Display headlines are supposed to attract the reader's attention and encourage reading of the body copy. Using uppercase (all-cap) typography does not generally accomplish these objectives.

More than 95 percent of text is set in lowercase letters. Research has shown that readers are more comfortable reading lowercase letters than all caps. Studies have also proved that the varying heights of lowercase letters forming words create an outline shape that is stored in the reader's mind, which aids in recalling the words when they are seen. Words comprised of lowercase characters can be read faster than words set in all caps.

The ideal reading process occurs when the eye is able to scan across a line of copy, grasp groups of three or four words at a time, and then jump to another set of words, then another. The separate stops, or fixational pauses, take about one-quarter of a second each. Words in lowercase letters allow this process to take place. On the other hand, words set in all caps force the reader to read individual letters and mentally combine the letters into words, and the words into phrases and sentences. The result is a 10 to 25 percent slowdown in reading speed and comprehension.

[2]Halli Forcinio, "Let's get digital," *Brand Marketing*, October 2000, 46–48.

There are times when all-cap headlines or subheadlines are, graphically, the right thing to use. Design may take precedence over the "rules of communication," or you may not be able to convince a client or art director that lowercase is a better idea. In these instances, words and lines should be held to a minimum. More than four or five words on a line and more than a couple of lines of all caps become difficult to read.[3]

TYPEFACES

The typeface selected for a particular ad is very important. Exhibit 18.12 illustrates the major classifications of type: text, old Roman, modern Roman, square serif, sans serif, and decorative.

[3]Allan Haley, "Using all capitals is a graphic oxymoron," *U & lc*, Fall 1991, 14–15.

Text	Old English
Old Roman	Garamond
Modern Roman	Century
Square Serif	Lubalin
Sans Serif	Avant Garde
Decorative	Ransom

Exhibit 18.12

Examples of Families of Type

TYPE FONTS AND FAMILIES

A type font is all the lowercase and capital characters, numbers, and punctuation marks in one size and face (Exhibit 18.13). A font may be roman or italic. Roman (with a lowercase "r") type refers to the upright letter form, as distinguished from the italic form, which is oblique. Roman (capital "R") denotes a group of serifed typeface styles.

Type family is the name given to two or more series of types that are variants of one design (Exhibit 18.14). Each one, however, retains the essential characteristics of the basic letter form. The series may include italic, thin, light, semibold, bold, medium, condensed, extended, outline, and so forth. Some type families have only a few of these options, whereas others offer a number of styles. The family of type may provide a harmonious variety of typefaces for use within an ad.

Measurement of Type

Typographers have unique units of measurement. It is essential to learn the fundamental units of measure if you are going to interact with production people. The point and pica are two units of measure used in print production in all English-speaking countries. Let us take a closer look at these two units of measure.

point (pt) The unit of measurement of type, about 1/72 inch in depth. Type is specified by its point size, as 8 pt., 12 pt., 24 pt., 48 pt. The unit for measuring thickness of paper, 0.001 inch.

Point A **point (pt)** is used to measure the size of type (heights of letters). There are 72 points to an inch. It is useful to know that 36-point type is about 1/2 inch

Bookman
abcdefghijklmnopqrstuvwxyz
ABCDEFGHIJKLMNOPQRSTU
1234567890$(&?!%',;:)* VWXYZ

Bookman Bold
abcdefghijklmnopqrstuvwxyz
ABCDEFGHIJKLMNOPQRSTU
1234567890$(&?!%',;:)* VWXYZ

Exhibit 18.13

Examples of Two Bookman Type Fonts, Regular and Bold

Helvetica Thin
Helvetica Light
Helvetica Light Italic
Helvetica
Helvetica Italic
Helvetica Italic Outline
Helvetica Regular Condensed
Helvetica Regular Extended
Helvetica Medium
Helvetica Medium Italic
Helvetica Medium Outline
Helvetica Bold
Helvetica Bold Compact Italic
Helvetica Bold Outline
Helvetica Bold Condensed
Helvetica Bold Condensed Outline
Helvetica Bold Extended
Helvetica Extrabold Condensed
Helvetica Extrabold Condensed Outline
Helvetica Extrabold Ext.
Helvetica Compressed
Helvetica Extra Compressed
Helvetica Ultra Compressed

Exhibit
18.14

A family of type retains its basic letter form and style characteristics through all its variations. Some type families consist of only roman, italic and bold versions. Others, such as the popular Helvetica family, have many variations and different stroke thicknesses.

high and 18-point type is about 1/4 inch high. Exhibit 18.15 illustrates the major terms used in discussing the height of type. Type can be set from about 6 points to 120 points. Body copy is generally in the range of 6 to 14 points; most publications use type of 9, 10, or 11 points. Type sizes above 14 points are referred to as displays or headline type. However, these ranges are simply labels—in many newspaper ads, the body copy is 18 points or so, and there have been ads in which the headline was in the body-copy size range. Exhibit 18.16 provides a visual perspective on basic type sizes.

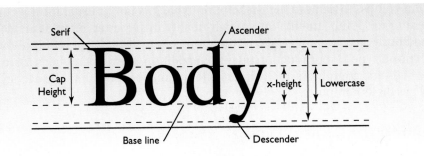

Exhibit
18.15

Major Terms for Type Height

Exhibit

18.16

A Visual Perspective of Type Sizes

9 point Garamond Condensed Book

10 point Garamond Condensed Book

11 point Garamond Condensed Book

18 point Garamond Condensed Book

36 point Garamond Conden

48 point Garamond

Points also are used to measure the height of space between lines, rules, and borders, as well as the height of the type.

pica The unit for measuring width in printing. There are 6 picas to an inch. A page of type 24 picas wide is 4 inches wide.

Pica A **pica** is a linear unit of measure. A pica equals 12 points of space, and there are 6 picas to an inch. Picas are used to indicate width or depth and length of line.

Em An em is a square of space of the type size and is commonly used for indentation of copy blocks and paragraphs. Traditionally, it is as wide as the height of the capital M in any type font.

Agate Line Most newspapers (and some small magazines) sell advertising space in column inches or by the agate line, a measure of the depth of space. There are 14 agate lines to a column inch, regardless of the width of the column. Newspaper space is referred to by depth (agate lines) and width (number of columns); for "100 × 2," read "one hundred lines deep by two columns wide."

Line Spacing Also called leading, line spacing is the vertical space between lines of type and is measured in points from baseline to baseline of type. Lines are said to be set solid when no additional line spacing has been added. Space is added to make type more readable. The rule of thumb is that the extra space should be no more than 20 percent of the type size. Thus, if you are using 10-point type, the maximum extra space between the lines is 2 points, for a 12-point leading.

TYPESETTING

Earlier in this chapter we said that almost all typesetting is performed on a desktop computer. The typographer of the future is an art director or designer—maybe even a copywriter—for whom type is more a means than an end.

Many agencies use low-end laser printers (usually 300 dots per inch [dpi]), which is not high enough resolution for reproduction. However, it is fine for doing layout comps. To achieve high-resolution type, it is not unusual for the computer operator to "dump" the file into a high-quality imagesetter, often at an electronic type house or typographer. There the more sophisticated typesetter (about 3,600 dpi) prints type of reproduction quality. In addition, the typographer's more expensive high-end computers and printers offer more type fonts than the agency generally has on its computer.

Guides for Digital Type

■ Use only original type. Don't assume the prepress service bureaus or printer has the exact same font.

- Remember that as a buyer of a type package you only license the usage rights. You have to acquire a multilicense if the font is to be used on more than one computer.

- Computer artists need to keep a running list of both screen fonts and printer fonts (screen fonts are used by computer for display on the screen; printer fonts are downloaded to the printer for output).

- Talk to your prepress service provider or printer about fonts being used in electronic mechanicals; otherwise, the ad or collateral piece may not look as intended.

- Avoid type smaller than 6 points, especially in serif typefaces (letters having "feet," such as Bodoni). The thin parts of small type characters can disappear when output is of high resolution making text difficult to read.

- When using reverse type, avoid type that is too small (6 point) or delicate. Sans serif and bold typefaces are better choices. Large blocks of reverse type are difficult to read.

- When possible, convert type to a graphic (vector objects) in EPS files. Common problems for prepress service providers are font substitution or PostScript errors caused by type in imported EPS graphics.

ELECTRONIC MECHANICAL AND ARTWORK

After the copy has been approved and placed in the ad on the desktop system with the rest of the ad's material (e.g., illustrations, logos), the advertiser will approve the electronic comp or rough. After approval, the digital file is sent to prepress.

Art for Prepress Services

Discuss the types of art being used—transparencies (like 35-mm slides, reflective art), line drawings or illustrations, digital photography—with the prepress service or printer. How are you going to supply the art: in hard copy, electronic files, or both? Agency production people need to ask (or check publication mechanical requirements) about what kind of electronic files are preferred.

As you can see, the right files, fonts, and technical requirements are necessary for prepress production to run smoothly. You can not assume the prepress, printer, or publication can run your material just because it looks good on your computer.

There are several types of art that the production people have to deal with, including line art and halftones in both black and white and color.

Line Art

Any art, type, or image that is made up of a solid color (and has no tonal value) is called line art. If you set type on your computer, it is line art (if it is in solid form). Artwork drawn in pen and ink is line art because the ink has no tonal value. Generally, such art is drawn larger than needed for the mechanical so as to minimize the art's imperfections when it is reduced and printed. Exhibit 18.17 contains an example of line art.

Linetint   You can give line art some variation in shades by breaking up the solid color with screen tints or benday screens. Exhibit 18.18 uses a screen tint to give the illusion of gray and contrast. This may be done on the computer layout, or the platemaker adds the screens during the film-stripping stage just prior to platemaking.

Line Color   Artwork does not need to be in color to produce line plates, in two, three, or more flat colors. Instead, each extra color is marked on a separate tissue or

continuous tone An
unscreened photographic picture
or image, on paper or film, that
contains all gradations of tonal
values from white to black.

acetate overlay on the base art as a guide for the platemaker, who then makes a separate plate for each color. Line color provides a comparatively inexpensive method of printing in color with effective results (see Exhibit 18.19A & B).

A solid color (flat or match color) is printed with the actual color. The color is specified with a Pantone Matching System (PMS) color reference number, and the printer mixes an ink that is literally that color. It is like going into a paint store and choosing a color swatch and having the clerk mix the paint to match your color. The ink is applied to the paper through printing, and the specified color is obtained.

Halftones

At the end of this chapter we discuss some of the new production technology (including stochastic screening), which may eventually change the way photos are reproduced. At present, the 100-year-old technology does the job reasonably well.

If you look at black-and-white photographs, you recognize they are different from line art—they have tonal value. Such photos have a range of tonal value between pure blacks and pure whites and are called **continuous-tone** artwork.

To reproduce the range of tones in continuous-tone art, the art (photo) must be broken up into dots. The art is then called a halftone. Halftones may be reproduced either with a printer's camera or digitally; either way breaks the image into dots. Exhibit 18.20 shows the reproduction of a black-and-white halftone. Remember that black ink is black ink and not shades of gray, so the production process must create an optical illusion by converting the tonal areas to different-size halftone dots on the printed paper that the eye perceives as gray. If you look at the printed halftone gray areas with a magnifying glass, you will see little black dots and not gray (Exhibit 18.21 shows a magnification). In the traditional process, the dots are formed on the negative during the camera exposure when a screen is placed between the film and photograph (or other kinds of continuous-tone copy). As the film is exposed, light passes through the screen's 50 to 200 hairlines per square inch, and the image reaching the film is in dot form. The size of the dots will vary according to the contrast of tone in the original; this simply means that dark areas in the original photo will give one size dot, medium tones another size dot, and lighter tones still another size dot. The result is a film negative with dots of varying sizes, depending on the tonal variations in the original.

After the halftone negative is made, it is placed on a metallic plate and is exposed to the plate. In letterpress printing, the engraving is splashed with acid that

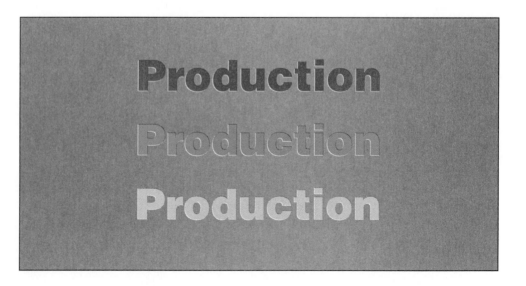

eats away the metal, leaving the dots as raised surfaces. In offset printing, the dots are transferred to the smooth flat plate photographically.

Halftone screens come in a variety of standard sizes. Each publication has its own requirement for the screen size, dictated somewhat by the printing process and paper being used. Newspapers, magazines, and promotional materials printed by offset use screens that generally range from 110 to 133 lines per square inch. In other words, a 133-line screen produces 133 dots to an inch. The more dots per inch, the greater the quality of detail reproduced from the original. The quality of the paper must also increase to accommodate the higher dot levels, which drives up paper costs.

The Halftone Finish If you want to make a halftone of a photograph, the computer artist or the platemaker can treat the background in a number of ways;

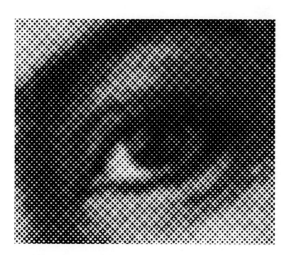

that treatment is called its finish. A few of the techniques that can be applied to halftones include the following:

- *Square halftone.* The halftone's background has been retained.
- *Silhouette.* The background in the photograph has been removed by the photo-platemaker or the computer operator.
- *Surprint.* This is a combination plate made by exposing line and halftone negatives in succession on the same plate.
- *Mortise.* An area of a halftone is cut out to permit the insertion of type or other matter.

Line Conversion   A line conversion transforms a continuous-tone original into a high-contrast image of only black-and-white tones similar to line art. The conversion transfers the image into a pattern of some kind: mezzotint, wavy line, straight line, or concentric circle. Most design software programs offer a number of line conversion choices.

Two-Color Halftone Plates   A two-color reproduction can be made from monochrome artwork in two ways. A screen tint in a second color can be printed over (or under) a black halftone. Or the artwork can be photographed twice, changing the screen angle the second time so that the dots of the second color plate fall between those of the first plate. This is called a duotone. It produces contrast in both colors of the one-color original halftone.

Four-Color Process Printing   Another printing system is needed when the job requires the reproduction of color photos (Exhibit 18.22). This system is called a **four-color process**. The four colors are cyan (blue), magenta (red), yellow, and black. (CMYK are the letters used to indicate these colors.) These are the least number of colors that can adequately reproduce the full spectrum of natural colors inherent in photography. The first three—cyan, magenta, and yellow—provide the range of colors; the black provides definition and contrast in the image.

Full-color or process color requires photographic or electronic scanner separation of the color in the photographs (or other continuous-tone copy) into four negatives, one for each of the process colors. This process of preparing plates of the various colors and black is called color separation (see Exhibit 18.23). If you examine any of the color ads in this text (or any other publication) with a magnifying glass, you will find the halftone dots in four colors.

four-color process
The process for reproducing color illustrations by a set of plates, one that prints all the yellows, another the blues, a third the reds, and the fourth the blacks (sequence variable). The plates are referred to as *process plates*.

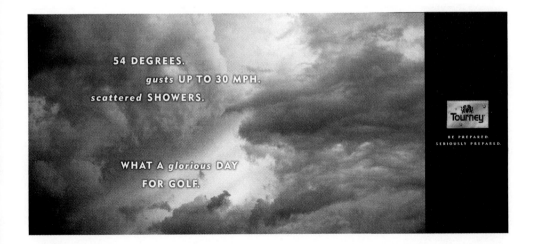

Exhibit
18.22

This ad has two color photos—logo and sky. To reproduce these you need a minimum of four process inks.
Courtesy: Howard, Merrell & Partners.

Digital Scanners   Transforming a photograph into a digital file is done by a device called a scanner. There are two basic types: flatbed and drum scanners. You probably have either seen or used a flatbed scanner. These require little training and their quality varies. Printers or agencies use professional scanners that are capable of creating high-quality images. In general, a drum scanner, in which the original photo or image wraps around a drum that rotates next to a light source, is capable of producing very high-quality results. They are the most expensive image-capturing device on the market. These machines digitally scan the photos to be used in ads. They create the dot pattern used in making a halftone by the traditional method. The important thing to remember is that photographs (whether color or black and white) must be broken up into a dot pattern to print.

red, yellow, blue, and black plates

yellow plate

red plate

yellow and red plates

blue plate

blue and yellow plates

blue, red, and yellow plates

black plate

Color Proofing

Achieving color reproduction that satisfies ad agencies and advertisers is one of the most crucial roles of the magazine production manager. Agencies generally demand to see a proof before the job is printed. In today's electronic color production, traditional proofing systems seem to have taken a back seat to digital color proofers, color printers, networked color copiers, and short-run color production devices.

For the most accurate contact proofs—those requiring the best match to jobs printed by conventional offset lithography—nothing beats a film-based laminated, or single-sheet, off-press proof. An off-press proof ensures the separator that color separations have been made according to customer expectations.[4]

Press Proofs

For years, press proofs, or progressives, usually made on special proofing presses, were the standard proofs sent to agencies for checking. Prior to the development of off-press proofs, color separators used press proofs. Making a press proof involved stripping the separations on film, making plates, mounting the plates on a proof press, and printing the desired number of proofs. Press proofs are made with ink on paper—often the same paper that will be used for the job—rather than with a photographic simulation process of off-press systems. Today press proofs are still used by many ad agencies who are willing to pay the steep price for what they believe is the most accurate proof. In theory, press proofs provide a virtually exact representation of the final project.

Progressive Proofs (Progs) These proofs give the advertiser a separate proof for each color (red, yellow, blue, and black), as indicated in Exhibit 18.24 (also see Exhibit 18.23), as well as a proof for each color combination (red and yellow, red

Exhibit

18.24

There is more than one way for the agency to send this ad to multiple publications.
Courtesy: Howard, Merrell & Partners.

[4]Richard M. Adams II, "Color-proofing systems," *Pre,* March/April 1994, 55–59.

and blue, blue and yellow)—seven printings in all. After approval by the advertiser and agency, the proofs are sent to the printer to use as guides in duplicating the densities for each color.

Off-Press Proofs

These proofs are made from film negatives generated from the electronic file. The same films will be used to make printing plates. These proofs are less expensive and faster than press proofs, and they are adequate in most cases. Off-press proofs are the typical color proof today. No plate or printing is involved. There are numerous types of off-press (prepress) proofing systems. The most popular are overlay and adhesive proofs.

Overlay Proofs   The development of overlay proofing enabled color proofs to be made from film without using a proof press. The overlay proofs consist of four exposed sheets containing the cyan (blue), magenta (red), yellow, and black process colors, overlaid on a backing sheet. The four overlays (yellow, red, blue, and black) are then stacked to produce a composite image. Because they use multiple, separate, plastic layers, overlay proofs cannot be expected to accurately predict color on press; but they are still used today for checking color break, or general color appearance and position.

Adhesive or Laminate Proof   In 1972, DuPont introduced the first off-press proofing system that closely resembled printed images, the Cromalin system. Cromalin is a laminated or single-sheet proof, in which four (or more) layers are exposed separately and laminated together to reproduce the image of cyan, magenta, yellow, and black separations. Cromalins use dry pigments to produce images on photosensitive adhesive polymers or pretreated carrier sheets. Cromalin is generally considered the superior adhesive process. The proofs are keyed to SWOP (Specifications for Web Offset Publications)/GAA (Gravure Association of America) guidelines, which set standards for inks, density of tones, reverses, and other technical matters. Among the highest fidelity four-color proofs are the **MatchPrint** and the Signature proof, both very similar but from different suppliers.

matchprint   A high-quality color proof used for approvals prior to printing. Similar to a Signature print.

There are digital hard and soft copy systems that eliminate film to produce continuous-tone proofs. The soft proofing systems allow production and design people to call up a digitized color image and evaluate it before separations are made for an intermediate or position proof. The interactive proofing system gives the agency more flexibility with deadlines and saves time and money for clients.

Types of Proofs   The choices of types of proof are numerous. Production managers need to decide how accurate a proof is needed, or to put it another way, how much quality they need to pay for. Obviously, they don't want expensive proofs if they are not needed. Here are a number of proof types:

Proof Type	Color Accuracy	Cost
Black-and-white laser	Prints can show color breaks but no color. 300–600 dpi.	Inexpensive
Bluelines	Proofs made from exposing film to light-sensitive paper. They show only a single color image. Uses halftone film.	Inexpensive
Velox	Simple black-and-white proofs made from film on photographic paper. Uses halftone film.	Moderate

Digital high-end	Proofs made from an electronic file. Made by Kodak, 3M, among others. Several processes all meet industry standards. 1800 dpi and higher. Cannot proof actual film.	Moderate
Desktop digital	Usually uses ink jet or thermal wax and gives fairly accurate approximation of color. 300 dpi. Needs color management system to give close approximation of color.	Inexpensive
Laminate/ adhesive	Composite proofs are created by exposing the color separations in contact to proofing film and laminating the results. Uses halftone film. Very accurate in color match.	Moderate
Overlay	Made up of layers of acetate attached to a backing substrate. Each overlay film has an image from each separation color. Colors indicate color breaks, not very accurate. Uses halftone film.	Moderate
Press	Proof run on printing press. Uses halftone film. Uses actual printing inks to give most accurate proof.	Expensive

SENDING DUPLICATE MATERIAL

How do we get this Subdue ad (Exhibit 18.24) out of our computer to ten publications? Ten Zips? Maybe. Most print ads run in more than one publication. Frequently, advertisers have different publications on their schedules, or they need to issue reprints of their ads or send material to dealers for cooperative advertising. There are various means of producing duplicate material of magazine or newspaper ads. Keep in mind that this process is usually done by sending a digital file to the publication. A brief summary of the traditional processes still used by a number of publications follows.

Letterpress Duplicates   There are several kinds of letterpress duplicate plates because publishers may require a specific type of duplicate plate. Photopolymer plates are produced on photosensitive plastic and are molds. Electrotype is another duplicate plate produced from a plastic mold using a combination of metals; it is very durable and is capable of printing millions of impressions. Cronapress plates (called Cronars) can be made with a pressure-sensitive material capable of duplicating the original impression exactly.

Offset and Gravure Duplicates   Duplicate material for offset publication can consist of repro proofs (reproduction proofs) or 3M Scotchprints (a plasticized repro proofing material). Usually, photoprints or reproduction proofs are preferred for partial-page newspaper ads; film is often required for full-page newspaper insertions. Duplicate films can also be made from the original artwork or mechanicals. For color gravure magazines or Sunday supplements, duplicate positive films are usually supplied. For black-and-white offset or gravure ads, photographic prints are often substituted for films.

A number of publications use satellite transmission systems to send a facsimile of each page of the publication to a reception station, where it is recorded on page-size photofilm. The film is then used to make offset plates, which are placed on the presses to reproduce the publication in the usual way. Newspapers use his system permits to run different regional editions utilizing the main news items from headquarters while allowing for variations in advertising content within each regional edition. These services transmit an advertiser's ad by satellite to publications with reception stations in much the same way.

OTHER PRODUCTION ADVANCES

The rapid changes in technology during the past few years have been changing the prepress and printing processes. In the near future, production managers and art directors will have many new options for handling their projects. In all cases, the new technologies are beginning to make an impact on the production and printing processes as we know them. These new techniques range from color separation, color management, and proofing to printing. The following techniques are of particular interest.[5]

Stochastic Screening and Color Separations

Stochastic screening, or frequency modulation screening, is a process for producing incredible tone and detail that approximates photographic quality. With conventional screens, the dots are spaced equally on a grid (e.g., 110 or 133 lines per inch) and the tonal value is achieved by increasing or decreasing the size of the dots. On the other hand, stochastic screening has very tiny dots all of the same size, and their numbers vary according to the tonal value. Used by a quality printer, the image appears to be continuous tone or photographic quality and much better than any traditional process. At this time, few companies produce this process. These companies offer an advertiser the ability to produce higher-quality color separations, which in turn allows them to print sharper color ads.

HiFi Color   High-fidelity color is expanding what we know and can do with print reproduction techniques and processes. HiFi color was born out of the limitations of the conventional color printing gamut, which are only a fraction of what the human visual system can see. It is a group of emerging technologies that will expand this printed gamut and extend control by improving and increasing tone, dynamic range, detail, spatial frequency modulation, and other appearance factors of print and other visual media.

HiFi color comprises the technologies of stochastic, or frequency modulation screening, four-plus color process and waterless printing methods, specialty papers, films, coatings, and laminates, proofing systems, color management systems, software and hardware.

Color Management Systems (CMS)   The ideal—and we haven't yet gotten to this point in technology—is seeing an image on a screen and getting an exact printed image, or, as it is touted, what you see is what you get. This is very important in terms of quality control and design. As images go through the production process, the information is transformed in different ways; for example, as photographic data in the original; as pixels of red, green, and blue on the computer screen; as dots of cyan, magenta, yellow, and black on paper. Software color management systems can bring more consistency to this process, but designers need to know what they can and cannot control. It can be complex even with a color management system.

---

[5]Kurt Klein and Daniel Dejan, "New printing technology," *Communication Arts,* Design Annual 1993, 283–290.

Waterless Printing   The new technology of waterless printing is gaining popularity; however, the explanation here is kept simple. Most offset presses use a dampening system of water to cover the plate. Offset is based upon the fact that water and grease (ink) don't mix. In waterless printing, a silicone-coated plate is used that rejects ink in the nonimage areas. The result is spectacular detail, highline screens, richer densities, and consistent quality throughout the press run; in short, great quality.

Other Developments   Gamut color, in simplified terms, adds the computer pixel colors of red, green, and blue (actually closer to orange, green, and purple) to the process colors (magenta, cyan, yellow, and black) giving a much wider range of hues for printing. This system may offer expanded color options and quality.

In direct-digital printing, printers are connected to workstations, which take and send files to the press. Film is not used, and in some cases neither are plates. Digital information is transferred onto electrophotographic cylinders instead of plates, and these cylinders use toner to print process color. There are other presses that receive digitized pages onto special plates, often used where the printing runs are short. Presstek/Heidelberg created another waterless printing process that uses no film, no stripping, and no plate processing; has recyclable plates, faster makeready, and no ink/water balance problems; and is time saving and boasts a reduction in production costs. It has some problems, though; it is basically designed to run good short-run color for jobs in the 500 to 5,000 impression range.

The computer and digitization are spawning most of this advancement in printing and production technology. The day is not far off when the printing and production industry will have a completely filmless, digital process.

The student of advertising production will have to learn these advances in the field, many of which will be both revolutionary and evolutionary, complicating the decision as to which system to use.

SUMMARY

All advertising people need to understand the basics of production. The production terms, concepts, and processes are not easy to learn but are essential to know because they affect budgets, time, and efficiency issues.

Publishers set mechanical requirements for their publications. Advertising production people need to be familiar with sources of information pertaining to print production requirements.

Today most ads are created on the computer (digital). The comps presented to clients appear to be finished. The process from the computer screen to a finished ad in a publication may be completed in a digital or traditional fashion, or a mix of the two processes. The future will involve more computer-to-plate digital production.

There are three basic kinds of printing processes: letterpress (printing from a raised surface), offset lithography (printing from a flat surface), and gravure (printing from a depressed surface). In addition, silk screen or screen printing offers advertisers additional production applications. The form of printing may affect the type of material sent to the publication to reproduce the ad.

Advertisers may use new prepress digital technology or traditional means to prepare ads for production. The publication tells the advertiser what type of material is required or accepted. Each method of prepress has advantages and disadvantages, depending on the degree of quality desired. Typography concerns the style (or face) of type and the way the copy is set. Typefaces come in styles called families. The size is specified in points (72 points per inch). The width of typeset lines is measured in picas (6 picas to an inch). The depth of newspaper space is measured in lines. The space between the lines of type is called leading or line spacing.

The graphics and production processes can be complex because what you see isn't always what really is. Continuous-tone art (a photograph) must be converted into halftone dots (may be scanned or use traditional printer's darkroom procedure) so that the tonal values of the original can be reproduced. Line art has no tonal value; it is drawn in black ink on white paper using lines and solid black areas.

Production technology is constantly changing to produce printed materials faster, cheaper, and more efficiently. Achieving color reproduction that satisfies ad agencies and advertisers is one of the most crucial roles of the magazine production manager. There are a multitude of proofs for the production manager to choose from dictated by the need to match colors exactly and the expense involved. "How much quality do we need?" is an often-asked question in terms of which proof to use. Color management systems help advertisers get what you see.

REVIEW

1. Differentiate among the three basic printing processes.
2. What is a digital file?
3. What is continuous-tone copy?
4. What is line art?
5. What are color separations?
6. What are the colors used in printing press or four-color?
7. When is a laminate/adhesive proof used?

TAKE IT TO THE NET

We invite you to visit the Russell/Lane page on the Prentice Hall Web site at **www.prenhall.com/myphlip** for end-of-chapter exercises and applications.

Chapter 19

The Television Commercial

Television advertising remains a powerful and expensive medium. It is complicated by a number of factors including the fact that every viewer is a television advertising expert. Everyone knows what he or she likes and dislikes about TV spots. This creates a challenge for advertisers. After reading this chapter you will understand:

>> copy development
>> creating the commercial
>> producing the commercial
>> controlling the cost

There is no question that television is still the most powerful advertising medium because it blends sight, sound, and motion that can create emotional reactions. Maybe the Internet will rival TV as a marketing communications medium someday as an interactive person-to-person medium using sight, sound, motion, and emotion. But for now, television still reaches multitudes of potential consumers with great impact. It has power.

THE POWER OF THE TV IDEA

Here are a few convincing examples of television's marketing and communication power.

In 1999, Subway found their sales to be flat promoting low-fat benefits. In January 2000 their agency developed two television spots featuring Jared Fogle, who lost 245 pounds on a strictly Subway diet, and Tae Bo master Billy Blanks. "We've been doing low-fat for 3 1/2 years and did well generating about 5 percent sales increases, but using those two spots drove the business 15 to 20 percent," said Chris Carroll, director of marketing. In some stores sales were up as much as 40 percent. Initially, the client rejected the agency's commercial idea three times.[1]

In early 2001, Grey Poupon extended its product into the fastest-growing yellow mustard segment with a premium yellow mustard. The launch was aimed at Grey Poupon's premium-seeking "creative cook," typically consumers over 35 with household incomes of $55,000 or higher who use yellow mustard more than any other mustard flavor in cooking. The new variety attempted to bring Grey Poupon's upscale image to the yellow mustard category with a twist on their famous Grey Poupon Rolls Royce commercial.[2] The "Pardon Me," Rolls Royce campaign for Grey Poupon hadn't run on television since 1997, but it *still* has awareness levels of almost 70 percent and 63 percent of consumers recently claimed they've seen the commercial over the last two months. That's communication power.

Most top-tier banks sell product, BB&T preempts respect for the *individual* in their advertising. BB&T brand switching intentions increased 300 percent after exposure to their advertising. Exhibit 19.1 voiceover says, *I want to live to be a hundred and three. I will start each day with strong, hot coffee. I will never get tired of walking on the beach. And when I go to the bank, they will know my name. BB&T. You can tell we want your business.*

In their "traditional values" spot, the voiceover says, *While some people talk about bringing back traditional values, there are places where it never left. Places where a handshake is a contract. Where people take pride in a hard day's work. And because these people aren't rich or poor, but just sort of in the middle like most of us. They'll need a bank to help them. Through good times and bad, they'll hang in there and so will we. BB&T. You can tell we want your business* (see Exhibit 19.2).

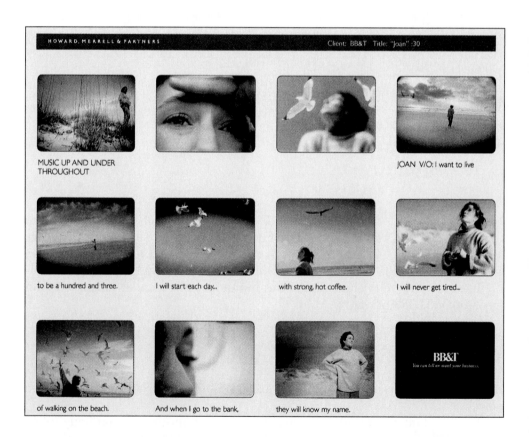

Exhibit

19.1

BB&T focused on consumer dreams instead of bank products.

Courtesy: Howard, Merrell & Partners.

---

[1]Kate MacArthur, "Subway sales so strong marketer delays new ads," *Advertising Age*, 19 June 2000, 8.
[2]Stephanie Thompson, "Grey Poupon rolls out yellow mustard variety," *Advertising Age*, 18 December 2000, 10.

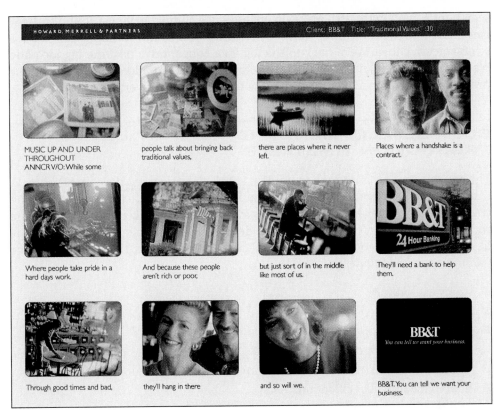

MUSIC UP AND UNDER THROUGHOUT
ANNCR V/O: While some

people talk about bringing back traditional values,

there are places where it never left.

Places where a handshake is a contract.

Where people take pride in a hard days work.

And because these people aren't rich or poor,

but just sort of in the middle like most of us.

They'll need a bank to help them.

Through good times and bad,

they'll hang in there

and so will we.

BB&T. You can tell we want your business.

Exhibit

19.2

This spot talks about the consumer's values and hopes and the fact that BB&T will be there to help them.

Courtesy: Howard, Merrell & Partners.

Ingalls Advertising self-promotion sums up some of the characteristics of goof TV, "there are a select few advertisements which cut through, appealing to consumers with humor, intelligence, charm and emotion. Yes, there are ads people actually like. Chances are, you like them too. Why? Because good ads are like good people. They're smart, funny, and engaging. You tend to remember them long after they're gone . . . . *Don't even think about getting into consumers' wallets unless you first get into their lives.*" If you knew how to do this, you wouldn't have to read the rest of this chapter. On the other hand, many people who are supposed to know this don't practice it.

THE PROBLEMS OF TV

Still the medium poses some problems discussed in earlier chapters: commercial clutter that leaves viewers confused about advertisers, loss of audiences, high production costs, and zapping. For example, according to Roper Reports, 38 percent of viewers say they often switch to another channel when ads come on, up 24 percent from 1985.[3] These problems are constant reminders to advertisers of the need to plan their messages very carefully. But it is precisely this adversity that breeds innovation—and creative innovation. Roper finds 31 percent of viewers say they are often amused by funny or clever commercials (up 5 percent from 1993); about 70 percent agree advertising is often fun or interesting to watch.

Artistic Fads

One of the things advertisers have to be aware of is that solutions to grab a viewer's attention come and go. Remember the shaky camera, claymation, morphing one object into another object, or using the oldies film footage? There is a continuing

---

[3]"Entertained by commercials," *American Demographics,* November 1997, 41.

search for some new way to wake up an audience. Simply having a sound strategy isn't enough to make a viewer watch. There must be a sound strategy wrapped in a strong creative idea. We're back to the big idea concept. We take the big idea and blend visuals, words, motion, and technology to create emotional reactions—done properly, this is what makes television the most powerful advertising medium.

COPY DEVELOPMENT AND PRODUCTION TIMETABLE

The creative process is difficult to predict. It isn't always easy to develop new breakthrough copy within the planned timetable or guess the client's reaction to the copy. The agency may love it; the client may hate it. It may take time to develop the right ideas. However, it is important to develop a reasonable timetable for copy development and production. A typical copy/development timetable sequence might include the following:

- Copy exploratory
- Present ideas to client
- Revisions to client for approval to produce
- Circulate copy for clearance (legal, R&D, management)
- On-air clearance (network/local stations)
- Prebid meeting (specifications/sets)
- Bid review/award job
- Preproduction meeting
- Shoot
- Postproduction
- Rough cut to client for approval
- Revisions
- Final to client
- Ship date

The responsibility for such a timetable is shared by the advertising agency and the client. How long does it take for a one- to five-day shoot with 2 to 10 actors to clear this process? Anywhere from 11 to 43 days. This range illustrates the complexity of the process. It isn't easy to generalize.

CREATING THE TELEVISION COMMERCIAL

Many creative people believe it is easier to create a good television commercial than it is to create a good print ad. After all, the TV creative person has motion to command more attention, sound, professional actors, producers, directors, and editors. They should be able to communicate with all that support if there is a grain of an idea.

The TV commercial has two basic segments: the video (the sight or visual part) and the audio (spoken words, music, or other sounds). The creation process begins with the video because television is generally better at showing than telling; however, the impact of the words and sounds must be considered.

Visual Techniques

Testimonials Testimonials can be delivered by known or unknown individuals. Viewers are fascinated with celebrities. A celebrity personality (Cindy Crawford,

Michael Jordan, Tiger Woods, for example) will grab a viewer's attention. About 20 percent of all TV commercials feature a celebrity. Athletes have outdistanced entertainers in the celebrity endorsement area since 1989.[4] Even coaches get into the act; Dan Reeves, coach of the Atlanta Falcons, has been spokeperson for Zocor cholesterol medication. There is always a risk with some celebrities getting into trouble or publicly saying the wrong thing or supporting the wrong cause, but it is worth it because of all the attention they get and the impact they have, says a vice president for Total Research Corp.[5] It costs an advertiser about $20,000 to research a celebrity to get diagnostic information of not only the personality, but whether the personality fits their product or service. Slim-Fast uses satisfied customers to show how much weight they have lost for credibility.

Serials   Serials are commercials created in a series where each commercial continues the previous story. MCI's serial campaign about a fictional publishing house, Gramercy Press, was a takeoff on the technique made popular by the Taster's Choice couple. There were 12 spots in the MCI series of commercials, which communicated a lot of information about products. Several beer companies have also tried the serial approach, as have Pacific Bell telephone, Ragu spaghetti sauce, and Energizer batteries.

Oldies Footage   Classic television and film sequences are now easily manipulated to create ads that target media-savvy viewers. Audiences have seen John Wayne selling Coors beer, Ed Sullivan introducing the Mercedes M-class sport-utility vehicle, Fred Astaire sweeping with a Dirt Devil, and Lucy Ricardo and Fred Mertz pushing tickets for the California lottery.

Spokesperson   This technique features a "presenter" who stands in front of the camera and delivers the copy directly to the viewer. The spokesperson may display and perhaps demonstrate the product. He or she may be in a set (a living room, kitchen, factory, office, or out of doors) appropriate to the product and product story, or in limbo (plain background with no set). The product should be the hero. Paul Silas, coach of the Charlotte Hornets became a logical spokesperson for the Charlotte Hornets. The spokesperson should be someone who is likable and believable but not so powerful as to overwhelm the product.

Demonstration   This technique is popular for some types of products because television is the ideal medium for demonstrating to the consumer how the product works: how a bug spray kills, how to apply eye pencils in gorgeous silky colors, or how easy it is to use a microwave to cook a whole meal quickly. When making a demonstration commercial, use close shots so the viewer can see clearly what is happening. Try to make it unexpected, if possible. You may choose a subjective camera view (which shows a procedure as if the viewer were actually doing whatever the product does), using the camera as the viewer's eyes. Make the demonstration relevant and as involving as possible. Do not try to fool the viewer for two important reasons: (1) Your message must be believable; and (2) legally, the demonstration must correspond to actual usage—most agencies make participants in the commercial production sign affidavits signifying that the events took place as they appeared on the TV screen.

Close-Ups   Television is basically a medium of close-ups. The largest TV screen is too small for extraneous details in the scenes of a commercial. A fast-food chain may use close-ups to show hamburgers cooking or the appetizing finished product

---

[4]Colin Bessonette, "Q&A on the news," *The Atlanta Journal,* January 1, 1996, A2.
[5]Cyndee Miller, "Celebrities hot despite scandals," *Marketing News,* 28 March 1994, 1–2.

ready to be consumed. With this technique, the audio is generally delivered off-screen (the voiceover costs less than a presentation by someone on the screen).

Story Line   The story-line technique is similar to making a miniature movie (with a definite beginning, middle, and end in 30 seconds), except that the narration is done offscreen. A typical scene may show a family trying to paint their large house with typical paint and brush. The camera shifts to the house next door, where a teenage female is easily spray-painting the house, the garage, and the fence in rapid fashion. During the scenes, the announcer explains the advantages of the spray painter.

Comparisons   Their soft drink has sodium. Our brand is sodium-free. Comparing one product with another can answer questions for the viewer. Usually, the comparison is against the leader in the product category. You could do a user lifestyle comparison between your brand and a competitive brand. In direct product comparisons, you must be prepared to prove in court that your product is significantly superior, as stated, and you must be credible in the way you make your claim, or the commercial may induce sympathy for the competitor.

Still Photographs and Artwork   By using still photographs and/or artwork, including cartoon drawings and lettering, you can structure a well-placed commercial. The required material may already exist, to be supplied at modest cost, or it can be photographed or drawn specifically for your use. Skillful use of the TV camera can give static visual material a surprising amount of movement. Zoom lenses provide an inward or outward motion, and panning the camera across the photographs or artwork can give the commercial motion (panning means changing the viewpoint of the camera without moving the dolly it stands on).

Slice-of-Life   Slice-of-life is an old dramatic technique where actors tell a story in an attempt to involve people with the brand. It is a short miniplay in which the brand is the hero. Most slice-of-life commercials open with a problem, and the brand becomes the solution.

The viewer must see the problem as real, and the reward must fit the problem. Because problem solving is a useful format in almost any commercial, slice-of-life is widely used. Brands selling largely emotional benefits (jeans, soft drinks, beer, greeting cards, athletic gear) have employed the format in great numbers. The humorous Budweiser "Whassup?" campaign promoted a new look at male bonding.

Customer Interview   Most people who appear in TV commercials are professional actors, but customer interviews involve nonprofessionals. An interviewer or offscreen voice may ask a housewife, who is usually identified by name, to compare the advertised kitchen cleanser with her own brand by removing two identical spots in her sink. She finds that the advertised product does a better job.

Vignettes and Situations   Advertisers of soft drinks, beer, candy, and other widely consumed products find this technique useful in creating excitement and motivation. The commercial usually consists of a series of fast-paced scenes showing people enjoying the product as they enjoy life. The audio over these scenes is often a jingle or song with lyrics based on the situation we see and the satisfaction the product offers. In many cases, it is the music that holds it all together. It can be used effectively to update a brand or sell a lifestyle. It is a challenge to link with the brand and can be costly to produce since you have to have shoot 15 or so vignettes.

Humor   Humor has long been a popular technique with both copywriters and consumers because it makes the commercial more interesting. The dangers are that the humorous aspects of the commercial will get in the way of the sell and that the viewer will remember the humor rather than the product or the benefit. The challenge is to make the humorous copy relevant to the product or benefit.

Pacific Bell Yellow Pages, as most yellow page directories, tried to reverse this trend with humorous spots. Directories sell usage to their advertisers, so the spots sold usage to consumers. The campaign, "Another problem solved courtesy of Pacific Bell Yellow Pages," featured a bratty kid sitting at his computer who talks back to his father, saying such things as "Talk to the hand. Jimmy isn't listening." A Yellow Page directory hits Jimmy on the head and is shown open to page 456, with the heading, "Military schools." Another spot has a man dressed up as a chicken making a delivery and singing a song at a sorority house and is embarrassed by two coeds who answer the door. Another Yellow Page book hits him in the head, "open to page 338" "Career Counseling."[6]

Animation   Animation consists of artists' inanimate drawings, which are photographed on motion-picture film one frame at a time and brought to life with movement as the film is projected. The most common form of animation is the cartoon. A favorite among children but popular with all ages, the cartoon is capable of creating a warm, friendly atmosphere both for the product and for the message. Animation can also be used to simplify technical product demonstrations. In a razor commercial, the actual product may be shown as it shaves a man's face, and an animated sequence may then explain how the blades of the razor remove whisker after whisker. The cost of animation depends on its style: With limited movement, few characters, and few or no backgrounds, the price can be low. As an executional format, animation has at least two basic "subforms": as a full, 30-second spot; and as a considerably shorter "middle cut-away." This middle may show up as line drawings, claymation, or computerized graphics, in each instance its purpose is to somehow demonstrate what apparently cannot be effectively demonstrated in "live action."[7]

> **animation (TV)**   Making inanimate objects appear alive and moving by setting them before an animation camera and filming one frame at a time.

Stop Motion   When a package or other object is photographed in a series of different positions, movement can be simulated as the single frames are projected in sequence. Stop motion is similar to artwork photographed in animation. With it, the package can "walk," "dance," and move as if it had come to life.

Rotoscope   In the rotoscope technique, animated and live-action sequences are produced separately and then optically combined. A live boy may be eating breakfast food while a cartoon animal trademark character jumps up and down on his shoulder and speaks to him.

Problem Solution   This technique has been around since the beginning of television. The purpose of many products is to solve the prime prospect's problem—a headache, poor communication, or plaque. You get the idea. The product is selling the solution. Problem solution is similar to slice-of-life, but lacks the depth of story line or plot development. But be sure to let the visuals tell the story. Solve the problem with visuals.

---

[6]Alice Z. Cuneo, "SBC Yellow Pages tries striking ad approach," *Advertising Age*, 15 May 2000, 4.
[7]Richard Czerniawski and Michael W. Maloney, *Creating Brand Loyalty* (New York: Amacom, 1999), 201–202.

Mood Imagery This technique is expensive and difficult. It often combines several techniques. The main objective is to set a certain mood and image for the product you are trying to sell. An example of this technique is the GE "We bring good things to life" campaign.

Split and Bookend Spots A variation on the serial commercial is the split spot: Two related (usually 15-second) spots run with a completely unrelated spot between them. For example, Post Grape-Nuts ran a split spot in which a woman asks a man how long the cereal stays crunchy in milk. The man does not want to find out, but she insists, and viewers are left hanging. Next is an unrelated 30-second commercial for another product. The couple then comes back, and she says, "After all this time it's still crunchy." The theory behind split and bookend commercials is that breaking out of the expected format will get your product remembered.

Infomercials As discussed in Chapter 8, the infomercial is a commercial that looks like a program. These commercials sell everything from woks to make-a-million-in-real-estate programs, and usually run for 30 minutes. The National Infomercial Marketing Association recommends that every infomercial begin and end with a "paid advertisement" announcement so that consumers understand what they are watching. The obvious advantage is that the advertiser has an entire program about its product.

Combination Most commercials combine techniques. A speaker may begin and conclude the message, but there will be close-ups in between. In fact, every commercial should contain at least one or two close-ups to show package and logo. Humor is adaptable to most techniques. Animation and live action make an effective mixture in many commercials, and side-by-side comparisons may be combined with almost any other technique. Exhibit 19.3 uses photomicrographs and

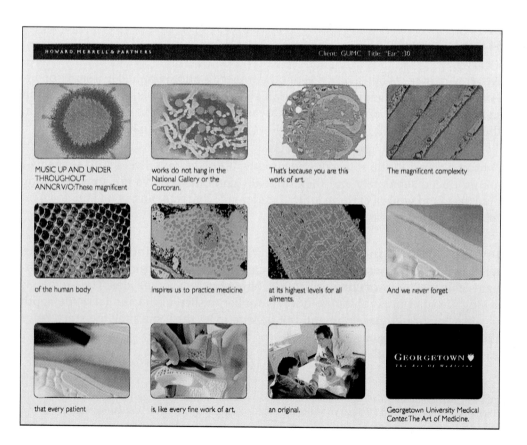

Exhibit
19.3

Photomicrographs are mixed with live action.
Courtesy: Howard, Merrell & Partners.

live action to create *The Art of Medicine* commercial for Georgetown University Medical Center. "And we never forget that every patient is, like fine art work, an original."

Video Influence

Many techniques used in commercials that were once unique to MTV have become the visual rules of today. These include hyperkinetic imagery, visual speed, and sophistication; ironic, wise-guy attitudes; unexpected humor; quick, suggestive cuts rather than slow segues; narrative implications rather than whole stories; attitudes, not explanations; tightly cropped, partial images instead of whole ones; mixtures of live action, newsreel footage, animation, typography, film speeds, and film quality; and unexpected soundtrack/audio relationships to video.

Which Technique?

Over the years there have been a number of studies to help advertisers make up their minds as to what kind of commercials to run. None provides all the answers, however. Ogilvy & Mather found that people who liked a commercial were twice as likely to be persuaded by it compared to people who felt neutral toward the advertising. Perhaps the single most striking finding was the fact that commercial liking went far beyond mere entertainment. People like commercials they feel are relevant and worth remembering, which could have an impact on greater persuasion. Original or novel approaches by themselves seem to have little to do with how well a commercial is liked. They also found that liking was a function of product category. A lively, energetic execution also contributed to liking, but was less important than relevance.

In other research findings, Video Storyboard tests reinforce that consumers like commercials with celebrities. In fact, consumer preference for this type of commercial has risen in the past 10 years. Such commercials are more persuasive than slice-of-life vignettes or product demonstrations. Exhibit 19.4 shows that celebrities are bested only by humor and kids as executional elements that characterize persuasive commercials.

"To me, technique has never been as interesting as ideas," says director Bob Giraldi, "and now that we're in this time when technique is as important if not more important than anything, I keep thinking how I can come up with techniques that are interesting."[8]

Video Storyboard Persuasion Results

	Women	Men	18–34	34–39	50+
Commercials with **humor**	57	**68**	58	63	64
Commercials with **children**	**61**	44	52	56	52
Commercials with **celebrities**	39	34	**44**	34	30
Real-life situations	34	30	**39**	33	24
Brand **comparisons**	32	23	**35**	31	20
Musical commercials	**29**	18	27	23	20
Product **demonstrations**	17	**26**	19	24	21
Endorsements from experts	**17**	13	16	16	14
Hidden-camera testimonials	12	10	**14**	10	9
Company **presidents**	6	**12**	**12**	9	7

Exhibit

19.4

Video storyboard persuasion results

Source: Adweek, 15 August 1994, 17.

---

[8]Anthony Vagnoni, "Back to the future," *Creativity,* June 1996, 19–20.

Planning the Commercial

In planning the TV commercial, there are many considerations: cost, medium (videotape or film), casting of talent, use of music, special techniques, time, location, and the big idea and its relationship to the advertising and marketing objectives and, of course, to the entire campaign.

Let us review some of the basic principles of writing the commercial script or thinking the idea through:

- You are dealing with sight, sound, and motion. Each of these elements has its own requirements and uses. There should be a relationship among them so that the viewer perceives the desired message. Make certain that when you are demonstrating a sales feature, the audio is talking about that same feature.

- Your audio should be relevant to your video, but there is no need to describe what is obvious in the picture. Where possible, you should see that the words interpret the picture and advance the thought.

- Television generally is more effective at showing than telling; therefore, more than half of the success burden rests on the ability of the video to communicate.

- The number of scenes should be planned carefully. You do not want too many scenes (unless you are simply trying to give an overall impression) because this tends to confuse the viewer. Yet you do not want scenes to become static (unless planned so for a reason). Study TV commercials and time the scene changes to determine what you personally find effective. If you do this, you will discover the importance of pacing the message—if a scene is too long, you will find yourself impatiently waiting for the next one.

- It is important to conceive the commercial as a flowing progression so that the viewer will be able to follow it easily. You do not have time for a three-act play whose unrelated acts can be tied together at the end. A viewer who cannot follow your thought may well tune you out. The proper use of opticals or transitions can add motion and smoothness to scene transitions.

- Television is basically a medium of close-ups. The largest TV screen is too small for extraneous detail in the scenes of a commercial. Long shots can be effective in establishing a setting, but not for showing product features.

- The action of the commercial takes more time than a straight announcer's reading of copy. A good rule is to purposely time the commercial a second or two short. Generally, the action will eat up this time, so do not just read your script. Act it out.

- You will want to consider the use of supers (words on the screen) of the basic theme so that the viewer can see, as well as hear, the important sales feature. Many times, the last scene will feature product identification and the theme line.

- If possible, show the brand name. If it is prominent, give a shot of the package; otherwise, flash its logotype. It is vital to establish brand identification.

- Generally, try to communicate one basic idea; avoid running in fringe benefits. Be certain that your words as well as your pictures emphasize your promise. State it, support it, and, if possible, demonstrate it. Repeat your basic promise near the end of the commercial; that is the story you want viewers to carry away with them.

- Read the audio aloud to catch tongue twisters.

- As in most other advertising writing, the sentences should usually be short and their structure uncomplicated. Use everyday words. It is not necessary to have something said every second. The copy should round out the thought conveyed by the picture.

- In writing your video description, describe the scene and action as completely as possible: "Open on husband and wife in living room" is not enough. Indicate where each is placed, whether they are standing or sitting, and generally how the room is furnished.

Writing the Script

It's probably obvious, but writing a TV commercial is very different from writing print advertising. First, you must use simple, easy-to-pronounce, easy-to-remember words. And you must be brief. The 30-second commercial has only 28 seconds of audio. In 28 seconds, you must solve your prime prospect's problems by demonstrating your product's superiority. If the product is too big to show in use, be certain to show the logo or company name at least twice during the commercial. Think of words and pictures simultaneously. You usually divide your script paper into two columns. On the left, you describe the video action, and on the right you write the audio portion, including sound effects and music. Corresponding video and audio elements go right next to each other, panel by panel (see Exhibit 19.5).

Write copy in a friendly, conversational style. If you use an off-camera announcer, make certain that his or her dialogue is keyed to the scenes in your video portion. Although it is not always possible, matching the audio with the video makes a commercial cohesive and more effective. The audio—words, sound effects, or music—in a script is as important as the video portion. They must work together to bring the viewer the message. You need strong copy and sound and strong visuals. All are vital for an effective commercial.

Some agencies add visuals to their scripts. They use specially designed sheets of paper 8 by 11 inches (usually), with boxes down the center for rough sketches of the video portion (Exhibit 19.6) called photoscripts. For presentations, most agencies use full-size TV storyboards.

VIDEO	AUDIO
	MUSIC: IN AND UNDER (George Winston quiet jazz)
1. MS: BEACH SCENE 3 PEOPLE IN CHAIRS SITTING OUTSIDE OF BEACH HOUSE. BEACH BLANKET IN SAND.	ANNCR: Pawleys is a great
2. CU: CHILD DIGGING IN SAND WITH OCEAN BACKGROUND.	family resort.
3. MS: PEOPLE WALKING ON ALMOST EMPTY BEACH. A FEW HOUSES ARE IN THE BACKGROUND.	It is nature at its best . . .
4. LS: LADY ALONE WALKING INLET WITH DISTANT HOUSE OR TWO.	a beautiful pristine beach
5. WIDE SHOT OF EMPTY BEACH, FEW HOUSES.	Don't come, we're having fun.
6. SLIDE.	
	Pawleys is OUR beach.

Exhibit 19.5

A Script for a TV Commercial

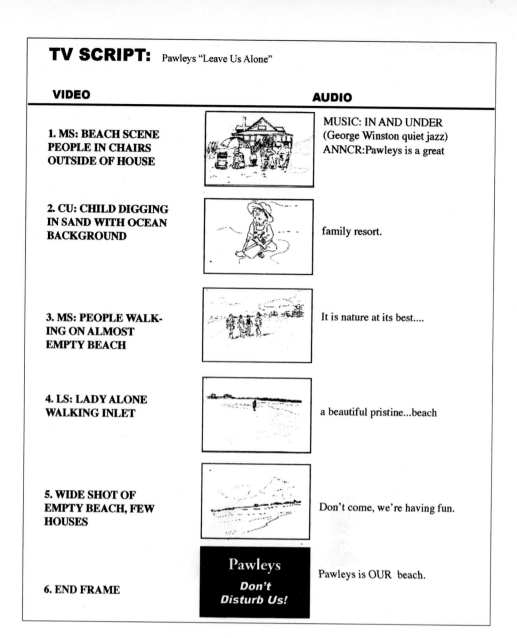

TV SCRIPT: Pawleys "Leave Us Alone"

VIDEO		AUDIO
1. MS: BEACH SCENE PEOPLE IN CHAIRS OUTSIDE OF HOUSE		MUSIC: IN AND UNDER (George Winston quiet jazz) ANNCR:Pawleys is a great
2. CU: CHILD DIGGING IN SAND WITH OCEAN BACKGROUND		family resort.
3. MS: PEOPLE WALK-ING ON ALMOST EMPTY BEACH		It is nature at its best....
4. LS: LADY ALONE WALKING INLET		a beautiful pristine...beach
5. WIDE SHOT OF EMPTY BEACH, FEW HOUSES		Don't come, we're having fun.
6. END FRAME	Pawleys *Don't Disturb Us!*	Pawleys is OUR beach.

Exhibit
19.6

A TV Script with Storyboard

Developing the Storyboard

storyboard Series of drawings used to present a pro-posed commercial. Consists of illustrations of key action (video), accompanied by the audio part. Used for getting advertiser approval and as a production guide.

Once the creative art and copy team has developed a script, the next step is to cre-ate a **storyboard,** which consists of a series of sketches showing key scenes devel-oped in the script. It is a helpful tool for discussing the concept with other agency or client personnel, who may not know the background or who may not be able to visualize a script accurately. Without a storyboard, each individual may interpret the script's visuals differently.

Storyboard Versus Finished Look   It is extremely difficult, if not impossi-ble, to visualize the look of a finished commercial from the storyboard. Director Jim Edwards says, "The hardest thing to do in directing is to make someone understand your vision before you actually make the pictures and then it's too late. Most people [clients, account people] are very literal minded and don't work well with their imaginations"—and that's what a storyboard is supposed to help you do. Of course, the quality of the storyboards varies from virtual stick figures in limbo to full-color drawings. Keep in mind, using this limited medium, it is a difficult task to show all the details that are necessary to understand for production purposes.

Storyboards consist of two frames for each scene. The top frame represents the TV screen (visual). The bottom frame carries a description of the video (as per script) and the audio for that sequence (some storyboards carry only the audio portion). The number of sets of frames varies from commercial to commercial and is not necessarily dictated by the length of the commercial. There may be 4 to 12 or more sets of frames, depending on the nature of the commercial and the demands of the client for detail.

The ratio of width to depth on the TV screen is 4 by 3. There is no standard-size storyboard frame, although a common size is 4 inches by 3 inches.

The storyboard is a practical step between the raw script and actual production. It gives the agency, client, and production house personnel a common visual starting point for their discussion. Upon client approval, the storyboard goes into production.

Assessing the storyboard requires answering a number of questions: Is there a campaign idea? Is it on strategy? Is the campaign idea meaningful? Credible? Provocative? Does the execution showcase the *campaign idea*? Is the benefit visualized? Does it tell a picture story? Is it clear, credible, and compelling? Does the board represent a commercial or a campaign? Are the ideas communicated clearly in visual-audio elements? Does it *sell* versus *tell*?

Exhibits 19.1, 19.2 and 19.3 are examples of photoboards. The photoboard is similar to the storyboard, but shows the *actual* frames (photos) that were shot. It is frequently used by companies as a sales tool to show merchants and dealers exactly what kind of advertising support they will be given.

Other Elements of the Commercial

Opticals   Most commercials contain more than a single scene. Optical devices or effects between scenes are necessary to provide smooth visual continuity from scene to scene. They are inserted during the final editing stage. The actual opticals may be one of the director's functions. However, these are used to aid in the transition of getting from one scene to the next scene or establishing a visual. Sometimes which technique depends on the importance of a particular scene or the detail that needs to be seen. Exhibit 19.7 illustrates some very basic optical decisions. Among the most common are the following:

opticals Visual effects that are put on a TV film in a laboratory, in contrast to those that are included as part of the original photography.

Cut   One scene simply cuts into the next. It is the fastest scene change because it indicates no time lapse whatsoever. A cut is used to indicate simultaneous action, to speed up action, and for variety. It keeps one scene from appearing on the screen too long.

Dissolve   An overlapping effect in which one scene fades out while the following scene simultaneously fades in. Dissolves are slower than cuts. There are fast dissolves and slow dissolves. Dissolves are used to indicate a short lapse of time in a given scene, or to move from one scene to another where the action is either simultaneous with the action in the first scene or occurring very soon after the preceding action.

Fade-in   An effect in which the scene actually "fades" into vision from total black (black screen).

Fade-out   This is opposite of a fade-in. The scene "fades" into total black. If days, months, or years elapse between one sequence of action and the next, indicate "Fade out . . . fade in."

Matte   Part of one scene is placed over another so that the same narrator, for example, is shown in front of different backgrounds.

Super   The superimposition of one scene or object over another. The title or product can be "supered" over the scene.

ECU - An Extreme Close Up shows, for example, person's lips, nose, eyes.

CU - The Close Up is a tight shot, but showing face on entire package for emphasis.

MCU - The Medium Close Up cuts to person about chest, usually showing some background.

MS - The Medium Shot shows the person from the waist up. Commonly used shot. Shows much more detail of setting or background than MCU.

LS - The Long Shot shows the scene from a distance. Used to establish location.

Exhibit
19.7

Examples of Camera Directions

Wipe The new scene "wipes" off the previous scene from top or bottom or side to side with a geometric pattern (Exhibit 19.8). A wipe is faster than a dissolve but not as fast as a cut. A wipe does not usually connote lapse of time, as a dissolve or fade-out does. There are several types of wipes: flip (the entire scene turns over like the front and back of a postcard), horizontal (left to right or right to left), vertical (top to bottom or bottom to top), diagonal, closing door (in from both sides), bombshell (a burst into the next scene), iris (a circle that grows bigger is an iris out), fan (fans out from center screen), circular (sweeps around the screen—also called clock wipe). Wipes are most effective when a rapid succession of short or quick scenes is desired, or to separate impressionistic shots when these are grouped together to produce a montage effect.

Zoom A smooth, sometimes rapid move from a long shot to a close-up or from a close-up to a long shot.

Soundtrack The audio portion of the commercial may be recorded either during the film or videotape shooting or at an earlier or later time in a recording studio. When the soundtrack is recorded during the shooting, the actual voices of the peo-

Exhibit
19.8

Example of Wipe

ple speaking on camera are used in the commercial. If the soundtrack is recorded in advance, the film or videotape scenes can be shot to fit the copy points as they occur; or if music is part of the track, visual action can be matched to a specific beat. If shooting and editing take place before the soundtrack is recorded, the track can be tailored to synchronize with the various scenes.

Music Not all commercials need music. But think about it early in the process. Music has the ability to communicate feelings and moods in a unique way. As a result, the use of music can make or break a TV commercial. In some commercials, it is every bit as important as the copy or visuals. It is often used as background to the announcer's copy or as a song or jingle that is integral to the ad.

"Music is the best means we have to automatically strike a chord," says Jeremy Miller, PR director for TBWA/Chiat/Day L.A., "it's better than any amount of words or even images. When we used Rod Stewart's 'Forever Young' for an Apple Computer ad, we were positioning the product precisely where we wanted it. We'll cut one ad to a dozen different songs just to see which one works the best. It's that important."[9]

Here are some ways you can put music to work:[10]

■ *Backgrounds.* In many commercials, background music is used primarily to contribute to the mood. Appropriate music can be used to establish the setting; then it can fade and become soft in the background.

■ *Transitions.* Music can be an effective transition device to carry viewers from one setting to another. For example, the music may start out being sedate as the

[9]Davin Seay, "The beat goes on as advertisers increase efforts to tag products with hip sound images," *BrandWeek*, 22 May 2000, 3–10.
[10]Music—How to Use It for Commerical Production, a publication of the Television Bureau of Advertising, New York.

scene is peaceful. As it switches to the product being used, the music changes to rock and the tempo builds, marking the transition from place to place.

- *Movement.* Sound effects (SFX), natural sounds, and music can contribute to movement. Music that moves up the scale, or down, supports something or someone moving up or down.
- *Accents.* Music can punctuate points or actions. The "beat" of the music and visuals can match to hold viewers' attention and drive the commercial. Musical sounds—as little as a single note—can attract attention.

New or Old Music Some advertisers pay big money to professional musicians to develop a special tune or lyrics for a commercial or campaign. Nike recently used original music throughout a commercial with Tiger Woods bouncing his golf ball on his head. In another recent Nike commercial, they used established music, "You Are So Beautiful," throughout the commercial. Using existing music can be expensive, but the licensing of an old song can be effective. When a great song is part of the creative equation, audiences can't get enough of it. "Night and Day" has been reborn and reborn again for Air France, Audi, Ford, and Maxwell House, as was "Stand by Me" for Buick, after years at Citibank. "Wild Thing" simply has too many credits to mention. What "Wild Thing" tells us is that classic songs gain, rather than lose, creative impact with multiple uses; and that they do so not only via network commercials but also via local ones; all of which reinforce one another in a seemingly endless cycle. Rick Lyon of Rick Lyon Music says, "In a certain sense, a song like 'Wild Thing' belongs to all of us. Maybe that's why audiences not only accept but enjoy its repeated use as they've enjoyed other visual advertising cons." It is similar to using the Statue of Liberty or the Mona Lisa. Royal Caribbean Cruise Line has used "Lust for Life," in a number of commercials. Superstar Sting was so enamoured with the new edition Jaguar, that he sought out the automaker's ad agency to volunteer his musical services.

Licensed music gains instant access to the listener's subconscious. It lets a brand such as Buick communicate trust and reliability when its "Stand by Me" had just done the same for Citibank. Or it lets McDonald's promote a folksiness with Randy Newman's "You've Got a Friend in Me," only months after it had gained fame in the popular family hit movie *Toy Story.*[11] The Gap's khaki love fest, set to the tune of Donovan's "Mellow Yellow," unites Baby Boomers and Gen Xers in a nirvana of perceived coolness.

Whether you're using country, rock, or Latin, the tone of the music can help transfer drama, love, happiness, or other feelings to the viewer. It is a tool to cue the viewer's feelings. Original music can be written and scored for the commercial, or licensing of old or popular songs can be obtained, which can be very expensive. The least expensive music is stock music sold by stock music companies. It is cheap because it is not exclusive.

PRODUCING THE TV COMMERCIAL

The job of converting the approved storyboard is done by TV production. There are three distinct stages to this process:

- Preproduction includes casting, wardrobing, designing sets or building props, finding a location or studio, and meeting with agency, client, and production house personnel.

---

[11]Rick Lyon, "The circle game," *Creativity,* September 1997, 18.

- Shooting encompasses the work of filming or videotaping all scenes in the commercial. In fact, several takes are made of each scene.
- Postproduction, also known as editing, completion, or finishing, includes selecting scenes from among those shots, arranging them in the proper order, inserting transitional effects, adding titles, combining sound with picture, and delivering the finished commercial.

Exhibit 19.9 shows a photoboard of a SAS Institute (software makers) ad that doesn't translate well in stills, but was excellent in production. This spot represents the harvesting of digital data. It was a challenge for the producer.

In charge of production is the producer, who combines the talents of coordinator, diplomat, watchdog, and businessperson. Some producers are on the staffs of large agencies or advertisers. Many work on a freelance basis. The work of a producer is so all-embracing that the best way to describe it is to live through the entire production process. Let us do that first and pick up the details of the producer's job in the section headed "Role of the Producer."

Let us begin with the problems of shooting the spot, for which a director is appointed by the producer.

The Director's Function

The key person in the shooting, the **director** takes part in casting and directing the talent, directs the cameraperson in composing each picture, assumes responsibility for the setting, and puts the whole show together. A director of a regional commercial will earn about $7,500 per day, and national commercial directors average about $13,000 per commercial; however, better-known directors may demand

TV director The person who casts and rehearses a commercial and is the key person in the shooting of the commercial.

Exhibit
19.9

Individual frames of a photoboard don't always translate a visually technical idea well.
Courtesy: Howard, Merrell & Partners.

$25,000 to $35,000 per spot. The Source Maythenyi, an advertising/production database service, recently estimated that there are 4,000 specialized commercial directors and that doesn't include a growing number of feature film directors.[12]

The Bidding Process

There is only one way to provide specifications for a commercial shoot when you are seeking bids from production companies, and that is in writing. There is an industry-accepted form (AICP Bid and Specification Form). Information for this form is provided by the agency and client. The use of this form ensures that all production companies are provided with identical job specifications for estimating production costs. It ensures that all bids are based on the same information.

The Preproduction Process

A preproduction meeting must be held prior to every production. The agency producer is expected to chair this meeting. The following agency, client, and production company personnel usually attend:

> Agency: producer, creative team, account supervisor
> Client: brand manager or advertising manager
> Production company: director, producer, others as needed

The following points should be covered at every preproduction meeting: direction, casting, locations and/or sets, wardrobe and props, product, special requirements, final script, legal claims/contingencies, and timetable update.

In addition to covering the points just listed, the creative team and the director will likely present shooting boards and the production thinking behind the commercial. The shooting boards should be used for the following purposes:

- to determine camera angles
- to determine best product angles
- to project camera and cast movement and help determine talent status (extra versus principal)
- to determine number of scenes to be shot
- to determine timing of each scene

ROLE OF THE PRODUCER

Agency Producer

The producer's role begins before the approval of the storyboard. Conferring with the copywriter and/or art director, the producer becomes thoroughly familiar with every frame of the storyboard.

1. The producer prepares the "specs," or specifications—the physical production requirements of the commercial—to provide the production studios with the precise information they require to compute realistic bids. Every agency prepares its own estimate form. In addition, many advertisers request a further breakdown of the cost of items such as preproduction, shooting, crew, labor, studio, location travel and expenses, equipment, film, props and wardrobe, payroll taxes, studio makeup, direction, insurance, and editing.

---

[12]Warren Burger, "Action fever," *Creativity*, June 2000, 47–49.

2. The producer contacts the studios that have been invited to submit bids based on their specialties, experience, and reputation; meets with them either separately or in one common "bid session"; and explains the storyboard and the specs in detail.

3. The production house estimates expenses after studying specs, production timetable, and storyboard. Generally, a 35 percent markup is added to the estimated out-of-pocket expenses to cover overhead and studio profit. Usually, the production company adds a 10 percent contingency fee to the bid for unforeseen problems. The bids are submitted. The producer analyzes the bids and recommends the studio to the client.

4. The producer arranges for equipment. The studio may own equipment, such as cameras and lights, but more often it rents all equipment for a job. The crew is also freelance, hired by the day. Although the studio's primary job is to shoot the commercial, it can also take responsibility for editorial work. For videotape, a few studios own their own cameras and production units; others rent these facilities.

5. Working through a talent agency, the producer arranges, or has the production company arrange, auditions. Associates also attend auditions, at which they and the director make their final choices of performers. The client may also be asked to pass on the final selection.

6. The producer then participates in the preproduction meeting. At this meeting the producer, creative associates, account executive, and client, together with studio representatives and director, lay final plans for production.

7. During the shooting, the producer usually represents both the agency and the client as the communicator with the director. On the set or location, the creative people and client channel any comments and suggestions through the producer to avoid confusion.

8. It is the producer's responsibility to arrange for the recording session. Either before or after shooting and editing, he or she arranges for the soundtrack, which may call for an announcer, actors, singers, and musicians. If music is to be recorded, the producer will have had preliminary meetings with the music contractor.

9. The producer participates in the editing along with the creative team. Editing begins after viewing the dailies and selecting the best takes.

10. The producer arranges screenings for agency associates and clients to view and approve the commercials at various editing stages and after completion of the answer print.

11. Finally, the producer handles the billings and approves studio and other invoices for shooting, editing, and payment to talent.

The "Outside" Producer

An **outside producer** is the person representing a production company whose entire business is filmmaking. He or she is hired by the agency producer to create the TV commercial according to agency specifications.

outside producer
The production company person who is hired by the agency to create the commercial according to agency specifications.

Shooting

Most productions consist of the following steps:

1. *Prelight.* This is simply the day (or days) used to set the lighting for specific scenes. To do this exclusively on shoot days would tie up the entire crew.

2. *Shooting.* This phase of the production process is the filming (or taping) of the approved scenes for the commercial. These scenes are then "screened" the next day (dailies) to ensure that the scene was captured as planned.

3. *Wrap.* This signals the completion of production. It is at this stage that most of the crew is released.

4. *Editing.* This takes place after the shoot is completed. Scenes are screened and selected for use in the commercial. The scenes are then merged with a sound track, titles, and opticals, composing a completed or finished commercial.

The role of the client and account service at the shoot is one of advisor. It is really the creative's day and it is their responsibility to deliver the spot. In situations where the client needs to provide input on the set, the prime contact is the account representative or agency producer. The producer is generally the liaison between the agency and the director. This chain of command is simple and direct and eliminates confusion on the set, which is an absolute necessity when shooting.

Postproduction Process

Postproduction begins after a production company exposes the film in the camera at the "shoot." The film that comes out of the camera must be developed in a chemical bath and then printed onto a new strip of positive film called the "dailies." The editor then screens these "dailies" and selects the good takes from the day's shooting.

The editor then physically splices the takes selected from each scene together with the next to create a "rough cut," which is a rough rendition of the finished commercial. Once the editor has cut this film and the agency and client approve the cut, the editor takes the original film that was shot and developed and pulls the takes from that film that matches the selected workprint takes.

Today, virtually all final edits, effects, and opticals are done on videotape. The original camera film takes (35 mm motion picture film) are transferred electronically to one-inch videotape. During this transfer of film to videotape, the color is corrected.

The editor then takes this material into a video edit, where each take is run on videotape and the "cut-in" through "cut-out" points for each take are laid down in sequence, from the first frame of the first scene to the end frame of that scene (to match the workprint), until the entire commercial is laid down from the color-corrected videotape matter (called the "unedited tape master"). Titles and other special effects are added during this final unedited-tape-to-edited-tape session. The sound (which the editor and agency had worked on along with the picture) is then electronically relayed onto the video-edited master, and the spot is finished. Sound complicated? It is.

Postdirectors are independent contractors in the production mix. They are in the business of cutting film and creatively supervising videotape transfers from film; supervising video edits and special effects; recording narration, sound, music, and sound effects; mixing these sounds together; relaying them onto the picture; and delivering a finished product to the agency.

Computer Postproduction Technology

The computer is, and has been, revolutionizing some aspects of print production and prepress activities and is also active in revolutionizing TV postproduction. Advances in hardware and software are continuing to change the creation and production of TV commercials. Names such as Silicon Graphics, Avid, Wavefront, Inferno, Flame, and Quantel's Henry and Harry have been mainstays for a number of years. Terms such as 3-D animation, compositing, morphing, 2-D animation, nonlinear editing, live-action compositing, and real-time are common among the professionals who generate visual images and special effects. The systems used in the early 1990s to produce the video magic could cost $25,000 to $250,000. Today, Macintosh offers many of the same video effects to more producers of commercials at lower costs. As usual, when discussing computer hardware and software, each system has a plus and a minus; but the availability offers more creative and production people more options to create unique visuals and commercials.

It is safe to say that today's **computer-generated imagery** (CGI) offers creative minds great new opportunities in production and postproduction. This technology allows creative people to squash, squeeze, stretch, and morph objects in less time than ever before. Computers are turning live action into cartoon action. At production facilities, creative talents can use digital-graphics/animation-compositing systems to top four or five layers of live action with five or six layers of graphics, all simultaneously, allowing the finished visual composite to be seen as it develops.

computer-generated imagery (CGI) Technology allowing computer operators to create multitudes of electronic effects for TV—to squash, stretch, or squeeze objects—much more quickly than earlier tools could. It can add layers of visuals simultaneously.

A recent Lexus commercial, dubbed "High Bank Track," featured a Lexus 300ES cruising up a futuristic Los Angeles freeway, around skyscrapers, and into the sky on an elevated, banked track. The computerized spot was pieced together out of dozens of bits and pieces. The people at A52 (imaging company) aligned hundreds of elements in Inferno and Flame (linking pieces of real road, model road, and CG road with real, CG, and model cars, for instance) which made the spot complicated. Many scenes were deeply layered composites, using elements from several different places that meant mixing elements from four or five different crews that were shooting simultaneously.[13]

CGI Wizardry Remember the Budweiser Clydesdale who held the pigskin for the point-after attempt in the Super Bowl? Or the beer-slurpin' frogs? These are largely computer generated (CG) or a mix of special techniques. The ability of animators and software engineers to imbue their characters with a greater sense of charm and warmth has made skeptics become computer converts. It doesn't hurt that the work from *Toy Story* to Coca-Cola polar bears has been embraced by audiences. Computer-animation people have been preoccupied with technical issues in the past. Technology has changed that. Now we have the ability to make photorealistic animals, for example. They look real, for the most part, only now they can do things no animal could be trained to do. Lowe came up with the idea of illustrating side-impact air bags by placing a new Mercedes in a herd of lumbering rhinos on New York streets. The digital crew worked with stock film footage to study how rhinos move.

CGI and cel animation both play big roles in television commercial production. Costs of both are dropping, software is improving, and the proliferation of computer-generated graphics has created a growing reservoir of artists, techniques, and trends. The classic Coca-Cola polar bears could exist only in CGI. Cost, however, is still a major factor in using CGI and is considerably higher than live action budgets. "National spots are rarely budgeted below $250,000 for a 30-second commercial; they can easily reach $1 to 2 million on the high end for clients like Coca-Cola, auto companies, and other large corporations," says executive producer Paul Golubovich.[14] BBDO-Mexico created a Mexican and South American spot for Pepsi, which featured animated morsels interacting with the soft drink. In "Chicken," the concept becomes *thinking food*—peas form a thought balloon that takes the shape of the Pepsi wave.

---

[13]"On Track," *Millimeter*, April 1999, 19.
[14]Michael Spier, "Why CGI?" *Millimeter*, May 1997, 93–100.

Recently, we have seen in television production an awareness that CGI can be used to help create things that couldn't otherwise be created. Taking different techniques and marrying them into one cohesive unit is difficult, but with developing software, and more skilled people, the process becomes easier and more creative.

The combination of elements from two or more photographic sources often produces a striking effect. With the advent of computers, the process of combining different layers became much easier, but at the same time it is more complex because the variety of combinations are now seemingly limitless. Filmed images can now be scanned into the computer by running compositing software, enabling the digital blending of several—or, literally hundreds—of layers of imagery. Exhibit 19.10 uses a number of techniques in this high-tech commercial.

You may have heard of some of the following electronic production tools and techniques:

- *Compositing.* In the digital realm, compositing is the umbrella term for many processes required to technically accomplish image combination in the computer.

- *Matte.* Essentially a silhouette in black and white, matte is the necessary signal for the computer to cut out the part of the image intended to be visible. It can also exist in many other physical forms, such as a painting on glass or a masked-off camera composition.

- *Keying.* Keying is electronically composing one picture over another. The two types of keying are luminance and chroma-keying. This term came from the

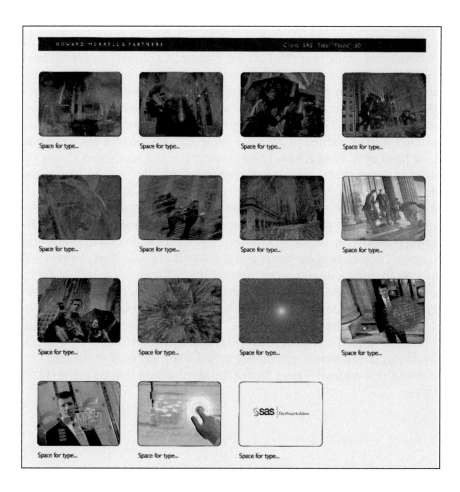

word "keyhole" and is interpreted by the computer as a signal enabling a hole to be cut in a clip layer.

- *Chroma-keying.* This is another matte derivation method in which the computer sources a specific color (usually green, blue, or red) to create a key signal. This is a way of performing automatic matte extraction, using the colored background. In a weather program that has a map and the weatherperson in front of the map, the map is an electronic image chroma-keyed off of a green screen. The weatherperson can't actually see the map without looking at a monitor. All that is actually behind them is a color screen. It is interpreted by the computer as a hole and is replaced with the layer behind, in this case a map.

- *Keyer.* A keyer is simply an electronic composer.

- *Morphing.* **Morphing** is an industry term for metamorphosing, which means transforming from one object to another. For example, in a Schick shaving spot, a man's head is turned into a 3-D cube, and for Exxon a car turns into a tiger. This computer graphics technique allows its operator to move between the real world and computer graphics by electronically layering visual transitions between live action.

  The cost of morphs varies. They can range from $5,000 for a "garage" job using a PC up to $70,000, depending on the complexity. But meticulous advance planning remains the key to a successful job. A Schick shaving heads commercial, which morphed a series of six talking shaving heads and upper torsos, required a two-day blue-screen shoot, composited over a bathroom background.[15]

- *Harry.* The Quantel Henry/Harry on-line system is an editing device with an optical device tied to it. It allows computer composites to mix with live video. Ninety percent of Harry work can now be created on a Macintosh. The Harry is faster and much more expensive, but the Mac appears to be closing the gap.

- *Flame.* On the other hand, Flame is an optical device with an editing device tied to it. It functions as a high-capacity, random-access, multilayer compositing system, with video editing/effects/digital-audio capacity. So you can see that you have to have the right technology for the right job. And, yes, it can be confusing to the nonproduction person in the advertising industry. A Bud Light commercial showed an invisible man breaking out of the "Secret Invisibility Lab" to get a six pack of Bud Light and astounds everyone he encounters. Aside from his floating six pack, the spot also featured hovering test tubes and another invisible character's bouncing paddle ball courtesy of some Harry and Flame effects.[16]

- *In-House Desktop.* During the early 1990s, agencies could use their in-house Macintosh computers to interface with video composers. This made video editing, long the domain of highly trained specialists, a viable in-house option. This allowed the agency personnel to cut and paste video images just as desktop computers cut-and-paste print graphics. The quality isn't quite the level of the production houses' hardware/software, but it is getting closer and allows agencies to cut costs and use them for producing the storyboard, the animatic for testing, and rough cuts, and then send the disk to the production company, where the spot is polished into a final commercial of broadcast quality. Those clients that do not need top-quality images can complete the entire commercial postproduction process on the system.

morphing An electronic technique that allows you to transform one object into another object.

---

[15]Beth Jacques, "The do's and don'ts of mixing animation and live action," *Millimeter,* April 1994, 77–82.

[16]Kristinha McCort, "Production review," *Millimeter,* April 1999, 27.

CONTROLLING THE COST OF COMMERCIAL PRODUCTION

The cost of producing a TV commercial is of deep concern to both the agency and the advertiser. The chief reason that money is wasted in commercials is inadequate preplanning. In production, the two major cost items are labor and equipment. Labor—the production crew, director, and performers—is hired by the day, and equipment is rented by the day. If a particular demonstration was improperly rehearsed, if a particular prop was not delivered, or if the location site was not scouted ahead of time, the shooting planned for one day may be forced into expensive overtime or into a second day. These costly mistakes can be avoided by careful planning.

Cost Relationship

Several areas that can have a dramatic impact on TV production costs are the following:

- *Location or studio.* Is the commercial planned for studio or location? Location shoots, outside geographic zones, mean travel time and overnight accommodations for the crew, adding a minimum average cost of $7,500 per away day.

- *Talent.* The number of principals on the storyboard is important and can be expensive. The more people on-camera in your commercials, the higher the talent residual bill. The rates for talent are based on the Screen Actors Guild (SAG) union contract. For national commercials, you can roughly estimate your talent cost per on-camera principal as .0015 of your media budget for the spot. That is, $15,000 per person per $10 million in exposure. If 20 on-camera people are involved in your spot, expect a $300,000 bill. That chunk of your budget may exceed the entire net cost of production. So it is important to discuss how many on-camera principals are planned for the spot and how many are absolutely necessary.

residual A sum paid to certain talent on a TV or radio commercial every time the commercial is run after 13 weeks, for the life of the commercial.

- *Residuals.* Another major expense is the **residual,** or reuse fee, paid to performers—announcers, narrators, actors, and singers—in addition to their initial session fees. Under union rules, performers are paid every time the commercial is aired on the networks, the amount of the fee depending upon their scale and the number of cities involved. If a commercial is aired with great frequency, a national advertiser may end up paying more in residuals than for the production of the commercial itself. This problem is less severe for the local advertiser because local rates are cheaper than national rates. The moral is: Cast only the number of performers necessary to the commercial and not one performer more.

  The use of extras presents less of a cost issue. The first 30 extras in a spot must be paid a session fee ($232/day) and are not entitled to residuals. Rates for use of extras beyond the first 30 can be negotiated.

- *Special effects.* If the board indicated the use of special effects or animation (either computer-generated or cel), ask how the special effect will be achieved. It is not unusual for complicated computer-generated effects to cost $6,000 to $12,000 per second and more! To prevent surprises, ask questions. What may appear to be a simple execution on the surface may in fact contain extremely expensive elements. Neither the agency nor client should be satisfied until everyone understands the project. Anything short of this can result in surprise creative and expenditures.

- *Estimate costs.* Given the potential complexity of shooting commercials due to a wide range of factors (location, special rigs, special effects, talent, set construction), it is not uncommon to believe a relatively "simple" looking spot presented in storyboard form will be "relatively" inexpensive. This is simply not the case. Both the client and the agency must always, always require a rough cost for each spot recommended. The number provided will help put the project into focus relative to the planned media support for the commercials. Generally, it is not uncommon for clients to spend 10 percent of their planned media budget in production. As this percentage escalates, the production decision becomes more difficult, particularly in today's economic climate.
- *Editorial fee cost.* There is a creative labor fee for the editor's service. This charge is for the editor's and assistant editor's time. Depending on the editor and the difficulty of the edit, a creative fee can range from $400 to $500 (to supervise sound only, for example, on a single-scene commercial) to more than $9,000 to cut a multi-image, complex spot with special effects manipulations and music.
- *The cost of film transfer and videotape conform or edit and finishing.* This cost can range from about $1,000 for this work, including tape stock and finished materials, to $7,500 for expensive and difficult treatments.
- *Special effects and titling.* This cost can range from $100 to make a title art card and include it in the edit session, to $10,000 to $30,000 for heavy design, frame-by-frame, picture manipulations.
- *Recording and mixing.* The cost of recording and mixing a voice-over, music, and sound effects together can range from $450 to $4,000 or more.

If you total all of these possibilities, from the combined lowest to the combined highest, the cost can be $2,136 to $67,100 to edit a 30-second commercial!

TV Production Cost Averages

According to the American Association of Advertising Agencies, the average cost of producing a 30-second commercial rose 16 percent in 1999 to $343,000.[17] Obviously, there is great variation in producing commercials: interviews/testimonials averaged $249,000; animation, $210,000; and tabletop/products, food averaged $111,000. These figures indicate the importance of producing a TV spot that is on target because the investment simply to get the idea on film or tape is significant. Historically, location shoots take more time than studio shoots; and in 1993, for the first time, more location shoots were done than studio shoots.

Unilever spent several million dollars producing three commercials for ThermaSilk shampoo. The spots featured a lush, dreamlike setting of mythical places: In each one, a princesslike woman tames a dragon or beast, and in doing so also transformed her hair into beautiful locks. J. Walter Thompson, the ThermaSilk agency, used some 90 special effects and animation experts, and employed a digital artist on the set. The settings dramatized an insight into the 25- to 35-year-old female target: that each morning women undergo a transformation when blow-drying their hair. "A lot of advertising in this category talks at women; it's not emotionally based," says Cathy Lennox of JWT. "We found heat-styling is an emotionally charged time, when a woman is transformed." Another reason the campaign resonated with women was its appeal of fantasy to escape the emotional world.[18]

---

[17]"Commercial production costs jump," *Advertising Age*, 20 November 2000, 2.
[18]Patricia Winters Lauro, "ThermaSilk commercials enter the big-budget realm of fairy tales, dragons and special effects," *The New York Times*, 8 May 2000, C–18.

Digital Links and Post Production

No sooner than we could send a voice from room to room, we wanted to send it from continent to continent. And if we could beam a voice, why not a piece of paper? And if paper works, well, why not commercials in progress? Long-distance transmissions and manipulation of commercials are not unusual. Agencies, production houses, and directors are using various forms of digital links. Of course, the purpose is for people in one location to communicate about the creative process and maintain control over the process without having to travel. Director Henry Sandbank used this technology on a Coca-Cola project that involved 40 scenes and took weeks to complete in postproduction; he could check in several times every day with the San Francisco effects production house from his New York office. The agency creatives didn't have to travel or hang around, either.

SUMMARY

Television remains the most powerful advertising medium because of its ability to blend sight, sound, and motion to create emotional reactions. The time to communicate is very short—usually 15 to 30 seconds—and creates a challenge for communicating the product story or position.

There are numerous creative techniques available to the creative team: testimonials, demonstrations, slice-of-life, interviews, humor, animation, serials, infomercials, and so forth. Research can aid the creative decision process in terms of which technique is appropriate for the strategy.

Storyboards are usually created to help communicate the idea to the advertiser and the production company. It is important that everyone clearly visualize the same commercial before time and money are invested in the idea.

Developing commercials requires some understanding of production terminology such as wipes, dissolves, and close-ups that help communicate the nature of a particular visual or transition from one scene to the next. Writing and visualizing the commercial in simple and easy-to-understand terms is essential to success—it is, after all, a visual medium. Because a good idea can be destroyed by bad production, producing the finished commercial is just as important as conceiving the "big idea."

Producing the commercial involves three distinct stages: preproduction, shooting, and postproduction. Computer-generated imagery allows creative people to do almost anything they can imagine—but at a high cost.

REVIEW

1. What is ad retention? What is the retention range for TV commercials?
2. What cost-relationship factors are involved in the making of a TV commercial?
3. John Wayne selling Coors beer is an example of which technique?
4. Who attends the preproduction meeting?
5. What is a Harry?

TAKE IT TO THE NET

We invite you to visit the Russell/Lane page on the Prentice Hall Web site at **www.prenhall.com/myphlip** for end-of-chapter exercises and applications.

This storyboard was the starting point. The finished computer commercial cost more than $1.5 million and took 6 months to complete.

Below is a typical production schedule.

Typical Production Schedule

Bidding Studio	Stage or Location Shoot without Special Effects	Special Effects Shoot
Includes:	2–3 Weeks	3–6 Weeks

Includes:
- Screening Directors' Reels
- Sending Job Specification
- Bids (AICP Form) Returned
- Bid Comparison by Agency
- Estimating Supplemental Costs (music, travel, etc.)

Pre-Production	Stage or Location Shoot without Special Effects	Special Effects Shoot
Includes:	2–3 Weeks	3–6 Weeks

Includes:
- Casting
- Location Search
- Set Design
- Wardrobe Fittings

Shoot	Stage or Location Shoot without Special Effects	Special Effects Shoot
Roll Camera	1–7 Days	1–7 Days

Post Production	Stage or Location Shoot without Special Effects	Special Effects Shoot
Includes:	2–3 Weeks	4–10 Weeks

Includes:
- Edit film
- Film color correction
- Post special effects
- Casting voice-over talent
- Recording voice-over talent
- Demo music
- Music recording
- Final audio mix & masters

SCRIPT

VIDEO	AUDIO
OPEN ON CU OF MAN AS HE CLIMBS OVER ROCKS. EAGLE FLIES BY.	MUSIC/SFX: (Up and Under)
CUT TO LONG SHOT OF LABYRINTH AS MAN APPROACHES ENTRANCE.	
CUT TO MS OF MAN SLOWLY ENTERING LABYRINTH.	

This is an example of a storyboard and script.
Courtesy: J. Walter Thompson.

SERIES OF DRAMATIC CUTS AS MAN
TRAVELS THROUGH LABYRINTH
OVERCOMING OBSTACLES: FLOOR, WALL,
FIRE.

CUT TO SHOT OF MAN ENTERING CHAMBER   ANNCR: It is a test. . .
CONTAINING SWORD EMBEDDED IN
GLOWING ORB.

CUT TO CU OF MAN'S HAND AS HE DRAWS   not just of strength,
THE SWORD FROM THE ORB.

CUT TO CU OF MAN, IN PROFILE, AS HE   but of the power of the mind.
HOLDS THE SWORD IN FRONT OF HIM.

CUT TO CU OF GUARDIAN WHO EMERGES
FROM CHAMBER WALL WITH SWORD IN
HAND. BATTLE ENSUES.

CUT TO MS OF MAN AS HE DEFEATS   And if you complete the journey,
GUARDIAN WHOSE BODY EXPLODES
INTO FRAGMENTS.

MAN RAISES SWORD SKYWARD IN   you will be changed. . .
VICTORY AND IS TRANSFORMED INTO
MARINE IN DRESS BLUE UNIFORM.   forever.

SERIES OF QUICK CUTS OF MARINE   The Few.
EXECUTING SWORD SALUTE.

    The Proud.

CUT TO CU OF MARINE. *SUPER*: MARINES.
1-800-MARINES.   The Marines.

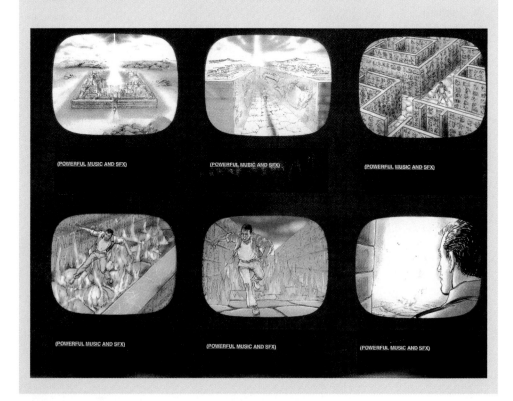

(POWERFUL MUSIC AND SFX)

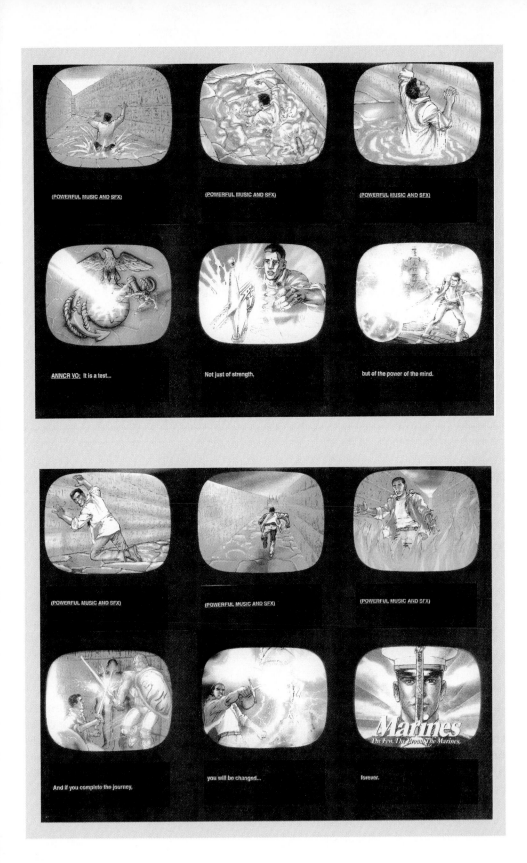

Chapter 20

The Radio Commercial

CHAPTER OBJECTIVES

In print and television, visuals are an integral part of communication. Radio is a different medium, one for ears alone. After reading this chapter you will understand:

>> the nature of the medium

>> how to create from a strategy

>> structuring the commercial

>> writing the commercial

>> musical commercials

>> producing radio commercials

>> unions and talent

Maybe it's because most radio ads are local where the copywriter hasn't time to really think about the ad, but much of radio advertising is bad. Writing radio should be easy. All you have to do is talk to someone about the product. Right? Well, maybe. Great radio advertising is very difficult. You need to be able to awaken images in the listeners' minds by using sound, music, and voices. You have the opportunity to play with their imagination in what is referred to as "the theater of the mind."

THE NATURE OF THE MEDIUM

Copywriter Tom Monahan says, "In radio there's no place to hide anything. No place for the mistakes, the poor judgement, the weakness. Everything is right there in front for all 30 or 60 seconds. Everything must be good for the spot to be good.

The concept, copy, casting, acting, production—everything. One of them goes wrong, sorry, but it's tune-out time."[1]

Radio expert, Phil Cuttino, president of Cuttino Communications, often refers to "watching radio—the most misunderstood medium." Let us take a closer look at the nature of the medium.

Before the beginning of widespread viewing of television in the mid-1950s, families used to "watch" the radio. We have all heard excerpts from radio's "**theater of the mind**"—*Superman, The Lone Ranger, Bulldog Drummon, Inner Sanctum*, and Orson Welles's fabulous spoof, *War of the Worlds*. People watched the radio because the mental imagery that came with every episode was breathtaking or scary or beautiful or just plain funny. However, television's combination of audio and visuals was very compelling and certainly effective as a storyteller and theater. TV also was, and is, a dynamic advertising medium. Unfortunately, radio was subordinated to the position of music, talk, and other audio-oriented programming.

Television is the darling of today's airwaves. Even television advertising has taken on a star quality. In major publications, there are commentaries on TV commercials, as well as an objective and subjective rating. TV is the closest that ad people come to "show biz." Another contributing factor to radio's lowly position in the creative pecking order is the fact that most creative teams consist of art directors, designers, and copywriters. Because radio has no material visuals, the visual arts people are out of business when it comes to radio. This tends to lead the creative team to either print or television advertising.

Over time, a new type of radio commercial has emerged, which Phil Cuttino calls "print radio." When radio is needed, some copywriters, who are experienced in print advertising but know little about radio, tend to fall back on a familiar copy format. As a result, we hear "print radio" all the time. There is a headline, a subhead, body copy, a logo, and a slogan—an audio newspaper ad.

To understand the importance of radio, you need to understand the cynical nature of the American consumer.

No one believes anyone anymore. American consumers are searching for an excuse to disbelieve what you are saying. All they need is a cue that you are trying to sell them something, and they will blank you out mentally. They may not change the dial; this is a case of "The lights are on, but nobody's home." Before you can tell the consumer your story, you must disarm him, entertain him, amuse him, get him on your side.

Radio, like magazines, is a very personal medium. Almost everyone has a favorite radio station. Many consumers listen to Net radio on-line where some stations use broadband and streaming video content. Consumers get to know the radio personalities; they attend events sponsored by their radio station. It is this kind of listener allegiance, this nonhostile environment, that makes it easier for marketers to approach the listenership. Remember, consumers are not waiting to hear your commercial. They are listening to the radio to be entertained, so entertain them, then sell them. Entertainment is your admission ticket to their consciousness.

The future is challenged for traditional radio. The Internet has challenged traditional radio in the home and office, but radio has maintained its dominance in the car. The prospects of direct-to-car digital satellite radio bring more challenges to local radio and advertisers.[2]

theater of the mind
In radio, a writer paints pictures in the mind of the listener through the use of sound.

---

[1] Tom Monahan, "Advertising," *Communication Arts*, July 1994, 198.
[2] Erik Gruenwedel, "Net radio daze," *Adweek*, 1 May 2000, IQ26–27.

FLEXIBILITY, MARKETABILITY, AND PROMOTIONABILITY

Radio offers more than other advertising media. It has the flexibility, the marketability, the promotionability, and the price to fit advertisers' needs to reach their targets—if they choose the right stations and use the right message.

- You have 60 seconds all to yourself. Print ads have to fight for attention with other ads on the page. TV has to contend with channel surfers because viewers have favorite TV programs, whereas radio listeners have favorite radio stations. In the time span of a 60-second radio commercial, no other advertising can interfere with your message. The main equalizer in radio is the ability of a locally produced radio spot to be on a level playing field with any national spot. The power of a radio commercial is the idea, the imagery. Unlike TV, national-quality production can be easily created for a reasonable cost. Your advertiser can be as big as any other marketer for 60 seconds.

- Radio has the most captive audience of any media. The advent of mass transit has not changed the fact that in most cities, to get from point A to point B, you still have to get in your car and drive. The heaviest radio listenership occurs in the morning and afternoon drive times. During that time, listeners cannot go to the kitchen for a beer, answer the door, or pick up a magazine. They are trapped in their cars, listening to the traffic report, the news, and, of course, your radio commercial.

- Listeners and advertisers have many programming formats to choose from: country, adult contemporary, news/talk/sports/business, oldies, top 40, religion, classic rock, urban rhythm and blues, easy listening, alternative rock, variety, ethnic, classical, gospel, jazz, new age, and preteen. This makes radio a highly selective medium for the advertiser. Reflecting the ethnic multinational nature of our society, there also are foreign-language stations in many markets available to advertisers.

CREATING THE COMMERCIAL

Even though radio requires a different style of advertising, ads are developed through a thought process similar to that used in other media. You have to understand your target. As Tom Little, award-winning creative director, once said, "People don't buy products. They buy solutions to problems." Last year people bought about 350,000 quarter-inch drill bits in this country. People didn't want quarter-inch drill bits. They wanted quarter-inch holes. The radio creative writer has to refer back to the objectives and strategy and describe the target in both demographic and psychographic terms before beginning the creative process. The writer needs to be sure the message is going to be believed—that it says the right things to the right people—and needs to ask if the copy strengthens the brand position, the place you want to occupy in the consumer's mind. Is it credible? Do you have all the copy points that your research indicates is needed? Is it human? Is it believable communication? Do people really talk like that? Or is it simply copy lingo? These are some of the things the radio copywriter must think about when sitting down to the blank page or the computer screen.

The writer for radio has the opportunity to develop an entire commercial alone (although in some agencies a creative team may work on a project). That means writing the script, picking the talent, and producing the commercial. In radio, the copywriter enjoys the freedom to create scenes in the theater of the listener's imagination by painting pictures in sound—a car starting or stopping, a phone ringing, water running, ice cubes falling into a glass, crowds roaring, a camera clicking. Remember, sound alone has an extraordinary ability to enter people's minds.

Spirit Mountain Casino enters the imagination in the beginning of this commercial:

Guy: As Sam left the house that morning he tripped over his cat.

SFX: (Thud)

SAM: Hey, Kitty.

GUY: The jolt shook loose a giant blob of peanut butter from his toast, which landed on his shirt. The shirt his mom had given him on her deathbed. Just then he noticed the cat wasn't moving. Now he was late to work. And that was the day they gave out free trips to Hawaii.

ANNC: Bad luck...........Luck Happens. Spirit Mountain Casino.

Let us look at the three elements the copywriter uses to create mental pictures, memorability, and emotion: words, sound, and music.

Words

Words are the basic building blocks of effective radio commercials. They are used to describe the product, grab attention, create interest, build desire, and evoke a response from the listener. The warmth of the human voice may be all that is needed to communicate your message.

HomeWarehouse.com's "Duct Tape" tongue-in-cheek commercial says,

ANNC: And now, a public apology to the women of America.

GUY: Dear women, we are sorry for being insensitive to your needs. We are sorry for the football season. We are sorry for not listening, even though we nod as if we are. We are sorry for looking in the general direction of really attractive women. And for the time in college we swore we'd never tell you about. We are sorry for not noticing when you highlight your hair. We are sorry for using the garage to store our tools, instead of your car. And we're sorry we didn't use HomeWarehouse.com like you said we should........

SFX: Hammer noise........

GUY: And we're sorry if we skipped anything.

Sound

Used properly, sound can unlock the listener's imagination and create feelings. Any sound effect used should be necessary and recognizable; you should never have to explain it for the audience.

The sound has to convey a special message or purpose; it has to attract attention and complement the words. Sound can be used to underscore a point; create feelings of suspense, excitement, or anger; and invoke almost any mood you desire.

There are three basic sources of sound effects: manual, recorded, and electronic. Manual effects are those that are produced live, either with live subjects or with studio props; opening doors, footsteps, and blowing horns are examples. Recorded effects are available from records, tapes, or professional sound libraries. They offer the copywriter almost every conceivable sound—dogs barking, cats meowing, leaves blowing, thunder crashing, cars racing. Electronic effects are sounds that are produced electronically on special studio equipment. Any sound created by using a device that generates an electrical impulse or other electronic sound is an electrical effect.

Music

Music can be very powerful in catching the listener's attention and evoking feelings. Thus music has been called the "universal language." Different kinds of music appeal to different emotions: A minor key is sadder than a major key; an increased tempo creates a sense of anticipation.

Commercials are often set to music especially composed for them or adapted from a familiar song. A few bars of distinctive music played often enough may serve to identify the product instantly. Such a musical logotype usually lasts from 4 to 10 seconds. **Jingles** are a popular means of making a slogan memorable—think of the music for Coca-Cola, Pepsi, Chevrolet, and McDonald's over the years. Exhibit 20.1 shows Folk's Southern Cous Cous jingle version.

Create from Strategy

What's brown, fuzzy, round on the outside, green on the inside, and tastes good? The California Kiwifruit Commission set an objective to increase awareness of their ugly little product. Their strategy was built around "Kiwifruit Is Fun." "The commission understands people's perception of the California kiwifruit and gave us permission to have fun with its outward appearance . . . knowing that it's what's inside that counts," says Christine Coyle, creative director of Dick & Chris Radio Ranch. The spots humorously played out two situations: a recognizable school food pageant and a California Kiwifruit audition. The ads were able to convince consumers who were suspect of the funny-looking fruit to go ahead and give it a try. The vertical integrated program combined radio with some print and some in-store services that helped educate grocery produce managers. Unit sales the first year of the campaign went up 67 percent, or an increase of about 5 million new households purchasing the product. The strategy worked.

DEVELOPING THE RADIO SCRIPT

You will find some differences in the formats used in the script examples in this chapter. This is because most agencies have their own format sheets for copywriters. Formats also vary according to how the script will be used: If you are going to be in the studio with the producers and talents, you can verbally explain how the script is to be read or answer any questions that come up. If, however, you are going to mail the script to DJs to be read live, you need to be certain that anyone reading it will understand exactly what you want. The guidelines shown in Exhibit 20.2 illustrate explicit script directions.

Radio, Theater of the Mind

According to Cuttino, one of the biggest mistakes you can make in creating radio is the failure to recognize the fact that everyone has mental images of sounds that they hear. When no material images exist, sound creates an image in the mind's eye.

**Exhibit
20.1**

**Example of a
Clever Jingle**

Courtesy: Folk's Restaurants.

*Now hold the capers and the sun dried tomatoes
Hold the Cous Cous and those tarragon potatoes
When I'm in the mood for some comfort food
Nobody knows me like my Folks*

LEFT SECTION OF PAGE IS FOR INFORMATION RELATING TO VOICES, ANNOUNCER, MUSIC, SOUND, USUALLY IN CAPS.	The right section of the script consists of copy and directions. It should be typed double-spaced. Pause is indicated by dots (. . .) or double dash (— —). Underline or use CAPS for emphasis.
MUSIC:	Music is usually indicated by all caps. WILLIAM TELL OVERTURE ESTABLISH AND FADE UNDER. In some cases, music is underlined. Directions may be indicated by parentheses ( ).
VOICE #1	(LAUGHING LOUDLY) Excuse me sir . . .
OLD MAN	Yes . . . (RAISING VOICE) What do you *want?*
SFX:	SUPERMARKET NOISES, CRASHING NOISES AS SHOPPING CARTS CRASH. Sound effects indicated by SFX: (:08) BUZZER
SINGERS:	He's bright-eyed and bushy-tailed . . .
ANNCR:	This indicates announcer talking.
VO:	Voice Over.

Exhibit

20.2

Example of Radio Form Directions

It is the duty of the radio writer/producer to take control of the listener's imagery and guide it to a positive reaction that seeds the memory with the targeted message and leads to the proper response. For instance, a writer creates a commercial featuring a car dealer who is screaming about a sale, assuming that the tactic will get the listener's attention and will eventually lead the consumer to the dealership because of the "incredible savings." Unfortunately, the mind's eye of the listener doesn't see a sleek new car or the money he is saving; he sees a middle-aged man in a garish plaid suit yelling at him. In communications, it is important to be concerned about what people feel about your advertisement.

The late Creative Director, Tom Little used to brag about radio's ability to paint pictures in the mind, "I had to spend $40,000 to build an air line set for our television ads, but I could build that same set in the minds of radio listeners for almost nothing."

The Elements of a Good Radio Commercial

- Be single-minded, focused. Don't ask the consumer to take on too much information at one time. Prioritize your copy points. Think of your commercial as a model of our solar system. The major copy point is the sun and all the other copy points are planets of varying degrees of importance, but they all revolve around and support the central idea.
- Research your product or service. Many clients keep tabs on their competition, but they rarely relate their features and benefits to factual data. Meaningful statistics can give substantial support to your message.
- Relate to the consumer. When you tell consumers your story, always relate the brand to their wants and needs. Do not assume they will come to the right conclusion.

- Generate extension. You can multiply the effect of your commercial many times over by achieving extension—consumers picking up phrases from the spot and using them. A clever phrase or execution can have consumers asking other people if they have heard the spot, people requesting the spot to be played on the radio, even getting mentions by DJs.

- Produce an immediate physical, emotional, or mental response. Laughter, a tug on the heart strings, or mental exercises of a consumer during a radio spot help seed the memory and aid message retention.

- Use plain, conversational English. Be a clear communicator. Don't force your characters to make unnatural statements. This is not the boardroom—no "execubabble," just clear, plain, and simple English. Valerie Bickley created a dialogue commercial using music and SFX for Downtown Nautilus (Exhibit 20.3). She also has significant repetition of the client's name.

WRITING THE COMMERCIAL

Some agencies have a special creative director in charge of radio advertising. For years, the feeling has been that agencies have assigned junior talent to write radio commercials. It is now hoped that having a specific person in charge of radio will generate enthusiasm for doing great radio. Others hire the expertise of people like Phil Cuttino of Cuttino Communications to generate strategic radio advertising.

There are radio boutiques that have been used for many years by clients and agencies to help create and produce radio commercials. Some of the most popular boutiques include Dick & Chris Radio Ranch, BarzRadio, Radio in the Nude, World Wide Wadio, Oink Ink Radio, Outer Planet, Radioland, Hungarian Radio, and Sarley, Bigg & Bedder.

MUSIC: JAZZ TYPE. MIX IN RHYTHMIC BREATHING NOISES SOUNDS FROM A GYM IN KEY SPOTS.

GUY TALKING WHILE WORKING OUT: HEAR NOISES IN BACKGROUND:

Here, you're your own boss. And all your hard work pays off.

FEMALE VO: Introducing Downtown Nautilus . . . Greenville's 14,000 square foot fitness center with all the latest in Nautilus equipment and free weights.

GUY: The routine never gets boring. And you make your *own* hours.

FEMALE VO: Downtown Nautilus has daily aerobics classes.

GUY: It's totally up to you. You can start your day early . . . put in a productive lunch hour . . .

FEMALE VO: Downtown Nautilus has over 30 state-of-the-art exercise bikes, stair climbers, and treadmills.

GUY: Or stay late and go for some serious overtime . . . And guess what? You'll always feel good about it.

FEMALE VO: Downtown Nautilus has saunas, tanning beds and certified trainers.

GUY: I work because I have to. I work out because I want to.

FEMALE VO: Downtown Nautilus has everything . . . except you.

GUY: Downtown Nautilus. A Cool Place to Sweat.

FEMALE VO: Join Greenville's most productive workers at Downtown Nautilus. Sign up by March 31 and get a Charter Membership at a special introductory price.

FEMALE VO TAG: 103 N. Main Street.

Exhibit
20.3

This commercial uses two actor voices, music, and SFX.
Courtesy: Valerie Bickley Creative.

The radio commercial, like the TV commercial, has as its basic ingredient the promise of a significant and distinctive benefit or position. Once the promise has been determined, you are ready to use the arsenal of words and sounds to communicate your product. Ways to vitalize the copy include the following:

- *Simplicity.* The key to producing a good radio commercial is to build around one central idea. Avoid confusing the listener with too many copy points. Use known words, short phrases, simple sentence structure. Keep in mind that the copy needs to be conversational. Write for the ear, not the eye. Get in the habit of reading your copy out loud.

- *Clarity.* Keep the train of thought on one straight track. Avoid side issues. Delete unnecessary words. (Test: Would the commercial be hurt if the words were deleted? If not, take them out.) Write from draft to draft until your script becomes unmistakably clear and concise. At the end of the commercial, your audience should understand exactly what you have tried to say. Despite having several facts in your commercial, make sure you have the big idea.

- *Coherence.* Be certain that your message flows in logical sequence from first word to last, using smooth transitional words and phrases for easier listening.

- *Rapport.* Remember, as far as your listeners are concerned, you are speaking only to them. Try to use a warm, personal tone, as if you were talking to one or two people. Make frequent use of the word you. Address the listeners in terms they would use themselves.

- *Pleasantness.* It is not necessary to entertain simply for the sake of entertaining, but there is no point in being dull or obnoxious. Strike a happy medium; talk as one friend to another about the product or service.

- *Believability.* Every product has its good points. Tell the truth about it. Avoid overstatements and obvious exaggerations; they are quickly spotted and defeat the whole purpose of the commercial. Be straightforward; you want to convey the impression of being a trusted friend.

- *Interest.* Nothing makes listeners indifferent faster than a boring commercial. Products and services are not fascinating in themselves; the way you present them makes them interesting. Try to give your customer some useful information as a reward for listening.

- *Distinctiveness.* Sound different from other commercials and set your product apart. Use every possible technique—a fresh approach, a musical phrase, a particular voice quality or sound effect—to give your commercial a distinct character.

Some Techniques

Basically a medium of words, radio—more than any other medium—relies heavily on the art of writing strong copy. However, just as print ads and TV commercials include pictures and graphics to add impact to the copy, radio creates mental pictures with other techniques. Radio copywriters can choose among many proven techniques to give more meaning to the copy, to help gain the attention of the busy target audience, and to hold that attention for the duration of the commercial. Some of these techniques parallel those used in television.

- *Humor.* Humor is an excellent technique for service and retail businesses. Consumers never relate an ad to the advertising agency that produced it; they only relate the spot to the advertiser. Therefore, humor can portray a company as friendly, likable, and easy when negotiating a sale.
    Many award-winning radio spots use humor. Tom Little, a creative director who has judged many award shows, once said humorous spots won awards

because they stood out from the hundreds that he had to listen to. If that's true, then the same probably works for consumers. Of course, humor may be part of any writing technique we have discussed. Humor is often appropriate for low-priced packaged products, products people buy for fun, products whose primary appeal is taste, or products or services in need of change-of-pace advertising because of strong competition. Be very careful about making fun of the product or the user or treat too lightly a situation that is not normally funny. Sprite successfully made fun of soft-drink advertising and what the product will do for you in its appeal to Generation Xers.

- *Emotion.* This is an effective method to use when the topic is indeed emotional. Family, health care, donations, mental care, security, and similar products and services use emotion to stimulate the targeted response.

- *Music/sound effects.* Music creates the mood and sound effects create the imagery in the consumer's mind. Jingles can be very memorable and effective when they relate directly to the product or service.

- *White space.* This is, of course, a term used in print advertising. However, white space in radio can be extremely compelling. A 60-second spot may start with music or sound effects with no copy for 45 seconds, bringing the consumers' curiosity into play and leaving them wide open to accept a provocative message.

- *Dialogue.* This is a great technique to use in many situations. Dialogue doesn't confront the consumer; it allows the listener to eavesdrop on the conversation. Dialogue is also very successful when the advertiser has a product that appeals to men and women. Dialogue between a man and a woman allows the commercial to play to both targets.

- *Sex.* It can sell very well.

- *Straight announcer.* Sometimes the simplest approach works best. In this commonly used and most direct of all techniques, an announcer or personality delivers the entire script. Success depends both on the copy and on the warmth and believability of the person performing the commercial. Tom Bodet for Motel 6 was all of these things and one of the reasons the commercials were so popular. This approach works particularly well when a positive image has previously been established and a specific event is being promoted, such as a sale.

- *Combination.* Radio techniques may be mixed in countless ways, as illustrated by the Greenville Mall spot in Exhibit 20.4 (combines music, sound effects, an announcer, and a person). You might notice that it uses the name of the product five times in interesting ways to gain brand recognition. To select the right technique for a particular assignment, follow the guidelines discussed in Chapter 19 for selecting TV techniques.

TIMING OF COMMERCIALS

Time is the major constraint in producing a radio commercial. Most radio stations accept these maximum word lengths for live commercial scripts:

- 10 seconds, 25 words
- 20 seconds, 45 words

In prerecorded commercials, of course, you may use any number of words you can fit within the time limit. However, if you use more than 125 words for a 60-second commercial, the commercial will have to be read so rapidly that it may sound unnatural or even unintelligible. Remember, if you insert sound effects, that will

Greenville Mall 60-second radio
Valentine's Day

NARRATOR: AH . . . Valentine's Day. The moment of truth for sweethearts.

TANGO MUSIC: DRAMATIC, UNDERNEATH REST OF THE SPOT

JANE: Hmmm . . . that was incredible . . .

NARRATOR: cooed a satiated Jane to her dashing beau Theodore . . . after sharing a sinfully delicious crème brûlée at their favorite restaurant.

THEODORE: For me too darling.

NARRATOR: replied Theodore gazing soulfully into her eyes as he placed a beautiful gift on the table

JANE: "Theodore, you shouldn't have!"

NARRATOR: lied the politically correct Jane. Quivering with excitement, she unwrapped the box, peeked inside and exclaimed passionately:

JANE: "Ohh honey! Where did you find this? Paris? Milan?

THEODORE: "Why shucks mam . . ."

NARRATOR: . . . said Theodore in his most humble John Wayne imitation.

THEODORE: "I mosied over to your favorite store at Greenville Mall and picked ya something out."

NARRATOR: Where upon an ecstatic Jane, having finally found a man who could *shop,* chose wisely to ignore the John Wayne thing, and instead pronounced:

JANE: "Darling, a toast to our future!"

SFX: HEAR GLASS CHINGING:

PAGE TWO
GREENVILLE MALL 60-second radio
VALENTINE'S DAY

THEODORE: "To Greenville Mall"

JANE: "Yes, to Greenville Mall. May you always shop there!"

UP WITH TANGO MUSIC . . .

NARRATOR: (AS IF MOVED TO TEARS) Sniff! For the most novel of romantic gifts this Valentine's Day, shop the stores of Greenville Mall.

NARRATOR/OR ALL THREE VOICES: Greenville Mall. Always Something New.

Exhibit
20.4

This spot uses two actor voices plus an announcer to communicate and entertain. Notice repetition of product.
Courtesy: Valerie Bickley Creative.

probably cut down on the number of words you can use. If you have footsteps running for five seconds, you are going to have to cut 10 to 12 words. You need to time the musical intros and endings or sound effects because each will affect the number of words allowable. It is not unusual to go into the recording studio with a script that is a couple of seconds short because the extra time allows the talents to sound more natural. Actors need some breathing room to sound sincere.

MUSICAL COMMERCIALS

Music can be a powerful tool for getting your product remembered. As musical writer Steve Karman has said: "People don't hum the announcer."[3]

In writing musical commercials, you have to start with an earthquake, then build to something really big. In other words, there is no room for subtlety. The thought process and strategy are different from those in regular songwriting.

There are three main elements to writing commercial music:

1. **Intro:** The beginning of the song. The tempo and lyrics may be established here.
2. **Verse:** The middle of the song. This is where the message is developed. There may be several verses.
3. Theme or chorus: May be the conclusion of the song.

Often you begin with the chorus to establish your theme, or you may repeat the theme throughout. The theme is what listeners remember. Some musical forms, such as blues, can be thought of as both verse and chorus. A theme may serve as a musical logotype for a product, lasting about 4 to 10 seconds. Copywriter David Rosen wrote a spot for Fila's Stack II shoe, named after basketball star Jerry Stackhouse. He explains that, "Stackhouse's first step and his agility is his big thing—but the lyrics are about his personality:"

> The way I feel,
> You know the love is real,
> With your leather and lace,
> You've got a tongue but not a face.
> Left and right,
> I like all the things you do.
> Just show me that you love me,
> 'Cuz I love both of you.
> Chorus: Jerry loves his Fila shoes.
> I know I'm gonna score with you.

And the off-beat chorus continues and ends with "I think the man is freaken' out, Ooh, I love it when you make that little squeaky noise."

Former Folks marketing director, Sheri Bevil says, "Folks restaurants hired Jack Turner to do an original score and lyrics for a number of jingles. Usually the radio opens with one of the jingles (see Exhibit 20.5). Then the promotional message goes over the bed of music (usually an announcer). Then, it ends with another jingle. The jingle takes up 28 to 30 seconds leaving another 30 seconds for the specific message." In some cases, Bevil says, "the spot would also end with a 5- to 10-second tag."

Many commercials are composed especially for the advertiser or product. Others are simply adapted from a familiar song. A melody is in the public domain, available for use by anyone without cost, after its copyright has expired. Many old favorites and classics are in the public domain and have been used as advertising themes. That is one of their detriments: They may have been used by many others.

Popular tunes that are still protected by copyright are available only by (often costly) agreement with the copyright owner. An advertiser can also commission a composer to create an original tune, which becomes the advertiser's property and gives the product its own musical personality.

---

[3] Bruce Bendinger, The Copy Workshop Workbook (Chicago: Bruce Bendinger Creative Communications, Inc., 1988), p. 214.

Southern Boy Version: Folks Southern Kitchen
I've been a Southern boy all of my life
Got a Southern drawl and a Southern wife
When I'm in the mood for some comfort food
Nobody knows me like my Folks

Tag. This fall at Folks we're offering chicken pot pie in a bread bowl, a 12 ounce, thick n' juicy pork porterhouse and savory meatloaf made from a fantastic new recipe. They're the season's best entrees and they're available at all nineteen Metro Folks locations.

Do you have the talent to write a jingle? Does the typical copywriter have the ability to do so? In general, the job of writing such copy is left to the music experts.

Audio Technology

Over the past 10 years there has been a radical change in the way music and sound are recorded. A little more than a decade ago, the world of high-fidelity multitrack recording and sync-to-picture belonged solely to record companies, postproduction houses, and commercial ventures.

In the early 1990s, software was created for the Macintosh that allowed true four-track recording and simultaneous MIDI (musical instrument digital interface) file playback. The simple interface was based on the integrated portable studio metaphor and required no sophisticated knowledge of the software. It looked and functioned like a four-track cassette mixer/recorder, but it turned any Macintosh with a Digidesign NuBus card into a CD-quality production environment. It has been used extensively in the past few years to produce albums and CDs and for basic sync work. Advances in hardware/software systems now turn a Macintosh into a true multitrack digital audio workstation.

You can record your basic ideas digitally from the very beginning, and add and edit digital audio tracks to your composition. You can then use the software to transfer the master digitally to a digital audio tape (DAT) or CD. Every step in the multitrack production of digital audio is in the hands of the individual.

Musicians can use it as a composition environment, and produce CDs or CD-quality demos from the original tracks. Video postproduction sound designers can use it for typical audio sweetening. MIDI studios can use it to record final audio tracks over existing tracks.

METHODS OF DELIVERY

There are three ways a radio commercial can be delivered: live, by station announcer, and prerecorded.

The Live Commercial

A live commercial is delivered in person by the studio announcer, disc jockey, newscaster, or other station personality; or perhaps by a sports reporter from another location. Although generally read from a script prepared by the advertiser, the commercial is sometimes revised to complement the announcer's style. If time allows, the revised script should be approved in advance by the advertiser. Ad-libbing (extemporizing) from a fact sheet should be discouraged because the

Exhibit

20.6

Example of a Prerecorded Jingle

announcer may inadvertently omit key selling phrases or, in the case of regulated products such as drugs, fail to include certain mandatory phrases.

Some commercials are delivered partly live and partly prerecorded. The prerecorded jingle, for example, can be played over and over with live-announcer copy added. Sometimes the live part (the dealer "tie-up") is left open for the tie-in ad of the local distributor.

One advantage of the live commercial is that the announcer may have a popular following, and listeners tend to accept advice from someone they like. The other big advantage is cost: Station announcers usually do your commercials free of extra talent costs.

Station Announcer

For a campaign dealing with a retail offer that will change frequently, advertisers often use a station announcer reading copy written by the agency. This is recorded at the station at no charge to the client—sometimes even with the client's musical theme in the background. This type of delivery allows for frequent changes in copy at no cost.

The Prerecorded Commercial

Advertisers undertaking a regional or national campaign will not know local announcers' capabilities. In any case, it would be impractical to write a separate script to fit each one's particular style. Commercials for these campaigns are therefore usually prerecorded. Not only does this assure advertisers that the commercial will be identical each time it is aired, but it also allows them to take advantage of myriad techniques that would be impractical in a live commercial. (Actually, in many instances, "live" commercials are recorded by the station so that they can run even when the announcer is not on duty.) Sheri Bevil Advertising produced commercials for Folks Home Fixins' promotion (see Exhibit 20.6) using Folks president and owner, Rick Pratt, as the announcer/spokesperson. As stated earlier, most radio commercials are 60-seconds, but at times an advertiser may buy a mix of times. Exhibit 20.7 is an example of a 15-second radio spot for the Atlanta Traffic Report using Rick Pratt. You'll notice that this promotional spot sells the price of the Lunch Combos. All of Folks commercials are usually prerecorded to guarantee control of message.

Exhibit

20.7

Example of a Short Radio Spot

Talent and Unions

As with television, the use and payment to performers appearing in radio commercials is dictated by the AFTRA (American Federation of Television and Radio Artists) commercial contract. Talent is paid a session fee when the commercial is recorded. There are other requirements for payment based upon usage, including spot, network, dealer, demo and copy testing, and foreign use. It is another cost the advertiser must consider.

PRODUCING THE RADIO COMMERCIAL

Although there are certain broad similarities, producing radio commercials is far simpler and less costly than producing TV commercials. First, the agency or advertiser appoints a radio producer, who converts the script into a recording ready to go on the air. After preparing the cost estimate and getting budget approval, the producer selects a recording studio and a casting director, if necessary. If music is called for, the producer calls a music "house" that usually composes, arranges, and takes all steps necessary to get the finished music. If the music is not a big-budget item, the producer may call for **"stock" music** (prerecorded and used on a rental basis).

> **stock music**   Existing recorded music that may be purchased for use in a TV or radio commercial.

After the cast has been selected, it rehearses in a recording studio, which can be hired by the hour. However, because most commercials are made in short "takes" that are later joined in the editing, a formal rehearsal is usually unnecessary. When the producer feels the cast is ready, the commercial is acted out and recorded on tape. Music and sound are taped separately and then mixed with the vocal tape by the sound-recording studio. In fact, by double- and triple-tracking music and singers' voices, modern recording equipment can build small sounds into big ones. However, union rules require that musicians and singers be paid extra fees when their music is mechanically added to their original recording. After the last mix, the master tape of the commercial is prepared. When final approval has been obtained, duplicates are made on audiocassettes or CDs for release to the list of stations.

Things to Remember During Production

Phil Cuttino has a bias against having the account executive or client at a recording session. He feels their presence creates too many problems, which can inhibit great production. Among these: the talent and engineer tighten up, and everyone is concerned about time instead of producing an effective spot. He suggests that you use a phone patch from the studio to play the spot for the account executive first. Then, with his or her blessing, call the client for the final approval. The engineer and talent should remain in the studio until the final approval is achieved. Cuttino also has some other production thoughts:

- *Call ahead.* Have the studio pull the music and sound effects selections.
- *Studio.* Find a studio that has several talented engineers that will quickly learn your style. Make sure the studio has a good SFX and music library and the latest technology.
- *Brain power.* During production, use everyone's brain to make the spot better. Ask for input from your engineer and voice talent. Remember, they probably have been involved in more spots in a week than you have in months.
- *Take your time.* Don't push the talent or engineer. Lead them to what you want.
- *Keep up with the technology.* New technology will always broaden your creative envelope.

■ *Casting.* Acting professionals usually have the best and most believable voices because they are visualizing the scene. This is particularly true with dialogue or group scenes. Go to plays often to find new talent. Do not look at the people who are auditioning for a part in the spot . . . they will try to sell you with facial expression, body language, and hand motions . . . all worthless on radio. At first, allow talent to give you their own interpretation of the scene. You may be inspired by their rendition.

Steps in Radio Production

We may summarize the steps in producing a commercial as follows:

1. An agency or advertiser appoints a producer.
2. The producer prepares cost estimates.
3. The producer selects a recording studio.
4. With the aid of the casting director, if one is needed, the producer casts the commercial.
5. If music is to be included, the producer selects a musical director and chooses the music or selects stock music.
6. If necessary, a rehearsal is held.
7. The studio tapes music and sound separately.
8. The studio mixes music and sound with voices.
9. The producer sees that the master tape is prepared for distribution on either tape or cassettes and shipped to stations.

You are on the air!

SUMMARY

Radio can be visual, despite its lack of visuals. It has the listener's mind to paint a picture within and is truly the theater of the mind. Words, sound effects, and music are the tools of the radio copywriter. The biggest limitation is that the radio copywriter is always working against the clock.

It is the duty of the radio writer/producer to take control of the listener's imagery and guide it to a positive reaction that seeds the memory with the targeted message and leads to the proper response. The power of a radio commercial is the idea imagery.

There has been a radical change in the way music and sound are recorded. Using a Macintosh computer, musicians and sound designers can record digital masters. So the computer and its innovative software are other creative tools—this time for broadcast. Music can be a powerful tool for getting products remembered.

When developing a commercial, it is important to keep it simple and concentrate on one main idea. Repetition of the main selling ideas is considered necessary, but the main thing is to get the brand and message remembered. Some of the writing techniques and formats include straight announcer, slice-of-life, jingle-announcer, customer interview, and humor.

As with television, all performers appearing in national commercials are subject to union compensation agreements.

REVIEW

1. Why is radio the theater of the mind?
2. Briefly summarize the elements of good radio commercials.

3. What is white space in radio?
4. Name four radio station programming formats.
5. What are the three main elements to writing commercial music?
6. What are the steps in radio production?

TAKE IT TO THE NET

We invite you to visit the Russell/Lane page on the Prentice Hall Web site at **www.prenhall.com/myphlip** for end-of-chapter exercises and applications.

Chapter 21

Trademarks and Packaging

Product names and trademarks are very important to brand equity, brand identity, and the marketing process. In today's market, advertising and packaging must support each other. After reading this chapter you will understand:

>> what a trademark is

>> protecting the trademark

>> forms of trademarks

>> general trademark rules

>> the process for developing memorable names

>> packaging and marketing

>> packaging and research

The brand is one of the most important assets of a company, and the trademark is the brand's asset. There are about 1,250,000 trademarks registered with the U.S. government alone in this global economy. Consider the financial investment in the name and trademark of Coca-Cola since 1886, when it was first developed. Think of the corporate and financial loss if Coca-Cola lost the exclusive right to its trademark. It is not impossible for them to lose that right. It is for this reason they go to great lengths to protect their trademark. They have a special group that monitors all use of the brand(s) to protect their investment. Companies such as Coca-Cola have become so concerned about their brand image, use, and reputation on the Web that they have taken steps to prevent, or at least monitor, what's going on in cyberspace. Coke has six brand cop lawyers. Some spend their time surfing the Web, tracking repeat offenders, and writing cease and desist letters centered on Coke brand abuses, on-line and off. Many of these cases are first investigated by Coke's trade research department. The nature of such infractions is studied to determine the need for legal action by the corporate legal department. They ask interlopers to stop using the Coke brand or trademark. Among the most common types of on-line brand abuses are the following:[1]

- Unauthorized use of logos and images
- Use of a company's name on a competitor's site
- Unauthorized framing, where a Web site appears within another site
- Domain abuse and parody sites
- Unauthorized use of a company's name or product in metatags
- Diverting users away from a Web site by hiding key words in background text

All companies face the same threat to their brand and trademark, which we talk about later in this chapter.

A LITTLE BACKGROUND

Lanham Act

There were few trademarks used on general merchandise prior to the Civil War. In 1870, the rapid growth in trade identity gave rise to the first federal trademark law. Lacking sufficient legislative safeguards, concerned manufacturers met in 1878 and founded The United States Trademark Association. Its name was changed to the International Trademark Association (INTA) in 1993. This organization promoted the enactment of the Trade-Mark Act of 1881, a revision in 1905 and 1920. In 1946, the Lanham Act was passed by Congress. It defined a trademark and expanded the concept of infringement, permitted the registration of service marks, provided incontestability status for marks in continuous use for five years, and provided that federal registration of a trademark would constitute "constructive notice of the registrant's claim of ownership thereof."

In 1996, President Clinton signed the Federal Trademark Dilution Act passed by Congress. It provided owners of famous trademarks with a federal cause of action against those who lessened the distinctiveness of such marks by the use of the same or similar trademarks on similar or dissimilar products or services. Unlike trademark infringement, a dilution action does not require proof or likelihood of consumer confusion. An amendment was added later that year in the form of the Anticounterfeiting Consumer Protection Act of 1996.[2]

Patent and Trademark Office and Technology

In 2000, the agency once known as the Patent and Trademark Office renamed itself the United States Patent and Trademark Office. The explosion in e-commerce has been followed by a boom in business method software patents, as more entrepreneurs and investors realize the value of owning a way of doing business on the Internet. In 1997, the agency created a separate department for processing those 920 patent applications. The next year the number of applications increased to 1,300, and they doubled in 1999 to 2,600. Each application takes an average of 26 months to process, compared to 18 months for general patents. The software patents were a fraction of the 161,000 issued in 1999.[3]

---

[1] Beth Snyder Bulik, "The brand police," *Business 2.0*, 28 November 2000, 144–148.
[2] "The Lanham Act: Alive and well after 50 years," International Trademark Association, www.inta.org/lanham.htm, 20 June 2000.
[3] Sabra Chartrand, "What's in a name? A sign of other changes at the United States Patent and Trademark Office," *The New York Times*, 3 April 2000, C6.

Understanding Corporate Identity

Joseph Sinel published the first book dedicated to trademarks in 1924. He outlined rules for corporate identity and recognized that a trademark established the character of a company and influenced the appearance of a product. Today, the corporate mark is still the cornerstone of an identity program, but it involves much more. Partially due to technology and expanding avenues of communication, corporate identity has become an all-encompassing discipline that embodies the corporate personality, history, reputation, and vision. SDRC, a 3-D software maker, changed its name to I-deas to have a more memorable name and reflect their best-selling product (see Exhibit 21.1). One of the driving forces in the corporate identity boom has been the skyrocketing mergers and acquisitions and increases in small business start-ups. Corporate identity solutions are not solved with a single medium, but are a strategically planned sum of its parts—print, display, packaging, the Web, broadcast, and a cross-media relationship—creates an exponentially more powerful whole.

All brands, like people, have a personality of one kind or another, but like the strongest individuals, the most powerful brands have more than personality—they have more character, more depth, more integrity. They stand out from the crowd, according to Ken Love, of Lippincott & Margulies, an international identity and image management firm.[4] Love also believes the United States is coming back to a more comprehensive approach to corporate identity for the first time since the early 1980s.[5]

Packaging is a very important part of the brand equity and integrated marketing equation. It has been labeled as the only truly international method of branding. A distinctive shape such as the Coca-Cola bottle or Johnson & Johnson's baby lotion is instantly recognized anywhere. What we are talking about in this chapter is the power of a strong effective image—a name, a symbol, a package—to build brand equity. Today, it goes beyond these basics of corporate marks and typeface

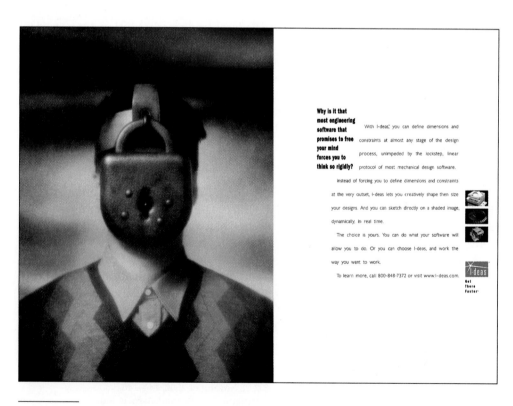

Exhibit 21.1

I-deas better reflects the software maker's name than SDRC.

Courtesy: Howard, Merrell & Partners.

---

[4]"Corporate identity rises on the tide of competition and change," *Graphic Design:USA*, April 2000, 62–72.
[5]"The new corporate identity," *Graphic Design:USA*, October 1997, 64–84.

and must carry seamlessly across many media landscapes from traditional print and broadcast to internal and external Web sites to virtual reality and other not-yet-thought-of forms of communicating. Here we focus primarily on trademarks and packaging.

There are those who believe that in an age of 500 TV channels, the retail shelf will become the only true mass medium. That notion has already produced greater attention to packaging a brand banner, widespread use of contemporary colors, and more senior marketing people getting involved in packaging. It is a product of twin forces that rule most marketing decisions: time and money. Consumers have less time to shop in a leisurely manner, so marketers are seeking new methods to attract their attention. And marketers are spending more money on putting the message where consumers make a purchase. Strategic design firms are constantly being told that packaging has to communicate the entire brand strategy, whereas not too long ago, packaging was simply a necessary evil. Herb Meyers of GerstmanMeyers says, "Packaging and advertising have to support each other, so people are putting more work into getting their brand message across and an increasing insistence by marketers on integrated campaigns."[6]

This need to protect the investment in a brand or company name and trademark has spawned a whole body of law. Getting legal protection is the province of the attorney; however, it begins with the creation of the trademark itself. We touch here on some of the ground rules.

WHAT IS A TRADEMARK?

We have said that brands are among the most valuable assets a marketer has. When a product is manufactured and a brand is created, it must be distinctive from the competition.

There are several types of company and product identifications. The **trademark**, also called a brand name, is the name by which people can speak of the product. Very often a trademark will include some pictorial or design element. If it does, the combination is called a **logotype** (or simply a **logo**).

Trademarks are proper terms that identify the products and services of a business and distinguish them from products and services of others. Specifically, a trademark is a word, design, or combination used by a company to identify its brand and to distinguish it from others, and it may be registered and protected by law. Trademark formats can include letters, numbers, slogans, geometric shapes, pictures, labels, color combinations, product and container shapes, vehicles, clothing, and even sound.

Trademarks can also be termed service marks when used to identify a service. In general, a trademark for goods appears on the product or its packaging, and a service mark is used in advertising to identify the services.

The logo design is an extremely important element in the successful marketing of a product. It is difficult to sell a product until a reasonable level of name recognition is achieved among consumers. In fact, the creation of a logo is so important that a number of firms have been established whose primary function is the design of logos, packages, and corporate identity. Most designers attempt to forge a compatible relationship among the package design, logo, and advertising for the product. A strong logo on the package and in product advertising creates an environment of recognition. Exhibit 21.2 reflects a number of design options that were presented to Folks restaurants when they were searching for a new logo. Exhibit 21.3 shows a version as it is used today.

trademark Any device or word that identifies the origin of a product, telling who made it or who sold it. Not to be confused with *trade name*.

logotype, or logo A trademark or trade name embodied in the form of a distinctive lettering or design. Famous example: Coca-Cola.

---

[6]Terry Lefton, "Packaging all they can get into what's on the shelf," *BrandWeek,* October 3, 1994, 34–35.

Clearly, the most successful packages are those that combine an intriguing design scheme with a provocative logotype. What we mean is a logo that is distinctive enough if it is extracted from the package that it will still project the visual personality of the product. After all, when pushing a shopping cart down a supermarket aisle, the consumer's first images will be recognizable brand names.

Trademarks should not be confused with trade names, which are corporate or business names. General Motors, for example, is the trade name of a company making automobiles whose trademark (not trade name) is Buick. The terms trademark and trade name are often confused. **Trade names** are proper nouns. Trade names can be used in the possessive form and do not require a generic form. Many companies, however, use their trade names as trademarks. For example, Reebok

trade name A name that applies to a business as a whole, not to an individual product.

International Ltd. is the corporate name, and Reebok may be used as a trade name, as "Reebok's newest line of athletic shoes is for children." Reebok also is used as a trademark: "Are you wearing Reebok athletic shoes or another brand?"

If you're confused, think of yourself as a new product. Your surname is your trade name (e.g., Lane, Smith, Bevil). Your gender is the product classification (Female Lane, Female Smith, or Female Bevil). Your given name then is the brand (Lois Lane, Judy Smith, Sheri Bevil) because it distinguishes you from other family members (like Sarah Bevil).

Some personal names (as with product names) may sound the same but may have different spellings—Sherry, Sherri, or Sheri, or even Cheri (Kwik-Draw, Quick-Draw, Kwic, Kwik, Quick). Or they may simply be very familiar names—Jennifer, Jane, Jessica, Sarah, Hanna, Emily—or clearly distinctive, like Ruhanna. Yet, distinctive may appear difficult to read or pronounce. Companies and products have a similar problem. They want names that can easily become familiar to consumers, yet be easy to read and pronounce and be memorable.

General Electric's Naming Process

General Electric has a simple procedure for developing trademarks for its brands. GE's branding strategy has a number of steps:[7]

1. *Pick a name.* General Electric, for example.
2. *Create a memorable trademark.* The GE monogram is recognized the world over.
3. *Make a promise.* For 60 years, GE promised better living through electricity, which became better living through technology, for the past 30 years.
4. *Effectively communicate the promise.* GE has always had highly imaginative and memorable work produced by its agencies.
5. *Be consistent.* Even as we grow and modify our business, we carefully manage the use of our identity worldwide.
6. *Don't get bored.* GE has kept the same strategic promise for 30 years.

If you follow this basic strategy, your brand should thrive.

For a firm to qualify for an exclusive trademark, several requirements must be met. If these criteria are not satisfied, the trademark is not legally protected and will be lost to the firm.

The use of a design in an ad does not make it a trademark, nor does having it on a flag over the factory. The trademark must be used in connection with an actual product. It must be applied to the product itself or be on a label or container of that product. If that is not feasible, it must be affixed to the container or dispenser of the product, as on a gas pump at a service station.

The trademark must not be confusingly similar to trademarks on comparable goods. It must not be likely to cause buyers to be confused, mistaken, or deceived as to whose product they are purchasing. The trademark must be dissimilar in appearance, sound, and significance from others for similar goods. Of course, it is up to a court to decide these issues. The products involved need not be identical. Air-O was held in conflict with Arrow shirts. The marks will be held in conflict if the products are sold through the same trade channels or if the public might assume that a product made by a second company is a new product line of the first company. The product Big Boy! powder for soft drinks was held in confusion with Big Boy stick candy.

---

[7]Richard A. Costello, "Focus on the brand," *The Advertiser,* Spring 1993, 11–18.

Trademarks must not be deceptive—that is, they must not indicate a quality the product does not possess. For instance, the word Lemon soap was barred because it contained no lemon; as was the word Nylodon for sleeping bags that contained no nylon.

Trademarks must not be merely descriptive. For example, when people ask for fresh bread, we cannot trademark our bread Fresh. When people ask for fresh bread, they are describing the kind of bread they want, not specifying the bread made by a particular baker. To prevent such misleading usage, the law does not protect trademarks that are merely descriptive and thus applicable to many other products.

Trademark Protection

Because a trademark is so valuable, companies go to great lengths to protect their brand names. In recent years, there have been a number of court cases involving allegations that one company has infringed on the trademark of another.

In deciding where trademark infringement has taken place, several factors are considered by the courts:

1. The distinctiveness of the complainant's mark
2. The similarity of the marks
3. The proximity of the parties' products
4. The likelihood of the complainant's bridging the gap between noncompeting products
5. The similarity of the parties' trade channels and advertising methods
6. The quality of the alleged infringer's products
7. The sophistication of the particular customers

Recently, a federal judge ruled that an Ohio-based Internet company infringed on copyrights held by BellSouth Corp. The judge held that the RealPages Web site owned by Don Madey did not have the right to use RealPages as its identification or as part of its Internet address. BellSouth has held a trademark on the phrase Real Yellow Pages since 1984. The Web site also used the phrase "let your mouse do the walking," but agreed to stop using that phrase. BellSouth also owns the copyright to the phrase "let your fingers do the walking." The company said they had no choice but to protect their marks. The company filed suit only after trying to discuss the issue with the Web site company.[8]

Beware if your trademark is based on a common word. It will be considered legally weak, and difficult to protect. Police unpermitted use of your trademark vigorously, and don't let any competitor use your mark even briefly. And, if you want to start a trademark infringement suit, don't do it unless you keep detailed records and can document lost profits accurately.

Trademark Loss

In short, if you don't use a trademark properly, you can lose the rights to it. What would happen to Pepsi if the courts ruled you or anyone could call a soft drink Pepsi? Some companies have seen the untimely demise of a trademark. That's right—untimely demise. Many familiar words today were once valid trademarks:

---

[8]Michael E. Kannell, "Judge sides with BellSouth on copyright," *Atlanta Journal-Constitution,* 10 September 1997, C2.

aspirin	cornflakes
yo-yo	nylon
escalator	thermos
lanolin	raisin bran
cellophane	linoleum

To protect a trademark, advertisers must use it with a generic classification so the trademark does not become the name of the product. Originally, Thermos was the trademark owned by the Aladdin Company, which introduced vacuum bottles. In time, people began asking, "What brand of thermos bottle do you carry?" The word "thermos" had come to represent all vacuum bottles, not just those made by Aladdin. The courts held that Thermos had become a descriptive word that any manufacturer of vacuum bottles could use because thermos (with a lowercase "t") was no longer the exclusive trademark of the originator.

Selecting Brand Names

A strong brand name will aid marketing objectives by helping create and support the brand image. There are several considerations in the brand name selection.[9]

■ The name should differentiate the product from the competition. In some product categories, there is a limit to how different brand images can be. In fragrances there has traditionally been one basic image—romance. There is great similarity among brand names—Caleche, Cacharel, and Chantilly. Consider more distinctive names such as Obsession, Charlie, Passion, Romance, and Tiffany. In either direction, creation and support of the brand image—abstract promise rather than actual benefit—are the dominant factors in name selection.

■ The name should describe the product, if possible. Brand names such as Post-it, Pudding Pops, Eraser Mate, and lastminutetravel.com are very descriptive. They communicate to consumers exactly what to expect.

■ The name should be compatible with the product. The product should be compatible with the brand name. In other words, do not name a sleeping tablet "Awake."

■ The name should be memorable and easy to pronounce. One-word, one-syllable brand names are often considered ideal—Fab, Tide, Dash, Bold, Surf, Coke, and Tab. Even though short names may be more memorable, they may be limiting in identifying the type of product or its use.

Al and Laura Ries, brand consultants, recommends the following considerations in naming a brand:[10]

■ The name should be short. For instance, Jell-O, Nilla, TheraFlu. Shortness is an attribute even more important for an Internet brand.

■ The name should be simple. Simple is not the same as short. A simple word uses only a few letters of the alphabet and arranges them in combinations that repeat themselves. Schwab is a short name, but not simple because it uses six letters of the alphabet. Coca-Cola is both a short and simple name. Autobytel.com suffers from being too complicated.

[9]Daniel L. Doden, "Selecting a brand name that aids marketing objectives," *Advertising Age*, 5 November 1990, 34.

[10]Al Ries and Laura Ries, *The Immutable Laws of Internet Branding* (New York: HarperBusiness, 2000), 59–70.

- The name should be unique. Unique is a key characteristic that makes a name memorable. No name is totally unique unless you create it from scratch, like Acura, Lexus, or Kodak. Remember, a common or generic name is not unique.
- The name should be alliterative. If you want people to remember something, rhyme it for them. Alliteration is another way to improve your brand's memorability: Bed, Bath & Beyond, Blockbuster, Volvo, and Weight Watchers.
- The name should be speakable. Try Abercrombie & Fitch and Concierge.com.

Forms of Trademarks

Branding experts agree that although still very relevant, the overall value of a *company's* name has diminished. Convergence, globalization, and the dot-com influx has caused a shift in the branding strategy. The vast majority of the words in the *Oxford English Dictionary* have been registered and trademarked. So there has been an effort to become more creative as demonstrated by dot-coms and technology companies, such as Cingular Wireless, Bcom3 Group, etc. But beware, because "creative" names sometimes dilute corporate image.[11] Below are examples of traditional trademark forms.

Dictionary Words   Many trademarks consist of familiar dictionary words used in an arbitrary, innovative, or fanciful manner. Many common words have already been used, causing the advertiser to seek other methods to name a product: Apple computers, Verbatim data disks, Deer Park spring water, Nature Made vitamins, Ivory soap, Dial soap, Equal sweetener, Whopper burgers, Glad plastic bags, Shell oil, Coach leather, Water Grabber plant water absorber, Target discount store, Folks restaurant, and Pert shampoo. This type of trademark must be used in a merely descriptive sense to describe the nature, use, or virtue of the product: Look at the word "natural" and related names such as Natural Blend, Natural Brand, Natural Impressions, Natural Light, Natural Man, Natural Silk, Natural Smoothe, Natural Stretch, Natural Suede, Natural Sun, Natural Touch, Natural Woman, and Natural Wonder; or the prefix "opti" as used in Opti Fonts, Opti Free, Opti-Fry, Opti-Grip, Opti Heat, Opti Pure, Opti-Ray, Opti-Tears, and Opti Twist.

The possible advantage of using dictionary words is that consumers will easily recognize them. Of course, the task is to get people to associate the word(s) with the product. Just think what the following real product names using two dictionary words are about: Healthy Choice, Skin Bracer, Budget Rent-A-Car, Drug Emporium, Wonder Bra, Big Mac, EarthLink, Action Plus, Hotmail, and AquaFresh.

At times, a name can be somewhat limiting. For instance, when Burger King moved into a breakfast menu, the name Burger King was a limitation because people do not think of burgers as breakfast.

coined word An original and arbitrary combination of syllables forming a word. Extensively used for trademarks, such as PoFolks, Mazola, Gro-Pup, Zerone. (Opposite of a dictionary word.)

Coined Words   When we run out of dictionary options, we sometimes make up words, such as Ticketron, Advil, Infiniti, Primerica, Kleenex, Xerox, NYNEX, UNUM, Norelco, Exxon, Delco, Keds, Kodak, Mazola, TransAir, and Tab. **Coined words** are made up of a new combination of consonants and vowels. The advantage of a coined word is that it is new; it can be made phonetically pleasing, pronounceable, and short. Coined words have a good chance of being legally protectable. The challenge is to create a trademark that is distinctive. Ocean Spray took the ingredients of cranberries and apples and created the name Cranapple, which is distinctive, descriptive, and relatively easy to pronounce. There is, however, a Cranberry Apple herb tea. Is this confusing? Probably not.

---

[11]Jenna Schnuer, "The name game," *Advertising Age*, 10 October 2000, 32.

The simpler coined words are one syllable. It is common to coin trademark words that have a vowel next to a hard consonant or a vowel between two hard consonants, such as Keds. This structure can be expanded—Kodak, Crisco, or Tab.

Personal Names   These may be the names of real people, such as Calvin Klein, Liz Claiborne, Anne Klein, Estee Lauder, Tommy Hilfiger, Perry Ellis, Pierre Cardin, Alexander Julian, Ralph Lauren, L.L. Bean, Jenny Craig, Forbes, and Sara Lee; fictional characters, such as Betty Crocker; historical characters, such as Lincoln cars; or mythological characters, such as Ajax cleanser. A surname alone is not valuable as a new trademark; others of that name may use it. Names such as Ford automobiles, Lipton teas, Heinz foods, and Campbell's soups have been in use for so long, however, that they have acquired what the law calls a "secondary" meaning—that is, through usage the public has recognized them as representing the product of one company only. However, a new trademark has no such secondary meaning.

There are a lot of names that use Mrs.—Mrs. Fields, Mrs. Winner's, Mrs. Richardson's, Mrs. Allison's, Mrs. Smith's, Mrs. Dash, Mrs. Baird's, Mrs. Butterworth's, Mrs. Lane's, and Mrs. Paul's.

Foreign names have been successfully used to endow a product with an exotic quality. Of course, because the market is now global, they are more and more common. The argument against creating foreign names may be the problem of pronunciation or remembering. However, foreign names are part of the global landscape: Toyota, Feni, Gianfranco Ferre, Corneliani, Lubiam, Bertolucci, Giorgia Brutini, Shiseido, Gucci, Volkswagen, Fila, Ferrari, and L'Aimant.

Geographical Names   A geographical name is really a place name: Nashua blankets, Utica sheets, Pittsburgh paints, and Newport cigarettes. These names are old trademarks and have acquired secondary meaning. Often the word "brand" is offered after the geographical name. The law does not look with favor on giving one person or company the exclusive right to use a geographical name in connection with a new product, excluding others making similar goods in that area. However, if the name was chosen because of a fanciful connotation of a geographical setting, rather than to suggest that the product was made there, it may be eligible for protection, as with Bali bras, and Klondike ice cream bars.

Geographical names can be combined with dictionary words to create trademark names such as Maryland Club coffee and Carolina Treat barbecue sauce. The options are many: Georgia Coffee, Texas Instruments, Texas Trails, New York Woman, Florida Queen, Newport Harbor, Georgia-Pacific, and Raleigh Community Hospital.

Initials and Numbers   Many fortunes and years have been spent in establishing trademarks such as IBM, IKEA furniture, RCA, GE, AC spark plugs, A&W root beer, J&B whiskey, A.1. steak sauce, and V8 vegetable juice. Hence, these are familiar. In general, however, initials and numbers are the most difficult form of trademark to remember and the easiest to confuse and imitate. How many of these sound familiar: STP, DKNY, S.O.S., AMF, M.O.M.S., S.A.V.E., A.S.A., A&P, 6-12, or 666? There are also combinations of initials and numbers: WD-40 lubricant; numbers and words: 9-Lives cat food, 4 in 1, Formula 44, Formula 109, Formula 28, Formula 36, 4 Most; or dictionary words and initials: LA Gear.

Pictorial   Many advertisers use some artistic device, such as distinctive lettering style or a design, insignia, or picture. The combination, as mentioned before, is called a logotype, or logo. It is important for the advertiser to make sure that any symbol or design is distinctive and will reproduce clearly when used in a small size. Vibe's, a Java tool, has a logo and ad that exhibits a modern technology image (Exhibit 21.4).

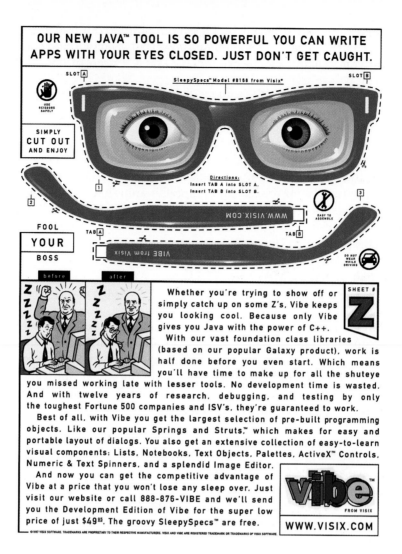

Exhibit

21.4

This Java tool has a modern logo.

Courtesy: West & Vaughan, Inc.

The Successful Trademark

Whatever the form of a specific trademark, it will be successful only if it is distinctive and complements the manufacturer's product and image. As we mentioned earlier in this chapter, the trademark cannot be considered an isolated creative unit. In most cases, it must be adaptable to a package. It must also be adaptable to many different advertising campaigns, often over a period of many years. The longer a trademark is associated with a brand, the more people recognize it and the greater its value.

Global Trademarks

Since the 1870s, trademark law has been based on use of the marks in commerce. "No trade, no trademark" was the law's basic premise. Since 1946, U.S. trademark owners have been required to submit proof of prior use when they apply to register their marks at the Patent and Trademark Office. Recently, the law was changed to permit companies to base trademark applications on an intent to use the mark. This change brought U.S. policy in harmony with worldwide standards.

The law permits an applicant with a bona fide intent to use a mark to apply to register it, for example, on January 1, and if the registration is issued eventually—say, on October 31—to trace its rights back to the application date. A registration is issued when the application is approved by the Patent and Trademark Office and confirmed when the applicant submits proof of use within six months of approval.

As many as five six-month extensions may be granted, giving the company several years to actually market a product under a particular mark. The registration period has been reduced from 20 to 10 years, but may be renewed indefinitely. This 10-year term is more in keeping with international standards and allows for clearing the trademark register of "deadwood." The law also includes prohibiting false statements in advertising about a competitor's product.[12]

General Trademark Rules

Putting a lock on the ownership of a trademark requires taking the following steps:

1. Always be sure the trademark word is capitalized or set off in distinctive type. KLEENEX, *Kleenex*, **Kleenex.**
2. Always follow the trademark with the generic name of the product, or by using the word "brand" after the mark: Glad disposable trash bags, Kleenex tissues, Apple computers, Tabasco brand pepper sauce.
3. Do not speak of the trademark word in the plural, as "three Kleenexes," but rather, "three Kleenex tissues."
4. Do not use the trademark name in a possessive form, unless the trademark itself is possessive, such as Levi's jeans (not "Kleenex's new features," but "the new features of Kleenex tissues"), or as a verb (not "Kleenex your eyeglasses," but "Wipe your eyeglasses with Kleenex tissues").

It is the advertising person's responsibility to carry out these legal strictures in the ads, although most large advertisers will have each ad checked for legal requirements including trademark protection.

DuPont promotes the correct use of their Teflon trademark (see Exhibit 21.5). "Protecting the Teflon trademark is critical to the successful management of a very valuable asset. Improper use of the trademark, or allowing others to use it improperly, lowers its value and can ultimately turn a respected trademark into a common generic term."

Registration Notice

Legal departments at some companies go to great lengths to protect their valuable trademarks. Some common ways of indicating trademark registration follow:

- The "®" symbol after the trademark as a superscript. Example: Mrs. Winner's®
- A footnote referenced by an asterisk in the text.
     Example: McDonald's*
     *A registered trademark of McDonald's Corporation.
     or
     *Reg. U.S. Pat. Tm. Off.
     or
     Registered in the U.S. Patent and Trademark Office.
- A notation of the registration in the text or as a footnote on the same page.
- If a trademark is repeated frequently in an ad, some firms require the registration notice only on the first use.

Most companies require notice of unregistered but claimed words and/or symbols as their trademark, by using the "TM" symbol.

---

[12]Vincent N. Palladino, "New trademark law aids U.S. in foreign markets," *Marketing News,* 13 February 1989, 7.

Rule 1: Show Registration.

Show registration status, by using the symbol "®" each and every time the trademark appears.

If there is no ® on a keyboard, as in some electronic mail systems, use parenthesis "R" parenthesis: (R). For countries where the registration symbol is not recognized, use an asterisk (*).

Acceptable	Unacceptable
Teflon® resin	No designation of registration status
Teflon(R) resin	
*Teflon** resin	Teflon resin

IMPORTANT: Regardless of whether "®", (R), or (*) is used, a footnote must be used at least once in each document. Examples of acceptable footnotes:

* *Teflon* is a registered trademark of DuPont.

Teflon® is a registered trademark of DuPont for its fluoropolymer resins.

Rule 3: Use Correct Generics.

Use the correct generic (common name) for the trademark at least once per package. Generic is the term for the class of goods for which the mark is registered.

Acceptable	Unacceptable
Teflon® resins	*Teflon*® president, *Teflon*® gasket, *Teflon*® cookware, *Teflon*® business
Other acceptable generics: films, fibers, finishes, fabric protector, fluoro-polymer, fluoro-additive, micro-powder, coating solutions, PTFE, PFA, FEP, ETFE	

NOTE: Although not generics, it is acceptable to refer to the *Teflon*® trademark and the *Teflon*® brand.

Rule 2: Be Distinctive.

Make the trademark distinctive from the surrounding text each and every time.

Acceptable	Unacceptable
Initial Cap: *Teflon*® resin	Any instance where the trademark is not distinguished from surrounding text, such as: "gaskets with teflon"
All Caps: TEFLON® resin	
Bold: *Teflon*® resin	
Italics: *Teflon*® resin	
Color: Teflon® resin	

Rule 3: Use Correct Generics.

The trademark is the trademark. Don't embellish upon it!

Acceptable	Unacceptable
Wear resistance of *Teflon*®	**Possessives:** *Teflon*®'s wear resistance
Coatings of *Teflon*®	**Hyphens:** *Teflon*®-coated
Fabrics using *Teflon*® wear longer	**Line Breaks** Fabrics using *Teflon*® wear longer
Coat pans with *Teflon*®	**Verbs:** Teflon® your pans
Teflon®	**Coined Words:** *Teflon*® ized

Exhibit

21.5

Guidelines on Use of Teflon Trademark

Courtesy: DuPont.

HOUSE MARKS

As mentioned earlier in this chapter, trademarks are used to identify specific products. However, many companies sell a number of products under several different trademarks. These companies often identify themselves with a **house mark** to denote the firm that produces these products. Kraft is a house mark, and its brand Miracle Whip is a trademark.

house mark A primary mark of a business concern, usually used with the trademark of its products. *General Mills* is a house mark; *Betty Crocker* is a trademark; *DuPont* is a house mark; *Teflon II* is a trademark.

SERVICE MARKS, CERTIFICATION MARKS

A company that renders services, such as an insurance company, an airline, or even Weight Watchers, can protect its identification mark by registering it in Washington as a **service mark**. It is also possible to register certification marks, whereby a firm certifies that a user of its identifying device is doing so properly. Teflon is a material sold by DuPont to kitchenware makers for use in lining their pots and pans. Teflon is DuPont's registered trademark for its nonstick finish; Teflon II is DuPont's certification mark for Teflon-coated cookware that meets DuPont's standards. Advertisers of such products may use that mark. The Wool Bureau has a distinctive label design that it permits all manufacturers of pure-wool products to use (Exhibit 21.6). Certification marks have the same creative requirements as trademarks—most of all, that they be distinctive.

service mark A word or name used in the sale of services, to identify the services of a firm and distinguish them from those of others, for example, Hertz Drive Yourself Service, Weight Watchers Diet Course. Comparable to trademarks for products.

COMPANY AND PRODUCT NAMES

Corporate Name Changes

Over the years, thousands of companies have undergone corporate name and identity changes. Corporations can spend millions of dollars to complete the process. Costs include hiring consultants, advertising, and changing logos and designs on such items as stationery, uniforms, trucks, and planes.

Anderson Consulting, a global management and technology consulting company spent $175 million to promote its new name—accenture. To come up with the new name, they hired Landor brand identity company, owned by Young & Rubicam, which sifted through 5,500 potential options. The original list was pared down to 550, then down to 50. Then 10 names. The new name was then blitzed in January of 2001 in college football bowl games, the Super Bowl, and in print (*The Wall Street Journal, Fortune, Forbes, Business Week*, etc.). Interestingly enough, the name didn't actually originate with the brand identity company. An employee from Oslo, Norway combined "accent" and "future." It also contains a "greater than" sign (>) hanging over the "t" like an accent mark, but the consonant isn't pronounced differently.[13]

Sometimes a company feels a need to distance itself from a name, as ValuJet did. The start-up airline was damaged from all the negative publicity surrounding the crash of one of its planes in the Florida Everglades in 1996. The newspaper ad

The Woolmark label on this blanket means that you're getting a quality-tested product made of the world's best . . . pure wool.

PURE WOOL

Exhibit
21.6

Certification Mark

---

[13]Richard Linnett, "Anderson's accenture gets $175 mil ad blitz," *Advertising Age*, 4 December 2000, 20.

announcing the name change said, "When ValuJet became AirTran, we decided to change everything (well almost)." In late 1997, the airline officially changed its name to AirTran Airways after a merger. For the most part, however, such changes are rarely based on a company's attempt to distance itself from a negative incident of image, according to Ruffell Meyer, a director of Landor Associates in San Francisco. As indicated in Exhibit 21.1, I-deas became the new name because it was easier to promote and more memorable than SDRC. Fueling the increase is a rise in mergers and acquisitions, new business formation, and further consolidations in industries such as telecommunications and banking.

Another ad said, "After all these years, we think it's time you call us by our first name: Bayer. Today Miles becomes Bayer." The copy started: "You know us as Miles, one of America's largest companies. But in nearly 150 countries, our name is Bayer. Bayer is one of the biggest health care, chemical and imaging technology companies in the world. . . . You already know Bayer for aspirin."

Corporate name changes and, accordingly, graphic identity programs have been on the rise since the mid-1990s, as reported by Interbrand Schechter, a subsidiary of the Omnicom Group, which looks at publicly traded companies on the New York, American, and NASDAQ stock exchanges. They found that a record 100 publicly listed companies changed their names during 1997. The study indicated that merger and acquisition activity continues to be the leading agent of change. Among the new names are the following:

Avaya	Lucent	PriceWaterhouseCoopers
Spherion	Verizon	Aventis
Ventor	Cingular	Novartis

The Process for Developing Memorable Names

There probably isn't a single procedure everyone accepts for selecting names. Ruffell Meyer of Landor Associates says, "The misconception is that you have a couple of people sitting around over a pizza lunch. The first step is to meet with senior management to talk about the direction of the company, its values and image. Does it want to be known for speedy or reliable service or reliability? Later employees and customers may be included in the discussion."

Once the information is gathered, the brand identity staff begins the name-generation and image-making processes. The tools are likely to include software packages that can morph word combinations. Landor has a database with more than 50,000 names. A typical list of possibilities can exceed a thousand names. Cingular, the result of the merger of SBC Communications and BellSouth Mobility, was created from a list of 6,000 names. When AT&T spun off what is now known as Lucent Technologies, the short list contained some 700 names including acronyms, name and number combinations, and coined words. Lucent was chosen because it implies clarity of thought and action.

A few years later, former Enterprise Network Group of Lucent Technologies that made office telephone systems became an independent company called Avaya Communication. The new company began business in 2000 in 90 countries, 30,000 employees, and nearly 1 million customers. These corporate expansions are one of the reasons for new corporate names. Another is the obvious growth of dot-com names and changes of names, for example.

Delta Air Lines missed out on their current URL, when former domain owner of DeltaComm Development, sold delta.com in June 1999 to Delta Financial. In 2000, Delta Air Lines bought the easier-to-remember URL and launched an ad campaign trumpeting the new URL. Delta Air Lines began on the Web in 1995, with

Skylinks.com at the URL delta-air.com. A Delta spokesperson said, "URL's now are an intrinsic part of a company's identity."[14]

A basic legal search should be made of each name to see if someone else owns the rights to it. This process reduces the possibilities by about 80 percent. You again analyze the remaining names against the objective and reduce them to a list of about a dozen or so. At this point, you would probably perform a linguistic analysis to determine what happens when the name is translated into foreign languages. Then you might test the names on consumers. You get the idea. Correctly done, the result is a memorable name that is adapted to a number of advertising formats. Now let us look at the specific steps. First, pull together the basic information:

- Describe what you are naming. In your description, include key features and characteristics, competitive advantages, and anything else that differentiates your company, product, or service from the rest of the field.

- Summarize what you want your name to do. Should it suggest an important product characteristic (e.g., Blokrot for treated lumber) or convey a particular image (e.g., Pandora's Secrets for an expensive perfume)? Write down the characteristics and images you want your name to convey.

- Describe whom you are targeting with the name. Identify your targets and their demographic and lifestyle characteristics. Would they react more positively to a traditional, conservative name or to a liberal, flashy one? List the name qualities you think would appeal to them (name length, sound, and image).

- List names that you like and dislike. Try to come up with a few dozen current names in both categories (include your competitors' names). Note words and roots that might work for your new name and jot them down.

- Build a list of new name ideas. Start with the list of names that you like and add to it by pulling ideas from a good thesaurus (e.g., *The Synonym Finder* by Jerome Rodale), a book of names (e.g., *The Trademark Register of the United States*), relevant trade journals, a book of root words (e.g., *Dictionary of English Word Roots* by Robert Smith), or other sources.

- Combine name parts and words. Take words, syllables, and existing name parts and recombine them to form new names.

- Pick your favorites. Select several names that meet all your criteria (just in case your top is unavailable or tests poorly).

Next, verify the name's availability and test your favorites:

- Conduct a trademark search. Check to make sure your names are not already in use. Thomson & Thomson in Boston, Corsearch, or Compu-Mark in Washington are companies that can help check state and U.S. patent and trademark records. The cost ranges from $300 to $800. The cost of having a lawyer do a search in the United States is $500 to $1,000 if you don't require a written opinion summarizing the findings, or $1,500 to $2,500 if you do. The search has to be analyzed for marks that are confusingly similar to your proposed name, and to make sure your proposed name doesn't dilute anyone else's trademark. Dilution refers to the injury to a trademark owner when a mark is used by another, even on goods that do not compete. There are state as well as federal statutes prohibiting dilution.[15]

[14]David Goetzl, "Delta flies toward $1 billion in web sales," *Advertising Age*, 11 September 2000, 54–56.
[15]Maxine Lans Retsky, "Don't change your name without proper clearance," *Marketing News*, 27 October, 1997, 7.

■ Test your name before using it. Regardless of how fond you are of the new name, others may have different opinions. Solicit reactions to your name from prospective customers, stockholders, and industry experts.

Coca-Cola ran into a controversy with Fruitopia's name. In 1991, students at Miami University in Ohio came up with a total marketing plan, which included a product name, for a sparkling water and juice drink in development for the Minute Maid brand at Coca-Cola Foods Canada. When they presented it to Coca-Cola, Coca-Cola thought the name Fruitopia was very "iffy." The product rolled out in the United States in 1994 with the Fruitopia name; although there was no question about the legal rights of ownership—Coca-Cola had paid the university a fee for all of the students' work—there was a question of who developed the name. Coca-Cola said that a marketing group, working independently with their advertising agency, came up with the name. This is a reason most companies don't take unsolicited proposals for new products, ads, or product names. If Coca-Cola had not paid for the rights for the students' work, there could have been a legal battle for the name Fruitopia.

Name Assistance   The naming of products may be developed by the advertiser or the advertising agency, working independently or together. There are companies and consultants that specialize in helping companies and agencies develop memorable names. The Namestormers use software to help develop product and company names such as CarMax (used-car dealer network), Pyramis (medical systems), AutoSource (auto parts network), Spider's Silk (lingerie), CareStream (health care company), and Wavemaker (notebook computer). Goldman & Young, Inc. uses Linguistic Architecture to define image strategy and positioning, then creates names such as Polaroid Captiva, Nissan Pathfinder, Oldsmobile Achieva, Clairol Affluence, Honda Fourtrax atv, and GMC Yukon. Namelab, another company that develops names, has used constructional linguistics to create the names Acura, Compaq, Geo, Lumina, and Zapmail. Then there are the brand identity companies who also develop names (Landor Associates, VSA Partners, etc.). Keep in mind that anyone in the process can create a name. Howard, Merrell & Partners creative director coined the word WRAITH for WRAITH Speakers (see Exhibit 21.7).

Protect the Usage of Corporate Symbol

Earlier we indicated that companies should control how the trademark is used in writing ads, and so forth. Many companies provide departments and units with written guidelines instructing the use of trademarks. For example, Kodak has a 10-page document for proper use, with examples of incorrect usage, of their trademarks. This includes trademark printing instructions for black-and-white and color usage.

Blockbuster Corporation warns its employees, "Always use the exact registration or trademark form." You should never change the word or design; never change the upper and lowercase letters; never change the colors; never change the plural or singular form; never add the word "the" to the word or design; never add a design to the word or vice versa; and never make the mark a possessive noun.

PACKAGING

Package design should be a holistic endeavor that requires looking at the entire environment the packaging is working within—the product's durability; manuals, instructions, and other printed materials that are stuffed into a package; and the package's ability to communicate on a retail shelf says designer, Wendy Jedlicka.[16]

---

[16]Wendy Jedlicka, "Packaging," *Communication Arts*, March/April 2000, 111.

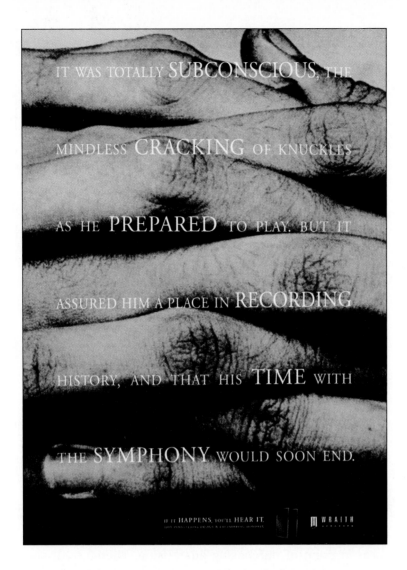

IT WAS TOTALLY SUBCONSCIOUS, THE

MINDLESS CRACKING OF KNUCKLES

AS HE PREPARED TO PLAY, BUT IT

ASSURED HIM A PLACE IN RECORDING

HISTORY, AND THAT HIS TIME WITH

THE SYMPHONY WOULD SOON END.

IF IT HAPPENS, YOU'LL HEAR IT.

WRAITH

Exhibit
21.7

The name for WRAITH speakers was created by a creative director at Howard, Merrell & Partners.
Courtesy: Howard, Merrell & Partners.

The product package is much more than a container. The package must be designed to take several factors into account. First, it must protect the package contents (see Exhibit 21.8); every other consideration is secondary to the function of the package as a utilitarian container. Second, the package must meet reasonable cost standards. Because the product package is a major expense for most firms, steps must be taken to hold down costs as much as possible.

Once these two requirements of package protection and cost are satisfied, we move to the marketing issues involved in packaging. These include adopting a package that is conducive to getting shelf space at the retail level. A unique package with strange dimensions or protruding extensions or nonflat surfaces is going to be rejected by many retailers. A package must be easy to handle, store, and stack. It should not take up more shelf room than any other product in that section, as a pyramid-shape bottle might. Odd shapes are suspect: Will they break easily? Tall packages are suspect: Will they keep falling over? The package should be soil-resistant. Does it have ample and convenient space for marking? The product should come in the full range of sizes and packaging common to the field.

For products bought upon inspection, such as men's shirts, the package needs transparent facing. The package can make the difference in whether a store stocks the item.

Small items are expected to be mounted on cards under plastic domes, called blister cards, to provide ease of handling and to prevent pilferage. Often these cards are mounted on a large card that can be hung on a wall, making profitable use of

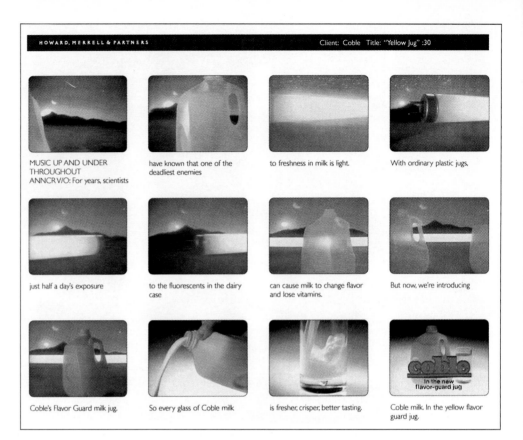

MUSIC UP AND UNDER THROUGHOUT ANNCR V/O: For years, scientists

have known that one of the deadliest enemies

to freshness in milk is light.

With ordinary plastic jugs,

just half a day's exposure

to the fluorescents in the dairy case

can cause milk to change flavor and lose vitamins.

But now, we're introducing

Coble's Flavor Guard milk jug.

So every glass of Coble milk

is fresher, crisper, better tasting.

Coble milk. In the yellow flavor guard jug.

Exhibit

21.8

This TV commercial touts the milk jug's value of protecting flavor and vitamins.

Courtesy: Howard, Merrell & Partners.

that space. Remember, the buyer working for the store judges how a product display will help the store, not the manufacturer.

Once we have considered the requirements of the retail trade, we can turn our attention to designing a container that is both practical and eye-catching. The package is, after all, the last chance to sell the consumer and the most practical form of point-of-purchasing advertising. Therefore, it should be designed to achieve a maximum impact on the store shelf. Striving for distinctiveness is particularly critical in retail establishments such as grocery stores, where the consumer is choosing from hundreds of competing brands.

Changing Package Design and Marketing Strategies

Design firms redesign packages to suit changing market strategies for existing consumer products and develop new packaging concepts for product introductions. P&G created a new way to dry clean at home. The packaging had to attract attention and hold the different content items (see Exhibit 21.9). Several trends in package design can be cited. One is the increasing tendency to use packaging to shore up store brands. Another is the use of sophisticated design approaches or unique packaging to establish a high quality for upscale, private-label brands. There has also been a shift from packaging that suits the convenience of the manufacturer to packaging that is "consumer-friendly" in terms of opening and use, reclosing, and portions. In short, package design is responding to a more sophisticated, discerning consumer.

Most brand identity firms not only assist in product or company names, but also are product design and packaging experts.

Packaging and Marketing

Until this century, the role of product packages was generally confined to protecting the product. Only the package label was linked with promotional activities. The

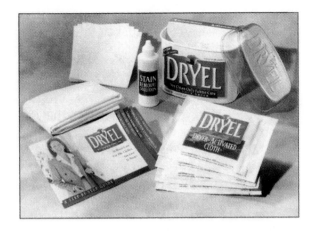

Exhibit

21.9

Dryel packaging must include a number of items combined as one.
Courtesy: Proctor & Gamble.

Uneeda Biscuit package introduced in 1899 is generally considered to be the first that was utilized for promotion. However, few companies followed Uneeda's lead.

During the depression of the 1930s, the role of packaging as a promotional tool changed dramatically. Most companies had limited advertising funds during this period, so they resorted to using the package as an in-store means of promotion. So successful were their efforts that the role of packaging in the marketing mix became routinely accepted by manufacturers.

The package design for most products is developed in much the same way as an advertising campaign. Although each package is developed, designed, and promoted in a unique fashion, there are some common approaches to the successful use of a package as a marketing tool.

1. *The type of product and function of the package.* Is the product extremely fragile? Do consumers use the product directly from the package? Are there special storage or shipping problems associated with the product?

2. *The type of marketing channels to be used for the product.* If the product is sold in a variety of outlets, will this require some special packaging considerations? Will the package be displayed in some special way at the retail level? Are there special point-of-purchase opportunities for the product?

3. *The prime prospects for the product.* Are adults, children, upper-income families, or young singles most likely to buy the product? What package style would be most appealing to the target market?

4. *Promotion and advertising for the product and its package.* Will the package be used to complement other promotional efforts? Are on-pack coupons or premiums being considered? Can standard package-design ideas be adapted to any special promotional efforts being considered?

5. *The relationship to other packages in a product line.* Will the product be sold in different sizes? Is the product part of a product line that is promoted together? Does the product line use the same brand name and packaging style?

6. *The typical consumer use of the product.* Will the package be stored for long periods in the home? Does the product require refrigeration or freezing? Are only portions of the product from the package used?

Obviously, the answers to these and other questions can be obtained only through careful research. The package designer must strive for a balance between creativity and function.

Packaging and Color Influence

Advertisers are very much aware that colors work on people's subconscious and that each color produces a psychological reaction. Reactions to color can be pleasant or unpleasant. Color can inform consumers about the type of product inside the package and influence their perceptions of quality, value, and purity. Thus, color in packaging is an important tool in marketing communications.

What kind of consumer perceptions would you encounter if you brewed the same coffee in a blue coffeepot, a yellow pot, a brown pot, and a red pot? Would the perceptions of the coffee be the same? Probably not. Studies indicate that coffee from the blue pot would be perceived as having a mild aroma, coffee from the yellow pot would be thought a weaker blend, the brown pot's coffee would be judged too strong, and the red pot's coffee would be perceived as rich and full-bodied.

In 1998, Pepsi moved toward a distinctively blue look to better compete against Coke's dominant red. The scope of the project included new designs for cans, bottles, vending machines, soda fountains, and vehicles, which in turn also triggered the need for graphic changes in collateral and signs. Pepsi changed to a heavier reliance on blue than in the past. The design supports this in several ways: the italicized logo, the use of a background with lots of depth and two blues, and an abstract ice background for the Pepsi logo that gives a "visceral representation of refreshment."

Kodak is yellow. Fuji is green. United Parcel service is brown. Think of how Tiffany's blue box has been burned into the consumer's mind. Color has strong influence and should be considered carefully.

Package Research

Today, effective packaging is a vital part of marketing a product. The only absolute in testing a package design is to sell it in a test-market setting. There are several aspects of assessing a package design, including recognition, imagery, structure, and behavior.

- *Recognition.* A package must attract attention to itself so that the consumer can easily identify it in the retail environment. The recognition properties of a package can be measured. Research can determine how long it takes a consumer to recognize the package and what elements are most memorable.
- *Imagery.* The package must be easily recognized, but it must project a brand image compatible with the corporate brand-imagery objectives. A package can reinforce advertising, or it can negate it.
- *Structure.* The objective is to determine any structural problems consumers pinpoint that may inhibit repeat purchases. Is the package easy to open? Is it easy to close? Is it easy to handle? Is it easy to use?
- *Behavior.* This can be the most expensive means of researching packages. Often, this approach presents simulated shelf settings to groups of people and monitors whether they pick up or purchase a product.

Package Differentiation

Twelve suburban women sit around a focus group table, psyching themselves up to talk about cat food for two hours. Through the course of the evening, only two things really perk them up: the chance to describe their cats, and a vacuum-packed foil bag of cat food.

Even before they have examined the nuggets of cat food, most have said they would buy it, intrigued by the high-tech, brick-like bag they have come to expect to see in the coffee aisle, certainly, but never spotted before among the cans, boxes, and bags of pet food.

It is a point increasingly driven home to marketers of food, health and beauty product lines, and over-the-counter drugs: The package is the brand.

Marketers are paying more attention to package design because products are so much more at parity these days. When differentiation through taste, color, and other

Exhibit
21.10

Does the label help differentiate this product from liquid detergents? It must to be successful.

Courtesy: Proctor & Gamble.

product elements has reached parity, packaging makes a critical difference.[17] A case in point is Pepsi-Cola's reaction to making their "plasticization" of the famous curved bottle. They couldn't duplicate the curved bottle, but they did create a stable of designs with monikers such as Fast Break or Big Slam. They found the bottles were a way to build excitement without changing the formula. Febreze Clean Wash laundry aid looks similar to liquid detergents and color-brighteners (Exhibit 21.10).

Brand Identity

Brand identity is a specific combination of visual and verbal elements that helps achieve the following attributes of a successful brand: create recognition; provide differentiation; shape the brand's imagery; link all brand communications to the brand; and—very important—be the proprietary, legal property of the company that owns the brand.

There are a surprisingly short number of components that make up a brand identity. These include name logos, which are the designed versions of a name; symbols; other graphic devices; color; package configuration (the physical structure of a package—see Exhibit 21.11); and permanent support messages—slogans and jingles.[18]

Exhibit
21.11

Packaging for new products must stand out on the store shelf.

Courtesy: Proctor & Gamble.

---

[17]Betsy Spethmann, "The mystique of the brand: Jarred, bagged, boxed, canned," *BrandWeek,* 27 June 1994, 25.

[18]Anita K. Hersh and John Lister, "Brand identity," *The Advertiser,* Spring 1993, 66–71.

Cotrends and Packaging

Cobranding, coadvertising, and copackaging are trends that enable companies with strong brand equities to team together to gain more market share at a lower cost. For example, Betty Crocker cobrands with Reese's Candy, Sunkist with Kraft, and Stayfree with Arm & Hammer. The challenge is to present the brand identities and brand communications in such a way that both brand names are strengthened by the visual association, while marketing costs are shared.

Package Design

A product's package is more than a necessary production expense. Therefore, much care needs to be given to the role of packaging in integrated marketing, relationship marketing with its emphasis on quality, and interactive media. In its promotion function, the package does everything a medium should. At the point-of-purchase, it alone informs, attracts, and reminds the consumer. At the point-of-use, it reinforces the purchase decision. Quality and value are viewed as relatively new marketing concepts, yet some 15 years ago the Design and Market Research Laboratory showed that quality perception was one of the key criteria for packaging assessment. But quality and value have always been part of the marketing and packaging equation.

Because packaging is such an important weapon in the marketing arsenal, it should be approached as other marketing elements, with marketing research, specifically user research with target consumers.

Frank Tobolski, president of JTF Marketing/Studios, says research techniques measure the communication strengths and weaknesses of package graphics. They answer such questions as: Do the graphics communicate well? Do the graphics reinforce and enhance the image positioning? Do the products and package sell? He reports on a case where a toy company developed new packaging for a line of products. Perceptual and imagery evaluation in diagnostic laboratory tests were performed, indicating some problems and potential negative sales effects. To obtain behavioral sales data, test quantities of packages were produced for a balanced store test. For six weeks during the Christmas season, 18 stores stocked the new test design and 18 stocked the existing control design. Toy specialty, discount, department store, and mass merchandiser stores were used for the matched store pairings. The bottom line after six weeks found the existing control packages sold 63 percent more units than the test packages. Even after adjusting the test stores, the new designs sold 35 percent less.[19] A major loss in sales was diverted by testing. Imagine the loss if there had been a full new-package rollout.

Today's packaged-goods marketing managers constantly face the critical task of justifying expenditures in terms of the potential return on investment (ROI). Although most can instantly give you current sales figures, few know the yield on their latest shelf media, or, specifically, packaging design.

Why? There is growing evidence that packaging design has a much stronger impact on sales than is realized.

As any brand manager will tell you, packaging represents a substantial portion of brand equity. When the word "Coke" is uttered, it is more than likely that an image of the trademarked, hourglass-shaped bottle comes to mind.

A Package Value survey suggests that marketers should benchmark new packaging proposals against their own brand equity. The study interviewed a total of 251 men and women, all primary grocery shoppers. Those polled were shown a card with a brand name printed on it and asked to rate the brand on a scale of 1 (agree

---

[19]Frank Tobolski, "Package design requires research," *Marketing News,* 6 June 1994, 4.

strongly) to 5 (disagree strongly). Using "top box" methodology, only respondents who said they "agreed strongly" with all statements were included in the final results.

The subjects were then shown photos of actual packaging. The difference between the scores recorded when people were supplied with a brand name and when they were influenced by actual packaging is what makes the study intriguing. For example, when asked to rate the quality of Procter & Gamble's Tide, both the brand name and the packaging got scores of 61.[20]

Package Look-Alikes

Procter & Gamble sued the 124-store F & M drug chain over the chain's P&G look-alike packages. P&G said the look-alike products confused people and were a disservice to their customers. One of the products, for example, cloned P&G's Pantene, using the same color scheme with a swirl symbol in a small rectangle. Many of the private-label knockoff packaging was displayed next to the brand name products in the store.[21] P&G's move was like a warning shot to everyone with look-alike packages. Of course, the burden of proof lies with P&G proving that knockoff packaging causes consumer confusion. Attorney Maxine Lans says, "You can't stop a competitor from bringing out a similar product, but you can prevent the consumer from buying another product by accident because it looks so much like yours."

Brand Identity Firms

Corporate identity, brand identity, packaging systems, research, brand equity management, naming, branded environments, retail design, and event branding—all of these often require firms that specialize in packaging and brand identity programs for corporations. Landor Associates is one of the firms that does all of these. These companies work with the agency or the corporation or both in developing packaging and may be involved with the total design concept of a corporation or brand. For example, when you think of McDonald's Corporation—the hamburger people—what comes to mind? Golden arches? Employee uniforms? Cup designs? Paper or box designs? Logo? Paper bags? Premiums? Letterheads? Publications? There are many elements that help identify McDonald's, and every element has its name or logo for starters. The corporate design people help the marketer and sometimes the agency develop strong corporate visual communications.

As most restaurants, Folks not only has to integrate logos for the company name, but also design all the products and collateral and packaging. In Exhibit 21.12, Their Good To Go cups and packages all reflect the corporate image.

Packaging and Special Markets

Herb Meyers of the Gerstman & Meyers design firm believes how a product is packaged plays a critical role in how a market responds to brands. He points to the maturing Baby Boomers. The first of them turned 50 in 1996. They have always been the darling of the marketing community. Meyers notes that the percentage of Americans over age 65 will increase more dramatically between from 2010 to 2030. The number of Americans over age 50 is estimated to soar over 80 percent, and the over-50 crowd will account for one-third of the population by the year 2025. This segment has as much discretionary income—$150 billion—as all other age groups combined.

[20]Terry Lofton, " If your brand's number two, get with the package program," *BrandWeek,* 27 June 1994, 26.
[21]Greg Erikson, "Seeing double," *BrandWeek,* October 17, 1994, 30–55.

Exhibit

21.12

All packaging must reflect the corporate image.

Courtesy: Folks, Inc.

Gerstman & Meyers has been doing research in exploring the structural, graphic, and usage issues of packaging that impact this segment of the population. Their survey found typefaces to be a pivotal issue. Almost all mature consumers found it difficult to read small type. Respondents wanted packaging to clearly communicate, to provide information, and to present words in sharp contrast to the background color on labels. Furthermore, respondents looked for cues such as color and graphics with which they were familiar and had exposure to from advertising or purchasing habit. Consumers responded favorably to graphics, photographs, and illustrations as a representation of the package contents, and branding icons helped them find and differentiate the products they wanted.

Among the structural/ergonomic issues that influence packaging are seals. Respondents said that tamper-proof seals need to be balanced with accessibility. Price was important to them, but they were willing to pay more for packages they perceive to have added value, such as convenience of storage or ease in opening. They liked flip-top caps; freshness-preserving inner wraps for cookies and crackers; portion packs for coffee, tea, and baked goods; can lid opening rings that accommodate two fingers, and large handles on bottles. Unique features that do not solve problems, however, were considered an expensive frill: The toothpaste pump was singled out as one such item. These consumers preferred transparent packaging through which they could view the product. They also liked easy-to-pour products.

Portion packages were considered to be a benefit for products not used frequently. The survey found that improvements driven by the needs and considerations of the aging market can be viewed as transgenerational packaging solutions.

Among those things the respondents didn't like were shrink wraps that are hard to open, tear tapes and tear tabs that are too small to grasp, gable-top milk and juice cartons that are difficult to open the first time, and heat-sealed cereal inner bags or potato chip bags that are difficult to open and reseal.[22]

SUMMARY

As we approach the millennium, packaging has become a very important part of the brand equity equation. It has been labeled as the only true method of international branding.

A product's trademark is like a person's name. It gives a product an identity and allows customers to be sure they are getting the same quality each time they purchase it. In addition, the trademark makes advertising and promotion activities possible. For established products, the trademark is one of the company's most valuable assets. It would be very difficult to estimate the value of trademarks such as Coca-Cola, Pepsi-Cola, IBM, or Mercedes. That is why companies take such pains to protect their trademarks.

The trademark can take the form of a word, a design, or a combination of both. Their formats can include letters, numbers, slogans, geometric shapes, color combinations, and so forth. When a trademark is a picture or other design, it is called a logotype. The same principle of trademark protection applies to logos as it does to brand names. Successful trademarks may take many forms; however, they should be easy to pronounce, have something in common with the product, and lend themselves to a variety of advertising and design formats.

The package design is developed in much the same way as an advertising campaign. Package research can help in assessing a number of factors, including recognition, imagery, structure, and behavior. Packaging is an important marketing tool and should be researched with target groups. Brand identity continues to be an important issue.

REVIEW

1. What is a trademark?
2. What is a service mark?
3. How can you lose a trademark?
4. What are the steps to putting a lock on the ownership of a trademark?
5. Name several marketing issues involved in packaging.

TAKE IT TO THE NET

We invite you to visit the Russell/Lane page on the Prentice Hall Web site at **www.prenhall.com/myphlip** for end-of-chapter exercises and applications.

---

[22]"Aging populace shapes package design needs, says Gerstman & Meyers Survey," *Graphic Design:USA,* March 1996, 21.

Chapter 22

The Complete Campaign

CHAPTER OBJECTIVES

Advertisers usually create campaigns that fit into an integrated marketing communication program. They don't create just an ad by itself. After reading this chapter you will understand:

>> situation analysis

>> creative objectives and strategy

>> media objectives and strategy

>> sales promotion plans

>> research posttests

A brand is usually not built overnight. Its success may be measured in years or decades. Coca-Cola wasn't built in a year. BMW has been the ultimate driving machine for almost 30 years. We don't get there with a single ad. Maybe, we get there with a strong campaign. More likely, we depend on all of the integrated communications from the company or brand to dovetail all other messages or impressions about the brand. We build brand equity from everything we do. These messages may include public relations, direct response, events, packaging, Web sites, and promotion among others. Jackie Reed, president and CEO of Fair Riley Call/Bozell, refers to thinking in terms of "media neutral." She defines this as the art and science of marketing communications that begins without a bias toward advertising or any other specific discipline, and systematically applies the right amount of each discipline to achieve the maximum return on investment. This may mean creating direct response or developing a Web site for a marketer, and not necessarily writing ads. In Chapter 3, we discussed a strategic marketing communication plan that could be applied to planning all marketing communications. Here we apply it specifically to advertising campaigns; campaign, as defined by Webster, being a "series of planned actions."

You've learned about the important components of the advertising process—development of strategy, media, research, print ads, and broadcast—all of which are extremely important. The truth is, we don't generally think in terms of individual ads because most brand advertising depends on a series of ads run over a period of time. In other words, a campaign. We should always think in terms of campaigns. In Exhibit 22.1, a pure creative personality turned an obscure ethical flea treatment into a mainstream consumer brand. This campaign won a Gold Effie Award for significant sales increases presented by the American Marketing Association to Howard, Merrell & Partners. Notice the continuity in message as well as the visuals. These ads reinforce each other. The ad campaign also doesn't work alone; it is integrated into the sales and marketing program. As a general rule, campaigns are designed to run over a longer period of time than an individual ad, although there are exceptions. The average length of a regional or national campaign is about 17 months, although it is not uncommon for a campaign to last three or four years, and a few campaigns have lasted much longer.

For example, in 1929 DuPont started using the campaign theme "Better Things for Better Living Through Chemistry." Fifty-five years later it was changed—"through chemistry" was dropped. That is building a lot of brand equity. Basically, the messages remained true to their original campaign premise. On the other hand, some campaigns need to change. In 2001, Ford Truck Division dropped its year-old "Ford Country" for a back-to-basics return to its reliable "Built Ford Tough." The automaker's truck division decided that "Built Ford Tough" carried a punch similar to Chevy's "Like A Rock," that Ford Country hadn't been able to deliver. Ford hadn't totally stopped using Tough, but it had faded somewhat during the Ford Country effort. The point is that advertisers must understand their product and consumers in a changing marketplace. There is no reason to change an advertising campaign for the sake of change.

There is never a guarantee that the next campaign will be as strong, let alone stronger, than the original. And some companies grope for a better campaign with little success. For example, in the mid-1970s, Burger King had perhaps its most famous campaign, "Have It Your Way," but decided it was time to change. So they followed with

America Loves Burgers, and We're America's Burger King
Who's Got the Best Darn Burger?
Make it Special. Make it Burger King.
Aren't You Hungry for Burger King Now?
Battle of the Burgers.
Broiling vs. Frying.
The Big Switch.

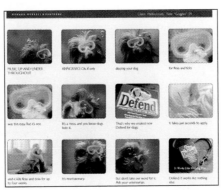

Exhibit 22.1

These ads show continuity even in different media.

Courtesy: Howard, Merrell & Partners.

Search for Herb.
This Is a Burger King Town.
We Do It Like You Do It When We Do It at Burger King.
Sometimes You Gotta Break the Rules.
Your Way. Right Away.
BK Tee Vee: I Love This Place.
Get Your Burgers Worth.
Got the Urge.

Any campaign needs to bring together all of the advertising elements we have discussed into a unified campaign. This calls for an advertising plan. As we have emphasized, good advertising starts with a clear understanding of marketing goals, both short- and long-term. These goals are often expressed as sales or share-of-market objectives to be accomplished for a given budget and over a specific time period.

With our marketing goals in mind, we begin to build the advertising plan with a situation analysis.

SITUATION ANALYSIS

To plan and create future advertising, we need to establish a current benchmark or starting point—this is the role of the situation analysis. It has two time orientations: the past and the present. In other words, it asks two basic questions: Where are we today, and how did we get here? The rest of the advertising plan asks the third basic question: Where are we going in the future?

The situation analysis is the first step in developing a campaign. Exhibit 22.2 reminds us of the planning process discussed earlier in Chapter 3. There are strategic steps that must be taken in the planning process. Campaigns are planned; they don't just happen.

The Product

Successful advertising and marketing begin with a good product. At this point, we need to analyze our product's strengths and weaknesses objectively. Most product failures stem from an overly optimistic appraisal of a product. Among the questions usually asked are the following:

1. What are the unique consumer benefits the product will deliver?

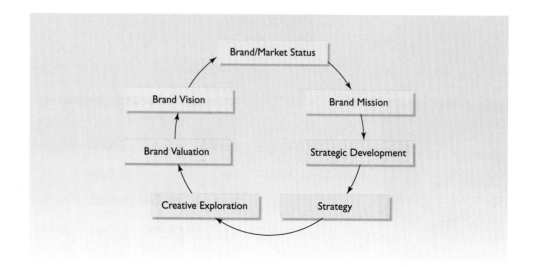

Exhibit

22.2

Planning Cycle

568   PART V   Creating the Advertising

2. What is the value of the product relative to the proposed price?

3. Are adequate distribution channels available?

4. Can quality control be maintained?

Prime-Prospect Identification

The next step is to identify our prime prospects and determine if there are enough of them to market the product profitably. As discussed in Chapter 4, there are a number of ways to identify the primary consumer of our product.

Who buys our product and what are their significant demographic and psychographic characteristics? Can we get a mental picture of the average consumer? Who are the heavy users of the product—the prime prospects? Remember the 80/20 rule; do we need to find those market segments that consume a disproportionate share of our product and determine what distinguishes them from the general population? Finally, we need to examine the prime-prospect's problem. What are their needs and wants in the product or product type?

Competitive Atmosphere and Marketing Climate

We carefully review every aspect of the competition, including direct and indirect competitors. Which specific brand and products compete with your brand, and in what product categories or subcategories do they belong? Is Mountain Dew's competition 7-Up or Sprite, Mellow-Yellow or Crush, or does it extend to colas, iced tea, and milk? If so, to what extent in each case?

With what does Neon directly compete? Indirectly? Neon's competitive subcompact set includes Honda Civic, Ford Escort, Saturn, Nissan Sentra, Toyota Corolla, Chevrolet Cavalier, Geo Prizm, Plymouth, and Dodge Shadow. When we examine the demographic competitive set, we find the typical subcompact buyers are 50 to 55 percent female, over half are married, 35 to 40 years of age, and less than half have a college degree. Honda Civic and Saturn models attract the most distinguishable buyer profiles—typically better educated, earning more income, and younger. The psychographic profile is the competitive set. The greatest fluctuations in psychographic profiles for this set exist between import and domestic buyers. Domestic buyers tend to be motivated by style over engineering; they prefer roomier cars and greater performance. Import buyers prefer engineering over style; they like compact cars and believe imports offer higher quality overall. Now we're beginning to scratch the surface. As you can see, there are numerous factors.

CREATIVE OBJECTIVES AND STRATEGY

At this point, we begin to select those advertising themes and selling appeals that are most likely to move our prime prospects to action. As discussed in Chapter 16, advertising motivates people by appealing to their problems, desires, and goals—it is not creative if it does not sell. Once we establish the overall objectives of the copy, we are ready to implement the copy strategy by outlining how this creative plan will contribute to accomplishing our predetermined marketing goals:

1. Determine the specific claim that will be used in advertising copy. If there is more than one, the claims should be listed in order of priority.

2. Consider various advertising executions.

3. In the final stage of the creative process, develop the copy and production of advertising.

Creative Criteria for Campaigns

Most advertising experts agree on the need for similarity between one advertisement and another in developing successful advertising campaigns. Another term, continuity, is used to describe the relationship of one ad to another ad throughout a campaign. This similarity or continuity may be visual, verbal, aural, or attitudinal.[1]

Visual Similarity All print ads in a campaign should use the same typeface or virtually the same layout format so that consumers will learn to recognize the advertiser just by glancing at the ads. This may entail making illustrations about the same size in ad after ad and/or the headline about the same length in each ad. A number of ads in campaigns have appeared throughout this book (e.g., BB&T, Subdue, Pennant, North Carolina Tourism, etc.). Each illustration in the Brookhill Steeplechase (Exhibit 22.3) ads are about the same size, heads are visually treated in the same manner, the body copy is in three lines, and there is a similar style illustration in the same location, borders, etc. For a different kind of client and reader, Loeffler Ketchum Mountjoy created similar visuals and verbal styles for North Carolina Tourism (Exhibit 22.4) using similar styles but not identical style illustrations and treatment of type; however, there is still definite continuity. You have the same visual feel from ad to ad. We are saying visual continuity—not sameness. These examples pertain to print, but the look could easily be carried over to television or direct marketing (see the BB&T television in Exhibit 22.5). Strong continuity from medium to medium can strengthen the communication. This also applies to all the elements of integrated communications (promotions, Web, etc.).

[1]Kenneth Roman and Jane Maas, *The New How to Advertise* (New York: St. Martin's Press, 1992), 71–78.

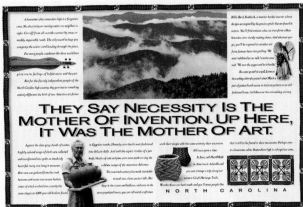

Another device is for all ads in a campaign to use the same spokesperson or continuing character in ad after ad. Still another way to achieve visual continuity is to use the same demonstration in ad after ad from one medium to the other.

Verbal Similarity   It is not unusual for a campaign to use certain words or phrases in each ad to sum up the product's benefits. It is more than a catchy phrase. The proper objective is a set of words that illuminates the advertising, encapsulates the promise, and can be associated with one brand only.

Here are a few campaign phrases that have worked:

For hair so healthy it shines.

PANTENE

Have you driven a Ford lately?

FORD

Where's your mustache?

MILK

From Sharp minds come Sharp products.

SHARP

From the French Alps.

EVIAN

For the skin that just has to be touched.

AVEENO

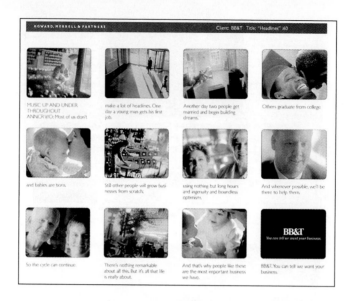

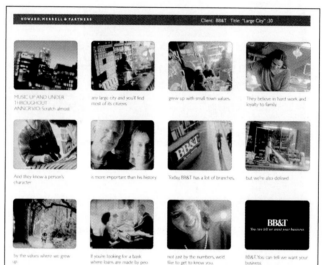

Pepsi used the words "You're in the Pepsi Generation" to help position it among a younger audience and make Coca-Cola appear to be an old-fashioned brand. But it didn't limit all the upbeat, self-assuring benefits of membership of being part of the Pepsi Generation to people between 13 and 24 years of age; it opened it up to everybody—everybody wanted to be in the Pepsi Generation. It wasn't a point of time in years, it was a point of view. No matter what your age, you could be part of the Pepsi Generation. Great words and great strategy make great campaigns. Here are a few other words and classic campaign strategies:

Aren't you glad you use Dial?
Don't you wish everybody did?

You're in good hands with Allstate.

American Express. Don't leave home without it.

Have it your way at Burger King.

Is it true blondes have more fun?
Be a Lady Clairol blonde and see!

You deserve a break today, at McDonald's.

Nike. Just do it.

Repeating the benefits, theme, and key copy points in ad after ad bestows continuity across all media and helps to build brand personality.

We have shown a number of Pennant ads throughout this text to give you a real taste of their campaign. These ads use visual, verbal, and attitude similarity (see Exhibit 22.6).

"Name that weed" is a simple concept. Mix that with the unexpected illustrations of bluegrass, yellow foxtail, crabgrass, and so on, and you have a simple visual verbal communication. Campaigns need to be flexible so they can carry from ad to ad. Baby Gap used a verbal concept that could be endless. Here's a few examples:

Baby Gap is gift
Baby Gap is newborn
Baby Gap is spring
Baby Gap is lux
Baby Gap is jeans

Aural Similarity   You can create aural continuity in broadcast, if you desire. You may use the same music or jingle in commercial after commercial. Using the same announcer's voice in each ad also helps build continuity—classic, "This is Tom Bodett for Motel 6." The same sound effect can make a campaign very distinctive. Avon used the sound of a doorbell for many years in its "Avon Calling" advertising. Maxwell House used the perking sound for its Master Blend commercials, giving an audible campaign signal.

Exhibit
22.6

Each body copy begins with the "Weed". . . and is just one of the weeds that Pennant prevents. So now you can choke out your worst weeds without beating up on ornamentals and warm-season turf.

Courtesy: Howard, Merrell & Partners.

Attitudinal Similarity   Each ad expresses a consistent attitude toward the product and the people using it. The commercial's attitude is an expression of brand personality. The Pepsi Generation campaign was more than words. It communicated an attitude to younger consumers and older consumers. Of course, we cannot leave out the Nike shoe campaign, which said, "Just Do It"—or their swoosh campaign.

Everyone agrees that Nike is one of the strongest brand names in the world, and not just because it sells great products. Its presence and identity are so strong that many people want to connect with the brand. It signifies status, glamour, competitive edge, and the myriad intricacies of cool. It is this description that is communicated in every message, no matter to whom it is directed. Their secret of success resides along a delicate and emotionally charged progression that connects the company, the consumers, and the abiding fantasies that are tethered to sports.[2] In true integrated marketing fashion, its personality is communicated to all—from employees, to stockholders, to consumers. It is conveyed through its corporate culture, as well as its advertising.

MEDIA OBJECTIVES

Although we have chosen to discuss creative strategy before media objectives, both functions are considered simultaneously in an advertising campaign. In fact, creative and media planning have the same foundations—marketing strategy and prospect identification—and cannot be isolated from each other. The media plan involves three primary areas.

media strategy
Planning of ad media buys, including identification of audience, selection of media vehicles, and determination of timing of a media schedule.

Media Strategy

At the initial stages of media planning, the general approach and role of media in the finished campaign are determined:

1. *Prospect identification.* The prime prospect is of major importance in both the media and the creative strategy. However, the media planner has the additional burden of identifying prospects. The media strategy must match prospects for a product with users of specific media. This requires that prospects be identified in terms that are compatible with traditional media audience breakdowns. You will recall that this need for standardization has resulted in the 4A's standard demographic categories discussed in Chapter 4.
2. *Timing.* All media, with the possible exception of direct-mail, operate on their own schedule, not that of advertisers. The media planner must consider many aspects of timing, including media closing dates, production time required for ads and commercials, campaign length, and the number of exposures desired during the product-purchase cycle.
3. *Creative considerations.* The media and creative teams must accommodate each other. They must compromise between using those media that allow the most creative execution and those that are most efficient in reaching prospects.

Media Tactics

At this point, the media planner decides on media vehicles and the advertising weight each is to receive. The reach-versus-frequency question must be addressed and appropriate budget allocations made.

---

[2]Lisa Siracuse, "Looks aren't everything: An examination of brand personality," *Integrated Marketing Communications Research Journal,* Spring 1997, 38–39.

Media Scheduling

Finally, an actual media schedule and justification are developed, as described in the example in Chapter 7.

The Sales Promotion Plan

As with any integrated communications planning, the sales-promotion plan for consumers is discussed very early, and its relationship to the advertising plan (and other communications activities) is determined. Sales-promotion activities may involve dealer displays, in-store promotions, premiums, cooperative advertising, and/or couponing offers.

Once a theme for communications has been established, creative work is begun on the sales-promotion material, which is presented along with the consumer advertising material for final approval. Naturally, advertising and sales-promotion materials would reinforce each other. Once the sales-promotion material is approved, the production is carefully planned so that all of the sales-promotion material will be ready before the consumer advertising breaks.

OTHER INTEGRATED ELEMENTS

Don't forget the importance of every aspect of your integrated marketing communication to function as one voice. You need to keep focused on the brand or positioning throughout the marketing mix. "The brand is all about exhilaration and energy, and you see that in all that we do," says Scott Moffitt, director of marketing, Mountain Dew, "whether it is advertising, events, endorsements, or simply premiums, conveying the 'Dew-x-perience' is paramount."[3] Not only does Dew have strong advertising, but they have grassroots marketing programs and a sports-minded focus.

GETTING THE CAMPAIGN APPROVED

We now have a complete campaign: the ads, the media schedule, sales-promotion material, and costs for everything spelled out, ready for management's final approval. For that approval, it is wise to present a statement of the company's marketing goals. The objectives may be to launch a new product, to increase sales by x percent, to raise the firm's share of the market by z percent, or to promote a specific service of a firm. Next, the philosophy and strategy of the advertising are described, together with the reasons for believing that the proposed plan will help attain those objectives. Not until then are the ads or the commercials presented, along with the media proposal and the plans for coordinating the entire effort with that of the sales department.

What are the reasons for each recommendation in the program? On what basis were these dollar figures calculated? On what research were any decisions based? What were the results of preliminary tests, if any? What is the competition doing? What alternatives were considered? What is the total cost? Finally, how may the entire program contribute to the company's return on its investment? Those people who control the corporate purse strings like to have definite answers to such questions before they approve a total advertising program.

---

[3]"Being true to Dew," *BrandWeek*, 24 April 2000, 28–31.

RESEARCH—POSTTESTS

The final part of the campaign entails testing its success. Posttesting falls into two related stages. In the first, the expected results are defined in specific and measurable terms. What do you expect the advertising campaign to accomplish? Typical goals of a campaign are to increase brand awareness by 10 percent or improve advertising recall by 25 percent.

In the second stage, the actual research is conducted to see if these goals were met. Regardless of what research technique is used (for example, test markets, consumer panels), the problem is separating the results of the advertising campaign from consumer behavior that would have occurred in any case. That is, if we find that 20 percent of the population recognizes our brand at the end of a campaign, the question arises as to what the recognition level would have been if no advertising took place. To answer this question, a research design is often used as a pretest. The pretest is intended not only to provide a benchmark for the campaign, but also to determine reasonable goals for future advertising.

A 10-year study by Information Resources Inc.'s BehaviorScan showed that advertising produces long-term growth even after a campaign ends. The study emphasized TV campaigns and concluded the following:

- Increased ad weight alone will not boost sales.
- Typically, advertising for new brands, line extensions, or little-known brands produced the best incremental sales results.
- Campaigns in which the "message in the copy is new" or the media strategy had changed also produced good sales results.
- Results of copy recall and persuasion tests were unlikely to predict sales reliably.

The study also suggested that discounting results in "training customers to buy only on a deal," and the trade promotion actually worked against TV advertising. However, couponing often helped a brand message and spurred a sale.

The test was conducted in 10 markets with household panels of 3,000 respondents in each market. The commercials were transmitted to two equal groups of homes. This study compared purchase information obtained through scanners and a card encoded with demographic and other information that was presented at supermarket checkout stands.[4]

Campaign Portfolio

Corcoran Parking Services (Exhibit 22.7) copy says: "For less than it costs to pay off a tow truck once, you could have your very own parking space 24 hours a day. For a month. For more info call 919–956–7843." It plays with no parking signs. . . . no nothing, but lots of visual continuity.

These classic Verbatim ads (Exhibit 22.8) use unexpected visuals and the same message, "Verbatim tapes, optical disks. Your best defense against data loss."

Miravant Medical Technologies use strong continuity in their print campaign (Exhibit 22.9) from ad to ad. These interesting visuals and compelling copy appeal to a professional audience. As you would expect the copy is technical, "PhotoPoint, being developed by Miravant, utilizes highly-purified synthetic drugs which are activated by a special non-thermal light. Applications as diverse as cancer and eye disease. . . ."

---

[4]Gary Levin, "Tracing ads' impact," *Advertising Age,* 4 November 1991, 49.

Exhibit

22.7

How do you sell parking spaces? This campaign uses clever "No Parking" signs.

Courtesy: West & Vaughan.

Exhibit

22.8

These ads use strong visual continuity and the unexpected.

Courtesy: Loeffler Ketchum Mountjoy.

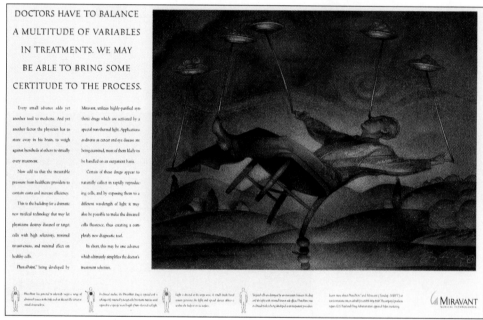

The steps in preparing a national campaign for a consumer product are the following:

1. Situation analysis
   a. Product analysis
   b. Prime-prospect identification
   c. Prime-prospects' problem analysis
   d. Competitive atmosphere and market climate
2. Creative objectives and strategy
   a. Determine specific copy claims
   b. Consider various advertising executions
   c. Begin creation of ads and commercials (and other integrated communications)

3. Media objectives
   a. Media strategy—includes prospect identification, timing, and creative considerations
   b. Media tactics
   c. Media scheduling

4. The sales-promotion plan (and/or other integrated programs)

5. Getting the campaign approved

6. Research posttests

In general, advertising campaigns need to have similarity from ad to ad. It may be visual, verbal, aural, or attitudinal. Campaigns should be designed to last and not be changed simply because you are bored with them.

REVIEW

1. What is the basic purpose of an ad campaign?

2. What is ad continuity?

3. What is involved in the situation analysis?

4. What are some of the means of guaranteeing continuity in a campaign?

TAKE IT TO THE NET

We invite you to visit the Russell/Lane page on the Prentice Hall Web site at **www.prenhall.com/myphlip** for end-of-chapter exercises and applications.

Case History

Mary Black Memorial Hospital

VASCULAR CENTER'S INTRODUCTORY CAMPAIGN

Mary Black Memorial Hospital in Spartanburg, South Carolina, opened their Vascular Center in October of 2000 with the hiring of two highly qualified vascular physicians from out of the area. Competitor Spartanburg Regional Hospital System had opened their Cardio-Vascular Center some time earlier with some awareness of their services available to the Upstate South Carolina community.

THE CHALLENGE

The marketing objective was to generate interest in the new Vascular Center from both potential patients and referring physicians in the Spartanburg community. A key part of the challenge was defining what vascular disease is when it is not connected with treatment of cardiac (heart) problems.

THE STRATEGY

Socoh Marketing LLC, a marketing consultancy to the hospital, recommended that Mary Black introduce this new service in a two-phase program. Phase One would define exactly what vascular disease is and some of the symptoms of this growing health care problem. Phase Two would introduce the two new physicians (and their team) as the "solution" to the problem. Importantly, the "newness" of the service was not to be emphasized as much as the fact that the new physicians were already busy fighting the effects of vascular disease.

THE CAMPAIGN

Two ads were chosen to define the "problem" of vascular disease to Spartanburg area residents. Headlines included, "263 arteries. 235 veins. Millions of capillaries. You've got one heck of a circulatory system." And, "Vascular Disease Will Leave You Without A Leg To Stand On. (Literally.)"

Phase Two, designed to provide a solution to the previously defined problem, featured a full-page ad with the headline, "Saving Lives. One day. One hour. One second at a time." A brochure, with additional information that an ad could not include for space limitation reasons, was available for those who inquired for more information. The brochure also included themes from the newspaper ads. Phase Two of the campaign also introduced the new campaign theme to be used hospital-wide: "The Hands of Healing at Mary Black."

Realistic photography was done during actual vascular procedures to demonstrate the "team approach" at Mary Black and to communicate that patients would experience a team that was already busy improving the health of those in the Spartanburg community.

RESULTS

Response to date has been very good. Telephone inquiries and interest in the free peripheral screening suggests that the Spartanburg community is not only interested in finding out more about this important health issue, but also equally interested in having Mary Black Memorial Hospital treat the disease for them. According to Cliff Floyd, public relations coordinator at Mary Black Memorial Hospital, "We brought in two high-profile physicians with national reputations to get this program started. The campaign allowed us to demonstrate the hospital had the solution to a problem that, although not as glamorous as open-heart surgery, affects thousands of local residents. And we did it in a way that showed we were experienced and competent in what we were doing—hitting the ground in full stride—even though it was a brand new department. With much credit to the campaign, referrals from other physicians are increasing and the physicians caseload continues to grow."

CREDITS:

Bill Fox, CEO/Mary Black Memorial Hospital
Cliff Floyd, Public Relations Coordinator/Mary Black Memorial Hospital
Brad Majors, President/Socoh Marketing LLC
Shannon Kohn, Copy/Design & Layout

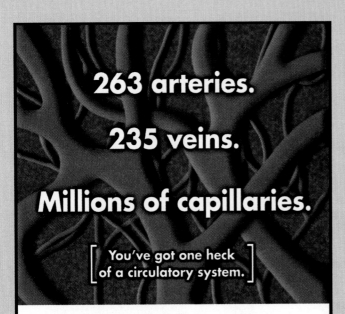

263 arteries.

235 veins.

Millions of capillaries.

[You've got one heck of a circulatory system.]

The Vascular Center at Mary Black Memorial Hospital wants to make sure every inch of it works perfectly.

As we age, the network of vessels that makes up our circulatory system can become narrowed or even blocked by years of fatty deposits. It's what doctors call vascular disease, and it's not pretty. The heart has to pump harder. All those blood vessels feel the strain, and even the smallest blockage can spell big trouble.

That's why the highly-skilled staff at Mary Black Memorial Hospital's new Vascular Center uses state-of-the-art diagnostic testing to locate potential problems early—before they become life-threatening—and help put patients back on the road to a long, healthy life.

Through the life-saving technology used each day at The Vascular Center, Mary Black Health System continues its commitment of providing the finest healthcare possible for our patients and our community. Call us for an appointment today—all those arteries, veins and capillaries of yours will be glad you did.

(864) 596-7428

THE VASCULAR CENTER
MARY BLACK HEALTH SYSTEM

1690 SKYLYN DRIVE, SUITE 350 • SPARTANBURG, SC 29307

VASCULAR DISEASE WILL LEAVE YOU WITHOUT A LEG TO STAND ON.

(LITERALLY.)

Each year in the US, over 100,000 amputations are performed on people who ignored the warning signs of vascular disease.

The folks at Mary Black Memorial Hospital's new Vascular Center want to make sure you're not one of them.

Pain and swelling in your legs. Cramps that keep you from a good night's sleep. Numbness. Tingling. These are all signs of vascular disease, and should never be ignored. What you might think is just "poor circulation" may in fact be a blockage that could lead to amputation, a heart attack or even a stroke.

The highly-skilled staff at Mary Black Hospital's new Vascular Center uses state-of-the-art diagnostic procedures to detect vascular problems early, and treat them in the least invasive way possible.

Through the life-saving technology used daily at The Vascular Center, Mary Black Health System continues its commitment of providing the finest healthcare possible for our patients and our community. Give us a call today for more information or to schedule an appointment. It could mean much more than just your legs. It could mean your life.

(864) 596-7428

THE VASCULAR CENTER
MARY BLACK HEALTH SYSTEM

1690 SKYLYN DRIVE, SUITE 350 • SPARTANBURG, SC 29307

FOR A FREE PERIPHERAL VASCULAR SCREENING, CALL (864) 573-3335.

The Hands of Healing
@ Mary Black

SAVING LIVES. ONE DAY. ONE HOUR. ONE SECOND AT A TIME.

Vascular disease never takes a vacation. Never rests. The highly-skilled team of physicians, nurses and technologists at Mary Black Memorial Hospital's new Vascular Center knows this all too well. That's why they work long and hard, fighting the causes and effects of vascular disease—and saving lives.

Leading The Vascular Center's team approach to patient care are two veterans in the field of vascular medicine—vascular surgeon, Dr. Jeffrey Rubin, and interventional radiologist, Dr. Neal Simmons. Both board-certified and extremely experienced, these doctors come well-equipped with the knowledge needed to diagnose problems early, and the guidance needed to help their team treat these problems in the least-invasive way possible.

Ever mindful of patient care, Drs. Rubin and Simmons don't think twice about asking other physicians from Mary Black Health System—like Wound Center and internal medicine physicians—to lend their expertise when the situation calls for it. They call it teamwork, and it makes a big difference in the lives of their patients.

The battle against vascular disease is a never-ending one. But through the use of the latest vascular technology and state-of-the-art diagnostic procedures, the Hands of Healing at Mary Black's new Vascular Center hope to change that. Call today for a free brochure that'll show you first-hand why they'll never stop fighting. And why they'll keep saving lives—one day, one hour, one second at a time.

(864) 596-7428

THE VASCULAR CENTER
MARY BLACK HEALTH SYSTEM

1690 SKYLYN DRIVE, SUITE 350 • SPARTANBURG, SC 29307

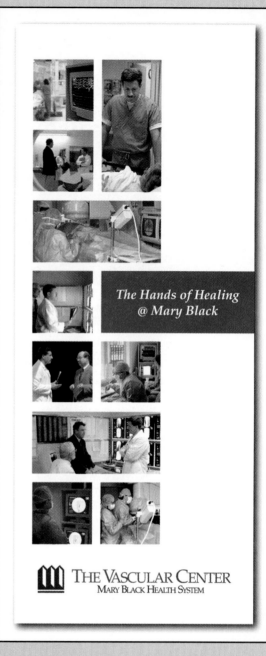

The Hands of Healing
@ Mary Black

THE VASCULAR CENTER
MARY BLACK HEALTH SYSTEM

Case History

Folks Southern Kitchens

Courtesy: Sheri Bevil Advertising

BACKGROUND

Folks Southern Kitchen is a restaurant chain in Atlanta and north Georgia that operates in one of the nation's most competitive restaurant environments. Their marketing budget is a fraction of Outback, Chili's, Applebees, etc., as a result, their share of voice is low in the marketplace. As a result, they must get more bang for their buck to compete.

The strategic analysis raised a number of issues to be considered. The need to build a sense of place; break the perception of parity; exploit the "home replacement" market; develop a strong acceptance among women, etc. There were a number of strengths.

- aided awareness of the brand was very high
- high percentage of repeat customers
- 26 percent of guests eat 2 to 3 times per month

There were weaknesses.

- many people still think of the chain's old name
- unaided awareness lower than that of major chains

COMPETITION

New competition literally opens weekly in the metro area. A few years ago Folks repositioned itself from competing with the family dining restaurants such as Shoney's, Ryan's, etc. to competing with Chili's and Applebee's.

TARGET

Historically, each store pulls a different mix of consumers—some a little older, a little better educated, more ethnic, etc. Their lunch attracts business and working people. Their dinner attracts families—from young families to grandparents in the middle income range. Extensive research indicated the need to target women 25–49.

CREATIVE

This quarterly campaign promoted, *Folks Home Fixins' . . . .our house or yours*. In addition to their regular menu, they promoted "Take Out" special meals, *Meal for 4*, which include choice of two vegetables, bread and a gallon of tea. Ads for catering and a Holiday Meal (for up to 16 people) were also needed.

MEDIA

Folks primarily uses radio, direct marketing, newspaper, outdoor, and a little television. Being a small chain, Folks isn't able to compete with the larger advertising budgets of many of their competitors. For this campaign, they didn't have the money to be in TV. Television has been used as part of a branding effort in previous campaigns. They also used FSI's and some 200,000 targeted direct mail. Since the restaurants aren't uniformly distributed through the DMA, a custom DMA was created from zip codes housing the restaurants and a ranker was run on this geography to determine which radio stations to use. Rankers were also run on the broader DMA because of its larger, more reliable sample size and because a number of the restaurant visitors come from the broader area. The Atlanta Journal–Constitution is used primarily for inserts, and suburban newspapers and smaller dailies are used as needed to support specific stores.

TOTAL PROGRAM

Currently, the advertising supports quarterly promotions. The marketing and promotion efforts include more than ads. The restaurant business demands a multitude of communications including: quarterly promotions, menu designs, table tents, kids coloring pieces, in-store promotions, employee motivation programs, public relations activities, etc.

RESULTS

The restaurant continues to keep their core customer and are aggressively seeking a broader customer base. Despite the increase in competition, Folks continues to steadily grow.

PART VI

Other Environments of Advertising

Chapter 23

Retail Advertising

CHAPTER OBJECTIVES

Both retailers and consumers have changed and are changing the way they do business and shop. The local media have responded to these changes. After reading this chapter you will understand:

>> retail trends

>> changes in retailing

>> differences in national and retail advertising

>> media in retailing

>> use of cooperative advertising

What is your idea of a retailer? Stores found in or near regional shopping malls: major department stores such as Lord & Taylor, JCPenney, Neiman-Marcus, Rich's, Bloomingdale's, Nordstrom, Marshall Fields, Macy's, and Parisian; specialty stores such as Victoria's Secret, The Limited, Casual Corner, Pottery Barn, Crate & Barrel, GAP, the Disney Store; discounters such as Target, Kmart, Wal-Mart, Books-A-Million, Stein-Mart, Best Buy, Circuit City, and Toys "R" Us; supermarkets such as Publix, Kroger, and A&P; and convenience stores such as 7-Eleven and Circle K. Or, do you include Cold Water Creek, Victoria's Secret catalog or Amazon.com, PlanetRx, and WebVan? This is only scratching the surface. There are thousands of independent clothing, shoe, grocery, drug, camera, and specialty shops that also come to mind. You probably don't always think of warehouse clubs such as Sam's; service retailers such as banks, restaurants, quick-service restaurants, video stores, and beauty salons as retailers.

Retailing has been defined as all activities in selling goods or services directly to consumers for their personal use. Most retailing takes place in retail stores, of course, but don't forget that nonstore retailing—mail, telephone, door-to-door, vending machines, CD-ROM catalogs. Southern States Volkswagen (Exhibit 23.1) uses the famous VW ad style of the original beetle in this "Deja vw." The message is basically, "Take one for a test drive and we think you'll agree."

Today's consumers have all kinds of retail outlets—category killers (superstores), Internet, CD-ROM catalogs, outlet malls, interactive television—all in a battle with department stores, specialty shops, and mom-and-pop stores. Printed catalogs and Web purchases are growing rapidly as consumers are finding they are pressed for time. It seems like retailing is "schizophrenic."

RETAIL BRANDING

National retail companies have refocused themselves to become more competitive and profitable or just to survive. Recently, Montgomery Ward department stores threw in the towel and closed. The popular GAP Inc. stumbled. It's a tough environment. It's a changing environment as consumer shopping patterns change. Talbot's sales started slowing in 1995. In response it tried to win younger customers, but the changes were too extreme and it turned off long-loyal customers. In 2000, Talbot's became a retailing darling with a stunning 21.9 percent increase in sales (Wal-Mart was less than 5 percent). To take care of core customers, Talbot's increased in-store focus groups, required managers to provide weekly summaries of customer comments—the message, "give us classic merchandise that is a little fashion-forward, but not so much that it crosses the line." They significantly increased marketing spending to $89 million. Their catalog continued to be the core vehicle and was mailed to

58 million customers. The ads were as understated as their clothes, one featured a woman in a red Talbot's suit at a voting machine with a young daughter in tow, "Clothes designed for models," the caption read. "Role models."[1]

Wendy Liebmann, partner in WSL Strategic Retail said research shows that consumers are shopping at more outlets per week. Since 1996, the *How America Shops* study found that consumers have doubled the number of stores they patronize during their weekly shopping trips. However, they are not making more trips (3.5 per week remains constant). They are making more stops on each trip.[2]

As we said, it is a tough environment. There are too many choices and too many stores. Retailers are now in the same position as packaged goods. Retailers must rise above the marketplace clutter and go to the emotional relationship with the customer. Retailers are beginning to understand that they can't tell consumers they have 40 percent off this week, and come back with the same message next week. JCPenney has developed a new formula to balance branding and sales by using a broadcast branding campaign supplemented by an increased use of radio to drive immediate sales. Titus MacDuff, a discount clothier, communicates luxury in their newspaper with, "If you don't have time to buy one of these suits, send your butler," and the body copy talks value and quality (Exhibit 23.2).

Retailers are constantly having to reinvent themselves whether they are brick-and-mortar or dot-com operations. Recently, the Disney Store redesigned their ail-

Exhibit 23.2

What do consumers want? Luxury, value and quality.

Courtesy: Howard, Merrell & Partners.

---

[1]"Talbots heats up by cooling down," *Business Week*, 18 December 2000, 98–104.
[2]Ira P. Scheiderman, "Niche marketers should follow old rules," *BrandMarketing*, August 2000, 6.

ing stores. The newer store was brighter, containing more merchandise that can be changed quickly to promote new products. Despite being about the same size as the old stores, the new ones have 40 percent more selling space by eliminating large backrooms. The stores are significantly less expensive to run. For example, new lighting costs were reduced by $40,000 per year over the old. This is another reminder that successful companies must have more than marketing to be successful.[3]

If we mention JCPenney or Lord & Taylor ads, images of their ad formats probably come to mind. Retail advertising takes on all forms and involves all media.

Retailers' Own Brands

A lot of retailers continue making more room in their stores for their own branded lines of clothes. There is more profit from selling their own brands—2 percent to 8 percent more on average—because they cut out the middleman. These private labels are attempts by department stores to differentiate themselves from competitors:

Saks: The Works, Essentials, and Real Clothes;
Carson Pirie Scott: Hasting & Smith, Great Lakes Recreation, and Architect;
Federated: INC, Charter Club, Alfani, and Badge;
JCPenney: Arizona;
Barney's: New York Collection.

"Private label is an important part of our strategy," says Joseph Feczko, senior vice president of marketing at Federated. "Before it was a commodity opportunity. Now, we are building brands with a personality. Five years ago only 5 percent of Federated's apparel was made up of its own brands, but that number is closer to 15 percent today."

Another factor in the equation is that many designer brands have opened their own stores in competition with department stores. Kurt Salmon Associates, a management consulting firm, says that every department store has Tommy Hilfiger and DKNY, and so there is no reason to go to Macy's over Bloomingdale's. The key is to make the private labels "branded." Advertising can help provide the proper image by evoking a certain mood or attitude. For example, the notion is that it will make wearers feel sexy (Calvin Klein) or sporty (Abercrombie & Fitch) or wealthy (Ralph Lauren). As Penney's vice president of brand development says, "You've got to get into people's head. You have to project an image." In 1990, JCPenney came up with the Arizona jeans line, which competes right next to Levi's. Sales have grown from $50 million a year to more than $1 billion.

Most retailers admit that their bread and butter is still among the established brands. They will establish a significant percentage of private label, but the dominant factor will always be the so-called market brands.

Before we discuss the advertising, let us take a look at retail trends and the nature and scope of the business. Marketing research indicates continued change in supermarkets, discount department stores, traditional department stores, megastores, specialty apparel shops, and shopping centers:[4]

Supermarkets are the most-shopped type of retail store, which probably isn't surprising. Despite their success, supermarkets are beset with two main competitive alternatives: discount super centers (e.g., Super Kmart, Super Wal-Mart, Super Target) and warehouse clubs (e.g., Sam's). Without more efficient operating procedures, supermarkets might be overtaken in the low-margin grocery business by wholesale clubs and super centers.

---

[3]Gary Gentile, "Disney unveils new store design and retail strategy," *The Atlanta Journal-Constitution,* 6 October 2000, D-9.
[4]Howard L. Green, "New consumer realities for retailers," *Marketing News,* 25 April 1994, 4.

Discount department stores continue to attract more shoppers every year, as they have for 20 years. Elements that will contribute to their continued growth in the next decade include operating efficiencies due to extensive use of technologies, emphasis on low prices, wide selections, and service.

Traditional department stores have experienced a steady decline in shopping frequency since 1974. Stores are attempting to be more consumer-service oriented.

Wholesale clubs have attracted close to 20 percent of shoppers, but have recently stumbled. Basically, warehouse clubs have moved away from their original concepts by adding bakeries and perishables because of increased competition from expanded format supermarkets and combination superstores. There is a saturation of wholesale clubs.

Big-box destination retailers, or mega warehouses, continue to boom in almost every category: computers, office supplies, children's toys, building materials, pet supplies, sporting goods, baby supplies, books, crafts, and so forth. In each category there has been a rush of expansion and market share, followed by consolidation to establish format dominance.

Specialty apparel retailers have been losing customers for the past 20 years as demographics and shopping habits have changed. The result has been a significant decline in shopping frequency over these years. The future will bring closings and consolidation as competition for apparel specialists in outlet centers and power strip centers intensifies.

Shopping centers have seen sales per square foot decline over the past 25 years. Customer visits to shopping centers have declined since 1980, and the number of stores visited per trip also declined. Trips to regional malls are declining almost as rapidly as visits to downtown areas. The future is bright only for those with superior regional access, densely populated trade areas, and economically strong anchors.

The Science of Shopping

What do shoppers love? Here are a few things that Paco Underhill, credited with being a founder of the science of shopping research, learned:[5]

- *Touch.* We live in a tactile-deprived society. Almost all unplanned buying is a result of touching, hearing, smelling, or tasting something on the premises of a store—which is why merchandising is so powerful.
- *Mirrors.* Mirrors slow shoppers in their tracks, which is very good for whatever merchandise is near.
- *Talking.* Stores that attract lots of couples, friends, or groups of shoppers usually do well.
- *Recognition.* Small, locally owned stores can learn customers' names. Given a choice, people will shop where they feel wanted and generally they'll pay a little more for the privilege.
- *Bargains.* At Victoria's Secret underwear is frequently piled on a table and marked four pair for $20, which sounds a lot better than the $5 a pair normally charged. At even the poshest stores, the clearance racks get shopped avidly.
- *Lines.* The memory of a good shopping trip can be wiped out at the checkout line.
- American shoppers automatically move to the right, the front right of any store is its prime real estate.
- All shoppers reach right, most of them being right-handed. If you're stocking cookies, for instance, the most popular brand goes dead center and the brand you're trying to build goes just to the right of it.

---

[5]Paco Underhill, *Why We Buy?* (New York: Simon & Schuster, 1999), 83–159.

- Getting customers to the back wall is a challenge. Blockbuster Video has trained its customers to go directly to the back wall to get the new releases.

Retailing Trend Capsule

People's shopping patterns have changed as the percentage of working women increased, and their lives have gotten busier. The rise of off-price and warehouse clubs as well as superstores has influenced the way people shop. Many traditional retailers can expect to wither away if they do not learn to adapt to the new environment. Let us examine a few trends in retailing.

- *Traditional retailers.* There is little doubt that typical smaller stores and retailers will continue to feel pressure from high-volume deep-discount competitors. Many will not be able to compete on price, but they can build their reputations in specific areas—as JCPenney did with quality, value-priced goods. Traditional retailers should consider adopting new strategies that combine traditional retail business with mail-order, Web-site, or transactional television components. The direct-response option should inspire more interest in the retailer.

- *Restaurants.* Competition will intensify as many markets have reached saturation. It is predicted that there will be a continuing boom in ethnic chains and broader menus. Established chains from Pizza Hut to Taco Bell have been successful in the "Americanization" of Italian and Mexican fare. Current growth areas include Chinese and possibly Thai or Indian. Biscuitville uses off-beat retro ads to compete with the larger chains. It promotes its niche benefits, "Before you eat that biscuit, maybe we should tell you where it's been"(see Exhibit 23.3).

- *Grocery stores.* The future of local grocery stores and chains may well depend on their ability to create individual store personalities, making geodemographic targeting essential.

Exhibit

23.3

This retro ad is so crowded it begs to be read.

Courtesy: Howard, Merrell & Partners.

- *Home shopping.* From the Internet to the home shopping networks on cable television, sales will climb. Although, the brick-and-mortar stores won't be replaced as some have predicted.
- *Fashion.* People will demand that clothing fit their style and lifestyle rather than fitting themselves into the latest styles. Office wear will continue to be the more functional and less formal trend. Evening wear will err on the side of simplicity and flexibility. This shift does not mean an abandonment of high style. But it will take less ornamentation to impress. Vanity will give way to value: A dress that goes to work should also be adaptable for dinner—either at home or on the town. The trend will favor clothing with lasting, go-anywhere, flexible, interchangeable lines, but distinction will not disappear.
- *Entertainment and freedom products.* The boom in home entertainment and personal technology products will expand. The electronic hearth will be the center of fun and family recreation for the Baby Boomer generation. The convenience these products give is their greatest selling point. Nomadic products empower consumers—or at least executives and professionals—by granting them control of the use of their time. Just think of the impact of cell phones and beepers.

CONSUMER ATTITUDES

Truthfulness of Ads

A recent Better Business Bureau study found a high degree of skepticism about truthfulness of local retail and sale ads. Only 6.6 percent of respondents from midwestern cities said retail ads were truthful; only about 13 percent thought sale ads were very truthful.

Among consumers' objections are the following:

- Insults to one's intelligence
- False and exaggerated savings claims
- False and exaggerated product claims

Consumers found car dealerships, appliance retailers, furniture dealers, and discount stores among those thought most guilty of deception.

Retail Satisfaction Profiles

Frequency Marketing, Inc. identifies the household member who does the most department store shopping by demographics, values and attitudes, and shopping behavior. The five classifications for women are as follows:[6]

- *Fashion Statements.* This is the most affluent and educated women's group. Because of their household incomes (average, $73,400), they have a high index of planned purchases and like being on the cutting edge of fashion. They account for 13.2 percent of primary department store shoppers.
- *Wanna-Buys.* This group has some of the same attitudes as the Fashion Statements, but don't have as much money (average, $40,600). They account for 18.6 percent of shoppers and buy on impulse.
- *Family Values.* This group accounts for one in six shoppers, and a large percentage have children living at home. Half have college degrees, and nine in ten are

---

[6]Susan Krafft, "How shoppers get satisfaction," *American Demographics,* October 1993, 13–16.

professionals. They are most likely to be planning to buy children's clothing, sporting goods, and a new washer or dryer.

- *Down to Basics.* This group has more children than the other groups (about 60 percent have children), a median age of 34, and an average household income of $32,600. Only 3 percent graduated from college. Despite having less money, they have attitudes similar to those in the Family Values group. They are careful spenders and buy little on credit. They check for sales and buy little other than for children. They account for roughly 16 percent of primary shoppers.

- *Matriarchs.* These are older women often living in retired households, and they are the most conservative group. Their favorite place to shop is in department stores; however, they have fewer planned purchases, and feel things change too fast these days.

Men fall into three classifications:

- *Patricians.* Just one in five in this group are married; they have the most money (average, $57,500) and are good targets for men's clothing, electronics, and sporting goods.

- *Practicals.* This group has an average income of $39,500. Members of this group are likely to be single. They prefer to pay with cash and are more likely to shop in discount stores. They are good targets for men's clothing, and even better for electronics and sporting goods.

- *Patriarchs.* This group is the lowest educated and has the lowest household incomes of male clusters. They are the oldest of the male clusters and buy primarily to replace worn-out items; however, they replace them with top-of-the-line items.

Integrated Marketing Includes P-O-P

Today's emphasis on integrated marketing and consistency of message means more involvement of point-of-purchase (P-O-P) at the early stages of creative planning. A Point-of-Purchase Advertising Institute study of brand management found that 40 percent of all in-store media is purchased from or developed by sales promotion and advertising agencies. Ad agencies were responsible for recommending 36.8 percent of temporary P-O-P and 27.8 percent of permanent in-store programs.

A Kmart study found that P-O-P merchandising increased sales of coffee by 567 percent, paper towels by 773 percent, and toothpaste by 119 percent.

A retailer survey indicated the greatest weaknesses of P-O-P displays provided by manufacturers include that they were inappropriate for the channel of trade (26.1 percent), the wrong size (22.6 percent), poorly built (19.2 percent), and unattractive (13.3 percent). The survey indicated that specialty stores, supermarkets, and department stores were the most receptive to P-O-P displays.

New research, "In-Store-Advertising Becomes Measured Medium," being conducted by the Point-of-Purchase Advertising Institute (POPAI) and the Advertising Research Foundation, hopes to put P-O-P on par with print and television.[7]

RETAILING IN THE LATE 1990s

Frequency Marketing's director of customer relations research says, "Retailing in the 1990s is all about understanding customers and catering to their specific needs regarding merchandise, quality, value, and customer service."

[7]Dick Blatt, "New research to transform the advertising industry," *BrandMarketing,* January 2000, 26.

The growth of discount retailing illustrates the changing value systems of today's shoppers. Shoppers can no longer be identified by a single value concept. They display multiple values. For example, consumers still prefer traditional department stores for adult fashions, but even the most upscale shoppers look to discount stores for children's clothing.[8]

NATIONAL AND RETAIL ADVERTISING

The primary difference between consumer product advertising and retail advertising is that product advertising is generally feature and benefit oriented, whereas much of retail advertising is price and availability oriented. As we said earlier in this chapter, more national retailers are running image advertising to develop the public's perceptions about the store as a brand, but the bulk of retail advertising features a number of products promoting price. In national advertising, the advertising says, "Buy this brand or product at any store." In retail advertising, the ad says, "Buy this product here. Better come early."

In national advertising, it is difficult to trace the sales effect of a single insertion of an ad. Even tracing the effect of a series of ads takes time and is difficult unless the series runs exclusively in one medium. In retail advertising, on the other hand, an advertiser can usually tell how effective it is by noon of the day after the ad appeared.

TYPES OF RETAIL ADVERTISING

Retail advertising is as diverse as the establishments that use it. However, there are certain patterns of retail advertising that reflect the character and goals of various retailers. The Newspaper Advertising Bureau has suggested six categories of retail advertising:[9]

- *Promotional.* Here the emphasis is on sales and high sale volume at a reduced price. Discount stores such as Kmart are the primary users of this type of advertising.

- *Semipromotional.* In this type of advertising, sale offerings are interspersed with many regular-priced items. Most department stores and supermarkets use this advertising strategy.

- *Nonpromotional.* Many small shops and specialty stores adopt a no-sale advertising strategy. Their advertising plays down price and emphasizes dignified appeals featuring the quality of the merchandise and the expertise of their sales staffs.

- *Assortment ads.* The intent of these ads is to show the large variety of products. The ads have an institutional aspect in that they promote the store as a place for one-stop shopping.

- *Omnibus ads.* Similar to assortment ads, omnibus ads are usually more clearly sales oriented. These ads may feature related items or a variety of nonrelated items from several departments.

- *Institutional ads.* Many stores use advertising that emphasizes their unique character. Institutional ads must be careful to tell a story of importance to a store's customers.

---

[8]Dayton's is top retailer in customer satisfaction survey," *Marketing News,* 6 June 1994, 8.
[9]The I-Wonder-How-to-Set-Up-an-Advertising-Program-and-How-Much-to-Budget Book, a publication of the Newspaper Advertising Bureau.

	JAN	FEB	MAR	APR	MAY	JUN	JUL	AUG	SEP	OCT	NOV	DEC
All stores and services (%)	10.0	7.2	7.0	8.2	8.1	8.7	8.5	8.4	8.8	8.2	8.3	8.6
Appliance stores	7.2	6.6	7.7	7.7	8.6	8.7	8.9	8.5	7.7	8.3	9.1	10.9
Auto dealers (new domestic)	7.1	7.5	7.4	8.8	8.6	9.2	9.1	8.9	9.2	8.5	8.2	7.6
Auto dealers (new import)	7.4	7.2	9.0	8.6	9.3	9.1	8.8	9.6	8.1	8.2	7.4	7.3
Beer	7.7	7.3	8.4	8.2	9.2	9.3	9.4	9.6	8.1	8.3	7.6	7.0
Bookstores	9.4	6.4	6.5	6.4	6.9	6.9	6.9	10.0	10.1	7.9	8.6	14.0
Bridal market	5.0	5.8	6.4	7.6	9.8	11.4	9.3	10.5	9.6	9.0	7.7	8.0
Department stores	5.5	5.9	7.8	7.6	7.9	7.6	7.1	8.5	7.6	8.2	10.4	16.0
Discount stores	5.8	5.9	7.6	7.7	8.2	8.1	7.6	8.4	7.6	8.2	10.2	14.7
Drugstores	7.8	7.5	8.2	7.9	8.3	8.1	8.0	8.4	8.0	8.4	8.5	11.0
Fabric and sewing stores	7.5	7.2	8.3	7.7	7.7	7.2	7.9	8.5	8.2	10.0	10.6	9.2
Fast food	7.3	7.2	8.3	8.2	8.6	8.9	9.1	9.2	8.3	8.4	8.1	8.4
Jewelry stores	5.6	6.7	6.5	6.6	8.5	7.4	6.9	7.3	6.6	7.1	9.2	21.5
Restaurants	7.5	7.3	8.2	8.3	8.7	8.8	8.9	9.2	8.3	8.5	8.1	8.2
Shoe stores	6.4	6.1	8.8	8.5	8.5	8.1	7.6	9.9	8.4	7.9	8.6	11.2
Women's wear stores	6.3	6.1	8.1	8.1	8.5	7.8	7.7	8.5	8.0	8.3	9.4	13.1

Exhibit 23.4

Advertisers' Seasonal Business Cycles

Courtesy: Radio Advertising Bureau.

Retailer's Business Cycles

Retailers don't sell the same amount of merchandise every month. Selling cycles vary according to the product or service category. Exhibit 23.4 shows that August is the best month for restaurants, followed by July and June; new domestic auto dealers' best months are May and August; November is the month for carpet; December sales are double any other month for jewelry stores; November is tops for fabric and sewing stores; and May tops hardware store sales. Retailers use this information in planning their advertising and promotional efforts.

Special Promotion Times

It is no surprise that there are special promotions for Christmas, Mother's Day, President's Day, Memorial Day, and Father's Day. The Folks Southern Kitchen ad (Exhibit 23.5) promotes Father's Day for one of their stores, "Dad, Father, Daddy, Papa, Pop." But there are many, many other promotional opportunities, including Boss's Day, National Singles Week, Pancake Day, National Stress Awareness Day, National Lingerie Week, Take Our Daughters to Work Day, National Hugging Day, National Library Week, Girl's Club Week, Jewish Heritage Month, Senior Citizens Month, National Pet Week, National Diabetes Month, National Pie Day, Better Sleep Month, National Decorating Month, National Barbecue Month, Nurse's Day, International Pickle Week, Chocolate Awareness Month, and National Anti-Boredom Month—you get the idea. There are lots of advertising and promotional opportunities.

In June alone, the promotional opportunities include the following:

Bridal fairs/weddings
Belmont Stakes racing
Summer begins
Adopt-A-Shelter Cat Month

National Skin Safety Month
National Fragrance Week
National Fishing Week
Pet Appreciation Week

Exhibit 23.5

Special days deserve special ads or promotions.

Courtesy: Sheri Bevil Advertising.

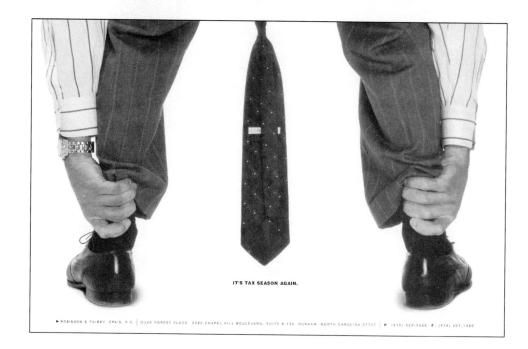

IT'S TAX SEASON AGAIN.

Dairy Month

National Beef Steak Month

National Fresh Fruit/Vegetable Month

National Frozen Yogurt Month

National Iced Tea Month

National Rose Month

National Little League Week

Flag Day

Father's Day

Turkey Lover's Month

National Pest Control Month

THE RETAIL ADVERTISING MIX

Like other styles of advertising, retail advertising must (1) determine overall goals and objectives to the marketing and advertising programs, (2) identify target markets, and (3) develop a copy and media strategy to reach these targets. But the way in which retail advertising strategy is carried out differs markedly from that in which national advertising (which we discussed earlier) is carried out. Even tax preparers and fitness programs can reach consumers through retail advertising (Exhibit 23.6).

A retail advertising campaign usually includes media other than newspapers. Radio advertising is used frequently with great success because it is reasonable in cost and easy to produce, and it can be changed within hours if necessary. Television is also used more frequently now, although not as often as radio. Many successful campaigns use brochures and catalogs. Frequently, the catalogs are distributed with Sunday newspapers. Outdoor and shelter ads may also be used effectively. OfficeMax.com promotes their benefit of "taking control" (see Exhibit 23.7).

Selecting local media is a "How best to . . . ?" problem: how best to use newspapers, radio, television, outdoor, direct-mail—the chief media—alone or in combination to sell merchandise and attract store traffic.

Newspapers in Retailing

Newspapers are the primary local advertising vehicle, although they don't have the dominance among retailers they once enjoyed. Research indicates that consumers as well as retailers regard newspapers as the prime medium for local advertising.

Exhibit
23.7

Retailers also use
out-of-home media to
promote their services.
Courtesy: OfficeMax.com.

Many retailers may advertise in several newspapers in a metro area—the suburban papers could be dailies or weeklies. Folks Southern Kitchens advertises in a number of papers (for example, Atlanta, Gainesville, Rome, Marietta, Cartersville, etc.). Exhibit 23.8 shows an ad for one of the suburban papers that is slightly different from those run in Atlanta. One difference in the ad is promoting a specific store location.

Today's newspapers offer a retailer more than just retail advertising space. For example, the *Atlanta Journal-Constitution*'s services are typical of metro newspapers:

■ *Preprinted inserts.* A Zoned Area Preprints program offers select or total market coverage. Advertising preprints are inserted directly into the newspaper and are distributed to subscribers and single-copy purchasers.

■ *Direct-mail.* The ZIP program allows advertisers to reach nonsubscribers by mailing their preprint to selected zip codes. This program enables advertisers to take advantage of less-expensive newspaper distribution to reach subscribers while using direct-mail for nonsubscribers. Shared mail, solo mail, and

a variety of targeting options are also available. Exhibit 23.9 is an example of a flyer telling consumers about a store location change.

■ *Extra editions.* Some seven extra community editions with 11 advertising zones cover the metro area, enabling advertisers to target primary market areas.

■ AJC Direct. The most desirable households are targeted with their carrier program to deliver advertising, product samples, magazines, catalogs and other material targeted to some 350,000 upscale households. The paper can also merge the advertiser's customer names and credit card lists with the newspaper's subscriber list and eliminate any duplication.

As you can see, these newspaper services can be tailored to the advertiser's needs.

Starch Research found that the average adult newspaper ad-noted score for a full-page ad was 42 percent (men scored 34; women, 48); the half-page score was 34 percent (men, 32; women, 35); and the quarter-page score was 23 percent (men, 23; women, 29). The noted score for all ads was 28 percent (men, 24; women, 31). Remember that a noted score indicates the percentage of newspaper readers who reported seeing the ad being measured.

Exhibit 23.10 shows a chart indicating product categories. You can see that the noted scores vary by product category. To use this chart, choose the business type and move across the chart to the appropriate ad size. The numbers show the percentage of male and female adult newspaper readers seeing ads of that size and business category. By multiplying this percentage times the circulation of the newspaper, you can calculate how many newspaper readers will likely see an ad.

Thank You for Twenty Years!

We're moving to a new location very soon.
The good news - the new location is
only a few miles down the road:

**2590 Spring Road
at Cumberland Parkway**

Y'all be sure to come see us real soon!

As you await the new opening in just a few days,
please visit our other nearby Folks locations:

Mableton • 5400 Floyd Rd. • 770-739-5180
Marietta • 2031 Cobb Pkwy. at Windy Hill • 770-952-5111

Cooking Soon in Your Neighborhood!

Until then, enjoy one of our other 19 locations:

Atlanta
North Druid Hills at I-85
404-321-0300

Cartersville
904 Joe Frank Harris Pkwy.
770-382-6311

Conyers
1081 Iris Drive
770-922-2830

Cumming
Hwy. 20 at GA 400
770-844-9633

Decatur
Lawrenceville Hwy.
at Market Square
404-321-3948

Douglasville
Hwy. 5 at I-20
770-949-8400

Gainesville
1500 Browns Bridge Rd.
770-534-1300

Jonesboro
6564 Tara Blvd.
770-968-8965

Mableton
5400 Floyd Road
770-739-5180

Marietta
Cobb Pkwy. at Windy Hill
770-952-5111

Marietta
Sandy Plains Rd. at
Canton Hwy.
770-425-2322

Norcross
5119 Jimmy Carter Blvd.
770-446-8266

Rome
Shorter Ave. at
Gala Shopping Center
706-235-4666

Roswell
Alpharetta Hwy. at
Holcomb Bridge Rd.
770-998-2100

Smyrna
Concord Rd. at
South Cobb Dr.
770-432-7333

Snellville
2277 East Main St.
770-972-3060

Stockbridge
Hwy. 138 at
Hannover Pkwy.
770-474-6668

Tucker
LaVista Rd. at
Northlake Pkwy.
770-493-6925

Woodstock
Hwy. 92 at I-575
770-516-0308

**Exhibit
23.9**

These flyers tell of
location change.
Courtesy: Sheri Bevil Advertising.

Product	Men (%)				Women (%)			
	1 Page	3/4 Page	1/2 Page	All Ads	1 Page	3/4 Page	1/2 Page	All Ads
Appliance	33	33	25	23	31	30	28	25
Department stores	31	32	26	26	58	55	47	48
Drugstores	40	41	34	27	56	51	47	39
Food stores	28	20	24	22	50	42	41	42
Lawn/garden	46	27	39	28	33	38	37	32
Shoe stores	28	—	22	18	56	—	59	36
Sporting goods	51	40	38	29	50	27	19	20

Exhibit

23.10

Newspaper Ad Noted Scores

Source: Roper Starch.

Radio in Retailing

Radio spot scheduling is very flexible. Promotions can easily be adapted to radio. Folks Restaurants has used radio-remote broadcasts for new store openings in the Atlanta area with great results, in addition to their regular radio scheduled promotions (Exhibit 23.11). Retailers often use radio to supplement ads in other media because it is a good reminder medium. As indicated earlier, radio is a segmented medium enabling a retailer to reach certain targeted consumers. On the negative side, in large markets a retailer may have to buy a number of different stations to reach their prospects because the share of audience of a single station is relatively small.

Television in Retailing

Television became a major force in retailing during the 1980s. Much of the retail advertising dollars spent has been a result of the growth of independent TV station and cable outlets with relatively low advertising rates.

Most major markets have more than one cable system, which means an advertiser with stores on one side of town can simply target prospects by buying only the cable system(s) that reach their prospective customers. At the same time, there are companies that will allow an advertiser to make one buy and reach multiple cable systems. Advertisers can buy cable networks such as CNN, ESPN, USA, CNN's Headline News, the Weather Channel, MTV, VH-1, and so forth because of the availability of time for local advertisers, usually at rates significantly lower than network stations in the same market. The audience is probably significantly smaller at any given time on a specific cable network than the number of households hooked to cable, which means a high cost per thousand, but the cost is within the budgets of even the smallest retail advertiser.

Database Marketing

Database-driven direct marketing can target specific consumers. Instead of targeting all teens, it may allow a marketer to target teens who have purchased a video

Exhibit

23.11

Folks Southern Kitchen
Radio.

Courtesy: Sheri Bevil Advertising.

Home Fixins' 60-sec. Radio (Open with jingle, announcer, end with jingle.)

Announcer: Rick Pratt

Hi, I'm Rick Pratt, the one and only original owner of all 19 Folks Southern Kitchen Restaurants, locally owned and operated since 1978. Unlike a lot of chain restaurants, my Folks take pride in serving quality Southern food and heaps of Southern hospitality. Right now, Folks has some great new Home Fixins' for you and your family. You can enjoy them in our home or pick them up to eat at yours. Complete meals include Homemade Meat Loaf, slow-cooked Pot Roast, savory Pork Tenderloin with a rich gravy, or oven-baked Turkey and Cornbread Dressing . . . Home Fixins' by Folks will satisfy your family's appetite.

game worth more than $50 in the last 90 days. Most major retailers have a program to make better use of their customer database. Building customer loyalty through retention and upgrading of most-valued customers is a major item for most retailers. One-to-one marketing is another rising tool. Many retailers are participating in the direct-to-buyer market; with never-before available opportunities and mass marketing taking a back seat, efforts such as permission marketing and direct-mail take off. Lands' End has said there was a tendency when e-business started to think business would shift away from telemarketing call centers, but people are saying customers will contact us however they want to.

Measured marketing, a term used by supermarkets that issue plastic cards to their customers so they can build a database, permits the stores to identify their best customers and treat them differently. Customers in the top 10 percent group make 1.8 visits per week and spend $3,674 per year—double what the next best decile spends. The top 30 percent of the cardholders accounts for roughly 75 percent of the store's total sales.[10]

Retail On-Line

Amazon.com is one of the e-tail giants, but retail on-line success stories have been few and far between. Dell became the computer leader by realizing that it was cost-effective to configure machines to each buyer's specs, and ever since, brands have been communicating to consumers that they're the boss. Gateway also could be bought on-line, and then came a brick-and-mortar company too. Other commodity products that appeal to the Web's demographics, such as books and music, also have been successful. Some ticketing and travel services routinely do well. Sellers of broad-based consumer goods have been slow to grow. GAP has had success with their Web site games and promotions and began developing a selling presence in 1997. They found that people stayed on their site 50 percent longer than the average site. An analyst commented that GAP had an excellent demographic fit with Web users, and many of their products, such as T-shirts and socks, don't usually require trying on for size. But GAP continues to struggle on and off-line.[11] "One year as an e-tailer on the Internet is like dogs years," says Jane Saltzman who managed the private label programs at Macy's before jumping to eToys. Internet brands are just beginning to build familiarity and reputation and are moving to more private labels to increase profits.[12]

Enriched e-mails. Enriched e-mail offers retailers and e-tailers immediacy, response tracking, and generation of leads. A number of companies will ask people in their on-line database if they can send them e-mails about special deals. E-mail is getting more popular with marketers as it gets better. If response to enriched e-mails is 10 percent, according to Forrester Research, marketers using enriched e-mail would see a response rate increase to 12.5 percent, according to Grey Email Group.[13]

Cinema Commercials

Retailers, realizing that prospective customers frequently are nearby in a shopping center's adjoining cinema complexes, have moved into that medium.

Rod Eaton, Target's director of sales promotion, says that the idea should be a movie and not a commercial. Many advertisers are reluctant to enter the medium

[10]Arthur Middleton Hughes, "The real truth about supermarkets—and customers," *DM News*, 3 October 1994, 40.

[11]Alice Z. Cuneo, "The GAP readies electronic commerce plan for web site," *Advertising Age*, 23 June 1997, 18.

[12]Elaine Underwood, "Storebrands, without the store," *Superbrands*, 19 June 2000, 32.

[13]Eileen P. Gunn, "Marketers keen on enriched e-mail," *Advertising Age*, 16 October 2000, s12.

for that reason, because they believe messages should stick with soft sell, or risk incurring the ire of moviegoers.[14] Target has run spots in Screenvision Cinema Network consisting of 8,200 screens in 2,000 theaters. Target has run shorter versions of the cinema advertising on TV. Target, GAP, Sears, and food retailers such as McDonald's and Outback, have used cinema.

Outdoor Out-of-Home

Retailers have always used outdoor advertising as a reminder or to tell consumers that a store is down the street. Often it is used in conjunction with other media. Exhibit 23.7 shows a shelter ad promoting the convenience of a dot-com business of a brick-and-mortar company.

Cooperative Advertising

The simplest definition of cooperative advertising is a joint promotion of a national advertiser (manufacturer) and a local retailer on behalf of the manufacturer's product or service in the retail store. Co-op advertising is prepared by the advertiser and is available for the local merchant to advertise and share as much as 50 percent of the advertising cost. Therefore, a retailer that uses a lot of cooperative advertising could double its advertising budget.

Chief advantages are the following:

- Cooperative advertising helps the buyer stretch his or her advertising capability.
- It may provide good artwork, with good copy of the product advertised—which is especially important to the small store.
- It helps the store earn a better volume discount for all its advertising.

Cooperative advertising works best when the line is highly regarded and is either a style or some other kind of leader in its field.

Chief disadvantages are the following:

- Although the store pays only 50 percent of the cost, that sum may be disproportionate for the amount of sales and profit the store realizes.
- Most manufacturers' ads emphasize the brand name at the expense of the store name.

Co-op requires a lot of paperwork. Most newspapers and some radio stations have co-op advertising departments that help retailers seek co-op allowances from manufacturers and supply affidavits and other documentation required by a manufacturer. Many small advertisers find the paperwork prohibitive, and the media try to make it easier in hopes of getting their share of the advertising. In some cases, the retailer may have a business department inside their advertising department to make sure the store collects all the money due it.

SUMMARY

More retailers are turning to branding to compete with the competition. The media mix has expanded for retailers over recent years. Newspapers still account for the majority of retail advertising, but retailers use virtually every medium to promote

---

[14]Alice Z. Cuneo, "Now playing: GAP, Target take retail to the movies," *Advertising Age*, 9 June 1997, 18.

their stores, products, and services. Consumers are looking for ways to save time and money. As a result, direct marketing and on-line buying are increasing. As with business in general, the retail business has been and is significantly changing. Part of the change is driven by the way consumers shop—from supermarkets, discount department stores, wholesale clubs, shopping centers, and malls, to big-box category killers—shopping patterns have changed.

These changes have given rise to sophisticated segmentation and niche marketers. Retail advertising is done by local merchants or service organizations to attract customers. Retailers use business-cycle information to decide when to advertise. Cooperative advertising offers retailers allowances from manufacturers that can actually double the advertising budgets.

As retailers get more sophisticated marketing information, the media have responded with services. For example, newspapers offer many extra services (direct-mail, zones, research, and other services) to compete with the broadcast media and direct-mail.

REVIEW

1. Define retailing.
2. What is the primary difference between consumer product advertising and retail advertising?
3. What are the three best months of sales for bookstores?
4. What is a zoned area preprint?
5. What are the advantages of cooperative advertising to a retailer?

TAKE IT TO THE NET

We invite you to visit the Russell/Lane page on the Prentice Hall Web site at **www.prenhall.com/myphlip** for end-of-chapter exercises and applications.

Case History

Morgan Imports Retail Branding Magazine Campaign

Eran Thomson and Robert Shaw West of West & Vaughan indicated that Morgan Imports wanted a less retail approach, more of a brand image. They felt they were starting to blend in with the big "imports" chains you see shouting, "Baskets. From just $5.99." Morgan wanted to be known for offering a bit of foreign intrigue, not a bargain on some cheap-looking thing made in New Jersey.

Morgan stocks unique, hand-crafted items usually in very limited supply, from around the world. West & Vaughan wanted to create the atmos-

phere of a warehouse full of surprising things, all fresh off the boat, just waiting to be discovered. They decided to shoot only four base photos—two crates, a carton and a sack—and put headlines on them digitally.

West says in future ads, "we can do frequent, inexpensive copy changes to accommodate new inventory and keep the campaign from becoming repetitive."

Exhibit
23.12

This branding approach is clearly different from the competition. These Morgan import ads will stand out from the crowd.
Courtesy: West & Vaughan.

(a)

(b)

(c)

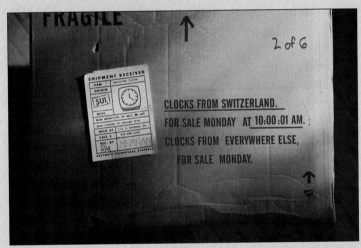

(d)

Chapter 24

International Advertising

CHAPTER OBJECTIVES

Not long ago, international advertising was considered a specialized and separate marketing category. Major corporations had distinct international divisions with their own sales forces, marketing and advertising executives, and distribution channels. Today, international marketing is more likely to be part of the mainstream of business operations as American companies look abroad for new customers. At the same time, these firms are developing strategies to compete with hundreds of foreign-based multinational corporations that have invaded the United States. After reading this chapter, you will understand:

>> American advertising in a global economy

>> how marketing strategy must adapt to multinational competition

>> the cultural and political components of international business

>> how advertising agencies organize to serve multinational clients

>> centralized versus localized marketing strategy and management

International marketing and advertising are expanding during an interesting period in global politics. The following lead to a news story offers some insight into the current state of global marketing.

> Coca-Cola Co., a symbol for capitalism around the world, entered North Korea on Wednesday, just two days after the U.S. government lifted most economic sanctions.[1]

---

[1] Henry Unger, "Coca-Cola's in North Korea," *The Atlanta Journal*, 22 June 2000, G-1.

THE MULTINATIONAL CORPORATION

The keystone of the global economy is the multinational corporation. The concept of the multinational corporation is largely a post–World War II creation that consists of companies that offer products and services around the world, taking advantage of opportunities to increase sales and profits on behalf of their stockholders. At one time, multinational marketing was largely confined to American companies, with few competitors headquartered outside the United States. While America still provides the majority of multinational firms, it is a stage shared with companies located in a number of countries.

A review of the "Fortune Global 500" over the last few years shows that the list of companies is becoming more and more diverse in terms of their country of origin. As recently as 20 years ago, the United States was home to more than half of these multinational corporations. Today, only 36 percent of the world's largest companies are U.S. corporations. Similar situations are found in Europe where 30 percent of the top 500 are located (down from 35 percent in 1995), and Japan where 23 percent of these companies are headquartered as contrasted to 21 percent in 1998. Overall, 40 percent are headquartered in North America, 35 percent in countries of the European Union, and 23 percent in Japan.[2]

In 1990, the rest of the world outside these three areas contributed about 2 percent to the list of "Fortune 500" companies. Today, China and South Korea have more than 4 percent of these multinationals. The trend will continue as more and more corporations in emerging economies gain the economic power to compete for world markets. Regardless of their location, the size and scope of these companies are truly staggering. For example, these 500 companies account for more $12 trillion in sales—40 percent of the world's Gross Domestic Product—and employ some 44 million people. As we discuss global marketing and advertising, we need to keep in mind the control exerted by these relatively few companies and the concentration of economic power they represent.

Despite their importance, multinational companies are finding they indeed live in interesting times. Clearly, communication technology, diplomacy, and improved transportation are making international marketing and advertising more efficient. On the other hand, a growing sense of nationalism and an increasing protectionism of local customs and traditions are impeding foreign expansion into many markets. Perhaps people are reacting to a communication revolution that threatens to merge and blur the differences in nations. Whatever the reason, a prevailing sense of isolationism is a factor that international marketing must consider with great care.

Procter & Gamble operates in almost 150 countries and sells its 300 brands to millions of people each day. Executives at Procter & Gamble and their counterparts operating on the same stage must be anthropologists and sociologists as well as marketers. Success at this level relates as much to a sensitivity to other people, a willingness to learn, and an openness to new ideas and cultures as it does to business expertise. In the global arena, it is important to view differences in lifestyle and traditions, as well as consumer behavior, objectively rather than making judgments about customs or cultures in other parts of the world. "Marketing across borders requires specialized skills to meet the diverse challenges of language, culture, economics, regulation and distribution. Worldwide expansion of brands is essential to the continued growth of companies [in the] 21st century."[3]

---

[2]"The global 500 list," *Fortune*, 24 July 2000, 227.
[3]*Advertising Age International*, Asia-Pacific Media Map.

In a book entitled *Global Literacies: Lessons on Business Leadership and National Culture*, the authors examine many of the problems and opportunities for international business. Decisions facing the multinational marketer range from dietary differences—in India McDonald's makes hamburgers from lamb instead of beef in deference to Hindu religious beliefs—to language—"Finger lickin' good" translates to "Eat your fingers off" in Chinese. But as important as these details are, the overall theme of the book is that American businesses should prepare for a new style of management in a global economy. A style that rewards those who are willing to become a citizen of the new worldwide environment.

The changing complexion of global advertising and marketing is readily apparent from the diversification of ownership of multinational companies throughout the world. At the end of World War II, international business was largely confined to the exportation of American products, management expertise, and marketing and advertising know-how to other countries. Today, the United States is a net importer of goods by a significant margin and a number of major industries such as textiles and electronics, once dominated by American companies, are virtually all foreign owned.

While the United States remains the principal producer and consumer of advertising, the expansion of advertising abroad is growing rapidly. This expansion will be accelerated as more and more countries of the Far East, Middle East, and Latin America increase individual consumption of a variety of goods and services. Today, three of the top six advertising agencies are headquartered outside the United States. Advertising's global presence is demonstrated by the location of major advertising centers. As measured by the value of advertising created and placed from agencies in a city, the top advertising markets are:

1. New York
2. Tokyo
3. London
4. Chicago
5. Paris
6. Los Angeles
7. Detroit
8. Sao Paulo
9. Minneapolis
10. San Francisco
11. Milan
12. Frankfurt[4]

Clearly, this list shows that advertising success and expertise are not confined to any country or region.

Another indicator of the worldwide reach of multinational companies and their marketing efforts can be seen in the percentage of United States versus worldwide advertising spending. For example, traditional American businesses such as Coca-Cola, Procter & Gamble, and Colgate-Palmolive spend more than 50 percent of their advertising budgets abroad. Close behind are other American industrial giants such as General Motors, Johnson & Johnson, and Ford that spend as much as 40 percent of their advertising abroad.

The advertising dollars allocated by these international companies to overseas markets are impressive. However, they don't tell the full story of the genesis of this economic expansion. It can be argued that the global business revolution of the last decade is fundamentally a communication revolution. Around the world, even in emerging countries, ownership of communication devices far outweighs any other appliances or household convenience. For example, in the Netherlands, 22 percent of households have a microwave oven, compared to 95 percent with a television set and 50 percent with a video recorder. Similarly, in Spain 5 percent of households own a clothes dryer while 98 percent own a television and 67 percent have a cassette recorder. These statistics are duplicated throughout the world. In some coun-

---

[4]"Agency report," *Advertising Age*, 19 April 1999, S16.

tries household television ownership is ahead of homes with bathrooms or even running water. From a political and social standpoint, communication allows people throughout the world, most especially in formerly totalitarian countries, to see what is taking place in democratic, economically advanced countries. In country after country, communication has resulted in demands for more open political systems, which inevitably turn to demands for more economic freedom and choice. Without an expansion of communication, it is doubtful that the current political and economic environment would exist.

THE INTERNET AND INTERNATIONAL COMMUNICATION

While a number of factors have played a role in the emergence of international marketing, we can expect an accelerated pace as the Internet and other new communication technology become commonplace around the world. For a number of years, Internet usage was overwhelmingly located in the United States. However, that is quickly changing as household Internet usage increases in country after country. Projections are that by 2005 Web users will be non-English speaking by a wide majority (see Exhibit 24.1) and the U.S. share of the worldwide on-line population will drop from 43 percent in 1999 to approximately 25 percent in 2005.

While the Internet can provide businesses with instantaneous worldwide communication, the potential for a truly integrated world marketing community is probably some time in the distance, if it happens at all. The distinct character and preferences within the Japanese, German, Brazilian, and American markets are not going to disappear overnight regardless of technology. Multinational firms realize that to be successful on-line communication must relate to the interests of consumers in specific countries. "[The Internet] should give the advantage to firms that understand the subtleties of particular national markets. Smart U.S. firms will hire the local talent they need to get this kind of understanding. . . ."[5]

A significant area where the United States lags behind many other developed countries is wireless technology. Ironically, the fact that most countries do not have the sophisticated technical infrastructure of the United States meant that they had to establish Internet over wireless systems. Most experts think that it is wireless technology and communication that will ultimately fuel the next generation of e-commerce and e-media. In recent years, wireless technology, such as cell phones mutating into all-purpose, two-way communication devices, show that the wireless revolution is quickly moving to the United States.

The Internet provides the means to reach international market segments based on both language and local preferences. So-called cultural Internet is being developed where a core service may provide information and advertising in Spanish to a worldwide Hispanic market. However, within this larger service, there will be numerous opportunities for targeting. For example, StarMedia provides on-line

Exhibit

24.1

Get Ready for Non-English-Speaking Web Users

Does your Web site offer visitors the choice to view its pages in multiple languages? Come 2002, the majority of Internet users will speak a language other than English. This trend is expected to continue and by 2005, non-English speakers will account for six out of 10 Internet users, predicts Computer Economics, a Carlsbad, CA-based independent research firm that supports IT decision makers.

From: Target Marketing, September 1999, 30.

Internet Usage According to Language

	1999	2001	2003	2005
English-Speaking	91,969,151 (54%)	108,282,662 (51%)	124,265,453 (46%)	147,545,824 (43%)
Non-English Speaking	79,094,449 (46%)	104,480,528 (49%)	143,733,527 (54%)	198,008,511 (57%)
Total Worldwide	171,168,600	212,889,190	268,150,180	345,735,835

---

[5]Jonathan Weber, "The Net world order," www.thestandard.com, 13 June 2000.

services to both Latin America and the United States. "The service targets Hispanics by the nation they live in. Similarly, services operating in the U.S. can provide content based on the city in which the user lives and their historical or cultural context."[6]

As permission marketing becomes more common throughout the world and issues such as privacy and legal and regulatory standards are addressed, international on-line marketing will achieve some of the same efficiencies that we are beginning to witness in the United States. For example, the problem of whether or not an ethnic population prefers English or their native language, a major headache for direct-mailers and traditional media, is easily addressed by offering Web visitors their choice of language.

The Internet and other technology will come into different markets at varying rates, an issue that companies know they have to confront in the short term. The rate of new media adoption is becoming faster and faster as one technology builds on the basic platform of its predecessor. Radio took 30 years to gain 50 million listeners in the United States; television took 13 years to achieve the same level; the Internet reached 100 million users in only six years, and when wireless and broadband technologies agree on compatibility issues, they will probably reach even higher penetration levels in half the time.[7]

THE DEVELOPMENT OF GLOBAL MARKETING AND ADVERTISING

International advertising and marketing have been greatly influenced by the global environment in the last 20 years. The success of American business is more and more dependent on exporting products abroad. At the same time, American consumers are increasingly familiar with products from around the world. Just as important, the methods, organization, strategy, and execution of advertising is remarkably different because of the advent of international marketing.

During the years shortly after World War II, international business meant American products, marketing, and advertising carried abroad. American companies exported a variety of goods to Europe and Asia as these regions began the difficult recovery from the war. Today, America no longer dominates global commerce, and advertising and marketing are truly worldwide. As multinational companies compete on an international stage, we see the effects through the development of universal brands and even a similarity of product usage among people in diverse cultures and societies.

A major challenge of international business is dealing with a world that is expanding in terms of marketing opportunity and simultaneously becoming more individualistic. As we view the various challenges facing international marketers, we will find that both companies and multinational advertising agencies are adopting management styles that emphasize a two-way flow of communication between headquarters and individual markets. Marketing employees of the future will be valued as much for the information and insights they provide top management as for the sales and marketing skills they provide at the local level.

The need for international exports by American companies is obvious from the numbers. The United States with only 5 percent of the world's population accounts for 20 percent of global Gross Domestic Product (GDP) and both of those percentages, especially the U.S. share of the world's population, will continue to decrease

---

[6]Jeffery D. Zbar, "Powering up internet en Espanol," *Advertising Age*, 29 November 1999, S2.
[7]"Web gets even faster," *Parade*, 11 June 2000.

in coming years. However, there are several trends that bode well for international expansion by U.S. firms:[8]

1. Countries throughout the world are becoming stronger economically. These countries offer opportunities for American companies to market a number of goods and services that would not have been possible only a few years ago. For example, Georgia-based AFLAC insurance receives 80 percent of its revenues abroad, with Japan being its primary market.

2. Not only are international sales increasing, but many American firms are finding higher profits outside the United States. Often competitive factors are not as strong abroad and the costs of promotion are significantly lower than in this country. In many instances, better financed American companies will be able to take market share from local businesses and other multinationals.

3. Many foreign countries are demonstrating huge demand for U.S. goods, services, and technology. As many of these countries continue to see increases in their standard of living they will provide significant profit centers for U.S. companies. In many cases, companies are investing heavily in these countries to establish a presence in anticipation of greater sales and profits in the future.

International marketing involves many elements from organizational management to advertising execution. One of the appealing advantages of globalization is the efficiencies of doing business on a worldwide basis. Indeed, as we examine the major marketers of the various regions of the world, many of the same companies and brands—Ford, Sony, Nestle, Unilever, Coca-Cola—appear again and again. Even though a one-size-fits-all strategy for international marketing will rarely work, significant economies of scale do exist for these companies.

However, elements such as country-by-country media usage sometimes mitigate full exploitation of the advantages of global advertising. In fact, a relatively small number of agencies and media-buying companies have worldwide media directors because of the vast differences found in media planning from country to country. Exhibit 24.2 shows the top three countries in terms of advertising spending: the United States, Japan, and Germany. Japanese television expenditures are almost double those in Germany. On the other hand, Germans invest 69 percent of their advertising budgets in print compared to 46 percent in the United States and only 35 percent in Japan. These differences become more pronounced as additional countries are added to a media schedule. Yet, media is only one of dozens of advertising decisions that must be addressed by international marketers on a individual country basis.

GLOBAL MARKETING AND ADVERTISING

One of the catch phrases of multinational business is **global marketing.** The term, attributed to Theodore Levitt of Harvard University, suggests that companies can develop worldwide advertising and marketing strategies for their products. At the heart of the concept is the assumption that consumer needs are basically alike all over the world and they will respond to similar appeals regardless of cultural differences. Like most marketing concepts, global marketing must be adapted to the unique circumstances faced by each business. A major challenge of international marketing is to develop an organization that gives a sense of corporate identity to a company and its brands, but one that also allows some degree of local autonomy in dealing with the special character of each country.

global marketing
Term that denotes the use of advertising and marketing strategies on an international basis.

---

[8]Greg Paulette, "Our oyster," *Georgia trend*, February 2000, 20.

RANKING

I. UNITED STATES

Projected 2000 total ad spending: $134.3 billion
1998 ad spending per capita: $437.60
1999 population: 274.9 million
1999 GNP per capita: $33,946

Ad Spending by Medium by %
(2000 estimates)

Radio
13.0%

Outdoor
1.8%

Magazines
12.2%

Newspapers
34.3%

Television
38.7%

2. JAPAN

Projected 2000 total ad spending: $33.2 billion
1998 ad spending per capita: $262.60
1999 population: 127.4 million
1999 GNP per capita: $30,720

Ad Spending by Medium by %
(2000 estimates)

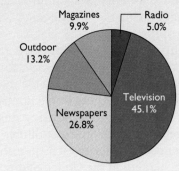

Magazines
9.9%

Radio
5.0%

Outdoor
13.2%

Television
45.1%

Newspapers
26.8%

2. GERMANY

Projected 2000 total ad spending: $21.6 billion
1998 ad spending per capita: $237.50
1999 population: 82.7 million
1999 GNP per capita: $27,337

Ad Spending by Medium by %
(2000 estimates)

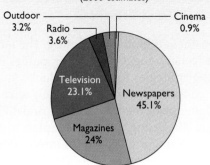

Outdoor
3.2%

Cinema
0.9%

Radio
3.6%

Television
23.1%

Newspapers
45.1%

Magazines
24%

Exhibit

24.2

Selected countries' media
usage patterns.

From: www.Adageinternational.com
Sources: Zenith Media; *The Economist*

The importance of branding and brand equity can't be overemphasized in global marketing. It is the identity and reputation of a specific brand that make the efficiencies of multinational marketing possible. It has been estimated that as much as 90 percent of the value of some companies is linked directly to their brands. Without their high-profile trademarks and logos Coca-Cola is just flavored water, Kellogg is baked grain, and Swatch is just another timepiece. Instead, these companies have established their brands as standing for quality, consistency, and leadership in their respective product categories. Companies, as never before, are recognizing the inherent value in their brands as they begin to expand throughout the world.[9]

To develop a successful multinational marketing organization there are a number of areas that must be addressed:

1. Management

Regardless of the scope of a marketing strategy, it is usually coordinated at top management levels. A number of companies have initiated very sophisticated control centers to market worldwide. Nestle has long been viewed as a master of multinational marketing. From its headquarters in Vevey, Switzerland, it manages 10 worldwide corporate brands (e.g., Nestle, Carnation, Perrier) and approximately 7,000 local brands (e.g., KitKat, Polo).

A typical management approach by multinational companies is to consolidate strategic management decisions at corporate headquarters and give local managers flexibility to develop specific tactics within this strategy. Not unexpectedly, management centralization has resulted in a consolidation of advertising agencies. Even the largest companies tend to have no more than four agencies—some only one—to create and manage their worldwide promotions (although it is common for local agencies to be retained for a specific advertising project). This trend in turn has led to the development of huge multinational advertising agencies, agency holding companies, and worldwide agency networks to service these accounts. McCann-Erickson Worldwide, Young & Rubicam, and BBDO Worldwide are among a handful of agencies with the personnel, offices, and expertise to provide full service to these multinational clients.

Regardless of the overall structure of a company, sound management principles demand that some flexibility must be accessible to executives in specific locations. In fact, "despite a centralization trend, few marketers stay faithful to one structure; many opt for a hybrid system of strong central strategic direction and local execution."[10]

Coca-Cola is an example of a company that has developed significant changes in its management organization to accommodate a hybrid model for its multinational structure. At one time even the most inconsequential decisions had to go through the company's Atlanta headquarters. This management style served it well as it dominated the world soft drink market after World War II. However, in a more competitive environment, it ignored the reality that regional differences in politics, economics, and culture were difficult to discern from a perspective on North Avenue in Atlanta. In applauding his company's adoption of a more liberal management style, a European Coke executive said, "Norway, Belgium and Ireland have three very different cultures, and we (Coke) were trying to manage them out of the

[9]"The power of the brand," *Fortune*, 24 July 2000, S19.
[10]Joy Dietrich, "Global ad decisions centralized," *Advertising Age*, 14 June 1999, 70.

same division. Before, we tried to fit a lot of very diverse cultures into organizational structures that were convenient for us. Now we've got an organizational structure to match the natural cultural clusterings of the countries."[11]

It is important that we don't view centralized management as a totally top-down approach with a manager dictating decisions from a seat at the headquarters building to far-flung branch offices around the world. While this may have been the case among some companies in the past, it rarely exists today except among the smallest international players. Instead, most companies regard local managers as their "eyes and ears" to provide current information that allows central management to function efficiently on a global basis.

2. Advertising Execution

It is important to remember that a marketing organization must have as its fundamental goal the accomplishment of a task rather than striving for simplicity to the organization. Regardless of the management approach used by a company, the key marketing and advertising elements are the same as for domestic marketing, that is to enhance brand identity, increase share-of-mind, and so forth. The less standardized elements such as product quality, advertising themes, and marketing tactics become, the more difficult it is to establish a global personality.

When considering global marketing and advertising management, companies and their agencies normally consider three basic organizational options.[12] As we discuss these alternatives, it is important to realize that each has a number of variations and most companies will use some aspects of each in one or more countries or for particular products. There are few absolutes in the changing field of international business.

■ *Standardization.* Advertising strategy and execution are handled globally with changes in creative or other elements of a campaign kept to a minimum. Under this plan, advertising agency account and creative teams interact with a centralized marketing vice president to determine overall global strategy. A major advantage of this approach is that it insures consistent advertising execution and quality. More importantly, it allows the promotion for a company or brand to speak with a single voice throughout the world and establish global themes.

pattern standardization An advertising plan where overall strategy is controlled centrally, but local offices have flexibility in specific advertising executions.

■ *Pattern standardization.* Under **pattern standardization**, a global advertising agency controls overall strategy and general creative and media approaches while advertising execution is handled locally or regionally. Each country handles its own media selection and tailors campaigns to meet local needs. From an intuitive standpoint, this approach is the most reasonable one and, indeed, some version of pattern standardization is most popular with both companies and agencies. For example, the Golden Arches offer McDonald's instant identification in London, Phoenix, and Madrid.

Problems that arise with pattern standardization tend not to be with the concept, but instead in the execution and management of the various advertising plans. The question is how much country-to-country autonomy is practical and when does pattern standardization shift to a fully localized approach? Obviously, there are no definitive answers, but companies and agencies undertaking this management philosophy will find that training and indoctrination

---

[11]Bert Roughton, Jr., "Independence adds marketing oomph to Coke abroad," *The Atlanta Journal-Constitution,* 11 June 2000, G-1.
[12]"Three model approaches," *Target Marketing,* February 1996, 12.

into the foundation business and advertising and creative principles of the brand are the key to long-term success.

■ *Localization.* At the other end of the management spectrum from standardization is localization. Under this management philosophy, each country manages the strategy and execution of campaigns in that locale. Local advertising agencies tailor campaigns to each area's culture and needs. Tactical control is decentralized, but strategic planning at the corporate level provides an overall emphasis to local country marketing efforts.

It is clear that technology is becoming more readily available to make the *idea* of international advertising and global marketing a reality. However, it is impossible to accommodate all the cultural and national differences in any single marketing strategy. Global marketing is such an appealing concept from a cost and efficiency standpoint that companies are tempted to adopt it even when it has obvious pitfalls. It can be argued that the misapplication of global marketing places the well-being of the firm ahead of the consumer. Exhibit 24.3 demonstrates the continuum of a one-strategy, one-execution global marketing approach versus a consumer-oriented marketing concept with a different strategy, a different execution in each country approach.

3. Sensitivity

A final consideration of globalization and effective management is the development of a sensitivity to the host countries. In a strict adherence to centralized management, it is sometimes difficult to envision either customers or employees from the same perspective as a local executive who shares a common culture and perspective as consumers. In recent years, there has been a heightened sensitivity to the responsibilities of companies operating as guests in host countries.

This responsibility can take the form of an awareness of how advertising copy, themes, slogans, and brands should be displayed and promoted. Critics point out that major multinational corporations should not look to developing nations as only a source of cheap labor and additional sales and profits. Instead, international businesses should use their economic leverage to help raise economic standards in emerging countries where they operate. There is no expectation that companies should forego the profit motive and stockholder equity as they go abroad. But, as many companies are demonstrating, there is an important balance to be reached between maximizing shareholder equity and being a responsible marketer.

The opinions of how to conduct multinational business cover a wide spectrum. However, it is clear that a growing debate over the conduct of global business is creating a changing environment for multinational businesses. Many people are questioning the benefit of globalization to developing countries. As Lance Crain, Editor-in-Chief of *Advertising Age*, wrote in an editorial, "It could be that consumers in third world countries don't want world brands imposed on them. . . . In many parts of the world, consumers have become pickier, more penny-wise, or a little more

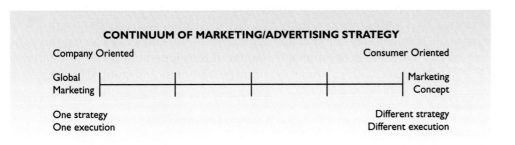

CONTINUUM OF MARKETING/ADVERTISING STRATEGY

Company Oriented   Consumer Oriented

Global Marketing |———————|———————|———————| Marketing Concept

One strategy   Different strategy
One execution   Different execution

Exhibit

24.3

Multinational firms usually develop marketing plans that represent a compromise between the needs of consumers and the firm.

nationalistic."[13] Clearly, the notion of global marketing has ethical and philosophical elements that cannot be ignored.

POLITICAL AND ECONOMIC MOVEMENTS TOWARD A WORLD ECONOMY

As discussed earlier in this chapter, communication technology such as the Internet and satellites have made traditional political borders irrelevant in terms of government control of communication. The availability of information in formerly closed societies has created demand for products and services that only a few years ago would have been unknown in much of the world.

North American Free Trade Agreement (NAFTA) A treaty designed to eliminate trade barriers among the United States, Mexico, and Canada.

This new openness has created a demand that fosters international trade. Steps toward removing artificial barriers to commerce are in place or at the discussion stage throughout the world. The opening of China, Vietnam, and South Africa to trade with the United States are only a few examples of multinational business opportunities that would have been considered unthinkable only a few years ago. In addition, agreements such as the **North American Free Trade Agreement** (NAFTA) and the **General Agreement on Tariffs** (GATT) have moved to open overseas markets by lowering or eliminating tariffs and giving impetus to a free-trade environment among an increasing number of countries. While these countries stand to benefit from a greater availability of goods, none of these agreements overcome cultural, language, and product usage differences among nations. The job of the multinational advertiser is made easier, but hardly solved by these alliances.

General Agreement on Tariffs and Trade (GATT) A treaty designed to lower trade barriers among 117 nations.

By far the most far-reaching and ambitious trade agreement is the economic unification of Europe. Since 1992, Europe has moved toward a unified market consisting of most of the countries of the region. Called the **European Community** (EU), it represents the largest and most important experiment in bringing the concept of a global market to fruition.

European Community (EC) The developing economic integration of Europe. Potentially a single market of some 300 million consumers in 1991.

The most significant step toward a unified Europe was the 1998 introduction of a single currency called the *euro*. Consistent monetary policy offers consumers a means for price comparisons, gives products a universal value, and makes currency conversion much easier among the 15 nations of the EU. If fully implemented, the EU will provide a common trade area larger in size and value than the United States that will function economically as a single nation with limited barriers to commerce.

Obviously, an undertaking of this magnitude is a tremendous task. Countries that have been political and economic rivals for centuries are being asked to set aside their differences and make significant compromises for the common good. There are numerous elements to be negotiated to provide a market in a traditional sense. They include issues as diverse as currency exchange to the manner in which products can be portrayed in television commercials. The detractors of the EU say that it will never be fully implemented because, in fact, there is no common European community. According to critics, to assume that geographic proximity can lead to economic cooperation on a scale suggested by EU is impractical.

Like global marketing itself, the EU concept will probably find its final place somewhere between its strongest supporters and its harshest critics. There is ample evidence that nationalism among the EU countries will not be swept away overnight. The EU does demonstrate the extent of the challenges facing the concept of pan-national economic agreements. If developed countries in relatively close proximity and with a number of common traditions and cultural heritages are

---

[13]Lance Crain, "Agencies press get-global plans but clients face local realities," *Advertising Age*, 14 February 2000.

having the difficulties demonstrated by the EU, it underscores the problems faced by all multinational marketers.

THE MULTINATIONAL ADVERTISING AGENCY

As marketing has become a multinational enterprise, advertising has had to follow. In the 1940s and 1950s when McCann-Erickson and J. Walter Thompson led American agencies into the international arena, they started foreign branches on a country-by-country basis. These branch agencies typically were responsible for the advertising of a few large U.S. clients in a limited number of countries.

This approach to international advertising was extremely expensive and did not guarantee that the foreign branches would adequately serve and coordinate the international marketing needs of their clients. During the 1970s, most U.S. agencies moved from full ownership of foreign offices to some form of joint venture or minority ownership of existing foreign agencies. This plan overcame the long start-up time involved in beginning a new agency and provided advertising plans that reflected local business practices and culture. Joint ventures also recognized the growing expertise of local advertising talent and the fact that around the world agencies were providing client services on a par with major American agencies.

In the last 20 years, two transformations have significantly altered international advertising. The first is the manner in which clients and their agencies manage the advertising function and the second is the manner in which they view their customers.

Management of the Advertising Function

While the basic advertising functions are essentially the same for multinational advertising agencies, the management and control of these functions can vary greatly from domestic clients. The key to success in the management of international agencies is to realize that they are client driven. In fact, international agencies usually must build parallel organizations to their clients. On the client side, marketing directors in countries around the world report to international brand management groups while local country account directors report to agency international account teams. To be successful, agency organizations must operate at both local and corporate levels.

> The international groups deal with brand strategy, asset allocation by market or region, trademark issues. . . . The local agency team, along with the local marketing team, ensures that shared ideas get executed appropriately for each market (which may involve creative or tactical modification), and that results get reported back to the international group for dissemination to other markets.[14]

The two-tier, local/corporate approach allows multinational marketers and their agencies to achieve beneficial efficiencies in building worldwide brands. The sharing of information and ideas from individual agency offices generates ideas and offers perspectives from a number of sources. Likewise, the organization gains from a more consistent approach to creativity and brand positioning and smooths out any discrepancies that might otherwise arise in local executions. Finally, it allows a pooling of resources (both financial and intellectual) to face the challenges of operating on a global scale.

---

[14]Robert Mazzuchelli, "The day of the global agency has arrived," *Promo*, August 1998, S20.

Research and the Multinational Consumer

Marketers, whose only experience is in U.S. markets, find that multinational research presents some unique challenges. Multinational research, especially in attempting to discern common purchase behavior involving a number of countries, deals with issues that gathering data within one country usually does not face. "Research across cultures requires an understanding of individual motivations, societal structures, and cultural patterns. Motivational research within one culture usually assumes that societal and cultural factors are constant. In cross-cultural studies, however, society and culture need to be taken into consideration to fully understand the meaning of behavior."[15] The key to reliable cross-cultural research is the insights and interpretation of data in addition to factual presentations.

It is the interpretation of the research that creates the major problems for international marketers. Even developing a logo that is both understood and effective across a number of countries can present major obstacles. At the heart of the research process is finding a means to effectively translate key advertising and marketing elements from one country to another. While traditional language translation is important, translation, in this sense, includes an identification of the subtle nuances of culture and traditions within a country.

marketing trans-lation Refers to the introduction and execution of a global marketing plan into a specific country as part of an international campaign.

Marketing translation refers to total introduction of the marketing plan to other countries. This translation involves not only language and the numerous shades of meaning that advertisers must deal with, but also accounting for differences in media usage and availability, legal restrictions on various types of promotion, and basic advertising practices from country to country. It is obvious that no advertising plan can be introduced worldwide without numerous adaptations.

A vital element in the translation process is the brand audit. Brand audits are designed to gain consumer perspectives about a specific brand. The brand audit attempts to define what a brand means to consumers worldwide and then develop market strategies that will enhance the brand's future sales potential. Often a brand audit demonstrates that the general perceptions that a company has of its brands don't match those of its customers in specific countries.

Regardless of the function, creative media or research, agencies face two major problems in developing organizations that will meet the demands of clients. First, they are basically accommodating the organizational structure of their clients. An agency with several multinational accounts often finds that the specific needs for account management will differ from one client to the other. In effect, some agencies find that they need different management organizations for each client. The second major problem faced by multinational agencies is how to manage centrally and communicate locally. The adage, "think globally, act locally," is a dilemma for every agency. Agencies must translate broad client marketing strategies to the level of the individual customer in each country they serve.

THE MULTINATIONAL ADVERTISING PLAN

The basic functions of advertising remain the same regardless of the arena. Successful advertising should be based on sound planning and marketing strategy. Consumer benefits must constitute the central themes of advertising messages, and all forms of marketing communication should be coordinated and integrated into a campaign rather than presented as a series of unrelated advertising and sales promotion messages.

---

[15]"Our thinking and research," *Hispanic & Asian Marketing Communication Research*, www.hamcr.com, 13 June 2000.

While advertising basics may be consistent, international advertising presents special problems in execution and practices from country to country. The multinational marketer will find that the use and receptivity of advertising as well as its objectives and basic goals demonstrate extraordinary diversity. As firms introduce products on a worldwide basis, their problems range from something as familiar as product category competition to the much more difficult problem of convincing buyers to change established habits or even reject previously held cultural prohibitions.

Regardless of the objective of a particular international campaign, advertisers must deal with a host of situations unique to each country. This section discusses three areas of primary concern to international agencies and their clients: (1) creative and cultural considerations, (2) media planning and buying procedures, and (3) legal restrictions and regulations.

Creative and Cultural Considerations

The creative process for international advertising needs to begin with an understanding of a particular society and its culture. Only after a marketer has a knowledge of the cultural environment of a country or region, can a business hope to create effective advertising. Determining the specific motivations for buying products and services is difficult enough for domestic advertisers. Multiply this problem by the dozens of countries in which American companies operate and the scope of the problems of international business and marketing become apparent.

Just as business practices don't translate directly from country to country, neither do advertising practices. However, knowing the business culture of a country offers helpful insights into the total buying and selling process that involves advertising. For example, in Holland business meetings adhere to a strict schedule, spend little time with small talk, and move directly to business decisions. In Mexico and Malaysia meetings are more informal and often conducted in social settings or at the host's home. In Brazil meetings are informal and often open with some general conversation, but move quickly to business and often conclude with a final decision.[16]

Taking a cue from personal business relationships, advertisers must take great care in the messages they send. For example, most international advertising executives warn against humorous advertising. ". . . styles can vary widely from country to country, even among those sharing borders and languages. Just as humor doesn't translate well, neither do many attitudes, assumptions and behaviors, no matter how normal or innocuous they may seem in one's home country."[17]

American advertising, of course, is extremely dependent on culture with its use of humor, puns, and twists on familiar words. Consequently, the literal translation of American advertising is filled with a number of disastrous pitfalls.

At one time U.S.-based multinational advertisers routinely used word-for-word translations and exported American advertising around the world. In recent years, they have found that while this process might be quick and inexpensive, it also is almost always unsatisfactory. Today, a number of firms have been established to work with international agencies and their clients to develop advertising that not only considers language differences, but the nuances of culture and the ways in which products are used and should be presented from one country to another.

The shorthand language of American advertising is often misunderstood or regarded as offensive in other countries. Potential land mines for the international marketer are many. Companies and advertising agencies find that reliance on research and resident employees are the two primary means of avoiding the problems inherent in dealing with international consumers. It is clear that even the

---

[16]"Business etiquette around the world," *Promo*, August 1998, S4.
[17]Julie Moline, "Behavior modification," *Meetings & Conventions*, November 1998, 38.

broadest advertising strategies must be translated to fit the local culture and customs. As we have discussed, the efficiencies of consistent creative themes, especially lower advertising production costs, make it important to try to develop creative campaigns that are exportable. More and more international campaigns seek to highlight similar consumer motivations and develop messages that emphasize the big idea rather than local differences among consumers.

MEDIA PLANNING PROCEDURES AND LEGAL CONSIDERATIONS

Multinational advertisers find many of the same problems in developing media plans from country to country as they experience with creative messages. In fact, international media planning is in some respects even more difficult than developing creative strategy. Despite the difficulty of finding common creative themes that will play well in a number of different countries, the problem is largely under the control of the advertiser. However, barriers to effective media planning are for the most part determined by factors within the host countries.

Media buying on an international basis can be as simple as buying media in a single country to developing a plan that will be executed in a hundred or more countries in every region of the world. However, regardless of the scope of a multinational media plan, there are a number of areas that the media planner must consider as part of the process:

1. *Media availability.* In many countries, both print and broadcast media are severely limited and nontraditional media such as direct-mail may be unavailable or impractical. Some countries permit television commercials to be aired only in certain dayparts or they may be limited to advertising blocks before or after programming. However, the situation is improving compared to the early 1990s.

   A number of factors have combined to create a more open media environment. In addition to technology, particularly satellites, there has been unprecedented economic expansion in the former communist countries of Eastern Europe, much of Asia, and selected areas of Central and South America. As governments seek more foreign investment, controls on media and commerce are often relaxed. Finally, a number of regimes recognize that it is in their political self-interest to encourage a rise in the domestic standard of living, which often requires some advertising of product availability.

2. *Legal requirements.* As in this country, products such as alcohol and tobacco as well as other product categories may be limited or excluded from all or certain media. There also are a number of restrictions about the way in which products can be promoted to children. Basically, the rules governing advertising to children differ widely, but focus on four primary areas:

   ■ Specific products that can be advertised. For example, the British Codes of Advertising and Sales Promotion specify that children should not be encouraged to eat or drink at or near bedtime nor to substitute snacks for main meals.
   ■ Appropriate media to reach children. Sweden does not allow direct-response marketing to children under 16.
   ■ The use of famous characters including actors, athletes, and cartoon figures is restricted in a number of countries. Other countries also have restrictions on the use of children in commercials.[18]

---

[18]Michael Plogell and Felix Hofer, "No-nos in Europe," *Promo*, April 2000, 23.

■ In this country, comparison advertising is quite common, but many countries impose tight restrictions on its use or ban it altogether.

One of the newer challenges for multinational advertisers is the Internet. As more and more businesses turn to the Internet as a means of product information, promotion, and customer research, it becomes difficult to stay within the rules of international commerce as they are interpreted from one country to another. You will recall that in Chapter 14, we discussed the popularity of online sweepstakes. The problem with these games, and other promotions, is that they are illegal in a number of countries. Since the Internet does not allow a marketer to limit geographic coverage, most businesses include a statement about who is eligible to enter. Another approach used in Internet promotion is to include a statement that all product claims meet United States (or whatever countries the promotion is intended for) legal and regulatory standards and are intended for persons residing in those countries. None of these steps provide a foolproof solution, but it does provide the company with some defense if challenges are made in foreign jurisdictions.

3. *Media and product usage.* Consumers in various countries demonstrate markedly different preferences for media and products. In Japan, television viewing averages more than eight hours a day per household, the figure is less than three hours in Great Britain. In other countries television is just now becoming a primary medium. In many regions, increases in television viewing seem to be at the expense of print media, especially newspapers. In most of the world, television is the primary advertising medium, held back only by regional restrictions on its use as an advertising vehicle.

One of the interesting features of the growth of worldwide television is that it exhibits some of the same nationalistic trends we have seen in other areas of international business. While shows like *E.R.* and *Baywatch, Friends,* and *Wheel of Fortune* have a worldwide following, there is a move to local programming in many countries. Americans watching an Egyptian soap opera or an Italian variety show might not appreciate the content or the production values, but that is just the point. As a cultural critic pointed out, ". . . it may seem paradoxical that television, perhaps the first truly global medium, turns out to be the one most responsive to the whims of local viewers."[19] Once again we underscore the difficulty of attempting to apply American standards of taste, television, or advertising to other cultures.

In addition to the differences in the use of traditional media, media planners also must consider nontraditional media, which are very important in some areas of the world. For example, cinema advertising, regarded as a very minor medium in America, is a primary vehicle in Asia and parts of Europe. Out-of-home advertising is also extremely important in many countries.

4. *Research.* Like all advertising executives, media planners must take a multinational perspective as clients and media move across borders to add market share and audiences. During the last two decades, the international media-buying function has changed dramatically. Searching for cost efficiencies and recognizing the unique problems of international media buying, multinational clients have demanded special expertise from their agencies. In this environment, the demands for cross-cultural media research have become crucial.

Reliable media and product usage data are just now becoming available in many countries. Media planners must be extremely careful in using research that lacks the reliability and validity that is taken for granted in the United States. Marketers also are finding that what many Americans view as legitimate

---

[19]A.O. Scott, "The whole world isn't watching," *New York Times Magazine*, 30 January 2000, 12.

market research is regarded in many countries as the height of bad manners and is in some cases illegal. For example, questions about income, product usage, or media habits would simply not be answered in many parts of the world.

Regardless of the media-planning problems faced by multinational marketers, advertisers must deal with the problems of developing and executing the media plan, which is much more intricate than those generated for a single country. Media buying is so complex for large multinational advertisers that the media function is increasingly concentrated in buying combines or brokers that buy for a number of agencies. These combines can afford to hire highly trained personnel, conduct multinational audience research, and establish databases that would be beyond the financial reach of most individual advertising agencies. The combines also can gain significant media discounts by buying for groups of clients instead of on the basis of single companies or brands.

U.S. media generally give agency discounts based on media placement for single brands or corporations. However, in many parts of the world, media allow agencies to combine media placement for all their clients to establish discounts. Discounts based on total agency placement mean that the larger the agency or media-buying company, the greater the financial advantage to their clients. Clients, of course, are well aware of these cost efficiencies, and are more likely to sign on with the biggest media-buying companies. Consequently, the big only get bigger, with small- and medium-size buying firms and agencies increasingly cut out of major business.

Many media executives are predicting that satellite and cable television and the Internet are going to have dramatic short-term effects on the process of international media planning. These new technologies are already offering programming and advertising that is simultaneously available in a number of countries. This development offers the potential for significant cost efficiencies in both international brand awareness and advertising, but with accompanying challenges of language, media, and legal restrictions.

CHALLENGES FOR ADVERTISING DIVERSITY IN THE UNITED STATES

When major league baseball began the 2000 season, 21 percent of players on opening-day rosters were born outside this country. If the minor leagues were included, 40 percent of professional baseball players were foreign born. Major league players come from 16 countries spanning the globe from Australia to the Dominican Republic. The "American pastime" is a microcosm of American society.

A U.S. business does not have to look abroad to find an ethnically diverse and quickly changing marketplace (see Exhibit 24.4). The minority population of the United States will grow steadily during the next 50 years. By the end of this decade, the non-Hispanic white population will be less than 70 percent of the total U.S. population and by 2050, it will be less than half. Putting aside the fact that multicultural inclusiveness is the right thing to do, American businesses are finding that ethnic advertising and marketing is a necessity in the twenty-first century.

Research shows that the growth in population diversity is more than matched by increases in purchasing power. From 1995–1998, average U.S. household spending increased 13.7 percent while multicultural family expenditures increased 17.8 percent.[20] To reach this growing market, major advertisers such as Procter &

---

[20]Jeffery D. Zbar, "With right touch, marketers can hit multiple cultures," *Advertising Age,* 16 November 1998, S25.

Exhibit

24.4

Advertising reflects the
diversity of American society.
Courtesy: Jacobs Outdoor.

Gamble, Sears, General Motors, and AT&T are developing targeted campaigns and engaging minority-owned advertising agencies.

These companies and their agencies are finding that multicultural advertising is a process that demands discipline and a great deal of strategic planning.

> Successful ethnic marketing is sometimes about language, but always about culture. Language is one aspect of culture that can aid in the development of compelling communications. Community, religious values, family, nationality, the immigrant or minority experience, history, tradition, mythology, and food also play roles. Simply put, culture is the intellectual and emotional context against which your message will be weighed.[21]

The Multicultural Marketplace

For the past 30 years, social scientists have been attempting to determine the degree to which immigrants have been assimilated into American society. A better question might be how American society is changing as a result of this multicultural environment. Take a trip down the typical grocery store aisle and you will find salsa, kimchi, couscous, bagels, and guava jelly. Banks have staffed their call centers with bilingual tellers and AT&T devised a successful promotion that encouraged ethnic minorities to place overseas calls.

Product differentiation is just as likely to be based on culture as on product benefits.

> Merchants of all kinds are anxious to attract and keep this growing market. That's why you can now choose from more than 300 Hallmark greeting cards en espanol, order a canister of jalapeno rugelach, pay for it with a Lunar New Year designer check and send it in an envelope with a Cinco de Mayo postage stamp. You can pick out your wedding dress at a Greek, Hispanic or African bridal show, or select from 147 different shades of Cover Girl makeup.[22]

---

[21]Carl J. Kravetz, "Speaking to America," *Agency*, Spring 2000, 32.
[22]Marilyn Halter, "America assimilating into its immigrants," *The Atlanta Journal-Constitution*, 30 July 2000, G5.

In broad terms, there are three major ethnic markets in the United States: Hispanic, Asian America, and Africa America. Each group presents special problems and opportunities for marketing and advertising. In discussing these emerging markets, we should keep in mind that there are many subcultures within each group. For example, an Asian-American prospect of Japanese heritage may have much different product preferences than a person coming from a Korean or Vietnamese background. The next section will discuss some of the primary elements in marketing to various groups.

The Hispanic Market In the near future, the Hispanic population will pass African Americans as the largest minority group in the United States. This market can be reached by a growing number of media outlets, which makes it somewhat easier than in the past to communicate with them. Univision and Telemundo television networks provide extensive news and entertainment to the Hispanic market. In fact, Univision is the fifth most watched network in this country. With a 92-percent share of the Spanish-speaking audience, it is bucking the trend of other networks by showing significant audience increases.

In addition to these networks, the growing Hispanic market has resulted in additional media outlets and substantial advertising investments directed to them by major advertisers. In particular, Spanish language vehicles have seen significant growth, with local market television, radio, and magazines joining newspapers to reach prospects in major Hispanic population centers. Spanish language television has been joined by magazines in the vein of *Latina*, and *Glamour en espanol*, and a host of radio outlets and newspapers.

U.S. advertisers attempting to reach the Hispanic market are finding that even selecting a language can be a problem in this market. There seems to be a significant difference between older and younger age groups in terms of language preference. In many cases teenagers and younger adults prefer English language content while their parents and older members of the community feel more comfortable with Spanish. As one marketing executive pointed out in discussing television, "Good programming pulls in viewers and since so many people are bilingual, it won't matter so much what language the program is in as long as it's compelling and reflects Latinos' lifestyles and their sense of humor."[23] The translation process must go beyond language. For example, General Motors found that in the Hispanic community trucks often provide family transportation and so they deleted the "Like a Rock" theme in their Hispanic advertising.

Marketers also are finding that product development as well as advertising is a key to reaching the ethnic market. Most major package-good companies have been slow to introduce specific brands for the Hispanic market. However, those companies that have done so have met with great success. Frito-Lay introduced a Doritos line extension in spicy flavors such as Salsa Verde and Flamin' Hot Sabrositos targeted to the Hispanic market. Within a year, this line extension had become a $100 million business. Likewise, General Mills profitably marketed a Para su Familia (For Your Family) line of cereal.

Other companies have been more conservative, but are still aggressively marketing to the Hispanic consumer. Kraft Food's research showed that a high percentage of Hispanic housewives prefer to cook from scratch. In response, the company distributed recipes that showed how various Kraft brands could be incorporated in basic food preparation. Procter & Gamble published a free bilingual magazine that included coupons for P&G products.[24]

---

[23]Jeffery D. Zbar, "Marketing to Hispanics," *Advertising Age*, 30 August 1999, S19.
[24]Roberta Bernstein, "Food for thought," *American Demographics*, May 2000, 39.

It is clear that investing money alone is not enough to successfully market to the ethnic population. These consumers have traditional purchasing habits and customs that must be reflected in any advertising and promotion. However, research shows that when a brand gains acceptance in the minority community, there is a significant level of brand and company loyalty that makes the effort extremely profitable.

The Asian-American Market   While Americans celebrated the year 2000 with great fanfare, Asian Americans were preparing for February 5 when the Asian Lunar calendar rolled to 4698, the Year of the Dragon. The event was marked by a number of "Year of the Dragon" promotions by major companies especially in California and New York. Also in California, the Asian community held its annual Asian-American Expo to observe the new year and recognize Asian arts and traditions. The event is sponsored by companies as diverse as Nestle, Sears, Bank of America, and GTE.[25]

The Asian-American market is the most diverse among the major minority segments. It is this diversity of demographics, language, and culture that makes the Asian-American community difficult to reach effectively with promotional messages. Statistics indicate that it is a market well worth the effort. It is an extremely affluent market with the highest household income and education levels of any major U.S. demographic segment. For example, 42 percent of Asian Americans hold bachelor's degrees compared to 25 percent of whites. It also is a market that demonstrates high levels of brand loyalty to those companies that make the effort to reach out to it.

According to Embassy Communications Corporation, a leading Asian-American marketing and advertising agency, there are 15 distinct subgroups of this market.[26] However, six groups comprise 77 percent of the total Asian-American community:

Chinese Americans	23.8 percent
Filipino Americans	20.4 percent
Japanese Americans	12.3 percent
Korean Americans	11.6 percent
Vietnamese Americans	8.9 percent

Even within these broad groups, there are a number of diverse clusters. For example, Chinese Americans immigrate from mainland China, Taiwan, and Hong Kong (prior to reunification). In addition, Chinese Americans born in this country classify themselves as "American-born Chinese" (or ABC).

The Asian-American population is concentrated heavily in urban areas of California, New York, and Hawaii. The market is younger, more innovative, and technology literate than the general population. The Asian-American market has among the highest percentage of households on-line, so the Internet offers promise as a means of reaching this diverse market as e-commerce becomes more popular.

One of the most important areas where the various segments of the Asian-American market demonstrates some important differences is in their assimilation into American culture. For example, almost 80 percent of Vietnamese in this country are foreign born, compared to less than one-third of Japanese Americans. Not surprisingly, more than 90 percent of Vietnamese Americans prefer their native language rather than English. They also are extremely committed to their culture and preservation of Vietnamese traditions. On the other hand, Filipino Americans are

---

[25]Bob Woods, "Asian persuasion," *Promo*, April 2000, 31.
[26]Information from Embassy Communications Corporation, www.embassyco.com, 18 June 2000.

very fluent in English and are more likely to live outside urban centers. While they place high values on their Filipino heritage, they demonstrate remarkable rates of assimilation into mainstream American life.

Research has shown that Chinese Americans are much more price conscious than Koreans who tend to be more brand driven in their purchase behavior. Because the Asian-American market has become such a major component of total buying power in recent years, we are only now obtaining the type of market research common among other demographic groups. The evidence is that the Asian-American market is one that businesses should devote more effort than has previously been the case.

The African-American Market   The African-American market is huge with approximately 34 million people and buying power of more than $500 billion. During the decade of the 1990s, African-American buying power grew 73 percent, far surpassing their population growth. It is anticipated that the African-American population will grow at a rate of more than 10 percent during the next decade with continuing increases in economic capacity.

More than any other demographic category, African-American consumers demonstrate extremely high levels of brand loyalty with less brand switching than most other consumer groups. It is this brand loyalty that rewards those businesses that reach out to this market with products and messages directed to their interests. Companies have begun to realize that these markets are most effectively reached with specialized media and advertising messages. For example, a number of marketers have recognized the African-American celebration of Kwanzaa with special promotions and merchandise.

Marketers realize that investing advertising dollars alone is not enough to engender a company or product to minority consumers. The investment must consider the special concerns of this community and the products and services that they are most likely to purchase. Research has indicated that African-American households are projected to spend a larger share of their incomes on clothing, entertainment, and health care. It is interesting to note that one of the categories where African Americans are projected to lower expenditures is rent as more and more of these households become home owners.[27]

Reaching the African-American market is a much easier task for marketers than either the Hispanic or Asian segments for two reasons:

■ There is no language barrier in reaching the African-American community so advertisers don't have to make decisions concerning English versus indigenous languages.

■ While there are differences of media and product preferences among African Americans, just as among the white majority, they represent a much more homogeneous and assimilated market than either Asian or Hispanic consumers.

While a common language makes reaching the African-American market easier than other ethnic minorities, marketers still face the real hurdle in communicating with sensitivity and understanding to people in this market. The key to success in the African-American market, as with other ethnic minorities, is to show an understanding and insight of their culture, traditions, and the basic product benefits they are seeking.

---

[27]Tom Maguire, "Ethnics outspend in areas," *American Demographics*, December 1998, 16.

SUMMARY

International advertising has moved from the specialized to the commonplace. It is rare that even the smallest company doesn't engage in some form of international marketing—either in the goods it sells or those it buys. As more and more countries improve both their economic position and their openness to trade with other countries, we will see even more business conducted on an international basis.

A major part of the growth of international marketing is the adoption of new forms of technology. First satellite transmission of television signals and, more recently, the emergence of the Internet have contributed to a faster pace of advertising and marketing on a worldwide basis. But the driving force behind multinational marketing is the search for new markets by the mature economies of the United States and Europe. These mature economies no longer offer the level of growth and expansion needed to sustain continuing growth by large corporations. In addition, sales in developed countries are made largely through brand switching rather than creating real growth.

The potential rewards of marketing in emerging countries can be substantially greater than the same effort invested in domestic marketing. However, multinational companies have learned that overseas marketing and advertising is very different than traditional American advertising. While the basic functions may be the same, the complexities of dealing in a global economy are testing the planning, research, and managerial abilities of both companies and their advertising agencies. The difficulties experienced by the European Community, a developed region with one of the highest standards of living in the world, reinforce the problems companies face as they introduce their products in emerging nations.

One thing is certain, advertising will play a much larger role in most international markets compared to the United States. The most successful brands often will be those that establish the first beachhead in emerging markets. The common criteria for U.S. advertising—CPMs, cost-per-point, audited circulation and verified ratings, and so forth—are simply not applicable in many foreign markets. Instead, experience and judgment must be used to deal with the intricacies of international marketing.

Moreover, even those businesses that do not participate in multinational advertising will be faced with the challenges of ethnic diversity in this country. The growth of Hispanic, Asian, and other cultures within American society will increasingly require the creative use of media, promotion, and sales messages to reach this evolving market. Not just marketing expertise, but a sensitivity to the culture, language, and values of other peoples will be a requirement in this new marketplace. However, for those willing to devote the time to learn how to operate in this diverse environment the rewards will be great. Clearly, multicultural advertising will continue to undergo a period of dramatic change throughout this decade.

TAKE IT TO THE NET

We invite you to visit the Russell/Lane page on the Prentice Hall Web site at **www.prenhall.com/myphlip** for end-of-chapter exercises and applications.

Chapter 25

Legal and Other Restraints on Advertising

CHAPTER OBJECTIVES

There is no area of business that faces more legal, regulatory, and public opinion restrictions and scrutiny than that applied to advertising. Given the level of visibility of advertising, it is not surprising that both regulators and the general public want to ensure that advertising is as truthful and ethical as possible. In recent years, the development of new media technology has raised a number of concerns about privacy because marketers are able to easily gather data about individuals. There is no question that advertising will operate in an even more litigious environment in the future. After reading this chapter you will understand:

>> the history of advertising regulation

>> the role of the Federal Trade Commission in advertising regulation

>> advertising and free-speech issues

>> advertising and the media clearance process

>> the relationship between federal and state regulation

>> the Better Business Bureau and advertising self-regulation

During most of the nineteenth century, the marketing exchange function was personal with buyers and sellers knowing one another and locally owned businesses providing the backbone of the retail distribution system. By the latter part of the century, business was becoming more complex and centralized and there was an increase in deceptive advertising. By the early 1900s a much needed examination and housecleaning of flagrant advertising abuses had begun. For the first time there was general agreement that formal regulation was needed to deal with illegal and unethical advertising practices.

This period also marked a rejection of the libertarian notion of **caveat emptor,** "let the buyer beware." This concept was based on the classical economic perception of a free marketplace of goods and ideas and perfect knowledge on the part of

caveat emptor Latin for "Let the buyer beware." Represents the notion that there should be no government interference in the marketplace.

the participants in that marketplace. Under this concept, buyers and sellers were presumed to have equal information, and it was assumed that both groups, being rational, would make correct economic choices without government interference into business transactions.

By the early 1900s, public sentiment had forced Congress to deal with the abuses of the industrial barons who created monopolies and amassed fortunes while driving smaller competitors into bankruptcy. In addition, the complexities of the marketplace led to the rejection of the principle of caveat emptor. It has been replaced by the idea that consumers cannot hope to have perfect knowledge of the marketplace and must be protected by legal guarantees of the authenticity of advertising claims and other marketing practices.

By the 1950s, a relatively simple and straightforward marketing process had begun to change dramatically. Manufacturer control of the distribution channel, so much a concern of the trust busters of the early 1900s, was being replaced by national retail chains exercising significant power over the marketing channel. In addition,

> . . . America was firmly on the road to a new kind of society where everyone could aspire to a lifestyle once available only to the privileged. A confluence of forces was creating markets of unprecedented size and richness. Advertising, already a valued member of the sales team, took on an additional role: legitimizing lifestyles that encouraged impulse buying by presold shoppers. Advertising also had become a lightning rod for those who felt aggrieved by an increasingly impersonal market.[1]

Today, we are facing another period of change in marketing and advertising. The growth of e-commerce, converging media technologies, even greater consolidation of retail outlets, and the emergence of direct-response promotion and selling are combining to create a much different marketing and promotion environment than we have experienced in the past. As we discuss the formal and informal regulations of advertising, it is important to keep in mind some basic guidelines of fair and honest advertising. These principles, as enunciated by the Council of Better Business Bureaus, are unchanging regardless of the means of advertising and marketing:

1. The primary responsibility for truthful and nondeceptive advertising rests with the advertiser. Advertisers should be prepared to substantiate any claims or offers made before publication or broadcast and, upon request, present such substantiation promptly to the advertising medium or the Better Business Bureau.
2. Advertisements that are untrue, misleading, deceptive, fraudulent, falsely disparaging of competitors, or insincere offers to sell shall not be used.
3. An advertisement as a whole may be misleading although every sentence separately considered is literally true. Misrepresentation may result not only from direct statements but by omitting or obscuring a material fact.[2]

As we will see throughout this chapter, these principles form the framework for virtually all the regulation of advertising as well as the guidelines used by advertisers and their agencies in preparing and placing advertising. Not only is misleading advertising wrong, it is bad business. Most products depend on repeat business for

---

[1]Stanley Cohen, "'Protecting' consumers," *Advertising Age Special Edition: The Advertising Century*, 1999, 120.
[2]From the "Better Business Bureau Code of Advertising," www.bbb.org.

their survival. When misleading advertising creates unreasonable customer expectations, it is unlikely that the product will enjoy future sales.

Despite the best efforts of most businesses, they know that they must deal with the reality of an often hostile atmosphere toward advertising. In this highly charged and controversial arena, it is imperative that advertisers avoid even the appearance of impropriety or deception. Advertisers must be extremely careful not to run afoul of the various laws and regulations applied to advertising.

There are three primary constraints on advertising:

1. Laws and regulations of legally constituted bodies such as Congress and the Federal Trade Commission
2. Control by the media through advertising acceptability guidelines
3. Self-regulation by advertisers and agencies through various trade practice recommendations and codes of conduct

You will notice that two of the three types of constraints are basically self-imposed. Both advertisers and the media that carry their messages are as concerned about misleading, false, or inappropriate advertising as any regulatory body. Advertising is not only a means of communicating with the public, but it also determines how the public perceives the companies, products, and services that advertise. Anything that damages the overall image of advertising hurts the efforts of each advertiser. The primary enforced of advertising regulation is the Federal Trade Commission Act, which we discuss first.

THE FEDERAL TRADE COMMISSION

The **Federal Trade Commission** (FTC) is the organization with the most significant and far-reaching control over advertising. Today, it is considered the consumer protection "police force." Ironically, when the FTC was first established, it had no mandate to regulate deceptive consumer advertising. The original intent of the Federal Trade Commission Act, passed in 1914, was to administer the congressional mandate that "unfair methods of competition are hereby declared unlawful." At the outset, unfair methods of competition were regarded as those involving disputes among businesses. A primary goal of the FTC during this period was to protect local retailers from large chains that were just beginning to become a major factor in some retail categories such as grocery stores.

During its early years, the FTC did not take action against a business unless it could be shown that competitors were being harmed by illegal trade practices. Business practices, including advertising, that injured the public were not considered within its jurisdiction. It was not until 1922, in *FTC* v. *Winsted Hosiery Company*, that the Supreme Court held that false advertising was an unfair trade practice. However, the FTC continued to function primarily as a means of protecting one business from another.

Then in 1938, passage of the **Wheeler-Lea Amendments** broadened this interpretation to include the principle that the FTC could protect consumers from deceptive advertising. This law also gave the FTC specific authority over false advertising in the fields of food, drugs, therapeutic devices, and cosmetics. Nevertheless, it was not until 1960 under the Kennedy administration that the FTC became a major force in consumer protection.

It was during the Kennedy presidency that the commission began to take primary leadership in protecting consumers from a number of trade, advertising, and product promotion practices. For example, the commission began to encourage public comment, which is now a common practice in FTC hearings. It also spearheaded the successful effort that led to the banning of broadcast cigarette advertising. Many of the procedures and proactive initiatives of recent years have their roots during the early 1960s. Today, the FTC exercises sweeping power over the advertising of all products sold or advertised across state lines.

Deceptive Advertising

At the heart of the FTC's enforcement mandate is the demand that advertising claims can be substantiated. The request for proof of product claims is the first step in the investigative process. Every marketer has an obligation to provide adequate substantiation for performance claims it makes in advertising and promotional messages. The FTC is particularly vigilant in the area of health, weight-loss, and exercise claims. In these product categories, substantiation must be based on acceptable and normal scientific standards and evaluated in an objective manner by qualified persons.

Advertisers must be prepared to prove, with objective and generally accepted evidence including scientific studies, that their claims are true. Often advertisers note in their advertising copy that some type of substantiation has taken place. Deceptive advertising has not been specifically defined by Congress, so the FTC operates through a series of guidelines developed over the years. Its judgment, in ruling an ad or claim deceptive, hinges on whether a consumer action was taken on the basis of advertising deception. In fact, general rules of deception are difficult to draft and must be considered on an ad-by-ad basis.

Currently the FTC uses a three-part test to determine if an advertisement is deceptive or untruthful:

1. There must be a representation, omission, or practice that is likely to mislead the consumer. For example, the FTC cited a telemarketing firm for having its callers represent themselves as law enforcement personnel. Even though the company had been hired by a police organization the FTC ruled that potential donors might react more favorably to a police officer than to a private solicitor.

2. The act or practice must be considered from the perspective of a consumer who is acting reasonably. In other words, the advertiser is not responsible for every possible interpretation, no matter how far fetched or unreasonable, that might be made by a consumer.

3. The representation, omission, or practice must be material. A claim or presentation, even if it is not true, must be judged to have had some influence over a consumer's decision. For example, it has been concluded that using plastic ice cubes in a soft drink commercial is not deceptive because no claims are being made about the ice cubes.

Methods of FTC Enforcement

The process of FTC enforcement is designed to protect the public, but also to ensure that marketers are given an opportunity for due process when disputes with the FTC cannot be resolved. Therefore, there is recourse in the courts for both parties if no resolution can be reached during the substantiation process.

1. The first step in the process is to file a claim of deceptive practices with the FTC. The complaint can come from consumers, competitors, or the FTC staff.

2. The FTC then begins its investigation. Normally, the inquiry starts with a request for **substantiation** from the advertiser.

3. If the commission finds the practice to be unsubstantiated and therefore deceptive, a complaint is issued. At this point, the advertiser is asked to sign a **consent decree** in which the firm agrees to end the deceptive advertising. Most complaints are settled in this manner. An advertiser who continues to engage

substantiation The key to FTC enforcement is that advertisers must be able to prove the claims made in their advertising.

consent decree Issued by the FTC. An advertiser signs the decree, stops the practice under investigation, but admits no guilt.

in deceptive advertising after signing a consent decree is liable for a fine of $10,000 per day.

4. If an advertiser refuses to sign a consent decree the commission issues a **cease and desist order.** Before such an order can become final, a hearing is held before an administrative law judge. The judge can dismiss the case and negate the cease and desist order. If it is upheld, the company may appeal the decision to the full commission.

5. Even if an advertiser agrees to abide by a cease and desist order, the commission may find that simply stopping a particular practice does not repair past damage to consumers. To counteract the residual effects of deceptive advertising, the FTC may require a firm to run **corrective advertisements.** They are designed to "dissipate the effects of that deception." The FTC often stipulates several requirements for corrective advertising such as content, format, frequency, and even the media schedule. The commission normally requires corrective advertising when deceptive advertising claims are judged to be the primary reason for consumer purchases.

6. If a company cannot reach agreement with the commission, its next recourse is the federal courts—first, to the Federal Court of Appeals and finally to the Supreme Court. It is extremely rare that a case goes beyond the cease and desist order. From a practical standpoint most advertising campaigns have run their course by the time an advertiser would go to court. Equally important is the fact that few firms want the adverse publicity that surrounds a protracted court battle.

In 2000, the FTC greatly expanded its enforcement capability through the FTC Consumer Sentinel program. The program consists of a database containing more than 250,000 complaints of consumer fraud that have been filed with federal, state, and local law enforcement agencies as well as private organizations such as the Better Business Bureau, the National Fraud Information Center, and Canada's Project Phone Busters.

The system allows various agencies to share information across jurisdictions as well as spotlighting trends that can help law enforcement agencies determine developing schemes that go beyond a single jurisdiction. As the Chief Postal Inspector commented, "The combined strengths of enforcement agencies . . . sharing complaint information and working together, provides us with a knockout punch against fraud."[3]

The FTC also works with government agencies such as the FCC in combating telemarketing fraud and deceptive long distance service advertising. As we have discussed throughout the text, technology has allowed advertisers to adopt a number of innovative approaches to reaching prospects. This same technology has aided law enforcement in identifying and prosecuting various attempts at consumer fraud and deception.

FTC Trade Regulation Rules and Industry Guides

Over the years, the FTC has developed a number of industry guidelines or FTC Rules that outline in some detail exactly what a business can and cannot do in terms of business practices. These rules are issued when the commission sees a pattern of industry-wide noncompliance with normal standards of advertising or other deceptive trade practices. Some examples of these rules include the following:

■ Funeral Rule requires funeral directors to disclose price and other information about funeral goods and services.

---

[3]Melissa Campanelli, "FTC expands fraud prevention program," *DM News*, 15 May 2000, 3.

cease and desist orders If an advertiser refuses to sign a consent decree, the FTC may issue a cease and desist order that can carry a $10,000-per-day fine.

corrective advertising To counteract the past residual effect of previous deceptive advertising, the FTC may require the advertiser to devote future space and time to disclosure of previous deception. Began around the late 1960s.

- Telemarketing Sales Rule compels telemarketers to disclose information that would affect a consumer's purchasing decision before the consumer agrees to pay for any goods or services the telemarketer is selling.

- Franchise and Business Opportunities Rule obligates sellers of franchises and business opportunities to give prospects a disclosure document containing specific information about the franchise and any earnings claims that are made.

- Children's Online Privacy Protection Rule requires that Web sites that collect information about children under the age of 13 must obtain parental consent and disclose the type of information they collect, how it will be used, whether it will be sent to other advertisers, and provide a contact person at the site.

These rules cannot cover every situation that might develop in these areas. However, they do address what the FTC considers the most important elements and those that experience has shown to be major problem areas in terms of non-compliance with FTC standards.

Major Concerns of FTC Enforcement

Over the years, a number of recurring advertising and marketing practices have resulted in countless complaints to the commission and other regulators. Among the most frequently cited examples are the following:

The Term "Free" in Advertising   The use of offers such as "buy one, get one free" or "two for one sale" have become so prevalent and their abuses so widespread that the FTC issued a four-page guide for nondeceptive usage of the term. The guide emphasizes that when the word "free" is used, a consumer has the right to believe that the merchant will not recoup any cost associated with the purchase of another item. A "two for one" deal requires that the first item is sold at regular price or the lowest price offered within the last 30 days. The commission also requires that any disclosure about the offer price must be made in a conspicuous manner in close conjunction with the offer. In other words, a fine print footnote in an advertisement is not acceptable disclosure.[4]

Advertising as a Contract   One of the many gray areas of advertising is the degree to which an ad constitutes a binding contractual agreement with consumers. For the most part the courts and the FTC have ruled that it is unreasonable to expect an advertisement or commercial to contain all the details of a formal contract. The commission expects that such a contract will be part of the final sales negotiation whereas advertising is normally the first step in the process of selling a product. To this end, the courts have been lenient on pricing errors in ads where no deception is intended.

However, under certain circumstances advertisements have been regarded as constituting binding offers. For example, when there is some language or commitment, no error in the ad, and the defendant has some control over potential liability, a court may find an obligation to provide a good or service at an advertised price. Since the issue is somewhat ill-defined, cautious advertisers would be well advised to treat every advertisement as if it were potentially a contract.

Fact Versus Puffery   One of the most difficult areas of advertising is the difference between legitimate **puffery** and deception. Most consumers realize that advertisers are intent on extolling the virtues of their products by highlighting the most positive features and benefits. It is very difficult to predict how the FTC or the courts will rule on a specific case. For example, a court ruled that Papa John's slogan

puffery Advertiser's opinion of a product that is considered a legitimate expression of biased opinion.

---

[4]Arthur Winston, "How to define the concept 'free' via the FTC," *DM News*, 24 June 1996, 15.

"Better Ingredients. Better Pizza." went beyond product puffery and was disparaging to competitive pizza makers. The court ruled that the term "better" must be proved in comparison to other brands, specifically Pizza Hut, which brought the suit.[5]

One of the most perplexing areas of puffery is so-called "implied uniqueness," "usurped benefit," or "preemptive claim." The terms refer to an advertiser promoting some feature of a product that is not distinctive to the brand, but may leave the impression that competing brands lack that quality or ingredient.[6] Taken to its extreme, a prohibition against this type of claim would eliminate any advertising unless a brand could demonstrate some unique product characteristic—something that most products lack. Again, the role of implied uniqueness is one where the specific message and advertising execution will determine if an advertiser has engaged in deceptive practices.

Some critics categorize any statement that is not literally true as deceptive. However, the legal definition of puffery is that it is ". . . an exaggeration or overstatement expressed in broad, vague, and commendatory language, and is *distinguishable* from misdescriptions or false representations of specific characteristics of a product and, as such, is not actionable." An important element in judging puffery is the FTC's view of the "average" consumer. If the typical person knows that a Chevrolet truck is not literally a "Rock," you are in good shape. However, as claims become more factual or provable, the advertiser begins to cross the line between puffery and misleading claims.

Testimonials At one time testimonial advertising, especially celebrity endorsements, were viewed very liberally by regulators. However, since the 1980s the FTC has developed some specific guidelines involving testimonial advertising. Among the primary considerations that the commission demands from testimonial endorsements are that they do the following:

- Reflect the honest opinions, beliefs, and experience of the endorser
- Cannot include any representations that would be deceptive or could not be substantiated if made directly by the advertiser

Most importantly, the FTC takes the position that in the absence of any disclaimer, the experience portrayed in a testimonial should be interpreted as what the average consumer would find when using a product or service. Notice that most testimonial advertisements, especially for health-related products, carry a statement to the effect that "Results are not typical" or "This result is not typical."[7]

The FTC also has taken the position that consumers can reasonably expect celebrities to be satisfied users of the products they endorse. To put teeth into this opinion, the courts have consistently held that endorsers who willfully engage in deception can be held liable along with the advertiser for damages. This ruling gives many would-be endorsers pause before they jump into a commercial.

Lotteries Lotteries are schemes for the distribution of prizes won by chance. In most states lotteries, except state-operated ones, are illegal if a person has to pay to enter them (legally known as consideration). Promotional sweepstakes are lotteries, but since they don't require an entry fee, they are not illegal. Both the United States Postal Service and the FTC move against illegal lotteries that either use the mail or are advertised across state lines.

---

[5]Jayson Blair, "O.K., so it's not literally a hut," *The New York Times*, 9 January 2000, C-1.
[6]Rance Crain, "How Wonder bread battle fueled a war over product 'uniqueness,'" *Advertising Age*, 20 April 1998, 25.
[7]Andrew B. Lustigman, "Can I say this? FTC urges caution," *DM News*, 7 June 1999, 14.

The Robinson-Patman Act and Cooperative Advertising

It is under the **Robinson-Patman Act** that the FTC gains much of its authority to enforce the payment of advertising allowances and other merchandising considerations including cooperative advertising. The Robinson-Patman Act is part of a three-law "package" that evolved over a period of almost 50 years. These laws and their purposes are as follows:

Robinson-Patman Act A federal law, enforced by the FTC. Requires a manufacturer to give proportionate discounts and advertising allowances to all competing dealers in a market. Purpose: to protect smaller merchants from unfair competition of larger buyers.

1. *1890 Federal Sherman Antitrust Act* was designed to prevent alliances of firms formed to restrict competition.
2. *1914 Clayton Antitrust Act* amended the Sherman Act. It eliminated preferential price treatment when manufacturers sold merchandise to retailers.
3. *1936 Robinson-Patman Act*, in turn, amended the Clayton Act. It prevents manufacturers from providing a "promotional allowance" to one retailer unless it is also offered to competitors on a proportionally equal basis. The basic intent of the act is to ensure that advertising allowances from manufacturers are not used as a substitute for an illegal pricing structure where large retailers are given an advantage over other retailers.

There are a number of provisions within the Robinson-Patman Act. Manufacturers use legal counsel to make sure that they are in compliance. However, this section will review some primary stipulations of the act to demonstrate the way in which it is enforced.

1. Competing retailers must be offered the same proportionate discounts and allowances, but a manufacturer can offer different programs in different trade areas.

    For example, manufacturer A, located in Wisconsin and distributing shoes nationally, sells shoes to three competing retailers that sell only in the Roanoke, Virginia area. Manufacturer A has no other customers selling in Roanoke or its vicinity. If manufacturer A offers its promotion to one Roanoke customer, it should include all three, but it can limit the promotion to them. The trade area should be drawn to include retailers who compete.

    This provision allows companies to selectively offer advertising support to retailers in trade areas of high sales potential without offering the same support throughout the country.
2. The seller has an obligation to take steps reasonably designed to provide notice to competing customers of the availability of promotional services and allowances. This notification must be made both to customers who purchase directly from the manufacturer and to those who buy through an intermediary.

    This section requires that manufacturers be proactive in making sure that all retailers have an equal opportunity to take advantage of any allowances.
3. Both retailers and media are in violation of the act if they provide bills, rate cards, or invoices that do not reflect the actual cost of advertising. You will recall that we discussed double billing in Chapter 10. The act specifically refers to double billing and FTC guidelines and offers the following example.

    A newspaper has a national rate and a lower local rate. A retailer places an advertisement with the newspaper at the local rate for a seller's product for which the retailer will seek reimbursement under the seller's cooperative advertising plan. The newspaper should not send the retailer two bills, one at the national rate and another at the local rate actually charged.
4. Robinson-Patman deals with merchandising allowances in addition to advertising discounts. One of the most common types of retail fees are payments by

manufacturers to gain display or shelf space. These payments are called *slotting fees* and when payments are charged on a discriminatory basis, they are in violation of the law.

In 2000, the FTC convened public hearings to examine the possibility that small manufacturers might be shut out of some retail chains by making them pay high charges for shelf space. An attorney, representing independent bakers and other small food businesses, alleged that "The marketplace discriminates against small firms. The [slotting fees] enable larger firms with more resources to foreclose against smaller companies."[8]

The regulation of co-op and other merchandising fees and allowances has evolved as the media environment has become more complex and the relationships between retailers and manufacturers have changed. Instead of protecting retailers from manufacturers, the commission finds that its emphasis has shifted in the past several years to examining the trade practices of large national chains. Regardless of the type of potential discrimination that might occur in the marketplace, Robinson-Patman is still a strong deterrent to antitrust practices and a major source of consumer protection.

THE FEDERAL FOOD, DRUG, AND COSMETIC ACT

In 1938 Congress passed the Federal Food, Drug, and Cosmetic Act, which established the Food and Drug Administration (FDA). The agency was empowered to enforce a number of requirements concerning labeling of food and drug products. The law also prohibits statements in food labeling that are false or misleading. This provision prevents manufacturers from including claims on their packaging that the FTC would not allow in advertising.

Throughout its history, the FDA's jurisdiction to control and regulate labeling and other elements relating to food and drugs has undergone a number of changes. FDA authority was enhanced with congressional passage of the Nutritional Labeling and Education Act of 1990. After passage of the act, the FDA became much more aggressive in the enforcement of regulations dealing with health claims on labels and packaging.

One of the most far-reaching actions of the FDA was the 1994 mandate for extensive nutrient content information in food labeling. Also many terms such as "extra lean" or "low" were specifically defined. The FDA Modernization Act of 1997 streamlined many of the procedures of the FDA, especially those dealing with drug labeling and testing. For example, if cosmetic or health food products imply that they "cure" some ailment or disorder, the FDA requires extensive substantiation and product testing before these claims are approved.

In recent times, the FDA gained its greatest notoriety in its fight with major tobacco companies. In 1996, FDA Chairman Dr. David Kessler asserted that cigarette and smokeless tobacco were delivery devices for nicotine and, as such, could be classified as a drug. Citing an immediate public health crisis, the FDA, with the support of President Clinton, issued broad based restrictions on tobacco marketing. However, on March 21, 2000, the Supreme Court ruled that Congress had not given the FDA authority to regulate tobacco products. Despite the Court's ruling, the FDA's aggressive stance, and the resulting negative publicity toward the tobacco industry, has been given a large measure of credit for the tobacco industry's multibillion dollar settlement with a majority of the states.

---

[8]Ira Teinowitz, "FTC urged to get tough on retail slotting fees," *Advertising Age*, 5 June 2000, 66.

THE UNITED STATES POSTAL INSPECTION SERVICE

The forerunner of The United States Postal Inspection Service was created by Benjamin Franklin in 1772 to regulate and audit colonial postal service functions. At the end of the Civil War there was a major outbreak of mail swindles and in 1872 Congress passed the Mail Fraud Statute, the nation's oldest federal consumer protection statute.

Mail fraud is any criminal scheme where the Postal Service is used to obtain money by offering a deceptive product, service, or investment opportunity. To obtain a conviction, postal inspectors must prove (1) the offer was intentionally misrepresented, and (2) the U.S. mail was used to carry out the fraud. Postal inspectors investigate a number of criminal activities that use the mail. In particular, the inspectors protect postal customers from mail advertising and promotion schemes involving the elderly and other susceptible groups.

For a number of years, the Postal Service has been empowered to obtain a mail stop order against a company sending false advertising. However, there was no penalty attached to the stop order. In 1999, passage of the Deceptive Mail Prevention and Enforcement Act (DMPEA) gave the Postal Service significantly more power to deal with mail fraud. The primary change brought about by DMPEA is that the Postal Service can impose civil penalties of up to $1 million for the first offense depending on the volume of mail.[9]

ADVERTISING AND THE FIRST AMENDMENT

The First Amendment of the Constitution makes no distinction between advertising or commercial speech and other types of communication. However, by tradition, advertising has never been allowed to fully participate in the open "marketplace of ideas." Whereas, noncommercial speech is offered the widest possible protection, advertising is held to a much stricter standard. In addition, the specific limits that can be placed on commercial speech is a constantly changing process open to continuing interpretation by the courts.

Not only have the courts been extremely reluctant to give advertising full constitutional protection, critics argue that the rationale for this discriminatory treatment has often been inconsistent and illogical. There is no question that in the last 50 years, advertising has gained some measure of judicial protection. Nevertheless, despite a trend toward a more liberal interpretation of commercial speech protection, advertising and other forms of commercial speech continue to be held to a higher standard than other forms of speech.

In order to understand the legal protection afforded commercial speech, it will be helpful to trace court opinions and attempts at regulation of commercial speech over the last several years.

The Development of the First Amendment and Advertising

The First Amendment protections afforded advertising have evolved over the last 60 years. Beginning with the opinion that the government had the right to impose virtually any restriction on advertising to a view that, at least in some cases, advertising deserves the full weight of constitutional protection. In order to examine the

---

[9]Andrew B. Lustigman, "DMPEA gives USPS sweeping powers," *DM News,* 6 December 1999, 14.

changing relationship between the First Amendment and advertising, we need to take a brief look at the development of the status of advertising and the historical protection of commercial speech by the courts.[10]

1942   The Supreme Court ruled that advertising was not entitled to First Amendment protection. The Court held that there were *no* restraints on government's right to prohibit commercial speech.

1964   The Court decided that an advertisement that expressed an opinion on a *public issue* was protected by the First Amendment, but only because it did not contain commercial speech.

1975   The Court gave advertising its first constitutional protection when it overturned a Virginia law making it a criminal offense to advertise out-of-state abortion clinics in Virginia newspapers. However, the ruling left open the question of protection for purely commercial speech that did not deal with opinion or some controversial public issue.

1976   In what many advertisers regard as the major breakthrough for commercially protected speech, the Court held in the case of *Virginia State Board of Pharmacy* v. *Virginia Citizens Consumer Council* that the state of Virginia could not prohibit the advertising of prescription drug prices. It said, in effect, that society benefits from a free flow of commercial information just as it benefits from a free exchange of political ideas.

1979   Advertisers' optimism that they had finally achieved full constitutional protection was short-lived. In the case of *Friedman* v. *Rogers* the Court upheld the right of the state of Texas to prevent an optometrist from using an "assumed name, corporate name, trade name or any other than the name under which he is licensed to practice optometry in Texas." In its decision, the Court said that First Amendment protection for commercial speech is not absolute and commercial speech can be regulated even when the restrictions would be unconstitutional "in the realm of noncommercial expression."

1980   Until this year, the Courts seemingly ruled on each case involving commercial speech on a purely ad hoc basis. Advertisers were left with little or no guidance or precedent as to how any particular case might be decided. However, in 1980 the Court articulated a set of general guidelines concerning constitutional protection that would be afforded commercial speech. These guidelines were set forth in the case of *Central Hudson Gas & Electric* v. *Public Service Commission of New York.*

This case concerned a prohibition by the New York Public Service Commission against utility advertising. The state's rationale was that the ban was compatible with public concerns over energy conservation. In overturning the prohibition, the Court established a four-part test to determine when commercial speech is constitutionally protected and when regulation is permissible. These guidelines known as the **Central Hudson Four-Part Test** are the following:

Central Hudson Four-Part Test
Supreme Court test to determine if specific commercial speech is protected under the Constitution.

1. *Is the commercial expression eligible for First Amendment protection?* That is, is it neither deceptive nor promoting an illegal activity? Obviously, no constitutional protection can be provided for commercial speech that fails this test.

2. *Is the government interest asserted in regulating the expression substantial?* This test requires that the stated reason for regulating the advertisement must be of primary interest to the state rather than of a trivial, arbitrary, or capricious nature.

---

[10]Stephen R. Bergerson, "Supreme Court strikes a blow for commercial speech," *American Advertising,* Summer 1993, 24.

3. *If the first two tests are met,* the Court then considers if *the regulation of advertising imposed advances the cause of the governmental interest asserted.* That is, if we assume that an activity is of legitimate government concern, will the prohibition of commercial speech further the government's goals?

4. *If the first three tests are met,* the Court must finally decide if *the regulation is more extensive than necessary to serve the government's interest.*

In the Central Hudson case, the Court ruled that the case met the first three guidelines, but that a total prohibition of utility advertising was more extensive than necessary. Thus, it failed the fourth part of the test and was ruled unconstitutional. The Central Hudson guidelines remain the foundation on which most commercial speech cases are considered.

1986 Most advertisers thought that Central Hudson had provided significant protection in limiting the right of states to ban legitimate advertising. However, in the case of *Posadas de Puerto Rico Associates* v. *Tourism Company of Puerto Rico* the Court seemed to once again strengthen the ability of states to regulate advertising. This case involved a Puerto Rican law banning advertising of gambling casinos to residents of Puerto Rico even though casino gambling is legal there. In a 5–4 decision, the Court ruled that the ban met all four standards of the Central Hudson Test.

1988 Many legal scholars see this as a watershed year in the Court's attitude toward advertising and, just as importantly, a change in its interpretation of Central Hudson. *Board of Trustees of the State University of New York* v. *Fox* dealt with a college regulation that restricted "private commercial enterprises" on campus. Students challenged the regulation, arguing that at events such as "Tupperware parties," noncommercial subjects were discussed. Since the regulation had the effect of prohibiting both noncommercial and commercial speech, it was too broad and, therefore, did not meet the fourth part of the Central Hudson Test.

In upholding the regulation, the Court ruled that regulations must be "narrowly tailored," but not necessarily the "least restrictive" option available. Critics of the decision point out that "narrowly tailored" is vague and may eliminate the protections of Central Hudson.

1993 In *City of Cincinnati* v. *Discovery Network*, the Court seemed to offer a clear victory for proponents of First Amendment protection of commercial speech. In a 6–3 decision the Court held that the Cincinnati City Council violated the First Amendment by banning newsracks for free promotional publications, but allowing them for traditional newspapers. The Court ruled that since the ban was based solely on the content of the publications in the racks, it did not meet the "narrowly tailored" test. The case was widely seen as a victory for commercial speech.

1995 Alcohol has long represented a product category in which state and federal legislation was extremely strict and rigid. Laws controlling the sale and promotion of alcohol have been traditionally more limiting than other categories of advertising. However, in 1995 the Supreme Court ruled in *Rubin* v. *Coors Brewing* that a federal law prohibiting alcohol content to appear on malt beverage container labels was unconstitutional. While the case did not address advertising directly, it did open the question of whether some restrictions regarding alcohol were too narrow.

1996 Legal scholars predict that two cases heard in this year may provide a significant step in affording more complete constitutional protection to commercial speech. In *44 Liquormart, Inc.* v. *Rhode Island* the Court ruled that a Rhode Island ban on price advertising for alcoholic beverages was unconstitutional. The Court referred to the Central Hudson Case and held that the Rhode Island law failed to prove that the ban on price promotions advanced the state's interest in promoting temperance (that is, it failed the third test of Central Hudson). Furthermore, the legislation was more extensive than necessary to accomplish the goals of the state (here, it failed the fourth test of Central Hudson).

Writing for the majority of the Court, Justice John Paul Stevens said, "... bans that target truthful, non-misleading commercial messages rarely protect consumers from such harms. Instead, such bans often serve only to obscure an 'underlying governmental policy' that could be implemented without regulating speech. ..."[11] Commenting for the advertising industry, Wally Snyder, president of the American Advertising Federation, noted, "the Supreme Court ruling represented the strongest opinion to date protecting truthful advertising from government censorship."[12]

In a subsequent case that year, the Court underscored the Rhode Island decision by returning to the Fourth Circuit U.S. Court of Appeals a case involving a Baltimore ban on alcoholic billboard advertising. In *Anheuser-Busch, Inc.* v. *Schmoke* the beer maker challenged the city ordinance on constitutional grounds of denial of First Amendment right to free speech. However, demonstrating the unpredictability of advertising and the law, the Appeals Court upheld its original verdict, ruling that since alcoholic beverage companies had other avenues for their advertising, the ban was not as broad as the Rhode Island law and therefore constitutional.

1999 The Greater New Orleans Broadcasters Association sought to overturn a ban on broadcast advertising of gambling that dated back to the Communications Act of 1934. Advocates of the ban argued that the government had a legitimate interest in protecting compulsive gamblers from the temptation that casino advertising fostered. In upholding the ban, the Fifth Circuit Court of Appeals commented that the restriction was appropriate because of the "... powerful sensory appeal of gambling conveyed by television and radio."[13]

In June 1999, when the case reached the Supreme Court, the lower court decisions were overturned using the earlier Central Hudson guidelines. According to Central Hudson, any government restrictions on truthful commercial speech had to be shown to advance some government interest and be no more extensive than necessary. The Court ruled that the casino-advertising ban does not sufficiently advance the government's stated interest to protect compulsive gamblers and does not do so in the least intrusive way.[14]

Some advertisers were encouraged that the New Orleans Broadcasters case might mean greater First Amendment protection for advertising, perhaps even a lifting of the prohibition against broadcast tobacco advertising. However, the Court was careful to write its decision narrowly. It "... focused on the irrationality of making distinctions among advertisers, while at the same time suggesting that a more uniform and coherent policy of advertising restrictions might well have been upheld. ... [It] left the door open for the Court to uphold, in future cases, restrictions on the advertising of other lawful products. ..."[15]

---

[11]"High court's hard line on ad bans," *Advertising Age*, 20 May 1996, 57.
[12]"Advertising alcoholic beverages," *Advertising Topics*, a publication of the Council of Better Business Bureaus, May 1996, 2.
[13]"High court overturns broadcasting ban on gambling advertising," *Advertising Topics*, July 1999, 1.
[14]Richard Carelli, "Supreme Court rejects ban on casino ads," www.nytimes.com, 14 June 1999.
[15]Linda Greenhouse, "Justices strike down ban on casino gambling ads," www.nytimes.com, 15 June 1999.

The New Orleans case, like a number of others since the Central Hudson guidelines, underscores the fact that each commercial speech case will be settled largely on its own merits. Still, there is no question that the Supreme Court will continue to demand that the government meets a high standard of public interest before agreeing to any prohibition of commercial speech.

Corporate Speech and Advertising

In recent years, we have seen a tremendous growth in corporate advertising espousing some idea or corporate philosophy as contrasted to selling a product or service. Like all forms of commercial speech, the protection afforded corporate advertising falls into a gray area. Similar to commercial speech, the Court has ruled that corporate advertising is protected under certain circumstances. In *First National Bank of Boston* v. *Bellotti* the Court overturned a state law that prohibited national banks from using corporate funds to advocate voting against a state constitutional amendment that would have allowed the legislature to impose a graduated income tax.

Over the years the Court has delineated several legal principles concerning corporate speech:

1. Spending money to speak does not, in itself, result in the loss of First Amendment rights.

2. Speaking on commercial subjects does not entail loss of First Amendment rights.

3. Speaking for economic interests does not entail loss of First Amendment rights.[16]

We should note that the Court is saying that a commercial aspect to speech does not *necessarily* remove that speech from the rights granted by the First Amendment. However, the converse of this view does not automatically grant these rights to either advertising or corporate speech.

Advertising and the Right of Privacy and Publicity

The right to privacy was given legal standing in 1905 when the Georgia Supreme Court ruled in favor of a plaintiff in a case involving the unauthorized use of an individual's photograph in a newspaper advertisement. Today, although state law varies, the prevailing opinion is that the use of a person's name or likeness without consent is misappropriation. For example, in several jurisdictions the use of a name or picture of a person without prior consent is a misdemeanor. However, civil liability, potentially involving significant judgments, is a much greater concern to advertisers.

Generally, the courts have ruled that public figures have far less protection than the general public in terms of their right of privacy. However, this distinction of public versus private is related to news, not advertising or other commercial uses. Legal precedent makes it clear that public figures are protected from commercial use of their name or likeness by a doctrine of the right of publicity.

The right of privacy protects a person from unwarranted and unnecessary intrusion by the press or commercial concerns. For example, the right of publicity protects a celebrity's commercial interest in the exploitation of his or her likeness.

---

[16]Candiss Baksa Vibbert, "Freedom of speech and corporations: Supreme Court strategies for the extension of the First Amendment," *Communications* 12 (1990): 26.

In some states, notably California, rights of publicity have been extended to the heirs of famous people. With the use of advanced technology, the value of a deceased person's likeness may have real value. In recent years, commercials have featured stars such as Fred Astaire and John Wayne long after their deaths. Because of the potential legal pitfalls, it would be rare for an advertiser to use a model, personality, or likeness without permission. Under the right of publicity doctrine, the courts also have ruled against a number of advertisers who used celebrity impersonators without permission. The key element in the right of publicity doctrine is that a person must show financial damage. Advertisers are extremely prudent in using a personality's name or likeness. Prevailing policy at virtually every agency is that a model, personality, or likeness will never be used without a written release.

ADVERTISING OF PROFESSIONAL SERVICES

One of the most controversial areas of commercial speech involves advertising by professionals, especially attorneys and health care providers. Until the mid-1970s virtually all forms of professional advertising were banned, often by trade associations such as state medical groups or bar associations. Critics of restrictions on legal advertising claim that one of the overriding concerns was to limit competition for established practitioners and, in fact, these restrictions constituted restraint of trade.

There is some validity to the charge. For example, surveys indicate that among doctors, those most likely to use advertising are physicians who have been in practice the least time; those who have smaller practices; and females.[17] In addition, the medical specialty most likely to advertise is plastic surgery. From a marketing perspective the data indicate that, as with any business, health care professions use advertising to gain market entry, increase market share, and gain patients (customers) in the most competitive market segments; that is, a majority of plastic surgery is elective.

Due in part to criticism that the bans constituted barriers to market entry and threatened antitrust lawsuits, the absolute prohibition of attorney (and by extension most other professions) advertising was lifted in 1977 in the case of *Bates* v. *State Bar* of *Arizona*. The Supreme Court ruled that state laws forbidding advertising by attorneys were unconstitutional on First Amendment grounds. The fourth test of the Central Hudson case, not an issue in 1977, seems to reinforce the Bates decision. That is, most legal scholars think that the total prohibition of a class of advertising will generally not meet the fourth test since any total ban will be considered broader than necessary. Bar associations and other professional groups still have regulatory powers over the accuracy and scope of their members' advertising, but they may not prohibit their members from advertising.

In 1988 the Supreme Court extended the right of attorneys to advertise professional services. A Kentucky lawyer, Richard Shapero, was cited for violating a Kentucky law prohibiting targeted mail solicitations to people who were in need of legal services because of some special circumstance. In this case Shapero had mailed an advertisement to homeowners facing foreclosure.

The Court ruled that although personal contact by an attorney could be prohibited, a letter posed no threat of undue influence to consumers who are under threat of legal action. In addition, the Court reasoned that a written proposal to a potential client could be more carefully regulated than a personal contact. The

[17]Boris Becker and Dennis O. Kaldenberg, "To advertise or not to advertise? Advertising expenditures by professionals," *Proceedings of the American Academy of Advertising, 1995*, Charles S. Madden, ed.

Shapero case had the immediate effect of lifting the ban on targeted letters in the 25 states that had previously prohibited them.

In 1993, the Court made an interesting distinction among various types of professional solicitations. The Florida board of accountancy banned personal solicitations for clients, either in person or by telephone. In *Edenfield* v. *Fane* the Court overturned the ban and, in doing so, made a clear distinction between lawyers and accountants. The Court held that, unlike lawyers, CPAs are not trained in the art of persuasion, are dealing with clients who probably have had a previous professional relationship with an accountant, and the client of a CPA is probably not under the stress that a lawyer's potential client might be. The Court found that it was unlikely that the potential clients of CPA would be subject to "uninformed acquiescence," which might be the case with a lawyer's client.

These recent court rulings are related in many respects to the issue of advertising and First Amendment protection. While the Court has eliminated sweeping bans against professional advertising, it has not given it the status of other forms of speech. Furthermore, *Edenfield* v. *Fane* demonstrates again the difficulty of anticipating how the Court may rule in any particular case involving commercial expression.

A 1995 case demonstrated that the courts consider a number of circumstances in ruling on professional solicitations and they are not prepared to issue blanket denial of any state regulations. For example, the Court upheld a Florida Bar Association rule prohibiting lawyers from sending direct-mail to accident victims. The Court took the position that an accident victim is in a more vulnerable state of mind than a person facing foreclosure—the circumstance of those solicited by Shapero. Again, referring to the Central Hudson guidelines, "The state had a substantial interest in protecting the integrity of its legal system."[18]

STATE AND LOCAL LAWS RELATING TO ADVERTISING

During the early years of the twentieth century, the advertising industry realized that something had to be done to stop the charlatans who were preying on an unsuspecting public. Led by major publishers, corporations, and advertising agencies, national pressure was brought against the worst offenders. Unfortunately, little was done to stop local, fly-by-night operators.

Printers' Ink, a leading trade magazine of the period, proposed state and local advertising regulations to address the growing problem of false advertising. Basically, it sought to regulate "untrue, deceptive, or misleading advertising." While *Printers Ink* has long ago ceased publication, its model statute, in its original or modified form, has influenced local advertising in virtually every state (see Exhibit 25.1).

Until recently, the roles of states and federal jurisdictions in regulating advertising were clearly separated. At the national level, the FTC had primary responsibility for regulating advertising in interstate commerce, while individual states were involved in local consumer protection legislation. State regulators usually dealt with retailers and smaller companies operating locally.

Currently, advertising regulation, even ordinances involving major national companies, is being aggressively pursued at the local level. The primary organization in this localized approach to advertising regulation is the National Association of Attorneys General (NAAG). The best example of the power of NAAG was the 1998 settlement with major U.S. tobacco companies. Known as the Master Settlement Agreement (MSA), it called for payments by the tobacco companies of more than

---

[18]Rosalind C. Truitt, "The cases for commercial speech," *Presstime*, March 1996, 31.

THE *PRINTERS' INK* MODEL STATUTE FOR STATE LEGISLATION AGAINST FRAUDULENT ADVERTISING

Any person, firm, corporation, or association, who with intent to sell or in any wise dispose of merchandise, securities, service, or anything offered by such person, firm, corporation, or association, directly or indirectly to the public for sale or distribution, or with the intent to increase the consumption thereof, or to induce the public in any manner to enter into any obligation relating thereto, or to acquire title thereto, or an interest therein, makes, publishes, disseminates, circulates, or places before the public, or causes, directly or indirectly, to be made, published, disseminated, circulated, or placed before the public, in this state, in a newspaper or other publication, or in the form of a book, notice, handbill, poster, bill, circular, pamphlet, or letter, or in any other way, an advertisement of any sort regarding merchandise, securities, service, or anything so offered to the public, which advertisement contains assertions, representation, or statement of fact which is untrue, deceptive, or misleading shall be guilty of a misdemeanor.

$200 billion through 2025. Compliance with the agreement will be monitored by the NAAG. While the tobacco settlement received the greatest publicity, the NAAG and other local and state law enforcement agencies have moved aggressively against a number of advertisers, even those that operate nationally.

In recent years, questions have been raised about the extent to which states will be permitted to go beyond or contradict national legislation. While the question is far from settled, it appears that in most areas the federal courts are asserting the superiority of federal law when a question arises.

COMPARISON ADVERTISING

An often-used sales technique is to compare one brand with its competitors. There are a number of approaches to comparison advertising, each with its own risks and benefits. J. Sterling Getchell is generally credited with the first major use of comparison advertising when the Getchell Agency introduced the Chrysler car in the 1930s by inviting customers to "Try all three." Ever since, it is rare that some automobile campaign does not feature comparative selling.

Despite the fact that advertisers have used comparative advertising for a number of years, many in the industry continue to view it with suspicion. For many years, conventional wisdom was that if you mentioned a competitor's name, you were giving away free advertising. However, when properly executed, comparative advertising can be an effective sales tool in competitive markets.

Comparative advertising began to be widely used after the FTC pushed for more comparative advertising in 1972. The commission urged ABC and CBS to allow commercials that named competitors. Until then, only NBC had permitted such messages, whereas ABC and CBS would allow only "Brand X" comparisons. Given this regulatory stamp of approval, the instances of comparative advertising increased dramatically over the next few years.

The FTC continues to aggressively support truthful and nondeceptive comparative advertising. In fact, the commission has warned trade associations and other industry-wide bodies that industry codes that prohibit or restrict comparative advertising are subject to investigation by the FTC. Likewise, when such organizations or self-regulatory groups demand a higher level of substantiation for comparative advertising than other forms of advertising, they also run the risk of challenges from the commission.

As competition within various product categories becomes more prevalent, comparative advertising seems to be on the rise. Where a number of brands compete in categories with little obvious product differentiation (e.g., paper towels, laundry and soap products) comparative advertising is commonplace. Still, there is a problem of giving competitors recognition. By featuring other brands by name there is a risk that consumers will remember the advertising, but not necessarily the details of the comparison. If not carefully executed, an advertiser may simply build brand awareness for a competitor or confuse consumers. Even in instances where consumers are not confused, they may regard the comparison as giving credibility to the competition. A consumer may legitimately ask, "Why would a company name a competing brand if it didn't have viable consumer benefits?"

Beyond problems of public perception of comparative advertising, both advertisers and their agencies may have legal problems if their advertising is ruled deceptive. The primary legal recourse open to companies are several provisions of the Lanham Act. As amended in 1988, the Lanham Act allows an advertiser to sue if a competitor "misrepresents the nature, characteristics, qualities, or geographic origin of his or her or another person's goods, services, or commercial activities." Under the act, companies may sue to stop advertisements in which false claims are made either about the advertiser's products or about the plaintiff's products. Naming competitors, either directly or by inference, is not without risk to both the agency and client. If a competitor can show damages (such as a decrease in market share) resulting from a dishonest or unfair comparison, it may collect multimillion dollar settlements under the act.

Comparative advertising is a growing problem in international advertising and especially among Internet promotions. While comparative advertising is generally accepted in the United States, it is relatively rare in other parts of the world. A multinational advertiser would find it extremely impractical to build a global campaign around product comparisons. In a study of 17 countries with established advertising industries, it was found that only Canada and the United States demonstrated high levels of comparison advertising. Seven other countries were found to have "very low" levels and in three countries comparison advertisements were illegal.[19]

The issue of comparative advertising is yet another area where technology has created a new set of concerns for marketers and advertisers. The type of usage and legal and/or regulatory restrictions of comparative advertising differ on a country-by-country basis. However, to give you an idea of the types of constraints on comparative advertising that a multinational company may encounter, consider the following:[20]

▪ Philippines	Specific product comparisons are prohibited
▪ Malaysia	Permitted, but the competitor cannot be named
▪ Switzerland	Permitted, but a full picture of the competitor's product must be shown
▪ Australia	Permitted, but must provide full information about products being compared

---

[19]Naveen Donthu, "A cross-country investigation of recall and attitude toward comparative advertising," *Journal of Advertising*, Summer 1998, 112.
[20]Stephen P. Durchslag, "Comparative advertising doesn't always work overseas," *Promo*, January 1999, 22.

Most advertising executives would advise against any type of product comparisons in multinational advertising and especially on a company Web site. Comparative advertising is another example of an American advertising technique that doesn't travel well.

THE ADVERTISING CLEARANCE PROCESS

advertising clearance process The internal process of clearing ads for publication and broadcast, conducted primarily by ad agencies and clients.

Each day, businesses must take great care to stay within the numerous laws and guidelines that affect their advertising and promotional activities. However, despite the litigious environment in which marketers ply their trade, among the primary forces advocating honest and truthful advertising are the business community, advertising agencies, and the media. There are several very practical reasons for marketers demanding high advertising standards.

1. Deceptive advertising may create initial sales, but not the continuing purchases on which most firms depend for their long-term survival.
2. False and deceptive advertising for a product diminishes a brand's equity—one of the most important assets of a company.
3. Misleading advertising, even by other companies and competitors, causes a loss of consumer confidence in all advertising.

The Media

Primary responsibility for truthful advertising lies with the advertiser. However the media that carry the millions of print and broadcast messages created by these advertisers are a major gatekeeper for the advertising process. The public has long expected the media to act on their behalf by prohibiting fraudulent and misleading advertising. However, the standards, scope, and diligence exercised by the media will vary a great deal from vehicle to vehicle. In recent years, the proliferation of media outlets and the fierce competition for advertising dollars has created an uneven landscape of media advertising standards.

The FTC recognizes the media's role in the enforcement of advertising standards and it has issued *Screen Advertisements: A Guide for the Media* to aid the media in determining the likelihood that an advertisement is fraudulent. The FTC has found that a disproportionate percentage of deceptive advertising is concentrated in categories such as weight-loss products, credit repair and loan offers, travel fraud, and get-rich-quick solicitations. As the FTC points out in the introduction to the guide, "Government agencies and self-regulatory groups can step in once the law has been violated, but only the media can stop false ads before they're disseminated."

SELF-REGULATION BY INDUSTRY-WIDE GROUPS

While most individual media and advertisers make every effort to disseminate truthful and fair advertising, a number of industry-wide groups provide guidelines and review advertising on both a national and local basis (see Exhibit 25.2). These efforts offer the public, competitors, and other interested parties a voluntary forum for negotiation before resorting to legal or regulatory bodies for the adjudication of disagreements.

Industry self-regulation serves two important purposes beyond insuring more informative and truthful advertising. First, it addresses public concerns about the practice of advertising by showing that there is a concerted attempt to foster responsible advertising. Second, strong self-regulation may ward off even stricter government controls.

Creative Code of the American Association of Advertising Agencies

ADOPTED APRIL 26, 1962

The members of the American Association of Advertising Agencies recognize:

1. That advertising bears a dual responsibility in the American economic system and way of life.

To the public it is a primary way of knowing about the goods and services that are the products of American free enterprise—goods and services that can be freely chosen to suit the desires and needs of the individual. The public is entitled to expect that advertising will be reliable in content and honest in presentation.

To the advertiser it is a primary way of persuading people to buy his goods or services, within the framework of a highly competitive economic system. He is entitled to regard advertising as a dynamic means of building his business and his profits.

2. That advertising enjoys a particularly intimate relationship to the American family.

It enters the home as an integral part of television and radio programs, to speak to the individual and often to the entire family. It shares the pages of favorite newspapers and magazines. It presents itself to travelers and to readers of the daily mails. In all these forms, it bears a special responsibility to respect the tastes and self-interest of the public.

3. That advertising is directed to sizable groups or to the public at large, which is made up of many interests and many tastes.

As is the case with all public enterprises, ranging from sports to education and even to religion, it is almost impossible to speak without finding someone in disagreement. Nonetheless, advertising people recognize their obligation to operate within the traditional American limitations: to serve the interests of the majority and to respect the rights of the minority.

Therefore we, the members of the American Association of Advertising Agencies, in addition to supporting and obeying the laws and legal regulations pertaining to advertising, undertake to extend and broaden the application of high ethical standards. Specifically, we will not knowingly produce advertising that contains:

    a. False or misleading statements or exaggerations, visual or verbal.
    b. Testimonials that do not reflect the real choice of a competent witness.
    c. Price claims that are misleading.
    d. Comparisons that unfairly disparage a competitive product or service.
    e. Claims insufficiently supported, or which distort the true meaning or practicable application of statements made by professional or scientific authority.
    f. Statements, suggestions, or pictures offensive to public decency.

We recognize that there are areas subject to honestly different interpretations and judgment. Taste is subjective and may even vary from time to time as well as from individual to individual. Frequency of seeing or hearing advertising messages will necessarily vary greatly from person to person.

However, we agree not to recommend to an advertiser and to discourage the use of advertising that is in poor or questionable taste or is deliberately irritating through content, presentation, or excessive repetition.

Clear and willful violations of this Code shall be referred to the Board of Directors of the American Association of Advertising Agencies for appropriate action, including possible annulment of membership as provided in Article IV, Section 5, of the Constitution and By-Laws.

Conscientious adherence to the letter and the spirit of this Code will strengthen advertising and the free enterprise system of which it is a part.

Exhibit

25.2

Advertising agencies take their responsibility for truthful advertising seriously.
Courtesy: American Association of Advertising Agencies.

Despite the best efforts of federal regulatory agencies, the media, and individual advertisers, the opinion persists among a large group of consumers that advertising is either basically deceptive or does not provide sufficient information. Given the investment that companies are making in advertising, this perception is a major problem and one that needs to be addressed with a united front by all honest businesses. As we will see in the next section, the advertising industry is making substantial investments in moving against deceptive advertising.

Better Business Bureaus

One of the best-known, aggressive, and successful organizations in the fight for honest and truthful advertising is the national network of Better Business Bureaus (BBBs) coordinated by the Council of Better Business Bureaus, Inc. (CBBB). The forerunners of the modern BBBs date to 1905, when various local advertising clubs formed a national association that today is known as the National Advertising Federation. In 1911, this association launched a campaign for truth in advertising coordinated by local vigilance committees. In 1916 these local committees adopted the name Better Business Bureaus and they became autonomous in 1926. Today, there are approximately 135 local bureaus in the United States and Canada.

Although the BBBs have no legal authority, they are a major influence on truth and accuracy in advertising. The BBBs are able to exert both the force of public opinion and peer pressure to set up voluntary efforts to address examples of potentially misleading or deceptive advertising.

THE NAD/NARB SELF-REGULATION PROGRAM

In 1971, in response to the many different consumer movements pushing for more stringent government regulation of advertising, the major advertising organizations—the American Advertising Federation, the American Association of Advertising Agencies, and the Association of National Advertisers—joined with the CBBB to form the National Advertising Review Council (NARC). NARC's primary purpose was to "develop a structure which would effectively apply the persuasive capacities of peers to seek the voluntary elimination of national advertising which professionals would consider deceptive." Its objective was to sustain high standards of truth and accuracy in national advertising through voluntary self-regulation.

NARC established a number of units that are administered by the CBBB (see Exhibit 25.3). The primary investigative unit is the **National Advertising Division** of the Council of Better Business Bureaus (NAD). The NAD is staffed by full-time lawyers who respond to complaints from competitors and consumers and referrals from local BBBs. They also monitor national advertising. The National Advertising Review Board (NARB) provides an advertiser with a jury of peers if it chooses to appeal an NAD decision. In 1974 the Children's Advertising Review Unit (CARU) was established to review the special advertising concerns of advertising directed to children. We will discuss the CARU later in this section.

In recent years, many within the advertising industry have encouraged the NARC to further expand the scope of self-regulation. Specifically, it has been asked to consider guidelines for self-regulation of alcohol and tobacco advertising as well as advertising to teenagers. What form such self-regulation would take remains to be seen. However, the fact that a number of advertising executives look to the NARC emphasizes the important place that the organization occupies in the advertising industry.

After a complaint is received, the NAD determines the issues, collects and evaluates data, and makes an initial decision on whether the claims are substantiated. If the NAD finds that substantiation is satisfactory, it announces that fact. If the NAD finds that the substantiation is not adequate, it will recommend that the advertiser modify or discontinue the offending claims. If the advertiser does not agree, it may appeal to the NARB. NAD decisions are released to the press and are also published in its monthly publication *NAD Case Reports*.

Exhibit 25.4 shows the case load for the NAD in a typical year. The data show that competitors are the primary source of complaints to the NAD. Peer pressure in a competitive marketplace is a significant deterrent against unfair or untruthful advertising. It also is interesting to note that only five (less than 5 percent) of the

National Advertising Division (NAD) The policy-making arm of the National Advertising Review Board.

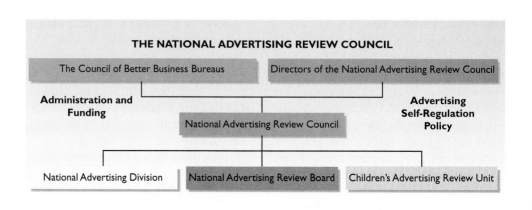

Exhibit
25.3

The NARC review process is established to ensure fairness.

Courtesy: National Advertising Division.

Exhibit

25.4

**Summary of
NAD/CARU/NARB
Case Work**

From: NAD Case Reports, January 2000, 1.
Courtesy: National Advertising Division,
Council of Better Business Bureaus, Inc.

Unit	Total Cases
NAD	155 (includes 58 pending cases)
CARU	43
NARB	5 (includes 1 pending case)

Source/Dispositions

NAD	Substantiated	Modified/Discontinued	Admin. Closed	Compliance	Referred to Government
Competitor	7	52	18	6	5
BBB	0	1	0	0	0
Consumer	0	2	1	0	0
Monitoring	1	1	3	0	0
Totals	8	56	22	6	5

CARU	Substantiated	Modified/Discontinued	Admin. Closed	Compliance	Referred to Government
Cases	0	8	0	0	2
Informal Inquiries	9	24	0	0	0
Totals	9	32	0	0	2

NARB	Requested	Granted	Upheld	Overturned	Remanded
Appeals	4		4		

total cases were referred to a government agency and the great majority of advertising claims were modified or discontinued.

The NARB is composed of 70 members—40 representing advertisers, 20 representing advertising agencies, and 10 from the public sector. Five members in the same proportion are assigned to hear an appeal. If the panel determines the NAD's decision is justified, but the advertiser still refuses to correct the deceptive element, the NARB may refer the advertising to the appropriate government agency. Underscoring the competitive nature of advertising claims, competitor challenges are by far the largest source of NAD cases. Over the years, product testing data has consistently ranked as the area resulting in the greatest number of complaints. In particular, comparative advertising is a source of a number of complaints. When test results are used to disparage a competitor, it is not surprising that a complaint to the NAD would be a likely outcome. In the most recent data, the following areas brought the greatest number of challenges to the NAD:

- Product testing/performance
- Disclosure
- Product demonstrations
- Puffery
- Ingredient/content/nutrition
- Taste/sensory claims

In our examination of the NAD/NARB process, we should understand that it cannot do the following:

- Order an advertiser to stop an ad
- Impose a fine
- Bar anyone from advertising
- Boycott an advertiser or a product

What it can do is bring to bear the judgment of an advertiser's peers that the company has produced advertising that is not truthful and is harmful to the industry, to the public, and to the offender. This judgment has great moral weight. It is reinforced by the knowledge that, if the results of an appeal to the NARB are not accepted, the matter can be referred to the appropriate government agency and at the same time will be released to the public. This step, unique in business self-regulation machinery, avoids any problem of violating antitrust laws, presents the entire matter to public view, and still leaves the advertiser subject to an FTC investigation.

The respect with which the advertising self-regulatory system is held was summed up by Robert Pitofsky, past chairman of the FTC, "I recognize that advertising today is more truthful and more informative than was the case 27 years ago [when NARB was founded]. Today, it has the best voluntary self-regulatory system of any industry in the country."[21]

The Children's Advertising Unit of the NAD

A 1999 study by the Kaiser Family Foundation found that children ages 2 to 18 spend an average of 40 hours per week with various forms of media. Respondents indicated that television dominated media usage and that almost half of children viewers had no parental supervision of their television viewing.[22] Other research has indicated that children have greater influence over family purchasing decisions than ever before.

The combination of children's media exposure and marketing influence has created an annual billion dollar business for television commercials alone. It also has created significant concerns among regulators, parents, public policy groups, and advertisers themselves. In 1998, the FCC mandated that networks program at least three hours a week of children's programming. The rule seems to have contributed to not only more, but better, children's televison fare.

In an environment dominated by Nickelodeon and Turner's Cartoon Network, competition for advertising dollars is keen. Children's programmers seek niche targets just as with adults in order to reach unique segments of the children's market. While traditional superhero animation such as *Batman Beyond* and *Spider-Man* still abounds, there also are examples of female superheroes (*The Power Puff Girls*), multi-ethnic urban morality plays (*Hey Arnold*), toddler educational shows (*Blue's Clues*), and science-oriented shows (*Squigglevisions* and *The Wild Thornberry's*) each directed at a different group of children.[23] However, despite an acknowledgment by most observers that television and other media directed toward children have improved in recent years, there is still considerable controversy about the propriety of overtly targeting sales messages to children.

Advertisers have long been aware that both the public and regulators demand a high standard of truthfulness and fairness for children's advertising. The notion of the "rational consumer" used in general advertising does not apply to messages directed at unsophisticated children, especially preteens. Advertising claims that would be perfectly suitable for adults might be unacceptable for children, especially preteens.

Because of this concern with children's advertising, the NAD, in cooperation with the advertising community, founded the **Children's Advertising Review Unit** (CARU) in 1974. The CARU's mission is similar to that of the NAD except it

Children's Advertising Review Unit (CARU) The CARU functions much as the NAD to review complaints about advertising to children.

[21]Robert Pitofsky, "NAD/CARU/NARB activity," *Advertising Topics*, April 1999, 1.
[22]Ann-Christine P. Diaz, "Kids use media nearly 40 hours a week: Study," *Advertising Age*, 29 November 1999, 28.
[23]Laurie Mifflin, "A growth spurt is transforming TV for children," www.nytimes.com, 19 April 1999.

considers the special circumstances of the younger audience reached by children-oriented advertising.

The principles of the CARU are contained in its *Self-Regulatory Guidelines for Children's Advertising*. In its introduction, the CARU enunciates the primary need for special treatment of children's advertising. "Because children are in the process of developing their knowledge of the physical and social world they are more limited than adults in the experience and skills required to evaluate advertising and to make purchase decisions. For these reasons, certain presentations and techniques which may be appropriate for adult-directed advertising may mislead children if used in child-directed advertising."

The CARU has found three areas of children's television advertising that present recurring problems:

1. *Product presentation.* Can the child gain a realistic sense of a product from the commercial?
2. *Adequacy of disclosures.* Do any of the parts of a product need to be purchased separately? Does the product require assembly?
3. *Sales pressure.* Are children given the impression that they will be superior to other children by buying the product or that their parents are more caring? Are cost considerations minimized by words such as "only" or "just"?[24]

Children and Interactive Media The Internet presents special problems for all marketers, but especially for those targeting children. In recognition of these concerns, the FTC has been given responsibility by Congress to implement enforcement of the Children Online Privacy Protection Act (COPPA). The rules took effect in April 2000 and dealt with a number of issues concerning how personal information could be collected on-line from children, requirements to gain parental consent for on-line activities, and mandates for disclosure of information by Web site operators.

The CARU has adopted a number of voluntary guidelines that complement COPPA. In addition, CARU also spells out appropriate methods for approaching children for on-line sales transactions and how to avoid unauthorized purchases of goods and services by children. For example, the guidelines call for a clear statement that children must have parental consent to make an order and that a cancellation mechanism should be available when such parental consent was not obtained. The CARU views ". . . the Internet as more than a new medium. It is more like a marketplace. Children on the Internet decide where to go, what to do, whom to talk with, just as if they were wandering around a market square in a small town. The difference is the town is the size of the world."[25]

Questions concerning children's advertising have few easy answers. Some critics think that no advertising should be directed to children. To these people only a total ban on such messages will be satisfactory. In fact, the United States has among the most liberal regulations in the world regarding promotion to children. However, given the economic support of the U.S. media through advertising, it is likely that America will continue to allow children's advertising that would probably be prohibited in many other countries. The role of children's advertising in this country makes it all the more imperative that everyone involved (media, advertisers, parents, special interest groups) work to ensure that children's advertising is appropriate for the audience to which it is intended.

---

[24]"An eye on children's advertising," a publication of the Children's Advertising Review Unit.
[25]Walter J. O'Brien, "An apple a day," *Agency*, Fall 1998, 48.

SUMMARY

In this chapter, we have been able to discuss only the highlights of the complex area of advertising regulation. However, it should be obvious that the legal, regulatory, and pubic opinion constraints concerning advertising will continue to demand a high level of performance from businesses and their agencies. The advertising community is aware of this concern and among the strongest proponents of fair and ethical marketing and promotion practices. Advertising executives know that the charlatans and scam artists make it difficult for all advertisers to maintain public confidence. They also invite greater scrutiny and government control of the industry.

Among major advertisers, there is no disagreement that advertising should be fair, truthful, and follow both the letter and the spirit of the law. The dollars invested in advertising substantiation, the media clearance process, and the industry-wide self-regulatory system are testimony to the fact that advertisers want to ensure fair and honest advertising. They know that even the appearance of impropriety can damage a brand's value—sometimes irreparably. Honest advertising not only is morally and ethically correct, but it is sound business practice as well.

REVIEW

1. What is the primary national governmental regulatory body for advertising?
2. What is the key element that the FTC requires in determining whether advertising is deceptive?
3. What is the concept of the "rational or reasonable consumer" in FTC enforcement?
4. What is meant by puffery?
5. What is the intent of the Central Hudson Four-Part Test?
6. What is the legal status of professional advertising?
7. What is corrective advertising?
8. What is a company's primary legal recourse when it has been harmed by deceptive comparison advertising?
9. What is the advertising clearance process?
10. What is the primary source of industry-wide advertising self-regulation?

TAKE IT TO THE NET

We invite you to visit the Russell/Lane page on the Prentice Hall Web site at **www.prenhall.com/myphlip** for end-of-chapter exercises and applications.

Chapter 26

Economic and Social Effects of Advertising

We have discussed the many roles that advertising plays in motivating buyers and distributing goods through the marketing channel. Implicit in this examination of advertising is its place in the overall society in which it functions. This chapter will examine the economic and social consequences of advertising. In doing so, we will see that some of these consequences are intended and some are coincidental. After reading this chapter you will understand:

» advertising as an economic force

» the societal implications of advertising

» responsible advertising is profitable advertising

» advertising and cause-related marketing

» the inadvertent social role of advertising

» the Advertising Council as an advocate for social goals

Advertising is regarded in a number of different ways. Economists, consumers, social advocates, and advertisers themselves have markedly different views of advertising as both a social and economic force. There is general agreement that advertising serves both the individual and the economy as a whole when it provides useful information that accurately describes the qualities of products, which in turn allow informed choices by consumers. However, reaching a consensus on what advertising concepts, practices, and executions achieve that goal is often difficult.

At one extreme, some economists believe that any advertising message beyond basic product descriptions is unnecessary and potentially misleading. At the other extreme, there are many in the business community who believe that advertising should have leeway for significant product puffery and emotional appeals as a means of creating product differentiation and a competitive selling environment.

Both economic and social critics were particularly vocal during the 1950s when motivational research and psychological testing started to be used in mainstream advertising. During this period psychologists teamed with advertisers in an attempt to determine the underlying (sometimes subconscious) reasons for product purchases. Advertising moved away from the tried and true "reason-why" copy approach with an emphasis on physical product benefits and began to focus ". . . on product features that implied social acceptance, style, luxury, and success . . . to create products with vivid personalities."[1] While the practice of motivational research and the application of psychological principles often created successful advertising, it was viewed with suspicion in many quarters, especially among consumer advocates. During the period there were endless debates over the use of subliminal advertising and other psychological techniques that critics claim would unconsciously coerce purchases from unwilling consumers.

While most people accept the fallacy of a good portion this research, the debate over the economic and social roles of advertising continues. Regardless of one's position, advertising occupies a primary position as a driving force in the sale and distribution of goods and services. The visibility of advertising in the marketing process has only increased the deliberations over the proper role of advertising. As consumers become more and more sophisticated about advertising, marketers realize they are under increasing scrutiny by the public, regulatory and public interest groups, and competitors.

In this environment, we should regard advertising, like most business functions, as simply a tool. It may be used for the best or worst of motives and it is practiced by those of high moral standards and charlatans. Effective advertising provides efficient and profitable communication for the firms that utilize it and reaches prospects with information that will aid consumers in making beneficial purchase decisions. However, to the extent that advertising has an important social component, advertisers have a greater responsibility to the public than most communicators.

As we begin our discussion of the effects of advertising, we should realize that marketing executives are sensitive to the dual role of balancing economic value and social responsibility and they work hard to fulfill both of these obligations. In the remainder of this chapter, we will discuss how advertising endeavors to achieve both economic efficiency and social responsibility for both buyers and sellers. However, we must remember that the social importance of advertising notwithstanding, its social goals must also consider the profit motive for the seller.

By the same token, we should understand that the social and economic elements of advertising are not mutually exclusive. For example, businesses are part of society and benefit from attention to environmental issues, better education, and other relevant societal issues that are brought to the public's attention through advertising. Likewise, to the extent that advertising can contribute to ending economic recession, gaining higher productivity and employment, and expanding the economy, the members of a society benefit from a higher standard of living.

This chapter will examine two major roles of advertising. First, we will discuss advertising's contribution to economic efficiency. That is, does advertising provide market information in a manner that could not be more effectively accomplished by other means? The second area of discussion is advertising's role in the social process as we examine its broad, noneconomic social effects.

---

[1]Juliann Sivulka, *Soap, Sex, and Cigarettes: A Cultural History of American Advertising* (Belmont, CA: Wadsworth Publishing Company, 1998), 266.

THE ECONOMIC ROLE OF ADVERTISING

One of the most controversial areas of advertising is the question of its contribution to the overall economy. To some it is a vital and extremely efficient means of introducing new products and maintaining brand awareness. However, in making a judgment about the benefits of advertising, we need to study its economic role of advertising from both the buyer's and seller's perspectives. From the view of the consumer, we want to know if advertising provides truthful, beneficial information that allows buyers to differentiate one product from another on a *meaningful basis*. And, if so, does it accomplish this objective in a more efficient manner than other means of consumer intelligence?

The second perspective is that of the seller. While these perspectives are not always mutually exclusive, obviously the motives of buyers and sellers are different. To be somewhat simplistic, the seller seeks maximum profits while the buyer seeks maximum satisfaction, often at the lowest cost. For example, in its mission statement for its Value of Advertising initiative, the 4As stated that it is "designed to understand and improve the process by which advertising budgets are set and approved by using advertising performance measurements credible to CEOs and CFOs."[2] Clearly, consumer satisfaction is of importance to CEOs, but it usually is secondary to other performance criteria such as profitability and stockholder equity.

ECONOMIC PERSPECTIVES ON ADVERTISING

As we mentioned earlier, there is a wide disparity of opinion concerning the economic contributions of advertising. To place the arguments in perspective, let's examine some of the most prevalent arguments for and against advertising.

The arguments in support of advertising are the following:

1. Advertising creates product improvements and new product development by promoting product quality. By doing so, competitors are compelled to provide consumers with matching or better product attributes. This process creates a spiral of product improvements to the benefit of consumers.

2. Advertising aids consumers in making informed product purchases by providing information about the newest products and product improvements. Mass advertising and promotion is the only practical means of keeping consumers informed of the multitude of products available in a dynamic economy.

3. Advertising revenues support a free press system. Advertising funds provide the public with access to a variety of media outlets that would otherwise be prohibitively expensive if available at all. The public gains economically by having access to inexpensive media supported by advertising and society gains through a readily available, democratic press system that is free from control by a small number of special interest groups or government.

4. By creating economies of scale, advertising actually reduces the cost of products to consumers. While advertising is obviously an expense to manufacturers and sellers of goods, by contributing to the creation of a mass market, consumers benefit from lower costs.

The arguments against advertising are the following:

---

[2] "Value of advertising," from www.aaaa.org, Web site of the American Association of Advertising Agencies.

1. Advertising is largely unproductive to the general economy. Most advertising, rather than creating real economic growth, is more likely to encourage consumers to switch brands. In such an environment, many firms utilize funds for advertising that might be better spent on research and development to produce superior products.

While there is no question that there is some validity to this criticism, economic productivity must be viewed from the perspective of both the individual firm and the total economy. In capitalism individual corporations must advertise to prevent brand share erosion even in the absence of overall sales increases in a product category. However, most economists are interested in advertising from a macroeconomic perspective. That is, does advertising contribute to the overall economic system as opposed to a specific firm?

Rather than trying to evaluate all advertising in terms of a single standard of productivity, we need to recognize that, like most business enterprises, advertising plays a number of roles on both a micro and macro level. With this in mind, we need to examine advertising economic productivity as a continuum rather than as an absolute:

- *Counterproductive.* That is, advertising is counterproductive when it raises prices or in some other way creates dissatisfaction with products that still have utility, thus causing unnecessary consumption. Critics often point out that advertising creates an environment in which social utility, as opposed to functional utility, is the motivation for an increasing number of purchases.

- *Unproductive.* Unproductive advertising is defined as advertising that does not increase generic demand, but causes no harm. Advertising designed to create brand switching among present consumers would fall into this category. Again, advertising that is judged to be unproductive on a macro level might have significant utility to an individual firm.

- *Somewhat productive.* Advertising in this category creates an increase in overall demand, but at a level lower than some other technique or at an unreasonably high cost.

- *Most productive.* The most productive advertising produces the greatest economic well-being at the lowest cost. In this category we assume that both buyers are informed of products that provide significant benefits and sellers are extending their sales and distribution in a profitable manner. Consequently, advertising is contributing to an ideal market situation in which buyers and sellers are both gaining significantly from the advertising investment.

It is difficult to deal in generalities when evaluating the economic value of advertising. Advertising's contribution to product sales is dependent on a host of circumstances unique to each product. The utility of advertising in a market for new products such as digital recording devices is much different than for the beer or cigarette industries whose products are characterized by flat sales and brand switching among most users. However, it is difficult to minimize advertising's contribution in the face of an annual investment of almost $200 billion.

2. Advertising's primary goal is to persuade rather than inform consumers. According to these critics an analysis of most advertising would provide messages that are heavy on exaggerated claims and light on useful information. By relying on emotional appeals, advertising often encourages consumers to purchase heavily advertised, but inferior products rather than creating an objective forum for product information.

No one would seriously debate that advertising's primary goal is to motivate prospects to buy products. However, the view that advertising alone can persuade to buy to fulfill some need gives advertising undue influence and underestimates the sophistication of most consumers.

Marketers know that advertising, no matter how effective, will not guarantee sales. Rather it works within an extremely complex framework of variables that ultimately determine purchase behavior. Product price, extent of distribution, quality of service, and perceived value relative to competition all play a role in making advertising effective and in turn are affected by advertising. Each company has unique problems associated with these factors and advertising may play a greater or lesser role in addressing a particular brand. As we discussed in Chapter 2, when advertising is unsuccessful, it is very likely that it was used inappropriately.

Advertising is flexible enough to speak to a number of marketing issues. It is the role of marketing and advertising departments to make sure that goals and objectives for the advertising program are clearly and realistically spelled out. For example, companies sometimes make the mistake of assuming that aggressive brand promotion is the only legitimate goal of advertising. However, advertisers must remember that advertising operates on two levels. Exhibit 26.1 shows how advertising moves the consumer vertically (**generic demand**) and horizontally (brand demand). A firm with very high market share might well engage in a generic demand strategy to increase product category spending. On the other hand, companies holding small shares of market will usually have to engage in aggressive brand advertising to maintain a competitive position with larger firms.

generic demand
The demand demonstrated for a product class rather than a specific brand.

3. Advertising does not affect the overall volume of spending, but rather redirects consumption with no net economic gain. That is, rather than increasing spending (which would increase output and increase employment), advertising simply moves money from one brand or category of products to another.

It is obvious that advertising does create brand switching and movement from one generic class of products to another. From a traditional macroeconomic point of view, advertising is not functioning in a productive role when engaging in these activities. However, we have to remember that we live in a competitive, capitalistic environment. Companies compete for consumers among a variety of very similar

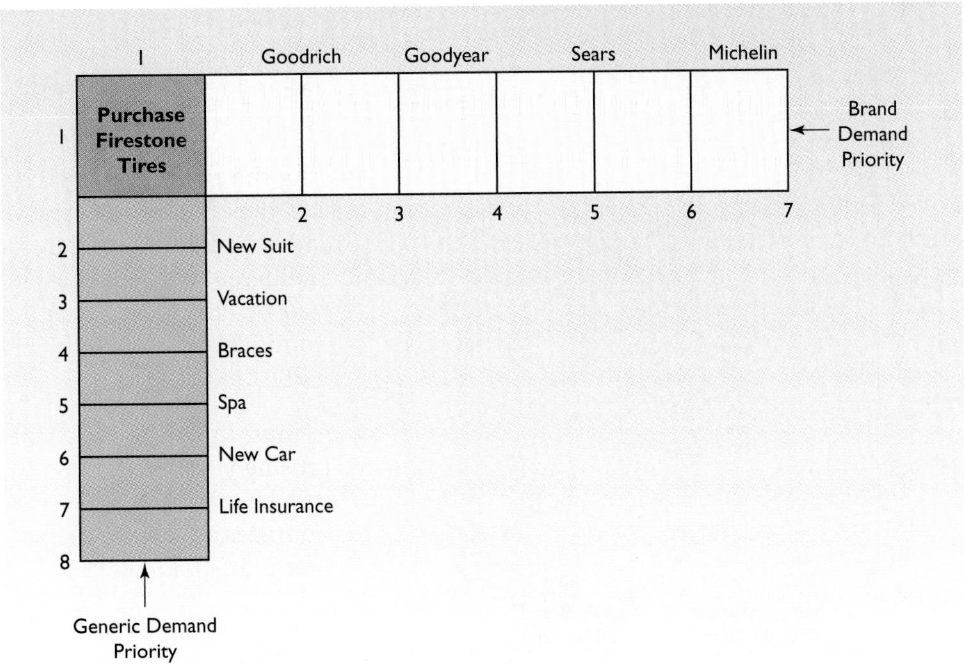

Exhibit 26.1

Effective advertising creates both brand and generic demand.

products. The huge expenditures for advertising and promotion is more testimony to the reality of the marketplace than any inherent deficiency of advertising as an economic tool.

Consensus concerning the economic role of advertising is extremely difficult to reach. The fact is that both the most vocal proponents and its harshest critics probably overstate the case. As in most debates the truth probably lies somewhere in the middle.

Effects of Advertising on Corporate Profits

Economists endlessly debate the role of advertising in terms of macroeconomic theory. Often these discussions center on the contributions of advertising within traditional models of pure competition, pure monopoly, and so forth. Advertising is often irrelevant in these models (e.g., in pure competition advertising is insignificant since the assumption is that most products are sold generically). However, companies use advertising in a world that rarely fits classical economic models. Rather, firms use advertising to gain greater profitability, greater market share, greater production efficiency, and even as a means of survival for the *individual firm*.

In a capitalistic environment, advertising operates in a framework of imperfect competition where product quality and price differ markedly among competing products. It is an environment where product distribution is often uneven, where service ranges from superior to awful, and where consumers are moved to purchase products based on emotional as well as rational motives.

Research has shown that consistent advertising for a product contributes to consumer perceptions that it is a quality brand (see Exhibit 26.2), that it is a good value (see Exhibit 26.3), and that it has a number of other positive attributes. Research shows that those companies committed to advertising's role in the marketing process tend to be more successful than other companies in the same product category. Among the findings are the following:

1. Advertising is not a frill activity, but rather it is a necessary and important part of a business's marketing operations. Without advertising, you are missing a vital link in the process that starts with brand awareness and leads through a

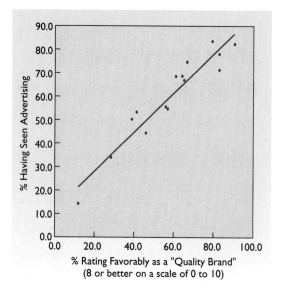

Exhibit

26.2

Percentage Rating Favorably the Product as a "Quality Brand" and Having Seen Its Advertising

From: Cahners Advertising Research Report, No. 130.2, October 1995, 2–3.

(graph axis labels) % Having Seen Advertising; % Rating Favorably as a "Quality Brand" (8 or better on a scale of 0 to 10)

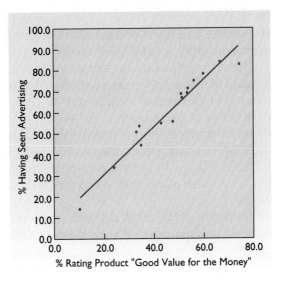

Exhibit

26.3

Percentage Rating the Product as a "Good Value for the Money" and Having Seen Its Advertising

From: Cahners Advertising Research Report, No. 130.2, October 1995, 2–3.

series of complex steps to increased sales, greater market share, and improved profitability.

2. There is a direct relationship between the amount of advertising a business does and its success in the marketplace. It isn't enough that a product is advertised. Of even greater importance is the amount of advertising. The businesses that advertise more than their competitors get better results. Token programs get token results.

3. Advertising enhances the way a product is perceived in the marketplace. To a large extent, the reputation that a product has for quality and for value are actually determined by the way and the degree to which the product is advertised and quality is the single most important factor in making a sale.

4. Finally, while advertising is an art, it is also a science. We know a great deal about the way it works, how it interacts with other aspects of the marketing operations of a business, and the way it helps to build profitability.[3]

Simply put, effective advertising enhances the consumer's image of a product, which in turn increases the likelihood that the product will be purchased. Advertising's contribution to product enhancement will often lead to significantly higher profits compared to products with lower customer esteem.

THE SOCIAL ROLE OF ADVERTISING

Whereas the economic contributions of advertising are typically the major concern of both companies and consumers, in recent years its social implications are coming under increasing scrutiny. There is little disagreement, even among advertising's harshest critics, that it serves a role in informing customers of new products, location, prices, and distribution outlets. These are the economic functions of the institution of advertising. However, the social and cultural roles of advertising are less clear and a topic of growing discussion in a number of quarters.

As we have discussed, advertising is primarily a communication tool and, as such, it functions within the basic models of communication theory developed over the last 75 years. As individuals are exposed to thousands of advertising mes-

---

[3]"How advertising drives profitability," *Cahners Advertising Research Report*, No. 2000.9, 6.

sages, these theories suggest that there are cumulative effects on both individuals and society as a result of this exposure. Later in this chapter, we will discuss some uses of advertising as an overt agent for social change.

Here, however, our interest is in the unintentional social role of advertising. A number of media researchers hypothesize that advertising contributes to the transmission of values and socialization of norms within a society. Depending on the perspective of the researcher, these values may be negative—a preoccupation with materialist acquisition—or positive—the encouragement of economic upward mobility. To some, advertising trivializes society by implying that all problems are solvable within a 30-second slice-of-life commercial. To others, advertising simplifies a complex marketplace by offering a variety of options to fulfill consumer needs.

In recent years, more research and attention has been devoted to these "secondary consequences" of advertising. If this research has shown us anything, it is that the study of advertising's social communication is multidimensional and not easily understood. For example, a body of research known as critical/cultural studies suggests that the interpretation of a mass communication message is in large part a matter of the prior preconceptions of the individual audience member.

As we discussed in Chapter 16, advertisers seek to communicate a central theme. The theme is product centered and, whatever the social setting of the ad or commercial, it is designed largely to create an interesting and relevant environment for a particular target market. The fact that individual members of the audience supply their own meanings, particularly to the social context, makes it very difficult for advertisers to avoid unintentional potholes.

Regardless of the intended advertising message, the implied, indirect communication conveyed by advertising is a topic that advertisers must deal with particularly in a multicultural society. Consumers are sophisticated in the way they view the media and advertising and are demanding more realistic and fair presentations of society. Addressing the problem is the first step in moving to solve a very complex issue. Addressing the portrayal of people of color in advertising, the Reverend Jesse Jackson pointed out that "Multi-cultural marketing . . . is good for business. It is a sign of respect for the growing prominence of minority consumers. To maintain and increase a competitive market share in the future, companies must earn customer loyalty within communities of color."[4]

In addressing the controversy over advertising's societal role, some argue that Americans are too ready to jump on any misstep, no matter how innocuous, in the name of political correctness. Others view it as a healthy trend that advertisers are becoming more sensitive to the potential harm done by inaccurate or unfair portrayals of people. For sure, the debate has brought advertising's social role to the forefront. This awareness of a social dimension long ignored by most advertisers is perhaps the most positive element to come out of these recent debates.

TYPES OF ADVERTISING CRITICISM

Surprisingly, given the primary economic function of advertising, the majority of contemporary advertising criticism centers on its role in society. Particularly in the popular press, the debate concerning the value and propriety of modern advertising is likely to concentrate on its effects on society as contrasted to any potential effects on the economy. Most social advertising criticism falls into one or more of the following four categories:

---

[4]The Rev. Jesse Jackson, "Rainbow imperative," *Advertising Age: The Next Century*, 1999, 56.

1. The Content of Advertising

A significant majority of advertising criticism concerns the content of specific ads and commercials. As we saw in Chapter 25, numerous complaints are brought by companies disturbed about competitor's claims, particularly in comparative advertising that they regard as unfair or deceptive. In addition, an array of alleged abuses from the use of sexual themes, exaggerated product claims, debasement of language by using purposely misspelled words and incorrect grammar, perpetuating of stereotypes, and manipulating children with unrealistic claims and promises are also cited.

A great deal of advertising criticism centers on its portrayal of some group in an unflattering or unrealistic manner. The 1960s marked a watershed in the fight to have more inclusive and realistic advertising treatment of women and African Americans. With the founding of the National Organization for Women (NOW) in 1966, an energized women's movement sought to eliminate traditional stereotypes of women as only wives and mothers.

Authors, such as Betty Friedan (*The Feminine Mystique*, 1963), created greater sensitivity to the role of women. As women moved into traditional male jobs, the 1960s saw women become corporate executives, lawyers, doctors, and engineers in greater and greater numbers. While advertising was slow to reflect the changing times, there was a notable change in the philosophy of some advertising portrayals of women during the period.

One of the most significant changes in advertising was the emergence of the female advertising executive. Women such as Mary Wells entered the executive suite and further accelerated the recognition of women in the advertising industry. Today, women occupy a prominent place in all areas of the communication industry, and they are not shy about making their views known about sexist advertising.

For example, Advertising Women of New York awards annual "Good, Bad and Ugly" Awards to advertisers they think are supportive and demeaning to women. The effort is an attempt by the advertising women to raise the sensitivity of their colleagues. As one of the members of the organization pointed out, ". . . the creative juices are flowing in the right direction, but I would say we're not out of the woods yet." Another woman executive said the purpose of the award was ". . . to say that someone's watching—and consumers are watching too."[5]

While advertising is making major strides to provide a more realistic portrayal of society in its messages, there is still more to do. During the 1990s, advertisers became more understanding of the roles of women and minorities. Despite advertising's heightened sensibility to women's issues and their portrayals in advertising, studies continue to show that many women remain unsatisfied with their depiction in advertising.

Not surprisingly, numerous studies show that women want to be realistically and fairly depicted in advertising. This research also underlines the changing nature of what is acceptable not only in advertising, but society in general. Astute advertisers must regard cultural issues as constantly changing and they must make every effort to implement steps to keep with these shifts.

Historically, the issue of fair treatment in advertising has been even worse for minorities than for women. In the past, many minority groups claim, with justification, that they were either ignored entirely or, when included in advertising, their roles were depicted as unequal to those of white models. This situation is slowly changing for two reasons. First, there is growing sensitivity to the issue by companies and advertising agencies. Second, faced with the diverse demographics of

---

[5]Stuart Elliott, "Women's group to present Good, Bad and Ugly Awards," www.newyorktimes.com, 28 September 1999.

American society, an advertiser would have to be extremely shortsighted to ignore minorities as potential prospects.

In recent years, a second minority-related advertising issue has come to the fore. For some time, there has been anecdotal evidence that minority media, especially radio, were being systematically excluded from corporate advertising schedules and, when included, advertisers were paying lower rates than for majority-owned stations.

In 1999, William E. Kennard, chairman of the FCC, brought the issue to public attention.[6] Citing a study entitled "When Being Number One is Not Enough," Kennard charged that minority broadcasters were being financially harmed by so-called "no urban/Spanish dictates." Basically, these were requirements by agencies and advertisers that no spots were to be purchased on urban music or Spanish-language stations. He saw these stipulations as being based on racial stereotypes rather than objective audience or marketing data. For example, one Hispanic broadcaster charged that a disposable diaper maker paid his stations less per spot than other stations even though Hispanics are among the heaviest users of the product.

In response to these allegations, Wally Snyder, president and CEO of the American Advertising Federation, a leading trade association, said, "Blanket policies like 'no urban and no Spanish dictates' do a disservice to everyone involved. . . . We urge advertisers and agencies to make decisions based on facts and not fiction. We urge them to value the contributions people of color can make to the bottom lines."[7]

Clearly the fair treatment and inclusion of minorities in advertising is a complex one. However, as the issues are increasingly discussed by advertisers and other interested groups, both the sensitivity to the issues and, ultimately, answers to the problems will be closer to solution.

Advertising and Senior Citizens   While not strictly speaking a minority group, seniors are another market that has been historically underrepresented in advertising. As we discussed in earlier chapters, advertisers continue to concentrate the bulk of their marketing efforts on 18- to 34-year-old consumers. However, as life spans and health care have improved during the last century, the 50-and-older population has shown significant growth. For example, U.S. Census estimates indicate that by 2020, Americans 50 or over will number 114 million (see Exhibit 26.4). This figure will increase to 124 million by the year 2030 when more than half of the population will be in this age group.

Of more importance to advertisers than the sheer number of older consumers is their financial well-being. According to the Federal Reserve, Americans with the highest level of financial assets are in the 65–74 age group, followed by those in the 55–64 segment.[8] In addition, these population groups rarely have children living at home (or in college) and often have no mortgage payments. Therefore, their income-to-debt ratio is more favorable than any other demographic segment. By virtually any financial measure, this group is one that marketers should increasingly attempt to reach (Exhibit 26.5).

As we have seen in our discussions of minority-related advertising, simple inclusion in an advertisement or commercial is not enough. The mature audience cannot be treated as a homogeneous group. Their interests, lifestyles, and product preferences cover a wide range of needs just as in any other market segment. As one

---

[6]Material in this section is from the FCC Web site, www.fcc.gov.
[7]Wally Snyder in testimony to the Federal Trade Commission, 13 January 1999.
[8]Cheryl Russell and Marcis Mogelonsky, "Riding high on the market," *American Demographics*, April 2000, 45–54.

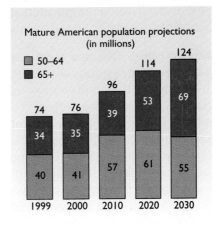

Mature American population projections
(in millions)

- 50–64
- 65+

Year	1999	2000	2010	2020	2030
Total	74	76	96	114	124
65+	34	35	39	53	69
50–64	40	41	57	61	55

Exhibit

26.4

Baby Boom's Encore

Source: U.S. Census Bureau.

From: Al Urbanski, "Grow up, already," *Promo,* October 1999, 23.

marketing executive pointed out, "Younger people marketing to older people tend to look at retirement as a 52-week vacation."[9] In fact, research shows that most mature adults have a need to find a purpose in their lives whether it is part-time or full-time employment, volunteer work, and so forth, and advertising should reflect this vitality.

Marketing to the Gay Community   We mentioned earlier in this chapter that advertising often lags behind reality in its portrayal of changes in lifestyle and society. Nowhere is this more apparent than in the conservative approaches made to the gay community. For years, marketing research has shown that this market segment has high disposable income, demonstrates significant brand loyalty, and constitutes an important market for a variety of brands. Yet, most mainstream advertisers have only recently openly targeted this market.

One company that has a long record of advertising to the gay market is Coors, which has placed advertisements in gay publications since the 1980s. Coors recently announced that future spending in gay magazines such as *The Advocate* and *Genre,* as well as a variety of other promotional vehicles, would increase 20 percent annually.[10] There is still reluctance on the part of many national corporations to advertise in gay-oriented publications or to direct mainstream media advertising to this market. However, the trend is toward greater inclusion of gays in the advertising plans of many major corporations. As more and more well-known brands

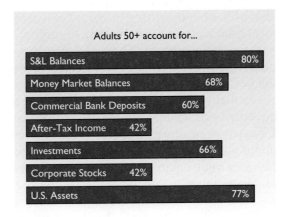

Adults 50+ account for...

Category	Percent
S&L Balances	80%
Money Market Balances	68%
Commercial Bank Deposits	60%
After-Tax Income	42%
Investments	66%
Corporate Stocks	42%
U.S. Assets	77%

Exhibit

26.5

Old Money

Source: The Senior Network.

From: Al Urbanski, "Grow up, already," *Promo,* October, 1999, 23.

---

[9]Al Urbanski, "Grow up, already," *Promo,* October 1999, 24.
[10]Hillary Chura, "Coors hikes spending on gay ads," *Advertising Age,* 27 March 2000, 16.

start to reach out to the gay market, we will see this type of advertising and promotion become more accepted by both advertisers and media.

Advertising Claims and Exaggeration   While various segments of the population are rightfully concerned about the attention and portrayals they receive in advertising, a second content-oriented criticism focuses on factors such as exaggeration and excessive puffery in advertising. Many critics charge that advertising is likely to provide misinformation that barely skirts basic legal requirements with negative appeals or, in some cases, outright falsehoods. As we discussed in Chapter 25, there are few business functions that undergo more governmental and regulatory scrutiny than advertising. But apart from these formal constraints, advertisers know that it is bad business to mislead consumers. While false or misleading advertising may influence a consumer to make an initial purchase, rarely will an unsatisfied consumer return. Putting aside the question of whether or not advertising is inherently less ethical than other business practices, we should at least give its practitioners credit for common sense.

2. The Product Being Advertised

Advertising is often caught in the crossfire between changing attitudes toward products and product categories and the legitimate interests of manufacturers to promote their brands. The controversy involved in this category of criticism centers on two issues.

The first issue is that the products are harmful or can be misused and therefore it is in the public interest to curtail their promotion. Sometimes, public opinion forces legal restrictions against the advertising of such products. As we discussed in Chapter 25, the Clinton administration, the Federal Drug Administration, and the Federal Trade Commission have been involved to one degree or another in limiting the promotion of tobacco. Many observers, especially those within the tobacco industry, see the latest round of restrictions as another indication that attempts will be made to expand current advertising restrictions to a total prohibition on any form of tobacco promotion.

Regardless of how one views these limitations for tobacco advertising and other legitimate products, it is obvious that advertising is being used as an indirect method to control the distribution. Alcohol is another category of products where advertising is almost as controversial as the products themselves. For a number of years, companies such as Seagram have tried to challenge the 60-year voluntary ban on broadcast advertising (this ban is limited to hard liquor, not beer or wine). To date liquor advertising has only been accepted by a few local cable systems and local broadcast stations. The ban continues to be enforced by most local stations and the major networks have a firm policy against liquor advertising. Industry observers cite a fear that widespread acceptance of liquor advertising would initiate FCC or congressional action as the reason for continuation of the ban.[11]

In many respects, those who oppose the use of tobacco and liquor are attacking advertising as a surrogate for these products. Many executives in the advertising industry, even those opposed to tobacco and liquor advertising, are concerned about government efforts to eliminate promotion of legal products. A number of industry trade organizations and individual agencies have spoken out on the issue and have joined to fight what they see as an infringement on the First Amendment rights of advertisers. They recognize that they are facing a major public relations battle as well as a legal one. In these types of controversies, the nuances are often lost on the general public and the advertising industry is portrayed as an advocate for big tobacco and liquor manufacturers.

---

[11]Hillary Chura, "Seagram ads drive cablers to drink again," *Advertising Age*, 24 April 2000, 97.

The second issue of advertising content is being waged over whether advertising that is "offensive" should be limited in some way. Based on personal preferences, there are those who would limit the promotion of personal hygiene items and other sensitive products. However, just as advertising may have a socialization effect on the audience, changing social mores about what is acceptable is constantly changing and these changes can often be seen in the content and creative execution of advertising messages.

Perhaps the most obvious indicator of the way advertising changes public attitudes is the advertising of birth control products and condoms. Despite pleas from the public health community, condom advertising traditionally has been banned from virtually every broadcast outlet. A decade ago, protest accompanied the first late-night condom advertising, even though it was largely confined to a few small independent stations.

During the 1990s, the seminudity on *NYPD Blue*, the sexually explicit story lines on shows like *Melrose Place*, and the various Lewinsky story lines in the news media may have desensitized the public to the point that commercials for birth control products seem tame by comparison. In any case, while a number of stations and cable networks will now accept condom commercials, the three major television networks will not. However, CBS has announced that it has the matter under advisement. Stay tuned.

3. Excessive Advertising Exposure

Many people say there is simply too much advertising regardless of its content. These critics often attack advertising as part of a commercialization of society that makes materialism a primary goal of our culture. Among the most controversial areas is the introduction of advertising and promotion into education. For the last two decades, companies have provided schools free instructional equipment, sponsorships of athletic teams, and other financial support in exchange for commercial opportunities to reach prime targets of school-aged children and their parents. While many parents and students are vocally opposed to the practice, fiscally strapped school systems look on these commercial opportunities as financial windfalls.

As we indicated in Chapter 13, both direct-mail and telemarketing are fighting a constant battle against those who wish to place legal restrictions against their use. However, in terms of mainstream advertising, most of the criticism in this category is directed toward television since print ads are more easily ignored by simply turning the page. A number of studies have shown that the commercialization of television has reached unprecedented levels in recent years.

The 1999 television season marked the first time that major networks expanded commercial breaks within shows to five minutes. Both NBC's *Law & Order: Special Victims Unit* and ABC's *West Wing* broke the five-minute barrier. In the past, these levels of commercialization had been largely confined to local stations during non-prime-time periods. While public complaints about clutter are increasingly heard, advertisers are equally concerned. As one media executive said, "Beyond just remembering the commercials, when you begin having commercial breaks last 4 or 5 minutes, people start switching channels."[12]

Indeed, research shows that the concerns of advertisers are well founded. In a study by Roper Starch Worldwide (see Exhibit 26.6), 52 percent of respondents were annoyed at the number of commercials. An alarming 39 percent of the audience switches to another channel during commercials (up almost 40 percent since 1990). Overall, only 19 percent of respondents said that they sit and watch commercials.

---

[12]Chuck Ross, "Now, many words from our sponsors," *Advertising Age*, 27 September 1999, 3.

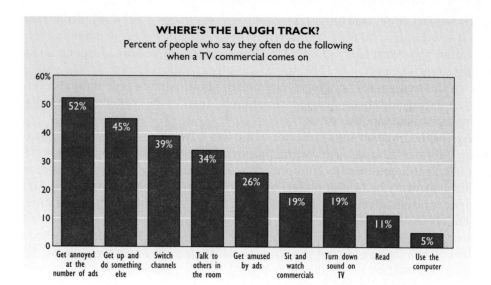

Exhibit

26.6

Research shows lack of audience attention to commercials.

Source: Roper Starch Worldwide.

From: American Demographics, September 1999, 20.

Many advertisers are concerned that the sheer number of advertising messages makes the public indifferent to them. As we paint buildings, glue messages to the floor of supermarkets, hang signs in elevators, and place stadium advertising that exists only in cyberspace, the question becomes when is enough really enough? In the 1970s, conventional wisdom said that the average person was exposed to 1,500 advertising messages each day. Now that estimate is more like 5,000. As one advertising agency president commented on the glut of messages, "It's the ultimate challenge. The greater the number of ads, the less people pay attention to them. One ad is the same as another now. People simply don't believe them anymore."[13]

It will be interesting to see what, if any, effect the introduction of new media technology and the fragmentation and interactive nature of future media vehicles will have on advertising exposure. Obviously, when interactive media allow consumers to accept or reject programming, advertising, or infomercials, there is much less likelihood that advertising will be regarded as intrusive.

4. Advertising's Unwanted Influences on Society

The final category of advertising criticism is in many respects related to the three we have already discussed. In this more general classification, critics dislike advertising basically because it exists. They disparage it on the grounds of content, motive, intrusiveness, and cost.

The charges range from advertising making people buy products they do not want or need, lowering morals, and generally exploiting the most susceptible segments of society, especially children. In fact, most research shows that mass communication, especially overtly persuasive communication such as advertising, has a very difficult time making even small changes in behavioral intentions or attitudes.

Likewise, common sense tells us that the advertising industry has little to gain by creating dissatisfied customers particularly when virtually all companies depend on return purchases for their existence. The best advertising are messages that provide factual product information that allows consumers to make reasoned choices among product options. As we have seen in Chapter 25, when the system fails there are a host of legal, regulatory, and self-regulation mechanisms available to rectify the situation.

---

[13]Charles Pappas, "Ad nauseam," *Advertising Age,* 10 July 2000, 16.

It is interesting that the overwhelming criticism in this fourth category is designed to protect other people, not the critics themselves. That is, most critics take the view that, while a particular advertising element will not fool them, they are duty bound to help those less intelligent who may be misled by some advertising ploy.

Advertising criticism is not a new phenomenon. However, a brief review of the history of advertising and its critics demonstrates that both have changed markedly over the last 130 years. Clearly, advertisers are asked to meet different standards than those of earlier years. The public view of advertising has changed over three major periods:

1. *The Era of Exaggerated Claims, 1865–1900* During this period most people accepted advertising as "buyer beware" communication where virtually any claim for a product was allowed. Some advertising claims, especially for patented medicine, were so outlandish that one wonders how anyone could have believed them.

2. *The Era of Public Awareness, 1900–1965* By the turn of the century, legislation such as the Pure Food and Drug Act of 1906 demonstrated a recognition that the public was demanding a truthful portrayal of products and services. Many responsible advertisers feared for the very existence of the industry as deceptive advertising became more and more prevalent during the closing years of the nineteenth century.

3. *The Era of Social Responsibility, 1965–present* During the last 30 years, advertisers have come to realize that literal truth is not sufficient to meet the demands of many consumers. Advertisers know that they must meet a standard of **social responsibility** in addition to providing truthful advertising. The consumer movement of the l960s, concerns with environmental safety, and a heightened awareness of social issues are reflected in modern advertising.

social responsibility The demand that advertising be aware of its responsibility to the public, i.e., it should do more than sell goods and services.

You will recall in Chapter 25, we discussed the formal regulatory constraints on advertising. In addition to these organizations, there are a number of consumer and public policy groups that seek to constrain deceptive or misleading advertising through publicity. Among the most well known is the Center for Science in the Public Interest, which presents the annual Harlan Page Hubbard Memorial Award to those advertisers who have failed to serve the public interest. The award "honors" the nineteenth century ad man who touted such products as Lydia Pinkham's Vegetable Compound, which promised cures for ailments ranging from cancer to arthritis. Meanwhile, organizations such as Mothers Against Drunk Driving (MADD) publicize advertising they think appeals to underaged drinkers and attempt to muster public opinion against these companies.

These are dozens of other consumer advocacy groups who have no official or legal authority. They do have the ability to muster negative public opinion and put a spotlight on questionable advertising. No reputable company wants to receive this type of notoriety and advertisers will usually respond to these consumer organizations in a positive manner if they think the criticism is justified.

Advertisers and their agencies also are sensitive to the content of media in which their messages appear. Some advertisers' policies are general in terms of media and programming that cannot be used by their agencies, and these restrictions usually gain little attention except from the sales reps who are denied commissions. For example, General Motors will not allow advertising to be placed in racier men's magazines.

Occasionally, the debate over media content becomes a major issue between advertisers and the media. For example, Procter & Gamble has been traditionally among the strictest advertisers in reviewing media content. In 2000, the company formed a "sex task force" to examine the company's advertising policy toward explicit magazine articles and covers. As one P&G executive said, "What we're doing is part of an ongoing dialogue with all different types of media . . . in order to encourage a positive environment in which to advertise our brands."[14]

No one challenges the right of an advertiser to choose the media outlets in which they want to advertise. However, media executives worry about the potential chilling effect when advertisers base media-buying decisions on editorial content. A legitimate fear is that publishers might be tempted to reconsider running certain stories if companies such as Procter & Gamble, which spends $500 million in magazines, complain about content.

Ironically, publishers, television producers, and others responsible for editorial and entertainment material find themselves in much the same position as those who are opposed to cigarettes, but view tobacco bans as an intrusion of the First Amendment. While media understand the motives of large companies to protect their image by advertising in media they find "acceptable," they worry about the long ramifications of the linkage between advertising and media content. We will discuss this problem in more detail later in this chapter.

OVERT USE OF ADVERTISING FOR SOCIAL CAUSES

In recent years, advertising has become an important component in persuading the public to embrace a number of social causes. The overt use of advertising to foster social causes is growing as more organizations, companies, and even individuals convey messages about some social cause through paid messages.

The same characteristics that make advertising such a beneficial tool in marketing products and services are also used to move people to adopt various social causes and gain support for nonprofit organizations. Social advertising is not an entirely new phenomenon. However, the number of diverse organizations using advertising to promote social causes has dramatically increased in the last two decades.

In recent years a number of civic, religious, and public policy organizations have increasingly used advertising to disseminate their messages to the widest possible audience (see Exhibit 26.7). The low cost and broad audiences reached by advertising will continue to make it a major means of circulating social messages. The most organized effort of social advocacy is the Advertising Council, which we mentioned briefly in Chapter 1.

THE ADVERTISING COUNCIL

advertising council
A non-profit network of agencies, media, and advertisers dedicated to promoting social programs through advertising.

For almost 60 years, the **Advertising Council** has created and distributed dozens of campaigns designed to stimulate public action and address major problems facing this country.[15] Council campaigns must be noncommercial, nondenominational, nonpolitical, and important to the general public. Since its beginnings dealing with wartime threats, the council continues to select, define, and confront some of the nation's most pressing problems.

Ad Council campaigns, in many respects, reflect contemporary society and its attitudes and concerns. While continuing to address issues concerning the environment, education, and public safety, the council has recently begun concentrated efforts to promote better family values and health care. Recognizing the number of single-parent families and the growing problem of children being raised

---

[14]Ann Marie Kerwin and Jack Neff, "Too sexy? P&G 'task force' stirs magazine debate," *Advertising Age,* 10 April 2000, 1.
[15]Information in this section was provided by the Advertising Council.

Exhibit
26.7

Advertising is used to communicate a number of diverse messages.
Courtesy: Jacobs Outdoor.

in less than ideal conditions, the council has emphasized child-oriented volunteerism through its "Give a Kid a Hand" campaign. It also has encouraged parental responsibility with messages in its "I Am Your Child" and "Child Abuse Prevention" initiatives. Similarly, the council's "Organ and Tissue Donor" campaign attempts to meet the serious shortfall in organ donors.

Council campaigns continue to be supported because research shows that they work. For a number of years, the council has measured the success of its campaigns. Results have shown that public service announcements can be an effective means of education and positive behavioral change. Some of the major campaigns and the results they have achieved include the following:

- **Colon Cancer**. A study conducted by the Advertising Research Foundation examined results of the council's "Inspiring Action and Saving Lives" campaign directed toward raising men's awareness of colon cancer. Research indicated that awareness of colon cancer among men increased almost 600 percent in the year after the initiation of the campaign. More importantly, the number of men tested for colon cancer showed an increase of 114 percent during the same period.

- **National Crime Prevention Council**. Another research study collected data from the council's long-running McGruff the Crime Dog campaign. The results showed that 80 percent of the public were aware of the campaign and 20 percent of respondents said they had taken specific actions as a result of what they had learned from the advertising.

While the success of Ad Council programs is undeniable, a number of issues face the organization as it enters the twenty-first century.[16]

1. Fragmented media. The Ad Council faces the same media-scheduling problems as its commercial counterparts. The sheer number of media outlets makes it more difficult to reach the majority of the population especially with general campaigns such as those encouraging use of seat belts. This fragmentation also increases the administrative costs of the council compared to the days when it dealt with three television networks and a relatively few mass circulation magazines.

---

[16]Stuart Elliott, "Advertising Council's new president is first from media business," www.nytimes.com, 28 September 1999.

2. The federal government's willingness to pay for some spots in its anti-drug campaign has created new competition for scarce air time for both the Ad Council and other social agencies seeking free exposure.

3. Related to the competition from government-sponsored advertising campaigns, there are now a host of corporate cause-related promotional enterprises that also vie for council placements with paid media schedules. We will discuss cause-related marketing in the next section.

Despite difficulties with placing their announcements, the Ad Council remains the single most important source of social advertising. Due in large measure to its efforts, the use of advertising to communicate social issues has been taken up by a number of other companies and organizations. For example, social institutions such as churches have turned to advertising, and advocacy advertising has also been used by corporations that think that media presentations of certain issues have been unfair and want to get their side of a story before the public. While some people have reservations about the role of advertising in promoting social institutions and issues, proponents argue that there is no more effective or inexpensive means of getting these messages before the public.

In the future, we can expect this type of advertising to increase as people accept the legitimate role of the mass media as a forum for public debate as well as product information. The availability of media with narrowly defined audiences, such as cable and specialized publications, will lead to even more advertising with social themes.

Advertising and Cause-Related Marketing

Only a few years ago, advertising for social causes, with the exception of some high visibility Ad Council campaigns, was a very minor part of total advertising messages. In 1971, Philip Kotler and Gerald Zaltman coined the term "social marketing," which they defined as "the design, implementation, and control of programs calculated to influence the acceptability of social ideas."[17] Today, so-called **cause-related marketing** has become an important part of advertising with its own practitioners, agencies, and research techniques. However, we need to distinguish between two categories of idea advertising:

cause-related marketing Marketing strategies that attempt to link a company to some social or charitable cause.

Social Marketing   The sophisticated marketing of concepts such as HIV prevention, anti-smoking initiatives, voter registration drives, and product recycling have become a major part of the advertising landscape. Unlike pro bono work with the Ad Council, a number of advertising agencies have concentrated their work in the area of social marketing and advertising. Millions of dollars are available to agencies from social service agencies, private organizations interested in social causes, and various levels of government.

Cause-Related Marketing   As contrasted with social marketing where good deeds are the expected outcome, cause-related marketing seeks to combine good works *and* profits. Cause-related marketing (also known as strategic philanthropy) attempts to associate a company or brand with some social cause. The idea is that this association with a social initiative of interest to a company's target market will create a brand differentiation, which unlike price or even product characteristics, cannot be easily matched by competitors. An example of this approach is Avon's campaign to heighten awareness and increase research funding for breast cancer.

The technique is an excellent value added, but rarely should it be the core strategy for selling a product. The most effective cause-related promotions are those

---

[17]Barry Schoenfeld, *Agency*, Spring 1999, 40.

that are based on long-term commitments to a single cause. Consumers grow to associate certain companies with specific philanthropies such as the Ronald McDonald Houses where families of hospitalized children can stay free of charge.

American Express is credited with introducing cause-related marketing in 1983 when it promised to make a donation to the renovation of the Statue of Liberty each time someone used its card. Cause-related marketing allows both companies and their customers to help some organization, while the company increases sales and builds customer goodwill. Like most promotional techniques, cause-related marketing has grown because it has been shown to work.

In the last decade, cause-related marketing has become a mainstay in the marketing programs of many companies. Long-term relationships between a company and a cause can build brand equity and strengthen relationships not only with customers, but with employees and other external public groups. According to surveys, 83 percent of Americans have a more positive image of a company that engages in meaningful cause-related marketing. Companies annually invest more than $600 million in cause-related sponsorships. As one media executive pointed out, "Cause marketing continues to grow because companies want to stand out, and having a social overlay to marketing campaigns has proven an effective way to do that."[18]

Environment Marketing

Environmental claims are primary elements in the advertising of a number of companies. In fact, the FTC has issued "Guides for the Use of Environmental Marketing Claims" to provide a framework for advertisers promoting environmental themes. Basically, the FTC holds advertisers to the same substantiation standards for environmental issues as it does with other product claims. The FTC warns that marketers must take care to qualify broad or vague environmental assertions. According to the FTC, ". . . marketers must be able to substantiate the reasonable interpretations that consumers draw from a [environmental] claim."[19]

Despite the FTC's interest and numerous news stories addressing environmental issues, are we really as "green" as we think? The year 2000 marked the thirtieth anniversary of Earth Day. As in every year since 1970, it was marked by Hollywood stars making speeches, press releases from environmental policy think tanks, and politicians exhorting their constituents to do their part for the environment. For all the rhetoric, the era of green marketing, so popular in the early 1990s, seems to have faded.

While a number of companies and products are still actively engaged in environmentally friendly endeavors, the public seems to be less interested than in earlier years. From the popularity of gas-guzzling sports utility vehicles to a significant growth in disposable diaper usage, consumers are voting against environmental products.

Some marketing executives think that the green marketing phenomenon of a decade ago was more talk than action anyway. While Earth Day and similar environmental awareness programs have raised public sensitivity, these educational campaigns have not been translated into significant lifestyle changes for the majority of American consumers. As one environmental activist observed, "Consumers want to have a clean conscience, but at the same time they're unwilling to pay more for environmentally responsible products that carry a significant price premium."[20]

---

[18]Barry Spethmann, "Contributions," *Promo*, February 1999, 31.
[19]From Federal Trade Commission, "Guide to environmental marketing claims," www.ftc.gov.
[20]Jack Neff, "It's not trendy being green," *Advertising Age*, 10 April 2000, 16.

When companies introduce environmentally oriented products and customers don't respond, both company executives and stockholders quickly lose interest. Despite the lack of general consumer interest in environmental marketing, we should not overlook the many companies and consumers who engage in and respond to green marketing. For example, sports clothing company Patagonia uses organic cotton in its products and donates substantial gifts to environmental concerns. Likewise, Swedish appliance maker Electrolux markets water-efficient washing machines and a solar lawn mower.[21] The question for marketers is how many consumers are interested in such products and are they willing to pay a higher price than traditional products to buy them?

ADVERTISING'S INFLUENCE ON EDITORIAL CONTENT

Historically, there have been three primary methods of supporting a press system: (1) government, (2) special interest groups such as religious denominations, and (3) a combination of advertising and the audience. In this country, depending on the medium, 50 to 100 percent of revenues are provided by advertising. Philosophically, advertising support is welcomed since it provides the media with revenues from many different companies and individuals so that no one entity has undue influence on editorial content.

Therefore, any threat of editorial influence by advertisers must be taken seriously. The traditional separation of advertising and editorial departments has become more problematic in recent years as the media have begun to adopt marketing strategies to promote all aspects of their operations. There are two primary areas of advertising influence that concern many observers:

1. *Direct influence by advertisers.* While anecdotal reports of advertisers' attempting to influence editorial decisions have circulated for years, recent surveys tend to offer evidence of the extent of this pressure. Studies indicate that a significant majority of editors report that advertisers have tried to influence news content, have withdrawn advertising because of editorial coverage, and have tried to kill specific stories. More alarming, in one study, it was reported that in 36 percent of cases advertisers were successful in influencing changes in editorial decisions.[22]

2. *Advertiser participation in advertorials and special issues.* In recent years, a number of media have created promotional ties with advertisers through the use of infomercials, advertorials, and special sections of magazines and newspapers. The concept of the advertorial is simple enough. A company, special interest group, or other organization places an ad to promote an idea rather than a product. The term **advertorial** suggests that the advertiser is placing a clearly identified sponsored message (or editorial) to bring some topic to the attention of readers or listeners. In principle, the idea is worthwhile and some would argue in the finest traditions of a free press. Since the early 1980s, the use of the advertorial has changed dramatically and its critics would say for the worst. Today, many advertorials are carried as special sections that look very much like the editorial content of the newspaper or magazine in which they appear.

advertorial The use of advertising to promote an idea rather than a product or service.

---

[21]"The green CEO," *Fortune*, 24 May 1999, 198.
[22]Patricia A. Curtin, "Newspaper editors' perceptions of advertising pressures on editorial content and practice," in *Proceedings of the 1998 Conference of the American Academy of Advertising*, Darrell D. Muehling, ed.

Many critics fear that the advertorial's editorial-like format blurs the boundaries between editorial and advertising. One magazine executive had this harsh comment about advertorials, "Confused? Advertisers want people to be confused. If readers think they are reading an objective article that just happens to praise a certain company, they are going to give it more credence than if it is perceived as advertising."[23] As we discussed in Chapter 11, the extreme example of the advertorial/special section is the custom-published magazine whose content is controlled and dictated by a single advertiser.

During the last decade, the use of advertising to promote ideas has grown significantly. Today, it is not unusual for more than 10 percent of the content of a business or news magazine to be devoted to such material. Many critics believe that current advertorial practices are likely to confuse and deceive readers or listeners and in the long run hurt the credibility of the media carrying them.

The problem of advertorials and special sections has become pervasive enough to move organizations such as the American Society of Magazine Editors (ASME) to develop guidelines for their use. Some common rules for advertorial use are the following:

1. Advertising supplements should not use the standard body type or headline type used by the news department.
2. The supplement's cover should carry clear identification that it is a sponsored piece, preferably above or below the nameplate.
3. The identification of the sponsor and who prepared the copy should be placed in a dominant position toward the front of the supplement.
4. Each page should be marked "Paid Advertising Supplement."

Despite these guidelines, research shows that more than one-third of advertorials are not properly labeled as advertisements. As one study of advertorial practices concluded, "Not only do readers need to be wary about the source of information in magazines, but magazine editors need to take stock of practices that might eventually alienate readers."[24]

Despite criticism of the practice, the use of special sections is not going to go away. In the current competitive advertising environment, it is unlikely that many publishers or station managers will bar infomercials and special sections. However, they do have an obligation to their readers and themselves to make sure that every precaution is taken to prevent the audience from being confused about the source of such advertising.

SUMMARY

It is fitting that we end our discussion of advertising by examining its economic and social effects. It is obvious that the primary reason for advertising's existence is its contribution to the profitability of the firms that use it. However, we must remember that it is a communication tool, as such, it functions in concert with other marketing functions to create product awareness, build brand equity, and provide consumer information as the basis for educated consumer decisions.

As advertising carries out its economic function, it also has a twofold social component. First, is the overt use of advertising to accomplish social goals. For

---

[23]Robert Johnson, "Special editorial section," *Pressed*, published by the College of Journalism and Mass Communication, University of Georgia, 1999, 21.
[24]Glen T. Cameron, Kuen-Hee Ju-Park, and Bong-Hyun Kim, "Advertorials in magazines: Current use and compliance with industry guidelines," *Journalism and Mass Communication Quarterly*, Autumn 1996, 722.

more than 60 years, the Advertising Council has marshaled the combined efforts of advertisers, agencies, and media to promote a number of social initiatives. Second, advertising carries out unintended socialization functions. Advertising is a mirror of society and the brands, logos, and images created by advertising are a reflection of the culture to which it communicates.

Advertising is increasingly coming to grips with a number of issues in our complex, multicultural economic and social environment. Questions from its economic productivity to matters of taste will continually be raised by a public that is becoming more sophisticated to the nuances of consumerism. The future of advertising will be one of change and adaptation as the public interest becomes an increasingly important part of the modern advertiser's agenda.

REVIEW

1. What is the primary advantage of advertising?
2. Why is it so difficult to trace the effects of advertising?
3. How is market share related to advertising?
4. What is the role of brand switching from a macro-advertising perspective?
5. What is meant by inadvertent social consequences of advertising?
6. Why do most advertisers oppose unethical advertising?
7. What were the three major periods of advertising from a social perspective?
8. Discuss the role of the Advertising Council.
9. What is the advertising clearance process?

TAKE IT TO THE NET

We invite you to visit the Russell/Lane page on the Prentice Hall Web site at **www.prenhall.com/myphlip** for end-of-chapter exercises and applications.

Glossary

A

Account planner. An outgrowth of British agency structure where a planner initiates and reviews research and participates in the creative process. In some agencies, the planner is considered a spokesperson for the consumer.

Advertising clearance process. The internal process of clearing ads for publication and broadcast, conducted primarily by ad agencies and clients.

Advertising Council. A non-profit network of agencies, media, and advertisers dedicated to promoting social programs through advertising.

Advertising goals. The communication objectives designed to accomplish certain tasks within the total marketing program.

Advertising objectives. Those specific outcomes that are to be accomplished through advertising.

Advertorial. The use of advertising to promote an idea rather than a product or service.

American Association of Advertising Agencies (AAAA, 4As). The national organization of advertising agencies.

Amplitude modulation (AM). Method of transmitting electromagnetic signals by varying the *amplitude* (size) of the electromagnetic wave, in contrast to varying its *frequency*. Quality is not as good as frequency modulation, but can be heard farther, especially at night. *See* Frequency modulation (FM).

Animation (TV). Making inanimate objects appear alive and moving by setting them before an animation camera and filming one frame at a time.

Appeal. The motive to which an ad is directed, it is designed to stir a person toward a goal the advertiser has set.

The Arbitron Company. Syndicated radio ratings company.

Audience fragmentation. The segmenting of mass-media audiences into smaller groups because of diversity of media outlets.

Audit Bureau of Circulations (ABC). The organization sponsored by publishers, agencies, and advertisers for securing accurate circulation statements.

Average quarter-hour estimates (AQHE). Manner in which ratio ratings are presented. Estimates include average number of people listening, rating, and metro share of audience.

B

Barter Acquisition of broadcast time by an advertiser or an agency in exchange for operating capital or merchandise. No cash is involved.

Barter syndication. Station obtains a program at no charge. The program has presold national commercials and time is available for local station spots.

Bleed. Printed matter that runs over the edges of an outdoor board or of a page, leaving no margin.

Block programming. A series of television shows that appeals to the same general audience.

Bounce-back circular. An enclosure in the package of a product that has been ordered by mail. It offers other products of the same company and is effective in getting more business.

Brand. A name, term, sign, design, or a unifying combination of them, intended to identify and distinguish the product or service from competing products or services.

Brand development index (BDI). A method of allocating advertising budgers to those geographic areas that have the greatest sales potential.

Brand equity. The value of how such people as consumers, distributors, and salespeople think and feel about a brand relative to its competition over a period of time.

Brand loyalty. Degree to which a consumer purchases a certain brand without considering alternatives.

Brand name. The written or spoken part of a trademark, in contrast to the pictorial mark; a trademark word.

Brand positioning. Consumers' perceptions of specific brands relative to the various brands of goods or services currently available to them.

Brand preference. When all marketing conditions are equal, a consumer will choose a preferred brand over another.

Building block strategy. A media concept that buys the medium that reaches the most prospects first and works down to those that reach the smallest number of prospects.

Business-to-business advertising. Advertising that promotes goods through trade and industrial journals that are used in the manufacturing, distributing, or marketing of goods to the public.

C

Cable networks. Networks available only to cable subscribers. They are transmitted via satellite to local cable operators for redistribution either as part of basic service or at an extra cost charged to subscribers.

Cable television. TV signals that are carried to households by cable. Programs originate with cable operators through high antennas, satellite disks, or operator-initiated programming.

Category manager. A relatively new corporate position. This manager is responsible for all aspects of the brands in a specific product category for a company including research, manufacturing, sales, and advertising. Each product's advertising manager reports to the category manager. Example: Procter & Gamble's Tide and Cheer detergent report to a single category manager.

Cause-related marketing. Marketing strategies that attempt to link a company to some social or charitable cause.

Caveat emptor. Latin for "Let the buyer beware," Represents the notion that there

should be no government interference in the marketplace.

Cease and desist orders. If an advertiser refuses to sign a consent decree, the FTC may issue a cease and desist order that can carry a $10,000-per-day fine.

Central Hudson Four-Part Test. Supreme Court test to determine if specific commercial speech is protected under the Constitution.

Children's Advertising Review Unit (CARU). The CARU functions much as the NAD to review complaints about advertising to children.

Classified advertising. Found in columns so labeled, published in sections of a newspaper or magazine set aside for certain classes of goods or services—for example, Help Wanted, Positions Wanted, Houses for Sale, Cars for Sale. The ads are limited in size and generally are without illustration.

Clearance. The percentage of network affiliates that carries a particular network program.

Closing date. Date when all advertising material must be submitted to a publication.

Clutter. Refers to a proliferation of commercials (in a medium) that reduces the impact of any single message.

Coined word. An original and arbitrary combination of syllables forming a word. Extensively used for trademarks, such as PoFolks, Mazola, Gro-Pup, Zerone. (Opposite of a dictionary word.)

Committee on Nationwide Television Audience Measurement (CONTAM). Industry-wide organization to improve the accuracy and reliability of television ratings.

Communications component. That portion of the media plan that considers the effectiveness of message delivery as contrasted to the efficiency of audience delivery.

Comparative advertising. It directly contrasts an advertiser's product with other named or identified products.

Compensation. The payment of clearance fees by a TV network to local stations carrying its shows.

Competitive stage. The advertising stage a product reaches when its general usefulness is recognized but its superiority over similar brands has to be established in order to gain preference. *See* Pioneering stage, Retentive stage.

Comprehensive. A layout accurate in size, color, scheme, and other necessary details to show how a final ad will look. For presentation only, never for reproduction.

Computer-generated imagery (CGI). Technology allowing computer operators to create multitudes of electronic effects for TV—to squash, stretch, or squeeze objects—much more quickly than earlier tools could. It can add layers of visuals simultaneously.

Concept testing. The target audience evaluation of (alternative) creative strategy. Testing attempts to separate good and bad ideas and provide insight into factors motivating acceptance or rejection.

Consent decree. Issued by the FTC. An advertiser signs the decree, stops the practice under investigation, but admits no guilt.

Consumer advertising. Directed to people who will use the product themselves, in contrast to trade advertising, industrial advertising, or professional advertising.

Consumer Franchise Building. Creating promotional messages that allow consumers to differentiate one brand from others in the product category.

Consumer price index. Comparative index that charts what an urban family pays for a select group of goods including housing and transportation.

Contest. A promotion in which consumers compete for prizes and the winners are selected strictly on the basis of skill.

Continuity. A TV or radio script. Also refers to the length of time given media schedule runs.

Continuous tone. An unscreened photographic picture or image, on paper or film, that contains all gradations of tonal values from white to black.

Controlled circulation magazines. Sent without cost to people responsible for making buying decisions. To get on such lists, people must state their positions in companies; to stay on it, they must request it annually. Also known as *qualified-circulation publications.*

Convergence. The blending of various facets of marketing functions and communication technology to create more efficient and expanded synergies.

Cooperative advertising. Joint promotion of a national advertiser (manufacturer) and local retail outlet on behalf of the manufacturer's product on sale in the retail store.

Copy approach. The method of opening the text of an ad. Chief forms: factual approach, imaginative approach, emotional approach.

Copy testing. Measuring the effectiveness of ads.

Corrective advertising. To counteract the past residual effect of previous deceptive advertising, the FTC may require the advertiser to devote future space and time to disclosure of previous deception. Began around the late 1960s.

Cost per rating point (CCP). The cost per rating point is used to estimate the cost of TV advertising on several shows.

Cost per thousand (CPM). A method of comparing the cost for media of different circulations. Also weighted or demographic cost per thousand calculates the CPM using

only that portion of a medium's audience falling into a prime-prospect category.

Coupon. Most popular type of sales-promotion technique.

Cross-media buys. Several media or vehicles that are packaged to be sold to advertisers to gain a synergistic communication effect and efficiencies in purchasing time or space.

Customer relationship marketing. A management concept that organizes a business according to the needs of the consumer.

D

Database marketing. A process of continually updating information about individual consumers. Popular techniques with direct-response sellers.

Direct houses. In specialty advertising, firms that combine the functions of supplier and distributor.

Direct marketing. Selling goods and services without the aid of wholesaler or retailer. Includes direct-response advertising and advertising for leads for sales people. Also direct door-to-door selling. Uses many media: direct mail, publications, TV, radio.

Direct Marketing Association (DMA). Organization to promote direct-mail and direct-response advertising.

Direct premium. A sales incentive given to customers at the time of purchase.

Direct-response advertising. Any form of advertising done in direct marketing. Uses all types of media: direct mail, TV, magazines, newspapers, radio. Term replaces *mail-order advertising. See* Direct marketing.

Disintermediation. The potential for online technology to eliminate all or part of the distribution channel by selling directly to customers.

Dot.coms. A generic designation that refers to companies engaged in some type of online commerce.

Drive time (radio). A term used to designate the time of day when people are going to, or coming from, work. Usually 6 A.M. to 10 A.M. and 3 P.M. to 7 P.M., but this varies from one community to another. The most costly time on the rate card.

E

Effective reach. The percentage of an audience that is exposed to a certain number of messages or has achieved a specific level of awareness.

Eight-sheet poster. Outdoor poster used in urban areas, about one-fourth the size of the standard 30-sheet poster. Also called *junior poster.*

End-product advertising. Building consumer demand by promoting ingredients in a product. For example, Teflon and Nutrasweet.

European Community (EC). The developing economic integration of Europe. Potentially a single market of some 300 million consumers in 1991.

Event marketing. A promotion sponsored in connection with some special event such as a sports contest or musical concert.

Everyday low pricing (EDLP). A marketing strategy that uses permanent price reductions instead of occasional sales promotion incentives.

Exclusionary zones (outdoor). Industry code of conduct that prohibits the advertising of products within 500 feet of churches, schools, or hospitals of any products that cannot be used legally by children.

Executional idea. It is a rendering in words symbols, sounds, colors, shapes, forms, or any combination thereof, of an abstract answer to a perceived desire or need.

F

Family life cycle. Concept that demonstrates changing purchasing behavior as a person or a family matures.

Fast-close advertising. Some magazines offer short-notice ad deadlines, sometimes at a premium cost.

Federal Communications Commission (FCC). The federal authority empowered to license radio and TV stations and to assign wavelengths to stations "in the public interest."

Federal Trade Commission (FTC). The agency of the federal government empowered to prevent unfair competition and to prevent fraudulent, misleading, or deceptive advertising in interstate commerce.

Flat rate. A uniform charge for space in a medium, without regard to the amount of space used or the frequency of insertion. When flat rates do not prevail, *time discounts* or *quantity discounts* are offered.

Flighting. Flight is the length of time a broadcaster's campaign runs. Can be days, weeks, or months—but does not refer to a year. A flighting schedule alternates periods of activity with periods of inactivity.

Focus group. A qualitative research interviewing method using in-depth interviews with a group rather than with an individual.

Four-color process. The process for reproducing color illustrations by a set of plates, one that prints all the yellows, another the blues, a third the reds, and the fourth the blacks (sequence variable). The plates are referred to as *process plates.*

Free-standing inserts (FSI). Preprinted inserts distributed to newspaper publishers, where they are inserted and delivered with the newspaper.

Frequency. In media exposure the number of times an individual or household is exposed to a medium within a given period of time.

Frequency discounts. Discounts based on total time or space bought, usually within a year. Also called *bulk discounts.*

Frequency modulation (FM). A radio transmission wave that transmits by the variation in the frequency of its wave, rather than its size (as in amplitude modulation [AM]). An FM wave is twenty times the width of an AM wave, which is the source of its fine tone. To transmit such a wave, it has to be placed high on the electromagnetic spectrum, far from AM waves with their interference and static, hence its outstanding tone.

Fulfillment. The tasks of filling orders, shipping merchandise, and back in marketing.

Fulfillment firm. Company that handles the couponing process including receiving, verification, and payment. It also handles contests and sweepstake responses.

Full-run editions. An advertiser who buys the entire circulation of a publication is buying the full-run circulation.

Full-service agency. One that handles planning, creation, production, and placement of advertising for advertising clients. May also handle sales promotion and other related services as needed by client.

G

General Agreement on Tariffs and Trade (GATT). A treaty designed to lower trade barriers among 117 nations.

Generic demand. The demand demonstrated for a product class rather than a specific brand.

Global marketing. Term that denotes the use of advertising and marketing strategies on an international basis.

Gross rating points (GRP). Each rating point represents 1 percent of the universe being measured for the market. In TV it is 1 percent of the households having TV sets in that area.

H

Highway Beautification Act of 1965. Federal law that controls outdoor signs in noncommercial, nonindustrial areas.

Hoarding. First printed outdoor signs—the forerunner of modern outdoor advertising.

House mark. A primary mark of a business concern, usually used with the trademark of its products. *General Mills* is a house mark; *Betty Crocker* is a trademark; *DuPont* is a house mark; *Teflon II* is a trademark.

I

Idea advertising. Advertising used to promote an idea or cause rather than to sell a product or service.

Illuminated posters. Seventy to 80% of all outdoor posters are illuminated for 24-hour exposure.

Imagery transfer research. A technique that measures the ability of radio listeners to correctly describe the primary visual elements of related television commercials.

Inadvertent social role of advertising. Advertising sometimes communicates social messages unintended by the advertiser. Stereotyping and less-than-flattering portrayals of individuals and ethnic or social audience segments can lead to negative perceptions of advertising.

Incentives. Sales promotion directed at wholesalers, retailers, or a company's salesforce.

Independent delivery companies. Private companies that contract with magazine publishers to deliver their publications.

Industrial advertising. Addressed to manufacturers who buy machinery, equipment, raw materials, and the components needed to produce goods they sell.

Infomercial. Long form television advertising that promotes products within the context of a program-length commercial.

In-house agency. An arrangement whereby the advertiser handles the total agency function by buying individually, on a fee basis, the needed, services (for example creative, media services, and placement, under the direction of an assigned advertising director.

Institutional advertising. Advertising done by an organization speaking of its work views, and problems as a whole, to gain public goodwill and support rather than to sell a specific product. Sometimes called *public-relations advertising.*

Integrated marketing communication (IMC). The joint planning, execution, and coordination of all areas of marketing communication.

Interactive era. Communication will increasingly be controlled by consumers who will determine when and where they can be reached with promotional messages.

Interconnects. A joint buying opportunity between two or more cable systems in the same market.

Internet. A worldwide system of computer links that provides instantaneous communication.

J

Jingle. A commercial or part of a commercial set to music, usually carrying the slogan or theme line of a campaign. May make a brand name and slogan more easily remembered.

Johann Gutenberg. Began the era of mass communication in 1438 with the invention of movable type.

L

Layout. A working drawing (may be computer developed) showing how an ad is to look. A printer's layout is a set of instructions accompanying a piece of copy showing how it is to be set up. There are also rough layouts, finished layouts, and mechanical layouts, representing various degrees of finish. The term *layout* is used also for the total design of an ad.

Letterpress. Printing from a relief, or raised, surface. The raised surface is inked and comes in direct contact with the paper, like a rubber stamp.

Lettershop. A firm that not only addresses the mailing envelope but also is mechanically equipped to insert material, seal and stamp envelopes, and deliver them to the post office according to mailing requirements.

Lifestyle segmentation. Identifying consumers by combining several demographics and lifestyles.

Lifetime value. An estimate of the long-term revenue that can be expected from a particular prospect.

List broker. In direct-mail advertising an agent who rents the prospect lists of one advertiser to another advertiser. The broker receives a commission from the seller for this service.

List manager. Promotes client's lists to potential renters and buyers.

Logotype, or logo. A trademark or trade name embodied in the form of a distinctive lettering or design. Famous example: Coca-Cola.

M

Magazine networks. Groups of magazines that can be purchased together using one insertion order and paying a single invoice.

Make-goods. When a medium falls short of some audience guarantee, advertisers are provided concessions in the form of make-goods. Most commonly used in television and magazines.

Market. A group of people who can be identified by some common characteristic, interest, or problem; use a certain product to advantage; afford to buy it; and be reached through some medium.

Marketing communication. The communication components of marketing, which include public relations, advertising, personal selling, and sales promotion.

Marketing concept. A management orientation that views the needs of consumers as primary to the success of a firm.

Marketing goals. The overall objectives that a company wishes to accomplish through its marketing program.

Marketing mix. Combination of marketing functions, including advertising, used to sell a product.

Marketing translation. The process of adapting a general marketing plan to multinational environments.

Market profile. A demographic and psychographic description of the people or the households of a product's market. It may also include economic and retailing information about a territory.

Market segmentation. The division of an entire market of consumers into groups whose similarity makes them a market for products serving their special needs.

Marketing translation. Refers to the introduction and execution of a global marketing plan into a specific country as part of a international campaign.

Mass communication era. From the 1700s to the early decades of this century, advertisers were able to reach large segments of the population through the mass media.

MatchPrint. A high-quality color proof used for approvals prior to printing. Similar to a Signature print.

M-commerce. Mobile technology that allows consumers to receive information, make purchases, and conduct business anywhere they happen to be.

Media buyers. Execute and monitor the media schedule developed by media planners.

Media imperatives. Based on research by Simmons Media Studies, showed the importance of using both TV and magazines for full market coverage.

Media plan. The complete analysis and execution of the media component of a campaign.

Media planners. Media planners are responsible for the overall strategy of the media component of an advertising campaign.

Media schedule. The detailed plan or calendar showing when ads and commercials will be distributed and in what media vehicles they will appear.

Media strategy. Planning of ad media buys, including identification of audience, selection of media vehicles, and determination of timing of a media schedule.

Merge/purge (merge & purge). A system used to eliminate duplication by direct-response advertisers who use different mailing lists for the same mailing. Mailing lists are sent to a central merge/purge office that electronically picks out duplicate names. Saves mailing costs, especially important to firms that send out a million pieces in one mailing. Also avoids damage to the goodwill of the public.

Mergenthaler linotype. Ottmar Mergenthaler invented the linotype, which replaced hand-set type by automatically setting and distributing metal type.

Message management. Utilizes database information to offer different messages to various consumer categories.

Morphing. An electronic technique that allows you to transform one object into another object.

Multinational advertising. The coordination and execution of advertising campaigns that are directed to a number of countries.

N

National advertising. Advertising by a marketer of a trademarked product or service sold through different outlets, in contrast to *local advertising.*

National Advertising Division (NAD). The policy-making arm of the National Advertising Review Board.

Negative option direct response. Technique used by record and book clubs whereby a customer receives merchandise unless the seller is notified not to send it.

Networks. Interconnecting stations for the simultaneous transmission of TV or radio broadcasts.

Newspaper Association of America (NAA). The marketing and trade organization for the newspaper industry.

Newspaper networks. Groups of newspapers that allow advertisers to buy several papers simultaneously with one insertion order and one invoice.

Niche marketing. A combination of product and target market strategy. It is a flanking strategy that focuses on niches or comparatively narrow windows of opportunity within a broad product market or industry. Its guiding principle is to pit your strength against their weakness.

Nonwired networks. Groups of radio and TV stations whose advertising is sold simultaneously by station representatives.

North American Free Trade Agreement (NAFTA). A treaty designed to eliminate trade barriers among the United States, Mexico, and Canada.

North American Industrial Classification System. System that uses six-digit identification numbers for classifying manufacturing firms.

O

Off-network syndication. Syndicated programs that previously have been aired by a major network.

Offset lithography. Lithography is a printing process by which originally an image was formed on special stone by a greasy material, the design then being transferred to the printing paper. Today the more frequently used process is *offset* lithography, in which a thin and flexible metal sheet replaces the stone. In this process the design is 9offset9 from the metal sheet to a rubber blanket, which then transfers the image to the printing paper.

On-line services. Refers to computer-accessed databases and information services for business and home use.

Open rate. In print, the highest advertising rate at which all discounts are placed.

Opticals. Visual effects that are put on a TV film in a laboratory, in contrast to those that are included as part of the original photography.

Optimizers. Computer model and software that allow media buyers to make decisions about the value of various audience segments in a media schedule.

Chapter 13 Direct Response and Internet

Opt-out. Procedures that recipients to notify advertisers that they no longer wish to receive advertising messages. A term usually associated with online promotions.

Outbound telemarketing. A technique that involves a seller calling prospects.

Outdoor Advertising Association of America (OAAA). Primary trade and lobbying organization for the outdoor industry.

Out-of-home. Outdoor and transportation advertising.

Outside producer. The production company person who is hired by the agency to create the commercial according to agency specifications.

P

Partial runs. When magazines offer less than their entire circulation to advertisers Partial runs include demographic, geographic, and split-run editions.

Pass-along readership. Readers who receive a publication from a primary buyer. In consumer publications, pass-along readers are considered inferior to the primary audience, but this is usually not the case with business publications.

Passive meters. Unobtrusive device that measures individual viewing habits through sensors keyed to household members.

Pattern standardization. An advertising plan where overall strategy is controlled centrally, but local offices have flexibility in specific advertising executions.

Penny press. Forerunner of the mass newspaper in the United States. First appeared in the 1830s.

People meter. Device that measures TV set usage by individuals rather than by households.

Per inquiry (PI). Advertising time or space where medium is paid on a per response received basis.

Personal drive analysis (PDA). A technique used to uncover a consumer's individual psychological drives.

Pica. The unit for measuring width in printing. There are 6 picas to an inch. A page of type 24 picas wide is 4 inches wide.

Pioneering stage. The advertising stage of a product in which the need for such a product is not recognized and must be established or in which the need has been established but the success of a commodity in filling those requirements has to be established. *See* Competitive stage, Retentive stage.

Pixel. The smallest element of a computer image that can be separately addressed. It is an individual picture element.

Plant. In outdoor advertising the local company that arranges to lease, erect, and maintain the outdoor sign and to sell the advertising space on it.

Point (pt). The unit of measurement of type, about 1/72 inch in depth. Type is specified by its point size, as 8 pt., 12 pt., 24 pt., 48 pt. The unit for measuring thickness of paper, 0.001 inch.

Point-of-purchase advertising. Displays prepared by the manufacturer for use where the product is sold.

Positioning. Segmenting a market by creating a product to meet the needs of a select group or by using a distinctive advertising appeal to meet the needs of a specialized group, without making changes in the physical product.

Poster panel. A standard surface on which outdoor posters are placed. The posting surface is of sheet metal. An ornamental molding of standard green forms the frame. The standard poster panel is 12 feet high and 25 feet long (outside dimensions).

Potential rating index by ZIP market (PRIZM). A method of audience segmentation developed by the Claritas Corporation.

Premarketing era. The period from prehistoric times to the eighteenth century. During this time, buyers and sellers communicated in very primitive ways.

Premium. An item, other than the product itself, given to purchasers of a product as an inducement to buy. Can be free with a purchase (for example, on the package, in the package, or the container itself) or available upon proof of purchase and a payment (self-liquidating premium).

***Printers' Ink* Model Statute (1911).** The act directed at fraudulent advertising, prepared and sponsored by *Printers' Ink*, which was the pioneer advertising magazine.

Product differentiation. Unique product attributes that set off one brand from another.

Product manager. In package goods, the person responsible for the profitability of a product (brand) or product line, including advertising decisions. Also called a brand manager.

Product user segmentation. Identifying consumers by the amount of product usage.

Professional advertising. Directed at those in professions such as medicine, law, or architecture, who are in a position to recommend the use of a particular product or service to their clients.

Psychographics. A description of a market based on factors such as attitudes, opinions, interests, perceptions, and lifestyles of consumers comprising that market.

Public relations. Communication with various internal and external publics to create an image for a product or corporation.

Puffery. Advertiser's opinion of a product that is considered a legitimate expression of biased opinion.

Q

Qualitative research. This involves finding out what people say they think or feel. It is usually exploratory or diagnostic in nature.

R

Radio Advertising Bureau (RAB). Association to promote the use of radio as an advertising medium.

Radio All Dimension Audience Research (RADAR). Service of Statistical Research, Inc., major source of network radio ratings.

Rate base. The circulation that magazines guarantee advertisers in computing advertising costs.

Rate differential. The controversial practice of newspapers charging significantly higher rates to national advertisers as compared to local accounts.

Rating point (TV). The percentage of TV households in a market a TV station reaches with a program. The percentage varies with the time of day. A station may have a 10 rating between 6:00 and 6:30 P.M. and a 20 rating between 9:00 and 9:30.

Rebate. The amount owed to an advertiser by a medium when the advertiser qualifies for a higher space discount.

Relationship marketing. A strategy that develops marketing plans from a consumer perspective.

Remnant space. Unsold advertising space in geographic or demographic editions. It is offered to advertisers at a significant discount.

Representative (rep). An individual or organization representing a medium selling time or space outside the city or origin.

Research era. In recent years advertisers increasingly have been able to identify narrowly defined audience segments through sophisticated research methods.

Residual. A sum paid to certain talent on a TV or radio commercial every time the commercial is run after 13 weeks, for the life of the commercial.

Response lists. Prospects who have previously responded to direct mail offers.

Retail advertising. Advertising by a merchant who sells directly to the consumer.

Retentive stage. The third advertising stage of a product, reached when its general usefulness is widely known, its individual qualities are thoroughly appreciated, and it is satisfied to retain its patronage merely on the strength of its past reputation. *See* Pioneering state, Competitive stage.

Return on investment (ROI). One measure of the efficiency of a company is the rate of return (profits) achieved by a certain level of investment on various business functions including advertising.

Reverse production timetable. Used in direct mail to schedule a job. The schedule starts with the date it is to reach customers and works backward to a starting date.

Ride-alongs. Direct-mail pieces that are sent with other mailings, such as bills.

Riding the boards. Inspecting an outdoor showing after posting.

Robinson-Patman Act. A federal law, enforced by the FTC. Requires a manufacturer to give proportionate discounts and advertising allowances to all competing dealers in a market. Purpose: to protect smaller merchants from unfair competition of larger buyers.

Rotary bulletins (outdoor). Movable painted bulletins that are moved from one fixed location to another one in the market at regular intervals. The locations are viewed and approved in advance by the advertiser.

Rotogravure. The method of printing in which the impression is produced by chemically etched cylinders and run on a rotary press; useful in long runs of pictorial effects.

S

Sales promotion. (1) Sales activities that supplement both personal selling and marketing, coordinate the two, and help to make them effective. For example, displays are sales promotions. (2) More loosely, the combination of personal selling, advertising, and all supplementary selling activities.

Sampling. The method of introducing and promoting merchandise by distributing a miniature or full-size trial package of the product free or at a reduced price.

Scatter plan. The use of announcements, over a variety of network programs and stations, to reach as many people as possible in a market.

Screen printing. A simple printing process that uses a stencil. It is economical but is limited in reproduction quality.

Secondary research. Research or data that is already gathered by someone else for another purpose.

Selective binding. Binding different material directed to various reader segments in a single issue of a magazine.

Self-liquidating premium. A premium offered to consumers for a fee that covers its cost plus handling.

Service advertising. Advertising that promotes a service rather than a product.

Service mark. A word or name used in the sale of services, to identify the services of a firm and distinguish them from those of others, for example, Hertz Drive Yourself Service, Weight Watchers Diet Course. Comparable to trademarks for products.

Share of audience. The percentage of households using TV tuned to a particular program.

Short rate. The balance advertisers have to pay if they estimated that they would run more ads in a year than they did and entered a contract to pay at a favorable rate. The short rate is figured at the end of the year or sooner if advertisers fall behind schedule. It is calculated at a higher rate for the fewer insertions.

Showing. Outdoor posters are bought by groups, referred to as *showings*. The size of a showing is referred to as a 100-GRP showing or a 75- or 50-GRP showing, depending on the gross rating points of the individual boards selected.

Simmons Market Research Bureau (SMRB). Firm that provides audience data for several media. Best known for magazine research.

Siquis. Handwritten posters in sixteenth- and seventeenth-century England—forerunners of modern advertising.

Situation analysis. The part of the advertising plan that answers the questions: Where are we today and how did we get here? It deals with the past and present.

Social responsibility. The demand that advertising be aware of its responsibility to the public, i.e., it should do more than sell goods and services.

Spam. Online advertising messages that are usually unsolicited by the recipient.

Specialty advertising. A gift given to a consumer to encourage a purchase.

Spectacular. Outdoor sign built to order, designed to be conspicuous for its location, size, lights, motion, or action. The costliest form of outdoor advertising.

Spot television. Purchase of time from a local station, in contrast to purchasing from a network.

Standard Advertising Unit (SAU). Allows national advertisers to purchase newspaper advertising in standard units from one paper to another.

Standard Rate and Data Service (SRDS). SRDS publishes a number of directories giving media and production information.

Stock music. Existing recorded music that may be purchased for use in a TV or radio commercial.

Storyboard. Series of drawings used to present a proposed commercial. Consists of illustrations of key action (video), accompanied by the audio part. Used for getting advertiser approval and as a production guide.

Stripping. Scheduling a syndicated program on a five-day-per-week basis.

Substantiation. The key to FTC enforcement is that advertisers must be able to prove the claims made in their advertising.

Sweepstakes. A promotion in which prize winners are determined on the basis of chance alone. Not legal if purchaser must risk money to enter.

Sweep weeks. During these periods, ratings are taken for all television markets.

Syndicated TV program. A program that is sold or distributed to more than one local station by an independent organization outside the national network standard.

Synergistic effect. In media buying, combining a number of complementary media that create advertising awareness greater than the sum of each.

T

Target audience. That group that composes the present and potential prospects for a product or service.

Target marketing. Identifying and communicating with groups of prime prospects.

Telemarketing. Contacting prospective buyers over the telephone. Major area of direct marketing.

Theater of the mind. In radio, a writer paints pictures in the mind of the listener through the use of sound.

Time-shift viewing. Recording programs on a VCR for viewing at a later time.

Total concept. The combining of all elements of an ad–copy, headline, and illustrations–into a single idea.

Total market coverage (TMC). Where newspapers augment their circulation with direct mail or shoppers to deliver all households in a market.

Total survey area. The maximum coverage of a radio or television station's signal.

Trade advertising. Advertising directed to the wholesale or retail merchants or sales agencies through whom the product is sold.

Trademark. Any device or word that identifies the origin of a product, telling who made it or who sold it. Not to be confused with *trade name.*

Trade name. A name that applies to a business as a whole, not to an individual product.

Trade paper. A business publication directed to those who buy products for resale (wholesalers, jobbers, retailers).

Traffic Audit Bureau for Media Measurement (TAB). An organization designed to investigate how many people pass and may see a given outdoor sign, to establish a method of evaluating traffic measuring a market.

Traffic-building premium. A sales incentive to encourage customers to come to a store where as a sale can be closed.

Translation management. The process of translating advertising from one culture to another.

TV director. The person who casts and rehearses a commercial and is the key person in the shooting of the commercial.

TvQ. A service of Marketing Evaluations that measures the popularity (opinion of audience rather than size of audience) of shows and personalities.

Typography. The art of using type effectively.

U

Up-front buying. Purchase of network TV time by national advertisers during the first offering by networks. Most expensive network advertising.

Up-selling. A telemarketing technique designed to sell additional merchandise to callers.

V

Values and lifestyles system (VALS). Developed by SRI International to cluster consumers according to several variables in order to predict consumer behavior.

Vendor program. Special form of co-op advertising in which a retailer designs the program and approaches advertisers for support.

Vertical publications. Business publications dealing with the problems of a specific industry: for example, *Chain Store Age, National Petroleum News, Textile World.*

W

War Advertising Council. Founded in 1942 to promote World War II mobilization. It later evolved into the Advertising Council.

Wheeler-Lea Amendments. Broadened the scope of the FTC to include consumer advertising.

Y

Yield management. A product pricing strategy to control supply and demand.

Z

Zoning. Newspaper practice of offering advertisers partial coverage of a market, often accomplished with weekly inserts distributed to certain sections of that market.

Index

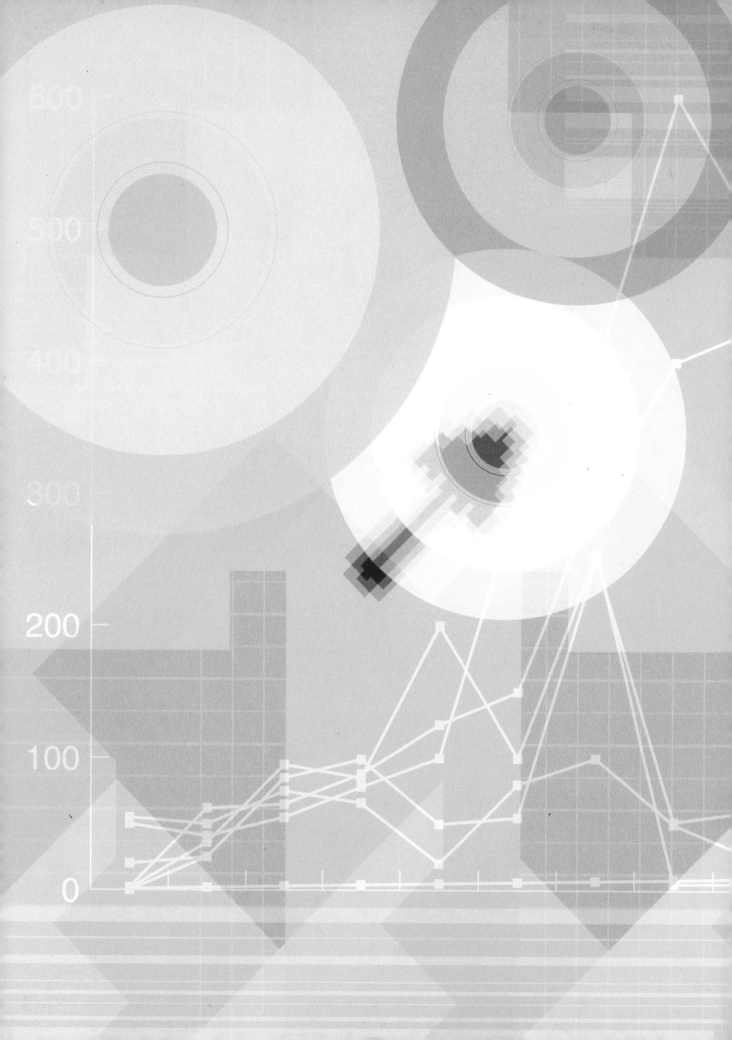